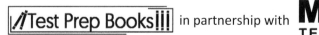 

FREE Test Taking Tips Video/DVD Offer

To better serve you, we created videos covering test taking tips that we want to give you for FREE. **These videos cover world-class tips that will help you succeed on your test.**

We just ask that you send us feedback about this product. Please let us know what you thought about it—whether good, bad, or indifferent.

To get your **FREE videos**, you can use the QR code below or email freevideos@studyguideteam.com with "Free Videos" in the subject line and the following information in the body of the email:

  a. The title of your product

  b. Your product rating on a scale of 1-5, with 5 being the highest

  c. Your feedback about the product

If you have any questions or concerns, please don't hesitate to contact us at info@studyguideteam.com.

Thank you!

Praxis Elementary Education Multiple Subjects Study Guide

3 Practice Tests and Praxis 5001 Prep
[6th Edition]

Joshua Rueda

Written and edited by TPB Publishing.

TPB Publishing is not associated with or endorsed by any official testing organization. TPB Publishing is a publisher of unofficial educational products. All test and organization names are trademarks of their respective owners. Content in this book is included for utilitarian purposes only and does not constitute an endorsement by TPB Publishing of any particular point of view.

Interested in buying more than 10 copies of our product? Contact us about bulk discounts:
bulkorders@studyguideteam.com

ISBN 13: 9781637750544
ISBN 10: 1637750544

Table of Contents

Quick Overview

As you draw closer to taking your exam, effective preparation becomes more and more important. Thankfully, you have this study guide to help you get ready. Use this guide to help keep your studying on track and refer to it often.

This study guide contains several key sections that will help you be successful on your exam. The guide contains tips for what you should do the night before and the day of the test. Also included are test-taking tips. Knowing the right information is not always enough. Many well-prepared test takers struggle with exams. These tips will help equip you to accurately read, assess, and answer test questions.

A large part of the guide is devoted to showing you what content to expect on the exam and to helping you better understand that content. In this guide are practice test questions so that you can see how well you have grasped the content. Then, answer explanations are provided so that you can understand why you missed certain questions.

Don't try to cram the night before you take your exam. This is not a wise strategy for a few reasons. First, your retention of the information will be low. Your time would be better used by reviewing information you already know rather than trying to learn a lot of new information. Second, you will likely become stressed as you try to gain a large amount of knowledge in a short amount of time. Third, you will be depriving yourself of sleep. So be sure to go to bed at a reasonable time the night before. Being well-rested helps you focus and remain calm.

Be sure to eat a substantial breakfast the morning of the exam. If you are taking the exam in the afternoon, be sure to have a good lunch as well. Being hungry is distracting and can make it difficult to focus. You have hopefully spent lots of time preparing for the exam. Don't let an empty stomach get in the way of success!

When travelling to the testing center, leave earlier than needed. That way, you have a buffer in case you experience any delays. This will help you remain calm and will keep you from missing your appointment time at the testing center.

Be sure to pace yourself during the exam. Don't try to rush through the exam. There is no need to risk performing poorly on the exam just so you can leave the testing center early. Allow yourself to use all of the allotted time if needed.

Remain positive while taking the exam even if you feel like you are performing poorly. Thinking about the content you should have mastered will not help you perform better on the exam.

Once the exam is complete, take some time to relax. Even if you feel that you need to take the exam again, you will be well served by some down time before you begin studying again. It's often easier to convince yourself to study if you know that it will come with a reward!

Test-Taking Strategies

1. Predicting the Answer

When you feel confident in your preparation for a multiple-choice test, try predicting the answer before reading the answer choices. This is especially useful on questions that test objective factual knowledge. By predicting the answer before reading the available choices, you eliminate the possibility that you will be distracted or led astray by an incorrect answer choice. You will feel more confident in your selection if you read the question, predict the answer, and then find your prediction among the answer choices. After using this strategy, be sure to still read all of the answer choices carefully and completely. If you feel unprepared, you should not attempt to predict the answers. This would be a waste of time and an opportunity for your mind to wander in the wrong direction.

2. Reading the Whole Question

Too often, test takers scan a multiple-choice question, recognize a few familiar words, and immediately jump to the answer choices. Test authors are aware of this common impatience, and they will sometimes prey upon it. For instance, a test author might subtly turn the question into a negative, or he or she might redirect the focus of the question right at the end. The only way to avoid falling into these traps is to read the entirety of the question carefully before reading the answer choices.

3. Looking for Wrong Answers

Long and complicated multiple-choice questions can be intimidating. One way to simplify a difficult multiple-choice question is to eliminate all of the answer choices that are clearly wrong. In most sets of answers, there will be at least one selection that can be dismissed right away. If the test is administered on paper, the test taker could draw a line through it to indicate that it may be ignored; otherwise, the test taker will have to perform this operation mentally or on scratch paper. In either case, once the obviously incorrect answers have been eliminated, the remaining choices may be considered. Sometimes identifying the clearly wrong answers will give the test taker some information about the correct answer. For instance, if one of the remaining answer choices is a direct opposite of one of the eliminated answer choices, it may well be the correct answer. The opposite of obviously wrong is obviously right! Of course, this is not always the case. Some answers are obviously incorrect simply because they are irrelevant to the question being asked. Still, identifying and eliminating some incorrect answer choices is a good way to simplify a multiple-choice question.

4. Don't Overanalyze

Anxious test takers often overanalyze questions. When you are nervous, your brain will often run wild, causing you to make associations and discover clues that don't actually exist. If you feel that this may be a problem for you, do whatever you can to slow down during the test. Try taking a deep breath or counting to ten. As you read and consider the question, restrict yourself to the particular words used by the author. Avoid thought tangents about what the author *really* meant, or what he or she was *trying* to say. The only things that matter on a multiple-choice test are the words that are actually in the question. You must avoid reading too much into a multiple-choice question, or supposing that the writer meant something other than what he or she wrote.

5. No Need for Panic

It is wise to learn as many strategies as possible before taking a multiple-choice test, but it is likely that you will come across a few questions for which you simply don't know the answer. In this situation, avoid panicking. Because most multiple-choice tests include dozens of questions, the relative value of a single wrong answer is small. As much as possible, you should compartmentalize each question on a multiple-choice test. In other words, you should not allow your feelings about one question to affect your success on the others. When you find a question that you either don't understand or don't know how to answer, just take a deep breath and do your best. Read the entire question slowly and carefully. Try rephrasing the question a couple of different ways. Then, read all of the answer choices carefully. After eliminating obviously wrong answers, make a selection and move on to the next question.

6. Confusing Answer Choices

When working on a difficult multiple-choice question, there may be a tendency to focus on the answer choices that are the easiest to understand. Many people, whether consciously or not, gravitate to the answer choices that require the least concentration, knowledge, and memory. This is a mistake. When you come across an answer choice that is confusing, you should give it extra attention. A question might be confusing because you do not know the subject matter to which it refers. If this is the case, don't eliminate the answer before you have affirmatively settled on another. When you come across an answer choice of this type, set it aside as you look at the remaining choices. If you can confidently assert that one of the other choices is correct, you can leave the confusing answer aside. Otherwise, you will need to take a moment to try to better understand the confusing answer choice. Rephrasing is one way to tease out the sense of a confusing answer choice.

7. Your First Instinct

Many people struggle with multiple-choice tests because they overthink the questions. If you have studied sufficiently for the test, you should be prepared to trust your first instinct once you have carefully and completely read the question and all of the answer choices. There is a great deal of research suggesting that the mind can come to the correct conclusion very quickly once it has obtained all of the relevant information. At times, it may seem to you as if your intuition is working faster even than your reasoning mind. This may in fact be true. The knowledge you obtain while studying may be retrieved from your subconscious before you have a chance to work out the associations that support it. Verify your instinct by working out the reasons that it should be trusted.

8. Key Words

Many test takers struggle with multiple-choice questions because they have poor reading comprehension skills. Quickly reading and understanding a multiple-choice question requires a mixture of skill and experience. To help with this, try jotting down a few key words and phrases on a piece of scrap paper. Doing this concentrates the process of reading and forces the mind to weigh the relative importance of the question's parts. In selecting words and phrases to write down, the test taker thinks about the question more deeply and carefully. This is especially true for multiple-choice questions that are preceded by a long prompt.

9. Subtle Negatives

One of the oldest tricks in the multiple-choice test writer's book is to subtly reverse the meaning of a question with a word like *not* or *except*. If you are not paying attention to each word in the question, you can easily be led astray by this trick. For instance, a common question format is, "Which of the following is...?" Obviously, if the question instead is, "Which of the following is not...?," then the answer will be quite different. Even worse, the test makers are aware of the potential for this mistake and will include one answer choice that would be correct if the question were not negated or reversed. A test taker who misses the reversal will find what he or she believes to be a correct answer and will be so confident that he or she will fail to reread the question and discover the original error. The only way to avoid this is to practice a wide variety of multiple-choice questions and to pay close attention to each and every word.

10. Reading Every Answer Choice

It may seem obvious, but you should always read every one of the answer choices! Too many test takers fall into the habit of scanning the question and assuming that they understand the question because they recognize a few key words. From there, they pick the first answer choice that answers the question they believe they have read. Test takers who read all of the answer choices might discover that one of the latter answer choices is actually *more* correct. Moreover, reading all of the answer choices can remind you of facts related to the question that can help you arrive at the correct answer. Sometimes, a misstatement or incorrect detail in one of the latter answer choices will trigger your memory of the subject and will enable you to find the right answer. Failing to read all of the answer choices is like not reading all of the items on a restaurant menu: you might miss out on the perfect choice.

11. Spot the Hedges

One of the keys to success on multiple-choice tests is paying close attention to every word. This is never truer than with words like almost, most, some, and sometimes. These words are called "hedges" because they indicate that a statement is not totally true or not true in every place and time. An absolute statement will contain no hedges, but in many subjects, the answers are not always straightforward or absolute. There are always exceptions to the rules in these subjects. For this reason, you should favor those multiple-choice questions that contain hedging language. The presence of qualifying words indicates that the author is taking special care with their words, which is certainly important when composing the right answer. After all, there are many ways to be wrong, but there is only one way to be right! For this reason, it is wise to avoid answers that are absolute when taking a multiple-choice test. An absolute answer is one that says things are either all one way or all another. They often include words like *every*, *always*, *best*, and *never*. If you are taking a multiple-choice test in a subject that doesn't lend itself to absolute answers, be on your guard if you see any of these words.

12. Long Answers

In many subject areas, the answers are not simple. As already mentioned, the right answer often requires hedges. Another common feature of the answers to a complex or subjective question are qualifying clauses, which are groups of words that subtly modify the meaning of the sentence. If the question or answer choice describes a rule to which there are exceptions or the subject matter is complicated, ambiguous, or confusing, the correct answer will require many words in order to be expressed clearly and accurately. In essence, you should not be deterred by answer choices that seem

4

excessively long. Oftentimes, the author of the text will not be able to write the correct answer without offering some qualifications and modifications. Your job is to read the answer choices thoroughly and completely and to select the one that most accurately and precisely answers the question.

13. Restating to Understand

Sometimes, a question on a multiple-choice test is difficult not because of what it asks but because of how it is written. If this is the case, restate the question or answer choice in different words. This process serves a couple of important purposes. First, it forces you to concentrate on the core of the question. In order to rephrase the question accurately, you have to understand it well. Rephrasing the question will concentrate your mind on the key words and ideas. Second, it will present the information to your mind in a fresh way. This process may trigger your memory and render some useful scrap of information picked up while studying.

14. True Statements

Sometimes an answer choice will be true in itself, but it does not answer the question. This is one of the main reasons why it is essential to read the question carefully and completely before proceeding to the answer choices. Too often, test takers skip ahead to the answer choices and look for true statements. Having found one of these, they are content to select it without reference to the question above. Obviously, this provides an easy way for test makers to play tricks. The savvy test taker will always read the entire question before turning to the answer choices. Then, having settled on a correct answer choice, he or she will refer to the original question and ensure that the selected answer is relevant. The mistake of choosing a correct-but-irrelevant answer choice is especially common on questions related to specific pieces of objective knowledge. A prepared test taker will have a wealth of factual knowledge at their disposal, and should not be careless in its application.

15. No Patterns

One of the more dangerous ideas that circulates about multiple-choice tests is that the correct answers tend to fall into patterns. These erroneous ideas range from a belief that B and C are the most common right answers, to the idea that an unprepared test-taker should answer "A-B-A-C-A-D-A-B-A." It cannot be emphasized enough that pattern-seeking of this type is exactly the WRONG way to approach a multiple-choice test. To begin with, it is highly unlikely that the test maker will plot the correct answers according to some predetermined pattern. The questions are scrambled and delivered in a random order. Furthermore, even if the test maker was following a pattern in the assignation of correct answers, there is no reason why the test taker would know which pattern he or she was using. Any attempt to discern a pattern in the answer choices is a waste of time and a distraction from the real work of taking the test. A test taker would be much better served by extra preparation before the test than by reliance on a pattern in the answers.

FREE Videos/DVD OFFER

Doing well on your exam requires both knowing the test content and understanding how to use that knowledge to do well on the test. We offer completely FREE test taking tip videos. **These videos cover world-class tips that you can use to succeed on your test.**

To get your **FREE videos**, you can use the QR code below or email freevideos@studyguideteam.com with "Free Videos" in the subject line and the following information in the body of the email:

     a. The title of your product

     b. Your product rating on a scale of 1-5, with 5 being the highest

     c. Your feedback about the product

If you have any questions or concerns, please don't hesitate to contact us at info@studyguideteam.com.

Thanks again!

Introduction to the Praxis II Elementary Education: Multiple Subjects Exam

Function of the Test

The Praxis Elementary Education: Multiple Subjects exam is one of the Educational Testing Service's (ETS's) Subject Assessment tests. The Subject Assessment tests are intended to measure knowledge of more than ninety specific subjects taught by educators in kindergarten through twelfth grade classrooms. These tests also aim to teach skills and knowledge in those subject areas. The tests are offered worldwide but are primarily used in the United States mostly as a required part of the certification and licensing procedure in certain individual states. They are also used as part of the licensing process by some professional associations and organizations.

The Elementary Education: Multiple Subjects exam covers four individual subjects: Reading and Language Arts, Mathematics, Social Studies, and Science. States that require the test typically require that a test-taker reach a minimum passing score on each of the four sub-tests in order to pass and receive the license or certification sought. Individuals taking the test are usually beginning teachers, either freshly out of college, having recently decided to seek a particular license or certification, or having recently moved to a state where the test is required or preferred.

Test Administration

The test is administered by computer through an international system of testing centers, including Prometric centers, some colleges and universities, and a variety of other locations. Although it is primarily used in the United States, the test is available at locations throughout the world. However, the test is not available at all times. Instead, there is a window of approximately two weeks per month during which the test may be taken. The individual subtests can be taken separately, but the fee for taking them together offers a significant discount from the combined cost of the four individual tests.

Accommodations for test-takers meeting the requirements of the Americans with Disabilities Act include extended testing time, additional rest breaks, a separate testing room, a writer/recorder of answers, a test reader, and large print test materials. Alternate forms of the test are available in sign language, Braille, or audio format.

Test takers may opt to retake the test at any time after twenty-one days have passed from the initial attempt. An individual wishing to retake one of the four tests that comprise the Multiple Subjects exam must also wait twenty-one days from the initial attempt of that exam.

Test Format

All questions are selected response (in which the test-taker chooses from multiple choice options or chooses a particular word, sentence or part of a graphic), and numeric entry (in which the test-taker gives a numeric answer). In all cases, the test-taker will receive a question from the computer and be prompted to select a response from the options on the screen or enter a number. Questions may be answered in any order, and test takers may mark questions to return to them later.

The four sub-tests of the exam break down as follows:

Subject	Minutes	Questions
Reading and Language Arts	90	80
Mathematics	65	50
Social Studies	50	55
Science	50	50
Total	255	235

Scoring

Raw scores are based on the number of correct responses with no penalty for incorrect answers or guesses. The raw scores are then converted to a scaled score from 100 to 200. The required passing scaled score varies from state to state and from sub-test to sub-test. On the Reading and Language Arts sub-test, the required score ranges from a low of 154 to a high of 165 with most states requiring at least a 157. The median score in 2015 was a 169. On the Mathematics sub-test, the required score ranges from a low of 143 to a high of 171 with most states requiring at least a 157. The median score in 2015 was a 170. On the Social Studies sub-test, the required score ranges from a low of 142 to 166 with most states requiring at least a 155. The median score in 2015 was a 163. Finally, on the Science sub-test, the required score ranges from a low of 144 to 170 with most states requiring at least a 159. The median score in 2015 was a 167.

ETS also offers a "Recognition of Excellence" to test takers who perform exceptionally well on the exam. The award is typically given to test takers whose scores fall in the top 15 percent of scores on the exam.

Recent/Future Developments

No recent or immediate future changes to the test have been announced by ETS.

Study Prep Plan for the Praxis II Elementary Education: Multiple Subjects Exam

1 **Schedule** - Use one of our study schedules below or come up with one of your own.

2 **Relax -** Test anxiety can hurt even the best students. There are many ways to reduce stress. Find the one that works best for you.

3 **Execute** - Once you have a good plan in place, be sure to stick to it.

One Week Study Schedule		
Day 1	Reading	
Day 2	Mathematics	
Day 3	Social Studies	
Day 4	Science	
Day 5	Practice Tests #1 & #2	
Day 6	Practice Test #3	
Day 7	Take Your Exam!	

Two Week Study Schedule			
Day 1	Reading	Day 8	Science
Day 2	Literature and Informational Texts	Day 9	Life Science
Day 3	Writing, Speaking, and Listening	Day 10	Physical Science
Day 4	Mathematics	Day 11	Practice Test #1
Day 5	Geometry & Measurement...	Day 12	Practice Test #2
Day 6	Solving Problems Involving Measurement	Day 13	Practice Test #3
Day 7	Social Studies	Day 14	Take Your Exam!

One Month Study Schedule							
Day 1	Reading	Day 11	Components of the Coordinate Plane	Day 21	Physical Science
Day 2	Literature and Informational Texts	Day 12	Statistical Concepts	Day 22	Energy
Day 3	Point of View	Day 13	Practice Questions	Day 23	Practice Questions
Day 4	Writing, Speaking, and Listening	Day 14	Social Studies	Day 24	Practice Test #1
Day 5	Language	Day 15	Geography, Anthropology, and Sociology	Day 25	Answer Explanations #1
Day 6	Practice Questions	Day 16	World History and Economics	Day 26	Practice Test #2
Day 7	Mathematics	Day 17	Practice Questions	Day 27	Answer Explanations #2
Day 8	Algebraic Thinking	Day 18	Science	Day 28	Practice Test #3
Day 9	Geometry & Measurement...	Day 19	Life Science	Day 29	Answer Explanations #3
Day 10	Perimeter, Area, Surface Area, and Volume	Day 20	Regulation and Behavior	Day 30	Take Your Exam!

Build your own prep plan by visiting:
testprepbooks.com/prep

Math Reference Sheet

Symbol	Phrase
+	added to, increased by, sum of, more than
-	decreased by, difference between, less than, take away
×	multiplied by, 3 (4, 5 . . .) times as large, product of
÷	divided by, quotient of, half (third, etc.) of
=	is, the same as, results in, as much as
x, t, n, etc.	a variable which is an unknown value or quantity
<	is under, is below, smaller than, beneath
>	is above, is over, bigger than, exceeds
≤	no more than, at most, maximum; less than or equal to
≥	no less than, at least, minimum; greater than or equal to
√	square root of, exponent divided by 2

Geometry	Description
$P = 2l + 2w$	for perimeter of a rectangle
$P = 4 \times s$	for perimeter of a square
$P = a + b + c$	for perimeter of a triangle
$A = \frac{1}{2} \times b \times h = \frac{bh}{2}$	for area of a triangle
$A = b \times h$	for area of a parallelogram
$A = \frac{1}{2} \times h(b_1 + b_2)$	for area of a trapezoid
$A = \frac{1}{2} \times a \times P$	for area of a regular polygon
$C = 2 \times \pi \times r$	for circumference (perimeter) of a circle
$A = \pi \times r^2$	for area of a circle
$c^2 = a^2 + b^2; c = \sqrt{a^2 + b^2}$	for finding the hypotenuse of a right triangle
$SA = 2xy + 2yz + 2xz$	for finding surface area
$V = \frac{1}{3}xyh$	for finding volume of a rectangular pyramid
$V = \frac{4}{3}\pi r^3; \frac{1}{3}\pi r^2 h; \pi r^2 h$	for volume of a sphere; a cone; and a cylinder

Radical Expressions	Description
$\sqrt[n]{a} = a^{\frac{1}{n}}; \sqrt[n]{a^m} = (\sqrt[n]{a})^m = a^{\frac{m}{n}}$	a is the radicand, n is the index, m is the exponent
$\sqrt{x^2} = (x^2)^{\frac{1}{2}} = x$	to convert square root to exponent
$a^m \times a^n = a^{m+n}$	multiplying radicands with exponents
$(a^m)^n = a^{m \times n}$	multiplying exponents
$(a \times b)^m = a^m \times b^m$	parentheses with exponents

Property	Addition	Multiplication
Commutative	$a + b = b + a$	$a \times b = b \times a$
Associative	$(a + b) + c = a + (b + c)$	$(a \times b) \times c = a \times (b \times c)$
Identity	$a + 0 = a; 0 + a = a$	$a \times 1 = a; 1 \times a = a$
Inverse	$a + (-a) = 0$	$a \times \frac{1}{a} = 1; a \neq 0$
Distributive		$a(b + c) = ab + ac$

Data	Description
Mean	equal to the total of the values of a data set, divided by the number of elements in the data set
Median	middle value in an odd number of ordered values of a data set, or the mean of the two middle values in an even number of ordered values in a data set
Mode	the value that appears most often
Range	the difference between the highest and the lowest values in the set

Graphing	Description
(x, y)	ordered pair, plot points in a graph
$y = mx + b$	slope-intercept form; m represents the slope of the line and b represents the y-intercept
$f(x)$	read as f of x, which means it is a function of x
(x_2, y_2) and (x_2, y_2)	two ordered pairs used to determine the slope of a line
$m = \frac{y_2 - y_1}{x_2 - x_1}$	to find the slope of the line, m, for ordered pairs
$Ax + By = C$	standard form of an equation, also for solving a system of equations through the elimination method
$M = (\frac{x_1 + x_2}{2}, \frac{y_1 + y_2}{2})$	for finding the midpoint of an ordered pair
$y = ax^2 + bx + c$	quadratic function for a parabola
$y = a(x - h)^2 + k$	quadratic function for a parabola with vertex
$y = ab^x; y = a \times b^x$	function for exponential curve
$y = ax^2 + bx + c$	standard form of a quadratic function
$x = \frac{-b}{2a}$	for finding axis of symmetry in a parabola; given quadratic formula in standard form
$f = \sqrt{\frac{\Sigma(x - \bar{x})^2}{n - 1}}$	function for standard deviation of the sample; where $\bar{x}$ = sample mean and n = sample size

Proportions and Percentage	Description
$\frac{\text{gallons}}{\text{cost}} = \frac{\text{gallons}}{\text{cost}} : \frac{7 \text{ gallons}}{\$14.70} = \frac{x}{\$20}$	written as equal ratios with a variable representing the missing quantity
$\frac{y_1}{x_1} = \frac{y_2}{x_2}$	for direct proportions
$(y_1)(x_1) = (y_2)(x_2)$	for indirect proportions
$\frac{change}{\text{original value}} \times 100 = percent\ change$	for finding percentage change in value
$\frac{new\ quantity - old\ quantity}{old\ quantity} \times 100$	for calculating the increase or decrease in percentage

Reading

Foundational Skills

Phonological Awareness

Importance of Phonological Awareness

Well before children are able to read and write, they begin to develop basic listening skills and gradually begin to imitate and produce the sounds they hear. Since **language** is used to communicate one's needs, react to situations, share experiences, and develop an understanding of the surrounding world, these beginning stages form the foundation of a child's literacy development. Before a child reaches the preschool years, they begin to develop the ability to recognize and manipulate the sounds in their environment.

Generally speaking, **phonological awareness** is the ability to identify and manipulate specific units of oral language, including words, syllables, onsets, and rimes. The beginning stages of phonological awareness occur when a child is able to listen to and understand the words that people speak and read and when they are further able to recognize the various sounds within these words. Phonological awareness is also defined as the ability to sound out various words by connecting the sounds heard to familiar sounds and to manipulate those sounds in order to create new sounds and words. A child is demonstrating phonological awareness when they are able to do the following:

- Appropriately recognize and apply words that rhyme—*cat, bat, sat*
- Identify initial letters—the *c* in *cat*
- Identify middle letters—the *a* in *cat*
- Identify ending letters—the *t* in *cat*
- Separate simple words into their individual sounds or phonemes—c/a/t *cat*

There are many strategies educators can use to strengthen a child's phonological awareness. One effective strategy to strengthen a child's awareness of word units is clapping out the number of syllables in a word. Familiar and enjoyable songs, such as "Bingo," help children to identify individual phonemes within a word and strengthen their spelling skills, listening comprehension, and rhythm. Other strategies may include word games that challenge children to think of rhyming words or words that share the same initial, middle, or ending sounds. Creating fun and engaging ways for children to strengthen their phonological awareness will build the framework for future literary success.

Phonemes, Syllables, Onsets, and Rimes

A **phoneme** is commonly referred to as a sound or a group of sounds that differentiate one word from another in a spoken language. Phonemes are language-specific sound units that do not carry inherent meanings but are simply known as the smallest unit in a language. For example, there are phonemes

12

unique to the English language that do not necessarily exist in other spoken languages. In English, although there are only twenty-six letters, there are forty-four phonemes:

Forty-Four Phonemes in English			
Consonant Sounds		**Vowel Sounds**	
/b/	boy	/a/	bat
/d/	desk	/e/	head
/f/	fall	/i/	dish
/g/	game	/o/	rock
/h/	hand	/u/	muck
/j/	joy	/a/	bake
/k/	king	/e/	meet
/l/	life	/i/	like
/m/	map	/o/	moat
/n/	nail	/yoo/	cube
/p/	park	/e/	alarm
/r/	run	/oo/	doom
/s/	sock	/oo/	nook
/t/	tail	/ou/	mouse
/v/	veil	/oi/	toy
/w/	water	/o/	call
/y/	yawn	/u/	herd
/z/	zebra	/a/	hair
/ch/	chalk	/a/	star
/sh/	shallow		
/th/	thorn		
/wh/	whale		
/zh/	leisure		
/ng/	sing		

Mastery of all forty-four phonemes in oral and written communication is a strong predictor of future reading readiness.

Syllables are defined as one complete unit of pronunciation. Every syllable contains only one vowel sound that can be created by one or more than one vowel. Syllables can consist of vowels that stand alone or combine with consonants. The study of syllables and how they operate help children to become stronger readers and will aid in spelling proficiency. Educators will often introduce new words that contain more than one syllable by teaching children to say and write the syllable. Segmenting a word into its individual syllables, as well as blending syllables into whole words, allows children to see the key parts of a word and provides opportunities for them to strengthen their reading skills.

In the English language, there are six different types of syllables, four of which are syllable combinations:

- Closed syllables: syllables that end in a consonant, as in *bat*, or *it*
- Open syllables: syllables that end with a vowel, as in *he*, *she*, or *we*
- Vowel-consonant-e syllables: syllables that end with a silent *e*, as in *ate*, *wife*, or *mile*

13

- Vowel team syllables: syllables that work in combination to create a new sound, as in *mouth* or *join*
- Consonant + le syllables: syllables that contain a consonant and end with an *le*, as in *turtle*
- R-Controlled syllables: syllables that contain a vowel followed by the letter *r*, where the *r* controls how the vowel is pronounced, as in *bird* or *word*

A word is broken up into two pieces: onset and rime. The **onset** is the initial phonological unit of any word, whether it is a consonant or a consonant cluster. The **rime** is the string of letters that follows the onset, usually consisting of a vowel or variant vowels along with one or more consonants. Many words in the English language share common features or patterns. These **word families** often share the same letter combinations that form the same or similar sounds. When introducing word families, educators will often initiate activities involving onsets and rimes to help children accurately recognize, read, and spell simple words. The study of onsets and rimes has shown to improve a child's overall literacy skills, increase reading fluency, and strengthen spelling skills. The following word family list illustrates words separated into onset and rime:

Word	Onset	Rime
sun	s	Un
sunny	s	unny
sunshine	s	unshine

Blending, Segmenting, Substituting, and Deleting Phonemes, Syllables, Onsets, and Rimes

The ability to break apart a word into its individual phonemes is referred to as **segmenting**. Segmenting words can greatly aid in a child's ability to recognize, read, and spell an entire word. In literacy instruction, **blending** is when the reader connects segmented parts to create an entire word. Segmenting and blending practice work together like pieces of a puzzle to help children practice newly-acquired vocabulary. Educators can approach segmenting and blending using a multi-sensory approach. For example, a child can manipulate letter blocks to build words and pull them apart. An educator may even ask the child to listen to the word being said and ask him or her to find the letter blocks that build each phoneme, one at a time:

/m/ /u/ /g/

/b/ /a/ /t/

/r/ /u/ /n/

Once children are able to blend and segment phonemes, they are ready for the more complex skill of blending and segmenting syllables, onsets, and rimes. Using the same multi-sensory approach, children may practice blending the syllables of familiar words on a word wall, using letter blocks, paper and pencil, or sounding them out loud. Once they blend the words together, students can then practice segmenting those same words, studying their individual syllables, letters, and sounds. Educators may again read a word out loud and ask children to write or build the first syllable, followed by the next, and so on. The very same practice can be used to identify the onset. Children can work on writing and/or

14

building this sound followed by the word's rime. Word families and rhyming words are ideal for this type of exercise so that children can more readily see the parts of each word. Using words that rhyme can turn this exercise into a fun and engaging activity.

Once children have demonstrated the ability to independently blend and segment phonemes, syllables, onsets, and rimes, educators may present a more challenging exercise that involves **substitutions** and **deletions**. As these are more complex skills, children will likely benefit from repeated practice and modeling. Using word families and words that rhyme when teaching this skill will make the activity more enjoyable, and it will also greatly aid in a child's overall comprehension.

Substitution and Deletion Using Onset and Rime				
Word	**Onset Deletion**	**Rime Deletion**	**Onset Substitution**	**Rime Substitution**
run	un	r	fun	rat
bun	un	b	gun	bat
sun	un	s	nun	sat

Substitution and Deletion Using Phonemes		
Word	**Phoneme Substitution**	**Phoneme Deletion**
sit	sat	si
bit	bat	bi
hit	hat	hi

Substitution and Deletion Using Syllables		
Word	**Syllable Substitution**	**Syllable Deletion**
cement	lament or, cedar	ce
moment	statement, or motive	mo
basement	movement, or baseball	base

Phonics and Word Analysis

Importance of Phonics and Word Analysis

Phonics is the study of sound-letter relationships in alphabetic writing systems, such as the English language, and it is paramount to a child's future ability to read and write. Phonics helps children recognize and identify letter symbols and translate these symbols into their corresponding sound units, phonemes. The study of phonics concerns itself with the **Alphabetic Principle**—the systematic relationships that exist between letters and sounds—as well as with **Phonemic Awareness**—the understanding that letters correspond with distinct sounds and that there are specific rules governing the placement of letters in the English language.

As children become more familiar with recognizing the names and shapes of each letter, called **graphemes**, they begin to verbally practice their corresponding sounds—the phonemes. Although this sounds straightforward, it can pose significant challenges to both the children and teachers.

For example, when children learn that the letter *y* is pronounced /wigh/, but that it can make other various sounds, including /ee/, /i/, and /igh/—depending on letter placement—it may take repeated practice in order for children to pronounce and read this one letter accurately. Some examples would be the words, *happy, gym,* and *cry.* Although each word contains the same vowel, *y,* the placement of the *y* in each word differs, which affects the letter's pronunciation.

For this reason, there is an ongoing debate in literacy circles regarding the appropriate instructional approach for teaching phonics. Should educators teach letter shapes with their corresponding names or letter shapes with their corresponding sound or sounds? Is it possible to combine instruction to include shapes, names, and sounds, or should each of these skills be taught in isolation with a cumulative approach—shape, sound/s, and name? Some experts believe that when children are introduced to letter names and shapes in isolation of their corresponding sounds, children can become quickly confused, which can delay reading acquisition. Therefore, the answer to what approach to take lies with a keen understanding of a student's background knowledge in English and each child's specific needs. In order to create effective phonics instruction and help students strengthen literacy development, it is strongly suggested that educators are sensitive and aware of these unique challenges to English language acquisition.

It is widely accepted that letter-sound relationships are best taught systematically, introducing one relationship at a time and gradually increasing in complexity. Effective instruction in the initial stages of phonics awareness involves explicit introduction of the most important and the most frequently used letter-sound relationships. For instance, short vowels should be introduced and practiced ahead of long vowels, and lower-case letters should be introduced ahead of upper case as they occur the most often. Letters that frequently appear in simple words, such as /a/, /m/, and /t/ would be logical starting points.

The following guide offers an introduction of phonics instruction:

Introduction	Examples
Initial consonants	s, t, m, n, p
Short vowel and consonant	-it, -in, -at, -an
Consonant blends	-st, -bl, -dr
Digraphs	-th, -ph, -sh, -ch
Long vowels	ear, eat, oar, oat
Final (silent) e	site, mine, lane
Variant vowels and diphthongs	-au, -oo, -ow, -ou, -oi
Silent letters and inflectional endings	-kn, -gn, -wr, es, s

Effective phonics instruction begins with focusing on the overall literacy experiences of the students and connecting these experiences to further their literacy development. Best practices in teaching will work to establish a student's prior phonics knowledge, if there is any at all. Educators can differentiate their instruction based on their students' unique needs and background knowledge of phonics. Creating phonics activities that ensure students are actively engaged and motivated is key to overall success in literacy development.

Once children have mastered the relationship that exists between the names, shapes, sounds of letters, and letter combinations, educators may begin a more implicit instructional approach by incorporating the children's current phonics awareness with simple basal readers that focus on basic monosyllabic words. Grouping monosyllabic words according to their initial sounds continues to be an effective approach to instruction as the students advance in their understanding and application of phonics. When educators combine or further this practice with that of identifying the names of the initial letters in the words, children are likely to have more success with overall literacy development. A word wall with simple consonant-vowel-consonant words in alphabetical order acts as a visual reference to help strengthen a child's literacy development:

Word Wall

A	B	C
add	ball	car
age	bean	clean
ant	black	cub

At this stage, educators begin laying the foundation for reading readiness. Children begin listening to others read and start to recognize familiar sounds within the words being read. They independently practice sounding out words and will soon learn how to independently segment, blend, and manipulate the individual sounds in each newly acquired word.

When a child demonstrates phonological awareness and a clear understanding of how phonics works, they are ready to further their literacy development with **word analysis**. Word analysis is an effective study that helps students acquire new vocabulary. **Morphemes** are when words are broken down into their smallest units of meaning. Each morpheme within words carry specific meanings, therefore adding to children's understanding of entire words. When children begin to recognize key morphemes—especially prefixes and suffixes—they are beginning to demonstrate word analysis skills, which is a critical foundation in literacy development.

Word analysis helps children to read and comprehend complex reading materials, including informational texts. It is essential for vocabulary development. Word analysis skills also help children clarify the meaning of unknown words, figurative language, word relationships, and nuances in word meaning with the use of context clues.

Some effective instructional strategies to teach word analysis skills include **Universal Design for Learning** (UDL), studying words according to a subject theme, using diagrams and graphic organizers, and pre-teaching and reviewing new vocabulary on a regular basis. UDL involves the modeling of how to analyze new words by breaking them down into their individual morphemes and studying each morpheme separately. Once each morpheme in a given word has been identified and defined, students put the morphemes back together in order to understand the word in its entirety. The following is a word analysis study of the word *astronaut*:

Word	Morpheme 1	Morpheme 2	Word Meaning
astronaut	astro—Greek origin, roughly translates to anything relating to the stars and outer space	naut—Greek origin, roughly translates to "sailor"	a sailor of outer space

Studying words according to a shared theme is another effective word analysis strategy. For instance, when studying mathematics, educators may focus on words that contain the same prefix, such as *kilometer*, *kilogram*, and *kilowatt*. Common suffixes in science include *microscope*, *telescope*, and *macroscope*.

Diagrams and graphic organizers provide students with visual clues to contrast and compare word meanings. From organizational charts and mind maps to Venn diagrams and more, visual aids help students readily see and analyze the similarities and differences in various word meanings.

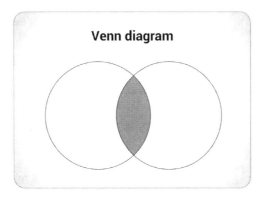

Venn diagram

With the introduction to new topics of discussion or a new theme to any subject area, it is likely that there will also be an introduction to new, unfamiliar words. Both educators and students will benefit from a formal introduction to these new words prior to the lesson. Pre-teaching new vocabulary increases vocabulary acquisition and allows children to become comfortable and familiar with new terms ahead of the lesson. Pre-teaching new vocabulary has also been shown to reduce unnecessary stress and time that would otherwise be taken to stop lessons in order to explain unfamiliar words.

Letter-Sound Correspondences

When children begin to learn the various letter-sound correspondences, their phonemic awareness begins to overlap with their awareness of orthography and reading. One of the widely accepted strategies to employ when introducing children to letter-sound correspondences is to begin with those correspondences that occur the most frequently in simple English words. In an effort to help build confidence in young learners, educators are encouraged to introduce only a few letter-sound combinations at a time and provide ample opportunities for practice and review before introducing new combinations. Although there is no formally established order for the introduction of letter-sound correspondences, educators are encouraged to consider the following general guidelines. However, they should also keep in mind the needs, experiences, and current literacy levels of the students. The following is intended as a general guide only:

1. a	6. n	11. g	16. l	21. x
2. m	7. c	12. h	17. e	22. v
3. t	8. d	13. i	18. r	23. y
4. p	9. u	14. f	19. w	24. z
5. o	10. s	15. b	20. k	25. j
				26. q

As a generally accepted rule, short vowels should be introduced ahead of long vowels, and lowercase letters should be mastered before the introduction of their upper-case counterparts.

Spelling conventions in the English language are primarily concerned with three areas: mechanics, usage, and sentence formation.

Mechanics

For primary students who are just beginning to master the alphabetic principle, educators should first concentrate on proper letter formation, the spelling of high-frequency words and sight words and offer classroom discussions to promote the sharing of ideas. When children begin to write in sentences to share their thoughts and feelings in print, educators may consider the introduction of an author's chair, in which students read their writing out loud to their classmates.

Although the phonetic spelling or invented spelling that primary students employ in these early stages may not be the conventional spelling of certain words, it allows primary students to practice the art and flow of writing. It works to build their confidence in the writing process. This is not the time for educators to correct spelling, punctuation, or capitalization errors as young learners may quickly lose interest in writing and may lose self-confidence.

One strategy to employ early on to help students with proper spelling is to ensure there is an easily accessible and updated word wall that employs high-frequency words and sight words. Students should be encouraged to refer to the word wall while they write.

Usage

Usage concerns itself with word order, verb tense, and subject-verb agreement among other areas. As primary children often have a basic knowledge of how to use oral language effectively in order to communicate, this area of spelling conventions may require less initial attention than the mechanics of spelling. During read-aloud and shared reading activities, educators may wish to point out punctuation marks found in print, model how to read these punctuation marks, and periodically discuss their importance in the reading and writing process.

When children begin to engage in writing exercises, educators may wish to prompt self-editing skills by asking if each sentence begins with a capital and ends with a period, question mark, or exclamation point.

Sentence Formation

Verbs, nouns, adverbs, and adjectives all play significant roles in the writing process. However, for primary students, these concepts are fairly complex to understand. One instruction approach that may prove effective is to categorize a number of simple verbs, nouns, adverbs, and adjectives on index cards by color coordination. Educators can then ask one child to choose a noun card and another student to choose a verb card. The children can then face the class and read their words starting with the noun and then the verb. The students can even try reading the verb first followed by the noun. A class discussion can follow, analyzing whether or not the sentences made sense and what words might need to be added to give the sentence more meaning.

Distinguishing High-Frequency Sight Words from Decodable Words

Beginning readers enter primary school years with many challenges involving literacy development. Tackling the alphabetic principle and phonemic awareness helps children to recognize that specific sounds are usually comprised of specific letters, or a combination thereof, and that each letter or combination of letters carries a specific sound. However, these young readers are also faced with the challenge of sight word mastery. **Sight words** do not necessarily follow the alphabetic principle and appear quite often in primary reading material. Some sight words are decodable, but many are not, which requires the additional challenge of memorizing correct spelling. Some of these non-decodable

20

sight words include words such as *who, the, he, does,* and so on. There are approximately one hundred sight words that appear throughout primary texts.

The goal for primary teachers is to help emergent readers to recognize these sight words automatically, in order to help strengthen reading fluency. One effective instructional approach is to provide children daily opportunities to practice sight words in meaningful contexts and to establish a clearly visible, large print word wall that children can freely access throughout the day. **Dr. Edward William Dolch** was a well-known and respected children's author and professor who, in the late 1940s, published a list of sight words he believed appeared most frequently in children's literature for grades kindergarten through second grade.

Now known as the **Dolch Word List**, these sight words are still widely used in primary classrooms throughout the United States. Organized by grade and frequency, the Dolch Word List consists of 220 words in total, with the first one hundred known as the "Dolch 100 List." **Dr. Edward Fry**, a university professor, author, and expert in the field of reading, published another commonly used high-frequency word list approximately a decade later. Although similar in many ways to the Dolch List, the Fry Word List primarily focuses on sight words that appear most frequently in reading material for third to ninth grade. Other high-frequency word lists now exist, but the Dolch and Fry word lists are still widely used in today's elementary classrooms. The debate, however, is whether to teach high-frequency sight words in isolation or as part of the integrated phonics program.

Unlike many sight words, **decodable words** follow the rules of phonics and are spelled phonetically. They are spelled precisely the way they sound—as in words like *dad* and *sit*. When a child has mastered their phonics skills, these decodable words can also be easily mastered with continued opportunities to practice reading. Activities involving segmenting and blending decodable words also help to strengthen a child's decoding skills. Some educators will find that it is beneficial to integrate lessons involving decodable words and high-frequency sight words, while others may see a need to keep these lessons separate until children have demonstrated mastery or near mastery of phonemic awareness. Some activities that encourage the memorization of sight words and strengthen decoding skills involve the use of flash cards, phonemic awareness games, air writing, and card games, such as *Bingo* and *Go Fish*.

Both Dolch and Fry word lists are organized according to frequency and grade level. It is widely accepted that educators follow a cumulative approach to reading instruction, introducing high-frequency sight words that are also phonetically decodable. Should words appear in the lesson that are not phonetically decodable, educators may wish to use this as an opportunity to evaluate the children's phonemic awareness skills and determine whether or not students are ready for lessons that integrate non-decodable sight words. For instance, an educator might challenge a student to study the parts of the non-decodable sight word by asking whether or not there are parts of the word that are phonetically decodable and parts that are not. This approach gives students the opportunity for guided word study and acts as a bridge between phonemic awareness skills and sight word memorization.

Determining what lists of words to introduce to students varies greatly and depends on an initial and ongoing spelling assessment of each child to determine their current spelling and reading levels. Effective instructional approaches also involve the intentional selection of words that demonstrate a specific spelling pattern, followed by multiple opportunities to read, spell, segment, and blend these word families. Students will benefit the greatest with ongoing formative and summative assessments of their decoding skills as well as their ability to apply their word knowledge to and memorize non-decodable sight words.

With the reinforcement of high-frequency word walls, daily opportunities to read, write, and engage in meaningful word games and activities, children will gradually begin to develop their reading and spelling skills and learn to become more fluent and capable readers.

Roots and Affixes

The study of **morphology** concerns itself with the segmenting of words into their respective affixes and roots. It also involves the studying of a word's origins. Children who study morphology expand their vocabulary knowledge as they begin to understand that words are connected by similar spelling patterns and similar meaning.

Affixes are parts of words that are bound to the root word either in front, following, or in the middle of the word itself. Since affixes do contain meanings, they are considered morphemes, but they are unable to exist without being attached to the root words.

Prefixes are affixes that appear in front of root words, such as *dis*appear or *un*able. Generally speaking, prefixes denote negation, direction, or intensity. For example, in the word *disappear*, the prefix *dis* means *not* or *opposite of*. Therefore, *disappear* can be defined as *to not appear*. In the word *inject*, the prefix *in* refers to *inside* or *towards*, and in the word *excruciate*, the *ex* works as an intensifier referring to the pain as being *thorough*.

Suffixes are affixes that appear at the end of root words. There are two types of suffixes: inflectional and derivational. **Inflectional suffixes** can change the number, tense, or degree of the word, such as the word *loud* changing to *loudest*. **Derivational suffixes** change the parts of speech of a given word. The word *slow* functions as an adjective in this sentence: *The slow turtle walks*. When the suffix *-ly* is added to the end of *slow*, the part of speech is automatically changed to an adverb: *The turtle walks slowly*.

Infixes—affixes that appear in the middle of a word—are the least conventional and most rare of all affixes. An example is the word *cupful*. This consists of the root word, *cup*, and the suffix, *-ful*. In order to pluralize this word, an *s* would need to be strategically placed directly following the letter *p* to form *cupsful*. The *s* acts as an infix, inserting itself and its meaning in the middle of the word.

Root words are referred to as free morphemes that can stand alone and carry an independent meaning without the need of any affixes. Some examples are the root words *help*, *kind*, and *shy*, which clearly hold their own meaning, but can also be attached to affixes, as in *helpful*, *unkind*, and *shyness*.

When students are invited to become word detectives, the study of root words and affixes is of prime importance. There are several instructional approaches to the study of root words and affixes, including a multi-sensory guided approach in which children can physically pull apart the affixes to be left with the root word and then manipulate the root word by playing with a variety of suffixes and prefixes. The following table begins with the original word containing both a prefix and suffix. The word is pulled

apart into its individual components—root, prefix, and suffix. Then, it is given a new prefix and suffix to form a new word, carrying a completely new meaning:

Original Word	Root Word	Prefix	Suffix	New Prefix	New Suffix	New Word
inactive	act	in	ive	de	ate	deactivate
disbelieving	believe	dis	ing	un	able	unbelievable
unbearable	bear	un	able	for	ing	forbearing

Effective instruction for root, prefix, and suffix study should involve the active exploration of words, with ample opportunity for children to read the words in meaningful context. Typically, a formal study of root words and affixes is introduced by the 4th grade, but it may be introduced earlier, depending on the students' understanding of basic phonics and spelling patterns. It is important for educators to keep in mind that new vocabulary terms, verb forms, plurals, and compound words may present a challenge for some students.

A formal study of root words, prefixes, and suffixes strengthens a child's knowledge of word meanings, expands vocabulary knowledge, and advances their understanding and application of various spelling patterns. Children will learn more about how affixes affect the spelling of the root word and can completely alter its meaning, which ultimately strengthens their ability to read, write, and spell accurately and effectively. As children become familiar with various affixes, they will begin to decipher the meaning of unfamiliar words that share the same affixes and roots.

Stages of Language Acquisition

There are many factors that influence a child's language acquisition. A child's physical age, level of maturity, home and school experiences, general attitudes toward learning, and home languages are just

some of the many influences on a child's literacy development. However, a child's **language acquisition** progresses through the following generalized stages:

Stage	Examples	Age
Preproduction	does not verbalize/ nods yes and no	zero to six months
Early production	one to two word responses	six to twelve months
Speech emergence	produces simple sentences	one to three years
Intermediate fluency	simple to more complex sentences	three to five years
Advanced fluency	near native level of speech	five to seven years

While this applies to language acquisition in one's home language, the very same stages apply to English language learners (ELLs). Since effective communication in any given language requires much more than a mere collection of vocabulary words that one can accurately translate, paying particular attention to each stage in language acquisition is imperative. In addition to vocabulary knowledge, language acquisition involves the study and gradual mastery of intonation, a language's dialects—if applicable—and the various nuances in a language regarding word use, expression, and cultural contexts. With time, effort, patience, and effective instructional approaches, both students and educators will begin to see progress in language acquisition.

Second language acquisition does not happen overnight. When educators take the time to study each stage and implement a variety of effective instructional approaches, progress and transition from one stage to the next will undoubtedly be less cumbersome and more consistent. In the early stages of language acquisition, children are often silently observing their new language environment. At these early stages, listening comprehension should be emphasized with the use of read aloud, music, and visual aids. Educators should be mindful of their vocabulary usage by consciously choosing to speak slowly and to use shorter, less complex vocabulary. Modeling during these beginning stages is also very effective. If the educator has instructed the class to open a book for instance, they can open a book as a visual guide. If it is time to line up, the educator can verbally state the instruction and then walk to the door to begin the line.

During the **pre-production stage**, educators and classmates may assist ELLs by restating words or sentences that were uttered incorrectly, instead of pointing out errors. When modeling the correct language usage instead of pointing out errors, learners may be less intimidated to practice their new language.

As students progress into the **early production stage**, they will benefit from exercises that challenge them to produce simple words and sentences with the assistance of visual cues. The educator should ask students to point to various pictures or symbols and produce words or sentences to describe the images they see. At the early production and speech emergent stages, ELL students are now ready to answer more diverse questions as they begin to develop a more complex vocabulary. Working in

24

heterogeneous pairs and small groups with native speakers will help ELL students develop a more advanced vocabulary.

At the **beginning and intermediate fluency stages**, ELLs may be asked questions that require more advanced cognitive skills. Asking for opinions on a certain subject or requiring students to brainstorm and find ways to explain a given phenomenon are other ways to strengthen language proficiency and increase vocabulary.

When a child reaches the **advanced fluency stage**, he or she will be confident in social and academic language environments. This is an opportune time to introduce and/or increase their awareness of idiomatic expressions and language nuances.

World-Class Instructional Design and Assessment (WIDA) is a consortium of various departments of education throughout the United States that design and implement proficiency standards and assessments for English and Spanish language learners. Primarily focusing on listening, speaking, reading, and writing, WIDA has designed and implemented English language development standards and offers professional development for educators, as well as educational research on instructional best practices.

The five English language proficiency standards according to WIDA are as follows:

English Language Proficiency Standards—WIDA
1. Within a school environment, ELL students require communication skills for both social and instructional purposes.
2. Effective communication involving information, ideas, and concepts is necessary for ELL students to be academically successful in the area of Language Arts.
3. Effective communication involving information, ideas, and concepts is necessary for ELL students to be academically successful in the area of Mathematics.
4. Effective communication involving information, ideas, and concepts is necessary for ELL students to be academically successful in the area of Science.
5. Effective communication involving information, ideas, and concepts is necessary for ELL students to be academically successful in the area of Social Studies.

According to WIDA, mastering the understanding, interpretation, and application of the four language domains—listening, speaking, reading, and writing—is essential for language proficiency. Listening requires ELL students to be able to process, understand, interpret, and evaluate spoken language. Speaking proficiently allows ELL students to communicate their thoughts, opinions, and desires orally in a variety of situations and for a variety of audiences. The ability to read fluently involves the processing, understanding, interpreting, and evaluating of written language with a high level of accuracy, and writing proficiency allows ELL students to engage actively in written communication across a multitude of disciplines and for a variety of purposes.

Since language acquisition involves the ELL students, their families, their classmates, educators, principals and administrators, as well as test and curriculum developers, WIDA strives to ensure that the English Language Proficiency Standards reflect both the social and academic areas of language development.

Common Phonics and Word-Recognition Approaches for ELLs

Phonics instruction and word-recognition exercises involve a number of skills, including print awareness, alphabetic knowledge, phonological and phonemic awareness, the alphabetic principle, decoding, the memorization of high-frequency words, and reading practice. As language acquisition is highly complex, there seems to be some debate in the educational field regarding the best instructional approaches for ELL students. Some educators argue that phonics should be taught in isolation and not in context, while others stress the need for a more integrated approach. When faced with what instructional approach to implement, educators who take the time to learn about each child's home language, literacy development, and exposure to the English language will be in the best position to decide on whether a student would benefit from an isolated phonics approach or one that is more integrated.

The following are the three different instructional approaches to phonics:

Synthetic Phonics

Educators implement an explicit approach, teaching individual letter-sound correspondence and helping students to blend letters into words.

Embedded Phonics

Educators teach letter-sound correspondence during the reading of a text.

Analogy-Based Phonics

Educators teach students to use parts of words that they already know to help decode words that they don't know. **Analogy-Based phonics** involves the use of story time, tutoring in small groups, and various language-based activities. Educators share various books and stories with decodable words with students and provide opportunities for children to spell words and write simple sentences with letter-sound correspondence.

The amount of time allotted for phonics and word recognition instruction varies greatly from classroom to classroom. Educators who pay particular attention to the ages of the ELL students and their current level of English language proficiency will be in the best position to decide on an appropriate approach to phonics instruction. However, generally speaking, younger ELL students in the primary grades will benefit from explicit practice with phonemic awareness and the alphabetic principle. Exposure to print awareness will increase in complexity as the child progresses in their understanding and application of phonemic awareness skills. Decoding practice, exposure to word families, spelling patterns, onsets and rimes, and structural analysis—including affixes and root words—should be gradually introduced as the child becomes more able to read simple words and simple sentences independently.

When working with ELL students, educators must be sensitive to each child's background knowledge, home language, and experiences involving literacy. In order to become proficient in the English language, ELL students must develop a clear understanding of the relationship that exists between letters and sounds in the English alphabetic system, and this may be in complete opposition to the rules they have already mastered in their home language. For example, some languages use the same or similar alphabet as English, but some of the phonemes might be pronounced differently, causing

26

confusion. The English language may also have letter combinations that do not exist in the student's home language, adding to the confusion. Complicating matters even further, some languages do not utilize an alphabetic writing system, such as the Chinese language, which is **logographic**, relying on characters that represent a word or idea, rather than relying on letters to produce a sound. Therefore, a formal study of phonics is critical to ELL students' literacy development.

One approach for educators to consider is the highlighting of similarities and differences between the student's home language and that of English. For instance, many **cognates** exist between English and Spanish that can act as a bridge to strengthen a child's English language acquisition. Since cognates share the same or similar meaning, spelling, and pronunciation in two different languages, ELL students can quickly add these new words to their vocabulary inventory. Some effective approaches to integrate cognate awareness into lessons include read aloud, student reading activities, and word sorts.

As children read aloud, ELL students are encouraged to raise their hand when they think they've come across a cognate. The reading can momentarily stop while the class discusses the similarities and differences between the pronunciation, spelling, and meaning of each cognate. During a student reading activity, ELL students are encouraged to locate two, three, or more cognates they encounter in their reading and to write them down in their notebooks. These cognates can then be added to the classroom's word wall and further explored. In pairs, students can be given a number of cards with Spanish and English cognates. The students then sort the cards appropriately and discuss their meaning, spelling, and pronunciation. These approaches not only build vocabulary knowledge and confidence for ELL students by actively including their home language in lessons, but they also help to build social bonds in the classroom. Since language acquisition is also very social, when children develop and strengthen positive friendships within and outside the classroom, language acquisition will likewise develop and strengthen. Other effective classroom approaches to help ELL students with phonics and word-recognition skills include the use of word walls and posters throughout the classroom.

As children progress with their phonemic awareness skills, educators may introduce word studies by helping children classify and sort words according to the same or similar spelling patterns. Word study increases children's vocabulary and acts as a bridge from reading to writing as children transfer their newly-acquired words into print. Introducing children to a variety of reading and writing genres and formats will also help to strengthen their reading and writing skills. For example, learning to follow recipes provides children with opportunities to read and engage in hands-on activities to demonstrate their understanding by following a recipe's steps. Personal journals continue to be an effective practice that stimulates creative writing and helps children to express their thoughts and opinions in writing, without worrying too much about grammar, spelling, and punctuation. Personal journals can also be used as reading practice as children pick and choose sections to read aloud to the entire class, in pairs, or in small groups.

It is important for educators to recognize that some written languages are not read from left to right, and some are not even read from top to bottom. Therefore, it is also important for educators to teach print conventions and book awareness, including the direction in which the words in books are read and how to handle and hold a book. These lessons can be taught explicitly or may be simply modeled by the educator during shared reading time.

Syllabication Patterns

A **syllable** is defined as a unit of spoken language that consists of one vowel sound that may or may not be surrounded by consonants. Syllables form part of a word or may even form the entire word itself.

There are both **monosyllabic words** that contain only one syllable, such as the word *sit*, and **polysyllabic words** containing more than one syllable, such as the words *today* or *yesterday*.

Generally speaking, there are six **syllable-spelling conventions** in the English language. Learning these conventions will help to strengthen a student's spelling and pronunciation accuracy. The study of syllables also helps to strengthen their literacy development in many other ways. It allows students to chunk longer words into manageable parts, instead of simply guessing at the word or ignoring it altogether, thereby strengthening reading fluency. Children who are exposed to syllable study will also have a better understanding of short and long vowel sounds, diphthongs and consonant blends, r-controlled vowels, prefixes, suffixes, and compound words.

Syllabication Patterns	Examples
1. Open—Syllables that stand by themselves, or that have a single vowel at the end of the syllable	he, my, apron
2. Closed—Syllables containing short vowel sounds that are spelled with a single vowel letter and end with one or more consonants	am, dog, rabbit
3. Vowel + Consonant + e—Syllables that contain one-letter long vowels, followed by one consonant and a silent e	base, nose, shake
4. Vowel Team—Comprised of two, three, or four letters that create long vowels, short vowels, or diphthongs	thieves, boil, suit
5. R-Controlled—Vowels that are followed by the letter r, with the r controlling the vowel's pronunciation	bird, word, herd
6. Consonant + le—Found exclusively at the end of words in which the vowel or combination of vowels is followed by a consonant, and the consonant is followed by an le	tackle, title, puzzle

Syllabication is the process of separating a word into its individual syllables. It is an essential skill in learning how to accurately pronounce words. Syllabication involves learning various syllabic patterns and rules in the English language; therefore, repeated practice is best. Since every syllable has one vowel sound, the study of syllabication must be preceded with a firm understanding of how English vowel sounds operate. For instance, short vowels sound much different than long vowels, and some vowel sounds are formed using more than one vowel, as in the sounds *ou* or *oi*.

To help children master syllabication, educators will need to introduce and practice the various **syllabication patterns**:

Rule/Pattern	Examples
1. Monosyllabic words are never divided.	house, car, eat, run
2. Compound words are divided between the individual words that make up the compound word.	base/ment; up/stairs; out/side
3. Divide a word directly after its prefix.	pre/view; de/text; un/seen
4. Divide a word directly before its suffix.	ac/tion; trac/tion
5. If a word ends in a consonant + le, divide directly before this consonant.	tur/tle; cy/cle
6. If there are two consonants directly in the middle of the word, divide between the consonants.	rab/bit; sis/ter
7. Keep consonant blends and digraphs together.	fast/ing; bun/ches
8. In words containing the letter combinations ck or the letter x, syllables are generally divided directly before the ck or the x.	ni/ckel; ta/xi
9. If a single consonant is positioned between two vowels and the first vowel is short, divide directly after the consonant.	nev/er; hab/it
10. If a single consonant is positioned between two vowels and the first vowel is long, divide directly before the consonant.	ma/jor; lat/er;
11. When two vowels in a word make individual sounds, divide between the two vowels.	ri/ot; li/on

While these syllabication patterns are helpful in order to gain a clearer understanding of how syllables operate, they are by no means exhaustive. As children gradually strengthen their awareness and application of syllables, educators may introduce them to more complex patterns.

Fluency

<u>Fluency Related Terms</u>

Reading fluency has been traditionally defined as a student's ability to read accurately, quickly, and with appropriate expression. This definition only accounts for reading aloud, however, so it has been expanded to include silent reading. **Silent reading fluency** is the ability to read more than one word at a time without having to vocalize one's reading. If readers are able to derive the accurate meaning and message from a reading passage without involving too much labor of reading mechanics, they are said to be reading with fluency. Reading fluency is automatic, with less attention and effort spent on decoding, allowing the reader to concentrate fully on reading comprehension. When a reader reaches the fluency stage, reading becomes much more of an enjoyable activity.

Generally, fluent readers do not require the need to reread passages for understanding and have developed a fairly large inventory of sight-word vocabulary. Fluent readers are usually able to self-correct and employ a number of reading strategies. Signs that a child is having difficulty with reading fluency include reading slowly, focusing on only one word at a time, needing to reread the passage for understanding, and stopping often to decipher and decode unknown words. There are three main focus areas that relate to reading fluency: accuracy, rate, and prosody. When children read accurately with steady, consistent speed and appropriate expression, reading comprehension is likely to strengthen.

Areas of Fluency:

Accuracy

Accuracy refers to the frequency of pronunciation errors a student might make when reading. When students make frequent pronunciation errors while reading, guess at the pronunciation of unknown words, or ignore words altogether, they are showing signs of **dysfluency**. Reading accurately requires the reader to read words correctly with minimal to no errors. When errors do occur, readers who read with accuracy are generally able to self-correct and continue reading without interrupting the flow of the reading.

Rate

Rate refers to a student's ability to recognize words automatically without having to spend any time on decoding them. This manifests in their ability to read texts at a steady and consistent rate. Both accurate reading and reading at a consistent rate greatly strengthen a reader's overall reading comprehension.

Prosody

Prosody refers to appropriate expression when reading—showing emotions, such as excitement, panic, or sorrow that accurately matches the intended emotions of the text. Readers may be able to read texts with accuracy and at a steady and consistent rate, but if they are unable to vocalize any expression in their reading or if the expression used does not match the intended expression of the text, their overall comprehension will be negatively affected. Readers who engage in an emotional or personal level with the text will experience greater reading comprehension and fluency.

<u>Impact of Fluency on Comprehension</u>

In reading fluency, specific instructional strategies will help strengthen a student's ability to read text accurately, at a consistent rate, and with appropriate expression, and they will also help to strengthen reading comprehension. When students experience dysfluency in their reading, their overall

comprehension will be negatively impacted. With an inability to make connections in their reading, children are unable to grasp the meaning in the text. When children are more focused on decoding individual words rather than on comprehending the text's message, much of their cognitive efforts are spent on deciphering the pronunciation of individual words, with little left to devote to comprehension of the text itself.

As children's reading fluency strengthens, they are able to interact on a much higher level with a variety of texts. It is important for educators to recognize that reading fluency acts as a bridge to reading comprehension and that time devoted to the individual components of reading fluency benefits a child's overall reading comprehension.

Literature and Informational Texts

Key Ideas and Details

Moral and/or Theme of a Literary Text

Literary analysis of a fictional text involves the study of character development, setting, mood, plot, point(s) of view, figurative language, and other literary elements. The **study of informational text** involves nonfictional elements, such as the author's purpose, major ideas or concepts, and more. All of these individual components in a text often interrelate and form the text's overall theme or message. Some common universal themes found in literature include disappointment, courage, overcoming obstacles, loneliness, and good triumphing over evil. In informational texts, the themes or messages vary greatly, but they usually involve subjects that pertain to the natural or social world. When children reach the stage in their literacy development that allows them to begin literary analysis exercises, they are beginning to take their reading comprehension beyond the surface details to arrive at an even deeper understanding of the text by studying these individual themes and messages.

When first introducing literary analysis, it is important for educators to select texts that carry themes children can relate to. Educators are encouraged to consider themes that depict similar life experiences or interests. Although many themes in texts are universal in nature, the younger the students are, the more important it is to choose texts that have themes with which they can identify, that appeal to their interests, and that inspire discussion and debate. As children progress and strengthen their literacy skills, they will be able to apply these skills to a wider variety of themes.

An ideal strategy to introduce literary analysis is to hold class discussions at the beginning and ending of texts, as well as periodically throughout the reading of a given text. Educators may prompt these class discussions with key questions that help students to make connections between the events and characters in a fictional text and the students' life experiences. Class discussions allow children to hear multiple ideas, which works to strengthen overall comprehension and build an appreciation of alternate points of view. These key questions also prompt children to consider their own feelings as they read the text, helping them to connect on a personal or emotional level, which strengthens overall comprehension. Class discussions should also challenge children a little further by asking them to explain why they feel a certain way about a message in the text. Once children have had ample opportunity to practice and master this skill, the next step is to teach children how to support their thoughts, feelings, and ideas by finding textual evidence that supports their views.

Learning to find supporting evidence within a text is a very complex skill that can initially cause some confusion and frustration. One strategy to employ that may assist children in learning how to find key

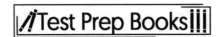

information is the introduction of graphic organizers. The following is an example of a graphic organizer that is split into three sections:

Student Answer	Text Evidence (quotation and page number)	Explanation

Searching for supportive evidence involves more than merely finding a quotation. The above graphic organizer guides students to connect the specific quotation(s) to their interpretation and further provides students the opportunity to explain, in their own words, how their answers and the quotations are connected. Forming credible and logical responses to questions and supporting those responses with appropriate quotations from the text are considered very advanced literary skills, which take students to a much deeper understanding of literature.

Central Idea of an Informational Text

Informational texts appear in several forms, including expository texts, persuasive texts, procedural texts, and nonfiction narratives. As early as kindergarten, children are encouraged to read a variety of informational texts. Placing an assortment of texts in the classroom library, hanging posters on classroom walls that promote a wide range of topics, and providing children with ample time and opportunity to explore any number of subjects, has shown to have a very positive impact on reading comprehension and overall literacy skill development. Informational texts provide children an opportunity to explore and develop a better understanding of the world around them. Taking this one step further, by allowing children to choose topics of informational texts that pique their curiosity, educators help children develop a more positive attitude toward reading and writing. All informational texts typically include five key elements:

- The author's purpose(s)
- A major idea(s)
- Supporting detail(s)
- Visual or graphic aid(s)
- Vocabulary

Author's Purpose

Expository texts typically share information about a given topic. **Persuasive texts** aim to convince readers to think or act a certain way, and **procedural texts** generally give step-by-step or "how-to" instructions in a given discipline. **Nonfiction narratives** tell a true story, perhaps to inspire, educate, bring awareness to a subject, or simply chronicle an important historical event. In order for students to become independent readers and draw their own conclusions about what they read, it is critical that they learn to discern the **author's purpose**.

One obvious approach to teaching children how to reveal an author's purpose is to simply ask children why they think the author wrote this information. These types of open-ended class discussions allow children to express their ideas, explore theories, and consider what others have to say on the subject.

32

Educators can record various answers and then ask the children to return to the text as detectives, looking for clues that support each theory.

Another approach to uncovering the author's purpose is for students to take a closer look at the written structure of the text and the vocabulary usage. For example, is the text's structure written in chronological order, simply listing events as they occurred? Does the text open up with a problem that is then resolved? Is the author using cause/effect or compare/contrast vocabulary? Learning about the structure of the text gives great insight into the author's purpose.

When children develop reading fluency, they are able to read a text with minimal to no errors, with consistent speed, and with appropriate expression, and they learn to connect with what they are reading on a personal level. As children read through an informational text, educators may ask how the students are feeling. Did they begin feeling one way and end up feeling another by the end of the text? When children examine their own personal feelings with regard to what they have read, they will be in a better position to explore the author's purpose.

Once children have had several opportunities to explore the author's purpose using a variety of informational texts, prompting them to write their own informational texts will help them to develop and strengthen a better understanding about writing with a purpose. Perhaps they can write a procedural text that lists the steps in how to ride a bike, or they can write a persuasive paper to try to convince their teacher that extra free time during the school day stimulates learning.

Learning to identify an author's purpose connects children with their reading on a deeper level. Instead of believing everything they read, they will begin to understand that there are many reasons why authors write, and they will further understand that they possess the ability to draw their own conclusions and make their own decisions on any given topic.

Major Idea

Some children struggle with identifying the main idea of an informational text. Identifying the **main idea** of a text requires that the reader understand the entire text and is able to zero in on one central, overarching idea amongst a sea of other information. The ability to sort through the entire text and arrive at the main idea takes a considerable amount of effort and practice for beginning readers.

Before prompting students to locate the main idea of a given text or passage, educators must first explain what the main idea actually is. Here are some guidelines, tips, and tricks to follow that will help children identify the main idea:

Identifying the Main Idea
The most important part of the text
Text title and pictures may reveal clues
Opening sentences and final sentences may reveal clues
Key vocabulary words that are repeatedly used may reveal clues

Providing students with simple lists of related vocabulary may be a logical starting point when teaching how to recognize a main idea. For instance, on a large chart, educators may list several fruits, vegetables, snacks, and meals, and then prompt the children to explain what they have in common. This also works well with a set of images, pictures, or photographs that all represent the same idea. After repeated practice, children will begin to strengthen their ability to center in on the main idea that connects all the elements on the list.

Once children begin to identify and demonstrate a clear understanding of the main idea in simple lists, educators may wish to introduce simple texts that gradually increase in complexity.

Supporting Details

Supporting details of texts are defined as those elements of a text that help readers make sense of the main idea. They either qualitatively and/or quantitatively describe the main idea, strengthening the reader's understanding.

Using simple sentences is an effective instructional approach when introducing children to supporting details. Educators may write out a simple sentence and ask the children to underline the main idea, as in the sentence that follows:

The *apple* is hard, red, and juicy.

Once the main idea, the apple, is accurately identified, educators can now ask children to locate words that describe or support this main idea and highlight/circle each supporting word:

The *apple* is hard, red, and juicy.

Simple sentence exercises will gradually become simple paragraphs and, eventually, full texts in which children are challenged with the task of locating the main idea and the supporting details. Children must learn to differentiate between trivial and supporting details by evaluating whether or not the detail in question further quantifies or qualifies the main idea. If the detail does neither, it is likely not important enough to be considered a supporting detail and can be left alone.

Graphic organizers can also be a helpful tool when working with main ideas and supporting details. There are many graphic organizers that help students to organize their analysis into clear and visible representations. The following are examples of graphic organizers that are commonly used when teaching the main idea and supporting details.

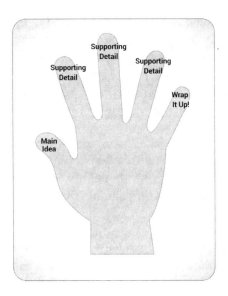

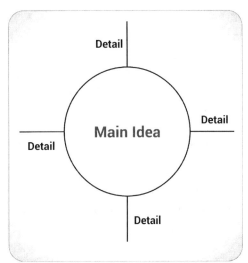

Children who demonstrate the ability to accurately identify a text's main idea and supporting details can further strengthen these skills by attempting to write their own texts with a main idea and supporting details. Likewise, graphic organizers can be used as tools that help children to organize their thoughts and ideas before they begin this writing process.

Visual or Graphic Aids

Authors of informational texts will often employ the use of visual or graphic aids in strategic locations throughout the text in order to strengthen the reader's understanding of the topic at hand. **Visual aids** can provide an overview of key information, illustrate relationships among important text elements, and summarize the main idea. Visual aids are generally colorful and catch students' attention; they help to simplify what could be potentially complicated information. There are a multitude of visual aids that are frequently used in informational texts, including models, graphs, charts, tables, maps, drawings,

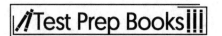

photographs, and time lines. Some visual aids also involve a side bar, which defines key vocabulary necessary to understand the topic.

In most instances, children merely need to look at the visual aid to make an instant connection. The implementation of graphic aids in writing reduces instructional time and strengthens comprehension. During read alouds and guided reading sessions, educators may wish to model how to extract meaning from visual aids by connecting the graphic to specific elements in the text. Before reading begins, educators have students skim through the pages to find the visual aids and predict what the text may be about based on the text's graphics. Therefore, visual aids may often help students to identify the text's main idea.

The time it requires to read and process the written text is considerably longer than the time it takes to derive meaning from the graph. Helping students to identify and derive meaning from visual aids will help to strengthen their reading comprehension skills and overall literacy development.

Vocabulary
Vocabulary used throughout informational texts is generally quite different than vocabulary found in fictional print. For this reason, it is imperative that educators help children strengthen and increase their vocabulary inventory so that they can eventually become successful at reading and understanding informational text.

For instance, educators can point out **signal words** throughout texts to help children more readily and accurately identify the author's purpose. Authors employ specific vocabulary that spotlight their intent. For instance, if authors wish to list examples to support a main idea, they may use vocabulary such as *for example*, *such as*, or *as illustrated*. When displaying the chronological order of events, authors may use *first*, *lastly*, *before*, and *finally*. Some common compare and contrast vocabulary words include *but*, *same as*, *similar to*, *as opposed to*, and *however*. There are several key phrases that signal cause and effect relationships, including *because of*, *as a result of*, and *in order to*.

By using word walls and personal dictionaries, sorting vocabulary words according to theme, introducing text maps, and teaching children to become familiar with sidebars and glossaries in informational texts, educators will help expand their students' vocabularies and strengthen their abilities to read and comprehend informational texts successfully.

Inferences Made from Text Supported with Appropriate Evidence
Although related to predictions and the finding of factual information, **inferences** refer to the ability to make logical assumptions based on contextual clues. People of all ages make inferences about the world around them on a daily basis but may not be aware of what they are doing. Even young children may infer that it is likely cold outside if they wake up and their bedroom is chilly or the floor is cold. While being driven somewhere on the highway and a child notices a person at the side of the road with a parked car, that child will likely infer that the individual is having car problems and is awaiting some assistance. Therefore, the challenge for educators is not necessarily teaching children how to infer, but rather demonstrating how this skill they already use can be transferred into the study of various texts.

One effective introductory strategy may be to set up scenarios within the classroom and challenge the children to infer what is happening. For instance, the educator may arrive at school pretending to have a cold without saying anything. By placing a personal box of tissues on the desk along with a nasal spray and frequently sneezing, the teacher is challenging the students to infer that he or she not feeling well.

36

Once the children begin to understand that making inferences is indeed similar to detective work by collecting key evidence, the educator can now introduce more inanimate objects like photographs, pictures, or diagrams void of explanatory language. The children's task would be to study the visual aids to try to infer what the subject is about. Educators can assist the children initially by asking questions aloud, modeling how to arrive at a logical inference. For example, the teacher might hold up a picture of a school in which all children are gathered in the playground and grouped according to their classes. Upon closer examination, the children might spot a fire truck parked at the side of the road and may infer that the school had a fire drill or an actual fire.

As the children progress in their ability to infer based on picture clues, it is time to transfer their new skill to texts. Educators may wish to begin with inference challenges in which students are prompted to write short stories about specific events—without directly mentioning the event. For instance, if a child is interested in swimming, they may write about the ideal temperature of the water, backstroke, freestyle, full laps, and so on without ever mentioning the word *swimming*. Other children in the class will then be prompted to read the short story and infer what the text is about. The children must examine the clues in the text, make an inference, and support the inference with evidence from the text:

> In the second paragraph, it says that the water was relatively warm, so it was easy to finish a full lap. This must mean that the person was swimming in the water.

The more initial practice children receive before moving into more complicated texts, the most success they will have in making accurate inferences and, in turn, the more fun they will have acting as text detectives.

Summarization of Information

While summarizing information from a text seems like an easy concept at first, it is more complex than one thinks. **Summarizing** involves the ability to extract the most important elements in writing, to eliminate elements of lesser importance, to reorganize the information, to rewrite information in one's own words, and, finally, to condense the writing into a significantly smaller text than that of the original. Thus, learning to summarize consists of many individual skills that all converge and overlap. There are two forms of summary: (1) summaries that aid the reader in understanding the text and (2) summaries that aid others in their understanding of the text.

Summarizing should be explicitly taught beginning in the primary school years with continual reinforcement and gradual introduction to more complex texts as students progress. In order to summarize effectively, children need to demonstrate the following abilities:

- Text comprehension
- Identification of main idea
- Elimination of inconsequential information
- Ability to condense
- Ability to paraphrase
- Ability to organize writing in a logical order

Personal Summaries

Educators are encouraged to first assist children in summarizing texts as a means to strengthen personal comprehension. For instance, when children are able to identify a text's main idea, state that idea in

their own words, and back up that main idea with supporting evidence, they are learning to summarize, and their comprehension undoubtedly strengthens.

Summarizing for oneself is also an invaluable tool for studying and memorizing, which children will use throughout their academic careers. When students summarize for themselves, the goal is to strengthen overall comprehension of the text, arrive at the author's point of view, and isolate the main idea. Since the summary is intended to be only for the student, there is no need to pay particular attention to spelling, grammar, or sentence structure. Students are learning to make personal notes for the purpose of comprehension strengthening and, possibly, memorization for upcoming tests.

Summaries for Others

Once children have demonstrated a clear ability to summarize a variety of texts for their own understanding, educators may begin to introduce them to the skill of **summarizing for others**. This involves a more complex approach to summarization. Now that students have ownership of the given text, they inherit the challenge of explaining the text's meaning to an audience. In addition to extracting the main idea, eliminating unimportant text elements, reorganizing and condensing the text, and paraphrasing, students must now pay close attention to the summary's length, the mechanics of writing, and the audience. For example, are students writing to classmates to help them better understand the text? Are they writing the summary for their teacher, in an effort to demonstrate their ability to summarize? Since this type of summarization involves a polished finish, children must also employ proofreading and revision skills.

Educators who are introducing summarization for the first time should focus on less complex texts that involve familiar subject matter, and the texts should be well organized, with titles, possible subtitles, and easily identifiable main ideas. Allowing children to refer to the text as often as possible while learning to summarize is also an important teaching strategy. Children at the early stages of summarizing should not be expected to have memorized and clearly understood what they have read. Sometimes children need to reread the same text several times before beginning a summarization. By explicitly teaching children how to recognize signaling devices, educators help them summarize and isolate a text's main idea. Some signaling devices may be found in an introductory or summary statement or specific words or phrases that have been placed in italics, bold print, or are underlined.

The more advanced students become with summarizing texts, the greater their comprehension and ability to apply what they learn will be.

Analysis of Characters, Setting, and Plot

When it comes to the study of stories or literary texts, it is important for children to gain an understanding and awareness of text structures and organization. All literary texts involve various story elements, including characters, setting, and plot. Being able to identify these elements and show their relationship to one another is key to understanding the story.

Characters

A story may have both main characters and minor characters, but all characters, regardless of their level of importance, work to provide the story's framework. Therefore, it is important for students to be able to list and describe all characters that appear throughout a story.

The following questions aid students in this endeavor:

- What do the characters look like?
- How old are they?
- What language or languages do they speak?
- What is their personality like?
- How do they relate to one another?
- Do you know of anyone like this in your life?
- Have you come across a similar character in another story?
- How are they the same?
- How are they different?

The more children identify with various characters in a story, the stronger their overall comprehension will be.

Setting

The setting is very important to a story's framework and may even change periodically as the story unfolds. Understanding when and where a story takes place helps children visualize the various scenes and relate the story's setting to a time and place in their own lives or to a similar setting in another story. Questions that aid in the understanding of setting include the following:

- What country are the characters in?
- What year or era is it?
- Does the story take place in a suburban, urban, or rural location?
- Is the setting similar or different to where you live?
- How is it similar?
- How is it different?
- Does this setting remind you of a setting in another story?
- How are the settings similar? How are they different?
- Would you like to visit this setting? Give clear reasons why or why not.

A story's setting is critical to helping children make sense of a character's language, dress, attitude, relationships with others, and character traits. Building a stronger understanding of each character within a story will assist young readers in their overall text comprehension.

Plot

Generally speaking, the **plot** of a literary text involves the introduction of a key problem at the beginning of a story, which is usually resolved by the story's end. Educators build a bridge that strengthens students' story comprehension by helping children connect the story's plot to a familiar scenario in another story or by helping children connect the problem in the text with a problem they have encountered in their own lives. For instance, the plot can involve dealing with a bully, battling the

elements of nature, or learning to overcome personal obstacles. The more children are able to relate to a story's plot, the greater their comprehension and appreciation of the story will be.

When teaching children about the various elements in literary texts, the use of visual aids, such as story maps, can provide invaluable assistance to a child's overall understanding:

STORY MAP

Name:_____ Book Title:_____

Characters

Setting

Problem

Solution

Relationships Among Individuals, Events, Ideas, and Concepts

Very rarely are elements within an informational text unrelated. Part of an author's responsibility is to connect a series of elements from the beginning of a text right through to the text's summary. The more successful an author is at relating the various elements, the easier the text is to comprehend. Educators may assist children in analyzing these relationships by first explaining that a relationship involves two or more characters, events, ideas, or concepts that have an impact on one another. There are key words or phrases in informational texts that may signal this relationship, including *therefore*, *because*, and *as a result*. Identifying these relationships will help children to comprehend the text's message, the author's point of view, and may even help to explain elements in the text that occur later on.

Features and Structures of Text

Structural Elements of Literature

There are several **genres** of literature including poetry, fiction, nonfiction, and drama. Each genre has specific structural elements. Although there are elements that are shared by more than one genre of literature—such as character, setting, and plot, which are found in both fiction and drama—there are also clear differences in other genres. For instance, the structural elements in nonfiction often consist of cause and effect, sequence, or compare and contrast.

Structural Elements in Drama

A drama, or a play, is almost exclusively delivered as a dialogue and performed live on a stage. The audience observes the story unfolding as opposed to reading it in a book. The actors or actresses in a

drama follow written scripts, which are divided into acts and further divided into scenes. The only written material generally given to the audience is the cast of characters, which lists all the character names with an accompanying brief description of their role in the play. This is the only written assistance the audience will receive, so it is imperative that they read through the cast of characters and then carefully follow each scene in the play to understand the story.

Stage directions in a drama refer to the directions or descriptions given to the actors in each scene. They are often presented in italics or in parentheses to differentiate the directions from the dialogue. Stage directions may tell actors where to stand, what direction to face, how to deliver lines, and whom to address.

Structural Elements in Poetry

Generally speaking, **rhyme** goes hand and hand with the study of poetry and involves the repetition of similar sounds. Sounds may rhyme at the end of every two or more lines, referred to as **end rhyme**, or may even rhyme in the middle of a line, referred to as **internal rhyme**. The following offers examples of both:

I went to school *today*,

Not wanting to leave the *house*,

And as I passed the *day*,

I remained as quiet as a *mouse*.

In rain or *shine*, your house or *mine*,

We'll meet *again*, my dear *friend*.

The first poem demonstrates the example of end rhyme. The second example demonstrates internal rhyme.

Meter is the rhythm of the syllables within a poem. Each type of meter equates to the specific number of syllables and, possibly, the way the syllables are stressed. There are five basic meters: *iambic*, *trochaic*, *spondaic*, *anapestic*, and *dactylic*. Recognizing the meter within poetry helps readers understand the poem's rhythm and guides the reader in how to read the poem with the poet's intended emphasis. Meter also helps poets develop and maintain the structural elements within the poem.

Text Features

In informational texts, certain features function to organize the information and also act as guides, which in turn supports the reader's overall comprehension.

Headings include titles and subtitles that identify the topic of study. They also help a reader to arrive at a clearer understanding with regard to the text's main idea. Headings can help readers make connections between background knowledge and the information in the text, which helps them make predictions before reading begins. Headings also strategically organize a text into sections so that one section at a time can be studied.

Sidebars are found in the right or left margins of informational texts. Sidebars often provide the reader with helpful, additional information about a topic that appears on that particular page. By providing examples, interesting facts, definitions of key terms, and more, sidebars emphasize important information that the author wishes to convey.

Hyperlinks are in-text links to specific website addresses that a reader may wish to visit to further their understanding of a specific topic. When authors insert hyperlinks into modern informational texts, they create a text that is more interactive, providing further resources for children to strengthen their comprehension of a given topic.

Organizational Structures of Informational Text

Organizational structures found in informational text differ from structures found in fictional works. It is important for educators to teach children how to recognize and use these structures to further their knowledge of a given discipline.

Cause and Effect

When an author unfolds a **cause-and-effect relationship** within a given text, readers must work to uncover what has happened and why. Sometimes, the cause and effect relationships are melancholy, but they can also be positive. Before asking children to locate the cause and effect relationship within an informational text, it is first important to define the terms and then provide key examples with which the students can relate. For instance, a teacher might ask the children what happens after it rains. There will undoubtedly be a variety of responses, from *the ground becomes wet* to *the flowers grow*. From this simple exercise, educators can begin to model the relationship between the *cause*—why something happened—and the *effect*—what happened as a result.

Showing pictures, photographs, and other visual aids, and gradually encouraging children to use key graphic organizers will also help them solidify their understanding of cause and effect relationships. Teaching key vocabulary words that specifically relate to cause and effect are also effective instructional strategies. Educators should ensure that these vocabulary lists become incorporated into classroom word walls and personal dictionaries.

Problem and Solution

Similar to cause and effect, the **problem and solution pairing** that often appears in informational texts refers to something that has happened that requires a solution. Although both cause and effect and problem and solution involve related events that occur before and after, cause and effect situations do not necessarily seek a solution to a problem. They seek to identify the impact one or more events have

42

had on something else. In contrast, the problem and solution pairing in a text refers specifically to a problem that has occurred that requires a solution:

Problem	Solution
Scraped a knee	Wash, dry, and apply bandage
Unprepared for upcoming test	Practice and study
No clean clothes to wear	Do some laundry

Contribution of Structural Elements to the Development of Literary Text
The structure or framework of any given literary text is significant to the overall quality of the work. **Structure** refers to how the literary work is organized by introduction, expansion of ideas, and interrelation of all the literary elements. If the structure of a literary work is inexistent or poorly developed, the individual elements will appear chaotic, which makes the challenge of comprehending and enjoying the literary work difficult.

Although there are different elements in literature depending on the genre, generally an author will introduce and develop characters, establish a theme, provide a plot, develop the setting, establish the conflict, and present the resolution. These elements must be strategically introduced and developed, paying particular attention to placement within the story's framework. A properly developed structure connects these individual elements so that the reader develops a deep appreciation for the story and arrives at a clear understanding of the author's message. A well-organized structure also helps readers connect background knowledge to new information as it unfolds, and it helps strengthen a reader's retention of important literary details.

Point of View

Author's Point of View
An important reading comprehension skill is identifying the points of view that exist in literature. In literature, the **point of view** refers to the lens through which readers see the story unfold. Readers are often able to understand the overall story more fully when they are able to determine from what angle the story is told. The point of view of the main character or of several characters helps readers interpret character traits, understand how each character relates to the other, and determine how those relationships relate to the story's plot. In literary works, there are four main points of view to consider:

- Third person omniscient
- Third person limited
- First person
- Objective

Third Person Omniscient
Third person refers to the use of the third person singular in writing, as in *he* or *she*. **Omniscient** is defined as all knowing. When the author employs **third person omniscient**, each character's perspective is revealed, allowing readers to consider and evaluate the points of view of all the characters within a story.

43

Third Person Limited

The difference between this point of view and third person omniscient is that **third person limited** only reveals the thoughts, feelings, and opinions of one character, thereby creating a more intimate impact on the reader and leaving the points of view of other characters a mystery to uncover. This point of view also employs the third person singular forms of *he* and *she* when speaking directly about a specific character.

First Person

Regarded in literature as the most intimate approach to point of view development, **first person** is written in first person singular, using the pronouns *I, me,* and *my*. When authors apply this point of view, readers develop a clear understanding of the true inner feelings of that particular character and strengthen their understanding of how the character relates to the story's plot and to supporting characters.

Objective

The **objective point of view** reveals no feelings, thoughts, or opinions of characters; it remains void of emotional elements. This point of view focuses on facts, data, historical information, and quotations for reference. Authors who write in the objective point of view write as outside observers describing events as they happen.

To help students develop an awareness of which point of view the author is applying, educators may wish to model the thinking process required to locate point of view evidence. Beginning with a character analysis in chart form, for instance, educators and students can list all characters within a story and discuss the character traits of each one. Teachers may then ask the students why they believe characters possess certain traits and may then facilitate this understanding by referring to specific areas in the story that reveal these traits.

Using various excerpts from familiar stories to develop a character analysis also helps children strengthen point of view awareness. Working as literary detectives, students should be prompted to look for the pronouns *he, she,* and *I* and then focus on the key vocabulary surrounding these pronouns.

The ability to identify key vocabulary used to evoke emotion, as well as vocabulary used to simply state facts, will be very useful in developing a student's ability to recognize points of view within a story:

Emotional Vocabulary	Factual Vocabulary
Fear: apprehensive, cautious, concerned, hesitant, uneasy, watchful	Facts: details, knowledge, information, proof
Anger: annoyed, cranky, critical, frustrated, irritated	Data: as evidenced by statistics
Sadness: disappointed, heartbroken, gloomy, depressed	Historical Information: recorded, an account of
Happy: amused, inspired, joyful, pleased	Quotations: testimony, witness, verification, affidavit

Identifying Similarities and Differences

By taking character analysis one step further, students can compare and contrast the similarities and differences between the points of view of two or more characters in a story. The ability to consider various points of view helps children strengthen their critical thinking skills in both academic and social settings.

Educators should consider using a variety of instructional approaches when comparing and contrasting points of view. One strategy educators can implement is a class debate or partner debate. A debate brings students to center stage as they learn to defend the point of view of various characters within a story while listening to classmates defend the points of view of other characters. Friendly debating has been proven to strengthen a student's ability to reason, apply logic, communicate with self-expression, listen to others, and organize thoughts and opinions. Debating also helps children develop an appreciation for opposing points of view and, therefore, works to build stronger bonds both in and out of the classroom. By taking on the point of view of a character in a story with the added responsibility of defending that point of view with evidence, students broaden their own thought processes and challenge the world around them in more depth.

Visual aids are another strategy that educators use when comparing and contrasting points of views, especially when examining characters in stories. Venn diagrams are especially effective as they provide a clear space for unique perspectives, with a common overlapping section for similarities. There are several visual aids available for use in the classroom depending on the age and ability of the students. From the earliest of primary education to the upper level high school grades, visual aids continue to be a

powerful instructional tool. The visual aid below demonstrates opposing and shared characteristics of characters:

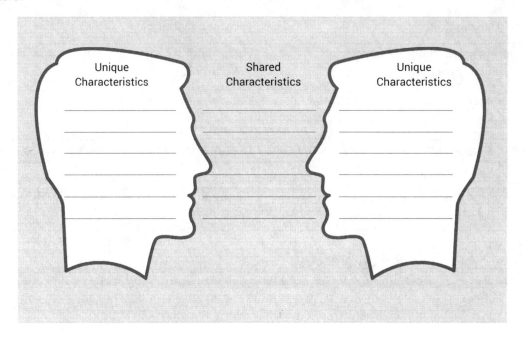

Impact of Point of View on Overall Structure of Texts

Generally speaking, the majority of informational texts involves a third person point of view. It is widely accepted in academic circles that the use of any other point of view for information purposes is likely to have a negative impact on the text's quality. Third person point of view removes the author from associating the information with a personal bias and allows the reader to evaluate the content objectively. Third person point of view strengthens informational texts with the use of validated research, facts, and statistics from a variety of credible sources. The more factual evidence that is presented in informational texts along with the employment of third person points of view, the more likely the work will be accepted as a reliable informational resource.

However, there are informational texts that use first person points of view for specific reasons. For example, informational texts that are written with the intent to persuade a reader's feelings, opinions, actions, or reactions will often use first person points of view. By giving the text a personal connection, authors can stress their expertise and experience with regard to the event or topic, which may carry weight on how readers relate to the information. Although this may prove to be advantageous to the author, the drawbacks to employing first person point of view include the potential for readers to evaluate the work as too subjective and, therefore, unreliable.

In contrast, first person point of view is the most frequently used in literary works. With the narrator playing an active role in the story's plot, readers are able to connect on an intimate level with the thoughts, emotions, and opinions being expressed.

It is important for authors to consider the main intent of their writing. The messages they wish to convey, the emotions they may wish to evoke, and the overall impressions they want to leave on their readers should ultimately guide authors toward the employment of a specific point of view.

Written, Visual, and Oral Information

Students in a modern classroom have access to a wide variety of instructional resources. From teacher-led instruction and classroom activities, traditional textbooks, encyclopedias, nonfiction magazines, and customized classroom libraries to desktop computers, iPads, tablets, laptops, online tutorials, and smart boards, there is a plethora of information waiting to be discovered. Learning how to integrate traditional written, visual, and oral information to other information provided on a multimedia platform can prove challenging, but it is well worth the effort. Since the vast majority of children from the primary school years and older are well equipped at using a variety of technology-based resources, educators who integrate technology in the classroom will likely succeed in helping children to progress both academically and socially. The classroom is as much a social setting as it is academic, and as society changes, so must the instructional approaches.

Time management is one of the initial tasks facing educators when setting up their academic year. Educators are responsible for teaching a wide range of subjects, specific domains within each subject, and numbers of skills within each domain. Designing long-range plans that take all of this into account and forming a framework for the academic year is the most logical starting point.

From this framework, educators can determine how to teach each discipline with an effective, time management approach. Taking the number of students, the possible varying academic and social levels, socioeconomic differences, and language barriers into account, teachers can begin to develop differentiated instructional approaches that cater to all the needs in the classroom. It is at this stage that both traditional resources and technology must find a way to complement each other in the classroom.

For instance, one effective approach is to instruct children to ensure that every research project involves a minimum of two textbook sources as well as a minimum of two technology-based sources. When introducing new topics or reinforcing a lesson, educators are still highly encouraged to use visual aids in the classroom, including word walls, personal dictionaries, and classroom labels. Modeling the effective use of hand-held books, reference guides, and magazines also provides children the opportunity to see how valuable written information continues to be in the world of education.

In order for children to experience a well rounded, quality education, instructional days should be divided between effective, quality instruction, independent exploration and learning, and positive social interaction. Since the needs of children vary in each classroom, as well as their academic and social levels, each educator's decision on how to divide instructional time will also vary. However, having access to technology is paramount in every classroom and at every grade level.

Technology in the classroom helps children to become more actively engaged and encourages independent learning with the use of student-centered, project-based activities. From virtual math tools to collaborative class blogs, there are many ways for students to effectively engage in technology in the classroom.

Although technology plays an important role in the modern classroom, it is still important for educators to guide children, helping them use the technology in an effective, efficient, and responsible manner. Teaching children about cyber-bullying, copyright, plagiarism, and digital footprints will inevitably strengthen their ability to responsibly and safely conduct themselves online.

Educators also use technology for lesson planning, assessments, and evaluation. With a number of online programs available, educators are able to provide students, colleagues, administration, and

parents with effective feedback and to develop and evaluate high-quality formative and summative assessments in an efficient manner.

By combining the use of technology along with teacher-centered instruction and traditional textbooks, educators will undoubtedly help to create a classroom with children who are actively engaged throughout the instructional day.

Visual and Oral Elements

Depending on home life and first language acquisition, children generally enter the primary years of school with a basic foundation of oral development as well as basic phonemic awareness. It is imperative to a young child's continued success in language development that educators provide students with language-rich lessons and activities throughout the instructional day.

Visual Instructional Techniques

Studies continue to show a strong correlation between language development and the use of visual aids. From the primary years of education through the post-secondary years, the use of visual aids as a way to enhance reading comprehension has proven to be very effective. In the primary grades, picture books provide students with visual cues that help them to decode unknown words and strengthen reading comprehension. Visual aids support and clarify meaning, helping to make the learning and reading process more enjoyable and more interactive. When educators engage the students in a **picture walk**, skimming through picture books prior to reading, children become more motivated to read. Even reluctant readers, struggling readers, and English language learners are more apt to pick up a picture book and attempt to read it from cover to cover, enjoying the graphics and using them as powerful clues to the text's overall meaning.

Graphic novels are also becoming a popular addition to classroom and school libraries. With a structural approach that is similar to comic books, graphic novels have a strong appeal to children in the middle school years, teen years, and beyond. The visual images within graphic novels help children to make immediate connections to a story's plot and help them to understand potentially more challenging information.

As a universal learning tool, visual aids help all learners to comprehend the meaning behind the words and strengthen their ability to retain information over a longer period of time.

Oral Instructional Techniques

When children are just learning to read, they benefit greatly from shared reading and oral reading experiences. Having a teacher or a classmate read a book aloud helps emergent readers connect their phonemic awareness skills to a growing understanding and application of print awareness. This will begin to form the foundation for more advanced reading skills in later years.

Oral reading also helps children strengthen their use of vocabulary and advances their vocabulary inventory. Educators and more advanced readers who model oral reading fluency—including rate, accuracy, and prosody—demonstrate to young readers that the process of reading is highly interactive and meaningful. Educators who spend significant time engaging in classroom discussions and asking and answering questions help children develop social interaction skills, listening comprehension skills, and oral communication skills. When early and intensive instruction focuses on oral language development, educators set the groundwork for future reading success.

48

Oral and Visual Instructional Techniques

Multimedia presentations, such as PowerPoint or SlideShare, have been traditionally most effective at the higher education levels. However, as young children are more and more exposed to a world of technology, educators at the primary years are beginning to employ multimedia presentations in the classroom.

If carefully planned out, multimedia presentations can be used to enhance comprehension on virtually any subject. Using powerful graphic imagery that is directly relevant to the topic—coupled with effective textual language or audio—has been particularly effective in a growing number of classrooms.

Presenting students with the challenge of creating their own multimedia presentations can also be very rewarding for educators and students alike. Either independently, in pairs, or in groups, children take the learning process into their own hands with the opportunity to demonstrate the knowledge of a given subject by employing relevant written text and graphics.

Literary Text vs. Oral, Staged, or Filmed Version

Many of today's students are saturated with technology in their everyday lives. With the availability of iPads, iPods, personal computers, and smartphones, children as early as the primary grades are not only familiar with modern technology, but are becoming confident practitioners. Therefore, integrating technology in the classroom is a logical approach to helping children connect to the learning process and engage their interests.

With regard to English language arts instruction, technology can provide ample opportunities for educators to help strengthen students' critical thinking, oral communication, and reading comprehension skills. Since stories have always been used as a way of helping to explain the world and our place in it, they continue to be an integral part of any society's culture. The same story can be shared orally, in print, in film, or onstage, and each presentation provides similarities and differences with regard to the story's elements and to the audience's interpretation. By allowing children to compare and contrast various presentations of the same story, educators can increase students' motivation in English language arts.

Isolated scenes in films or documentaries can be used to begin a class discussion on a given topic. Children can openly discuss what version of the story they prefer and why. They can become detectives as they watch carefully for differences and similarities in the story's elements, such as setting, plot, and character traits. Educators who introduce a film or stage version of a literary work may wish to introduce the elements of lighting, dialogue, or special effects and begin a class discussion about how these elements, much like points of view, setting, and details in print, are critical to a film's structure.

If used strategically and with careful planning, the use of films, plays, and various technology-based story presentations can prove to be a very effective instructional strategy that strengthens students' understanding and appreciation of English language arts.

Multiple Literary Texts Addressing the Same Theme

Introducing children to similar themes in literature can increase motivation in even the most reluctant of readers. Consider the classic children's book, *Alice in Wonderland*, written in the 1800s. Children are introduced to a young girl who is bored with her life and discovers a secret rabbit hole that brings her on an exciting adventure in another world. The excitement quickly turns into danger, as she must work to escape the evil queen and find her way back to safety. Near the end of the book, readers discover that

Alice was dreaming all along. In the novel, *Coraline*, written in 2002, the heroine, Coraline, feels neglected by her parents and discovers a secret door to a hidden world. Much like Alice, Coraline finds herself in peril and must try to outwit her evil "other" mother in order to return safely to her real parents.

Comparing two literary texts that address the same theme, whether it is human versus nature, human versus human, or rags to riches, can prove to be effective instructional techniques that prompt student engagement and strengthen interest in English language arts.

Multiple Informational Texts Addressing the Same Topic

When children begin to research topics for formal reports, presentations, or class discussions, it is important that they understand that information on a given topic comes in a variety of formats and is presented by many different points of view. Information is shared orally and is found in print and digital format, but not all information on a given topic will be the same. For instance, one text about the benefits of farming may completely contradict information found in another text. There are many reasons why contradictory information is found in two or more texts. Helping students consider the time period the text was written, the level of expertise of the author or authors, cultural points of view, and the author's purpose will help them strengthen their critical thinking skills, as well as allow them to develop their own interpretation and evaluation of the information.

It is critical that children begin to critique information found in print, online, or told orally and not just accept it at face value. These critical thinking skills will serve them well throughout their academic career and will play a fundamental role in their personal and professional lives.

Visual and Multimedia Elements in Texts

Graphic novels, comic books, fiction, folktales, myths, and poetry often include visual elements in the story. Whether in the form of drawings, photographs, sound, video, or animation, these visual elements work to strengthen the reader's understanding and interpretation of the author's message, help to set the story's tone, bring characters into perspective, and, possibly, provide the reader with alternative interpretations of the story's main idea.

Hyperlinks included in informational texts provide the reader with additional sources of information that strengthen the author's message. Informational texts also employ the use of graphs, charts, diagrams, and maps, which either work to compare and contrast information, demonstrate cause and effect, show a chronological timeline of events, or display trends and patterns.

Effective instructional approaches to literature incorporate how to interpret the various forms of visual and multimedia elements that exist within literary and informational texts. Modeling how to use visuals in various texts appropriately will undoubtedly strengthen students' reading comprehension and critical thinking skills.

Key Claims from Textual Evidence

The ability to identify significant claims made by the author and to support those claims with evidence found within the text is integral to the development of reading comprehension and critical thinking skills. Educators need to introduce key vocabulary words and phrases that authors use when stating and supporting claims. These vocabulary terms can be added to an ever-changing and expanding classroom word wall, incorporated into personal dictionaries and captured on charts to further classroom

discussions. Once children begin to identify key words and phrases as indicators of claims and claim evidence, they are ready to begin the more complex task of evaluating these claims.

When children can identify claims and show evidence that supports the claims, educators may wish to initiate a class discussion on whether or not these claims are valid. For instance, prompting a reader's background knowledge and personal experiences on the topic, examining the author's expertise on the subject, weighing any possible cultural or personal bias the author may have, and comparing/contrasting the author's claims to claims made by other authors on the same subject will help children develop objectivity as they read.

Role of Text Complexity

Three Factors to Measure Text Complexity

When selecting texts for classroom reading, it is imperative that educators consider the three main factors that measure complexity, which will best predict a child's reading success:

- Quantitative
- Qualitative
- Reader and Task

Quantitative Measures

When selecting appropriate texts for the classroom, educators must consider the type of words used throughout the text, the number of syllables in each word, and the spelling complexity of the words. Educators should also ask themselves if the text mostly contains decodable words or a significant number of sight word vocabulary. Finally, educators must consider the sentence lengths and the level of sentence complexity, since sentences vary from simple sentences to compound-complex sentences that may be too advanced for the students.

Qualitative Measures

Educators must also take into account the age of their students and whether or not certain subject matter is developmentally appropriate. Do children tend to have background knowledge in the subject, or will they likely be introduced to this new concept for the first time? Does the author employ the use of explicit language or figurative language that may be too complicated for younger students?

Reader and Task Measures

When educators go a step further in their planning by considering the needs of their individual students, reading instruction will be more effective. Educators should consider the various reader variables, such as level of reading fluency, the number of reluctant and motivated readers in the classroom, and the degree of home support for reading.

All of these factors combined significantly impact the type of text, level of complexity, and the tasks children are given to accomplish based on the reading material. Considering these factors that measure text complexity will also assist educators in choosing instruction and evaluation techniques.

Features of Text-Leveling Systems

For educators to apply quantitative, qualitative, and reader and task considerations effectively prior to introducing a reading assignment, they must first understand and consider the unique features of text-leveling systems:

Quantitative Measures	Qualitative Measures	Student and Task Measures
Total word count	Text predictability	Reluctant readers
Number of different words	Text structure and organization	Motivated readers
Number of high-frequency words	Visual aid, illustration, and info graphics support	Struggling readers
Number of low-frequency words	Background knowledge of topic	Interest in topic
Sentence length	Single theme vs. multi-themes	
Sentence complexity		

Writing, Speaking, and Listening

Writing

Characteristics of Common Types of Writing

Distinguishing Among Common Types of Writing
Opinion/Argument

In the early elementary grades, students begin to write simple **opinion pieces**. Acting as a precursor to argumentative and persuasive writing, opinion pieces allow children to express how they feel on a certain subject based on preferences, express their likes and dislikes, and use personal knowledge, without relying too heavily on supporting evidence. Educators encourage children to write opinion pieces with the use of personal journals as well as reflective pieces, connecting personal experiences to various stories read.

In the middle school years and beyond, students will be required to write **argumentative** or **persuasive** pieces of writing, which must involve logical and relevant proof for a claim or an assertion. Regarded as a more sophisticated form of writing, argumentative or persuasive writing works to change the point of view of the readers or ignite a call-to-action response. This form of writing does not shy away from contradicting points of view but, instead, brings them to light and then works to disprove or discredit each opposing claim. Some examples of argumentative or persuasive writing include essays, reviews, and letters to the editor.

Informative

Informative writing comes in many forms, including directions, instructions, definitions, summaries, and more. **Informative writing** works to relay information and advance the reader's understanding of a given subject. If written correctly, the vast majority of informative writing is written in third person to distance the author from relying on personal bias, instead relying on objective facts, historical evidence, and statistics.

Narrative

Almost always written in first person, **narratives** include autobiographies, memoirs, and even fictional stories. Their general purpose is to entertain readers, but some also focus on morals, values, or life lessons. By conveying personal experiences on a given subject or by opening up one's life to the audience, narrative writers create a more intimate connection with readers.

Purpose, Key Components, and Subgenres of Writing
Effective writing, whether for the purpose of persuading, entertaining, or advancing a reader's knowledge, must be well planned and organized. In order to create a powerful piece of writing, authors must adhere to specific structural designs, apply a functional and logical order to their writing, and employ key elements.

53

The following chart outlines three types of writing and their respective purposes, the structural elements unique to each type of writing, and some examples of subgenres:

	Opinion/Persuasive	**Narrative**	**Informative**
Purpose	To persuade, influence, or prompt a call-to-action response	To entertain or to share a moral when writing fictional narratives To share factual information when writing nonfiction narratives	To convey information and advance a reader's knowledge of a given topic
Key components	Opening statement and point of view Well organized paragraphs with supportive evidence and/or examples Strong concluding statement that reinforces point of view	Fictional narratives: plot, characters, setting, point of view, tone Nonfictional Narratives: introductory paragraph Body: including details and descriptions of events and individuals Conclusion	Introduction Headings and Subheadings Body Conclusion Works Cited
Subgenres	Speeches, letters, reviews, advertisements, essays	Fictional narratives: folktales, fantasy, science-fiction, mystery, drama Nonfictional narratives: autobiographies, biographies, memoirs	How-to books, cookbooks, instructional manuals, textbooks

Effectiveness of Writing Samples

The ultimate goal in every English language arts classroom is to advance students' ability to write coherently and effectively with relative ease. The process of writing begins in the very primary stages and continues throughout a student's academic career. With each passing year, students who receive effective writing instruction and constructive feedback will be able to practice and apply their writing skills to more complex writing assignments. To help students advance in their writing skills, evaluation and assessment of a student's writing should be ongoing and occur during and after instruction of each writing unit.

In order to evaluate the effectiveness of a student's writing, educators should continuously focus on formative and summative assessments that outline clear expectations for the student and the educator. **Formative assessments** allow both the student and the educator to monitor the student's writing progress with ongoing feedback, discussion, and guidance. For example, after formative assessments, educators may recognize that some students need further instruction on a given skill or would benefit from a modified writing assignment. **Summative assessments** should only be employed at the very end of an instructional unit and should be used to evaluate how well the student was able to apply specific writing skills to the assigned and completed task. Praising each student's writing progress and allowing time for one-to-one conferences are also valuable instructional techniques that build a student's confidence in the writing process.

The following are examples of assessment practices that help drive instruction and strengthen a student's understanding and application of writing skills for different types of writing.

Effective writing assessments:

- Rating scales and rubrics
- Student logs: student evaluation of writing exercises
- Small groups and peer evaluations
- POWER method: Plan, Organize, Write, Edit, Rewrite (self-assessment)
- Standardized and diagnostic assessments
- Formative assessments
- Summative assessments

Educators who give clear expectations at the beginning, throughout, and at the end of a writing task help students advance their writing skills and become more proficient writers across a number of disciplines and genres. Since there are different types of writing, and considering that writing occurs in all subjects and disciplines, all educators should plan and develop several opportunities for students to practice various types of writing. For example, depending on the students' age and grade level, short, creative, daily writing exercises at the beginning or end of class can be used as an effective opening or closing routine. One day, students can practice narrative writing and the next, persuasive. Teachers can offer an author's chair in which children can read excerpts of their informative, persuasive, or narrative writing, and answer questions from peers relevant to their writing.

Dedicating time to the writing process—with a variety of writing exercises and assignments that occur in every discipline—is paramount to a child's writing acquisition. Effective instructional and assessment practices help foster an appreciation of writing that will continue throughout a student's lifetime.

Characteristics of Effective Writing

Writing Pieces for Specific Purposes
Aristotle's Rhetorical Triangle is perhaps the best visual representation to demonstrate the importance of effective writing. Three key areas require the writer's full attention and should be balanced accordingly throughout the writing process:

Ethos refers to the writer's credibility: What are the writer's qualifications regarding the subject of the writing? Is the author using an objective or subjective approach? Are the sources, evidence, and examples in the writing relevant and credible?

Pathos refers to the writer's ability to engage and connect with the intended audience: What details and imagery does the author use to ignite and excite the emotions, imagination, values, and beliefs of the audience?

Logos refers to the validity of the author's message: Is the author's message clearly discernible? Is it logical and well organized?

Each of these three areas are critical to the quality of the writing and require the author's full attention and consideration throughout the writing process, from the preliminary stages to the final published work. Writers are tasked with the responsibility of choosing appropriate language to connect with an audience and choosing a style that maintains interest, which helps the audience understand the writer's purpose and accept the writer's intent. Did the writer succeed, for instance, in entertaining, informing, or persuading the audience?

Evaluation of a Piece of Writing

Traditionally, evaluating a student's writing has been a one-sided affair performed by the educator at the end of the writing process. This is no longer the customary practice since research has clearly shown the importance of formative assessments, as well as the importance of including the students as welcomed and respected self-evaluators. However, no evaluation or assessment should take place unless the instructions given for a particular writing assignment have been made clear, and the students have received quality, comprehensive writing instruction, in general. Assuming these requirements have been met, assessment and evaluation can take on many forms.

Formative assessments help keep the students focused and on task, and they also help to drive instruction. For example, educators are able to determine a child's individual needs, as well as common errors made by many students in the class. During formative assessments, children receive constructive feedback, and educators focus on the individual needs of each student. Formative assessments may also require students to perform self-evaluation using a guided rubric, which helps advance writing skills and develop autonomy. Summative assessments are equally important and also come in many forms. Some summative assessments are curriculum-based to ensure the appropriate standards are being met. Others may be anecdotal, wherein educators write endnotes that highlight areas that require improvement, praise the student's effort and progress, and provide next-step instructions.

Regardless of the type of assessments used, it is critical to a student's continued success that each assessment be personal, meaningful, well understood, and constructive, providing a clear pathway for their continued advancement in the writing process.

Appropriate Revisions to Writing

Writing is a multi-step process in which a student must consider the message and the audience. Likewise, revisions should focus on specific areas. If revision requirements are too vague or all requirements are combined into one task, students can become confused and overwhelmed. Breaking up revisions into specific categories will help students to recognize, understand, and correct specific errors.

One revision task should focus solely on the conventions of the English language, including spelling, punctuation, and grammar. Another task should focus on language usage, wherein students consider the writing style chosen and evaluate whether or not this style is appropriate for delivering the intended message to the intended audience. The writing structure is another area of focus that allows the student

56

to evaluate the introduction, body, and conclusion. Does the writing clearly introduce the topic, does the body gradually strengthen the writer's point of view with relevant and reliable sources and examples, and does the conclusion restate the writer's message in a concise and effective manner? Students should be actively involved in all revisions along with the educators in order for the revisions to make sense.

Clear and Coherent Writing

Coherent Writing

Coherent writing uses a logical order and consists of information that is both relevant to the topic and reliable. Coherent writing ensures that the language usage appropriately activates the audience's background knowledge and keeps the audience interested. For writing to be considered coherent, the author must also consider the structure and its relevance to the writing goal.

Writing Clarity

Although separate and distinct in definition, both coherent writing and writing clarity are interrelated and impact each other. For writing to be fully coherent, it must also be written clearly and for writing to be written clearly, it needs to be coherent. **Writing clarity** refers to the conventions of the English language. Has the author paid considerable attention to the spelling, grammar, and punctuation? For example, the misspelling of a word can confuse a reader and negatively impact writing clarity. The use of visual aids in the form of graphs, diagrams, maps, and charts can also greatly strengthen the writing clarity by allowing students to see examples of what they are reading.

Planning, Revising, and Editing

Planning is the precursor to writing. This brainstorming stage is when writers consider their purpose and think of ideas that they can use in their writing. Graphic organizers are excellent tools to use during the planning stage. Graphic organizers can help students connect the writing purpose to supporting details, and they can help begin the process of structuring the writing piece. Brainstorming can be done independently, in partners, or as a whole-class activity.

As students begin writing their first draft of a writing piece, they need to continuously revise and edit their work. **Revisions** take place during and after the writing process. As students revise their writing, they are encouraged to frequently refer back to the planning stage. This helps ensure that they are staying focused and are remaining on topic. During the revising and editing stage, educators prompt students to reread their work several times and to focus on one aspect of their writing each time.

For example, the first review may be to examine the writing content, while the second review may focus on spelling, grammar, and punctuation. Another helpful strategy during this stage is to have students display the graphic organizers they used during the planning stage and read their work aloud to the class, in small groups, or with a partner to receive constructive feedback and to welcome other perspectives and ideas. Students are able to refer to the planning stage as the classmate reads and can make connections as to whether or not the writer has stayed on topic.

Developmental Stages of Writing	Description	Grade-Appropriate Continuum
Scribbling	Random marks, circles, and lines that may not resemble print, but represent ideas for the young writer	Praise the children's creativity and ask them to explain their work to you. Consider adding a sentence at the bottom of their work based on the children's ideas.
Letter-like symbols	Letter-like symbols start to randomly appear and may be mixed in with numbers and scribbles.	Praise the children's creativity and point to the letter-like symbols for discussion. Consider adding a sentence at the bottom of the work based on the children's ideas.
Strings of letters	Using strings of letters in a row, children are demonstrating the preliminary understanding of letter-to-sound relationships.	Praise the children's efforts in attempting to use letters to represent sounds. Ask the children to tell you the story or to read you the sentences and consider writing what they say at the bottom.
The emergence of beginning sounds	Children begin to use letters to represent actual words and may string the letters together in a row that can tell a story.	Praise the children's efforts in attempting to use letters to represent actual words. Help with spacing, building sound-letter correspondence, and expanding vocabulary.
Words represented by consonants	Children begin to leave spaces between words with a possible mixture of uppercase and lowercase letters.	Praise children's work as a prompt for further explanation of the story. Prompt children to use more details and to build more sentences.

Initial, middle, final sounds	Children begin to write some basic sight words and familiar names, but all other words are spelled the way they sound.	Praise children's progress and continue to build vocabulary. Help children to organize writing with structure and sentence variety.
Transitional phase	Writing is beginning to approach conventional spelling.	Praise children's progress and model the use of effective wording by using specific vocabulary to expand ideas.
Standard spelling	Children begin to spell most words correctly, with a basic understanding that the spelling of many words is connected to the meaning.	Praise children's progress and challenge them to begin writing more complex sentences, expand ideas, and establish a clear purpose for writing.

Digital and Publishing Tools

Characteristics of a Variety of Tools

Students and educators alike are living in a digital era. By incorporating technology into the classroom, educators can find ways to better connect with students, encourage students to become more actively engaged in the learning process, and embrace the many benefits of digital tools that enhance the learning and teaching experience.

Digital tools come in several forms, including images, video, animation, sound, and text, and they are used for a variety of functions. For the purpose of writing, digital tools can be used to further communicate a writer's point of view or even to publish a piece of writing. Digital tools in the classroom facilitate the learning process and prompt collaboration among students and teachers, as well as among the students themselves.

Digital Tools for Interacting with Others

The Internet is a virtual highway of information that can be used to enhance both the learning and teaching experiences in the classroom. There are digital tools that allow children to interact and collaborate through strategic and critical thinking games, digital tools for messaging children, teachers, and parents, digital tools for creating visual effects, content sharing, feedback, grading, and so much more.

It is imperative, however, that educators thoroughly review sites before implementing their use in the classroom and that they further emphasize to children the importance of Internet safety, the impact of a digital footprint, and the concept of plagiarism. When used responsibly and effectively, digital tools

59

actively work to engage children, teachers, and the parent community in the learning process both in and out of the classroom.

Research Process

Steps in the Research Process
The following list depicts the steps relevant to the research process. Each step should be performed in chronological order, as they depend on each other for optimal work. For example, without the "Revise and edit" step, step 8 would be a poorly written first draft.

- Step 1: Decide on a topic to research
- Step 2: Set the purpose of the research
- Step 3: Locate sources of information—print, digital, experts
- Step 4: Evaluate the sources
- Step 5: Summarize information and cite sources
- Step 6: Write draft
- Step 7: Revise and edit
- Step 8: Publish writing

Primary and Secondary Sources
Primary sources refer to first-hand accounts of events, a subject matter, an individual, or a time period. Primary sources also include original works of art. They can also be non-interpretive, factual pieces of information. Some examples include diaries, journals, letters, government records, maps, plays, novels, and songs.

Secondary sources refer to the analysis or interpretation of primary sources and are, therefore, usually considered more subjective than objective. In other words, researchers may discover contradictory information on the same subject from different secondary sources. Some examples include literary and film reviews, newspaper articles, and biographies.

Both primary and secondary sources of information are useful. They both offer invaluable insight that helps the writer learn more about the subject matter. However, researchers are cautioned to examine the information closely and to consider the time period as well as the cultural, political, and social climate in which accounts were given. Learning to distinguish between reliable sources of information and questionable accounts is paramount to a quality research report.

Reliable and Unreliable Sources
When conducting research, students must be able to distinguish between reliable and unreliable sources in order to develop a well-written research report. When choosing print sources, typically published works that have been edited and clearly identify the author or authors are considered credible sources. Peer-reviewed journals and research conducted by scholars are likewise considered to be credible sources of information.

When deciding on what Internet sources to use, it is also a sound practice for researchers to look closely at each website's universal resource locator, the *URL*. Generally speaking, websites with.edu, .gov, or .org as the Top Level Domain are considered reliable, but the researcher must still question any possible political or social bias. Personal blogs, tweets, personal websites, online forums, and any site that clearly demonstrates bias, strong opinions, or persuasive language are considered unreliable sources.

60

Paraphrasing and Plagiarizing

Paraphrasing: The restating of one's own words, text, passage, or any information that has already been heard, read, or researched

Plagiarizing: The copying of a text, passage, or any other information in print or digital format, and claiming the work as one's own

Credible Print and Digital Sources

Credible **print sources** are those that have been edited and published, reveal the author or authors, and clearly identify their expertise on the subject matter. Scholarly reviews are typically very reliable sources as they are written by experts in the field and, more often than not, have been evaluated by their respective peers. Credible **digital sources** may sometimes prove a little more difficult to discern, and researchers must employ due diligence to ensure the sources are reliable. Distinguishing between biased and unbiased websites, objective versus subjective information, as well as informative versus persuasive writing can prove confusing at times. By paying attention to a website's URL and carefully considering the language and tone applied to the writing, researchers should be able to evaluate the website's reliability.

Learning how to locate key information within sources requires a basic understanding of written structure. If the source of information is written well, there should be titles, subtitles, headings, and subheadings that researchers can use to zero in on key information. Additionally, informational texts often employ the use of an index and table of contents, which helps them locate specific information. Similarly, digital sources often employ titles, subtitles, headings, and subheadings, and they will generally offer a search box to look for specific information or key terms within the website.

Citing sources at the end of a research paper is critical to the overall quality of work. If sources are not cited or poorly cited, a researcher's work risks losing credibility. There are various accepted methods to use when citing information. The method used often depends on the preferences of the authority that has assigned the research. The most generally accepted methods for citing sources are MLA, APA, and Chicago style. Although each citation format is distinct in structure, order, and requirements, they all identify key information. Citation formats also ensure that published authors of given works receive full credit.

Language

Conventions of Standard English Grammar, Usage, Mechanics, and Spelling

When learning to speak, listen, read, or write in any language, students are tasked with multiple challenges. The study of the English language is no exception. The conventions of Standard English are complex and require comprehensive study and continual practice.

Parts of Speech

Words within the English language play very unique roles in the formation of coherent sentences. Each English word is categorized into a specific part of speech that carries a unique function. For instance, in order to create simple English language sentences, writers are required to incorporate a noun and a verb. However, when sentences become more complex, additional parts of speech are required.

The following chart outlines the parts of speech, along with a brief description of their function within an English sentence and concrete examples.

Part of Speech	Function	Examples
Noun	Identifies a person, place, or thing—can be concrete or abstract	Love, thought, man, woman, child, school, home, integrity, America
Pronoun	Replaces a noun	He, she, it, they
Verb	Depicts an action or state of being	Run, jump, fly, is, are
Adjective	Modifies nouns	Great idea, interesting thought, tall girl
Adverb	Modifies verbs, other adverbs, and adjectives	He has an *extremely* shy demeanor. She *quickly* ran away. They walked *very* clumsily together.
Preposition	Almost always combined with other key words in a sentence in order to indicate a time, location, or movement	*At* nine o'clock, *beside* the nightstand, *toward* the door
Conjunction	Connects words, clauses, or sentences, with related meaning	She *and* I have similar tastes in food. The teacher handed us the assignment, *but* we refused to accept it. The dogs ran and played, *while* the cats sat and stared.
Interjection	Brief exclamations that are added to sentences for emphasis or effect	*Wow*! I had no idea you could sing! *"Boo!"* she screamed, as she jumped out from behind the door.

Although an explicit approach to teaching the various parts of speech plays an integral role in the primary grades, it is equally as important that a child learns to recognize these parts of speech when reading and gradually learn to apply them to writing tasks. Being able to recognize and appropriately use various parts of speech demonstrates a growing command of the English language and its conventions.

Correction of Errors

Usage and mechanics are often mistakenly used as interchangeable terms in the educational field. In writing, **usage** refers to a student's ability to choose appropriate words that clearly express an idea, thought, or opinion, or accurately summarize information. Therefore, usage is a very important component of learning to be an effective writer. **Mechanics** involve the writer's ability to use capitalization, ending punctuation, apostrophes, and commas properly. For writing to be both coherent and fluent, mechanics play an important role. **Spelling** is a little less complicated to understand, as it refers to the student's ability to spell decodable and non-decodable words accurately. Learning how and when to correct errors in usage, mechanics, and spelling can be a source of frustration for educators, but it need not be. By creating a logical balance and manageable plan for correcting student writing, educators will help children to be more effective, lifelong writers. The key is balance.

Traditionally, English language educators have focused a great deal of evaluation and feedback on correcting mistakes in usage, mechanics, and spelling alone. Although it is widely accepted that these components are necessary in order to write fluent and coherent sentences, too much focus on correcting these areas—and not enough attention paid to the creative side of writing—may have a negative impact on the writing process.

For example, instead of emphasizing or highlighting every spelling error, educators should ensure that their corrections reflect the task. In other words, if children are given a writing assignment that must incorporate their spelling words, they will undoubtedly expect the educator to correct and evaluate how well they spelled these key words. However, since the assignment also asked the children to use a creative approach to this writing assignment, educators would be doing students a disservice if they did not also offer praise and feedback on the children's writing creativity.

Developing a writing checklist with well-defined goals and sharing this checklist with the class helps educators keep the correction process clear and specific, and it provides children with the opportunity to self-correct and edit their work prior to submission. Using a standardized system of symbols that helps children focus on spelling, capitalization, or word choice is also an effective strategy. Displaying these symbols in a readily-accessible place in the classroom will allow them to self-correct and help their peers with the correction process.

For writing to be meaningful and for students to advance in their writing skills, educators should follow a balanced approach to correcting student work with frequent, timely, and appropriate feedback that reflects the task.

Sentence Types

When children begin to connect letters to words and, gradually, words to sentences, those sentences are generally very simple, consisting of one subject and one verb. However, as children advance in their writing fluency, it is paramount to introduce more complex sentences.

Simple sentences are sentences that consist of one subject and one verb:

I run.

She eats.

They play.

At this stage, educators may prompt children to add some more detail to the simple sentences with adjectives or adverbs:

I run *quickly*.

She eats *very well*.

They play *together*.

Compound sentences contain two independent clauses connected by a conjunction:

I run, but she runs marathons.

I run is an **independent clause**. *She runs marathons* is another independent clause. Each clause could be a complete sentence that stands on its own. However, they are connected with the coordinating conjunction, *but*.

Complex sentences are structures in which two clauses exist, but one clause is **dependent** on the other—that is, it cannot form a sentence in its own right and requires the assistance of the independent clause in order for the sentence to be coherent. Here's an example:

Although he passed the exam, he remained very sad.

He remained very sad is an independent clause, but *Although he passed the exam* is not, as it is dependent on the second part of the sentence in order for the sentence to be coherent.

Compound-complex sentences are structures that employ two or more independent clauses along with at least one dependent clause:

Though I preferred long distance running, I started speed walking, and I enjoyed it very much.

Though I preferred long-distance running is a dependent clause that relies on the independent clause *I started speed walking*. The second independent clause is *I enjoyed it very much*, making this sentence compound-complex.

English Used in Stories, Dramas, or Poems
Register
Despite the fact that a standardized form of English is used in published academic and scientific language, several varieties of spoken and written English also exist. There are differences in how one speaks at home, with friends, to teachers, and to colleagues. In each social setting, a person's **register**—their level of formality—will likely change in order to appropriately address the audience. Written registers also vary, depending on a number of factors. For instance, when writing a research paper for professional purposes, formal language will be used, but when writing a letter to a friend, a person is more apt to employ a more casual register. The following statements indicate differences in register:

Call me back when you get this message.

I look forward to hearing back from you at your earliest convenience.

Although both statements express the writer's desire to further communicate with the receiver of the message, the degree of formality, the register, is strikingly different.

Dialect

A language also has several dialects, which are dependent on a great many factors. **Dialects** have specific grammatical rules and patterns that often differ from the standard rules of the language. For instance, within Britain, Canada, and the United States, there are several dialects of the English language. One need only travel from Newfoundland, in eastern Canada, to Louisiana, in the southern United States, to witness a striking difference in how the English language is spoken.

Written dialects and registers also exist. They vary, based on the type of written work, when it was created, where it was written, by whom it was written, for what purposes, and for what audience it was intended. Authors of dramas, stories, and poetry employ the use of dialect for a multitude of reasons. For instance, when authors wish to develop a clear picture of the setting and characters within a drama, dialect plays a significant role. Here are some examples of dialect:

"Bess, you is my woman now…"—from George Gershwin's opera, *Porgy and Bess*

"That ain't no matter."—from Mark Twain's novel, *Huckleberry Finn*

With the careful and skillful placement of written dialect, the author conveys the character's personality, situation, and social class.

Determining the Meanings of Words and Phrases

Literal Meaning of Unknown Words

As children advance in their reading fluency, written material will likewise become more complex. Students transition from reading works in which the meaning is literal and direct, to works that require a more critical thinking approach. Educators can facilitate this transition by modeling and demonstrating how to use context clues, syntax, roots, and suffixes to derive meaning from texts.

Context Clues

There are many types of clues found within sentences that help to clarify the meaning of unfamiliar words. Sometimes sentences provide a clear and direct definition of an unfamiliar word:

<u>Anglophones</u>, *also known as native English speakers,* are found in every corner of the globe.

Teaching children phrases that are used to compare and contrast can also be an effective instructional approach:

The workday today was <u>laborious</u> *as opposed to* yesterday, which was relaxed and easy going.

If children were unfamiliar with the word *laborious*, they would quickly decipher that it means the opposite of *relaxed* and *easy going*, thanks to the use of the phrase *as opposed to*.

Syntax

There is a certain order to the way in which words are placed in a sentence. For instance, many English sentences follow the pattern of noun + verb + object. The more acquainted children become with syntax, the stronger their ability to recognize parts of speech and how they are interrelated.

65

Roots and Affixes

Having even a rudimentary understanding of root words and affixes can greatly increase a reader's ability to decipher unknown words. The study of word origins helps children to understand that words are not just arbitrarily put together, but they are often formed like pieces of a puzzle. The following are examples:

- Astronaut
    - Astro: star or celestial body (Greek)
    - Naut: sailor (Greek origin)
- Portable
    - Port: carry
    - Able: ability, capacity

Figurative Language

Figurative language is a specific style of speaking or writing that uses tools for a variety of effects. It entertains readers, ignites imagination, and promotes creativity. Instead of writing in realistic terms or literal terms, figurative language plays with words and prompts readers to infer the underlying meaning. There are seven types of figurative language:

Type	Definition	Example
Personification	Giving animate qualities to an inanimate object	The tree stood tall and still, staring up at the sky.
Simile	The comparison of two unlike things using connecting words	Your eyes are as blue as the ocean.
Metaphor	The comparison of two unlike things without the use of connecting words	She was in the twilight of her years.
Hyperbole	An over-exaggeration	I could eat a million of these cookies!
Alliteration	The patterned repetition of an initial consonant sound	The bunnies are bouncing in baskets.
Onomatopoeia	Words that are formed by using the very sound associated with the word itself	"Drip, drip, drip" went the kitchen faucet.
Idioms	Common sayings that carry a lesson or meaning that must be inferred	That math work was a piece of cake!

66

Interpretation

Since idioms and hyperboles are commonly used in everyday speech, educators may wish to introduce them early.

I'm so tired that I could sleep forever!—Hyperbole

He's not playing with a full deck!—Idiom

Other forms of figurative language can be found in poetry and in children's stories. As educators come across figurative speech, they can prompt children's critical thinking skills by asking what they think the author meant by those words or that particular sentence. Giving concrete examples of each style and challenging children to attempt writing their very own creative sentences will strengthen their understanding and application of figurative language.

Relationship Between Word Choice and Tone

The words authors choose to use must always be well thought out. Although words carry specific meanings, they also carry **connotations**—emotional feelings that are evoked by the words. Connotation creates the tone of the writing. Some words can be said to be loaded words or trigger words that ignite strong emotional responses in readers. These two sentences offer examples:

My grandfather is a robust, elderly man.

My grandfather is a chubby, old man.

In the first sentence, the adjectives used to describe the grandfather instill positive emotions in the reader. However, in the second sentence, the adjectives instill negative emotions. The **mood** of a writing piece refers to the emotions—positive or negative—the reader feels during and after reading. **Tone** refers to the author's purposeful choice of words, designed to evoke those feelings.

Characteristics of Conversational, Academic, and Domain-Specific Language

Three Tiers of Vocabulary

Language is used for effective communication and can be thought of as a social tool. However, since communication is also used in educational and professional circles, language must be flexible enough to meet the challenges of each social structure.

Conversational language is the everyday language spoken at home, with family, and with friends. It is a relaxed form of communication that may carry regional dialects, slang, and even sayings that may only be known by those who are part of those intimate social circles.

Academic language refers to the understanding and application of key vocabulary terms in order to achieve academic success. From their introduction to formal education, students become acquainted with this language tier. It prompts higher-level thinking and challenges students to research, analyze, and push the boundaries of thought, belief, and imagination.

Domain-specific languages are now widely used to refer to computer-based languages—called DSLs—but they are also known as any language system that has been specifically designed to perform a task in a given domain. In domain-specific languages, people are able to communicate concepts unique to that particular domain, avoid redundancy, and stay focused and on target.

67

Word Choice, Order, and Punctuation

Language is a powerful communication tool that advances thought and facilitates social change. Some features of language that play key roles in communication include word choice, order, and punctuation.

For example, an author can write two sentences that carry a similar meaning but evoke opposing emotions based on word choice. For instance, to write that a person is *intelligent* is a compliment, but to rewrite that sentence and replace *intelligent* with *smart aleck* changes the compliment to an insult. The order of words can also be effective in writing. Instead of beginning a sentence with the subject, authors can begin with the predicate, which instills a sense of mystery and wonder in the reader. The same can be true of fictional stories in which the author begins at the end or in the middle and works backward to unravel the tale. These writing styles create a powerful, dramatic effect on the stories.

Punctuation can also play a key role in how a reader interprets a passage:

He did do his homework?

He did do his homework!

With the mere change in ending punctuation, the author changes the reader's interpretation of the sentence. Although both sentences use identical words and order, the first sentence infers nothing more than an innocent inquiry, whereas the second infers an emotional, perhaps defensive response.

Speaking and Listening

Effective Collaboration

Communicating with Diverse Partners

Communication is never one-sided. There are always at least two individuals engaged in a conversation, and both acts of speaking and listening are often interchangeable. In the classroom, educators communicate with all students, and students communicate with one another. Some forms of communication are intended for instructional purposes, while other forms may be solely for entertainment. To be an effective communicator, it is critical that the purpose for speaking is clear to both the presenter and the audience. It is also important that the mode of communication is culturally sensitive and age appropriate. The presenter should use language that best suits their audience. For example, if an educator wishes to speak to a primary class about the importance of homework, domain-specific language may not be appropriate, but that same conversation with educational colleagues may

require domain-specific language. Here are some key techniques to consider when developing strong communication skills:

Effective Speaking	Effective Listening
Check for understanding and interest—ask key questions	Offer relevant information to the topic
Repeat important information in a variety of ways	Ask poignant questions, clarify understanding
Use nonverbal forms of communication—body language for effect	Use nonverbal forms of communication—body language for effect
Remain observant—maintain eye contact	Remain observant—maintain eye contact
Develop a healthy sense of humor	Develop a healthy sense of humor
Strive for honesty	Strive for honesty
Consider language choices	Develop active listening skills—not simply waiting to respond
Develop cultural sensitivity	Strengthen patience

Active Listening

To develop active listening skills, several important areas require focus and conscious effort. Before a speech or dialogue even begins, removing any distractions sets a positive and respectful tone. Those with active listening skills offer undivided attention, acknowledge the presenter's message by asking relevant questions and provide encouraging feedback when appropriate. Maintaining eye contact, smiling, and using posture that signifies respect are also effective characteristics of active listening, but perhaps one of the most important ways to improve active listening skills is to keep an open mind and defer judgment until the speaker has completed the entire message.

Active listening skills are an important part of children's family, social, and academic life, and they will eventually become an equally important part of their professional lives. Recognizing the importance of active listening and strengthening these skills assists students in achieving personal, academic, and professional success.

Engaging Oral Presentations

Elements of Engaging Oral Presentations

Oral presentations can cause panic in a classroom as children scramble to figure out how, when, where, why, and what to speak about. However, if given proper guidance, appropriate time, and constructive feedback, the panic will soon fade, and in turn, students will learn how to give powerful oral presentations.

In order to be effective, educators should follow best practices, including sharing a well-designed rubric with the class, discussing the importance of each skill listed, answering any questions the children might have, and providing ongoing and constructive feedback while children develop their presentations.

Key areas to develop oral presentations:

Volume

Children should consider where the presentation would be held. Will it be indoors, outdoors, in an auditorium, or in the classroom? Learning to match the volume of the presentation with the location and size of the audience will greatly improve the presentation.

Articulation

Pronouncing words clearly is another aspect of effective communication, especially during an oral presentation. Slurred words, rushed words, mumbling, or leaving out the beginning or ending of sentences will have a negative impact on the message, and the presenter risks losing the interest of the audience.

Awareness of Audience

Facing the audience at all times is paramount to the success of an oral presentation. If possible, walking around the room and maintaining eye contact with the audience have proven to be effective techniques. Welcoming questions from the audience, restating questions for everyone to hear, and providing honest and thoughtful responses, also play a key role in ensuring a successful oral presentation.

Practice Questions

1. When does scaffolded reading occur?
    a. A student hears a recording of herself reading a text in order to set personal reading goals.
    b. A student receives assistance and feedback on strategies to utilize while reading from someone else.
    c. A student is given extra time to find the answers to predetermined questions.
    d. A student is pulled out of a class to receive services elsewhere.

2. What are the three interconnected indicators of reading fluency?
    a. Phonetics, word morphology, and listening comprehension
    b. Accuracy, rate, and prosody
    c. Syntax, semantics, and vocabulary
    d. Word exposure, phonetics, and decodable skills

3. A teacher needs to assess students' accuracy in reading grade-appropriate, high frequency, and irregular sight words. Which of the following strategies would be most appropriate for this purpose?
    a. The teacher gives students a list of words to study for a spelling test that will be administered the following week.
    b. The teacher allows each student to bring their favorite book from home and has each student read their selected text aloud independently.
    c. The teacher administers the Stanford Structural Analysis assessment to determine students' rote memory and application of morphemes contained within the words.
    d. The teacher records how many words each student reads correctly when reading aloud a list of a teacher-selected, grade-appropriate words.

4. What type of texts are considered nonfiction?
    a. Folktales
    b. Memoirs
    c. Fables
    d. Short stories

5. How are typographic features useful when teaching reading comprehension?
    a. Typographic features are graphics used to illustrate the story and help students visualize the text.
    b. Typographic features give the answers in boldfaced print.
    c. Typographic features are not helpful when teaching reading comprehension and should not be used.
    d. Typographic features are print in boldface, italics, and subheadings, used to display changes in topics or to highlight important vocabulary or content.

See answers on next page.

Answer Explanations

1. B: Scaffolded opportunities occur when a teacher helps students by giving them support, offering immediate feedback, and suggesting strategies. In order to be beneficial, such feedback needs to help students identify areas that need improvement. Much like oral reading feedback, this advice increases students' awareness so they can independently make needed modifications in order to improve fluency.

Scaffolding is lessened as the student becomes a more independent reader. Struggling readers, students with reading difficulties or disabilities, and students with special needs especially benefit from direct instruction and feedback that teaches decoding and analysis of unknown words, automaticity in key sight words, and correct expression and phrasing.

2. B: Key indicators of reading fluency include accuracy, rate, and prosody. Phonetics and decodable skills aid fluency. Syntax, semantics, word morphology, listening comprehension, and word exposure aid vocabulary development.

3. D: Accuracy is measured via the percentage of words that are read correctly with in a given text. Word-reading accuracy is often measured by counting the number of errors that occur per 100 words of oral reading. This information is used to select the appropriate level of text for an individual.

4. B: Nonfiction texts include memoirs, biographies, autobiographies, and journalism. Choices A, C, and D are all examples of fictional prose.

5. D: Typographic features are important when teaching reading comprehension as the boldfaced, highlighted, or italics notify a student when a new vocabulary word or idea is present. Subtitles and headings can also alert a student to a change in topic or idea. These features are also important when answering questions, as a student may be able to easily find the answer with these typographic features present.

Mathematics

Numbers and Operations

Place Value System

Base-10 Numerals, Number Names, and Expanded Form
Numbers used in everyday life are constituted in a base-10 system. Each digit in a number, depending on its location, represents some multiple of 10, or quotient of 10 when dealing with decimals. Each digit to the left of the decimal point represents a higher multiple of 10. Each digit to the right of the decimal point represents a quotient of a higher multiple of 10 for the divisor. For example, consider the number 7,631.42. The digit one represents simply the number one. The digit 3 represents 3×10. The digit 6 represents $6 \times 10 \times 10$ (or 6×100). The digit 7 represents $7 \times 10 \times 10 \times 10$ (or 7×1000). The digit 4 represents $4 \div 10$. The digit 2 represents $(2 \div 10) \div 10$, or $2 \div (10 \times 10)$ or $2 \div 100$.

A number is written in **expanded form** by expressing it as the sum of the value of each of its digits. The expanded form in the example above, which is written with the highest value first down to the lowest value, is expressed as:

$$7,000 + 600 + 30 + 1 + 0.4 + .02$$

When verbally expressing a number, the **integer** part of the number (the numbers to the left of the decimal point) resembles the expanded form without the addition between values. In the above example, the numbers read "seven thousand six hundred thirty-one." When verbally expressing the decimal portion of a number, the number is read as a whole number, followed by the place value of the furthest digit (non-zero) to the right. In the above example, 0.42 is read "forty-two hundredths." Reading the number 7,631.42 in its entirety is expressed as "seven thousand six hundred thirty-one and forty-two hundredths." The word *and* is used between the integer and decimal parts of the number.

Composing and Decomposing Multi-Digit Numbers
Composing and decomposing numbers aids in conceptualizing what each digit of a multi-digit number represents. The standard, or typical, form in which numbers are written consists of a series of digits representing a given value based on their place value. Consider the number 592.7. This number is composed of 5 hundreds, 9 tens, 2 ones, and 7 tenths.

Composing a number requires adding the given numbers for each place value and writing the numbers in standard form. For example, composing 4 thousands, 5 hundreds, 2 tens, and 8 ones consists of adding as follows: $4,000 + 500 + 20 + 8$, to produce 4,528 (standard form).

Decomposing a number requires taking a number written in standard form and breaking it apart into the sum of each place value. For example, the number 83.17 is decomposed by breaking it into the sum of 4 values (for each of the 4 digits): 8 tens, 3 ones, 1 tenth, and 7 hundredths. The decomposed or "expanded" form of 83.17 is:

$$80 + 3 + 0.1 + 0.07$$

Place Value of a Given Digit

The number system that is used consists of only ten different digits or characters. However, this system is used to represent an infinite number of values. The place value system makes this infinite number of values possible. The position in which a digit is written corresponds to a given value. Starting from the decimal point (which is implied, if not physically present), each subsequent place value to the left represents a value greater than the one before it. Conversely, starting from the decimal point, each subsequent place value to the right represents a value less than the one before it.

The names for the place values to the left of the decimal point are as follows:

...	Billions	Hundred-Millions	Ten-Millions	Millions	Hundred-Thousands	Ten-Thousands	Thousands	Hundreds	Tens	Ones

Note that this table can be extended infinitely further to the left.

The names for the place values to the right of the decimal point are as follows:

Decimal Point (.)	Tenths	Hundredths	Thousandths	Ten-Thousandths	...

Note that this table can be extended infinitely further to the right.

When given a multi-digit number, the value of each digit depends on its place value. Consider the number 682,174.953. Referring to the chart above, it can be determined that the digit 8 is in the ten-thousands place. It is in the fifth place to the left of the decimal point. Its value is 8 ten-thousands or 80,000. The digit 5 is two places to the right of the decimal point. Therefore, the digit 5 is in the hundredths place. Its value is 5 hundredths or $\frac{5}{100}$ (equivalent to .05).

Value of Digits

In accordance with the base-10 system, the value of a digit increases by a factor of ten each place it moves to the left. For example, consider the number 7. Moving the digit one place to the left (70), increases its value by a factor of 10 ($7 \times 10 = 70$). Moving the digit two places to the left (700) increases its value by a factor of 10 twice ($7 \times 10 \times 10 = 700$). Moving the digit three places to the left (7,000) increases its value by a factor of 10 three times ($7 \times 10 \times 10 \times 10 = 7,000$), and so on.

Conversely, the value of a digit decreases by a factor of ten each place it moves to the right. (Note that multiplying by $\frac{1}{10}$ is equivalent to dividing by 10). For example, consider the number 40. Moving the digit one place to the right (4) decreases its value by a factor of 10 ($40 \div 10 = 4$). Moving the digit two places to the right (0.4), decreases its value by a factor of 10 twice ($40 \div 10 \div 10 = 0.4$) or ($40 \times \frac{1}{10} \times \frac{1}{10} = 0.4$). Moving the digit three places to the right (0.04) decreases its value by a factor of 10 three times ($40 \div 10 \div 10 \div 10 = 0.04$) or ($40 \times \frac{1}{10} \times \frac{1}{10} \times \frac{1}{10} = 0.04$), and so on.

Exponents to Denote Powers of 10

The value of a given digit of a number in the base-10 system can be expressed utilizing powers of 10. A **power of 10** refers to 10 raised to a given exponent such as $10^0, 10^1, 10^2, 10^3$, etc. For the number 10^3, 10 is the base and 3 is the exponent. A base raised by an exponent represents how many times the base is multiplied by itself. Therefore, $10^1 = 10$, $10^2 = 10 \times 10 = 100$, $10^3 = 10 \times 10 \times 10 = 1,000$, $10^4 = 10 \times 10 \times 10 \times 10 = 10,000$, etc. Any base with a zero-exponent equals one.

Powers of 10 are utilized to decompose a multi-digit number without writing all the zeroes. Consider the number 872,349. This number is decomposed to $800,000 + 70,000 + 2,000 + 300 + 40 + 9$. When utilizing powers of 10, the number 872,349 is decomposed to:

$$(8 \times 10^5) + (7 \times 10^4) + (2 \times 10^3) + (3 \times 10^2) + (4 \times 10^1) + (9 \times 10^0)$$

The power of 10 by which the digit is multiplied corresponds to the number of zeroes following the digit when expressing its value in standard form. For example, 7×10^4 is equivalent to 70,000 or 7 followed by four zeros.

Rounding Multi-Digit Numbers

Rounding numbers changes the given number to a simpler and less accurate number than the exact given number. Rounding allows for easier calculations which estimate the results of using the exact given number. The accuracy of the estimate and ease of use depends on the place value to which the number is rounded. Rounding numbers consists of:

- Determining what place value the number is being rounded to
- Examining the digit to the right of the desired place value to decide whether to round up or keep the digit
- Replacing all digits to the right of the desired place value with zeros

To round 746,311 to the nearest ten thousands, the digit in the ten thousands place should be located first. In this case, this digit is 4 (7<u>4</u>6,311). Then, the digit to its right is examined. If this digit is 5 or greater, the number will be rounded up by increasing the digit in the desired place by one. If the digit to the right of the place value being rounded is 4 or less, the number will be kept the same. For the given example, the digit being examined is a 6, which means that the number will be rounded up by increasing the digit to the left by one. Therefore, the digit 4 is changed to a 5. Finally, to write the rounded number, any digits to the left of the place value being rounded remain the same and any to its right are replaced with zeros. For the given example, rounding 746,311 to the nearest ten thousand will produce 750,000.

To round 746,311 to the nearest hundred, the digit to the right of the three in the hundreds place is examined to determine whether to round up or keep the same number. In this case, that digit is a one, so the number will be kept the same and any digits to its right will be replaced with zeros. The resulting rounded number is 746,300.

Rounding place values to the right of the decimal follows the same procedure, but digits being replaced by zeros can simply be dropped. To round 3.752891 to the nearest thousandth, the desired place value is located (3.75<u>2</u>891) and the digit to the right is examined. In this case, the digit 8 indicates that the number will be rounded up, and the 2 in the thousandths place will increase to a 3. Rounding up and replacing the digits to the right of the thousandths place produces 3.753000 which is equivalent to 3.753. Therefore, the zeros are not necessary, and the rounded number should be written as 3.753.

When rounding up, if the digit to be increased is a 9, the digit to its left is increased by 1 and the digit in the desired place value is changed to a zero. For example, the number 1,598 rounded to the nearest ten is 1,600. Another example shows the number 43.72961 rounded to the nearest thousandth is 43.730 or 43.73.

 **Mathematics**

Understanding Operations

Solving Multistep Mathematical and Real-World Problems
Problem Situations for Operations
Addition and subtraction are **inverse operations**. Adding a number and then subtracting the same number will cancel each other out, resulting in the original number, and vice versa. For example, $8 + 7 - 7 = 8$ and $137 - 100 + 100 = 137$. Similarly, multiplication and division are inverse operations. Therefore, multiplying by a number and then dividing by the same number results in the original number, and vice versa. For example, $8 \times 2 \div 2 = 8$ and $12 \div 4 \times 4 = 12$. Inverse operations are used to work backwards to solve problems. In the case that 7 and a number add to 18, the inverse operation of subtraction is used to find the unknown value ($18 - 7 = 11$). If a school's entire 4th grade was divided evenly into 3 classes each with 22 students, the inverse operation of multiplication is used to determine the total students in the grade ($22 \times 3 = 66$). Additional scenarios involving inverse operations are included in the tables below.

There are a variety of real-world situations in which one or more of the operators is used to solve a problem. The tables below display the most common scenarios.

Addition & Subtraction

	Unknown Result	**Unknown Change**	**Unknown Start**
Adding to	5 students were in class. 4 more students arrived. How many students are in class? $5 + 4 =?$	8 students were in class. More students arrived late. There are now 18 students in class. How many students arrived late? $8+? = 18$ Solved by inverse operations $18 - 8 =?$	Some students were in class early. 11 more students arrived. There are now 17 students in class. How many students were in class early? $? + 11 = 17$ Solved by inverse operations $17 - 11 =?$
Taking from	15 students were in class. 5 students left class. How many students are in class now? $15 - 5 =?$	12 students were in class. Some students left class. There are now 8 students in class. How many students left class? $12 - ? = 8$ Solved by inverse operations $8+? = 12 \rightarrow 12 - 8 =?$	Some students were in class. 3 students left class. Then there were 13 students in class. How many students were in class before? $? - 3 = 13$ Solved by inverse operations $13 + 3 =?$

	Unknown Total	Unknown Addends (Both)	Unknown Addends (One)
Putting together/ taking apart	The homework assignment is 10 addition problems and 8 subtraction problems. How many problems are in the homework assignment? $10 + 8 = ?$	Bobby has $9. How much can Bobby spend on candy and how much can Bobby spend on toys? $9 = ? + ?$	Bobby has 12 pairs of pants. 5 pairs of pants are shorts, and the rest are long. How many pairs of long pants does he have? $12 = 5 + ?$ Solved by inverse operations $12 - 5 = ?$

	Unknown Difference	Unknown Larger Value	Unknown Smaller Value
Comparing	Bobby has 5 toys. Tommy has 8 toys. How many more toys does Tommy have than Bobby? $5 + ? = 8$ Solved by inverse operations $8 - 5 = ?$ Bobby has $6. Tommy has $10. How many fewer dollars does Bobby have than Tommy? $10 - 6 = ?$	Tommy has 2 more toys than Bobby. Bobby has 4 toys. How many toys does Tommy have? $2 + 4 = ?$ Bobby has 3 fewer dollars than Tommy. Bobby has $8. How many dollars does Tommy have? $? - 3 = 8$ Solved by inverse operations $8 + 3 = ?$	Tommy has 6 more toys than Bobby. Tommy has 10 toys. How many toys does Bobby have? $? + 6 = 10$ Solved by inverse operations $10 - 6 = ?$ Bobby has $5 less than Tommy. Tommy has $9. How many dollars does Bobby have? $9 - 5 = ?$

Multiplication and Division

	Unknown Product	Unknown Group Size	Unknown Number of Groups
Equal groups	There are 5 students, and each student has 4 pieces of candy. How many pieces of candy are there in all? $5 \times 4 = ?$	14 pieces of candy are shared equally by 7 students. How many pieces of candy does each student have? $7 \times ? = 14$ Solved by inverse operations $14 \div 7 = ?$	If 18 pieces of candy are to be given out 3 to each student, how many students will get candy? $? \times 3 = 18$ Solved by inverse operations $18 \div 3 = ?$

	Unknown Product	Unknown Factor	Unknown Factor
Arrays	There are 5 rows of students with 3 students in each row. How many students are there? $5 \times 3 =?$	If 16 students are arranged into 4 equal rows, how many students will be in each row? $4 \times ? = 16$ Solved by inverse operations $16 \div 4 =?$	If 24 students are arranged into an array with 6 columns, how many rows are there? $? \times 6 = 24$ Solved by inverse operations $24 \div 6 =?$

	Larger Unknown	Smaller Unknown	Multiplier Unknown
Comparing	A small popcorn costs $1.50. A large popcorn costs 3 times as much as a small popcorn. How much does a large popcorn cost? $1.50 \times 3 =?$	A large soda costs $6 and that is 2 times as much as a small soda costs. How much does a small soda cost? $2 \times ? = 6$ Solved by inverse operations $6 \div 2 =?$	A large pretzel costs $3 and a small pretzel costs $2. How many times as much does the large pretzel cost as the small pretzel? $? \times 2 = 3$ Solved by inverse operations $3 \div 2 =?$

Remainders in Division Problems

If a given total cannot be divided evenly into a given number of groups, the amount left over is the **remainder**. Consider the following scenario: 32 textbooks must be packed into boxes for storage. Each box holds 6 textbooks. How many boxes are needed? To determine the answer, 32 is divided by 6, resulting in 5 with a remainder of 2. A remainder may be interpreted three ways:

- Add 1 to the quotient
  How many boxes will be needed? Six boxes will be needed because five will not be enough.

- Use only the quotient
  How many boxes will be full? Five boxes will be full.

- Use only the remainder
  If you only have 5 boxes, how many books will not fit? Two books will not fit.

Strategies and Algorithms to Perform Operations on Rational Numbers

A rational number is any number that can be written in the form of a ratio or fraction. Integers can be written as fractions with a denominator of 1 ($5 = \frac{5}{1}$; $-342 = \frac{-342}{1}$; etc.). Decimals that terminate and/or repeat can also be written as fractions ($47 = \frac{47}{100}$; $.\overline{33} = \frac{1}{3}$). For more on converting decimals to fractions, see the section *Converting Between Fractions, Decimals,* and *Percent*.

When adding or subtracting fractions, the numbers must have the same denominators. In these cases, numerators are added or subtracted, and denominators are kept the same. For example, $\frac{2}{7} + \frac{3}{7} = \frac{5}{7}$ and $\frac{4}{5} - \frac{3}{5} = \frac{1}{5}$. If the fractions to be added or subtracted do not have the same denominator, a common denominator must be found. This is accomplished by changing one or both fractions to a different but equivalent fraction. Consider the example $\frac{1}{6} + \frac{4}{9}$. First, a common denominator must be found. One

78

method is to find the least common multiple (LCM) of the denominators 6 and 9. This is the lowest number that both 6 and 9 will divide into evenly. In this case the LCM is 18. Both fractions should be changed to equivalent fractions with a denominator of 18.

To obtain the numerator of the new fraction, the old numerator is multiplied by the same number by which the old denominator is multiplied. For the fraction $\frac{1}{6}$, 6 multiplied by 3 will produce a denominator of 18. Therefore, the numerator is multiplied by 3 to produce the new numerator $\left(\frac{1 \times 3}{6 \times 3} = \frac{3}{18}\right)$. For the fraction $\frac{4}{9}$, multiplying both the numerator and denominator by 2 produces $\frac{8}{18}$. Since the two new fractions have common denominators, they can be added:

$$\frac{3}{18} + \frac{8}{18} = \frac{11}{18}$$

When multiplying or dividing rational numbers, these numbers may be converted to fractions and multiplied or divided accordingly. When multiplying fractions, all numerators are multiplied by each other and all denominators are multiplied by each other. For example,

$$\frac{1}{3} \times \frac{6}{5} = \frac{1 \times 6}{3 \times 5} = \frac{6}{15}$$

and

$$\frac{-1}{2} \times \frac{3}{1} \times \frac{11}{100} = \frac{-1 \times 3 \times 11}{2 \times 1 \times 100} = \frac{-33}{200}$$

When dividing fractions, the problem is converted by multiplying by the reciprocal of the divisor. This is done by changing division to multiplication and "flipping" the second fraction, or divisor. For example, $\frac{1}{2} \div \frac{3}{5} \rightarrow \frac{1}{2} \times \frac{5}{3}$ and $\frac{5}{1} \div \frac{1}{3} \rightarrow \frac{5}{1} \times \frac{3}{1}$. To complete the problem, the rules for multiplying fractions should be followed.

Note that when adding, subtracting, multiplying, and dividing mixed numbers (ex. $4\frac{1}{2}$), it is easiest to convert these to improper fractions (larger numerator than denominator). To do so, the denominator is kept the same. To obtain the numerator, the whole number is multiplied by the denominator and added to the numerator. For example, $4\frac{1}{2} = \frac{9}{2}$ and $7\frac{2}{3} = \frac{23}{3}$. Also, note that answers involving fractions should be converted to the simplest form.

Rational Numbers and Their Operations
Irregular Products and Quotients
The following shows examples where multiplication does not result in a product greater than both factors, and where division does not result in a quotient smaller than the dividend.

If multiplying numbers where one or more has a value less than one, the product will not be greater than both factors. For example, $6 \times \frac{1}{2} = 3$ and $0.75 \times 0.2 = .15$. When dividing by a number less than

one, the resulting quotient will be greater than the dividend. For example, $8 \div \frac{1}{2} = 16$, because division turns into a multiplication problem:

$$8 \div \frac{1}{2} \rightarrow 8 \times \frac{2}{1}$$

Another example is $0.5 \div 0.2$, which results in 2.5. The problem can be stated by asking how many times 0.2 will go into 0.5. The number being divided is larger than the number that goes into it, so the result will be a number larger than both factors.

Composing and Decomposing Fractions

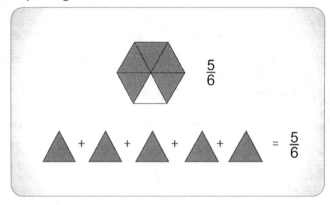

Fractions can be broken apart into sums of fractions with the same denominator. For example, the fraction $\frac{5}{6}$ can be decomposed into sums of fractions with all denominators equal to 6 and the numerators adding to 5. The fraction $\frac{5}{6}$ is decomposed as: $\frac{3}{6} + \frac{2}{6}$; or $\frac{2}{6} + \frac{2}{6} + \frac{1}{6}$; or $\frac{3}{6} + \frac{1}{6} + \frac{1}{6}$; or $\frac{1}{6} + \frac{1}{6} + \frac{1}{6} + \frac{2}{6}$; or:

$$\frac{1}{6} + \frac{1}{6} + \frac{1}{6} + \frac{1}{6} + \frac{1}{6}$$

A **unit fraction** is a fraction in which the numerator is 1. If decomposing a fraction into unit fractions, the sum will consist of a unit fraction added the number of times equal to the numerator. For example, $\frac{3}{4} = \frac{1}{4} + \frac{1}{4} + \frac{1}{4}$ (unit fractions $\frac{1}{4}$ added 3 times). **Composing fractions** is simply the opposite of decomposing. It is the process of adding fractions with the same denominators to produce a single fraction. For example,

$$\frac{3}{7} + \frac{2}{7} = \frac{5}{7}$$

and

$$\frac{1}{5} + \frac{1}{5} + \frac{1}{5} = \frac{3}{5}$$

Decrease in Value of a Unit Fraction

A unit fraction is one in which the numerator is 1 ($\frac{1}{2}, \frac{1}{3}, \frac{1}{8}, \frac{1}{20}$, etc.). The **denominator** indicates the number of *equal pieces* that the whole is divided into. The greater the number of pieces, the smaller each piece will be. Therefore, the greater the denominator of a unit fraction, the smaller it is in value. Unit fractions can also be compared by converting them to decimals. For example, $\frac{1}{2} = 0.5$, $\frac{1}{3} = 0.\overline{3}$, $\frac{1}{8} = 0.125$, $\frac{1}{20} = 0.05$, etc.

Use of the Same Whole when Comparing Fractions

Fractions all represent parts of the same whole. Fractions may have different denominators, but they represent parts of the same one whole, like a pizza. For example, the fractions $\frac{5}{7}$ and $\frac{2}{3}$ can be difficult to compare because they have different denominators. The first fraction may represent a whole divided into seven parts, where five parts are used. The second fraction represents the same whole divided into three parts, where two are used. It may be helpful to convert one or more of the fractions so that they have common denominators for converting to equivalent fractions by finding the LCM of the denominator. Comparing is much easier if fractions are converted to the equivalent fractions of $\frac{15}{21}$ and $\frac{14}{21}$. These fractions show a whole divided into 21 parts, where the numerators can be compared because the denominators are the same.

Order of Operations

When reviewing calculations consisting of more than one operation, the order in which the operations are performed affects the resulting answer. Consider $5 \times 2 + 7$. Performing multiplication then addition results in an answer of 17 ($5 \times 2 = 10$; $10 + 7 = 17$). However, if the problem is written $5 \times (2 + 7)$, the order of operations dictates that the operation inside the parentheses must be performed first. The resulting answer is 45:

$$2 + 7 = 9, \text{so } 5 \times 9 = 45$$

The order in which operations should be performed is remembered using the acronym **PEMDAS**. PEMDAS stands for parentheses, exponents, multiplication/division, and addition/subtraction. Multiplication and division are performed in the same step, working from left to right with whichever comes first. Addition and subtraction are performed in the same step, working from left to right with whichever comes first.

Consider the following example: $8 \div 4 + 8(7 - 7)$. Performing the operation inside the parentheses produces $8 \div 4 + 8(0)$ or $8 \div 4 + 8 \times 0$. There are no exponents, so multiplication and division are performed next from left to right resulting in: $2 + 8 \times 0$, then $2 + 0$. Finally, addition and subtraction are performed to obtain an answer of 2. Now consider the following example: $6x3 + 3^2 - 6$. Parentheses are not applicable. Exponents are evaluated first, $6 \times 3 + 9 - 6$. Then multiplication/division forms $18 + 9 - 6$. At last, addition/subtraction leads to the final answer of 21.

Properties of Operations

Properties of operations exist that make calculations easier and solve problems for missing values. The following table summarizes commonly used properties of real numbers.

Property	Addition	Multiplication
Commutative	$a + b = b + a$	$a \times b = b \times a$
Associative	$(a + b) + c = a + (b + c)$	$(a \times b) \times c = a \times (b \times c)$
Identity	$a + 0 = a; \ 0 + a = a$	$a \times 1 = a; \ 1 \times a = a$
Inverse	$a + (-a) = 0$	$a \times \dfrac{1}{a} = 1; \ a \neq 0$
Distributive	$a(b + c) = ab + ac$	

The **commutative property of addition** states that the order in which numbers are added does not change the sum. Similarly, the commutative property of multiplication states that the order in which numbers are multiplied does not change the product. The **associative property of addition and multiplication** state that the grouping of numbers being added or multiplied does not change the sum or product, respectively. The commutative and associative properties are useful for performing calculations. For example, $(47 + 25) + 3$ is equivalent to $(47 + 3) + 25$, which is easier to calculate.

The **identity property of addition** states that adding zero to any number does not change its value. The **identity property of multiplication** states that multiplying a number by one does not change its value. The **inverse property of addition** states that the sum of a number and its opposite equals zero. **Opposites** are numbers that are the same with different signs (ex. 5 and -5; $-\frac{1}{2}$ and $\frac{1}{2}$). The **inverse property of multiplication** states that the product of a number (other than zero) and its reciprocal equals one. **Reciprocal numbers** have numerators and denominators that are inverted (ex. $\frac{2}{5}$ and $\frac{5}{2}$). Inverse properties are useful for canceling quantities to find missing values (see algebra content). For example, $a + 7 = 12$ is solved by adding the inverse of 7 (which is -7) to both sides in order to isolate a.

The **distributive property** states that multiplying a sum (or difference) by a number produces the same result as multiplying each value in the sum (or difference) by the number and adding (or subtracting) the products. Consider the following scenario: You are buying three tickets for a baseball game. Each ticket costs $18. You are also charged a fee of $2 per ticket for purchasing the tickets online. The cost is calculated: $3 \times 18 + 3 \times 2$. Using the distributive property, the cost can also be calculated $3(18 + 2)$.

Representing Rational Numbers and Their Operations

Concrete Models

Concrete objects are used to develop a tangible understanding of operations of rational numbers. Tools such as tiles, blocks, beads, and hundred charts are used to model problems. For example, a hundred chart (10×10) and beads can be used to model multiplication. If multiplying 5 by 4, beads are placed across 5 rows and down 4 columns producing a product of 20. Similarly, tiles can be used to model division by splitting the total into equal groups. If dividing 12 by 4, 12 tiles are placed one at a time into 4 groups. The result is 4 groups of 3. This is also an effective method for visualizing the concept of remainders.

Representations of objects can be used to expand on the concrete models of operations. Pictures, dots, and tallies can help model these concepts. Utilizing concrete models and representations creates a foundation upon which to build an abstract understanding of the operations.

Rational Numbers on a Number Line

A **number line** typically consists of integers (...3,2,1,0,-1,-2,-3...), and is used to visually represent the value of a rational number. Each rational number has a distinct position on the line determined by comparing its value with the displayed values on the line. For example, if plotting -1.5 on the number line below, it is necessary to recognize that the value of -1.5 is .5 less than -1 and .5 greater than -2. Therefore, -1.5 is plotted halfway between -1 and -2.

Number lines can also be useful for visualizing sums and differences of rational numbers. Adding a value indicates moving to the right (values increase to the right), and subtracting a value indicates moving to the left (numbers decrease to the left). For example, $5 - 7$ is displayed by starting at 5 and moving to the left 7 spaces, if the number line is in increments of 1. This will result in an answer of -2.

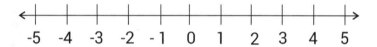

Multiplication and Division Problems

Multiplication and division are inverse operations that can be represented by using rectangular arrays, area models, and equations. Rectangular arrays include an arrangement of rows and columns that correspond to the factors and display product totals.

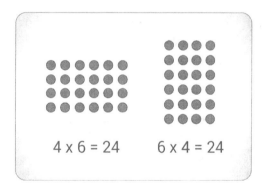

$4 \times 6 = 24$ $6 \times 4 = 24$

Another method of multiplication can be done with the use of an **area model**. An area model is a rectangle that is divided into rows and columns that match up to the number of place values within each number. Take the example 29×65. These two numbers can be split into simpler numbers: $29 = 25 + 4$ and $65 = 60 + 5$. The products of those 4 numbers are found within the rectangle and then summed up to get the answer. The entire process is:

$$(60 \times 25) + (5 \times 25) + (60 \times 4) + (5 \times 4) = 1,500 + 240 + 125 + 20 = 1,885$$

Here is the actual area model:

	25	**4**
60	60x25 1,500	60x4 240
5	5x25 125	5x4 20

$$
\begin{array}{r}
1,500 \\
240 \\
125 \\
+ \quad 20 \\
\hline
1,885
\end{array}
$$

Dividing a number by a single digit or two digits can be turned into repeated subtraction problems. An area model can be used throughout the problem that represents multiples of the divisor. For example, the answer to $8580 \div 55$ can be found by subtracting 55 from 8580 one at a time and counting the total number of subtractions necessary.

However, a simpler process involves using larger multiples of 55. First, $100 \times 55 = 5,500$ is subtracted from 8,580, and 3,080 is leftover. Next, $50 \times 55 = 2,750$ is subtracted from 3,080 to obtain 380. $5 \times 55 = 275$ is subtracted from 330 to obtain 55, and finally, $1 \times 55 = 55$ is subtracted from 55 to obtain zero. Therefore, there is no remainder, and the answer is:

$$100 + 50 + 5 + 1 = 156$$

Here is a picture of the area model and the repeated subtraction process:

$$8580 \div 55$$

	55
100	5500
50	2750
5	275
1	55

$$
\begin{array}{r}
55 \overline{)8580} \\
-5500 \quad \text{(100 x 55)} \\
\hline
3080 \\
-2750 \quad \text{(50 x 55)} \\
\hline
330 \\
-275 \quad \text{(5 x 55)} \\
\hline
55 \\
-55 \quad \text{(1 x 55)} \\
\hline
0
\end{array}
$$

Comparing, Classifying, and Ordering Rational Numbers

A **rational number** is any number that can be written as a fraction or ratio. Within the set of rational numbers, several subsets exist that are referenced throughout the mathematics topics. Counting numbers are the first numbers learned as a child. Counting numbers consist of 1,2,3,4, and so on. **Whole numbers** include all counting numbers and zero (0,1,2,3,4,...). **Integers** include counting numbers, their opposites, and zero (...,-3,-2,-1,0,1,2,3,...). Rational numbers are inclusive of integers, fractions, and decimals that terminate, or end (1.7, 0.04213) or repeat ($0.136\bar{5}$).

When comparing or ordering numbers, the numbers should be written in the same format (decimal or fraction), if possible. For example, $\sqrt{49}$, 7.3, and $\frac{15}{2}$ are easier to order if each one is converted to a decimal, such as 7, 7.3, and 7.5 (converting fractions and decimals is covered in the following section). A number line is used to order and compare the numbers. Any number that is to the right of another number is greater than that number. Conversely, a number positioned to the left of a given number is less than that number.

Converting Between Fractions, Decimals, and Percent

To convert a fraction to a decimal, the numerator is divided by the denominator. For example, $\frac{3}{8}$ can be converted to a decimal by dividing 3 by 8 ($\frac{3}{8} = 0.375$). To convert a decimal to a fraction, the decimal point is dropped, and the value is written as the numerator. The denominator is the place value farthest to the right with a digit other than zero. For example, to convert .48 to a fraction, the numerator is 48, and the denominator is 100 (the digit 8 is in the hundredths place). Therefore,

$$0.48 = \frac{48}{100}$$

Fractions should be written in the simplest form, or reduced. To reduce a fraction, the numerator and denominator are divided by the largest common factor. In the previous example, 48 and 100 are both divisible by 4. Dividing the numerator and denominator by 4 results in a reduced fraction of $\frac{12}{25}$.

To convert a decimal to a percent, the number is multiplied by 100. To convert .13 to a percent, .13 is multiplied by 100 to get 13 percent. To convert a fraction to a percent, the fraction is converted to a decimal and then multiplied by 100. For example, $\frac{1}{5} = 0.20$ and 0.20 multiplied by 100 produces 20 percent.

To convert a percent to a decimal, the value is divided by 100. For example, 125 percent is equal to 1.25 ($\frac{125}{100}$). To convert a percent to a fraction, the percent sign is dropped, and the value is written as the numerator with a denominator of 100. For example, $80\% = \frac{80}{100}$. This fraction can be reduced ($\frac{80}{100} = \frac{4}{5}$).

Understanding Proportional Relationships and Percent

Applying Ratios and Unit Rates

A **ratio** is a comparison of two quantities that represent separate groups. For example, if a recipe calls for 2 eggs for every 3 cups of milk, this is expressed as a ratio. Ratios can be written three ways:

- With the word "to"

85

- Using a colon
- As a fraction.

In the previous example, the ratio of eggs to cups of milk is written as 2 to 3, 2:3, or $\frac{2}{3}$. When writing ratios, the order is very important. The ratio of eggs to cups of milk is not the same as the ratio of cups of milk to eggs, 3:2.

In simplest form, both quantities of a ratio should be written as integers. These should also be reduced just as a fraction is reduced. For example, 5:10 is reduced to 1:2. Given a ratio where one or both quantities are expressed as a decimal or fraction, multiply both by the same number to produce integers. To write the ratio $\frac{1}{3}$ to 2 in simplest form, both quantities are multiplied by 3. The resulting ratio is 1 to 6.

A problem involving ratios may give a comparison between two groups. The problem may then provide a total and ask for a part, or provide a part and ask for a total. Consider the following: The ratio of boys to girls in the 11th grade class is 5:4. If there are a total of 270 11th grade students, how many are girls? The total number of **ratio pieces** should be determined first. The total number of 11th grade students is divided into 9 pieces. The ratio of boys to total students is 5:9, and the ratio of girls to total students is 4:9. Knowing the total number of students, the number of girls is determined by setting up a proportion:

$$\frac{4}{9} = \frac{x}{270}$$

A **rate** is a ratio comparing two quantities expressed in different units. A unit rate is a ratio in which the second quantity is one unit. Rates often include the word *per*. Examples include miles per hour, beats per minute, and price per pound. The word per is represented with a / symbol or abbreviated with the letter *p* and units abbreviated. For example, miles per hour is written as mi/h. When given a rate that is not in its simplest form (the second quantity is not one unit), both quantities are divided by the value of the second quantity. If 99 heartbeats were recorded in $1\frac{1}{2}$ minutes, both quantities are divided by $1\frac{1}{2}$ to determine the heart rate of 66 beats per minute.

Percent
The word **percent** means per hundred. Similar to a unit rate in which the second quantity is always one unit, a percent is a rate where the second quantity is always 100 units. If the results of a poll state that 47 percent of people support a given policy, this indicates that 47 out of every 100 individuals polled were in support. In other words, 47 per 100 support the policy. If an upgraded model of a car costs 110 percent of the cost of the base model, for every $100 that is spent for the base model, $110 must be spent to purchase the upgraded model. In other words, the upgraded model costs $110 per $100 for the cost of the base model.

When dealing with percentages, the numbers can be evaluated as a value in hundredths. For example, 15 percent is expressed as fifteen hundredths and is written as $\frac{15}{100}$ or 0.15.

Unit-Rate Problems
A rate is a ratio in which two terms are in different units. When rates are expressed as a quantity of one, they are considered **unit rates**. To determine a unit rate, the first quantity is divided by the second.

Knowing a unit rate makes calculations easier than simply having a rate. For example, suppose a 3-pound bag of onions costs $1.77. To calculate the price of 5 pounds of onions, a proportion could show:

$$\frac{3}{1.77} = \frac{5}{x}$$

However, by knowing the unit rate, the value of pounds of onions is multiplied by the unit price. The unit price is calculated:

$$\frac{\$1.77}{3 \text{ lb}} = \$0.59/\text{lb}$$

Multiplying the weight of the onions by the unit price yields:

$$5 \text{ lb} \times \frac{\$0.59}{\text{lb}} = \$2.95$$

The *lb.* units cancel out.

Similar to unit-rate problems, unit conversions appear in real-world scenarios including cooking, measurement, construction, and currency. Given the conversion rate, unit conversions are written as a fraction (ratio) and multiplied by a quantity in one unit to convert it to the corresponding unit. To determine how many minutes are in $3\frac{1}{2}$ hours, the conversion rate of 60 minutes to 1 hour is written as $\frac{60 \text{ min}}{1 \text{ h}}$. Multiplying the quantity by the conversion rate results in:

$$3\frac{1}{2}\text{h} \times \frac{60 \text{ min}}{1\text{h}} = 210 \text{ min}$$

(The *h* unit is canceled.)

To convert a quantity in minutes to hours, the fraction for the conversion rate is flipped to cancel the *min* unit. To convert 195 minutes to hours, $195 \text{ min} \times \frac{1 \text{ h}}{60 \text{ min}}$ is multiplied. The result is $\frac{195 \text{ h}}{60}$ which reduces to $3\frac{1}{4}$ h.

Converting units may require more than one multiplication. The key is to set up conversion rates so that units cancel each other out and the desired unit is left. To convert 3.25 yards to inches, given that 1 yd = 3 ft and 12 in = 1 ft, the calculation is performed by multiplying:

$$3.25 \text{ yd} \times \frac{3\text{ft}}{1\text{yd}} \times \frac{12\text{in}}{1\text{ft}}$$

The *yd* and *ft* units will cancel, resulting in 117 in.

Using Proportional Relationships

A **proportion** is a statement consisting of two equal ratios. Proportions will typically give three of four quantities and require solving for the missing value. The key to solving proportions is to set them up

properly. Consider the following: 7 gallons of gas costs $14.70. How many gallons can you get for $20? The information is written as equal ratios with a variable representing the missing quantity:

$$\left(\frac{gallons}{cost} = \frac{gallons}{cost}\right) : \frac{7}{14.70} = \frac{x}{20}$$

To solve for x, the proportion is cross-multiplied. This means the numerator of the first ratio is multiplied by the denominator of the second, and vice versa. The resulting products are shown equal to each other. Cross-multiplying results in:

$$(7)(20) = (14.7)(x)$$

By solving the equation for x (see the algebra content), the answer is that 9.5 gallons of gas may be purchased for $20.

Percent problems can also be solved by setting up proportions. Examples of common percent problems are:

    a. What is 15% of 25?
    b. What percent of 45 is 3?
    c. 5 is $\frac{1}{2}$% of what number?

Setting up the proper proportion is made easier by following the format: $\frac{is}{of} = \frac{percent}{100}$. A variable is used to represent the missing value. The proportions for each of the three examples are set up as follows:

    a. $\dfrac{x}{25} = \dfrac{15}{100}$
    b. $\dfrac{3}{45} = \dfrac{x}{100}$
    c. $\dfrac{5}{x} = \dfrac{\frac{1}{2}}{100}$

By cross-multiplying and solving the resulting equation for the variable, the missing values are determined to be:

    a.   3.75
    b. $6.\overline{6}$%
    c.   1,000

Basic Concepts of Number Theory

Prime and Composite Numbers

Whole numbers are classified as either prime or composite. A **prime number** can only be divided evenly by itself and one. For example, the number 11 can only be divided evenly by 11 and one; therefore, 11 is a prime number. A helpful way to visualize a prime number is to use concrete objects and try to divide them into equal piles. If dividing 11 coins, the only way to divide them into equal piles is to create 1 pile of 11 coins or to create 11 piles of 1 coin each. Other examples of prime numbers include 2, 3, 5, 7, 13, 17, and 19.

A **composite number** is any whole number that is not a prime number. A composite number is a number that can be divided evenly by one or more numbers other than itself and one. For example, the number 6 can be divided evenly by 2 and 3. Therefore, 6 is a composite number. If dividing 6 coins into equal piles, the possibilities are 1 pile of 6 coins, 2 piles of 3 coins, 3 piles of 2 coins, or 6 piles of 1 coin. Other examples of composite numbers include 4, 8, 9, 10, 12, 14, 15, 16, 18, and 20.

To determine if a number is a prime or composite number, the number is divided by every whole number greater than one and less than its own value. If it divides evenly by any of these numbers, then the number is composite. If it does not divide evenly by any of these numbers, then the number is prime. For example, when attempting to divide the number 5 by 2, 3, and 4, none of these numbers divide evenly. Therefore, 5 must be a prime number.

Factors and Multiples of Numbers

The **factors of a number** are all integers that can be multiplied by another integer to produce the given number. For example, 2 is multiplied by 3 to produce 6. Therefore, 2 and 3 are both factors of 6. Similarly, $1 \times 6 = 6$ and $2 \times 3 = 6$, so 1, 2, 3, and 6 are all factors of 6. Another way to explain a factor is to say that a given number divides evenly by each of its factors to produce an integer. For example, 6 does not divide evenly by 5. Therefore, 5 is not a factor of 6.

Multiples of a given number are found by taking that number and multiplying it by any other whole number. For example, 3 is a factor of 6, 9, and 12. Therefore, 6, 9, and 12 are multiples of 3. The multiples of any number are an infinite list. For example, the multiples of 5 are 5, 10, 15, 20, and so on. This list continues without end. A list of multiples is used in finding the least common multiple, or LCM, for fractions when a common denominator is needed. The denominators are written down and their multiples listed until a common number is found in both lists. This common number is the LCM.

Prime factorization breaks down each factor of a whole number until only prime numbers remain. All composite numbers can be factored into prime numbers. For example, the prime factors of 12 are 2, 2, and 3 ($2 \times 2 \times 3 = 12$). To produce the prime factors of a number, the number is factored, and any composite numbers are continuously factored until the result is the product of prime factors only. A factor tree, such as the one below, is helpful when exploring this concept.

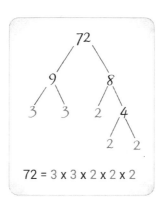

$72 = 3 \times 3 \times 2 \times 2 \times 2$

Determining the Reasonableness of Results

Reasonableness of Results within a Context

When solving math word problems, the solution obtained should make sense within the given scenario. The step of checking the solution will reduce the possibility of a calculation error or a solution that may be *mathematically* correct but not applicable in the real world. Consider the following scenarios:

A problem states that Lisa got 24 out of 32 questions correct on a test and asks to find the percentage of correct answers. To solve the problem, a student divided 32 by 24 to get 1.33, and then multiplied by 100 to get 133 percent. By examining the solution within the context of the problem, the student should recognize that getting all 32 questions correct will produce a perfect score of 100 percent. Therefore, a score of 133 percent with 8 incorrect answers does not make sense, and the calculations should be checked.

A problem states that the maximum weight on a bridge cannot exceed 22,000 pounds. The problem asks to find the maximum number of cars that can be on the bridge at one time if each car weighs 4,000 pounds. To solve this problem, a student divided 22,000 by 4,000 to get an answer of 5.5. By examining the solution within the context of the problem, the student should recognize that although the calculations are mathematically correct, the solution does not make sense. Half of a car on a bridge is not possible, so the student should determine that a maximum of 5 cars can be on the bridge at the same time.

Mental Math Estimation

Once a result is determined to be logical within the context of a given problem, the result should be evaluated by its nearness to the expected answer. This is performed by approximating given values to perform mental math. Numbers should be rounded to the nearest value possible to check the initial results.

Consider the following example: A problem states that a customer is buying a new sound system for their home. The customer purchases a stereo for $435, 2 speakers for $67 each, and the necessary cables for $12. The customer chooses an option that allows him to spread the costs over equal payments for 4 months. How much will the monthly payments be?

After making calculations for the problem, a student determines that the monthly payment will be $145.25. To check the accuracy of the results, the student rounds each cost to the nearest ten ($440 + 70 + 70 + 10$) and determines that the total is approximately $590. Dividing by 4 months gives an approximate monthly payment of $147.50. Therefore, the student can conclude that the solution of $145.25 is very close to what should be expected.

When rounding, the place-value that is used in rounding can make a difference. Suppose the student had rounded to the nearest hundred for the estimation. The result ($400 + 100 + 100 + 0 = 600$; $600 \div 4 = 150$) will show that the answer is reasonable but not as close to the actual value as rounding to the nearest ten.

Algebraic Thinking

Evaluating and Manipulating Algebraic Expressions and Equations

Differentiating between Algebraic Expressions and Equations

An **algebraic expression** is a statement about an unknown quantity expressed in mathematical symbols. A **variable** is used to represent the unknown quantity, usually denoted by a letter. An **equation** is a statement in which two expressions (at least one containing a variable) are equal to each other. An algebraic expression can be thought of as a mathematical phrase and an equation can be thought of as a mathematical sentence.

Algebraic expressions and equations both contain numbers, variables, and mathematical operations. The following are examples of algebraic expressions: $5x + 3$, $7xy - 8(x^2 + y)$, and $\sqrt{a^2 + b^2}$. An expression can be simplified or evaluated for given values of variables. The following are examples of equations: $2x + 3 = 7$, $a^2 + b^2 = c^2$, and $2x + 5 = 3x - 2$. An equation contains two sides separated by an equal sign. Equations can be solved to determine the value(s) of the variable for which the statement is true.

Adding and Subtracting Linear Algebraic Expressions

An algebraic expression is simplified by combining like terms. A **term** is a number, variable, or product of a number and variables separated by addition and subtraction. For the algebraic expression $3x^2 - 4x + 5 - 5x^2 + x - 3$, the terms are $3x^2$, $-4x$, 5, $-5x^2$, x, and -3. **Like terms** have the same variables raised to the same powers (exponents). The like terms for the previous example are $3x^2$ and $-5x^2$, $-4x$ and x, 5 and -3. To combine like terms, the coefficients (numerical factor of the term including sign) are added, and the variables and their powers are kept the same. Note that if a coefficient is not written, it is an implied coefficient of 1 ($x = 1x$). The previous example will simplify to:

$$-2x^2 - 3x + 2$$

When adding or subtracting algebraic expressions, each expression is written in parentheses. The negative sign is distributed when necessary, and like terms are combined. Consider the following: add $2a + 5b - 2$ to $a - 2b + 8c - 4$. The sum is set as follows:

$$(a - 2b + 8c - 4) + (2a + 5b - 2)$$

In front of each set of parentheses is an implied positive one, which, when distributed, does not change any of the terms. Therefore, the parentheses are dropped and like terms are combined:

$$a - 2b + 8c - 4 + 2a + 5b - 2 = 3a + 3b + 8c - 6$$

Consider the following problem: Subtract $2a + 5b - 2$ from $a - 2b + 8c - 4$. The difference is set as follows:

$$(a - 2b + 8c - 4) - (2a + 5b - 2)$$

The implied one in front of the first set of parentheses will not change those four terms. However, distributing the implied -1 in front of the second set of parentheses will change the sign of each of those three terms:

$$a - 2b + 8c - 4 - 2a - 5b + 2$$

91

Combining like terms yields the simplified expression:

$$-a - 7b + 8c - 2$$

Distributive Property

The **distributive property** states that multiplying a sum (or difference) by a number produces the same result as multiplying each value in the sum (or difference) by the number and adding (or subtracting) the products. Using mathematical symbols, the distributive property states:

$$a(b + c) = ab + ac$$

The expression $4(3 + 2)$ is simplified using the order of operations. Simplifying inside the parentheses first produces 4×5, which equals 20. The expression $4(3 + 2)$ can also be simplified using the distributive property:

$$4(3 + 2) = 4 \times 3 + 4 \times 2 = 12 + 8 = 20$$

Consider the following example: $4(3x - 2)$. The expression cannot be simplified inside the parentheses because $3x$ and -2 are not like terms and therefore cannot be combined. However, the expression can be simplified by using the distributive property and multiplying each term inside of the parentheses by the term outside of the parentheses: $12x - 8$. The resulting equivalent expression contains no like terms, so it cannot be further simplified.

Consider the expression:

$$(3x + 2y + 1) - (5x - 3) + 2(3y + 4)$$

Again, there are no like terms, but the distributive property is used to simplify the expression. Note there is an implied one in front of the first set of parentheses and an implied -1 in front of the second set of parentheses. Distributing the 1, -1, and 2 produces:

$$1(3x) + 1(2y) + 1(1) - 1(5x) - 1(-3) + 2(3y) + 2(4)$$

$$3x + 2y + 1 - 5x + 3 + 6y + 8$$

This expression contains like terms that are combined to produce the simplified expression:

$$-2x + 8y + 12$$

Algebraic expressions are tested to be equivalent by choosing values for the variables and evaluating both expressions. For example, $4(3x - 2)$ and $12x - 8$ are tested by substituting 3 for the variable x and calculating to determine if equivalent values result.

Simple Expressions for Given Values

An **algebraic expression** is a statement written in mathematical symbols, typically including one or more unknown values represented by variables. For example, the expression $2x + 3$ states that an unknown number (x) is multiplied by 2 and added to 3. If given a value for the unknown number, or variable, the value of the expression is determined. For example, if the value of the variable x is 4, the value of the expression 4 is multiplied by 2, and 3 is added. This results in a value of 11 for the expression.

92

When given an algebraic expression and values for the variable(s), the expression is evaluated to determine its numerical value. To evaluate the expression, the given values for the variables are substituted (or replaced), and the expression is simplified using the order of operations. Parentheses should be used when substituting. Consider the following: Evaluate $a - 2b + ab$ for $a = 3$ and $b = -1$. To evaluate, any variable a is replaced with 3 and any variable b with -1, producing:

$$(3) - 2(-1) + (3)(-1)$$

Next, the order of operations is used to calculate the value of the expression, which is 2.

Parts of Expressions

Algebraic expressions consist of variables, numbers, and operations. A **term** of an expression is any combination of numbers and/or variables, and terms are separated by addition and subtraction. For example, the expression $5x^2 - 3xy + 4 - 2$ consists of 4 terms: $5x^2$, $-3xy$, $4y$, and -2. Note that each term includes its given sign ($+$ or $-$). The **variable** part of a term is a letter that represents an unknown quantity. The coefficient of a term is the number by which the variable is multiplied. For the term $4y$, the variable is y, and the coefficient is 4. Terms are identified by the power (or exponent) of its variable.

A number without a variable is referred to as a **constant**. If the variable is to the first power (x^1 or simply x), it is referred to as a **linear term**. A term with a variable to the second power (x^2) is quadratic, and a term to the third power (x^3) is cubic. Consider the expression $x^3 + 3x - 1$. The constant is -1. The linear term is $3x$. There is no quadratic term. The cubic term is x^3.

An algebraic expression can also be classified by how many terms exist in the expression. Any like terms should be combined before classifying. A **monomial** is an expression consisting of only one term. Examples of monomials are: 17, $2x$, and $-5ab^2$. A **binomial** is an expression consisting of two terms separated by addition or subtraction. Examples include $2x - 4$ and $-3y^2 + 2y$. A **trinomial** consists of 3 terms. For example, $5x^2 - 2x + 1$ is a trinomial.

Verbal Statements and Algebraic Expressions

An algebraic expression is a statement about unknown quantities expressed in mathematical symbols. The statement *five times a number added to forty* is expressed as $5x + 40$. An equation is a statement in which two expressions (with at least one containing a variable) are equal to one another. The statement *five times a number added to forty is equal to ten* is expressed as:

$$5x + 40 = 10$$

Real world scenarios can also be expressed mathematically. Suppose a job pays its employees $300 per week and $40 for each sale made. The weekly pay is represented by the expression $40x + 300$ where x is the number of sales made during the week.

Consider the following scenario: Bob had $20 and Tom had $4. After selling 4 ice cream cones to Bob, Tom has as much money as Bob. The cost of an ice cream cone is an unknown quantity and can be represented by a variable (x). The amount of money Bob has after his purchase is four times the cost of an ice cream cone subtracted from his original $20 → $20 - 4x$. The amount of money Tom has after his sale is four times the cost of an ice cream cone added to his original $4 → $4x + 4$. After the sale, the amount of money that Bob and Tom have is equal:

$$→ 20 - 4x = 4x + 4$$

93

When expressing a verbal or written statement mathematically, it is vital to understand words or phrases that can be represented with symbols. The following are examples:

Symbol	Phrase
$+$	Added to; increased by; sum of; more than
$-$	Decreased by; difference between; less than; take away
$\times$	Multiplied by; 3(4, 5...) times as large; product of
$\div$	Divided by; quotient of; half (third, etc.) of
$=$	Is; the same as; results in; as much as; equal to
x, t, n, etc.	A number; unknown quantity; value of; variable

Use of Formulas

Formulas are mathematical expressions that define the value of one quantity, given the value of one or more different quantities. Formulas look like equations because they contain variables, numbers, operators, and an equal sign. All formulas are equations, but not all equations are formulas. A formula must have more than one variable. For example, $2x + 7 = y$ is an equation and a formula (it relates the unknown quantities x and y). However, $2x + 7 = 3$ is an equation but not a formula (it only expresses the value of the unknown quantity x).

Formulas are typically written with one variable alone (or isolated) on one side of the equal sign. This variable can be thought of as the *subject* in that the formula is stating the value of the *subject* in terms of the relationship between the other variables. Consider the distance formula: $distance = rate \times time$ or $d = rt$. The value of the subject variable d (distance) is the product of the variable r and t (rate and time). Given the rate and time, the distance traveled can easily be determined by substituting the values into the formula and evaluating.

The formula $P = 2l + 2w$ expresses how to calculate the perimeter of a rectangle (P) given its length (l) and width (w). To find the perimeter of a rectangle with a length of 3 ft and a width of 2 ft, these values are substituted into the formula for l and w:

$$P = 2(3 \text{ ft}) + 2(2 \text{ ft})$$

Following the order of operations, the perimeter is determined to be 10 ft. When working with formulas such as these, including units is an important step.

Given a formula expressed in terms of one variable, the formula can be manipulated to express the relationship in terms of any other variable. In other words, the formula can be rearranged to change which variable is the *subject*. To solve for a variable of interest by manipulating a formula, the equation may be solved as if all other variables were numbers. The same steps for solving are followed, leaving operations in terms of the variables instead of calculating numerical values. For the formula $P = 2l + 2w$, the perimeter is the subject expressed in terms of the length and width. To write a formula to calculate the width of a rectangle, given its length and perimeter, the previous formula relating the three variables is solved for the variable w. If P and l were numerical values, this is a two-step linear equation solved by subtraction and division. To solve the equation $P = 2l + 2w$ for w, $2l$ is first subtracted from both sides:

$$P - 2l = 2w$$

Then both sides are divided by 2:

$$\frac{P - 2l}{2} = w$$

Dependent and Independent Variables

A variable represents an unknown quantity and, in the case of a formula, a specific relationship exists between the variables. Within a given scenario, variables are the quantities that are changing. If two variables exist, one is dependent and one is independent. The value of one variable depends on the other variable. If a scenario describes distance traveled and time traveled at a given speed, distance is dependent and time is independent. The distance traveled depends on the time spent traveling. If a scenario describes the cost of a cab ride and the distance traveled, the cost is dependent and the distance is independent. The cost of a cab ride depends on the distance travelled. Formulas often contain more than two variables and are typically written with the dependent variable alone on one side of the equation. This lone variable is the *subject* of the statement. If a formula contains three or more variables, one variable is dependent and the rest are independent. The values of all independent variables are needed to determine the value of the dependent variable.

The formula $P = 2l + 2w$ expresses the dependent variable P in terms of the independent variables, l and w. The perimeter of a rectangle depends on its length and width. The formula $d = rt$ ($distance = rate \times time$) expresses the dependent variable d in terms of the independent variables, r and t. The distance traveled depends on the rate (or speed) and the time traveled.

Solutions to Linear Equations and Inequalities

Multistep One-Variable Linear Equations and Inequalities

Linear equations and linear inequalities are both comparisons of two algebraic expressions. However, unlike equations in which the expressions are equal, linear inequalities compare expressions that may be unequal. **Linear equations** typically have one value for the variable that makes the statement true. **Linear inequalities** generally have an infinite number of values that make the statement true.

When solving a linear equation, the desired result requires determining a numerical value for the unknown variable. If given a linear equation involving addition, subtraction, multiplication, or division, working backwards isolates the variable. Addition and subtraction are inverse operations, as are multiplication and division. Therefore, they can be used to cancel each other out.

The first steps to solving linear equations are distributing, if necessary, and combining any like terms on the same side of the equation. Sides of an equation are separated by an *equal* sign. Next, the equation is manipulated to show the variable on one side. Whatever is done to one side of the equation must be done to the other side of the equation to remain equal. Inverse operations are then used to isolate the variable and undo the order of operations backwards. Addition and subtraction are undone, then multiplication and division are undone.

For example, solve $4(t - 2) + 2t - 4 = 2(9 - 2t)$

Distributing: $4t - 8 + 2t - 4 = 18 - 4t$

Combining like terms: $6t - 12 = 18 - 4t$

Adding $4t$ to each side to move the variable: $10t - 12 = 18$

Adding 12 to each side to isolate the variable: $10t = 30$

Dividing each side by 10 to isolate the variable: $t = 3$

The answer can be checked by substituting the value for the variable into the original equation, ensuring that both sides calculate to be equal.

Linear inequalities express the relationship between unequal values. More specifically, they describe in what way the values are unequal. A value can be greater than (>), less than (<), greater than or equal to (≥), or less than or equal to (≤) another value. $5x + 40 > 65$ is read as *five times a number added to forty is greater than sixty-five*.

When solving a linear inequality, the solution is the set of all numbers that make the statement true. The inequality $x + 2 \geq 6$ has a solution set of 4 and every number greater than 4 (4.01; 5; 12; 107; etc.). Adding 2 to 4 or any number greater than 4 results in a value that is greater than or equal to 6. Therefore, $x \geq 4$ is the solution set.

To algebraically solve a linear inequality, follow the same steps as those for solving a linear equation. The inequality symbol stays the same for all operations *except* when multiplying or dividing by a negative number. If multiplying or dividing by a negative number while solving an inequality, the relationship reverses (the sign flips). In other words, > switches to < and vice versa. Multiplying or dividing by a positive number does not change the relationship, so the sign stays the same. An example is shown below.

Solve $-2x - 8 \leq 22$ for the value of x.

Add 8 to both sides to isolate the variable:

$$-2x \leq 30$$

Divide both sides by -2 to solve for x:

$$x \geq -15$$

Solutions of a linear equation or a linear inequality are the values of the variable that make a statement true. In the case of a linear equation, the solution set (list of all possible solutions) typically consists of a single numerical value. To find the solution, the equation is solved by isolating the variable. For example, solving the equation $3x - 7 = -13$ produces the solution $x = -2$. The only value for x which produces a true statement is -2. This can be checked by substituting -2 into the original equation to check that both sides are equal. In this case, $3(-2) - 7 = -13 \rightarrow -13 = -13$; therefore, -2 is a solution.

Although linear equations generally have one solution, this is not always the case. If there is no value for the variable that makes the statement true, there is no solution to the equation. Consider the equation:

$$x + 3 = x - 1$$

There is no value for x in which adding 3 to the value produces the same result as subtracting one from the value. Conversely, if any value for the variable makes a true statement, the equation has an infinite number of solutions. Consider the equation:

$$3x + 6 = 3(x + 2)$$

Any number substituted for x will result in a true statement (both sides of the equation are equal).

By manipulating equations like the two above, the variable of the equation will cancel out completely. If the remaining constants express a true statement (ex. $6 = 6$), then all real numbers are solutions to the equation. If the constants left express a false statement (ex. $3 = -1$), then no solution exists for the equation.

Interpreting Solutions on a Number Line

Solving a linear inequality requires all values that make the statement true to be determined. For example, solving $3x - 7 \geq -13$ produces the solution $x \geq -2$. This means that -2 and any number greater than -2 produces a true statement. Solution sets for linear inequalities will often be displayed using a number line. If a value is included in the set ($\geq$ or $\leq$), a shaded dot is placed on that value and an arrow extending in the direction of the solutions. For a variable $>$ or $\geq$ a number, the arrow will point right on a number line, the direction where the numbers increase. If a variable is $<$ or $\leq$ a number, the arrow will point left on a number line, which is the direction where the numbers decrease. If the value is not included in the set ($>$ or $<$), an open (unshaded) circle on that value is used with an arrow in the appropriate direction.

Like this:

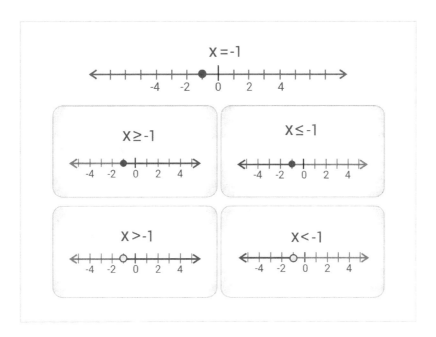

Similar to linear equations, a linear inequality may have a solution set consisting of all real numbers, or can contain no solution. When solved algebraically, a linear inequality in which the variable cancels out and results in a true statement (ex. $7 \geq 2$) has a solution set of all real numbers. A linear inequality in which the variable cancels out and results in a false statement (ex. $7 \leq 2$) has no solution.

Linear Relationships

Linear relationships describe the way two quantities change with respect to each other. The relationship is defined as linear because a line is produced if all the sets of corresponding values are graphed on a coordinate grid. When expressing the linear relationship as an equation, the equation is often written in the form $y = mx + b$ (slope-intercept form) where m and b are numerical values and x and y are variables (for example, $y = 5x + 10$). Given a linear equation and the value of either variable (x or y), the value of the other variable can be determined.

Suppose a teacher is grading a test containing 20 questions with 5 points given for each correct answer, adding a curve of 10 points to each test. This linear relationship can be expressed as the equation $y = 5x + 10$ where x represents the number of correct answers, and y represents the test score. To determine the score of a test with a given number of correct answers, the number of correct answers is substituted into the equation for x and evaluated. For example, for 10 correct answers, 10 is substituted for x:

$$y = 5(10) + 10 \rightarrow y = 60$$

Therefore, 10 correct answers will result in a score of 60. The number of correct answers needed to obtain a certain score can also be determined. To determine the number of correct answers needed to score a 90, 90 is substituted for y in the equation (y represents the test score) and solved:

$$90 = 5x + 10 \rightarrow 80 = 5x \rightarrow 16 = x$$

Therefore, 16 correct answers are needed to score a 90.

Linear relationships may be represented by a table of 2 corresponding values. Certain tables may determine the relationship between the values and predict other corresponding sets. Consider the table below, which displays the money in a checking account that charges a monthly fee:

Month	0	1	2	3	4
Balance	$210	$195	$180	$165	$150

An examination of the values reveals that the account loses $15 every month (the month increases by one and the balance decreases by 15). This information can be used to predict future values. To determine what the value will be in month 6, the pattern can be continued, and it can be concluded that the balance will be $120. To determine which month the balance will be $0, $210 is divided by $15 (since the balance decreases $15 every month), resulting in month 14.

Similar to a table, a graph can display corresponding values of a linear relationship.

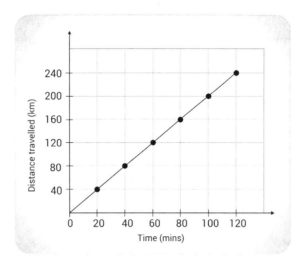

The graph above represents the relationship between distance traveled and time. To find the distance traveled in 80 minutes, the mark for 80 minutes is located at the bottom of the graph. By following this mark directly up on the graph, the corresponding point for 80 minutes is directly across from the 150 kilometer mark. This information indicates that the distance travelled in 80 minutes is 160 kilometers. To predict information not displayed on the graph, the way in which the variables change with respect to one another is determined. In this case, distance increases by 40 kilometers as time increases by 20 minutes. This information can be used to continue the data in the graph or convert the values to a table.

Recognizing and Representing Patterns

Number and Shape Patterns

Patterns within a sequence can come in 2 distinct forms: the items (shapes, numbers, etc.) either repeat in a constant order, or the items change from one step to another in some consistent way. The core is the smallest unit, or number of items, that repeats in a repeating pattern. For example, the pattern ○○▲○○▲○... has a core that is ○○▲. Knowing only the core, the pattern can be extended. Knowing the number of steps in the core allows the identification of an item in each step without drawing/writing the entire pattern out. For example, suppose the tenth item in the previous pattern must be determined. Because the core consists of three items (○○▲), the core repeats in multiples of 3. In other words, steps 3, 6, 9, 12, etc. will be ▲ completing the core with the core starting over on the next step. For the above example, the 9th step will be ▲ and the 10th will be ○.

The most common patterns in which each item changes from one step to the next are arithmetic and geometric sequences. An **arithmetic sequence** is one in which the items increase or decrease by a constant difference. In other words, the same thing is added or subtracted to each item or step to produce the next. To determine if a sequence is arithmetic, determine what must be added or subtracted to step one to produce step two. Then, check if the same thing is added/subtracted to step two to produce step three. The same thing must be added/subtracted to step three to produce step four, and so on.

Consider the pattern 13, 10, 7, 4 . . . To get from step one (13) to step two (10) by adding or subtracting requires subtracting by 3. The next step is checking if subtracting 3 from step two (10) will produce step

99

three (7), and subtracting 3 from step three (7) will produce step four (4). In this case, the pattern holds true. Therefore, this is an arithmetic sequence in which each step is produced by subtracting 3 from the previous step. To extend the sequence, 3 is subtracted from the last step to produce the next. The next three numbers in the sequence are 1, -2, -5.

A **geometric sequence** is one in which each step is produced by multiplying or dividing the previous step by the same number. To determine if a sequence is geometric, decide what step one must be multiplied or divided by to produce step two. Then check if multiplying or dividing step two by the same number produces step three, and so on. Consider the pattern 2, 8, 32, 128 . . . To get from step one (2) to step two (8) requires multiplication by 4. The next step determines if multiplying step two (8) by 4 produces step three (32), and multiplying step three (32) by 4 produces step four (128). In this case, the pattern holds true. Therefore, this is a geometric sequence in which each step is produced by multiplying the previous step by 4. To extend the sequence, the last step is multiplied by 4 and repeated. The next three numbers in the sequence are 512; 2,048; 8,192.

Although arithmetic and geometric sequences typically use numbers, these sequences can also be represented by shapes. For example, an arithmetic sequence could consist of shapes with three sides, four sides, and five sides (add one side to the previous step to produce the next). A geometric sequence could consist of eight blocks, four blocks, and two blocks (each step is produced by dividing the number of blocks in the previous step by 2).

Conjectures, Predictions, or Generalizations Based on Patterns

An arithmetic or geometric sequence can be written as a formula and used to determine unknown steps without writing out the entire sequence. (Note that a similar process for repeating patterns is covered in the previous section.) An arithmetic sequence progresses by a **common difference**. To determine the common difference, any step is subtracted by the step that precedes it. In the sequence 4, 9, 14, 19 . . . the common difference, or d, is 5. By expressing each step as a_1, a_2, a_3, etc., a formula can be written to represent the sequence. a_1 is the first step. To produce step two, step 1 (a_1) is added to the common difference (d):

$$a_2 = a_1 + d$$

To produce step three, the common difference (d) is added twice to a_1:

$$a_3 = a_1 + 2d$$

To produce step four, the common difference (d) is added three times to a_1:

$$a_4 = a_1 + 3d$$

Following this pattern allows a general rule for arithmetic sequences to be written. For any term of the sequence (a_n), the first step (a_1) is added to the product of the common difference (d) and one less than the step of the term ($n - 1$):

$$a_n = a_1 + (n - 1)d$$

Suppose the 8th term (a_8) is to be found in the previous sequence. By knowing the first step (a_1) is 4 and the common difference (d) is 5, the formula can be used:

$$a_n = a_1 + (n - 1)d \rightarrow a_8 = 4 + (7)5 \rightarrow a_8 = 39$$

100

In a geometric sequence, each step is produced by multiplying or dividing the previous step by the same number. The **common ratio**, or (r), can be determined by dividing any step by the previous step. In the sequence 1, 3, 9, 27 . . . the common ratio (r) is 3 ($\frac{3}{1} = 3$ or $\frac{9}{3} = 3$ or $\frac{27}{9} = 3$). Each successive step can be expressed as a product of the first step (a_1) and the common ratio (r) to some power. For example:

$$a_2 = a_1 \times r$$

$$a_3 = a_1 \times r \times r \text{ or } a_3 = a_1 \times r^2$$

$$a_4 = a_1 \times r \times r \times r \text{ or } a_4 = a\_1 \times r^3$$

Following this pattern, a general rule for geometric sequences can be written. For any term of the sequence (a_n), the first step (a_1) is multiplied by the common ratio (r) raised to the power one less than the step of the term $(n - 1)$:

$$a_n = a_1 \times r^{(n-1)}$$

Suppose for the previous sequence, the 7th term (a_7) is to be found. Knowing the first step (a_1) is one, and the common ratio (r) is 3, the formula can be used:

$$a_n = a_1 \times r^{(n-1)} \rightarrow a_7 = (1) \times 3^6 \rightarrow a_7 = 729$$

Corresponding Terms of Two Numerical Patterns

When given two numerical patterns, the corresponding terms should be examined to determine if a relationship exists between them. **Corresponding terms** between patterns are the pairs of numbers that appear in the same step of the two sequences. Consider the following patterns 1, 2, 3, 4 . . . and 3, 6, 9, 12 . . . The corresponding terms are: 1 and 3; 2 and 6; 3 and 9; and 4 and 12. To identify the relationship, each pair of corresponding terms is examined and the possibilities of performing an operation $(+, -, \times, \div)$ to the term from the first sequence to produce the corresponding term in the second sequence are determined.

In this case:

$1 + 2 = 3$ or $1 \times 3 = 3$

$2 + 4 = 6$ or $2 \times 3 = 6$

$3 + 6 = 9$ or $3 \times 3 = 9$

$4 + 8 = 12$ or $4 \times 3 = 12$

The consistent pattern is that the number from the first sequence multiplied by 3 equals its corresponding term in the second sequence. By assigning each sequence a label (input and output) or variable (x and y), the relationship can be written as an equation. If the first sequence represents the inputs, or x, and the second sequence represents the outputs, or y, the relationship can be expressed as: $y = 3x$.

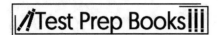

Consider the following sets of numbers:

a	2	4	6	8
b	6	8	10	12

To write a rule for the relationship between the values for a and the values for b, the corresponding terms (2 and 6; 4 and 8; 6 and 10; 8 and 12) are examined. The possibilities for producing b from a are:

$$2 + 4 = 6 \quad \text{or} \quad 2 \times 3 = 6$$

$$4 + 4 = 8 \quad \text{or} \quad 4 \times 2 = 8$$

$$6 + 4 = 10$$

$$8 + 4 = 12 \quad \text{or} \quad 8 \times 1.5 = 12$$

The consistent pattern is that adding 4 to the value of a produces the value of b. The relationship can be written as the equation $a + 4 = b$.

Geometry & Measurement, Data, Statistics, and Probability

Classifying One-, Two-, and Three-Dimensional Figures

Lines, Rays, and Line Segments

The basic unit of geometry is a **point**. A point represents an exact location on a plane, or flat surface. The position of a point is indicated with a dot and usually named with a single uppercase letter, such as point A or point T. A point is a place, not a thing, and therefore has no dimensions or size. A set of points that lies on the same line is called **collinear**.

A set of points that lies on the same plane is called **coplanar**.

 B

● C

 A

The image above displays point A, point B, and point C.

A **line** is as series of points that extends in both directions without ending. It consists of an infinite number of points and is drawn with arrows on both ends to indicate it extends infinitely. Lines can be

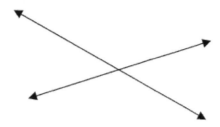
named by two points on the line or with a single, cursive, lower case letter. The two lines below could be named line AB or line BA or $\overleftrightarrow{AB}$ or $\overleftrightarrow{BA}$; and line m.

Two lines are considered parallel to each other if, while extending infinitely, they will never intersect (or meet). **Parallel lines** point in the same direction and are always the same distance apart. Two lines are considered perpendicular if they intersect to form right angles. Right angles are 90°. Typically, a small box is drawn at the intersection point to indicate the right angle.

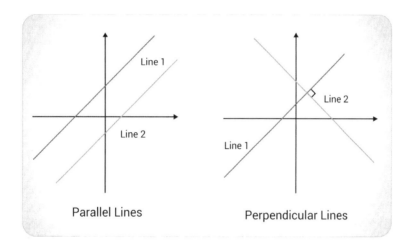

Line 1 is parallel to line 2 in the left image and is written as line 1 || line 2. Line 1 is perpendicular to line 2 in the right image and is written as line 1 ⊥ line 2.

A **ray** has a specific starting point and extends in one direction without ending. The endpoint of a ray is its starting point. Rays are named using the endpoint first, and any other point on the ray. The following ray can be named ray AB and written $\overrightarrow{AB}$.

A **line segment** has specific starting and ending points. A line segment consists of two endpoints and all the points in between. Line segments are named by the two endpoints. The example below is named segment KL or segment LK, written $\overline{KL}$ or $\overline{LK}$.

Classification of Angles

An **angle** consists of two rays that have a common endpoint. This common endpoint is called the **vertex of the angle**. The two rays can be called **sides of the angle**. The angle below has a vertex at point B and the sides consist of ray BA and ray BC. An angle can be named in three ways:

1. Using the vertex and a point from each side, with the vertex letter in the middle.
2. Using only the vertex. This can only be used if it is the only angle with that vertex.
3. Using a number that is written inside the angle.

The angle below can be written $\angle ABC$ (read angle ABC), $\angle CBA$, $\angle B$, or $\angle 1$.

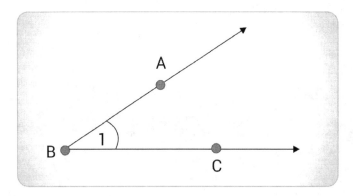

An angle divides a plane, or flat surface, into three parts: the angle itself, the interior (inside) of the angle, and the exterior (outside) of the angle. The figure below shows point M on the interior of the angle and point N on the exterior of the angle.

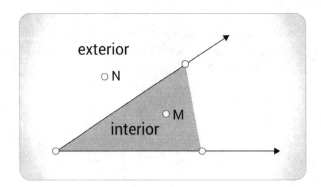

Angles can be measured in units called **degrees**, with the symbol °. The degree measure of an angle is between 0° and 180° and can be obtained by using a protractor.

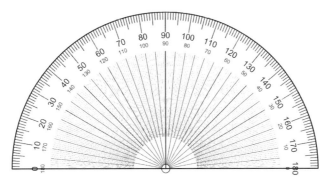

A **straight angle** (or simply a line) measures exactly 180°. A right angle's sides meet at the vertex to create a square corner. A **right angle** measures exactly 90° and is typically indicated by a box drawn in the interior of the angle. An **acute angle** has an interior that is narrower than a right angle. The measure of an acute angle is any value less than 90° and greater than 0°. For example, 89.9°, 47°, 12°, and 1°. An **obtuse angle** has an interior that is wider than a right angle. The measure of an obtuse angle is any value greater than 90° but less than 180°. For example, 90.1°, 110°, 150°, and 179.9°.

- Acute angles: Less than 90°
- Obtuse angles: Greater than 90°
- Right angles: 90°
- Straight angles: 180°

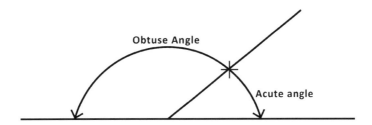

Two- and Three-Dimensional Shapes

A **polygon** is a closed geometric figure in a plane (flat surface) consisting of at least 3 sides formed by line segments. These are often defined as **two-dimensional shapes**. Common two-dimensional shapes

105

include circles, triangles, squares, rectangles, pentagons, and hexagons. Note that a circle is a two-dimensional shape without sides.

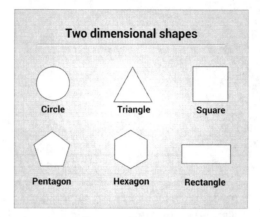

A solid figure, or simply solid, is a figure that encloses a part of space. Some solids consist of flat surfaces only while others include curved surfaces. Solid figures are often defined as **three-dimensional shapes**. Common three-dimensional shapes include spheres, prisms, cubes, pyramids, cylinders, and cones.

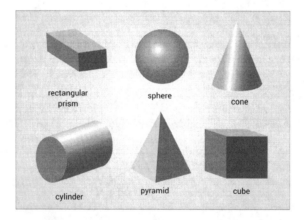

Composing two- or three-dimensional shapes involves putting together two or more shapes to create a new larger figure. For example, a semi-circle (half circle), rectangle, and two triangles can be used to compose the figure of the sailboat shown below.

Similarly, solid figures can be placed together to compose an endless number of three-dimensional objects.

Decomposing two- and three-dimensional figures involves breaking the shapes apart into smaller, simpler shapes. Consider the following two-dimensional representations of a house:

This complex figure can be decomposed into the following basic two-dimensional shapes: large rectangle (body of house); large triangle (roof); small rectangle and small triangle (chimney). Decomposing figures is often done more than one way. To illustrate, the figure of the house could also be decomposed into: two large triangles (body); two medium triangles (roof); two smaller triangles of unequal size (chimney).

Polygons and Solids

A **polygon** is a closed two-dimensional figure consisting of three or more sides. Polygons can be either convex or concave. A polygon that has interior angles all measuring less than 180° is **convex**. A **concave** polygon has one or more interior angles measuring greater than 180°. Examples are shown below.

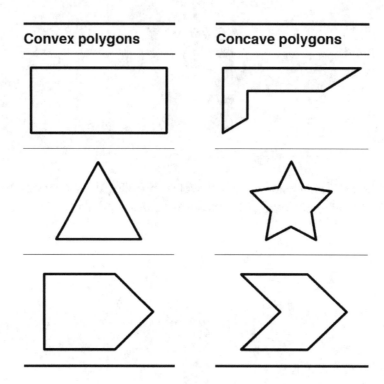

Polygons can be classified by the number of sides (also equal to the number of angles) they have. The following are the names of polygons with a given number of sides or angles:

# of sides	3	4	5	6	7	8	9	10
Name of polygon	Triangle	Quadrilateral	Pentagon	Hexagon	Septagon (or heptagon)	Octagon	Nonagon	Decagon

Equiangular polygons are polygons in which the measure of every interior angle is the same. The sides of **equilateral polygons** are always the same length. If a polygon is both equiangular and equilateral, the polygon is defined as a **regular polygon**. Examples are shown below.

Triangles can be further classified by their sides and angles. A triangle with its largest angle measuring 90° is a **right triangle**. A triangle with the largest angle less than 90° is an **acute triangle**. A triangle with the largest angle greater than 90° is an **obtuse triangle**. Below is an example of a right triangle.

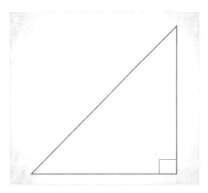

A triangle consisting of two equal sides and two equal angles is an **isosceles triangle**. A triangle with three equal sides and three equal angles is an **equilateral triangle**. A triangle with no equal sides or angles is a **scalene triangle**.

Isosceles triangle:

Equilateral triangle:

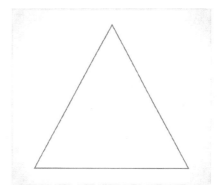

Scalene triangle:

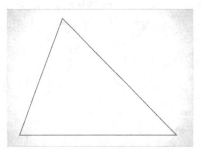

Quadrilaterals can be further classified according to their sides and angles. A quadrilateral with exactly one pair of parallel sides is called a **trapezoid**. A quadrilateral that shows both pairs of opposite sides parallel is a **parallelogram**. Parallelograms include rhombuses, rectangles, and squares. A **rhombus** has four equal sides. A **rectangle** has four equal angles (90° each). A **square** has four 90° angles and four equal sides. Therefore, a square is both a rhombus and a rectangle.

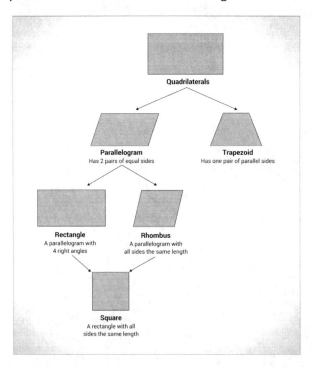

A **solid** is a three-dimensional figure that encloses a part of space. Solids consisting of all flat surfaces that are polygons are called **polyhedrons**. The two-dimensional surfaces that make up a polyhedron are called **faces**. Types of polyhedrons include prisms and pyramids. A **prism** consists of two parallel faces that are congruent (or the same shape and same size), and lateral faces going around (which are parallelograms).

A **prism** is further classified by the shape of its base, as shown below:

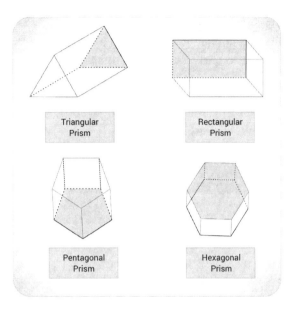

A **pyramid** consists of lateral faces (triangles) that meet at a common point called the **vertex** and one other face that is a polygon, called the **base**. A pyramid can be further classified by the shape of its base, as shown below.

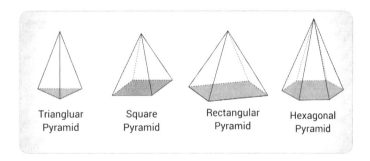

A **tetrahedron** is another name for a triangular pyramid. All the faces of a tetrahedron are triangles.

Solids that are not polyhedrons include spheres, cylinders, and cones. A **sphere** is the set of all points a given distance from a given center point. A sphere is commonly thought of as a three-dimensional circle. A **cylinder** consists of two parallel, **congruent** (same size) circles and a lateral curved surface. A **cone** consists of a circle as its base and a lateral curved surface that narrows to a point called the vertex.

Similar polygons are the same shape but different sizes. More specifically, their corresponding angle measures are congruent (or equal) and the length of their sides is proportional. For example, all sides of one polygon may be double the length of the sides of another. Likewise, similar solids are the same shape but different sizes. Any corresponding faces or bases of similar solids are the same polygons that are proportional by a consistent value.

Perimeter, Area, Surface Area, and Volume

Three-Dimensional Figures with Nets

A **net** is a construction of two-dimensional figures that can be folded to form a given three-dimensional figure. More than one net may exist to fold and produce the same solid, or three-dimensional figure. The bases and faces of the solid figure are analyzed to determine the polygons (two-dimensional figures) needed to form the net.

Consider the following triangular prism:

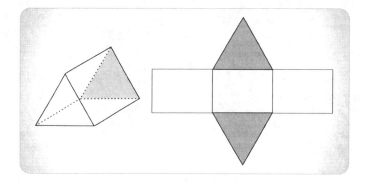

The surface of the prism consists of two triangular bases and three rectangular faces. The net beside it can be used to construct the triangular prism by first folding the triangles up to be parallel to each other, and then folding the two outside rectangles up and to the center with the outer edges touching.

Consider the following cylinder:

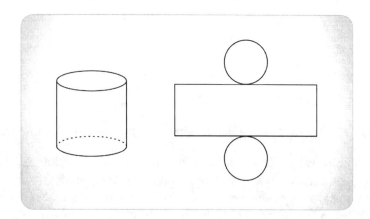

The surface consists of two circular bases and a curved lateral surface that can be opened and flattened into a rectangle. The net beside the cylinder can be used to construct the cylinder by first folding the circles up to be parallel to each other, and then curving the sides of the rectangle up to touch each other. The top and bottom of the folded rectangle should be touching the outside of both circles.

Consider the following square pyramid below on the left. The surface consists of one square base and four triangular faces. The net below on the right can be used to construct the square pyramid by folding each triangle towards the center of the square. The top points of the triangle meet at the vertex.

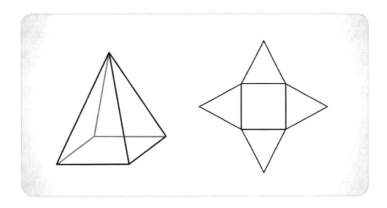

Surface Area of Three-Dimensional Figures

The **area of a two-dimensional figure** refers to the number of square units needed to cover the interior region of the figure. This concept is similar to wallpaper covering the flat surface of a wall. For example, if a rectangle has an area of 10 square centimeters (written 10 cm^2), it will take 10 squares, each with sides one centimeter in length, to cover the interior region of the rectangle. Note that area is measured in square units such as: square centimeters or cm^2; square feet or ft^2; square yards or yd^2; square miles or mi^2.

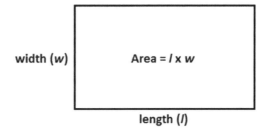

width (*w*)   Area = *l* x *w*

length (*l*)

The **surface area of a three-dimensional figure** refers to the number of square units needed to cover the entire surface of the figure. This concept is similar to using wrapping paper to completely cover the outside of a box. For example, if a triangular pyramid has a surface area of 17 square inches (written 17 in^2), it will take 17 squares, each with sides one inch in length, to cover the entire surface of the pyramid. Surface area is also measured in square units.

Many three-dimensional figures (solid figures) can be represented by nets consisting of rectangles and triangles. The surface area of such solids can be determined by adding the areas of each of its faces and bases. Finding the surface area using this method requires calculating the areas of rectangles and triangles. To find the area (A) of a rectangle, the length (l) is multiplied by the width:

$$(w) \rightarrow A = l \times w$$

The area of a rectangle with a length of 8 cm and a width of 4 cm is calculated:

$$A = (8 \text{ cm}) \times (4 \text{ cm}) \rightarrow A = 32 \text{ cm}^2$$

113

To calculate the area (A) of a triangle, the product of $\frac{1}{2}$, the base (b), and the height (h) is found:

$$A = \frac{1}{2} \times b \times h$$

Note that the height of a triangle is measured from the base to the vertex opposite of it forming a right angle with the base. The area of a triangle with a base of 11 cm and a height of 6 cm is calculated:

$$A = \frac{1}{2} \times (11 \text{ cm}) \times (6 \text{ cm}) \rightarrow A = 33 \text{ cm}^2$$

Consider the following triangular prism, which is represented by a net consisting of two triangles and three rectangles.

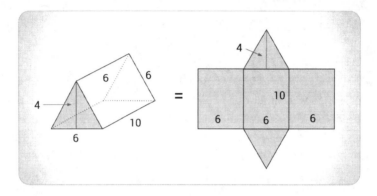

The **surface area of the prism** can be determined by adding the areas of each of its faces and bases. The surface area:

$$SA = area\ of\ triangle + area\ of\ triangle + area\ of\ rectangle$$
$$+ area\ of\ rectangle + area\ of\ rectangle$$

$$SA = \left(\frac{1}{2} \times b \times h\right) + \left(\frac{1}{2} \times b \times h\right) + (l \times w) + (l \times w) + (l \times w)$$

$$SA = \left(\frac{1}{2} \times 6 \times 4\right) + \left(\frac{1}{2} \times 6 \times 4\right) + (6 \times 10) + (6 \times 10) + (6 \times 10)$$

$$SA = (12) + (12) + (60) + (60) + (60)$$

$$SA = 204 \text{ square units}$$

Area and Perimeter of Polygons

Perimeter is the measurement of a distance around something or the sum of all sides of a polygon. Think of perimeter as the length of the boundary, like a fence. In contrast, **area** is the space occupied by a defined enclosure, like a field enclosed by a fence.

When thinking about perimeter, think about walking around the outside of something. When thinking about area, think about the amount of space or **surface area** something takes up.

Squares

The **perimeter of a square** is measured by adding together all of the sides. Since a square has four equal sides, its perimeter can be calculated by multiplying the length of one side by 4. Thus, the formula is $P = 4 \times s$, where s equals one side. For example, the following square has side lengths of 5 meters:

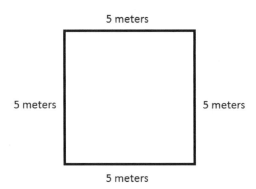

The perimeter is 20 meters because 4 times 5 is 20.

The **area of a square** is the length of a side squared. For example, if a side of a square is 7 centimeters, then the area is 49 square centimeters. The formula for this example is $A = s^2 = 7^2 = 49$ square centimeters. An example is if the rectangle has a length of 6 inches and a width of 7 inches, then the area is 42 square inches:

$$A = lw = 6(7) = 42 \text{ square inches}$$

Rectangles

Like a square, a **rectangle's perimeter** is measured by adding together all of the sides. But as the sides are unequal, the formula is different. A rectangle has equal values for its lengths (long sides) and equal values for its widths (short sides), so the perimeter formula for a rectangle is:

$$P = l + l + w + w = 2l + 2w$$

l equals length
w equals width

The area is found by multiplying the length by the width, so the formula is $A = l \times w$.

For example, if the length of a rectangle is 10 inches and the width 8 inches, then the perimeter is 36 inches because:

$$P = 2l + 2w = 2(10) + 2(8) = 20 + 16 = 36 \text{ inches}$$

Triangles

A **triangle's perimeter** is measured by adding together the three sides, so the formula is $P = a + b + c$, where a, b, and c are the values of the three sides. The area is the product of one-half the base and height so the formula is:

$$A = \frac{1}{2} \times b \times h$$

115

It can be simplified to:

$$A = \frac{bh}{2}$$

The base is the bottom of the triangle, and the height is the distance from the base to the peak. If a problem asks to calculate the area of a triangle, it will provide the base and height.

For example, if the base of the triangle is 2 feet and the height 4 feet, then the area is 4 square feet. The following equation shows the formula used to calculate the area of the triangle:

$A = \frac{1}{2}bh = \frac{1}{2}(2)(4) = 4$ square feet

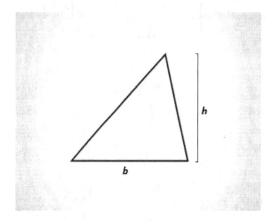

Circles

A circle's perimeter—also known as its **circumference**—is measured by multiplying the diameter by π.

Diameter is the straight line measured from a point on one side of the circle to a point directly across on the opposite side of the circle.

π is referred to as **pi** and is equal to 3.14 (with rounding).

So, the formula is $\pi \times d$.

This is sometimes expressed by the formula $C = 2 \times \pi \times r$, where r is the radius of the circle. These formulas are equivalent, as the radius equals half of the diameter.

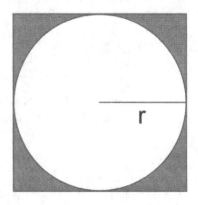

The area of a circle is calculated through the formula:

$$A = \pi \times r^2$$

The test will indicate either to leave the answer with π attached or to calculate to the nearest decimal place, which means multiplying by 3.14 for π.

Arc

The **arc of a circle** is the distance between two points on the circle. The length of the arc of a circle in terms of **degrees** is easily determined if the value of the central angle is known. The length of the arc is simply the value of the central angle. In this example, the length of the arc of the circle in degrees is 75°.

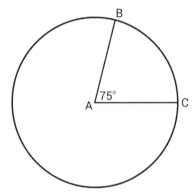

To determine the length of the arc of a circle in distance, the values for both the central angle and the radius must be known. This formula is:

$$\frac{central\ angle}{360°} = \frac{arc\ length}{2\pi r}$$

The equation is simplified by cross-multiplying to solve for the arc length. In the following example, to solve for arc length, substitute the values of the central angle (75°) and the radius (10 inches) into the equation above.

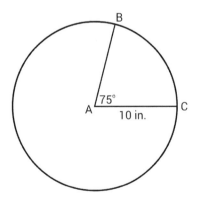

$$\frac{75°}{360°} = \frac{arc\ length}{2(3.14)(10\ in)}$$

To solve the equation, first cross-multiply: $4{,}710 = 360(arc\ length)$. Next, divide each side of the equation by 360. The result of the formula is that the arc length is 13.1 (rounded).

Parallelograms

Similar to triangles, the height of the parallelogram is measured from one base to the other at a 90° angle (or perpendicular).

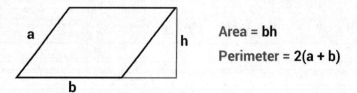

Area = bh

Perimeter = 2(a + b)

Trapezoid

The **area of a trapezoid** can be calculated using the formula: $A = \frac{1}{2} \times h(b_1 + b_2)$, where h is the height and b_1 and b_2 are the parallel bases of the trapezoid:

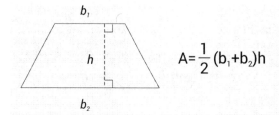

$$A = \frac{1}{2}(b_1 + b_2)h$$

Regular Polygon

The area of a regular polygon can be determined by using its perimeter and the length of the apothem. The **apothem** is a line from the center of the regular polygon to any of its sides at a right angle. (Note that the perimeter of a regular polygon can be determined given the length of only one side.) The formula for the area (A) of a regular polygon is $A = \frac{1}{2} \times a \times P$, where a is the length of the apothem, and P is the perimeter of the figure. Consider the following regular pentagon:

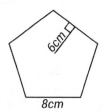

6cm

8cm

To find the area, the perimeter (P) is calculated first: $8 \text{ cm} \times 5 \rightarrow P = 40 \text{ cm}$. Then the perimeter and the apothem are used to find the area (A):

$$A = \frac{1}{2} \times a \times P \rightarrow A = \frac{1}{2} \times (6 \text{ cm}) \times (40 \text{ cm}) \rightarrow A = 120 \text{ cm}^2$$

Note that the unit is:

$$\text{cm}^2 \rightarrow \text{cm} \times \text{cm} = \text{cm}^2$$

Irregular Shapes

The perimeter of an irregular polygon is found by adding the lengths of all of the sides. In cases where all of the sides are given, this will be very straightforward, as it will simply involve finding the sum of the provided lengths. Other times, a side length may be missing and must be determined before the perimeter can be calculated.

Consider the example below:

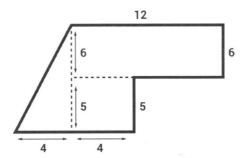

All of the side lengths are provided except for the angled side on the left. Test takers should notice that this is the hypotenuse of a right triangle. The other two sides of the triangle are provided (the base is 4 and the height is $6 + 5 = 11$). The Pythagorean Theorem can be used to find the length of the hypotenuse, remembering that:

$$a^2 + b^2 = c^2$$

Substituting the side values provided yields:

$$(4)^2 + (11)^2 = c^2$$

Therefore,

$$c = \sqrt{16 + 121} = 11.7$$

Finally, the perimeter can be found by adding this new side length with the other provided lengths to get the total length around the figure:

$$4 + 4 + 5 + 8 + 6 + 12 + 11.7 = 50.7$$

Although units are not provided in this figure, remember that reporting units with a measurement is important.

The area of irregular polygons is found by decomposing, or breaking apart, the figure into smaller shapes. When the area of the smaller shapes is determined, the area of the smaller shapes will produce the area of the original figure when added together. Consider the earlier example:

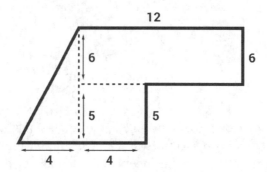

The irregular polygon is decomposed into two rectangles and a triangle. The area of the large rectangle ($A = l \times w \rightarrow A = 12 \times 6$) is 72 square units. The area of the small rectangle is 20 square units ($A = 4 \times 5$). The area of the triangle ($A = \frac{1}{2} \times b \times h \rightarrow A = \frac{1}{2} \times 4 \times 11$) is 22 square units. The sum of the areas of these figures produces the total area of the original polygon:

$A = 72 + 20 + 22 \rightarrow A = 114$ square units

Here's another example:

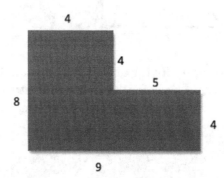

This irregular polygon is decomposed into two rectangles. The area of the large rectangle ($A = l \times w \rightarrow A = 8 \times 4$) is 32 square units. The area of the small rectangle is 20 square units ($A = 4 \times 5$). The sum of the areas of these figures produces the total area of the original polygon:

$A = 32 + 20 \rightarrow A = 52$ square units

Right Rectangular Prisms

A **right rectangular prism** consists of:

- Two congruent (same size and shape) rectangles as the parallel *bases* (top and bottom).
- Two congruent rectangles as the *side* faces.
- Two congruent rectangles as the *front and back* faces.

It is called a right prism because the base and sides meet at right angles.

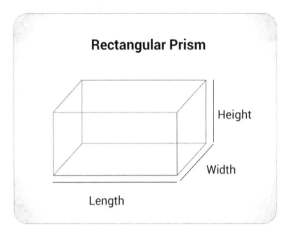

The length and width of the prism is the length and width of the rectangular base. The height of the prism is the measure from one base to the other.

The surface area of three-dimensional figures can be found by adding the areas of each of its bases and faces. The areas of a right rectangular prism are found as follows: two bases → $A = l \times w$; front and back faces → $A = l \times h$; two side faces → $A = w \times h$. The sum of these six areas will equal the surface area of the prism.

$$Surface\ area\ =\ area\ of\ 2\ bases\ +\ area\ of\ front\ and\ back\ +\ area\ of\ 2\ sides$$

This is true for all right rectangular prisms leading to the formula for surface area:

$$SA = 2 \times l \times w + 2 \times l \times h + 2 \times w \times h$$

$$SA = 2(l \times w + l \times h + w \times h)$$

Given the right rectangular prism below, the surface area is calculated as follows:

$$SA = 2\left(3\frac{1}{2}\text{ft}\right)\left(2\frac{1}{2}\text{ft}\right) + 2\left(3\frac{1}{2}\text{ft}\right)\left(1\frac{1}{2}\text{ft}\right) + 2\left(2\frac{1}{2}\text{ft}\right)\left(1\frac{1}{2}\text{ft}\right) \rightarrow SA = 35.5\text{ ft}^2$$

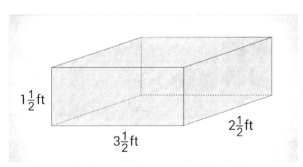

The **volume of a solid** (three-dimensional figure) is the number of cubic units needed to fill the space that the figure occupies. This concept is similar to filling a box with blocks. Volume is a three-dimensional measurement. Therefore, volume is expressed in cubic units such as cubic centimeters

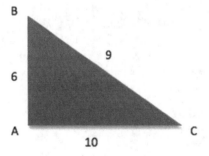
(cm^3), cubic feet (ft^3), and cubic yards (yd^3). If a rectangular prism has a volume of 30 cubic meters (30 m^3), it will take 30 cubes, each with sides one meter in length, to fill the space occupied by the prism. A simple formula can be used to determine the volume of a right rectangular prism. The area of the base of the prism ($l \times w$) will indicate how many "blocks" are needed to cover the base. The height (h) of the prism will indicate how many "levels" of blocks are needed to construct the prism.

Therefore, to find the volume (V) of a right rectangular prism, the area of the base ($l \times w$) is multiplied by the height (h):

$$V = l \times w \times h$$

The volume of the prism shown above is calculated:

$$V = \left(3\frac{1}{2}\text{ft}\right) \times \left(2\frac{1}{2}\text{ft}\right) \times \left(1\frac{1}{2}\text{ft}\right) \rightarrow V = 13.125 \text{ ft}^3$$

Effects of Changes to Dimensions on Area and Volume

Similar polygons are figures that are the same shape but different sizes. Likewise, similar solids are different sizes but are the same shape. In both cases, corresponding angles in the same positions for both figures are congruent (equal), and corresponding sides are proportional in length. For example, the triangles below are similar. The following pairs of corresponding angles are congruent: $\angle A$ and $\angle D$; $\angle B$ and $\angle E$; $\angle C$ and $\angle F$. The corresponding sides are proportional:

$$\frac{AB}{DE} = \frac{6}{3} = 2$$

$$\frac{BC}{EF} = \frac{9}{4.5} = 2$$

$$\frac{CA}{FD} = \frac{10}{5} = 2$$

In other words, triangle ABC is the same shape but twice as large as triangle DEF.

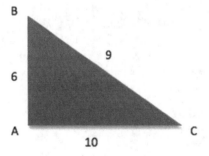
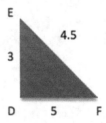

An example of similar triangular pyramids is shown below.

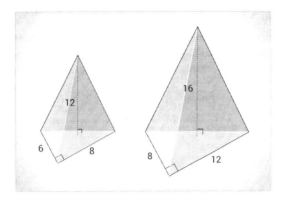

Given the nature of two- and three-dimensional measurements, changing dimensions by a given scale (multiplier) does not change the area of volume by the same scale. Consider a rectangle with a length of 5 centimeters and a width of 4 centimeters. The area of the rectangle is 20 cm^2. Doubling the dimensions of the rectangle (multiplying by a scale factor of 2) to 10 centimeters and 8 centimeters *does not* double the area to 40 cm^2. Area is a two-dimensional measurement (measured in square units). Therefore, the dimensions are multiplied by a scale that is squared (raised to the second power) to determine the scale of the corresponding areas. For the previous example, the length and width are multiplied by 2. Therefore, the area is multiplied by 2^2, or 4. The area of a 5 cm × 4 cm rectangle is 20 cm^2. The area of a 10 cm × 8 cm rectangle is 80 cm^2.

Volume is a three-dimensional measurement, which is measured in cubic units. Therefore, the scale between dimensions of similar solids is cubed (raised to the third power) to determine the scale between their volumes. Consider similar right rectangular prisms: one with a length of 8 inches, a width of 24 inches, and a height of 16 inches; the second with a length of 4 inches, a width of 12 inches, and a height of 8 inches. The first prism, multiplied by a scalar of $\frac{1}{2}$, produces the measurement of the second prism. The volume of the first prism, multiplied by $(\frac{1}{2})^3$, which equals $\frac{1}{8}$, produces the volume of the second prism. The volume of the first prism is 8 in × 24 in × 16 in which equals 3,072 in^3. The volume of the second prism is 4 in × 12 in × 8 in which equals 384 in^3:

$$3{,}072 \text{ in}^3 \times \frac{1}{8} = 384 \text{ in}^3$$

The rules for squaring the scalar for area and cubing the scalar for volume only hold true for similar figures. In other words, if only one dimension is changed (changing the width of a rectangle but not the length) or dimensions are changed at different rates (the length of a prism is doubled and its height is tripled) the figures are not similar (same shape). Therefore, the rules above do not apply.

Components of the Coordinate Plane

X-Axis, Y-Axis, Origin, and Four Quadrants

The **coordinate plane**, sometimes referred to as the **Cartesian plane**, is a two-dimensional surface consisting of a horizontal and a vertical number line. The horizontal number line is referred to as the **x-axis**, and the vertical number line is referred to as the **y-axis**. The x-axis and y-axis intersect (or cross) at a point called the **origin**. At the origin, the value of the x-axis is zero, and the value of the y-axis is zero.

The coordinate plane identifies the exact location of a point that is plotted on the two-dimensional surface. Like a map, the location of all points on the plane are in relation to the origin. Along the x-axis (horizontal line), numbers to the right of the origin are positive and increasing in value $(1, 2, 3,...)$ and to the left of the origin numbers are negative and decreasing in value $(-1, -2, -3,...)$. Along the y-axis (vertical line), numbers above the origin are positive and increasing in value and numbers below the origin are negative and decreasing in value.

The x- and y-axis divide the coordinate plane into four sections. These sections are referred to as quadrant one, quadrant two, quadrant three, and quadrant four, and are often written with Roman numerals I, II, III, and IV.

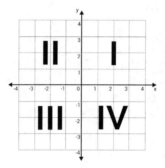

The upper right section is **Quadrant I** and consists of points with positive x-values and positive y-values. The upper left section is **Quadrant II** and consists of points with negative x-values and positive y-values. The bottom left section is **Quadrant III** and consists of points with negative x-values and negative y-values. The bottom right section is **Quadrant IV** and consists of points with positive x-values and negative y-values.

Solving Problems in the Coordinate Plane

The location of a point on a coordinate grid is identified by writing it as an ordered pair. An **ordered pair** is a set of numbers indicating the x-and y-coordinates of the point. Ordered pairs are written in the form (x, y) where x and y are values which indicate their respective coordinates. For example, the point $(3, -2)$ has an x-coordinate of 3 and a y-coordinate of -2.

Plotting a point on the coordinate plane with a given coordinate means starting from the origin $(0, 0)$. To determine the value of the x-coordinate, move right (positive number) or left (negative number) along the x-axis. Next, move up (positive number) or down (negative number) to the value of the y-coordinate. Finally, plot and label the point. For example, plotting the point $(1, -2)$ requires starting from the origin and moving right along the x-axis to positive one, then moving down until straight across from negative 2 on the y-axis. The point is plotted and labeled. This point, along with three other points, are plotted and labeled on the graph below.

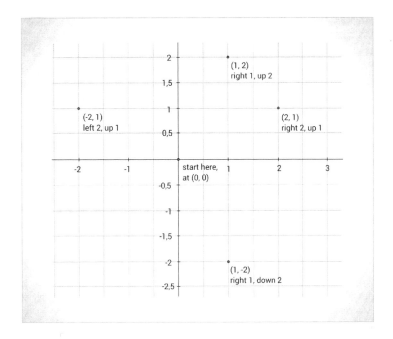

To write the coordinates of a point on the coordinate grid, a line should be traced directly above or below the point until reaching the x-axis (noting the value on the x-axis). Then, returning to the point, a line should be traced directly to the right or left of the point until reaching the y-axis (noting the value on the y-axis). The ordered pair (x, y) should be written with the values determined for the x- and y-coordinates.

Polygons can be drawn in the coordinate plane given the coordinates of their vertices. These coordinates can be used to determine the perimeter and area of the figure. Suppose triangle RQP has

vertices located at the points: $R(-4, 2)$, $Q(1, 6)$, and $P(1, 2)$. By plotting the points for the three vertices, the triangle can be constructed as follows:

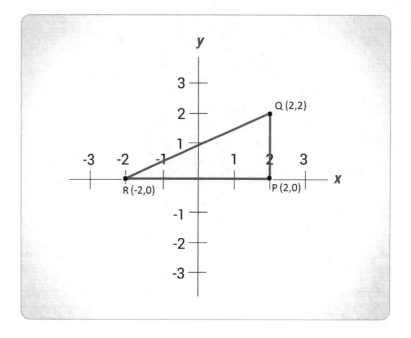

Because points R and P have the same y-coordinates (they are directly across from each other), the distance between them is determined by subtracting their x-coordinates (or simply counting units from one point to the other): $2 - (-2) = 4$. Therefore, the length of side RP is 4 units. Because points Q and P have the same x-coordinate (they are directly above and below each other), the distance between them is determined by subtracting their y-coordinates (or counting units between them): $2 - 0 = 2$. Therefore, the length of side PQ is 2 units. Knowing the length of side RP, which is the base of the triangle, and the length of side PQ, which is the height of the triangle, the area of the figure can be determined by using the formula $A = \frac{1}{2}bh$.

To determine the perimeter of the triangle, the lengths of all three sides are needed. Points R and Q are neither directly across nor directly above and below each other. Therefore, the distance formula must be used to find the length of side RQ.

The distance formula is as follows:

$$d = \sqrt{(x_2 - x_1)^2 + (y_2 - y_1)^2}$$

$$d = \sqrt{(2 - (-2))^2 + (2 - 0)^2}$$

$$d = \sqrt{(4)^2 + (2)^2}$$

$$d = \sqrt{16 + 4}$$

$$d = \sqrt{20}$$

The perimeter is determined by adding the lengths of the three sides of the triangle.

Solving Problems Involving Measurement

Elapsed Time, Money, Length, Volume, and Mass

Word problems involving elapsed time, money, length, volume, and mass require determining which operations (addition, subtraction, multiplication, and division) should be performed, and using and/or converting the proper unit for the scenario.

The following table lists key words that can be used to indicate the proper operation:

Addition	Sum, total, in all, combined, increase of, more than, added to
Subtraction	Difference, change, remaining, less than, decreased by
Multiplication	Product, times, twice, triple, each
Division	Quotient, goes into, per, evenly, divided by half, divided by third, split

Identifying and utilizing the proper units for the scenario requires knowing how to apply the conversion rates for money, length, volume, and mass. For example, given a scenario that requires subtracting 8 inches from $2\frac{1}{2}$ feet, both values should first be expressed in the same unit (they could be expressed $\frac{2}{3}$ ft & $2\frac{1}{2}$ ft, or 8 in and 30 in). The desired unit for the answer may also require converting back to another unit.

Consider the following scenario: A parking area along the river is only wide enough to fit one row of cars and is $\frac{1}{2}$ kilometers long. The average space needed per car is 5 meters. How many cars can be parked along the river? First, all measurements should be converted to similar units: $\frac{1}{2}$ km = 500 m. The operation(s) needed should be identified. Because the problem asks for the number of cars, the total space should be divided by the space per car. 500 meters divided by 5 meters per car yields a total of 100 cars. Written as an expression, the meters unit cancels and the cars unit is left: $\frac{500\ m}{5\ m/car}$ the same as 500 m $\times \frac{1\ car}{5\ m}$ yields 100 cars.

When dealing with problems involving elapsed time, breaking the problem down into workable parts is helpful. For example, suppose the length of time between 1:15pm and 3:45pm must be determined. From 1:15pm to 2:00pm is 45 minutes (knowing there are 60 minutes in an hour). From 2:00pm to 3:00pm is 1 hour. From 3:00pm to 3:45pm is 45 minutes. The total elapsed time is 45 minutes plus 1 hour plus 45 minutes. This sum produces 1 hour and 90 minutes. 90 minutes is over an hour, so this is converted to 1 hour (60 minutes) and 30 minutes. The total elapsed time can now be expressed as 2 hours and 30 minutes.

Measuring Lengths of Objects

The length of an object can be measured using standard tools such as rulers, yard sticks, meter sticks, and measuring tapes. The following image depicts a yardstick:

Choosing the right tool to perform the measurement requires determining whether United States customary units or metric units are desired, and having a grasp of the approximate length of each unit and the approximate length of each tool. The measurement can still be performed by trial and error without the knowledge of the approximate size of the tool.

For example, to determine the length of a room in feet, a United States customary unit, various tools can be used for this task. These include a ruler (typically 12 inches/1 foot long), a yardstick (3 feet/1 yard long), or a tape measure displaying feet (typically either 25 feet or 50 feet). Because the length of a room is much larger than the length of a ruler or a yardstick, a tape measure should be used to perform the measurement.

When the correct measuring tool is selected, the measurement is performed by first placing the tool directly above or below the object (if making a horizontal measurement) or directly next to the object (if making a vertical measurement). The next step is aligning the tool so that one end of the object is at the mark for zero units, then recording the unit of the mark at the other end of the object. To give the length of a paperclip in metric units, a ruler displaying centimeters is aligned with one end of the paper clip to the mark for zero centimeters.

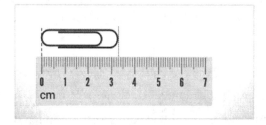

Directly down from the other end of the paperclip is the mark that measures its length. In this case, that mark is two small dashes past the 3 centimeter mark. Each small dash is 1 millimeter (or .1 centimeters). Therefore, the length of the paper clip is 3.2 centimeters.

To compare the lengths of objects, each length must be expressed in the same unit. If possible, the objects should be measured with the same tool or with tools utilizing the same units. For example, a ruler and a yardstick can both measure length in inches. If the lengths of the objects are expressed in different units, these different units must be converted to the same unit before comparing them. If two lengths are expressed in the same unit, the lengths may be compared by subtracting the smaller value from the larger value. For example, suppose the lengths of two gardens are to be compared. Garden A has a length of 4 feet, and garden B has a length of 2 yards. 2 yards is converted to 6 feet so that the measurements have similar units. Then, the smaller length (4 feet) is subtracted from the larger length (6 ft): 6 ft − 4 ft = 2 ft. Therefore, garden B is 2 feet larger than garden A.

Relative Sizes of United States Customary Units and Metric Units

The United States customary system and the metric system each consist of distinct units to measure lengths and volume of liquids. The U.S. customary units for length, from smallest to largest, are: inch (in), foot (ft), yard (yd), and mile (mi). The metric units for length, from smallest to largest, are: millimeter (mm), centimeter (cm), decimeter (dm), meter (m), and kilometer (km). The relative size of each unit of length is shown below.

U.S. Customary	Metric	Conversion
12 in = 1 ft	10 mm = 1 cm	1 in = 2.54 cm
36 in = 3 ft = 1 yd	10 cm = 1 dm(decimeter)	1m ≈ 3.28 ft ≈ 1.09 yd
5,280 ft = 1,760 yd = 1 mi	100 cm = 10 dm = 1 m	1 mi ≈ 1.6 km
	1,000 m = 1 km	

The U.S. customary units for volume of liquids, from smallest to largest, are: fluid ounces (fl oz), cup (c), pint (pt), quart (qt), and gallon (gal). The metric units for volume of liquids, from smallest to largest, are: milliliter (mL), centiliter (cL), deciliter (dL), liter (L), and kiloliter (kL). The relative size of each unit of liquid volume is shown below.

U.S. Customary	Metric	Conversion
8 fl oz = 1 c	10 mL = 1 cL	1 pt ≈ 0.473 L
2 c = 1 pt	10 cL = 1 dL	1 L ≈ 1.057 qt
4 c = 2 pt = 1 qt	1,000 mL = 100 cL = 10 dL = 1 L	1 gal ≈ 3.785 L
4 qt = 1 gal	1,000 L = 1 kL	

The U.S. customary system measures weight (how strongly Earth is pulling on an object) in the following units, from least to greatest: ounce (oz), pound (lb), and ton. The metric system measures mass (the quantity of matter within an object) in the following units, from least to greatest: milligram (mg), centigram (cg), gram (g), kilogram (kg), and metric ton (MT). The relative sizes of each unit of weight and mass are shown below.

U.S. Measures of Weight	Metric Measures of Mass
16 oz = 1 lb	10 mg = 1 cg
2,000 lbs = 1 ton	100 cg = 1 g
	1,000 g = 1 kg
	1,000 kg = 1 MT

Note that weight and mass DO NOT measure the same thing.

Time is measured in the following units, from shortest to longest: second (sec), minute (min), hour (h), day (d), week (wk), month (mo), year (yr), decade, century, millennium. The relative sizes of each unit of time is shown below.

- 60 sec = 1 min
- 60 min = 1 h
- 24 hr = 1 d
- 7 d = 1 wk
- 52 wk = 1 yr
- 12 mo = 1 yr

- 10 yr = 1 decade
- 100 yrs = 1 century
- 1,000 yrs = 1 millennium

Conversion of Units

When working with different systems of measurement, conversion from one unit to another may be necessary. The conversion rate must be known to convert units. One method for converting units is to write and solve a proportion. The arrangement of values in a proportion is extremely important. Suppose that a problem requires converting 20 fluid ounces to cups. To do so, a proportion can be written using the conversion rate of 8 fl oz = 1 c with x representing the missing value. The proportion can be written in any of the following ways:

$$\frac{1}{8} = \frac{x}{20} \left(\frac{c\ for\ conversion}{fl\ oz\ for\ conversion} = \frac{unknown\ c}{fl\ oz\ given} \right)$$

$$\frac{8}{1} = \frac{20}{x} \left(\frac{fl\ oz\ for\ conversion}{c\ for\ conversion} = \frac{fl\ oz\ given}{unknown\ c} \right)$$

$$\frac{1}{x} = \frac{8}{20} \left(\frac{c\ for\ conversion}{unknown\ c} = \frac{fl\ oz\ for\ conversion}{fl\ oz\ given} \right)$$

$$\frac{x}{1} = \frac{20}{8} \left(\frac{unknown\ c}{c\ for\ conversion} = \frac{fl\ oz\ given}{fl\ oz\ for\ conversion} \right)$$

To solve a proportion, the ratios are cross-multiplied and the resulting equation is solved. When cross-multiplying, all four proportions above will produce the same equation:

$$(8)(x) = (20)(1) \rightarrow 8x = 20$$

Divide by 8 to isolate the variable x, the result is $x = 2.5$. The variable x represented the unknown number of cups. Therefore, the conclusion is that 20 fluid ounces converts (is equal) to 2.5 cups.

Sometimes converting units requires writing and solving more than one proportion. Suppose an exam question asks to determine how many hours are in 2 weeks. Without knowing the conversion rate between hours and weeks, this can be determined knowing the conversion rates between weeks and days, and between days and hours. First, weeks are converted to days, then days are converted to hours. To convert from weeks to days, the following proportion can be written:

$$\frac{7}{1} = \frac{x}{2} \left(\frac{days\ conversion}{weeks\ conversion} = \frac{days\ unknown}{weeks\ given} \right)$$

Cross-multiplying produces: $(7)(2) = (x)(1) \rightarrow 14 = x$. Therefore, 2 weeks is equal to 14 days. Next, a proportion is written to convert 14 days to hours:

$$\frac{24}{1} = \frac{x}{14} \left(\frac{conversion\ hours}{conversion\ days} = \frac{unknown\ hours}{given\ days} \right)$$

Cross-multiplying produces:

$$(24)(14) = (x)(1) \rightarrow 336 = x$$

130

Therefore, the answer is that there are 336 hours in 2 weeks.

Statistical Concepts

Identifying Statistical Questions

The field of **statistics** describes relationships between quantities that are related, but not necessarily in a deterministic manner. For example, a graduating student's salary will often be higher when the student graduates with a higher GPA, but this is not always the case. Likewise, people who smoke tobacco are more likely to develop lung cancer, but, in fact, it is possible for non-smokers to develop the disease as well. Statistics describes these kinds of situations, where the likelihood of some outcome depends on the starting data.

Descriptive statistics involves analyzing a collection of data to describe its broad properties such average (or mean), what percent of the data falls within a given range, and other such properties. An example of this would be taking all of the test scores from a given class and calculating the average test score. Inferential statistics attempts to use data about a subset of some population to make inferences about the rest of the population. An example of this would be taking a collection of students who received tutoring and comparing their results to a collection of students who did not receive tutoring, then using that comparison to try to predict whether the tutoring program in question is beneficial.

Measures of Center and Range

The center of a set of data (statistical values) can be represented by its mean, median, or mode. These are sometimes referred to as **measures of central tendency**.

Mean

The first property that can be defined for this set of data is the **mean**. This is the same as the average. To find the mean, add up all the data points, then divide by the total number of data points. For example, suppose that in a class of 10 students, the scores on a test were 50, 60, 65, 65, 75, 80, 85, 85, 90, 100. Therefore, the average test score will be:

$$\frac{50 + 60 + 65 + 65 + 75 + 80 + 85 + 85 + 90 + 100}{10} = 75.5$$

The mean is a useful number if the distribution of data is normal (more on this later), which roughly means that the frequency of different outcomes has a single peak and is roughly equally distributed on both sides of that peak. However, it is less useful in some cases where the data might be split or where there are some outliers. **Outliers** are data points that are far from the rest of the data. For example, suppose there are 10 executives and 90 employees at a company. The executives make $1000 per hour, and the employees make $10 per hour.

Therefore, the average pay rate will be:

$$\frac{\$1000 \times 10 + \$10 \times 90}{100} = \$109 \text{ per hour}$$

In this case, this average is not very descriptive since it's not close to the actual pay of the executives or the employees.

Median

Another useful measurement is the **median**. In a data set, the median is the point in the middle. The **middle** refers to the point where half the data comes before it and half comes after, when the data is recorded in numerical order. For instance, these are the speeds of the fastball of a pitcher during the last inning that he pitched (in order from least to greatest):

$$90, 92, 93, 93, 95, 96, 97, 97, 97$$

There are nine total numbers, so the middle or *median* number is the 5th one, which is 95.

In cases where the number of data points is an even number, then the average of the two middle points is taken. In the previous example of test scores, the two middle points are 75 and 80. Since there is no single point, the average of these two scores needs to be found.

The average is:

$$\frac{75 + 80}{2} = 77.5$$

The median is generally a good value to use if there are a few outliers in the data. It prevents those outliers from affecting the "middle" value as much as when using the mean.

Since an outlier is a data point that is far from most of the other data points in a data set, this means an outlier also is any point that is far from the median of the data set. The outliers can have a substantial effect on the mean of a data set, but they usually do not change the median or mode, or do not change them by a large quantity. For example, consider the data set (3, 5, 6, 6, 6, 8). This has a median of 6 and a mode of 6, with a mean of $\frac{34}{6} \approx 5.67$. Now, suppose a new data point of 1000 is added so that the data set is now (3, 5, 6, 6, 6, 8, 1000). The median and mode, which are both still 6, remain unchanged. However, the average is now $\frac{1034}{7}$, which is approximately 147.7. In this case, the median and mode will be better descriptions for most of the data points.

Outliers in a given data set are sometimes the result of an error by the experimenter, but oftentimes, they are perfectly valid data points that must be taken into consideration.

Mode

One additional measure to define for X is the **mode**. This is the data point that appears most frequently. If two or more data points all tie for the most frequent appearance, then each of them is considered a mode. In the case of the test scores, where the numbers were 50, 60, 65, 65, 75, 80, 85, 85, 90, 100, there are two modes: 65 and 85.

The **range of a data set** is the difference between the highest and the lowest values in the set. The range can be considered the span of the data set. To determine the range, the smallest value in the set is subtracted from the largest value. The ranges for the data sets A, B, and C above are calculated as follows: A: $14 - 7 = 7$; B: $51 - 33 = 18$; C: $173 - 151 = 22$.

Best Description of a Set of Data

Measures of central tendency, namely mean, median, and mode, describe characteristics of a set of data. Specifically, they are intended to represent a *typical* value in the set by identifying a central

132

position of the set. Depending on the characteristics of a specific set of data, different measures of central tendency are more indicative of a typical value in the set.

When a data set is grouped closely together with a relatively small range and the data is spread out somewhat evenly, the mean is an effective indicator of a typical value in the set. Consider the following data set representing the height of sixth grade boys in inches: 61 inches, 54 inches, 58 inches, 63 inches, 58 inches. The mean of the set is 58.8 inches. The data set is grouped closely (the range is only 9 inches) and the values are spread relatively evenly (three values below the mean and two values above the mean). Therefore, the mean value of 58.8 inches is an effective measure of central tendency in this case.

When a data set contains a small number of values either extremely large or extremely small when compared to the other values, the mean is not an effective measure of central tendency. Consider the following data set representing annual incomes of homeowners on a given street: $71,000; $74,000; $75,000; $77,000; $340,000. The mean of this set is $127,400. This figure does not indicate a typical value in the set, which contains four out of five values between $71,000 and $77,000. The median is a much more effective measure of central tendency for data sets such as these. Finding the middle value diminishes the influence of outliers, or numbers that may appear out of place, like the $340,000 annual income. The median for this set is $75,000 which is much more typical of a value in the set.

The **mode of a data set** is a useful measure of central tendency for categorical data when each piece of data is an option from a category. Consider a survey of 31 commuters asking how they get to work with results summarized below.

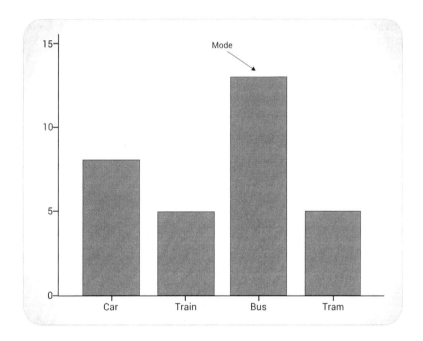

The mode for this set represents the value, or option, of the data that repeats most often. This indicates that the bus is the most popular method of transportation for the commuters.

Effects of Changes in Data

Changing all values of a data set in a consistent way produces predictable changes in the measures of the center and range of the set. A linear transformation changes the original value into the new value by

133

either adding a given number to each value, multiplying each value by a given number, or both. Adding (or subtracting) a given value to each data point will increase (or decrease) the mean, median, and any modes by the same value. However, the range will remain the same due to the way that range is calculated. Multiplying (or dividing) a given value by each data point will increase (or decrease) the mean, median, and any modes, and the range by the same factor.

Consider the following data set, call it set P, representing the price of different cases of soda at a grocery store: \$4.25, \$4.40, \$4.75, \$4.95, \$4.95, \$5.15. The mean of set P is \$4.74. The median is \$4.85. The mode of the set is \$4.95. The range is \$0.90. Suppose the state passes a new tax of \$0.25 on every case of soda sold. The new data set, set T, is calculated by adding \$0.25 to each data point from set P. Therefore, set T consists of the following values: \$4.50, \$4.65, \$5.00, \$5.20, \$5.20, \$5.40. The mean of set T is \$4.99. The median is \$5.10. The mode of the set is \$5.20. The range is \$.90. The mean, median and mode of set T is equal to \$0.25 added to the mean, median, and mode of set P. The range stays the same.

Now suppose, due to inflation, the store raises the cost of every item by 10 percent. Raising costs by 10 percent is calculated by multiplying each value by 1.1. The new data set, set I, is calculated by multiplying each data point from set T by 1.1. Therefore, set I consists of the following values: \$4.95, \$5.12, \$5.50, \$5.72, \$5.72, \$5.94. The mean of set I is \$5.49. The median is \$5.61. The mode of the set is \$5.72. The range is \$0.99. The mean, median, mode, and range of set I is equal to 1.1 multiplied by the mean, median, mode, and range of set T because each increased by a factor of 10 percent.

Describing a Set of Data

A set of data can be described in terms of its center, spread, shape and any unusual features. The **center of a data** set can be measured by its mean, median, or mode. Measures of central tendency are covered in the *Measures of Center and Range* section. The **spread of a data set** refers to how far the data points are from the center (mean or median). The spread can be measured by the range or by the quartiles and interquartile range. A data set with all its data points clustered around the center will have a small spread. A data set covering a wide range of values will have a large spread.

When a data set is displayed as a histogram or frequency distribution plot, the shape indicates if a sample is normally distributed, symmetrical, or has measures of skewness or kurtosis. When graphed, a data set with a normal distribution will resemble a bell curve.

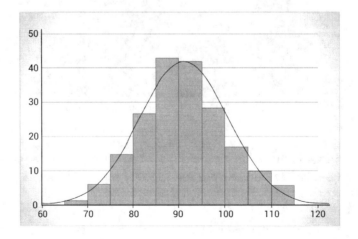

If the data set is symmetrical, each half of the graph when divided at the center is a mirror image of the other. If the graph has fewer data points to the right, the data is skewed right. If it has fewer data points to the left, the data is skewed left.

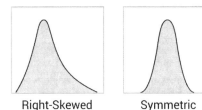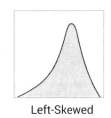

| Right-Skewed | Symmetric | Left-Skewed |

Kurtosis is a measure of whether the data is heavy-tailed with a high number of outliers, or light-tailed with a low number of outliers.

A description of a data set should include any unusual features such as gaps or outliers. A **gap** is a span within the range of the data set containing no data points. An outlier is a data point with a value either extremely large or extremely small when compared to the other values in the set.

Representing and Interpreting Data

Interpreting Displays of Data

A set of data can be visually displayed in various forms allowing for quick identification of characteristics of the set. **Histograms**, such as the one shown below, display the number of data points (vertical axis) that fall into given intervals (horizontal axis) across the range of the set. The histogram below displays the heights of black cherry trees in a certain city park. Each rectangle represents the number of trees with heights between a given five-point span. For example, the furthest bar to the right indicates that two trees are between 85 and 90 feet. Histograms can describe the center, spread, shape, and any unusual characteristics of a data set.

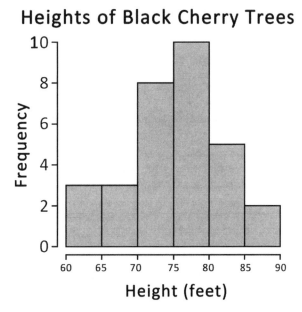

Heights of Black Cherry Trees

135

A **box plot**, also called a **box-and-whisker plot**, divides the data points into four groups and displays the five-number summary for the set as well as any outliers. The five-number summary consists of:

- The lower extreme: the lowest value that is not an outlier
- The higher extreme: the highest value that is not an outlier
- The median of the set: also referred to as the second quartile or Q_2
- The first quartile or Q_1: the median of values below Q_2
- The third quartile or Q_3: the median of values above Q_2

Calculating each of these values is covered in the next section, *Graphical Representation of Data*.

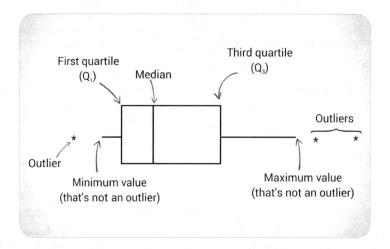

Suppose the box plot displays IQ scores for 12th grade students at a given school. The five number summary of the data consists of: lower extreme (67); upper extreme (127); Q_2 or median (100); Q_1 (91); Q_3 (108); and outliers (135 and 140). Although all data points are not known from the plot, the points are divided into four quartiles each, including 25% of the data points. Therefore, 25% of students scored between 67 and 91, 25% scored between 91 and 100, 25% scored between 100 and 108, and 25% scored between 108 and 127. These percentages include the normal values for the set and exclude the outliers. This information is useful when comparing a given score with the rest of the scores in the set.

A **scatter plot** is a mathematical diagram that visually displays the relationship or connection between two variables. The independent variable is placed on the x-axis, or horizontal axis, and the dependent variable is placed on the y-axis, or vertical axis. When visually examining the points on the graph, if the points model a linear relationship, or if a line of best-fit can be drawn through the points with the points relatively close on either side, then a correlation exists. If the line of best-fit has a positive slope (rises from left to right), then the variables have a positive correlation. If the line of best-fit has a negative slope (falls from left to right), then the variables have a negative correlation. If a line of best-fit cannot

be drawn, then no correlation exists. A positive or negative correlation can be categorized as strong or weak, depending on how closely the points are graphed around the line of best-fit.

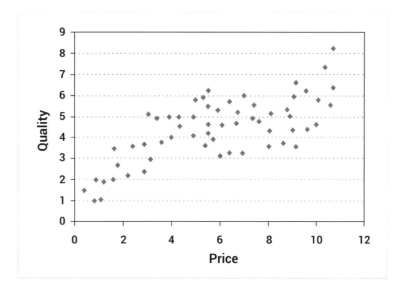

Graphical Representation of Data

Various graphs can be used to visually represent a given set of data. Each type of graph requires a different method of arranging data points and different calculations of the data. Examples of histograms, box plots, and scatter plots are discussed in the previous section *Interpreting Displays of Data*. To construct a histogram, the range of the data points is divided into equal intervals. The frequency for each interval is then determined, which reveals how many points fall into each interval. A graph is constructed with the vertical axis representing the frequency and the horizontal axis representing the intervals. The lower value of each interval should be labeled along the horizontal axis. Finally, for each interval, a bar is drawn from the lower value of each interval to the lower value of the next interval with a height equal to the frequency of the interval. Because of the intervals, histograms do not have any gaps between bars along the horizontal axis.

A scatter plot displays the relationship between two variables. Values for the independent variable, typically denoted by x, are paired with values for the dependent variable, typically denoted by y. Each set of corresponding values are written as an ordered pair (x, y). To construct the graph, a coordinate grid is labeled with the x-axis representing the independent variable and the y-axis representing the dependent variable.

137

Each ordered pair is graphed.

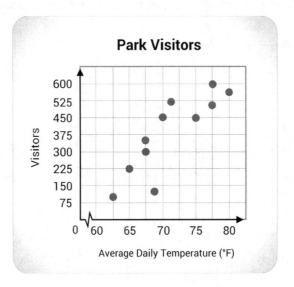

Like a scatter plot, a **line graph** compares variables that change continuously, typically over time. Paired data values (ordered pairs) are plotted on a coordinate grid with the x- and y-axis representing the variables. A line is drawn from each point to the next, going from left to right. The line graph below displays cell phone use for given years (two variables) for men, women, and both sexes (three data sets).

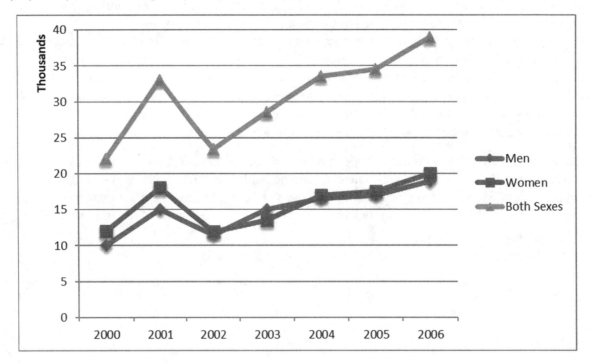

A **line plot**, also called **dot plot**, displays the frequency of data (numerical values) on a number line. To construct a line plot, a number line is used that includes all unique data values. It is marked with x's or dots above the value the number of times that the value occurs in the data set.

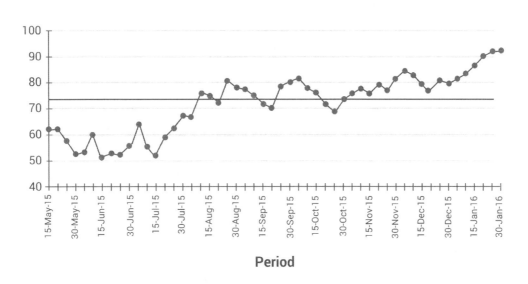

A **bar graph** looks similar to a histogram but displays categorical data. The horizontal axis represents each category and the vertical axis represents the frequency for the category. A bar is drawn for each category (often different colors) with a height extending to the frequency for that category within the data set. A **double bar graph** displays two sets of data that contain data points consisting of the same categories. The double bar graph below indicates that two girls and four boys like Pad Thai the most out of all the foods, two boys and five girls like pizza, and so on.

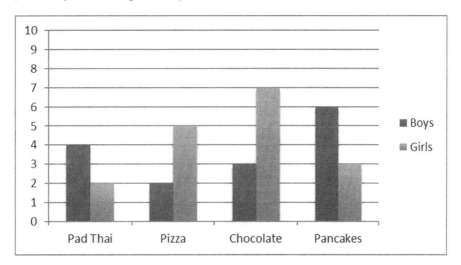

A circle graph, also called a **pie chart**, displays categorical data with each category representing a percentage of the whole data set. To construct a circle graph, the percent of the data set for each category must be determined. To do so, the frequency of the category is divided by the total number of data points and converted to a percent. For example, if 80 people were asked their favorite pizza topping and 20 responded cheese, then cheese constitutes 25% of the data ($\frac{20}{80} = 0.25 = 25\%$). Each category in a data set is represented by a *slice* of the circle proportionate to its percentage of the whole.

INCOME

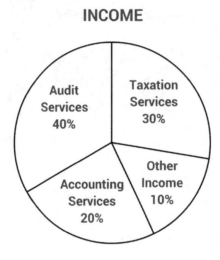

Choice of Graphs to Display Data

Choosing the appropriate graph to display a data set depends on what type of data is included in the set and what information must be displayed. Histograms and box plots can be used for data sets consisting of individual values across a wide range. Examples include test scores and incomes. Histograms and box plots will indicate the center, spread, range, and outliers of a data set. A histogram will show the shape of the data set, while a box plot will divide the set into quartiles (25% increments), allowing for comparison between a given value and the entire set.

Scatter plots and line graphs can be used to display data consisting of two variables. Examples include height and weight, or distance and time. A correlation between the variables is determined by examining the points on the graph. Line graphs are used if each value for one variable pairs with a distinct value for the other variable. Line graphs show relationships between variables.

Line plots, bar graphs, and circle graphs are all used to display categorical data, such as surveys. Line plots and bar graphs both indicate the frequency of each category within the data set. A line plot is used when the categories consist of numerical values. For example, the number of hours of TV watched by individuals is displayed on a line plot. A bar graph is used when the categories consists of words. For example, the favorite ice cream of individuals is displayed with a bar graph. A circle graph can be used to display either type of categorical data. However, unlike line plots and bar graphs, a circle graph does not indicate the frequency of each category. Instead, the circle graph represents each category as its percentage of the whole data set.

Interpreting the Probability of Events

Probabilities Relative to Likelihood of Occurrence

Probability is a measure of how likely an event is to occur. Probability is written as a fraction between zero and one. If an event has a probability of zero, the event will never occur. If an event has a

probability of one, the event will definitely occur. If the probability of an event is closer to zero, the event is unlikely to occur. If the probability of an event is closer to one, the event is more likely to occur. For example, a probability of $\frac{1}{2}$ means that the event is equally as likely to occur as it is not to occur. An example of this is tossing a coin. To calculate the probability of an event, the number of favorable outcomes is divided by the number of total outcomes. For example, suppose you have 2 raffle tickets out of 20 total tickets sold. The probability that you win the raffle is calculated:

$$\frac{number\ of\ favorable\ outcomes}{total\ number\ of\ outcomes} = \frac{2}{20} = \frac{1}{10}$$

Therefore, the probability of winning the raffle is $\frac{1}{10}$ or 0.1.

Chance is the measure of how likely an event is to occur, written as a percent. If an event will never occur, the event has a 0% chance. If an event will certainly occur, the event has a 100% chance. If an event will sometimes occur, the event has a chance somewhere between 0% and 100%. To calculate chance, probability is calculated, and the fraction is converted to a percent.

The probability of multiple events occurring can be determined by multiplying the probability of each event. For example, suppose you flip a coin with heads and tails, and roll a six-sided die numbered one through six. To find the probability that you will flip heads AND roll a two, the probability of each event is determined, and those fractions are multiplied. The probability of flipping heads is $\frac{1}{2}\left(\frac{1\ side\ with\ heads}{2\ sides\ total}\right)$, and the probability of rolling a two is $\frac{1}{6}\left(\frac{1\ side\ with\ a\ 2}{6\ total\ sides}\right)$. The probability of flipping heads AND rolling a 2 is:

$$\frac{1}{2} \times \frac{1}{6} = \frac{1}{12}$$

The above scenario with flipping a coin and rolling a die is an example of independent events. Independent events are circumstances in which the outcome of one event does not affect the outcome of the other event. Conversely, dependent events are ones in which the outcome of one event affects the outcome of the second event. Consider the following scenario: a bag contains 5 black marbles and 5 white marbles. What is the probability of picking 2 black marbles without replacing the marble after the first pick?

The probability of picking a black marble on the first pick is $\frac{5}{10}\left(\frac{5\ black\ marbles}{10\ total\ marbles}\right)$. Assuming that a black marble was picked, there are now 4 black marbles and 5 white marbles for the second pick. Therefore, the probability of picking a black marble on the second pick is $\frac{4}{9}\left(\frac{4\ black\ marbles}{9\ total\ marbles}\right)$. To find the probability of picking two black marbles, the probability of each is multiplied:

$$\frac{5}{10} \times \frac{4}{9} = \frac{20}{90} = \frac{2}{9}$$

141

Practice Questions

1. If $-3(x + 4) \geq x + 8$, what is the value of x?
   a. $x = 4$
   b. $x \geq 2$
   c. $x \geq -5$
   d. $x \leq -5$

2. Which inequality represents the values displayed on the number line?

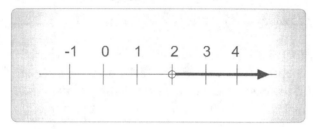

   a. $x < 2$
   b. $x \leq 2$
   c. $x > 2$
   d. $x \geq 2$

3. What is the 42nd item in the pattern: ▲○○□ ▲○○□ ▲ ...?
   a. ○
   b. ▲
   c. □
   d. None of the above

4. If a car can travel 300 miles in 4 hours, how far can it go in an hour and a half?
   a. 100 miles
   b. 112.5 miles
   c. 135.5 miles
   d. 150 miles

5. Greg buys a $10 lunch with 5% sales tax. He leaves a $2 tip after paying his bill. How much money does he spend?
   a. $12.50
   b. $12
   c. $13
   d. $13.25

See answers on next page.

Answer Explanations

1. D: Solve a linear inequality in a similar way to solving a linear equation. First, start by distributing the -3 on the left side of the inequality.

$$-3x - 12 \geq x + 8$$

Then, add 12 to both sides.

$$-3x \geq x + 20$$

Next, subtract x from both sides.

$$-4x \geq 20$$

Finally, divide both sides of the inequality by -4. Don't forget to flip the inequality sign because you are dividing by a negative.

$$x \leq -5$$

2. C: $x > 2$. The open dot on one indicates that the value is not included in the set. The arrow pointing right indicates that numbers greater than two (numbers get larger to the right) are included in the set. Therefore, the set includes numbers greater than two, which can be written as $x > 2$.

3. A: ○. The core of the pattern consists of 4 items: ▲○○□. Therefore, the core repeats in multiples of 4, with the pattern starting over on the next step. The closest multiple of 4 to 42 is 40. Step 40 is the end of the core (□), so step 41 will start the core over (▲) and step 42 is ○.

4. B: 300 miles in 4 hours is $\frac{300}{4} = 75$ miles per hour. In 1.5 hours, the car will go 1.5×75 miles, or 112.5 miles.

5. A: The tip is not taxed, so he pays 5% tax only on the $10.

The tax is 5% of $10, or $0.05 \times 10 = \$0.50$. Add up $\$10 + \$2 + \$0.50$ to get $12.50.

Social Studies

United States History, Government, and Citizenship

Colonization and Expansion in U.S. History

When examining how Europeans explored what would become the United States of America, one must first examine why Europeans came to explore the New World as a whole. In the fifteenth century, tensions increased between the Eastern and Mediterranean nations of Europe and the expanding Ottoman Empire to the east. As war and piracy spread across the Mediterranean, the once-prosperous trade routes across Asia's Silk Road began to decline, and nations across Europe began to explore alternative routes for trade.

Italian explorer **Christopher Columbus** proposed a westward route. Contrary to popular lore, the main challenge that Columbus faced in finding backers was not proving that the world was round. In fact, much of Europe's educated elite knew that the world was round; the real issue was that they rightly believed that a westward route to Asia, even assuming a lack of obstacles, would be too long to be practical. Nevertheless, Columbus set sail in 1492 after obtaining support from Spain and arrived in the West Indies three months later.

Spain launched further expeditions to the new continents and established **New Spain**. The colony consisted not only of Central America and Mexico, but also the American Southwest and Florida. France claimed much of what would become Canada, along with the Mississippi River region and the Midwest. In addition, the Dutch established colonies that covered New Jersey, New York, and Connecticut. Each nation managed its colonies differently, and thus influenced how they would assimilate into the United States. For instance, Spain strove to establish a system of Christian missions throughout its territory, while France focused on trading networks and had limited infrastructure in regions such as the Midwest.

Even in cases of limited colonial growth, the land of America was hardly vacant, because a diverse array of Native American nations and groups were already present. Throughout much of colonial history, European settlers commonly misperceived native peoples as a singular, static entity. In reality, Native Americans had a variety of traditions depending on their history and environment. Additionally, their culture continued to change through the course of interactions with European settlers; for instance, tribes such as the Cheyenne and Comanche used horses, which were introduced by white settlers, to become powerful warrior nations. However, a few generalizations can be made: many, but not all, tribes were matrilineal, which gave women a fair degree of power, and land was commonly seen as belonging to everyone. These differences, particularly European settlers' continual focus on land ownership, contributed to increasing prejudice and violence.

Situated on the Atlantic Coast, the Thirteen Colonies that would become the United States of America constituted only a small portion of North America. Even those colonies had significant differences that stemmed from their different origins. For instance, the Virginia colony under John Smith in 1607 started with male bachelors seeking gold, whereas families of Puritans settled Massachusetts. As a result, the Thirteen Colonies—Virginia, Massachusetts, Connecticut, Maryland, New York, New Jersey, Pennsylvania, Delaware, Rhode Island, New Hampshire, Georgia, North Carolina, and South Carolina— had different structures and customs that would each influence the United States.

Competition among several imperial powers in eastern areas of North America led to conflicts that would later bring about the independence of the United States. The French and Indian War from 1754 to 1763, which was a subsidiary war of the Seven Years' War, ended with Great Britain claiming France's Canadian territories as well as the Ohio Valley. The war was costly for all the powers involved, which led to increased taxes on the Thirteen Colonies. In addition, the new lands to the west of the colonies attracted new settlers, and they came into conflict with Native Americans and British troops that were trying to maintain the boundaries laid out by treaties between Great Britain and the Native American tribes. These growing tensions with Great Britain, as well as other issues, eventually led to the American Revolution, which ended with Britain relinquishing its control of the colonies.

Britain continued to hold onto its other colonies, such as Canada and the West Indies, which reflects the continued power of multiple nations across North America, even as the United States began to expand across the continent. Many Americans advocated expansion regardless of the land's current inhabitants, but the results were often mixed. Still, events both abroad and within North America contributed to the growth of the United States. For instance, the rising tumult in France during the French Revolution and the rise of Napoleon led France to sell the Louisiana Purchase, a large chunk of land consisting not only of Louisiana but also much of the Midwest, to the United States in 1803. Meanwhile, as Spanish power declined, Mexico claimed independence in 1821, but the new nation became increasingly vulnerable to foreign pressure. In the Mexican-American War from 1846 to 1848, Mexico surrendered territory to the United States that eventually became California, Nevada, Utah, and New Mexico, as well as parts of Arizona, Colorado, and Wyoming.

Even as the United States sought new inland territory, American interests were also expanding overseas via trade. As early as 1784, the ship **Empress of China** traveled to China to establish trading connections. American interests had international dimensions throughout the nation's history. For instance, during the presidency of Andrew Jackson, the ship **Potomac** was dispatched to the Pacific island of Sumatra in 1832 to avenge the deaths of American sailors. This incident exemplifies how U.S. foreign trade connected with imperial expansion.

This combination of continental and seaward growth adds a deeper layer to American development, because it was not purely focused on western expansion. For example, take the 1849 Gold Rush; a large number of Americans and other immigrants traveled to California by ship and settled western territories before more eastern areas, such as Nevada and Idaho. Therefore, the United States' early history of colonization and expansion is a complex network of diverse cultures.

American Revolution and the Founding of the Nation

The **American Revolution** largely occurred as a result of changing values in the Thirteen Colonies that broke from their traditional relationship with England. Early on in the colonization of North America, the colonial social structure tried to mirror the stratified order of Great Britain. In England, the landed elites were seen as intellectually and morally superior to the common man, which led to a paternalistic relationship. This style of governance was similarly applied to the colonial system; government was left to the property-owning upper class, and the colonies as a whole could be seen as a child dutifully serving "Mother England."

However, the colonies' distance from England meant that actual, hereditary aristocrats from Britain only formed a small percentage of the overall population and did not even fill all the positions of power. By the mid-eighteenth century, much of the American upper class consisted of local families who acquired

status through business rather than lineage. Despite this, representatives from Britain were appointed to govern the colonies. As a result, a rift began to form between the colonists and British officials.

Tensions began to rise in the aftermath of the French and Indian War of 1754 to 1763. To recover the financial costs of the long conflict, Great Britain drew upon its colonies to provide the desired resources. Since the American colonists did not fully subscribe to the paternal connection, taxation to increase British revenue, such as the **Stamp Act of 1765**, was met with increasing resistance. Britain sent soldiers to the colonies and enacted the **1765 Quartering Act** to require colonists to house the troops. In 1773, the new **Tea Act**, which created a monopoly, led some colonists to raid a ship and destroy its contents in the **Boston Tea Party**.

Uncertain about whether they should remain loyal to Britain, representatives from twelve colonies formed the First Continental Congress in 1774 to discuss what they should do next. When Patriot militiamen at Lexington and Concord fought British soldiers in April 1775, the **Revolutionary War** began. While the rebel forces worked to present the struggle as a united, patriotic effort, the colonies remained divided throughout the war. Thousands of colonists, known as **Loyalists** or **Tories**, supported Britain. Even the revolutionaries proved to be significantly fragmented, and many militias only served in their home states. The Continental Congress was also divided over whether to reconcile with Britain or push for full separation. These issues hindered the ability of the revolutionary armies to resist the British, who had superior training and resources at their disposal.

Even so, the **Continental Army**, under **General George Washington**, gradually built up a force that utilized Prussian military training and backwoods guerrilla tactics to make up for their limited resources. Although the British forces continued to win significant battles, the Continental Army gradually reduced Britain's will to fight as the years passed. Furthermore, Americans appealed to the rivalry that other European nations had with the British Empire. The support was initially limited to indirect assistance, but aid gradually increased. After the American victory at the Battle of Saratoga in 1777, France and other nations began to actively support the American cause by providing much-needed troops and equipment.

In 1781, the primary British army under **General Cornwallis** was defeated by an American and French coalition at Yorktown, Virginia, which paved the way for peace negotiations. The **Treaty of Paris in 1783** ended the war, recognized the former colonies' independence from Great Britain, and gave America control over territory between the Appalachian Mountains and Mississippi River. However, the state of the new nation was still uncertain. The new nation's government initially stemmed from the state-based structure of the Continental Congress and was incorporated into the Articles of Confederation in 1777.

The **Articles of Confederation** emphasized the ideals of the American Revolution, particularly the concept of freedom from unjust government. Unfortunately, the resulting limitations on the national government left most policies—even ones with national ramifications—up to individual states. For instance, states sometimes simply decided to not pay taxes. Many representatives did not see much value in the National Congress and simply did not attend the meetings. Some progress was still made during the period, such as the **Northwest Ordinance of 1787**, which organized the western territories into new states; nevertheless, the disjointed links in the state-oriented government inhibited significant progress.

Although many citizens felt satisfied with this decentralized system of government, key intellectuals and leaders in America became increasingly disturbed by the lack of unity. An especially potent fear among

them was the potential that, despite achieving official independence, other powers could threaten America's autonomy. In 1786, poor farmers in Massachusetts launched an insurrection, known as **Shays' Rebellion**, which sparked fears of additional uprisings and led to the creation of the **Constitutional Convention in 1787**.

While the convention initially intended to correct issues within the Articles of Confederation, speakers, such as **James Madison**, compellingly argued for the delegates to devise a new system of government that was more centralized than its predecessor. The Constitution was not fully supported by all citizens, and there was much debate about whether or not to support the new government. Even so, in 1788, the Constitution was ratified. Later additions, such as the **Bill of Rights**, would help protect individual liberty by giving specific rights to citizens. In 1789, **George Washington** became the first president of the newly created executive branch of the government, and America entered a new stage of history.

U.S. History from Founding to Present

One early development was the growth of political parties—something that Washington tried and failed to stop from forming. Federalists, such as **Alexander Hamilton**, wanted to expand the national government's power, while Democratic-Republicans, such as **Thomas Jefferson**, favored states' rights. The United States suffered multiple defeats by Britain in the War of 1812, but individual American victories, such as the **Battle of New Orleans**, still strengthened nationalistic pride.

In the aftermath of the war, the Federalists were absorbed into the Democratic-Republicans, which began the **Era of Good Feelings**. However, two new parties eventually emerged. The Democrats, whose leader **Andrew Jackson** became president in 1828, favored "Jacksonian" democracy, which emphasized mass participation in elections. However, Jackson's policies largely favored white male landowners and suppressed opposing views. The Whigs supported Federalist policies but also drew on democratic principles, particularly with marginalized groups such as African Americans and women.

At the same time, settlers continued to expand west in search of new land and fortune. The Louisiana Purchase of 1803 opened up large amounts of land west of the Mississippi River, and adventurers pushed past even those boundaries toward the western coast. The vision of westward growth into the frontier is a key part of American popular culture, but the expansion was often erratic and depended on a combination of incentives and assurances of relative security. Hence, some areas, such as California and Oregon, were settled more quickly than other areas to the east. Some historians have pointed to the growth of the frontier as a means through which American democracy expanded.

However, the matter of western lands became an increasingly volatile issue as the controversy over slavery heightened. Not all northerners supported abolition, but many saw the practice as outdated and did not want it to expand. Abolitionists formed the Republican Party, and their candidate, **Abraham Lincoln**, was elected as president in 1860. In response, southern states seceded and formed the **Confederate States of America**. The ensuing **Civil War** lasted from 1861 to 1865 and had significant consequences. Slavery was abolished in the United States, and the power of individual states was drastically curtailed. After being reunified, southern states worked to retain control over freed slaves, and the Reconstruction period was followed by **Jim Crow** segregation. As a result, blacks were barred from public education, unable to vote, and forced to accept their status as second-class citizens.

After the Civil War, the United States increasingly industrialized and became part of the larger Industrial Revolution, which took place throughout the western world. Steps toward industrialization had already

begun as early as Jackson's presidency, but the full development of American industry took place in the second half of the nineteenth century. Railroads helped link cities like Chicago to locations across the West, which allowed for rapid transfer of materials. New technologies, such as electricity, allowed leisure time for those with enough wealth. Even so, the **Gilded Age** was also a period of disparities, and wealthy entrepreneurs rose while impoverished workers struggled to make their voices heard.

The late nineteenth and early twentieth century not only marked U.S. expansion within North America but also internationally. For instance, after the **Spanish-American War in 1898**, the United States claimed control over Guam, Puerto Rico, and the Philippines. Rivalries in Europe culminated in World War I, in which great powers ranging from France to Russia vied for control in a bloody struggle. Americans did not enter the war until 1917, but we had a critical role in the final phase of the war. During the peace treaty process, **President Woodrow Wilson** sought to establish a **League of Nations** in order to promote global harmony, but his efforts only achieved limited success.

After World War I, the United States largely stayed out of international politics for the next two decades. Still, American businesses continued overseas ventures and strengthened the economy in the 1920s. However, massive speculation in the stock market in 1929 triggered the **Great Depression**—a financial crisis that spread worldwide as nations withdrew from the global economy. The crisis shepherded in the presidency of **Franklin D. Roosevelt**, who reformed the Democratic Party and implemented new federal programs known as the **New Deal**.

The Great Depression had ramifications worldwide and encouraged the rise of fascist governments in Italy and Germany. Highly dictatorial, fascism emphasized nationalism and militarism. World War II began when the Axis powers of Germany, Italy, and Japan built up their military forces and launched invasions against neighboring nations in 1939. As part of the Allies, which also included Britain, France, and the Soviet Union, America defeated the Axis powers in 1945 and asserted itself as a global force.

The **Union of Soviet Socialist Republics** had emerged through the **Bolshevik Revolution in 1917** in Russia and militantly supported **Communism**—a socialist system of government that called for the overthrow of capitalism. Although the Soviet Union formed an alliance with the United States during World War II, relations chilled, and the Cold War began in 1947. Although no true war was declared between the two nations, both the Union of Soviet Socialist Republics and the United States engaged in indirect conflict by supporting and overthrowing foreign governments.

Meanwhile, the **Civil Rights Movement** began to grow as marginalized groups objected to racial segregation and abuse by whites across the nation. Civil rights leaders, such as **Martin Luther King Jr.**, argued for nonviolent resistance, but others, such as **Malcolm X**, advocated more radical approaches. Civil rights groups became increasingly discontented during the Vietnam War because they felt they were being drafted for a foreign war that ignored domestic problems. Even so, significant reforms, such as the **Voting Rights Act of 1965**, opened up new opportunities for freedom and equality in America.

In 1991, the Soviet Union collapsed, leaving the United States as the dominant global power. However, as the United States struggled to fill the void left by the Soviet Union, questions arose about America's role in the world. Terrorist acts, such as the 9/11 attack on the World Trade Center in 2001, have shed doubt on the United States' ability to enforce its authority on an international scale.

Twentieth-Century Developments in the United States

Although the United States began industrializing in the second half of the nineteenth century, American technology continued to develop in new directions throughout the course of the twentieth century. A key example was the invention of the modern assembly line. Assembly lines and conveyor belts had already become a prominent part of industrial work, but **Henry Ford** combined conveyor belts with the system of assembly workers in 1913 in order to produce Model T automobiles. This streamlined production system, in which multiple parts were assembled by different teams along the conveyors, allowed industries in the United States to grow ever larger.

Ford's assembly lines also promoted the growth of the automobile as a means of transportation. Early cars were an expensive and impractical novelty and were primarily the toys of the rich. The Model T, on the other hand, was relatively affordable, which made the car available to a wider array of consumers. Many of the automobiles' early issues, such as radiator leaks and fragile tires, were gradually corrected, and this made the car more appealing than horses. With the support of **President Eisenhower**, the **Federal Aid Highway Act of 1956** paved the way for a network of interstates and highways across the nation.

At the same time, a revolutionary approach to transportation was emerging: flight. Blimps and balloons were already gaining popularity by the turn of the twentieth century, but aviators struggled to create an airplane. The first critical success was by the **Wright Brothers** in 1903, and they demonstrated that aircrafts did not need to be lighter than air. In time, airplanes surpassed the popularity of balloons and blimps, which tended to be more volatile. Aircraft also added a new dimension to warfare, and aircraft carriers became an integral piece of the American navy during World War II.

Furthermore, by demonstrating that heavier-than-air vehicles could actually carry passengers upward, the stage was set for the space race in the second half of the twentieth century. In 1958, the U.S. government created the **National Aeronautics and Space Administration (NASA)** to head the budding initiative to extend American power into space. After the Soviet Union successfully launched the **Sputnik satellite** into Earth's orbit in 1957 and sent the first human in space in 1961, the United States intensified its own space program through the **Apollo missions**. **Apollo 11** successfully landed on the moon in 1969 with **Buzz Aldrin** and **Neil Armstrong**. Later ventures into space would focus on space shuttles and satellites, and the latter significantly enhanced communications worldwide.

Indeed, the twentieth century also made considerable advancements in communications and media. Inventions such as the radio greatly boosted communication across the nation and world, such that news could be reported immediately rather than take days. Furthermore, motion pictures evolved from black-and-white movies at theaters to full-color television sets in households. From animation to live films, television matured into a compelling art form in popular culture. Live-action footage gave a new layer to news broadcasts and proved instrumental in the public's reaction to events, such as the Civil Rights Movement and the Vietnam War. With the success of the space program, satellites became a fundamental piece of Earth's communications network by transmitting signals across the planet instantaneously.

Further communications advancements resulted from the development of computer technology. The early computers in the twentieth century were enormous behemoths that were too bulky and expensive for anything but government institutions. However, computers gradually became smaller while still storing large amounts of data. A turning point came with the 1976 release of the Apple computer by

entrepreneurs **Steve Wozniak** and **Steve Jobs**. The computer had a simplistic design that made it marketable for a mass consumer audience, and computers eventually became household items. Similarly, the networks that would become the Internet originated as government systems, but in time they were extended to commercial avenues that became a vibrant element of modern communications.

However, other advancements in American science during the twentieth century were aimed toward more lethal purposes. In response to the multiple wars throughout the century, the United States built up a powerful military force, and new technologies were devised for that purpose. One of the deadliest creations was the **atomic bomb**, which split molecular atoms to produce powerful explosions; in addition to the sheer force of the bombs, the aftereffects included toxic radiation and electronic shutdowns. Developed and used in the last days of World War II, the nuclear bomb was the United States' most powerful weapon during the Cold War.

On the other hand, the twentieth century also marked new approaches to the natural environments in America. In reaction to the depletion of natural habitats by industrialization and overhunting, **President Theodore Roosevelt** helped preserve areas for what would become the National Parks in 1916. Laws, such as the **Clean Water Act of 1972**, helped improve the health of ecosystems, which benefitted not only wildlife but people across the nation. This also led to the development of alternative energy sources such as wind and solar power.

America continues to change and grow into the twenty-first century by building on preexisting ideas but also pioneering new concepts. As globalization becomes an increasingly prominent phenomenon, American businesses strive to adapt their products to consumers worldwide while also funneling in new ideas from other nations. Yet many of the current developments in American enterprises stem in part from earlier events in American history. For instance, the environmental movement has expanded to address new issues such as global warming. NASA continues its space exploration endeavors, but entrepreneurs hope one day to travel to Mars. Therefore, the history of technology within the United States remains an engaging and relevant subject in the present.

Connections between Causes and Effects

When examining the historical narratives of events, it is important to understand the relationship between causes and effects. A **cause** can be defined as something, whether an event, social change, or other factor, that contributes to the occurrence of certain events; the results of causes are called **effects**. Those terms may seem simple enough, but they have drastic implications on how one explores history. Events such as the American Revolution or the Civil Rights Movement may appear to occur spontaneously, but a closer examination will reveal that these events depended on earlier phenomena and patterns that influenced the course of history.

For example, although the battles at Concord and Lexington may seem to be instantaneous eruptions of violence during the American Revolution, they stemmed from a variety of factors. The most obvious influences behind those two battles were the assortment of taxes and policies imposed on the Thirteen Colonies following the French and Indian War from 1754 to 1763. Taxation without direct representation, combined with the deployment of British soldiers to enforce these policies, greatly increased American resistance. Earlier events, such as the Boston Massacre and the Boston Tea Party, similarly stemmed from conflicts between British soldiers and local colonists over perceived tyranny and rebelliousness. Therefore, the start of the American Revolution progressed from preceding developments.

150

Furthermore, there can be multiple causes and effects for any situation. The existence of multiple causes can be seen through the settling of the American West. Many historians have emphasized the role of manifest destiny—the national vision of expanding across the continent—as a driving force behind the growth of the United States. Yet there were many different influences behind the expansion westward. Northern abolitionists and southern planters saw the frontier as a way to either extend or limit slavery. Economic opportunities in the West also encouraged travel westward, as did the gradual pacification of Native American tribes.

Even an individual cause can be subdivided into smaller factors or stretched out in a gradual process. Although there were numerous issues that led to the Civil War, slavery was the primary cause. However, that topic stretched back to the very founding of the nation, and the existence of slavery was a controversial topic during the creation of the Declaration of Independence and the Constitution. The abolition movement as a whole did not start until the 1830s, but nevertheless, slavery is a cause that gradually grew more important over the following decades. In addition, opponents of slavery were divided by different motivations—some believed that it stifled the economy, while others focused on moral issues.

On the other end of the spectrum, a single event can have numerous results. The rise of the telegraph, for example, had several effects on American history. The telegraph allowed news to travel much quicker and turned events into immediate national news, such as the sinking of the USS Maine, which sparked the Spanish-American War. In addition, the telegraph helped make railroads run more efficiently by improving the links between stations. The faster speed of both travel and communications led to a shift in time itself, and localized times were replaced by standardized time zones across the nation.

The importance of grasping cause-and-effect relationships is critical in interpreting the growth and development of the Civil Rights Movement. Historical narratives of the movement often focus on charismatic individuals, such as Martin Luther King Jr., and they certainly played a key leadership role. Even so, elements of the movement had already emerged in previous decades through the growth of the **National Association for the Advancement of Colored People (NAACP)** and other organizations. Several factors proved critical to the formation of civil rights organizations during the 1950s. African American veterans returning from World War II, as well as those continuing to serve in the military, called for equal rights. Furthermore, the United States' role as a key member of the United Nations, which included African countries, required the federal government to take racial discrimination seriously.

A specific example in the Civil Rights Movement is the sit-ins during 1960, in which black and white students defied segregation policies in restaurants and other establishments. The wave is often thought to originate from spontaneous activism by students in Greensboro, North Carolina. However, there had already been other sit-ins, such as at **Royal Ice Cream Parlor** in Durham, North Carolina, in 1957. In fact, the sit-ins would not have spread as quickly without a preexisting network of activists across the nation, which in part stemmed from the growth of organizations through various local and national movements. By looking at such cases closely, it becomes clear that no event occurs without one—if not multiple—causes behind it, and that each historical event can have a variety of direct and indirect consequences.

One of the most critical elements of cause-and-effect relationships is how they are relevant not only in studying history but also in contemporary events. Much of the current political debate about social security and health care stems from FDR's New Deal in the 1930s, and at the time some people criticized

the programs for being too extensive, while others argued that he did not go far enough with his vision. Current environmental concerns have their origins in long-term issues that reach back centuries. The United States' mixed history of global isolation and foreign intervention continues to influence foreign policy approaches today. Most of all, people must realize that events and developments today will likely have a number of consequences later on. Therefore, the study of cause and effect remains vital in understanding the past, the present, and the future.

Nature, Purpose, and Forms of Government

The United States of America's government, as outlined by the **Constitution**, is designed to serve as a compromise between democracy and preceding monarchical systems. The American Revolution brought independence from Britain and freedom from its aristocratic system of governance. On the other hand, the short-lived Articles of Confederation revealed the significant weaknesses of state-based governance with limited national control. By dividing power between local, state, and federal governments, the United States can uphold its value of individual liberties while, nevertheless, giving a sense of order to the country.

The **federal government**, which is in charge of laws that affect the entire nation, is split into three main branches: executive, judicial, and legislative. It is important to realize that the three segments of the federal government are intended to stand as equal counterparts to the others, and that none of them are "in charge." The **executive branch** centers on the president, the vice president, and the cabinet. The president and vice president are elected every four years. Also known as the **commander-in-chief**, the **president** is the official head of state and serves as the nation's head diplomat and military leader. The **vice president** acts as the president of the Senate in the legislative branch, while the president appoints members of the cabinet to lead agencies, including the Treasury and Department of Defense. However, the president can only sign and veto laws and cannot initiate them himself.

Instead, the **legislative branch**, specifically Congress, proposes and debates laws. **Congress** is bicameral because it is divided into two separate legislative houses. Each state's representation in the **House of Representatives** is determined proportionally by population, with the total number of voting seats limited to 435. The **Senate**, in contrast, has only two members per state and a total of one hundred senators. Members of both houses are intended to represent the interests of the constituents in their home states and to bring their concerns to a national level while also being consistent with the interests of the nation as a whole. Drafts of laws, called **bills**, are proposed in one chamber and then are voted upon according to that chamber's rules; should the bill pass the vote in the first house of Congress, the other legislative chamber must approve it before it can be sent to the president. Congress also has a variety of other powers, such as the rights to declare war, collect taxes, and impeach the president.

The **judicial branch**, though it cannot pass laws itself, serves to interpret the laws. At the federal level, this is done through several tiers of judicial bodies. At the top, the **Supreme Court** consists of judges appointed by the president; these judges serve for life, unless they resign from their position or are removed by Congress for improper behavior. The Supreme Court's decisions in trials and other judgments rest on the justices' interpretations of the Constitution and enacted laws. As the Constitution remains fundamental to the American legal system, the Supreme Court's rulings on how laws follow or fail to uphold the Constitution have powerful implications on future rulings. Beneath the Supreme Court, there are a number of other federal judicial bodies—courts of appeals, district courts, and courts of special jurisdiction.

While the federal government manages the nation as a whole, state governments address issues pertaining to their specific territory. In the past, states claimed the right, known as **nullification**, to refuse to enforce federal laws that they considered unconstitutional. However, conflicts between state and federal authority, particularly in the South in regard to first, slavery, and later, discrimination, have led to increased federal power, and states cannot defy federal laws. Even so, the **Tenth Amendment** limits federal power to those specifically granted in the Constitution, and the rest of the powers are retained by the states and citizens. Therefore, individual state governments are left in charge of decisions with immediate effects on their citizens, such as state laws and taxes. Like the federal government, state governments consist of executive, judicial, and legislative branches, but the exact configuration of those branches varies between states. For instance, while most states follow the bicameral structure of Congress, Nebraska has only a single legislative chamber. **State governments** have considerable authority within their states, but they cannot impose their power on other states, nor can they secede from the United States.

Local governments, which include town governments, county boards, library districts, and other agencies, are especially variable in their composition. They often reflect the overall views of their state governments but also have their own values, rules, and structures. Generally, local governments function in a democratic fashion, although the exact form of government depends on its role. Depending on the location within the state, local government may have considerable or minimal authority based on the population and prosperity of the area; some counties may have strong influence in the state, while others may have a limited impact.

Native American tribes are treated as dependent nations that answer to the federal government but may be immune to state jurisdiction. As with local governments, the exact form of governance is left up to the tribes, which ranges from small councils to complex systems of government. Other U.S. territories, including the District of Columbia (site of Washington, D.C.) and acquired islands, such as Guam and Puerto Rico, have representation within Congress, but their legislators cannot vote on bills.

As members of a democracy, U.S. citizens are empowered to elect most government leaders, but the process varies between branch and level of government. Presidential elections at the national scale use the **Electoral College system**. Rather than electing the president directly, citizens cast their ballots to select electors, who generally vote for a specific candidate, that represent each state in the college. Legislative branches at the federal and state level are also determined by elections, albeit without an Electoral College. In some areas, judges are elected, but in other states judges are appointed by elected officials. It should also be noted that the two-party system was not built into the Constitution but gradually emerged over time.

Key Documents and Speeches in U.S. History

With more than two hundred years of history, American leaders have produced a number of important documents and speeches. One of the most essential is the **Declaration of Independence**, which the **Second Continental Congress** ratified on **July 4, 1776**. Although many historians and politicians have drawn upon the words of the Declaration to demonstrate the American ideal of freedom, most of them focus on the **preamble**, which focuses on the necessity of fair government and the right to overthrow tyrants. The main body of the document consists of a set of grievances against **King George III**. Still, this document was instrumental in American history because it asserted American independence from Great Britain. Even so, it is important to note that the Declaration did not immediately lead to the United

States; the document does not outline the government of the soon-to-be independent colonies, and independence would not become reality until Britain agreed.

The colonies' first blueprint for government was the **Articles of Confederation**, which was ratified in 1777. The document declared that the confederacy would be called the United States of America and that the individual states would have "a firm league of friendship" with each other. The emphasis on friendship and cooperation highlights how the confederation was a voluntary effort that states could follow or ignore as they saw fit. Still, the document also revealed the importance of obeying decisions made by Congress as a whole; while this was not very effective during the confederation period, the framework would live on to a degree in the following Constitution.

Much like the Declaration of Independence, the **1787 Constitution of the United States** is most remembered for the preamble, which takes a more philosophical approach. However, the body of the Constitution is highly complex, and it covers the framework and responsibilities of the different branches of the federal government and the limits to state power. These details are very important and help to define the key institutions within the government. To resolve later issues not addressed in the Constitution, the fifth article in the document establishes a process to modify the government, and the first ten amendments are known as the **Bill of Rights**. Under the Tenth Amendment, powers not specifically allotted to Congress by the Constitution are reserved for the people and to individual states.

George Washington was the first president of the United States, and his administration set many precedents for the nation, particularly with his **Farewell Address**. In it, he noted the rise of regional feelings, and he urged citizens to uphold their duty to the nation above sectionalism because he felt that America was strongest when united. The issue of regional conflicts and national identity would become increasingly important in years to come, especially during the Civil War. Washington also argued against intervention in European affairs, and this warning would become the cornerstone for advocates of American isolation. On the other hand, his advice that political parties are detrimental to democracy failed to halt the development of the party system.

Washington's fears about sectional conflict were confirmed at the start of the Civil War, when the southern states violently seceded from the Union. As the president during that tumultuous time, Abraham Lincoln was seen by many to embody the Union as a whole. This can be demonstrated through his **Gettysburg Address** in November of 1863. After the difficult and bloody **Battle of Gettysburg** ended in a Union victory, crowds gathered for the dedication of the Soldiers' National Cemetery. Although he was not the main speaker of the event, Lincoln's short yet eloquent speech proved to be the most significant. Drawing upon the Declaration of Independence's assertion that "all men are created equal," he argued that the current war was a test of that ideal. More than that, he emphasized the importance of the United States as a whole and argued that it must endure as a Union for the sake of the world.

Earlier that year in January, Lincoln had already indicated his opposition to slavery through the **Emancipation Proclamation**. Although it was an executive order instead of a law passed by Congress, this document was not challenged by the courts and helped determine the objectives of the Civil War. The proclamation asserted that all slaves in Confederate territories were free. One must note that some southern states remained in the Union, and therefore, were not affected by this proclamation. Even so, the order helped establish a basis for later laws and amendments that would end slavery in the United States.

Another presidential attempt to set a new precedent for American policy was **Woodrow Wilson's Fourteen Points**, which were outlined in a speech he gave to Congress in 1918 after the United States had entered World War I. Wilson saw the United States as a protector of democracy in the world and said that we could reform world policy by fighting in the war. For instance, Wilson called for an end to private negotiations, which had contributed to the secret alliances behind the war. Most of all, he argued for nations to come together in an international body to determine world policies. The negotiations after the war only partially fulfilled Wilson's ambitions by creating a weak League of Nations, but his vision of U.S. involvement in global affairs would become a key aspect of American foreign policy.

Even as the United States began playing a more active role on the international stage of politics, internal issues such as civil rights remained important, as shown in **Martin Luther King Jr.**'s "I Have a Dream" speech. A leader in the civil rights movement, King gave his speech as part of the 1963 March on Washington. Drawing on Lincoln's past speech at Gettysburg, King argued that America's journey to true equality was not over. His references to biblical passages gave the speech a spiritual tone, but he also mentioned specific locations across the nation to emphasize that local struggles were tied with national consequences. Through its optimistic tone, Dr. King's speech reflects not only civil rights activism but also the American dream of freedom and progress.

Rights and Responsibilities of Citizenship in a Democracy

Citizens living in a democracy have several rights and responsibilities to uphold. The first duty is that they uphold the established laws of the government. In a democracy, a system of nationwide laws is necessary to ensure that there is some degree of order. Therefore, citizens must try to obey the laws and also help enforce them because a law that is inadequately enforced, such as early civil rights laws in the South, is almost useless. Optimally, a democratic society's laws will be accepted and followed by the community as a whole.

However, conflict can occur when an unjust law is passed. For instance, much of the civil rights movement centered around **Jim Crow laws** in the South that supported segregation between black and whites. Yet these practices were encoded in state laws, which created a dilemma for African Americans who wanted equality but also wanted to respect the law. Fortunately, a democracy offers a degree of protection from such laws by creating a system in which government leaders and policies are constantly open to change in accordance with the will of citizens. Citizens can influence the laws that are passed by voting for and electing members of the legislative and executive branches to represent them at the local, state, and national levels.

This, however, requires citizens to be especially vigilant in protecting their liberties because they cannot depend solely on the existing government to meet their needs. To assert their role in a democracy, citizens should be active voters and speak out on issues that concern them. Even with these safeguards, it is possible for systems to be implemented that inhibit active participation. For instance, many southern states had laws that prevented blacks from voting. Under such circumstances, civil rights leaders felt that they had no choice but to resist the laws in order to defend their personal rights. Once voting became possible, civil rights groups strove to ensure that their votes counted by changing state and national policy.

An extension of citizens' voting rights is their ability to run as elected officials. By becoming leaders in the government, citizens can demonstrate their engagement and help determine government policy.

The involvement of citizens as a whole in the selection of leaders is vital in a democracy because it helps to prevent the formation of an elite cadre that does not answer to the public. Without the engagement of citizens who run for office, voters are limited in their ability to select candidates that appeal to them. In this case, voting options would become stagnant, which inhibits the ability of the nation to grow and change over time. As long as citizens are willing to take a stand for their vision of America, America's government will remain dynamic and diverse.

These features of a democracy give it the potential to reshape itself continually in response to new developments in society. In order for a democracy to function, it is of the utmost importance that citizens care about the course of politics and be aware of current issues. Apathy among citizens is a constant problem that threatens the endurance of democracies. Citizens should have a desire to take part in the political process, or else they simply accept the status quo and fail to fulfill their role as citizens.

Moreover, they must have acute knowledge of the political processes and the issues that they can address as citizens. A fear among the Founding Fathers was the prevalence of mob rule, in which the common people did not take interest in politics except to vote for their patrons; this was the usual course of politics in the colonial era, as the common people left the decisions to the established elites. Without understanding the world around them, citizens may not fully grasp the significance of political actions and thereby fail to make wise decisions in that regard. Therefore, citizens must stay informed about current affairs, ranging from local to national or global matters, so that they can properly address them as voters or elected leaders.

Furthermore, knowledge of the nation's history is essential for healthy citizenship. History continues to have an influence on present political decisions. For instance, Supreme Court rulings often take into account previous legal precedents and verdicts, so it is important to know about those past events and how they affect the current processes. It is especially critical that citizens are aware of the context in which laws were established because it helps clarify the purpose of those laws. For instance, an understanding of the problems with the Articles of Confederation allows people to comprehend some of the reasons behind the framework of the Constitution. In addition, history as a whole shapes the course of societies and the world; therefore, citizens should draw on this knowledge of the past to realize the full consequences of current actions. Issues such as climate change, conflict in the Middle East, and civil rights struggles are rooted in events and cultural developments that reach back centuries and should be addressed.

Therefore, education is a high priority in democracies because it has the potential to instill generations of citizens with the right mind-set and knowledge required to do their part in shaping the nation. Optimally, education should cover a variety of different subjects, ranging from mathematics to biology, so that individuals can explore whatever paths they wish to take in life. Even so, social studies are especially important because students should understand how democracies function and understand the history of the nation and world. Historical studies should cover national and local events as well because they help provide the basis for the understanding of contemporary politics. Social studies courses should also address the histories of foreign nations because contemporary politics increasingly has global consequences. In addition, history lessons should remain open to multiple perspectives, even those that might criticize a nation's past actions, because citizens should be exposed to diverse perspectives that they can apply as voters and leaders.

Geography, Anthropology, and Sociology

World and Regional Geography

Geography is essential in understanding the world as a whole. This requires a study of spatial distribution, which examines how various locations and physical features are arranged in the world. The most common element in geography is the **region**, which refers to a specific area that is separate from surrounding ones. Regions can be defined based on a variety of factors, including environmental, economic, or political features, and these different kinds of regions can overlap with each other.

It is also important to know the difference between location and place. A **location**, defined either through its physical position or through its relation to other locations, determines where something is, and this characteristic is static. A **place**, on the other hand, describes a combination of physical and human elements in relation to each other; the determination of place is therefore changeable depending on the movement of individuals and groups.

Geography is visually conveyed using maps, and a collection of maps is called an **atlas**. To illustrate some key points about geography, please refer to the map below.

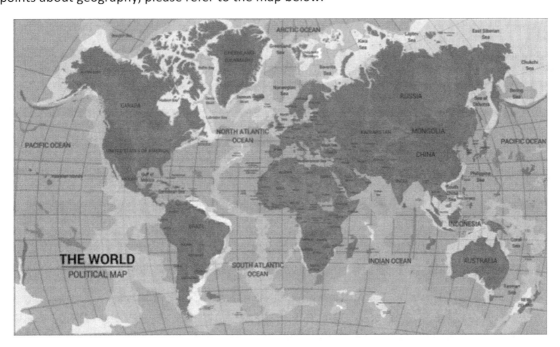

This is a traditional map of the world that displays all of the countries and six of the seven continents. **Countries**, the most common approach to political regions, can be identified by their labels. The **continents** are not identified on this map, with the exception of Australia, but they are larger landmasses that encompass most of the countries in their respective areas; the other five visible continents are North America, South America, Europe, Africa, and Asia. The seventh continent, Antarctica, is found at the South Pole and has been omitted from the map.

The absence of Antarctica leads into the issues of distortion, in which geographical features are altered on a map. Some degree of distortion is to be expected with a two-dimensional flat map of the world because the earth is a sphere. A map projection transforms a spherical map of the world into a flattened

perspective, but the process generally alters the spatial appearance of landmasses. For instance, Greenland often appears, such as in the map above, larger than it really is.

Furthermore, Antarctica's exclusion from the map is, in fact, a different sort of distortion—that of the mapmakers' biases. Mapmakers determine which features are included on the map and which ones are not. Antarctica, for example, is often missing from maps because, unlike the other continents, it has a limited human population. Moreover, a study of the world reveals that many of the distinctions on maps are human constructions.

Even so, maps can still reveal key features about the world. For instance, the map above has areas that seem almost three-dimensional and jut out. They represent mountains and are an example of **topography**, which is a method used to display the differing elevations of the terrain. A more detailed topographical map can be viewed below.

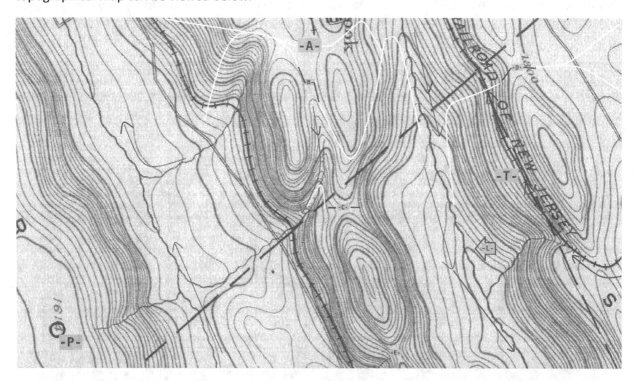

On some colored maps, the oceans, represented in blue between the continents, vary in coloration depending on depth. The differences demonstrate **bathymetry**, which is the study of the ocean floor's depth. Paler areas represent less depth, while darker spots reflect greater depth.

Please also note the many lines running horizontally and vertically along the map. The horizontal lines, known as **parallels**, mark the calculated latitude of those locations and reveal how far north or south these areas are from the equator, which bisects the map horizontally. Generally, with exceptions depending on specific environments, climates closer to the equator are warmer because this region receives the most direct sunlight. The **equator** also serves to split the globe between the Northern and Southern hemispheres.

Longitude, as signified by the vertical lines, determines how far east or west different regions are from each other. The lines of longitude, known as **meridians**, are also the basis for time zones, which allocate different times to regions depending on their position eastward and westward of the prime meridian. As

158

one travels west between time zones, the given time moves backward accordingly. Conversely, if one travels east, the time moves forward.

There are two particularly significant longitude-associated dividers in this regard. The **prime [Greenwich] meridian**, as displayed below, is defined as zero degrees in longitude, and thus determines the other lines. The line, in fact, circles the globe north and south, and it therefore divides the world into the Eastern and Western hemispheres. It is important to not confuse the Greenwich meridian with the **International Date Line**, which is an invisible line in the Pacific Ocean that was created to represent the change between calendar days. By traveling westward across the International Date Line, a traveler would essentially leap forward a day. For example, a person departing from the United States on Sunday would arrive in Japan on Monday. By traveling eastward across the line, a traveler would go backward a day. For example, a person departing from China on Monday would arrive in Canada on Sunday.

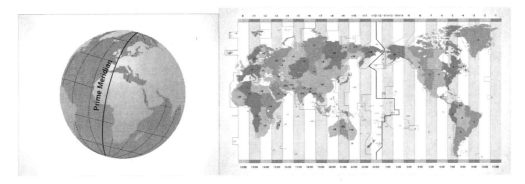

Although world maps are useful in showing the overall arrangement of continents and nations, it is also important at times to look more closely at individual countries because they have unique features that are only visible on more detailed maps.

For example, take the following map of the United States of America. It should be noted that the country is split into multiple states that have their own culture and localized governments. Other countries are often split into various divisions, such as provinces, and while these features are ignored for the sake of clarity on larger maps, they are important when studying specific nations. Individual

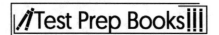
states can be further subdivided into counties and townships, and they may have their own maps that can be examined for closer analysis.

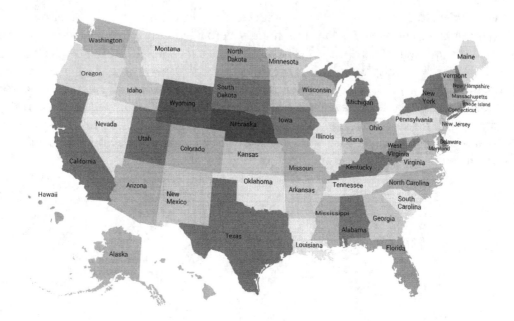

Finally, one of the first steps in examining any map should be to locate the map's key or legend, which will explain what features different symbols represent on the map. As these symbols can be arbitrary depending on the maker, a key will help to clarify the different meanings.

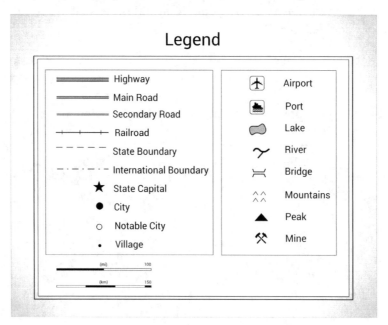

Interaction of Physical and Human Systems

Humans have always interacted with nature, and humanity has been shaped by, and, in turn, reshaped environments. Using tools to accomplish things they cannot do on their own, humans have proven highly adaptable to different environments. However, the specific ecosystems have helped to shape

160

human development as individuals and as groups. The earth is highly diverse and has many different ecosystems, each with its own flora and fauna. The specific resources available in different places have, therefore, influenced how humans develop.

Water, in particular, has proved vital in determining the course of human civilizations. As humans require water daily to survive, even more than they do food, proximity to water has always been of utmost necessity. Many human settlements originated adjacent to sources, and only in time expanded to other areas. Water is also essential for the growth of plants, which form a considerable portion of the human diet. In the wild, edible plants grow in places where they can thrive but may not be conveniently located for harvesting by humans. Therefore, humans gradually learned to grow plants themselves in places of their own choice. Humans also diverted water sources to new areas for themselves and to irrigate crops, thus transforming ecosystems.

Another important factor in the relationships between humans and nature has been the role of other animals. From small pests, such as weevils and rodents, to predators, including crocodiles and bears, many species of animals have often posed threats to humans, and conflict increased as humans expanded into environments inhabited by other creatures. On the other hand, animals are invaluable to humans because they can provide sustenance and clothing. This led to hunting and domestication of animal species. Domestication of both plants and animals involves humans breeding species to fit their own needs, which leads to new qualities that would normally not appear in the wild.

However, despite the considerable role that humans can play in altering environments, these changes have remained limited to local levels for much of human history. This does not mean that humans did not affect their ecosystems; some Native American tribes, for instance, used regular fires or hunting methods to maintain environments suitable for their needs. Even so, for much of human existence, nature was seen not simply as an obstacle but rather a power of its own right that was above human interference. **Natural phenomena** such as severe weather, diseases, and famine all kept human populations in check. Many pantheons of deities center on the gods' roles as arbitrary powers in the natural world, which reflects the lack of influence that humans had in the larger course of environmental changes.

Therefore, **natural resources** such as water and food were often seen as forces to be respected. Natural environments were recognized as vital regions, and alterations to fully exploit the resources were limited so that the resources could remain adequately sustainable. **Riparian customs** meant that water was the right of those with immediate access to it, and ownership changed accordingly with who lived nearby. However, increasing **industrialization** meant that natural resources such as water and lumber became resources that could be commoditized. In addition, appropriation gave water rights to those individuals or businesses that had first used the resource instead of being based on physical proximity.

Another instrumental change in the relationship between humans and nature is the increasing global connections worldwide. In many cases, earlier changes to environments occurred at local levels, with travel between different regions requiring considerable time and effort. The ability to travel around the world quickly has sharply altered that dynamic. Many local ecosystems, and the human cultures that developed accordingly, originated in separate circumstances that created unique plants and animals. Now products from one part of the world can be transported to entirely different environments and create new exchanges of goods. In some cases, the transferred species escape into the wild, and they often have traits for which the local environments are not prepared. This can result in invasive species that quickly grow and overpower native species.

A key symbol of artificial environments created by humans since early civilization has been the city, which is a human center of habitation that exists separate from the countryside around it. The creation of cities usually requires significant changes to the environment in which it is located, and the city must provide for the needs of residents without being compromised by nature. Yet the city has always remained connected to the rest of the world and to nature. Because a city generally lacks the capacity for agriculture and few natural resources are located within its confines, urban populations rely on resources from outlying areas for nourishment. The city, in turn, acts as a processing center for nearby settlements and offers rural workers and farmers the opportunity to sell their goods to a larger market.

Furthermore, the city, while an artificial construct, is still an environment in its own right. Although many species of animals have perished with the creation of cities, others, such as coyotes and pigeons, have adapted to urban life, thereby creating new ecosystems within cities. Natural connections within cities used to be stronger and more common because people would raise livestock within the city and regularly reuse garbage for livestock feed. While less hygienic, this helped stimulate natural cycles within the city. Recent efforts in many cities to create natural pockets, such as parks and community gardens, have also strengthened the ties between cities and the natural world. In a sense, the city reflects humanity's mixed relationship with nature as a whole: while humans continue to reshape the environment, they also remain linked to nature.

Uses of Geography

Geography helps people better understand the role that location plays in the past, present, and future. Historians make frequent use of maps in their studies to get a clearer picture of how history unfolded. Since the beginning of history, many different groups have fought conflicts that originated from struggles for land or other resources; therefore, knowing the location and borders of different empires and kingdoms helps reveal how they interacted with each other. In addition, environmental factors, such as access to water and the proximity of mountains, often help to shape the course of civilizations. Even single events and battles make more sense with maps that show how the warring sides met and maneuvered.

Furthermore, determining the geography of historical events, in particular geographical change over time, is essential due to the role that physical settings play in the present. Many important geographic landmarks continue to exist in the world, and they are often commemorated for their roles in history. Yet the physical geography has sometimes changed significantly. For instance, the **Aswan Dam** significantly reshaped the flow of the **Nile River**, which was the heart of ancient Egyptian society; without knowledge of the past geography, it is difficult to fully understand the civilization's context and how it differs from the present reality.

History also depends on archaeology, the study of human artifacts, for the evidence necessary to make conclusions about cultures. These items are generally buried, which helps preserve the artifacts yet makes it difficult to locate them. Historical geography helps in that regard by ascertaining key sites of human activity that could potentially retain artifacts. These insights help archaeologists discover new aspects of ancient cultures, which in turn strengthen historical arguments. Maps themselves sometimes serve as artifacts in their own right because they help reveal how humans of earlier periods viewed the world.

Along with the historical implications, knowledge of the world's geography remains important for people in the present day. The most immediate use of geography is in navigation. Tools such as Global

Positioning Systems have helped improve navigation, but they too represent an approach to geography that demonstrates how it continues to have a fundamental role in human society. Humans have even begun mapping the trajectories of planets and even their individual terrains.

However, beyond the direct uses for navigation, geography is invaluable in comprehending modern cultures and events. Whether through their proximity to other nations or their relation to environmental features, such as forests and deserts, societies remain deeply connected to their geographical settings. Therefore, to fully understand current affairs, such as wars and poverty, people must have a firm grasp on geographic settings. For instance, a study of nations in Africa, many of which continue to suffer from poverty, would require a close examination of geographic factors. The borders of many African countries were arbitrarily determined during the colonial period, and the conflicts of ethnic groups divided by these borders have influenced current struggles. On the environmental end, some nations have been significantly affected by desertification and deforestation, which makes studies of their ecological geography important as well.

Two recent key developments have made geography more important than ever before. The first change is the globalization of culture, economics, and politics. For much of human history, geography was most important at localized scales. Many people spent their entire lives in isolated communities, with intermittent trade between different centers. Geography was still important, but many people did not need to be familiar with anything other than their immediate locations. Today, on the other hand, places around the world are intricately connected to each other. Travel is relatively easy and quick and enables people to venture between different regions like never before. Areas that used to be geographically isolated from each other can now exchange ideas and products on an unprecedented scale.

In addition, due to the multinational relationship of politics, conflicts that would have been geographically isolated in the past can have international ramifications. Latin American revolutions, such as in Nicaragua during the Cold War, were seen as having larger implications in the struggle between American democracy and Soviet communism, which led to foreign interventions and wars that affected multiple countries. Therefore, geography is critical to not only addressing the current effects of globalization but also understanding how global interactions may influence international politics and economics in the future.

The second major factor in geography's role in modern events is the rising importance of environmental policies and climate change. Scientific developments have increasingly revealed how the planet as a whole can be considered a large ecosystem in its own right, with its own strengths and frailties. A change in one part of the environment, such as industrialization in India and China, can have larger consequences for neighboring regions and for the world as a whole. Geographical insights help to show how the world functions and how humans can work to improve their relationship with the natural world.

Moreover, as climate changes become more evident in the world, geography helps illustrate the effects of new environmental phenomena. For instance, scientists have studied the topography of nations to determine how rising sea levels will alter the land via flooding, and local and national governments are using these findings to prepare for the coming changes. Furthermore, the continued scrutiny of the state of the earth's geography reveals how climate change is transforming the planet at this very moment, as regional climates shift and islands vanish under the sea. As a result, geography will continue to have a role in future developments.

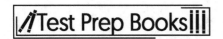

Different Cultural Backgrounds

When studying different cultures, it is important to realize that cultures are always changing in response to individuals and groups within it. Therefore, one must avoid stereotyping members of a certain culture or overgeneralizing. For example, American culture is highly diverse with multiple ethnic groups. Many ethnic communities have resided in the United States for generations, so it is incorrect to label them as a foreign culture, yet each group must be closely examined to understand American culture as a whole.

This diversity within larger classifications of cultures can be seen with Native Americans. There are many different tribes of Native Americans, and each has its own unique history and characteristics. Nevertheless, a few general qualities describe most Native American groups. First of all, Native Americans continue to struggle to escape the poverty that they were historically forced into during white settlement of the United States. Many, but not all, tribes have been traditionally matrilineal—with ancestry defined through female lineage—and emphasized communal sharing and a sustainable relationship with nature, but the American government often suppressed these customs. This has led many Native Americans to begin protecting their surviving heritage, including their rights to traditional religious practices and access to historical artifacts.

South of the United States, Mexico has a vibrant yet troubled culture. Mexico was one of the principal colonies of Spain, and the culture is therefore a diverse blend of Spanish and native customs. One enduring legacy of Spain's rule is the prominence of Roman Catholicism, albeit mixed with pre-Spanish concepts; for instance, the traditional Day of the Dead embodies both pre-Columbian and Christian ideals. On the other hand, the Spanish system of large estates created significant class disparities. Furthermore, Mexico's war for independence and conflicts with other nations drastically destabilized its government, and the nation continues to struggle with corruption and violence. Still, Mexico retains a rich culture that celebrates its complex history. Mexican families are generally large and cooperate to help each other.

French national identity is relatively new because regional ties were prevalent until the French Revolution in the 1790s. A rising sense of nationalism unites French culture today, but various regions maintain their own local traditions. Much of France has been traditionally agricultural, but the globalization of the food trade has disrupted local markets and led to mass migration to cities. Reflecting Catholic values, most of France's families follow a nuclear model of a two-parent household with children.

South Africa is culturally and ethnically diverse, but historically white settlers used apartheid to oppress and isolate other groups. However, previously marginalized ethnic groups are now actively working to assert their own identity within South Africa. Rural communities tend to be more traditional, while people within cities have adopted new values. South Africa is largely patriarchal with defined gender roles that give men dominance over women. Efforts to strengthen South Africa's industries have depleted many of its natural resources and created a growing environmental crisis that is particularly devastating to rural populations.

Laying claim to the legacies of ancient Persia, Iran's culture was at the crossroads of trade routes between multiple continents for centuries, which gave it a long and diverse background. Iran is primarily Islamic, with the majority of Muslims belonging to the Shi'a faith. They believe that their religious leaders, imams, are divinely appointed as the religious successors, known as **caliphs**, to the prophet Muhammad; even so, other religions such as Judaism and Zoroastrianism are also practiced in the

country. Iran's patriarchal culture generally restricts the role of women, but women have nevertheless become more involved in the civil service, sciences, and other fields.

Russia's culture is built on a rich history but has been especially influenced by the dominance of communism until the Soviet Union's dissolution in 1991. The use of state police and other agents to enforce government policies led to a sense of paranoia and distrust of anyone outside the family. On the other hand, this situation created strong support networks within families that led to strong relationships with relatives. The Soviet Union's drive to industrialize also led to numerous current environmental issues across Russia.

As with Russia, the People's Republic of China's modern culture is deeply influenced by decades of Communist rule. Under the leadership of Mao, China enacted massive efforts to strengthen Chinese industry and agriculture at the cost of environmental damage; China continues to undergo intense industrial operations in the present, which has caused pollution in the cities. On the other hand, China takes great pride in its long traditions and history that date back thousands of years. China has been traditionally patriarchal, and children have been expected to respect and care for their elders. Chinese culture is not monolithic, and there are many different ethnic groups within the country, including the Han, Manchu, and Uyghur. However, the one-child policy from 1978 to 2015 has destabilized long-term family dynamics by putting considerable pressure on single children to look after their parents.

Japan's family structure has also been disrupted in the modern era. Japanese culture is built on a sense of interdependence within families and the community as a whole, but a low birthrate has led to a rising number of elderly relatives and few children, which has unsettled the traditional foundation. Even so, Japan embraces a blend of modern advancements and traditional customs. Japanese culture is built on multiple layers of social status, and people use different forms of language depending on their relationship with others. As a result, traditional Japanese society is highly formal, but recent generations have become more open to new ideas. As Japan's islands have limited space and resources, it has been at the forefront of many natural conservation efforts, although some controversial traditions, such as whaling, still persist.

World History and Economics

Major Contributions of Classical Civilizations

There were a number of powerful civilizations during the classical period. **Mesopotamia** was home to one of the earliest civilizations between the Euphrates and the Tigris rivers in the Near East. The rivers provided water and vegetation for early humans, but they were surrounded by desert. This led to the beginning of irrigation efforts to expand water and agriculture across the region, which resulted in the area being known as the **Fertile Crescent**.

The organization necessary to initiate canals and other projects led to the formation of cities and hierarchies, which would have considerable influence on the structure of later civilizations. For instance, the new hierarchies established different classes within the societies, such as kings, priests, artisans, and workers. Over time, these city-states expanded to encompass outside territories, and the city of Akkad became the world's first empire in 2350 B.C. In addition, Mesopotamian scribes developed systemized drawings called **pictograms**, which were the first system of writing in the world; furthermore, the creation of wedge-shaped **cuneiform tablets** preserved written records for multiple generations.

Later, Mesopotamian kingdoms made further advancements. For instance, **Babylon** established a sophisticated mathematical system based on numbers from one to sixty; this not only influenced modern concepts, such as the number of minutes in each hour, but also created the framework for math equations and theories. In addition, the Babylonian king Hammurabi established a complex set of laws, known as the **Code of Hammurabi**, which would set a precedent for future legal systems.

Meanwhile, another major civilization began to form around the Nile River in Africa. The Nile's relatively predictable nature allowed farmers to use the river's water and the silt from floods to grow many crops along its banks, which led to further advancements in irrigation. Egyptian rulers mobilized the kingdom's population for incredible construction projects, including the famous pyramids. Egyptians also improved pictographic writing with their more complex system of **hieroglyphs**, which allowed for more diverse styles of writing. The advancements in writing can be seen through the Egyptians' complex system of religion, with documents such as the **Book of the Dead** outlining not only systems of worship and pantheons of deities but also a deeper, more philosophical concept of the afterlife.

While civilizations in Egypt and Mesopotamia helped to establish class systems and empires, other forms of government emerged in Greece. Despite common ties between different cities, such as the Olympic Games, each settlement, known as a **polis**, had its own unique culture. Many of the cities were oligarchies, in which a council of distinguished leaders monopolized the government; others were dictatorships ruled by tyrants. Athens was a notable exception by practicing an early form of democracy in which free, landholding men could participate, but it offered more freedom of thought than other systems.

Taking advantage of their proximity to the Mediterranean Sea, Greek cities sent expeditions to establish colonies abroad that developed their own local traditions. In the process, Greek merchants interacted with Phoenician traders, who had developed an alphabetic writing system built on sounds instead of pictures. This diverse network of exchanges made Greece a vibrant center of art, science, and philosophy. For example, the Greek doctor Hippocrates established a system of ethics for doctors called the **Hippocratic Oath**, which continues to guide the modern medical profession. Complex forms of literature were created, including the epic poem "The Iliad," and theatrical productions were also developed. Athens in particular sought to spread its vision of democratic freedom throughout the world, which led to the devastating Peloponnesian War between allies of Athens and those of oligarchic Sparta from 431 to 404 B.C.

Alexander the Great helped disseminate Greek culture to new regions. Alexander was in fact an heir to the throne of Macedon, which was a warrior kingdom to the north of Greece. After finishing his father's work of unifying Greece under Macedonian control, Alexander successfully conquered Mesopotamia, which had been part of the Persian Empire. The spread of Greek institutions throughout the Mediterranean and Near East led to a period of Hellenization, during which various civilizations assimilated Greek culture; this allowed Greek traditions, such as architecture and philosophy, to endure into the present day.

Greek ideas were later assimilated, along with many other concepts, into the **Roman Empire**. Located west of Greece on the Italian peninsula, the city of Rome gradually conquered its neighbors and expanded its territories abroad; by 44 B.C., Rome had conquered much of Western Europe, northern Africa, and the Near East. Romans were very creative, and they adapted new ideas and innovated new technologies to strengthen their power. For instance, Romans built on the engineering knowledge of

Greeks to create arched pathways, known as **aqueducts**, to transport water for long distances and devise advanced plumbing systems.

One of Rome's greatest legacies was its system of government. Early Rome was a republic, a democratic system in which leaders are elected by the people. Although the process still heavily favored wealthy elites, the republican system was a key inspiration for later institutions such as the United States. Octavian "Augustus" Caesar later made Rome into an empire, and the senate had only a symbolic role in the government. The new imperial system built on the examples of earlier empires to establish a vibrant dynasty that used a sophisticated legal code and a well-trained military to enforce order across vast regions. Even after Rome itself fell to barbarian invaders in fifth century A.D., the eastern half of the empire survived as the Byzantine Empire until 1453 A.D. Furthermore, the Roman Empire's institutions continued to influence and inspire later medieval kingdoms, including the Holy Roman Empire; even rulers in the twentieth century called themselves Kaiser and Tsar, titles which stem from the word "Caesar."

In addition, the Roman Empire was host to the spread of new religious ideas. In the region of Israel, the religion of **Judaism** presented a new approach to worship via **monotheism**, which is the belief in the existence of a single deity. An offshoot of Judaism called **Christianity** spread across the Roman Empire and gained popularity. While Rome initially suppressed the religion, it later backed Christianity and allowed the religious system to endure as a powerful force in medieval times.

Twentieth-Century Development in World History

At the turn of the twentieth century, imperialism had led to powers, such as France, the United States, and Japan, to establish spheres of influence throughout the world. The combination of imperial competition and military rivalries led to the outbreak of World War I when **Archduke Ferdinand of Austria** was assassinated in 1914. The war pitted **the Allies**, including England, France, and Russia, against the Central Powers of Austria-Hungary, Germany, and the **Ottoman Empire**—a large Islamic realm that encompassed Turkey, Palestine, Saudi Arabia, and Iraq. The rapid advances in military technology turned the war into a prolonged bloodbath that took its toll on all sides. By the end of the war in 1918, the Ottoman Empire had collapsed, the Austrian-Hungarian Empire was split into multiple countries, and Russia had descended into a civil war that would lead to the rise of the Soviet Union and Communism.

The **Treaty of Versailles** ended the war, but the triumphant Allies also levied heavy fines on Germany, which led to resentment that would be accentuated by the Great Depression of the 1930s. The **Great Depression** destabilized the global economy and led to the rise of fascism, a militarized and dictatorial system of government, in nations such as Germany and Italy. The rapid expansion of the Axis Powers of Germany, Italy, and Japan led to the outbreak of World War II. The war was even more global than the previous conflicts, with battles occurring in Europe, Africa, and Asia. World War II encouraged the development of new technologies, such as advanced radar and nuclear weapons, that would continue to influence the course of future wars.

In the aftermath of World War II, the **United Nations** was formed as a step toward promoting international cooperation. Based on the preceding League of Nations, the United Nations included countries from around the world and gave them a voice in world policies. The formation of the United Nations coincided with the independence of formerly colonized states in Africa and Asia, and those countries joined the world body. A primary goal of the United Nations was to limit the extent of future

wars and prevent a third world war; while the United Nations could not prevent the outbreak of wars, it nevertheless tried to peacefully resolve them. In addition to promoting world peace, the United Nations also helped protect human rights.

Even so, the primary leadership in the early United Nations was held by the United States and its allies, which contributed to tensions with the Soviet Union. The United States and the Soviet Union, while never declaring war on each other, fueled a number of proxy wars and coups across the world in what would be known as the **Cold War**. Cold War divisions were especially noticeable in Europe, where communist regimes ruled the eastern region and democratic governments controlled the western portion. These indirect struggles often involved interference with foreign politics, and sometimes local people began to resent Soviet or American attempts to influence their countries. For instance, American and Soviet interventions in Iran and Afghanistan contributed to fundamentalist Islamic movements. The Cold War ended when the Soviet Union collapsed in 1991, but the conflict affected nations across the globe and continues to influence current issues.

Another key development during the twentieth century, as noted earlier with the United Nations, was that most colonized nations broke free from imperial control and asserted their independence. Although these nations achieved autonomy and recognition in the United Nations, they still suffered from the legacies of imperialism. The borders of many countries in Africa and Asia were arbitrarily determined by colonists with little regard to the arrangement of native populations. Therefore, many former colonies have suffered conflicts between different ethnic groups; this was also the case with the British colony in India, which became independent in 1947. Violence occurred when it split into India and Pakistan because the borders were largely based on religious differences. In addition, former colonial powers continue to assert economic control that inhibits the growth of native economies. On the other hand, the end of direct imperialism has helped a number of nations, such as India and Iran, rise as world powers that have significant influence on the world as a whole.

Additionally, there were considerable environmental reforms worldwide during the twentieth century. In reaction to the growing effects of industrialization, organizations around the world protested policies that damaged the environment. Many of these movements were locally based, but others expanded to address various environmental threats across the globe. The United Nations helped carry these environmental reforms forward by making them part of international policies. For instance, in 1997, many members of the United Nations signed a treaty, known as the **Kyoto Protocol**, that tried to reduce global carbon dioxide emissions.

Most significantly, the twentieth century marked increasing globalization. The process had already been under way in the nineteenth century as technological improvements and imperial expansions connected different parts of the world, but the late twentieth century brought globalization to a new level. Trade became international, and local customs from different lands also gained prominence worldwide. Cultural exchanges occur on a frequent basis, and many people have begun to ponder the consequences of such rapid exchanges. One example of globalization was the 1993 establishment of the European Union—an economic and political alliance between several European nations.

Cross-Cultural Comparisons in World History Instruction

Cross-cultural interactions are the very heart of world history and must be closely examined to understand the world's historical patterns. One of the main reasons why cross-cultural studies are so important is because cultures are not necessarily synonymous with political entities, such as states.

168

Many countries, ranging from China to Greece, historically have many subcultures that should be considered individually. For example, a study of culture in the United States would need to consider multiple ethnic and regional groups. Even individual states and cities have their own traditions. On the other hand, these multiple cultures often coalesce into a larger, national culture that defines the overall society and politics of the nation. Therefore, cross-cultural studies of different subgroups in a larger body allow people to understand how the different parts of a culture interact and connect with each other.

Furthermore, cultures are not always restricted by the borders of nations, and cultural phenomena may extend through multiple countries. This can be seen in the spread of the Spanish language across Central and South America as well as other regions. The Spanish language and other various traditions tie the different countries together with a common culture. Even so, each nation changes the culture and gives it a unique style. A study of the culture in a single nation may be very insightful, but it would be incomplete if it failed to account for aspects of the culture beyond that country. In addition, this means that different cultures can overlap with each other and that the cultures of different countries may intersect in ways that their borders do not. By examining multiple cultures and how they are linked with each other, larger cultural patterns become apparent, which makes these studies critical in world history.

Throughout history, cultures have not existed in isolation but rather have been affected by other traditions. A key influence in how different cultures develop is not only their setting and history but how they interact with neighboring cultures. For instance, the conflict from 499 to 449 B.C. between the Persian Empire and the Greek city-states helped to influence the course of Greek culture as a whole by creating a national sense of dichotomy between the Greek ideal of freedom and Persian autocracy. Aside from direct impacts such as wars, cultures can influence each other through interactions that spread some concepts while also adopting new ideas from their neighbors. Pasta became a phenomenon in Italy in part because the Silk Road linked Italy with China, which already had similar foods.

The pervasiveness of globalization in the present day has increased the importance of cross-cultural comparison and made it a topic of immediate relevance. The world now has a truly global market in which travel, communications, and trade function on an international scale. This means that people of different cultures can now interact with each other much more easily than in earlier centuries, which allows for a rapid exchange of ideas and goods between cultures. Furthermore, despite the international scope of modern trade, many globalized markets strive to build on the appeal of local cultures. Doing so gives the products a genuine and unique quality that resonates with consumers. Yet it is critical to realize how local cultures are transformed and combined with concepts from other cultures in the global market. For example, sushi is a traditional food in Japan, but its export to other nations has led chefs to create new culinary fusions, such as sushi tacos.

Cross-cultural comparisons also help to reveal common patterns in human society. Sometimes different cultures develop similar concepts without directly interacting with each other. For instance, both the Mayan culture in Central America and the ancient Egyptians independently developed pyramid structures. Although the similarities have sparked rumors that these civilizations were connected, it is most likely that each version originated independently. Close examination of the two types of pyramids and their respective cultures reveals significant differences amidst the similarities. These comparisons are important because they show how human cultures converge and diverge in their patterns of growth. A key function of historical study is to gain a better understanding and appreciation of how humanity

develops. By examining the commonalities and differences between cultures, people can begin to theorize what factors influence the course of civilizations. However, such studies must account for the complex manners through which cultures interact with each other.

Terms and Concepts of Economics

Economics form a key component of human society. Studies of economies can be divided between **macroeconomics**, which considers the larger economy as a whole, and **microeconomics**, which focuses on the actions of smaller groups, households, and individuals. However, the most basic principle of economics comes down to resources. A **resource** can be defined as an object or material that can be used for some purpose. **Natural resources** come directly from the environment, whereas items altered through human activity are considered manufactured goods. Resources can be further divided into **renewable resources**, which are gradually replenished given enough time and proper circumstances, and **nonrenewable resources**, which regenerate slowly or not at all. In addition, there are four main types of economic resources: **land**, which includes most natural resources; **labor**, the services provided by individuals to create products; **capital**, which encompasses human-manufactured resources; and **entrepreneurship**, the process in which individuals utilize available resources for business ventures that generate new products.

Early on, human civilizations functioned using a **barter system**, where people would trade certain goods for other items. It remains common in some parts of the world today. However, the difficulty of storing and transporting products, such as livestock and minerals, for exchange, led to the development of monetary systems. **Money** is an object, such as a coin or a paper bill, which can be exchanged for any commercial product given enough money. It is important to note that money on its own often has no worth; **paper money**, for example, is a rather flimsy material with little actual use outside of its monetary worth. It only has value when members of a society agree that it can be used to make purchases.

Due to the artificial nature of money within societies, prices fluctuate depending on the supply and demand of products. **Supply** refers to the available quantity of a specific good or resource. In contrast, demand accounts for the quantity that buyers wish to obtain. These two factors influence several economic patterns. The **law of supply** states that the quantity available for purchase is directly related to the price, while the **law of demand** states that the price of an item is inversely related to the demand for the item. Thus, raising prices increases supply and reduces demand.

Furthermore, the value of money in part depends on the amount that is circulated in the market. A surplus of money has the potential to devalue the currency, which lowers the worth of each unit of money. This process, called **inflation**, has a detrimental effect on the economy as prices generally increase. However, the opposite trend, **deflation**, can also be detrimental; thus, political leaders usually strive to find a stable balance between the two ends of the spectrum. By finding equilibrium between supply and demand, an economy's prices remain relatively stable.

Economies, by nature, have limited access to certain resources, which creates a conflict between supply and demand. **Scarcity** occurs when the demand for a product exceeds its availability. Scarcity in part depends on the choices of individuals as they determine which products they want more than others. **Choices**, in turn, are influenced by the perceived costs of pursuing certain options over others. The costs and benefits of specific choices often differ depending on the individuals' perceptions of the options. When people believe that a certain service's or product's benefits outweigh its necessary costs, they

may choose to pay more for the desired benefits. It is important to realize that the laws of supply and demand are not absolute, and they may fluctuate depending on the situation.

Supply and demand can be further affected by **monopolies**, in which an individual or group holds sole or primary access to a given product or service. The individuals controlling a monopoly can limit the supply in a manner that best suits themselves but not necessarily the consumers. Monopolies are often asserted through the creation of barriers that limit access to the resources or services. For instance, patents give exclusive rights for inventions and discoveries to their respective creators or the firms that sponsored them. Without restraints, a monopoly can significantly limit economic development and prosperity of a society.

Effects of Economics on Population, Resources, and Technology

Economics are closely linked with the flow of resources, technology, and population in societies. The use of natural resources, such as water and fossil fuels, has always depended in part on the pressures of the economy. A supply of a specific good may be limited in the market, but with sufficient demand the sellers are incentivized to increase the available quantity. Unfortunately, the demand for certain objects can often be unlimited, and a high price or limited supply may prevent consumers from obtaining the product or service. If the sellers succumb to the consumers' demand and continue to exploit a scarce resource, supply could potentially be exhausted.

The resources for most products, both renewable and nonrenewable, are finite. This is a particularly difficult issue with nonrenewable resources, but even renewable resources often have limits: **organic products** such as trees and animals require stable populations and sufficient habitats to support those populations. Furthermore, the costs of certain decisions can have detrimental effects on other resources. For example, industrialization provides economic benefits in many countries but also has had the negative effect of polluting surrounding environments; the pollution, in turn, often eliminates or harms fish, plants, and other potential resources.

The control of resources within an economy is particularly important in determining how resources are used. While the demand may change with the choices of consumers, the range of supply depends on the objectives of the people producing the goods. They determine how much of their supply they allot for sale, and in the case of monopolies, they might have sole access to the resource. They might choose to limit their use of the resources or instead gather more to meet the demand. As they pay for the products, consumers can choose which sellers they rely on for the supply. In the case of a monopoly, though, consumers have little influence over the company's decision because there is no alternative supplier. Therefore, the function of supply within an economy can drastically influence how the resources are exploited.

The availability of resources, in turn, affects the human population. Humans require basic resources such as food and water for survival, as well as additional resources for healthy lifestyles. Therefore, access to these resources helps determine the survival rate of humans. For much of human existence, economies have had limited ability to extract resources from the natural world, which restricted the growth rate of populations. However, the development of new technologies, combined with increasing demand for certain products, has pushed resource use to a new level. On the one hand, this led to higher living standards that ensured that fewer people would die. However, this has also brought mass population growth. Admittedly, countries with higher standards of living often have lower birthrates. Even so, the increasing exploitation of resources has sharply increased the world's population as a whole

to unsustainable levels. The rising population leads, in turn, to more demand for resources that cannot be met. This creates poverty, reduced living conditions, and higher death rates. As a result, economics can significantly influence local and world population levels.

Technology is also intricately related to population, resources, and economics. The role of demand within economies has incentivized people to innovate new technologies that enable societies to have a higher quality of life and greater access to resources. Entrepreneurs expand technologies by finding ways to create new products for the market. The **Industrial Revolution**, in particular, illustrates the relationship between economics and technology because the ambitions of businessmen led to new infrastructure that enabled more efficient and sophisticated use of resources. Many of these inventions reduced the amount of work necessary for individuals and allowed the development of leisure activities, which in turn created new economic markets. However, economic systems can also limit the growth of technology. In the case of monopolies, the lack of alternative suppliers reduces the incentive to meet and exceed consumer expectations. Moreover, as demonstrated by the effects of economics on resources, technology's increasing ability to extract resources can lead to their depletion and create significant issues that need to be addressed.

Government's Role in Economics and the Impact of Economics on Government

Governments have considerable influence over the flow of economies, which makes it important to understand the relationships between them. When a government has full control over the economic decisions of a nation, it is called a **command system**. This was the case in many absolute monarchies such as eighteenth-century France; **King Louis XIV** built his economy on the concept of **mercantilism**, which believed that the state should manage all resources, particularly by accumulating gold and silver. This system of economics discouraged exports and thereby limited trade.

In contrast, the **market system** is guided by the concept of capitalism, in which individuals and businesses have the freedom to manage their economic decisions. This allows for private property and increases the opportunities for entrepreneurship and trade. Early proponents of capitalism emphasized **laissez-faire** policies, which means "let it be," and argued that the government should not be involved with the economy at all. They believe the market is guided by the concept of self-interest and that individuals will optimally work for their personal success. However, individuals' interests do not necessarily correlate with the needs of the overall economy. For instance, during a financial recession, consumers may decide to save up their money rather than make purchases; doing so helps them in the short run but further reduces demand in a slumping economy. Therefore, most capitalist governments still assert a degree of control over their economies while still allowing for private business.

Likewise, many command system economies, such as monarchical France, still relied heavily on private businesses maintained by wealthy businessmen. With the end of most absolute monarchies, communism has been the primary form of command system economies in the modern era. **Communism** is a form of socialism that emphasizes communal ownership of property and government control over production. The high degree of government control gives more stability to the economy, but it also creates considerable flaws. The monopolization of the economy by the government limits its ability to respond to local economic conditions because certain regions often have unique resources and needs. With the collapse of the Soviet Union and other communist states, command systems have been largely replaced with market systems.

The U.S. government helps to manage the nation's economy through a market system in several ways. First and foremost, the federal government is responsible for the production of money for use within the economy; depending on how the government manages the monetary flow, it may lead to a stable economy, deflation, or inflation. Second, state and federal governments impose taxes on individuals, corporations, and goods. For instance, a tariff might be imposed on imports in order to stimulate demand for local goods in the economy. Third, the government can pass laws that require additional regulation or inspections. In addition, the government has passed antitrust laws to inhibit the growth of private monopolies, which could limit free growth in the market system. Debates continue over whether the government should take further action to manage private industries or reduce its control over the private sector.

Just as governments can affect the direction of the economy, the state of the economy can have significant implications on government policies. Financial stability is critical in maintaining a prosperous state. A healthy economy will allow for new developments that contribute to the nation's growth and create jobs. On the other hand, an economic crisis, such as a recession or depression, can gravely damage a government's stability. Without a stable economy, business opportunities plummet, and people begin to lose income and employment. This, in turn, leads to frustration and discontent in the population, which can lead to criticism of the government. This could very well lead to demands for new leadership to resolve the economic crisis.

The dangers of a destabilized economy can be seen with the downfall of the French monarchy. The mercantilist approach to economics stifled French trade. Furthermore, regional aristocracies remained exempt from government taxes, which limited the government's revenues. This was compounded by expensive wars and poor harvests that led to criticism of King Louis XIV's government. The problems persisted for decades, and Louis XIV was forced to convene the **Estates-General**, a legislative body of representatives from across France, to address the crisis. The economic crises at the end of the eighteenth century were critical in the beginning of the French Revolution. Those financial issues, in turn, at least partially stemmed from both the government's control of the economy through mercantilism and its inability to impose economic authority over local regions.

Practice Questions

1. Which of the following civilizations developed the first democratic form of government?
   a. Roman Empire
   b. Ancient Greece
   c. Achaemenid Empire
   d. Zhou Dynasty

2. What is the difference between a primary source and a secondary source?
   a. Secondary sources are usually fictional, while primary sources are always true.
   b. Primary sources are context-specific, first-hand accounts, and secondary sources usually synthesize primary sources with some historical distance.
   c. Secondary sources are almost always first-hand accounts, while primary sources are second-hand fictional testimonies.
   d. There are no major differences between primary sources and secondary sources.

3. Which of the following was NOT a movement that was going on in the 1960s?
   a. Civil Rights Movement
   b. End the War Movement
   c. Women's Rights Movement
   d. LGBTQ Rights Movement

4. Which of the following is NOT one of the checks that individual branches have over another branch of government?
   a. The president may veto a bill passed by Congress
   b. The Supreme Court can try and remove the president for high crimes and misdemeanors committed in office
   c. Congress must approve all of the president's appointments to the Supreme Court
   d. Congress can pass a budget that limits what the president has to spend on defense

5. What was the Triple Entente?
   a. The Triple Entente was a free trade agreement between the United States, Britain, and France.
   b. The Triple Entente was a free trade agreement between Britain, France, and Germany.
   c. The Triple Entente was a military alliance between Austria-Hungary, Germany, and the Ottoman Empire.
   d. The Triple Entente was a military alliance between Britain, France, and Russia.

See answers on next page.

Answer Explanations

1. B: Ancient Greeks created many of the cultural and political institutions that form the basis of modern western civilization. Athens was an important Greek democracy, and all adult men could participate in politics after they had completed their military service. The Roman Empire, Choice *A,* evolved from the Roman Republic, but it was not democratic. The Achaemenid Empire and Zhou Dynasty, Choices *C* and *D*, were imperial monarchies that did not allow citizens to have much, if any, political voice.

2. B: Primary sources are context-specific, first-hand accounts, and secondary sources usually synthesize primary sources with some historical distance. Choice *A* is incorrect because both primary and secondary sources can be fictional or realistic. Choice *C* is wrong for two reasons. First, it confuses the fact that primary sources are first-hand accounts and secondary sources can be second-hand testimonies. Second, secondary sources aren't always fictional. Choice *D* is incorrect because primary sources and secondary sources are drastically different in scope and context.

3. B: End the War Movement. The 1960s were a time of growth for the United States. Everyone was pushing for rights and for changes to the system, and people were beginning to challenge the government. End the War was still a decade off, however, with Vietnam still around the corner. Choice A is incorrect because the Civil Rights Movement, led by leaders like Martin Luther King Jr., dominated the 1960s leading up to the Civil Rights Act. Choices C and D are incorrect because women's rights were also key throughout the decade, as well as the movement for LGBTQ rights.

4. B: By design, there are many checks and balances among the branches of government. The president does have the power to veto any law passed Congress, which Congress can override. Congress also has the power to consider and approve all of the president's picks for the Supreme Court and federal courts. Congress also controls the budget, which can limit what the president has to spend on the military. However, the Supreme Court does not get to try the president for high crimes and misdemeanors; that job belongs to Congress. The Chief Justice of the Supreme Court, however, does preside over the hearings.

5. D: During the early twentieth century, Britain sought military alliances with France and Russia after Germany militarized and expanded its colonies. The military alliance between Britain, France, and Russia was known as the **Triple Entente**, and it was one of the complex alliance systems that contributed to the start of World War I. Thus, Choice *D* is the correct answer. The Triple Entente was not a free trade agreement, so Choices *A* and *B* are both incorrect. The military alliance between Austria-Hungary, Germany, and the Ottoman Empire fought the Triple Entente as Central Powers during World War I. So, Choice *C* is incorrect.

Science

Earth Science

Structure of Earth System

Earth is a complex system of the **atmosphere** (air), **hydrosphere** (water), as well as continental land (land). All work together to support the **biosphere** (life).

The atmosphere is divided into several layers: the troposphere, stratosphere, mesosphere, and thermosphere. The **troposphere** is at the bottom and is about seven and a half miles thick. Above the troposphere is the 30-mile-thick **stratosphere**. Above the stratosphere is the **mesosphere**, a 20-mile layer, followed by the **thermosphere**, which is more than 300 miles thick.

The troposphere is closest to Earth and has the greatest pressure due to the pull of gravity on its gas particles as well as pressure from the layers above. 78 percent of the atmosphere is made of nitrogen. Surprisingly, the oxygen that we breathe only makes up 21 percent of the gases, and the carbon dioxide critical to insulating Earth makes up less than 1 percent of the atmosphere. There are other trace gases present in the atmosphere, including water vapor.

Although the stratosphere has minimal wind activity, it is critical for supporting the biosphere because it contains the ozone layer, which absorbs the sun's damaging ultra-violet rays and protects living organisms. Due to its low level of air movement, airplanes travel in the stratosphere. The mesosphere contains few gas particles, and the gas levels are so insignificant in the thermosphere that it is considered space.

Visible light is colors reflecting off particles. If all colors reflect, we see white; if no colors reflect, we see black. This means a colored object is reflecting only that color—a red ball reflects red light and absorbs other colors.

Because the thermosphere has so few particles to reflect light rays (photons), it appears black. The troposphere appears blue in the day, and various shades of yellow and orange at sunset due to the angle of the sun hitting particles that refract, or bend, the light. In certain instances, the entire visible spectrum can be seen in the form of rainbows. Rainbows occur when sunlight passes through water droplets and is refracted in many different directions by the water particles.

The **hydrosphere**, or water-containing portion of the Earth's surface, plays a major role in supporting the biosphere. In the picture below, a single water molecule (molecular formula H_2O) looks like a mouse head. The small ears of the mouse are the two hydrogen atoms connected to the larger oxygen atom in the middle.

176

Each hydrogen atom has one **proton** (positively charged, like the plus end of a magnet) in its **nucleus** (center), while oxygen has eight protons in its center. Hydrogen also has only one electron (negatively charged, like the minus end of a magnet) orbiting around the nucleus. Because hydrogen has only one proton, its electron is pulled more toward the oxygen nucleus (more powerful magnet). This makes hydrogen exist without an electron most of the time, so it is positively charged. On the other hand, oxygen often has two extra electrons (one from each hydrogen), so it is negatively charged. These bonds between the oxygen and hydrogen are called **covalent bonds**.

This charged situation is what makes water such a versatile substance; it also causes different molecules of water to interact with each other.

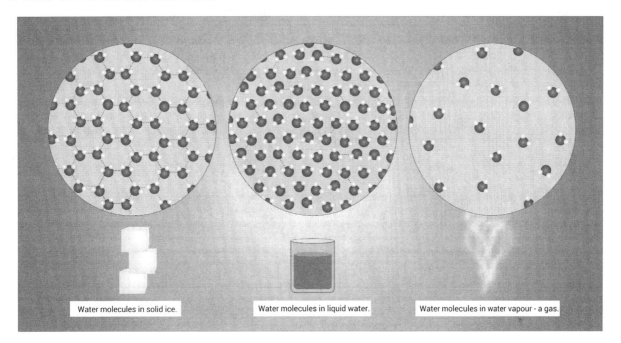

Water molecules in solid ice.   Water molecules in liquid water.   Water molecules in water vapour - a gas.

In a solid form (ice), water lines up in a crystal structure because the positive hydrogen atoms prefer to be next to the negative oxygen atoms that belong to other water molecules. These attractions are represented by the blue lines in the molecular picture of ice above. As heat is added and the ice melts, the water molecules have more kinetic energy and move faster; therefore, they are unable to perfectly arrange in the lattice structure of ice and turn into liquid. If enough heat is added, the water molecules will have so much kinetic energy they vaporize into gas. At this point, there are no bonds holding the water together because the molecules aren't close enough.

Notice how ice in its intricate arrangement has more space between the particles than liquid water, which shows that the ice is less dense than water. This contradicts the scientific fact that solids are denser than liquids. In water's case only, the solid will float due to a lower density! This is significant for the hydrosphere, because if temperatures drop to lower than freezing, frozen water will float to the surface of lakes or oceans and insulate the water underneath so that life can continue in liquid water. If ice was not less dense than liquid water, bodies of water would freeze from the bottom up and aquatic ecosystems would be trapped in a block of ice.

The hydrosphere has two components: **seawater** and **freshwater** (less than 5 percent of the hydrosphere). Water covers more than 70 percent of the Earth's surface.

177

The final piece of the biosphere is the **lithosphere**, the rocky portion of earth. **Geology** is the study of solid earth. Earth's surface is composed of elemental chunks called **minerals**, which are simply crystallized groups of bonded atoms. Minerals that have the same composition but different arrangements are called **polymorphs**, like graphite and diamonds. All minerals contain physical properties such as **luster** (shine), color, hardness, density, and boiling point. Their **chemical properties**, or how they react with other compounds, are also different. Minerals combine to form the rocks that make up Earth.

Earth has distinct layers—a thin, solid outer surface, a dense, solid core, and the majority of its matter between them. It is kind of like an egg: the thin crust is the shell, the inner core is the yolk, and the mantle and outer core that compose the space in between are like the egg white.

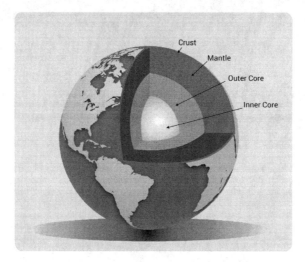

The outer crust of Earth consists of igneous or sedimentary rocks over metamorphic rocks (dense compacted rock underneath). The crust, combined with the upper portion of the mantle, forms the lithosphere, which is broken into several different plates, like puzzle pieces.

Major plates of the lithosphere

Major Plates of the Lithosphere

The **mantle** is divided in three zones. The thin zone adjacent to the crust is solid rock (the lower part of the lithosphere). Below that is the **asthenosphere**, which contains liquid magma (molten rock). The lower mantle is completely solid rock. Underneath the mantle is the outer core, a molten layer rich with iron and nickel, followed by the compact, solid, inner core.

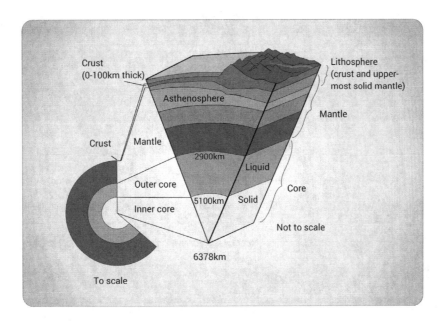

The inner and outer cores contain the densest elements (mostly iron with some nickel), which explains why they are at the center of earth: dense elements sink. Moving from outside in, Earth gets hotter and hotter, with inner core temperatures as hot as the surface of the sun. One source of this immense heat is **nuclear fission**, which occurs when a heavy element's nucleus breaks into smaller and smaller pieces and in the process produces huge amounts of energy. Some power plants that run on fission energy are used to produce electricity. The problem with fission is that it releases huge amounts of radiation. In Chernobyl, Ukraine in 1986, a power plant explosion killed thirty-one people and exposed hundreds to radiation, a known source of mutation and cancer.

Nuclear fusion is the opposite reaction, combining small elements into a larger atom. This process produces three to four times as much energy as fission. Nuclear fusion releases energy hotter than the sun, so some believe that finding a way to use it as an energy source may be a meaningful endeavor. Scientists haven't been able to construct a facility that can harness such high temperatures, but research is currently underway.

Even though the inner and outer cores contain the same elements, the inner core is solid while the outer core is liquid, indicating that they have different melting points. How can this be? This is because tremendous pressure (the weight of the world, literally) on the inner core is so forceful that the particles remain close together and stay in their solid form, making it harder to melt.

Processes of Earth

The **water cycle** is the cycling of water between its three physical states: solid, liquid, and gas. The sun is a critical component of the water cycle because its thermal energy heats up surface liquid water so much that parts of it evaporate. **Transpiration** is a similar process that occurs when the sun evaporates water from plant pores called **stomata**. As water vapor rises into the atmosphere through **evaporation** and transpiration, it eventually condenses and forms clouds heavy with liquid water droplets. The liquid (or solid ice or snow) will precipitate back to Earth, collect on land, and either be absorbed by soil or run-off to the oceans and lakes where it will accumulate, circulate, and evaporate once again.

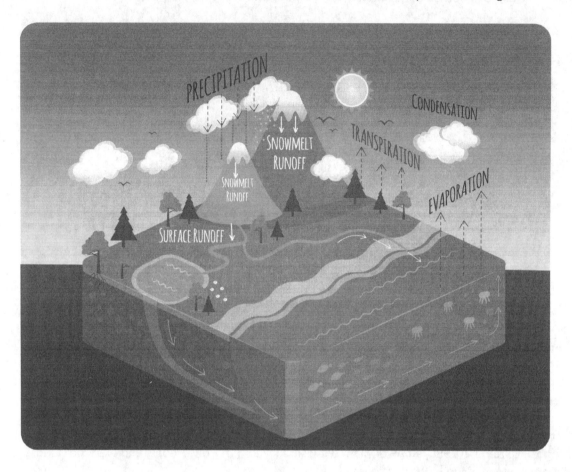

Clouds are condensed water vapor, which is water that has cooled from a gas to liquid, like the droplets on the outside of a glass of lemonade on a hot summer day. That water on the glass is water vapor that cooled enough to slow down the moving particles so that they become denser, forming a liquid. In the sky, water vapor combines in different ways so clouds appear in different forms. Cloud height, shape, and behavior results in a variety of different types:

- High-Clouds
    - Cirrus: wispy and thread-like
    - Cirrostratus: like cirrus clouds, but wider and thicker sheets. They have a halo effect where sunlight and moonlight refract through.
    - Cirrocumulus: a cross between cirrus and cirrostratus clouds. These have rows of round puffs like a cotton-ball stretched out.
    - Contrails: clouds made by jets
- Mid-Clouds
    - Altostratus: thick, stretched clouds that block sunlight and are blue-grayish in color
    - Nimbostratus: a thick altostratus cloud accompanied by rain

180

- o   Altocumulus: layered rolls of clouds
- Low-Clouds
  - o   Cumulus: white, round, puffy clouds
  - o   Stratus: wide, thick, stretched-out, gray clouds that may cause drizzle
  - o   Fog: lazy stratus clouds that have drooped so low that they reach Earth's surface
  - o   Cumulonimbus: the angry cloud that brings thunderstorms, hail, and tornadoes. It looks like a thick mountain.
  - o   Stratocumulus: stretched-out, grayish, puffy, cumulus clouds

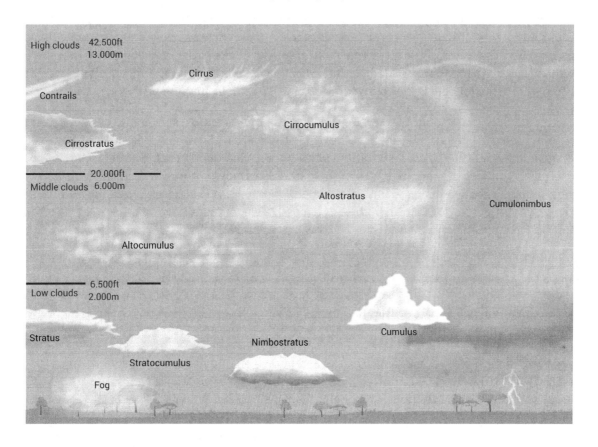

Precipitation comes in many different forms:

- **Rain** occurs due to water vapor condensing on dust particles in the troposphere. As more and more water condenses, the drops will eventually enlarge and accumulate mass, becoming so heavy that they fall to Earth.

- If the temperature is above the freezing point, the water falls as rain. Rain can freeze on the ground if the temperature on Earth's surface is colder than that of the troposphere. Freezing rain causes extremely dangerous driving conditions due to the slickness of the ice.

- **Sleet** freezes on its way down as opposed to freezing upon impact. Sleet starts as ice that melts as it falls through the atmosphere due to hitting spots of warmer temperature, and then it freezes again before hitting the ground.

- **Hail** is precipitation of balls of ice. Hail begins as ice at very cold temperatures in the atmosphere. Instead of precipitating sheets of ice like sleet storms, hailstorms precipitate ice that looks like rocks because hail is formed during thunderstorms. The massive winds throw hail up and down so more and more water vapor condenses and freezes on the original ice. Layer upon layer of ice combine, creating hail sometimes as large as golf balls.

- **Snow** forms as loosely packed ice crystals. Snow is less dangerous than the other frozen forms of precipitation and can produce beautiful snowflakes.

Even though seasons have predictable temperatures, there can be significant differences day to day. In the troposphere, the Sun's heat is trapped by the blanket of greenhouse gases and creates warm, low-pressure air. Because warm gas particles move faster and have less space between them, they are less dense than colder air, and they rise. Cool air moves below the warm air. This atmospheric movement is called **general circulation** and is the source of wind. Earth's spinning motion also causes wind.

Weather depends in a large part on temperature. Earth's equator is closest to the sun and receives more heat, so this area of earth is significantly warmer than the poles (Arctic and Antarctic). This warm air can form huge bubbles, as can the colder air at the poles. When warm air and cold air meet, the boundary is called a **front**. Fronts can be the site of extreme weather like thunderstorms, which are caused by water particles in clouds quickly rubbing against each other and transferring electrons, creating positive and negative regions. Lightning occurs when there is a massive electric spark due to the electrical current within a cloud, between two clouds, and even between a cloud and the ground.

While seasons are predictable trends in temperatures over a few months, **climate** describes the average weather and temperature patterns for a particular area over a long period of time, upwards of thirty years. While **fall** describes a season and **rain** describes weather, **rainforest** describes a climate. The climate of a rainforest, due to its proximity to the equator and oceans, consists of warm temperatures with humid air.

Even more extreme weather includes tornadoes and hurricanes. **Tornadoes** are spinning winds that can exceed 300 miles per hour and are caused by changing air pressure and quick winds. Hurricanes, typhoons, and tropical cyclones (the same phenomenon with different regional names) are storms with spinning winds that form over the ocean. **Hurricanes** are caused by warm ocean water quickly evaporating and rising to a colder, lower-pressure portion of the atmosphere. The fast movement of the warm air starts a cyclone around a central origination point (the eye of the storm). **Blizzards** are also caused by the clash of warm air and cold air. They occur when the cold Arctic air moves toward warmer air and involve massive amounts of snow.

Precipitation and run-off are constantly affecting the surface of Earth, as the run-off weathers rocks or breaks them down from the original bedrock into pieces called regolith. Regolith sizes range from microscopic to large and quickly form either soil or sediment. **Weathering** is the process of breaking rock while **erosion** is the process of moving rock. Weathering can be caused by both physical and chemical changes. Mechanical forces such as roots growing, animal contact, wind, and extreme weather cause weathering. Another cause is the water cycle, which includes flowing water, moving glaciers, and liquid ice seeping into rocks and cracking them as water freezes and expands. Chemical weathering actually transforms the regolith into clay and soft minerals. One consequence of chemical weathering is corrosive acid rain.

Rocks cover the surface of Earth. Igneous rock comes from the molten, hot, liquid magma circulating beneath Earth's surface in the upper mantle. Through vents called **volcanoes**, magma explodes or seeps onto the Earth's surface. Magma is not uniform; it varies in its elemental composition, gas composition, and thickness or viscosity. There are three main types of volcanoes: shield, cinder, and composite.

Shield volcanoes are the widest because their thin magma flows out of a central crater calmly and quietly, like a gentle fountain. This flowing magma results in layers of solid lava. The slow flow results in a convex hill that spans a wide area.

Like shield volcanoes, **cinder volcanoes** typically have a central crater and thin lava. In contrast to shield volcanoes, they are small, cone-shaped hills with steep sides. They are made of volcanic debris, or cinders. They are often found as secondary volcanoes near shield and composite volcanoes. In cinder volcanoes, the central vent spews lava that shatters into rock and debris and settles around it, resulting in its characteristic cone shape. Cinder volcanoes are surrounded by ashy, loose, magma dust.

Composite volcanoes (also called stratovolcanoes) are the most common and the tallest type of volcano. Their thick magma gets stuck at the vent, and as more and more builds up, the volcano eventually explodes and removes the clog. These eruptions generate loose debris, and once the plug has been violently expelled, the thick lava oozes out like a fountain. These volcanoes are the most dangerous with their extremely violent behavior and huge height. Most volcanoes are located around cracks in Earth's lithosphere.

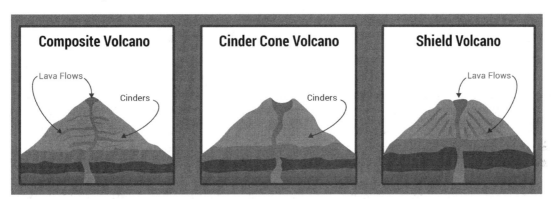

Once magma makes it to the surface, it is called **lava**. Once it cools, it solidifies into igneous rock. Common examples of igneous rock are obsidian, pumice, and granite. Weathering and erosion result in these rocks becoming soil or sediment and accumulating in layers mostly found in the ocean. These loose sediments settle over time and compress to become a uniform rock in a process called **lithification**. Examples of sedimentary rock include shale, limestone, and sandstone. As layers are piled atop each other, the bottom rock experiences an intense amount of pressure and transforms into metamorphic rock. Examples of metamorphic rocks are marble and slate. After long periods of time, the metamorphic rock moves closer to the asthenosphere and becomes liquid hot magma.

Magma's eventual fate is lava and igneous rock, and the cycle starts anew:

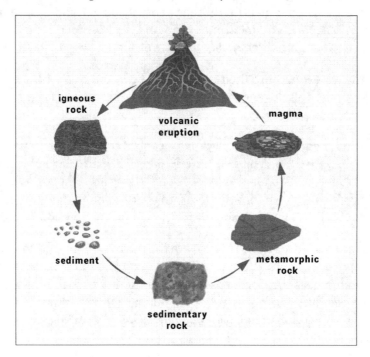

How does magma return to the surface if the lithosphere presses it down? Intense heat from the Earth's core travels to the upper mantle via **convection**. Convection involves thermal energy (heat) that converts into kinetic energy (movement), resulting in rapidly circulating molecules. Convection moves heat energy through fluids. In a pot of boiling water, the water closest to the burner becomes hot, causing its particles to move faster. Faster-moving molecules have more space between them and become less dense, so they rise. Some will vaporize, and some hit the cool air and slow down, becoming dense and sinking. Likewise, Earth's interior particles undergo convection (the heat source being the nuclear fission from the core), and the rock in the upper mantle will acquire so much kinetic energy that magma will be expelled from underneath Earth to the surface.

There are seven or eight major plates in the lithosphere and several minor plates. These tectonic plates explain the changing topography, or shape, of earth.

There are three types of boundaries between plates: divergent, convergent, and transform. All boundaries can be sites of volcanic activity. A **divergent boundary** occurs when plates separate. Lava fills in the space the plates create and hardens into rock, which creates oceanic crust. In a **convergent boundary**, if one of the plates is in the ocean, that plate is denser due to the weight of water. The dense ocean plate will slip under the land plate, causing a subduction zone where the plate moves underneath. Where plates converge on land, the continental crusts are both lighter with a similar density, and as a result they will buckle together and create mountains.

In **transform boundaries**, adjacent plates sliding past each other create friction and pressure that destroy the edges of the boundary and cause earthquakes. Transform boundaries don't produce magma, as they involve lateral movement.

Just as plates pushing together cause mountains, **canyons** are deep trenches caused by plates moving apart. Weather and erosion from rivers and precipitation run-off also create canyons. **Deltas** form when

rivers dump their sediments and water into oceans. They are triangular flat stretches of land that are kind of like a triangular spatula; the handle represents the river and the triangle represents the mouth of a delta.

Sand dunes are another landform caused by wind or waves in combination with the absence of plants to hold sand in place. These are found in sandy areas like the desert or the ocean.

Earth History

A popular theory about the beginning of the universe is called the **Big Bang Theory**. It proposes that about fourteen billion years ago, a dense ball of matter exploded, releasing particles and energy.

From there, many scientists propose:

- Earth formed 4.6 billion years ago, and life didn't appear until approximately 3.5 billion years ago.

- At Earth's birth, it was an inhospitable place of active volcanoes, intense heat, lightning, and constant bombardment with space debris (rocks and dust). Heat vaporized all liquid water, and the anaerobic atmosphere (without oxygen) was composed of poisonous gases.

- Over time, the landscape changed, and once organic molecules (proteins, fats, carbohydrates, and DNA) and organisms came on the scene, water and oxygen became available, and the biosphere began.

- The last 542 million years have been divided into three eras: Paleozoic, Mesozoic, and Cenozoic. The **Paleozoic era** started with the **Cambrian Explosion**, when the animal kingdom expanded and diversified from invertebrates (simple animals without backbones) in the Pre-Cambrian Era. The era ended with the Permian mass extinction, where most animal species disappeared, probably due to volcanic eruptions.

- After the Permian extinction, the **Mesozoic era** began the reign of the dinosaurs. **Angiosperm** (flowering plants) life also exploded in the Mesozoic Era. The Cretaceous mass extinction ended the era, when nearly half of marine life and large portions of terrestrial species were decimated.

- Our most recent era is the **Cenozoic era**, and life continues to proliferate.

Our insight into the development of Earth has been fueled by fossil evidence. **Paleontology** is the study of fossils, which requires the study of rock layers. Sedimentary rocks exist as layers called **strata** and contain remains of once-living organisms. The depth at which a fossil is found within a layer of rock indicates the fossil's age. The lower the layer, the older the fossil.

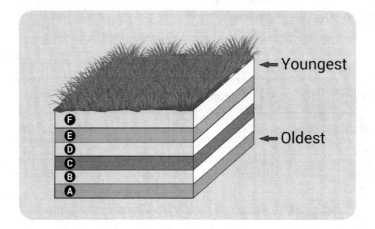

Fossils are remnants of organisms, such as teeth and bones. These structures, like petrified wood, have been preserved so well due to minerals seeping into the bone and acting as preservatives. Fossils can also be completely intact organisms found in glaciers or sap. Trace fossils are not actual parts of an organism but evidence that the organism was there, like a footprint or an imprint of a leaf.

Calculating the age of organisms in rock layers is based on the amounts of two different forms of radioactive elements like carbon. **Carbon-12** is the non-radioactive form, and **Carbon-14** is the radioactive form. In fossils, Carbon-12 won't decrease over time, but Carbon-14 will. Scientists can compare the amounts of Carbon-12 and Carbon-14 to estimate the age of fossils. The smaller the amount of Carbon-14, the older the fossil.

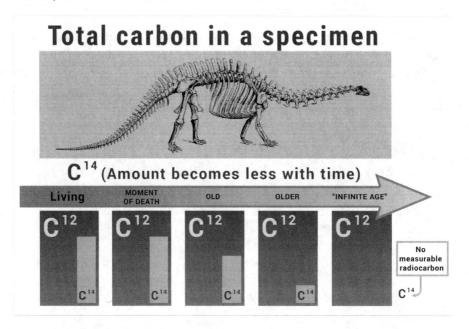

186

Earth and the Universe

Earth is part of a solar system that rotates around a star. Our solar system is a miniscule portion of the universe; the Sun is just one star, and there are more stars in the universe than there are grains of sands on Earth. Almost every existing star belongs to a galaxy, clusters of stars, rocks, ice, and space dust. Between galaxies there is nothing, just darkness. There could be as many as a hundred billion galaxies. There are three main types of galaxies: spiral, elliptical, and irregular.

The majority of galaxies are spiral galaxies, with a large, central galactic bulge, which is a cluster of older stars. They look like a disk with arms circulating stars and gas. Elliptical galaxies have no particular rotation pattern. They can be spherical or extremely elongated and do not have circulating arms.

Irregular galaxies have no pattern and can vary significantly in size and shape:

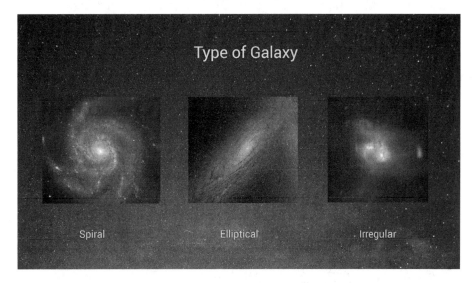

Earth's galaxy, the **Milky Way**, is a spiral galaxy and contains hundreds of billions of stars.

Pre-stars form from nebulas, clouds of gas and dust that can combine to form two types of small stars: brown and red dwarfs. **Stars** produce enormous amounts energy by combining hydrogen atoms to form helium via nuclear fusion. **Brown dwarfs** don't have enough hydrogen to undergo much fusion and fizzle out. **Red dwarfs** have plenty of gas (hydrogen) to undergo nuclear fusion and mature into white dwarfs. When they use all of their fuel (hydrogen), a burst of energy expands the star into a **red giant**. Red giants eventually condense into a **white dwarf**, which is a star approaching the end of its life.

Stars that undergo nuclear fusion will run out of gas quickly and burst in violent explosions called **supernovas**. This burst releases as much energy in a few seconds as the Sun will release in its entire lifetime. The particles from the explosion will condense into the smallest type of star, a **neutron star**; this will eventually condense into a **black hole**, which has such a high amount of gravity that not even light energy can escape.

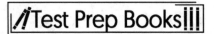
Earth's sun is currently a red dwarf; it is early in its life cycle. As the center of Earth's solar system, the Sun has planets and space debris (rocks and ice) orbiting around it. The various forms of space debris include:

- **Comet**: made of rock and ice with a tail due to the melting ice

- **Asteroid**: a large rock orbiting a star. The asteroid belt lies between Mars and Jupiter and separates the smaller rocky planets (Mercury, Venus, Earth, and Mars) from the larger, gassy planets (Jupiter, Saturn, Uranus, and Neptune). Pluto is not considered a planet anymore due to its small size and distance from the Sun.

- **Meteoroid**: a mini-asteroid with no specific orbiting pattern

- **Meteor**: a meteoroid that has entered Earth's atmosphere and starts melting due to the warmth provided by our insulating greenhouse gases. These are commonly known as "falling stars."

- **Meteorite**: a meteor that hasn't completely burned away and lands on Earth. One is believed to have caused the Cretaceous mass extinction.

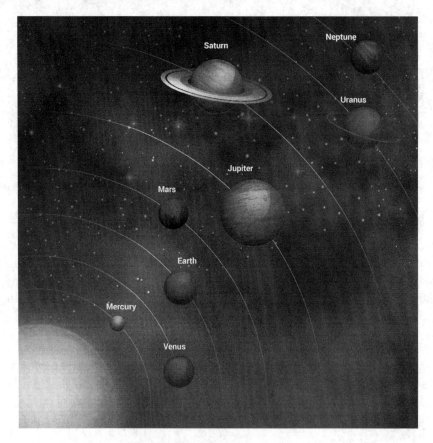

Each planet travels around the Sun in an **elliptic orbit**. The time it takes for one complete orbit is considered a year. The gravity of the massive Sun keeps the planets rotating, and the farther the planets are from the Sun, the slower they move and the longer their orbits. Earth's journey is little bit over 365 days a year. Because Mercury is so close to the Sun, one year for Mercury is actually only 88 Earth days. The farthest planet, Neptune, has a year that is about 60,255 Earth days long. Planets not only rotate

188

around the Sun, but they also spin like a top. The time it takes for a planet to complete one spin is considered one day. On Earth, one day is about 24 hours. On Jupiter, one day is about nine Earth hours, while a day on Venus is 241 Earth days.

Planets may have natural satellites that rotate around them called **moons**. Some planets have no moons and some have dozens. In 1969, astronaut Neil Armstrong became the first man to set foot on Earth's only moon.

Earth Patterns

The temperature on the sun varies from its core to its atmosphere. Its atmospheric temperature is predicted at over 1 million °F. The sun accounts for two types of energy reaching earth: light energy and thermal (heat) energy.

Plants absorb the light energy and they use it to perform photosynthesis.

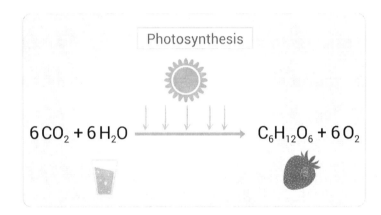

Photosynthesis

$$6\,CO_2 + 6\,H_2O \longrightarrow C_6H_{12}O_6 + 6\,O_2$$

The thermal energy is transferred to earth's atmosphere through radiation. Unlike the transfer of heat through convection, radiation is a direct transfer—there are no particles in space to transfer the sun's heat. Once thermal energy reaches earth, the carbon dioxide in the atmosphere acts as a blanket to trap the heat.

The heat from the sun as well as the orbit and position of earth cause seasons. As discussed, earth rotates around the sun and spins on an axis. Earth is slightly tilted on its side. An imaginary line around the middle called the **equator** splits the earth into the northern and southern hemispheres.

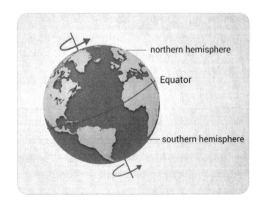

northern hemisphere

Equator

southern hemisphere

To understand seasons and the heating of the planet, refer to this picture:

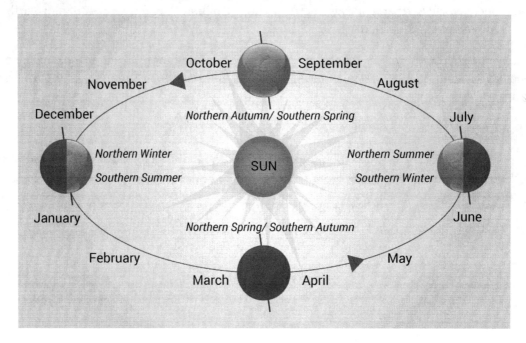

Observing July, these facts are apparent:

- Earth is tilted so that the northern hemisphere is pointing towards the sun. The southern hemisphere is pointed away.

- Because the north is tilted toward the sun, it gets more daylight in July than the southern hemisphere.

These observations explain why in July, the northern hemisphere experiences summer while the southern hemisphere experiences winter.

Notice in December that the opposite is true: the southern hemisphere gets more daylight compared to the northern hemisphere.

In spring and fall, both the north and the south get around the same sun exposure; therefore, those seasons have milder temperatures.

As the earth rotates, the distribution of light slowly changes, which explains why seasons gradually change. In June, the northern hemisphere experiences the summer solstice, the day with the most daylight. As the earth continues to orbit, its days will get shorter and shorter until the winter solstice, the shortest day of the year. Equinoxes occur in the fall and the spring and represent the days when the amount of daylight and darkness are relatively equal.

Just as the earth orbits the sun, the moon orbits the earth. The moon is much closer to earth than the sun. And even though the moon is so close to the earth, the moon contains no life because it lacks water and an atmosphere. Without greenhouse gases to blanket the sun's heat, temperatures on the moon are very low at night.

The moon is visible from the earth because it reflects sunlight at certain points in its orbit. The moon's orbit has a predictable pattern. It has two main phases, waxing and waning. When the moon is waxing, it goes from a new moon to a full moon. Notice that only the left side of the moon is dark during the waxing phase. The waning phase goes from full moon to new moon. Only the right side of the moon is dark when it is waning.

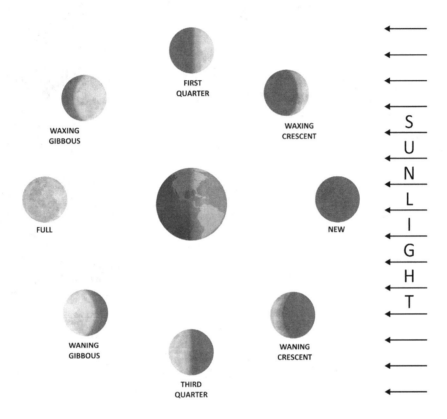

This picture shows that when the moon is behind the earth, then the moon's entire surface is reflected and we see a full moon. When the moon is between the earth and the sun, it is invisible at night, which is called a **new moon**.

Half-moons are visible when the moon and the earth are in a line that is perpendicular to the direction of sunlight. Only half of the moon reflects light to the earth at night, as seen in the figure above.

A moon that looks larger than a half moon is called a **gibbous moon**, and a moon that looks smaller is called a **crescent moon**.

Eclipses occur when the earth, the sun, and the moon are all aligned—the earth blocks the others from seeing each other. If they are perfectly lined up, a total eclipse happens, and if they are only a little lined up, there is a partial eclipse.

There are two types of eclipses: lunar and solar. A **lunar eclipse** occurs when the earth interrupts the sun's light reflecting off of the full moon. Earth will then cast a shadow on the moon, and particles in earth's atmosphere refract the light so some reaches the surface of the moon, causing the moon to look yellow, brown, or red.

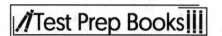
During a new moon, when the moon is between the earth and the sun, the moon will interrupt the sunlight, casting a shadow on earth. This is called a **solar eclipse**.

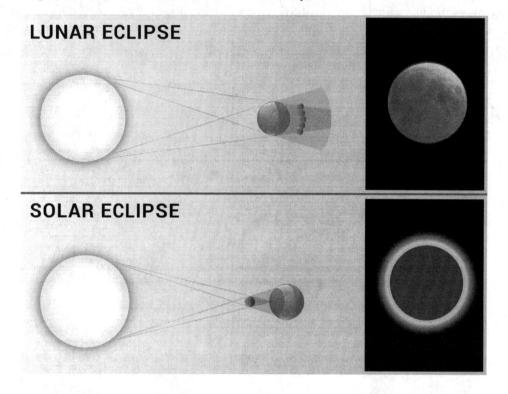

The moon also affects ocean tide due to gravity. Earth is much larger than the moon and has a very significant gravitational force that keeps us on the ground even though it is spinning very quickly. The moon is much smaller than earth, but because it is so close, it has a pulling effect on earth's oceans. When it is closest to earth, it pulls the water more, resulting in high tide. When the moon is farthest from earth, it pulls the ocean less and is called **low tide**.

Science as a Human Endeavor

Two of the worst earthquakes in history occurred in 1556 and 1976, causing 830,000 and 255,000 deaths, respectively. Earthquakes near the ocean cause massive tidal waves called tsunamis. In Indonesia in 2004, a tsunami resulted in 230,000 deaths. **Seismology** is the study of earthquakes. Understanding earthquakes can help predict them and possibly even prevent them.

Earthquakes have an initial source of plate movement called the **focus**. At the focus, there is a significant amount of tension, like the force of resistance generated by bending a wooden stick. Eventually, with enough pressure, there is so much tension that the stick breaks. The separate pieces that were once in a curved formation due to the strain will slip back into their original shape. This is called **elastic rebound** when it occurs at plate boundaries. After elastic rebound, the movement spreads outwards from the focus and causes waves of kinetic energy. These rolling vibrations are called **seismic waves**. Slipping back into place takes several adjustments called **aftershocks**, which are less severe than the initial movement but can still cause a significant amount of destruction. A logarithmic scale called the **Richter scale** measures the amplitude of seismic waves. An earthquake magnitude of 10 has the largest amplitude, and a magnitude of 1 has the smallest.

Science as an Inquiry

Science begins with questions—it is difficult to have an answer when there are no questions. A great source of inquiry for scientists has been weather. The study of weather is called **meteorology**. **Meteorologists** measure temperature, air pressure, wind speed, wind direction, and humidity, all in hopes of predicting how and where air and water vapor will move and behave. These questions inspire meteorologists to use weather balloons and satellites to study weather and make educated guesses. As knowledge grows, technologies also improve and facilitate better weather forecasting. The impressive **Doppler radar** has provided scientists with meaningful data since the 1980s, allowing them to better predict the weather with more certainty.

Research

Another aspect of science is **research**, which is the search for answers for a scientific inquiry. One of the largest areas of scientific research is space exploration. Of course, people have always wondered about the universe, but the United States didn't make space research a priority until the 1940s and 1950s "space race" with the Soviet Union. In 1957, Russia launched a satellite called **Sputnik**, which fueled the intense competition between the two countries. In space research, the question that accelerated space exploration was "How can man travel into space safely?" This question fueled the creation of NASA (the National Aeronautics and Space Administration) on October 1, 1958.

NASA research continues today. They observe the sky, launch satellites and telescopes into space, and study the data collected. Currently, there are a multitude of satellites and land vehicles or "rovers" on Mars collecting data with the hope of one day finding a way for humans to live there. In fact, the target date for human occupation on Mars is somewhere in the 2030s.

Process of Science

Theories are well-supported ideas that evolve from hypotheses and experimentation. A **hypothesis** is an educated guess about a scientific process or object. Once every angle of investigation has been examined and all evidence supports a hypothesis, only then can it be called a **theory**. It is important to know that theory development is a process. As technology advances and more aspects of science can be explored, evidence might no longer support a theory. With non-supportive data, either the theory can be modified or completely thrown out while new investigations are developed to examine other explanations.

For example, plate tectonic theory didn't appear until the early 20th century. People thought the earth was static and immobile. Only after many years of investigation and evidence did skeptics finally concede that the earth's surface was broken into plates. This theory wasn't universally accepted until the late 1960s and was considered revolutionary.

Early evidence that supported plate tectonics was publicized in the 1910s by Alfred Wegener, who observed that the South American and African borders to the Atlantic Ocean seemed like they could fit together like puzzle pieces. He proposed the idea of Pangaea, a massive supercontinent that existed long ago and must have broken into pieces due to a process called **continental drift**. Other evidence supporting plate tectonics were similar fossils found in Africa and South America, suggesting that they were once connected. But skeptics continued to scoff at the theory. Then, in the 1960s it was discovered, with the help of early computers, that a continental shelf (an underwater boundary

193

between plates) between the two continents had a remarkable fit that was very unlikely to be due to chance.

Life Science

Structure and Function of Living Systems

Prokaryotes, Viruses, and Eukaryotes

Every living organism is made up of **cells**, and these cells come in various shapes and sizes, depending on the organism. There are two types of cells: **prokaryotes** and **eukaryotes**. The big difference between them is that eukaryotes have a nucleus and prokaryotes do not. The structures that will be covered in this section will be bacteria, protist, fungus, plant, and animal cells:

Bacteria	Protist, Fungus, Plant, Animal
DNA Ribosomes Cytoplasm Cell Membrane Cell Wall	DNA Ribosomes Cytoplasm Cell Membrane Cell Wall (except animal cells) Unique structures Nucleus Mitochondria Chloroplasts (only autotrophs, or organisms that can produce their own food. Only protists and plants are producers).

Below is an example of a plant cell:

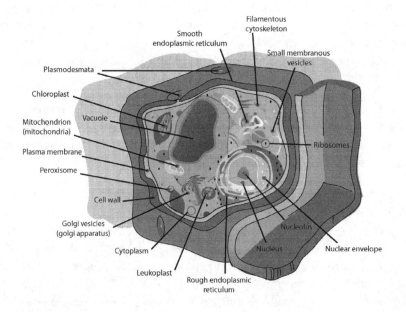

194

Animal cell

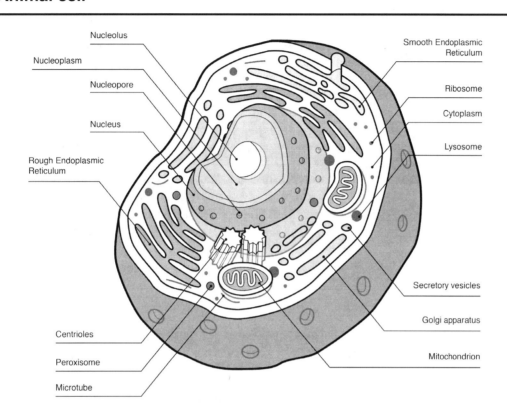

Below is an example of a bacteria cell:

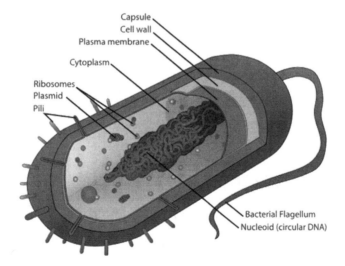

Like all cells, bacterial cells contain **DNA**, the genetic material that gives instructions for every single structure and process that the cell undergoes. DNA is a code made up of four letters: A (adenine), T (thymine), G (guanine), and C (cytosine). There are billions of these letters in DNA, and the order of these letters tells a cell exactly what to do and how to do it (just like reading a book of instructions).

Because DNA doesn't do anything on its own, all cells must have a means of decoding DNA and turning it into the structure, which is the function of **ribosomes**—they are protein-makers. If DNA is like a recipe, then the ribosomes are like the chef.

DNA and ribosomes sit in a fluid called **cytoplasm**, which contains a **cytoskeleton** (a network of proteins) that holds them in place. All cells need a covering to contain everything inside—these are called **cell membranes** in animals or cell walls for plant cells.

Bacteria can also have a capsule and a flagellum, which are all external structures. A **capsule** is sticky and causes bacteria to cluster with other cells or on food. Only about 50 percent of bacteria can move, and those that do often have a **flagellum**, which is a whip-like structure like a tadpole's tail.

Viruses are commonly thought of as living organisms, but many scientists argue they aren't for two reasons: (1) they are not cells, and (2) they cannot reproduce by themselves. Both qualities are required for an organism to be considered alive. Viruses are unique in that they require a host in order to make proteins and reproduce, because viruses don't have all of the complex tools of a living cell. When a virus has infected a host, it acts like a living organism—it moves and reproduces—but outside of a host, it does nothing. A virus can survive outside of a host, but it cannot reproduce. Scientists are still trying to properly define a virus, so we can currently say that viruses are not like bacteria or any other living thing.

Eukaryotic cells are more complex than prokaryotic cells. They make up all the organisms in the kingdoms protist, fungus, plant, and animal. Eukaryotic cells are also larger than prokaryotes and contain a nucleus and other organelles.

Eukaryotic cells hold their DNA inside a nucleus in pieces called chromosomes. **Chromosomes** are a cell's way of organizing long strands of DNA in twisted-up bundles. Imagine a room filled with rolls of toilet paper compared to a room that has all of those rolls unraveled and thrown everywhere; it would be a mess!

Other important organelles include chloroplasts and mitochondria. **Chloroplasts** can be found in cells called autotrophs, which can convert sunlight into energy. Plants are autotrophs. **Mitochondria** are little energy factories found in almost every type of cell. They use chemical reactions to make little packets of energy that can be used by other parts of the cell.

Energy

Energy is everywhere and is one of the few things in the universe believed to be constant. That means that in the whole universe, if all the energy could be measured (energy in all the stars, atoms, etc.), the amount of energy that was present at the beginning of time is exactly the same as it is now. The only difference is that energy has been converted into different forms. For example, a plant gets its energy from the Sun, using it to grow bigger and stronger; therefore, the Sun's energy is converted and stored inside the plant. Then a person eats the plant, using its stored energy. In this example, energy exists in the form of light, growth, and movement (picking the plant and chewing it).

Only with the energy food provides can organisms exist. Think of a construction team and a pile of bricks and mortar. The bricks are not going to just arrange themselves into a building. However, if a construction team uses their muscles and energy, the complex building can be built. If the construction team runs out of food, though, they will become exhausted and will be unable to construct the building.

196

The human body is the same way. Organs (heart, brain, stomach, etc.) are like the bricks. The chemical reactions in the body are like the workers. Energy is the food that the workers need to build the organism. The food of life is sugar, specifically glucose. A candy bar, soda, or a slice of birthday cake can provide a boost of energy because of all the sugar they contain. There are many bonds between the molecules of sugar, holding them in place (like the mortar holding the bricks in a building). When the bonds are broken in digestion, all that energy is released so that living things can invest that energy into chemical reactions.

Two chemical reactions are critical for living things: **photosynthesis** and **respiration**.

Any producer must have a chloroplast in order to convert light energy into food, usually in the form of a carbohydrate. **Chloroplasts** are organelles that look like little green beans because they contain the pigment **chlorophyll**, which is able to absorb the sunlight's energy in the form of photons, or light rays. Some prokaryotes are also photosynthetic, and although they don't have a chloroplast because they're too simple and don't contain organelles, they have a pigment in order to make their own food.

Plants need water and sunlight to live. Plants suck up water from their roots. The sunlight they need is absorbed by the chlorophyll in chloroplasts, which are clustered and concentrated in their leaves. Interestingly, the chlorophyll actually is able to absorb every color of light except for green, which is why leaves look green: they reflect green light. If the roots take in water and the leaves take in carbon dioxide and sunlight energy, why are stems important? The stems in plants are an example of how structure helps function. The stem is like a skeleton for plants; it holds the leaves high so they can be closer to the sun.

Plants are critical for life on earth because they absorb the energy from the sun and invest it in the bonds that make sugar. Sugar passes through the food chain to provide energy for all living organisms. Plants and other **autotrophs** can make their own energy, while **heterotrophs** (which cannot make their own energy) consume the sugar, break it down, and convert it into usable energy with their mitochondria.

Cellular Respiration in the Mitochondria

The **glucose** that provides energy does nothing by itself; it is the bonds between atoms holding these complex glucose molecules together that hold the energy. When the molecule is intact, the bonds between them hold energy in the form of potential energy. When the bonds are broken, that potential energy is released and becomes available to the workers in the cell to perform chemical reactions.

The process of cellular respiration breaks the bonds in an organelle called the **mitochondria** in eukaryotes (protists, fungi, plants, animals).

Note that the equation for cellular respiration is the almost exact opposite of photosynthesis:

$$C_6H_{12}O_6 + 6O_2 \rightarrow 6CO_2 + 6H_2O + 36ATP$$

The only difference between the above equation and photosynthesis is the new product: ATP. **ATP** is a conversion of light energy into usable pockets of energy that provide energy to all the workers in cells that do the chemical reactions. While glucose is like a $100 bill with lots of energy in its bonds, ATP is like one hundred $1 bills that can be invested here and there as needed.

Bacteria do not have mitochondria, so they perform different reactions in their cytoplasm that produce much less energy (2ATP).

Organisms Need Food for More than Just Energy

When we eat a hamburger, we're eating more than carbohydrates; we're also eating proteins and fats. Plants provide more than just carbohydrates when we eat them; they also are able to use the light energy to make proteins, fats, and, of course, their DNA, because if they didn't have DNA, they'd have no instructions to grow.

The following organic compounds and their atoms don't magically appear in organisms—life has to either grab the nutrients from soil or seeds or eat them.

- Carbohydrates, proteins, fats, and DNA/RNA have carbon, hydrogen, and oxygen
- DNA, proteins, and fats also have phosphorus
- DNA and proteins also have nitrogen
- Proteins also can have sulfur

Plants need all of these elements to make food. Where do they get them? Remember that earth's atmosphere is a conglomerate of different gases, including nitrogen. Bacteria in the soil are able to convert that nitrogen into a usable form, and the roots of plants absorb the critical nitrogen. Carbon and oxygen get into the plant via photosynthesis (carbon dioxide), as does the element hydrogen, because plants take in water, which contains hydrogen. Phosphorus and sulfur are absorbed in plants through soil. Since heterotrophs cannot make their own food, they have to eat an autotroph (or eat something that ate an autotroph) in order to obtain these critical elements.

Cycles are a recurring pattern in science, and making food is no exception. When living things die, fungi and bacteria act as decomposers and break down the material. That's actually why dead things and rotten meat smell bad; the decomposers have broken them down so much that gases containing carbon, oxygen, phosphorus, nitrogen, and even smelly sulfur are released. Remember that sulfur is heavy in protein, and eggs are protein-rich. It makes sense that rotten eggs have an unpleasant smell as they release sulfur because they're mostly protein. Once living things decompose, all the elements eventually recycle back to the atmosphere or to the soil, and the atoms are available to construct molecules once again.

Cellular Organization

Prokaryotes contain ribosomes, DNA, cytoplasm, a cell membrane, a cytoskeleton, and a cell wall. Eukaryotes vary between kingdoms but contain all of these structures except a cell wall because animal cells require so much mobility. Large, land-dwelling animals typically compensate with an exoskeleton (like insects) or an endoskeleton (like humans and other mammals, reptiles, and birds) for structure.

All bacterial cells are **unicellular** (existing as just one cell). Almost all types of protist and some species in fungi kingdom are unicellular, but they still have the complicated organelles of eukaryotes. A few protists, almost all fungi, and all plants and animals are multicellular. Multicellularity leads to development of structures that are perfectly designed for their function.

Cells combine to form **tissue**. Tissue combines to form **organs**. Organs combine to form **organ systems**, and organ systems combine to form one **organism**. The structures of all of these combinations allow for the maximum functionality of an organism, as demonstrated by the nervous system.

A **neuron** is a cell in the nervous system designed to send and receive electrical impulses. Neurons have dendrites, which are sensors waiting to receive a message. Neurons also have an **axon**, a long arm that sends the message to the neighboring neuron. The axon also has insulation known as **myelin** that speeds the message along. Many neurons combine to form a **nerve**, the tissue of the nervous system, which is like a long wire. The structure of this nerve is perfect—it is a long cable whose function is to send signals to the brain so the brain can process the information and respond. Nerve tissue combines with other tissue to form the **brain**, a complex structure of many parts.

The brain also has glands (epithelial tissue) that release hormones to control processes in our body. The brain and spinal cord together form the central nervous system that controls the stimulus/response signaling in our body. The nervous system coordinates with the circulatory system to make our heart beat, the digestive system to control food digestion, the muscular system to move an arm, the respiratory system to facilitate breathing, and all other body systems to make the entire organism functional. Cells are the basic building block in our bodies, and their structure is critical for their function and the function of the tissues, organs, and systems that they comprise.

In the graphic below, the left depicts a neuron, and the right depicts the nervous system. A neuron is a nerve cell, and it is the basic building block of the nervous system. Cell, tissue, organ, and organ system structure are critical for function.

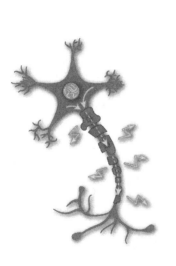
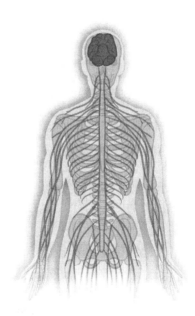

The following table lists organ systems in the human body:

Name	Function	Main organs
Nervous	Detect stimuli and direct response	Brain and spinal cord
Circulatory	Pump blood to deliver oxygen to cells so they can perform cellular respiration	Heart
Respiratory	Breathe in oxygen (reactant for cellular respiration) and release carbon dioxide waste	Lungs
Muscular	Movement	Heart and muscles
Digestive	Break down food so that glucose can be delivered to cells for energy	Stomach, small intestine, lots of others
Skeletal	Support and organ protection	All sorts of joints, skull, ribcage

Reproduction and Heredity

Cellular Reproduction

Unlike viruses, all living organisms can independently reproduce, but reproduction occurs differently between bacteria and the more complex kingdoms. Bacteria reproduce via **binary fission**, which is a simpler process than eukaryotic division because it doesn't involve splitting a nucleus and doesn't have a web of proteins to pull chromosomes apart. Prokaryotes have simpler DNA compared to cells that have a much larger number of individual chromosomes (humans have two sets of 23 chromosomes—one set from mom and one set from dad, for a total of 46 chromosomes). Think of going from class to class with two identical binders (like bacteria) versus going from class to class with 23 identical pairs of binders (humans); it would be much more difficult to organize the large set of binders than the smaller one.

Binary fission in bacteria is therefore relatively easy. Bacteria copy their DNA in a process called **DNA replication**, grow, and then the replicated DNA moves to either side, and two new cells are made.

Eukaryotic cell division is part of a well-defined cycle with the following phases:

- **G1 phase**: The cell is growing and working.

- **S phase**: The cell is getting too large, so it copies its DNA because it wants to make sure the two new cells have the full instruction manual that is DNA.

- **G2 phase**: The cell uses its workers to get ready for cell division.

- **M phase**: Chromosomes condense and line up in the middle of the cell. The copies are sent to either side.

- **Cytokinesis**: The moment when the cytoplasm is officially split in two, and then two identical daughter cells are produced and enter G1 phase.

200

The M phase has subdivisions because it quickly goes through a series of events. Each sub-phase of events is described and illustrated below.

PHASE	PHASE EVENTS	ANIMAL CELL DIAGRAM	PLANT CELL DIAGRAM
Interphase (G1, S, and G2)	DNA is loose and spread out and contained in nucleus. This is important because it is actively growing and needs access to its instructions to do chemical reactions correctly. Chromosomes are replicated (copied) in S phase so that they look like an X. Each side of the X has identical DNA.		
Prophase	Nucleus disappears and DNA condenses into chromosomes		
Metaphase	Chromosomes line up in center and proteins from either side of cell attach to them		
Anaphase	Proteins shorten and pull chromosomes apart so that one half (either left side of X or right side of X) of DNA goes to each new cell		
Telophase and Cytokinesis	Nuclei reform and chromosomes start to spread out **Animal cells**: cytoplasm to split in half **Plant cells**: cell plate (new cell wall) forms between daughter cells and extends (animal cells don't have a cell wall)		

Organism Reproduction

For bacteria, cell reproduction is the same as organism reproduction; **binary fission** is an asexual process that produces two new cells that are clones of each other because they have identical DNA.

Eukaryotes are more complex than prokaryotes and can go through **sexual reproduction**. They produce **gametes** (sex cells). Females make eggs and males make sperm. The process of making gametes is called **meiosis**, which is similar to mitosis except for the following differences:

- There are two cellular divisions instead of one.

- Four genetically different haploid daughter cells (one set of chromosomes instead of two) are produced instead of two genetically identical diploid daughter cells.

- A process called crossing over (**recombination**) occurs, which makes the daughter cells genetically different. If chromosomes didn't cross over and rearrange genes, siblings could be identical clones. There would be no genetic variation, which is a critical factor in the theory of evolution of organisms.

In sexual reproduction, a sperm fertilizes an egg and creates the first cell of a new organism, called the **zygote**. The zygote will go through countless mitotic divisions over time to create the adult organism.

Heredity: Passing Genes Across Generations

All living things are a product of their DNA, specifically portions of their DNA called genes that code for different characteristics.

Learned behavior is not affected by DNA and is not hereditable. Changes in appearance like a woman painting her toenails, a bird whose feathers accidentally fall out due to a tornado, or a person getting a scar are also not heritable. Heritable characteristics are those coded by DNA like eye color, hair color, and height.

A man named **Gregor Mendel** is considered the father of genetics. He was a monk and a botanist, and through extensive experiments with pea plants, he figured out a great deal about heredity.

Our genetic code comes in pairs. Each chromosome contains many genes, and since we have one chromosome from our mom and one chromosome from our dad, we have two copies of each gene. Genes come in different forms called **alleles**. The two alleles work together, and when the cell reads them and follows their instructions, the way an organism looks or behaves is called a **trait**. For some traits, there are only two alleles: a **dominant allele** and a **recessive allele**. Even though eye color is a bit more complicated, pretend that brown eyes are dominant over blue eyes, and there are the only two alleles:

- B = Brown eyes
- b = blue eyes

A child inherits these alleles from his parents. There are three possible combinations a child can inherit, dependent on his parents' alleles:

- BB (homozygous dominant)
- Bb (heterozygous)
- bb (homozygous recessive)

The combination of genes above will determine the trait in the offspring. If the child gets any combination with a B, the more powerful allele, his eyes will be brown. Only the bb combination will give the child blue eyes. In this example, the combination of alleles is called a **genotype**, and the actual eye color the child has is called a **phenotype**.

Change Over Time

The **theory of natural selection** is one of the fundamental tenets of evolution. It affects the **phenotype**, or visible characteristics, of individuals in a species, which ultimately affects the genotype, or genetic makeup, of those same individuals. **Charles Darwin** was the first to explain the theory of natural selection, and it is described by **Herbert Spencer** as favoring survival of the fittest.

202

Natural selection encompasses three assumptions:

- A species has heritable traits: All traits have some likelihood of being propagated to offspring.

- The traits of a species vary: Some traits are more advantageous than others.

- Individuals of a species are subject to differing rates of reproduction: Some individuals of a species may not get the opportunity to reproduce while others reproduce frequently.

Over time, certain variations in traits may increase both the survival and reproduction of certain individuals within a species. The desirable heritable traits are passed on from generation to generation. Eventually, the desirable traits will become more common and permeate the entire species.

Adaptation

The **theory of adaptation** is defined as an alteration in a species that causes it to become more well-suited to its environment. It increases the probability of survival, thus increasing the rate of successful reproduction. As a result, an adaptation becomes more common within the population of that species.

For examples, bats use reflected sound waves (echolocation) to prey on insects, and chameleons change colors to blend in with their surroundings to evade detection by its prey and predators. These adaptations are believed to be brought about by natural selection.

Adaptive radiation refers to the idea of rapid diversification within a species into an array of unique forms. It's thought to happen as a result of changes in a habitat creating new challenges, ecological niches, or natural resources.

Darwin's finches are often thought of as an example of the theory of adaptive radiation. Charles Darwin documented 13 varieties of finches on the Galapagos Islands. Each island in the chain presented a unique and changing environment, which was believed to cause rapid adaptive radiation among the finches. There was also diversity among finches inhabiting the same island. Darwin believed that as a result of natural selection, each variety of finch developed adaptations to fit into its native environment.

A major difference in Darwin's finches had to do with the size and shapes of beaks. The variation in beaks allowed the finches to access different foods and natural resources, which decreased competition and preserved resources. As a result, various finches of the same species were allowed to coexist, thrive, and diversify. Finches had:

- Short beaks, which were suited for foraging for seeds
- Thin, sharp beaks, which were suited for preying on insects
- Long beaks, which were suited for probing for food inside plants

Darwin believed that the finches on the Galapagos Islands resulted from chance mutations in genes transmitted from generation to generation.

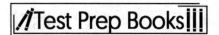

Life Cycle

Here's a look at the life cycles of many animals.

Chicken	Hens are female chickens, and they lay about one egg per day. If there is no rooster (male chicken) around to fertilize the egg, the egg never turns into a chick and instead becomes an egg that we can eat. If a rooster is around, he mates with the female chicken and fertilizes the egg. Once the egg is fertilized, the tiny little embryo (future chicken) will start as a white dot adjacent to the yolk and albumen (egg white) and will develop for 21 days. The mother hen sits on her clutch of eggs (several fertilized eggs) to incubate them and keep them warm. She will turn the eggs to make sure the embryo doesn't stick to one side of the shell. The embryo continues to develop, using the egg white and yolk nutrients, and eventually develops an "egg tooth" on its beak that it uses to crack open the egg and hatch. Before it hatches, it even chirps to let the mom know of its imminent arrival!
Frog	Frogs mate similar to the way chickens do, and then lay eggs in a very wet area. Sometimes, the parents abandon the eggs and let them develop on their own. The eggs, like chickens', will hatch around 21 days later. Just like chickens, a frog develops from a yolk, but when it hatches, it continues to use the yolk for nutrients. A chicken hatches and looks like a cute little chick, but a baby frog is actually a tadpole that is barely developed. It can't even swim around right away, although eventually it will develop gills, a mouth, and a tail. After more time, it will develop teeth and tiny legs and continue to change into a fully grown frog! This type of development is called **metamorphosis**.
Fish	Most fish also lay eggs in the water, but unlike frogs, their swimming sperm externally fertilize the eggs. Like frogs, when fish hatch, they feed on a yolk sac and are called **larvae**. Once the larvae no longer feed on their yolk and can find their own nutrients, they are called fry, which are basically baby fish that grow into adulthood.
Butterfly	Like frogs, butterflies go through a process called **metamorphosis,** where they completely change into a different looking organism. After the process of mating and internal fertilization, the female finds the perfect spot to lay her eggs, usually a spot with lots of leaves. When the babies hatch from the eggs, they are in the larva form, which for butterflies is called a **caterpillar**. The larvae eat and eat and then go through a process like hibernation and form into a **chrysalis**, or a **chrysalis**. When they hatch from the cocoon, the butterflies are in their adult form.
Bugs	After fertilization, other bugs go through incomplete metamorphosis, which involves three states: eggs that hatch, nymphs that look like little adults without wings and molt their exoskeleton over time, and adults.

All of these organisms depend on a proper environment for development, and that environment depends on their form. Frogs need water, caterpillars need leaves, and baby chicks need warmth in order to be born.

Regulation and Behavior

204

DNA is the instruction manual for every organism, including humans. It is identical in our cells (except for minor mutations); so why are neurons and heart muscles so different in function and appearance? The key is that in different cells, different parts of the DNA are read. Our DNA is an encyclopedia set with 46 volumes (chromosomes). The instructions for heart cells are different from instructions for neurons. And these instructions are scattered throughout the 46 volumes. It is still not completely understood how a cell chooses what parts of the encyclopedia to read, but it is known that different cells read different portions of our DNA.

Protein enzymes facilitate chemical reactions; they are the workers in the cell. Some unwind the DNA so that RNA can copy the genes in a process called **transcription**. **RNA** is similar to DNA except that it is single-stranded and has the base U, which stands for **uracil**, instead of the T in DNA. Another similarity between DNA and RNA is that they are both made of a base, a phosphate, and a sugar, though DNA is made of deoxyribose sugar and RNA is made of ribose sugar.

The final protein can have many destinations; it can become part of the cytoskeleton that holds the organelles in place, act as an enzyme, go to the cell membrane and act as a marker protein (a tag to identify the cell), act as a **transport protein** (allows materials to pass in and out of the cell), or as a **receptor protein** (can receive chemical messages like hormones and initiate reactions in the cell to respond), or leave the cell and become something else, like a person's hair and fingernails!

In the cell, processes are regulated at the DNA level because transcription and translation are tightly regulated. At the organism level, the entire nervous system controls activity. In humans, a stimulus is received by the sensory neuron, travels up the nerve to the brain, and a response travels down to whatever motor neuron is necessary for movement.

Sensory neurons detect environmental stimulus involving sight, sound, touch, taste, and smell.

Diversity of Life

Due to the speciation that has occurred over the last 3.5 billion years since life first appeared, the variety of organisms is astronomical. Scientists have identified about 2 million species, and they suspect that there are at least 8 million others out there.

A man named **Carolus Linnaeus** developed a naming system to try to create some order in classifying all species. For example, the classification of humans through the seven levels, from all-inclusive to the most specific, looks like this:

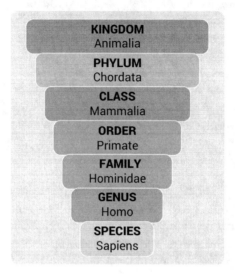

One benefit of this universal naming system is that because some organisms have different common names, like the roly-poly and doodlebug, or the cougar and panther, it allows scientists to have a common language. Due to the sheer magnitude of species, scientists need the seven levels, but when referring to organisms, their official names are just the last two: **genus** and **species**. Humans are simply referred to as **Homo sapiens**. This two-name system is called **binomial nomenclature**.

There are currently six kingdoms, although the prokaryotes (simpler cells) used to be lumped together into one kingdom called **Monera**. Currently, there are two prokaryotic kingdoms, **Archaebacteria** and **Eubacteria**.

Archaebacteria
Prokaryotes that have a cell membrane made of fats. They live in harsh places including extremely hot areas (volcanic vents or hot springs) and extremely salty locations (Utah's Salt Lake). These are the rarest prokaryotes.

Eubacteria
Common bacteria that have a cell membrane made of a protein-carbohydrate blend. They make up the vast majority of existing prokaryotes. An example is staphylococcus.

Protista
This kingdom consists of eukaryotes. Most are unicellular. This kingdom is the most diverse and can be divided into three types: fungus-like (including slime-molds), plant-like (including algae), and animal-like (including amoeba). Some scientists believe that there is so much diversity within the kingdom that they should be split into separate kingdoms, but so far they remain in one group.

Animal-like protists are **heterotrophs** (they do not make their own food), and plant-like protists are **autotrophs** (they make their own food). Fungus-like protists are heterotrophs. Like actual fungi, these

organisms externally digest their food by acting as parasites and decomposers. Animal-like protists ingest their food via phagocytosis (cell eating) or by absorbing it.

Depending on the particular protists, some produce asexually via mitosis and others reproduce sexually.

Fungi

Fungi are eukaryotic heterotrophs that digest their food externally. Many of them, including common mushrooms and toadstools, act as decomposers by breaking down dead organisms then absorbing the broken down nutrients. Other fungi accomplish ingestion as parasites feeding off of living organisms, as in the case of a yeast infection. All fungi are multicellular with one exception—**yeast**. Fungi have cell walls made of a complex carbohydrate called **chitin**. Most fungi reproduce sexually and asexually.

Plantae

Plants are multicellular autotrophs like daisies, roses, and pine trees. They are closely related to the aquatic producer, algae, but different in that algae don't contain true roots, stems, or leaves. Plants are **photosynthesizers**, and their cells have surrounding cell walls made of the starch cellulose.

Animalia

Animals are multicellular heterotrophs, like fungi, except that animals move and internally ingest their food by consuming it. Animals are the only kingdom to not have cells with cell walls due to their flexibility and ability to move. The animal kingdom is very diverse and includes humans, jellyfish, and spiders, as well as all sorts of other organisms.

Interdependence of Organisms

The biosphere has layers and layers of complexity:

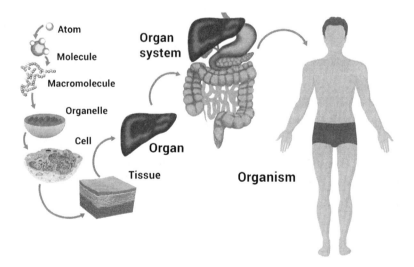

All organisms work together so that life can exist. An organism represents one of a species, like the fish below, and all organisms serve a particular function. The fish's niche is to eat aquatic producers and excrete waste that acts as fertilizer.

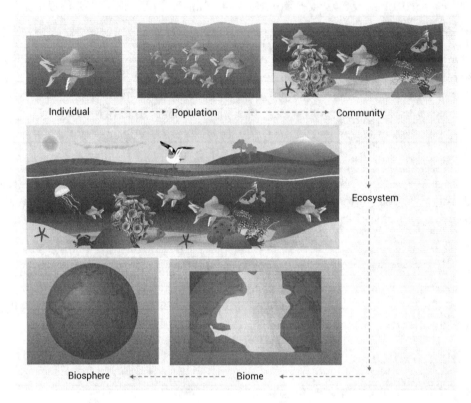

This fish is just one organism within a population. A **population** represents multiple individuals living in the same habitat. The community includes every biotic factor (living organism) within an ecosystem, in this case, the fish, jellyfish, algae, crab, bacteria, etc. An ecosystem includes all the biotic factors as well as the **abiotic**, which includes anything non-living—for the fish, that's a rock, a shipwreck, and a nearby glacier. For biomes, add weather and climate into the mix. The biosphere is all of Earth, which is the combination of all biomes.

We already discussed that producers (plants, protists, and even some bacteria) photosynthesize and make the food that provides energy required for all chemical reactions to occur and therefore all life to exist. A non-photosynthesizer must find and eat food, and this feeding relationship can be visualized in food chains. Consider this food chain:

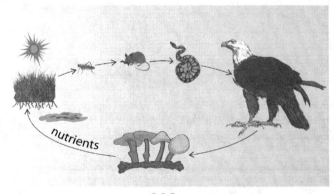

208

The true source of the energy for every living organism is the sun. Plants absorb the sun's energy to make glucose and are on the **first trophic level** (feeding level). The grasshopper on the **second trophic level** is an example of an herbivore and is a primary consumer, as he is the first eater in the food chain. Unfortunately, he receives only 10 percent of the energy that the plant absorbed (this is known as the 10 percent rule) because the other 90 percent of energy was either used by the plant to grow or will be lost as heat.

The mouse on the **third trophic level** is the secondary consumer, or second eater. Food chains are not as inclusive as **food webs**, which show all feeding relationships in an ecosystem. Looking at this food chain suggests that mice are carnivores (eaters of animals), but mice also eat berries and plants, so they are actually considered omnivores (eaters of both plants and animals). The mouse only gets 10 percent of the energy from the grasshopper, which is actually only 1 percent of the original energy provided by the Sun. The snake on the fourth trophic level is a carnivore, as is the hawk on the highest trophic level.

The arrows in the food chain show the transfer of energy, and fungi as well as bacteria act as decomposers, which break down organic material. Decomposers act at every trophic level because they feed on all organisms; they are non-discriminating omnivores. Decomposers are critical for life, as they recycle the atoms and building blocks of organisms.

Feeding relationships and **predator-prey relationships** (hunter-hunted, like the hawk and the rabbit in the food web above) are not the only relationships in an ecosystem. There also can be competition within and between species. For example, in the food chain above, the rabbit and snail both eat grass, showing a relationship called **competition**, when two organisms want the same thing. Other relationships include symbiotic relationships, which represent two species living together. Symbiosis comes in three varieties:

- **Mutualism**: an arrangement where both organisms help each other. An example is the relationship between birds and flowers. When birds consume the nectar that the flower produces, pollen rubs on the bird's body so that when it travels to a neighboring plant, it helps with fertilization. The plant helps the bird by providing food, and the bird helps the plant by helping it reproduce. This is a win-win.

- **Parasitism**: when one organism is hurt while the other is helped. Fleas and dogs are a prime example. Fleas suck the dog's blood, and dogs are itchy and lose blood. This is a win-lose.

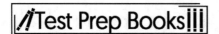

- **Commensalism**: when one organism is helped and the other is neither harmed nor helped. For example, barnacles are crusty little creatures that attach themselves to whales. They don't feed on the whale like a parasite. Instead, they use the whale to give them a free ride so they have access to food. The whales don't care about the barnacles. This is a win-do not care.

Personal Health

Humans appear to be the kings of nature, but unfortunately, disease can strike. Some protists (like the malaria-causing paramecium), fungi (yeast), and bacteria (strep) can make humans sick and can even be deadly.

The human body has an arsenal to help fight illness. Skin and the acid in our stomach are inhospitable to all sorts of disease-causing agents (pathogens) and fight them off without even trying. Eyebrows, eyelashes, nose hair, and cilia (tiny hairs) in the respiratory system trap any germs and prevent them from getting inside. Mucus is a defense to trap germs, which is why the human body overproduces it when sick—it acts like a spider web that catches germs, and when a person coughs or sneezes, the germs are expelled and unable to cause harm. If, however, the pathogen gets past these barriers, then the body has to start fighting them off. Inflammation and swelling, though annoying, actually help by increasing blood flow to an injured or infected area. And blood carries white blood cells that eat and destroy germs. Fevers are actually a body's natural response to killing pathogens.

If the germ is still not killed off, then the body makes massive amounts of white blood cells. One type of blood cell, the **plasma B-cell**, is particularly helpful because it makes structures called **antibodies**, little proteins that tag pathogens so that the other white blood cells can easily find and destroy them. Other types of white blood cells include **T-cells**, which destroy the pathogen as well as infected cells.

This picture shows how antibodies work:

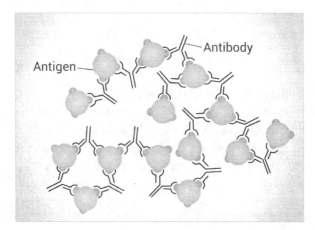

The **antigen** on the germ is the part that attaches to cells in our body and destroys them. Think of the antigen like the key that attaches to a protein on the outside of our cell, tricking the cell to let it in. The antibody perfectly binds to the antigen (the key), making it so that the germ cannot open and enter our cells. And the immune system produces killer T-cells that eat these tagged pathogens.

An amazing thing about antibodies is that they are completely fashioned to match each germ they come across. And antibodies stay circulating in blood so that if they ever encounter the disease again, they can tag it for destruction and block its harmful effects, making a person immune to the pathogen.

For this reason, scientists have developed vaccines, which can save lives. For example, **polio** is a disease that attacks the brain and spinal cord, causing paralysis and death. The vaccine for polio is given to children. It is given in the inactive form of the virus (dead virus) but it still carries the same antigen. A person vaccinated will develop antibodies that are exactly matched to the polio antigens, so if they ever encounter polio in real life, the immune system will eradicate it before it can do any damage.

When a person gets infected and their body starts making massive amounts of antibodies and killer cells, they can feel sick due to the energy expended to create such an army. Usually, after a few days, the body effectively fights off the germ, and life goes back to normal. In the case of bacterial infections that don't resolve themselves, antibiotics (bacteria killers) can be taken to help the body fight the germs. Antibiotics, unfortunately, don't help with viruses.

Interestingly enough, antibiotics were discovered by accident in 1928 by **Alexander Fleming**. He was performing research of an entirely different nature when he noticed mold had killed the cells he was trying to study. Upon further investigation, he realized that the effect of the mold was reproducible and effectively killed a variety of bacteria. His discovery laid groundwork for a new field of medicine, which targeted the destruction of bacteria. Since then, a variety of antibiotics have been developed, and some of them are uniquely designed for different diseases. Biological research is critical for disease prevention because bacteria are always changing, and there is a need to continually improve the antibiotics already available.

Science as a Human Endeavor

In addition to learning about bacteria and viruses to save lives, an example of how increased scientific knowledge has helped society can be seen in the field of botany. **Flowers** are the reproductive structure of plants and are very complex structures that allow plants to create genetic diversity.

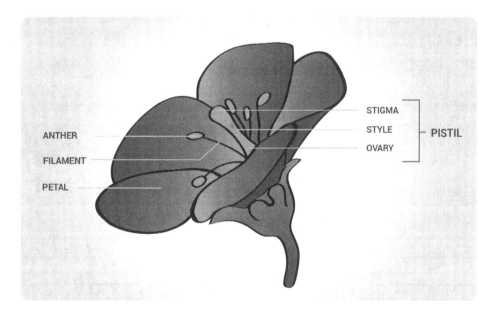

Scientists have determined the purpose for all of a flower's many parts:

- The **stamen** contains the pollen-holding **anther** (pollen is plant sperm) and the **filament** that holds it high.

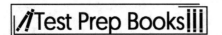

- The **pistil** contains the sticky **stigma** at the top to which pollen sticks; the **style**, which holds up the stigma; and the **ovary**, or egg that will eventually be fertilized.

- The petals are colored and even have infrared patterns we cannot see to attract pollinators like birds and bees.

Note how structure aids function in the flower: the pollen is lightweight and easily attaches to pollinators. The stigma is sticky and easily catches the pollen. The petals are beautiful landing pads designed to attract different animals.

Scientists are using their knowledge of flowers and genetics to genetically engineer flowers. They are working on creating pollen-free flowers that are easy on people with allergies, blue roses, and other flower varieties that don't exist in nature, and even glow-in-the-dark flowers by introducing foreign DNA.

Other botanists are also genetically engineering plants that provide our food, which is much more controversial, as many are worried about the consequences of consuming genetically modified organisms (GMOs). Some think GMOs are wonderful because they can provide massive amounts of food at low costs, while others fear introducing foreign food into the biosphere will alter ecosystems.

Science as Inquiry

As scientists have been able to visualize and decode DNA, they are also able to predict diseases. **Karyotypes** are pictures of individual's chromosomes, and even before birth, abnormalities such as Down syndrome (an extra chromosome 21) can be detected.

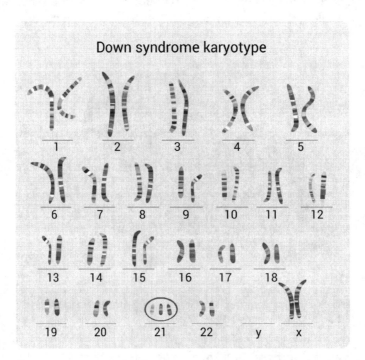

Adults can have blood tests to test their alleles and see if they have cancer-causing (or other disease-causing) genes. Being aware of possible diseases helps people to prevent and treat them.

As scientists ask more questions about disease detection, prevention, and treatment, quality of life continues to increase. For example, type 1 diabetes occurs when a person's pancreas fails to make insulin, and it is a deadly disease if left untreated. A few decades ago, scientists found a way to synthetically create insulin, and now diabetics can have long and prosperous lives.

Research

When the actor Johnny Depp flew to Australia to film a movie, he travelled with his two dogs. Australian officials immediately sanctioned him.

Australian law forbids anyone from bringing foreign species because one little change can disrupt an entire ecosystem. For example, in Hawaii, North American ducks were brought for hunting purposes, but they've endangered the native duck species. One new non-native organism can cause a natural species to become extinct.

Another danger to an ecosystem is human activity. As the human population grows and technology advances, our energy needs are polluting the atmosphere. And there are no doubts that global temperatures are climbing, which can change ecosystem dynamics. Increases in oil spills and ocean pollution is destroying aquatic ecosystems. Chopping down trees for wood as well as building parking lots and buildings is decimating terrestrial ecosystems. With these changes, biodiversity will dramatically drop. The list of endangered species continues to grow, and eventually many will become extinct. Altering populations of ecosystems can have dramatic effects.

Livestock overgrazing is also detrimental to the environment. If farms don't monitor grazing animals, plants simply lose the ability to rebound, often resulting in death. The lack of producers in an ecosystem, the start of the food chain, will have disastrous consequences for the entire community.

Research is important so that society can minimize activities that interfere with ecosystems. Developing non-renewable energy (such as wind, solar, and geothermal), deliberately planning a grazing schedule to prevent overgrazing, and protecting endangered species all should be primary focuses of research.

Process of Science

Scientific research always starts as a question, followed by a hypothesis, data collection, and conclusions. Conclusions lead to further questions, repeating the process.

This was the case with the study of insect development. Long ago, scientists noticed a strange phenomenon in insects, which we now know is a process called **metamorphosis**.

There are two types of metamorphosis in insects: incomplete metamorphosis, which has three stages, and complete metamorphosis, which has four stages.

Incomplete Metamorphosis: Grasshoppers	Complete Metamorphosis: Butterflies and Beetles
<ul><li>Egg</li><li>Nymph: a mini-adult with no wings</li><li>Adult: how the organism will look for the rest of its life</li></ul>	<ul><li>Egg</li><li>Larva: a wormy, six legged, massive eater</li><li>Pupa: a larva encased in a hard shell that dramatically develops and changes in appearance</li><li>Adult: how the organism will look for the rest of its life</li></ul>

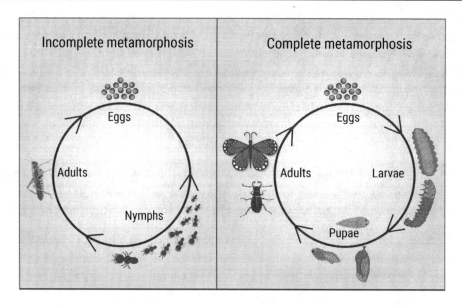

Insight into metamorphosis developed over centuries of research and goes through the scientific process, as shown below.

Problem/Question: What's happening to these insects that makes them look completely different from their younger selves?

Hypothesis: The prevailing hypotheses that were researched over the years were:

- These different creatures are from two different organisms.
- The worm-like creature is a younger version of the adult creature.

Data collection: A biologist named **Swammerdam** in the 1600s rejected the popular belief that the caterpillar and the butterfly were different organisms. Using observations from microscopic data, he confirmed that an insect (but not all insects) could go through an intermediate larval stage. Fossil evidence also confirmed the development of some insects through a larval stage. Scientists have even found genetic and protein differences from organisms that go through incomplete metamorphosis and complete metamorphosis. The insects with larval stage have a specific gene required for the process as well as differences in hormone production.

Conclusion: There is a complete metamorphosis cycle for many insects with larval and pupa stages between the egg and adult.

New problem: Why do insects go through complete metamorphosis?

New hypothesis: Complete metamorphosis is an adaptation. The intermediate "pupa egg" state between the larva and the adult stage arose so the juvenile and adult population don't compete for food, ensuring greater overall survival.

Physical Science

Physical and Chemical Properties

In the physical sciences, it is important to break things down to their simplest components in order to truly understand why they act and react the way they do. It may seem burdensome to separate out each part of an object or to diagram each movement made by an object, but these methods provide a solid basis for understanding how to accurately depict the motion of objects and then correctly predict their future movements.

Everything around us is composed of different materials. To properly understand and sort objects, we must classify what types of materials they comprise. This includes identifying the foundational properties of each object such as its reaction to chemicals, heat, water, or other materials. Some objects might not react at all and this is an important property to note. Other properties include the physical appearance of the object or whether it has any magnetic properties. The importance of being able to sort and classify objects is the first step to understanding them.

- **Matter**: anything that has mass and takes up space

- **Substance**: a type of matter that cannot be separated out into new material through a physical reaction

- **Elements**: substances that cannot be broken down by either physical or chemical reactions. Elements are in the most basic form and are grouped by identified properties using the Periodic Table. The periodic table groups elements based on similar properties. Metallic elements, inert elements, and transition elements are a few categories used to organize elements on the periodic table. New elements are added as they are discovered or created, and these newer elements tend to be heavier, fall into the metal section of the periodic table, and are often unstable. Examples of elements include carbon, gold, and helium.

- **Atoms**: the building blocks of all elements. Atoms are the smallest particles of matter that retain their identities during chemical reactions. Atoms have a central nucleus that includes positively charged protons, and neutrons, which carry no charge. Atoms are also surrounded by electrons that carry a negative charge. The amount of each component determines what type of atom is formed when the components come together. For example, two hydrogen atoms and one oxygen atom can bond together to form water, but the hydrogen and oxygen atoms still remain true to their original identities.

- **Mass**: the measure of how much of a substance exists in an object. The measure of mass is not the same as weight, area, or volume.

Physical Properties vs. Chemical Properties

Both physical and chemical properties are used to sort and classify objects:

- **Physical properties**: refers to the appearance, mass, temperature, state, size, or color of an object or fluid; a physical change indicates a change in the appearance, mass, temperature, state, size or color of an object or fluid.

- **Chemical properties**: refers to the chemical makeup of an object or fluid; a chemical change refers to an alteration in the makeup of an object or fluid and forms a new solution or compound.

Reversible Change vs. Non-Reversible Change

Reversible change (physical change) is the changing of the size or shape of an object without altering its chemical makeup. Examples include the heating or cooling of water, change of state (solid, liquid, gas), the freezing of water into ice, or cutting a piece of wood in half.

When two or more materials are combined, it is called a **mixture**. Generally, a mixture can be separated out into the original components. When one type of matter is dissolved into another type of matter (a solid into a liquid or a liquid into another liquid), and cannot easily be separated back into its original components, it is called a **solution**.

States of matter refers to the form substances take such as solid, liquid, gas, or plasma. **Solid** refers to a rigid form of matter with a flexed shape and a fixed volume. **Liquid** refers to the fluid form of matter with no fixed shape and a fixed volume. **Gas** refers to an easily compressible fluid form of matter with no fixed shape that expands to fill any space available. Finally, **plasma** refers to an ionized gas where electrons flow freely from atom to atom.

> Examples: A rock is a solid because it has a fixed shape and volume. Water is considered to be a liquid because it has a set volume, but not a set shape; therefore, you could pour it into different containers of different shapes, as long as they were large enough to contain the existing volume of the water. Oxygen is considered to be a gas. Oxygen does not have a set volume or a set shape; therefore, it could expand or contract to fill a container or even a room. Gases in fluorescent lamps become plasma when electric current is applied to them.

Matter can change from one state to another in many ways, including through heating, cooling, or a change in pressure.

Changes of state are identified as:

- **Melting**: solid to liquid
- **Sublimation**: solid to gas
- **Evaporation**: liquid to gas
- **Freezing**: liquid to solid
- **Condensation**: gas to liquid
- **Non-reversible change** (chemical change): When one or more types of matter change and it results in the production of new materials. Examples include burning, rusting, and combining solutions. If a piece of paper is burned it cannot be turned back into its original state. It has forever been altered by a chemical change.

216

Forces and Motion

People have been studying the movement of objects since ancient times, sometimes prompted by curiosity, and sometimes by necessity. On earth, items move according to specific guidelines and have motion that is fairly predictable. In order to understand why an object moves along its path, it is important to understand what role forces have on influencing an object's movements. The term **force** describes an outside influence on an object. Force does not have to refer to something imparted by another object. Forces can act upon objects by touching them with a push or a pull, by friction, or without touch like a magnetic force or even gravity. Forces can affect the motion of an object.

In order to study an object's motion, the object must be locatable and describable. When locating an object's position, it can help to locate it relative to another known object, or put it into a frame of reference. This phrase means that if the placement of one object is known, it is easier to locate another object with respect to the position of the original object.

The measurement of an object's movement or change in position (x), over a change in time (t) is an object's speed. The measurement of speed with direction is **velocity**. A "change in position" refers to the difference in location of an object's starting point and an object's ending point. In science, the Greek letter **Delta**, Δ, represents a change.

Equation:
$$velocity\ (v) = \frac{\Delta x}{\Delta t}$$

Position is measured in meters, and time is measured in seconds. The standard measurement for velocity is meters/second (m/s).

$$\frac{meters}{second} = \frac{m}{s}$$

The measurement of an object's change in velocity over time is an object's **acceleration**. **Gravity** is considered to be a form of acceleration.

Equation:
$$acceleration\ (a) = \frac{\Delta v}{\Delta t}$$

Velocity is measured in meters/second and time is measured in seconds. The standard measurement for acceleration is meters/second^2 (m/s^2).

$$\frac{\frac{meters}{second}}{second} = \frac{meters}{second^2} = \frac{m}{s^2}$$

For example, consider a car traveling down the road. The speed can be measured by calculating how far the car is traveling over a certain period of time. However, since the car is traveling in a direction (north, east, south, west), the distance over time is actually the car's velocity. It can be confusing, as many people will often interchange the words speed and velocity. But if something is traveling a certain distance, during a certain time period, in a direction, this is the object's velocity. Velocity is speed with direction.

The change in an object's velocity over a certain amount of time is the object's acceleration. If the driver of that car keeps pressing on the gas pedal and increasing the velocity, the car would have a change in velocity over the change in time and would be accelerating. The reverse could be said if the driver were

depressing the brake and the car was slowing down; it would have a negative acceleration, or be decelerating. Since acceleration also has a direction component, it is possible for a car to accelerate without changing speed. If an object changes direction, it is accelerating.

Motion creates something called **momentum**. This is a calculation of an object's mass multiplied by its velocity. Momentum can be described as the amount an object wants to continue moving along its current course. Momentum in a straight line is called **linear momentum**. Just as energy can be transferred and conserved, so can momentum.

For example, a car and a truck moving at the same velocity down a highway will not have the same momentum, because they do not have the same mass. The mass of the truck is greater than that of the car, therefore the truck will have more momentum. In a head-on collision, the vehicles would be expected to slide in the same direction of the truck's original motion because the truck has a greater momentum.

The amount of force during a length of time creates an **impulse**. This means that if a force acts on an object during a given amount of time, it will have a determined impulse. However, if the length of time can be extended, the force will be less, due to the conservation of momentum.

Consider another example: when catching a fast baseball, it helps soften the blow of the ball to follow through, or cradle the catch. This technique is simply extending the time of the application of the force of the ball, so the impact of the ball does not hurt the hand. As a final example, if a martial arts expert wants to break a board by executing a chop from their hand, they need to exert a force on a small point on the boards, extremely quickly. If they slow down the time of the impact from the force of their hand, they will probably injure their hand and not break the board.

Newton's Three Laws of Motion

Sir Isaac Newton spent a great deal of time studying objects, forces, and how an object's motion responds to forces. Newton made great advancements by using mathematics to describe the motion of objects and to predict future motions of objects by applying his mathematical models to situations. Through his extensive research, Newton is credited for summarizing the basic laws of motion for objects here on Earth. These laws are as follows:

First Law

The first law is the **law of inertia**. An object in motion remains in motion, unless acted upon by an outside force. An object at rest remains at rest, unless acted upon by an outside force. Simply put, inertia is the natural tendency of an object to continue along with what it is already doing; an outside force would have to act upon the object to make it change its course. This includes an object that is sitting still. The inertia of an object is relative to its momentum.

> Example: If a car is driving at a constant speed in a constant direction (also called a constant velocity), it would take a force in a different direction to change the path of the car. Conversely, if the car is sitting still, it would take a force greater than that of friction from any direction to make that stationary car move.

Second Law

The force (F) on an object is equal to the mass (m) multiplied by the acceleration (a) on that object. **Mass** (m) refers to the amount of a substance and **acceleration** (a) refers to a rate of velocity over time.

In the case of an object falling on Earth, the value of gravity will be placed in for acceleration (a). In the case of an object at rest on Earth, gravity is placed in for acceleration (a), and the force calculated by $F = ma$ is called **Weight** (W). It is important to discern that an object's mass (measured in kilograms, kg) is not the same as an object's weight (measured in Newtons, N). Weight is the mass times the gravity.

Example: The gravity on the earth's moon is considerably less than the gravity on earth. Therefore, the weight of an object on the earth's moon would be considerably less than the weight of the object on earth. In each case, a different value for acceleration/gravity would be used in the equation $F = ma$. Mass is used to calculate weight, and they are not the same.

Example: If a raisin is dropped into a bowl of pudding, it would make a small indentation and stick in the pudding a bit, but if a grapefruit is dropped into the same bowl of pudding, it would splatter the pudding out of the bowl and most likely hit the bottom of the bowl. Even though both items are accelerating at the same rate (gravity), the mass of the grapefruit is larger than that of the raisin; therefore, the force with which the grapefruit hits the bowl of pudding is considerably larger than the force from the raisin hitting the bowl of pudding.

Third Law

The third law of motion states that for every action there is an equal and opposite reaction. If someone pounds a fist on a table, the reactionary force from the table causes the person to feel a sharp force on the fist. The magnitude of the force felt on the fist increases the harder that they pound on the table. It should be noted that action/reaction pairs occur simultaneously. As the fist applies a force on the table, the table instantaneously applies an equal and opposite force on the fist.

Example: Imagine a person is wearing ice skates on ice and attempts to push on a heavy sled sitting in front of them. They will be pushed in the direction opposite of their push on the sled; the push the skater is experiencing is equal and opposite to the force they are exerting on the sled. This is a good example of how the icy surface helps to lessen the effects of friction and allows the reactionary force to be more easily observed.

Forces are anything acting upon an object either in motion or at rest; this includes friction and gravity. These forces are often depicted by using a force diagram or free body diagram. A **force diagram** shows an object as the focal point, with arrows denoting all the forces acting upon the object. The direction of the head of the arrow indicates the direction of the force. The object at the center can also be exerting forces on things in its surroundings.

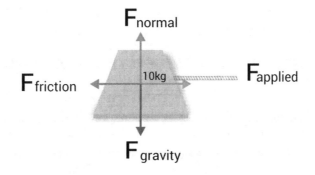

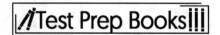
Equilibrium

If an object is in constant motion or at rest (its acceleration equals zero), the object is said to be in **equilibrium**. It does not imply that there are no forces acting upon the object, but that all of the forces are balanced in order for the situation to continue in its current state. This can be thought of as a "balanced"' situation.

Note that if an object is resting on top of a mountain peak or traveling at a constant velocity down the side of that mountain, both situations describe a state of equilibrium.

Falling Objects

Objects falling within the earth's atmosphere are all affected by gravity. Their rate of acceleration will be that of gravity. If two objects were dropped from a great height at the exact same time, regardless of mass, theoretically, they should hit the ground at the same time. This is due to gravity acting upon them at the same rate. In actuality, if this were attempted, the shape of the objects and external factors such as air resistance would affect their rates of fall and cause a discrepancy in when each lands.

Consider the traditional illustration of this principle: a feather and a rock are released at the same time in regular air versus being released at the same time in a vacuum. In the open atmosphere, the feather would slowly loft down to the ground, due to the effects of air resistance, while the rock would quickly drop to the ground. If the feather and the rock were both released at the same time in a vacuum, they would both hit the bottom at the same time. The rate of fall is not dependent upon the mass of the item or any external factors in a vacuum (there is no air resistance in a vacuum); therefore, all that would be affecting the rate of fall would be gravity. Gravity affects every object on the earth with the same rate of acceleration.

Circular Motion

An **axis** is an invisible line on which an object can rotate. This is most easily observed with a toy top. There is actually a point (or rod) through the center of the top on which the top can be observed to be spinning. This is called the axis.

When objects move in a circle by spinning on their own axis, or because they are tethered around a central point (also an axis), they exhibit circular motion. Circular motion is similar in many ways to linear (straight line) motion; however, there are a few additional points to note. A spinning object is always accelerating because it is always changing direction. The force causing this constant acceleration on or around an axis is called **centripetal force** and is often associated with centripetal acceleration. Centripetal force always pulls toward the axis of rotation. An imaginary reactionary force, called **centrifugal force**, is the outward force felt when an object is undergoing circular motion. This reactionary force is not the real force; it just feels like it is there. This has also been referred to as a "**fictional force**." The true force is the one pulling inward, or the centripetal force.

The terms centripetal and centrifugal are often mistakenly interchanged. If the centripetal force acting on an object moving with circular motion is removed, the object will continue moving in a straight line tangent to the point on the circle where the object last experienced the centripetal force. For example, when a traditional style washing machine spins a load of clothes in order to expunge the water from the load, it spins the machine barrel in a circle at a high rate of speed. A force is pulling in toward the center of the circle (centripetal force). At the same time, the wet clothes, which are attempting to move in a straight line, are colliding with the outer wall of the barrel that is moving in a circle. The interaction

220

between the wet clothes and barrel wall cause a reactionary force to the centripetal force and expel the water out of the small holes that line the outer wall of the barrel.

Conservation of Angular Momentum

An object moving in a circular motion also has momentum; for circular motion it is called **angular momentum**. This is determined by rotational inertia and rotational velocity and the distance of the mass from the axis of rotation or center of rotation. When objects are exhibiting circular motion, they also demonstrate the conservation of **angular momentum**, meaning that the angular momentum of a system is always constant, regardless of the placement of the mass. Rotational inertia can be affected by how far the mass of the object is placed with respect to the center of rotation (axis of rotation). The larger the distance between the mass and the center of rotation, the slower the rotational velocity. Conversely, if the mass is closer to the center of rotation, the rotational velocity increases. A change in one affects the other, thus conserving the angular momentum. This holds true as long as no external forces act upon the system.

For example, an ice skater spinning on one ice skate extends their arms out for a slower rotational velocity. When the skater brings their arms in close to their body (or lessens the distance between the mass and the center of rotation), their rotational velocity increases and they spin much faster. Some skaters extend their arms straight up above their head, which causes an extension of the axis of rotation, thus removing any distance between the mass and the center of rotation and maximizing their rotational velocity.

Another example is when a person selects a horse on a merry-go-round: the placement of their horse can affect their ride experience. All of the horses are traveling with the same rotational speed, but in order to travel along the same plane as the merry-go-round turns, a horse on the outside will have a greater linear speed, due to it being farther away from the axis of rotation. Another way to think of it is that an outside horse has to cover a lot more ground than a horse on the inside, in order to keep up with the rotational speed of the merry-go-round platform. Thrill seekers should always select an outer horse.

Energy

The term **energy** typically refers to an object's ability to perform work. This can include a transfer of heat from one object to another, or from an object to its surroundings. Energy is usually measured in Joules. There are two main categories of energy: renewable and non-renewable.

- **Renewable**: energy produced from the exhaustion of a resource that can be replenished. Burning wood to produce heat, then replanting trees to replenish the resource is an instance of using renewable energy.

- **Non-renewable**: energy produced from the exhaustion of a resource that cannot be replenished. Burning coal to produce heat would be an example of a non-renewable energy. Although coal is a natural resource found in/on the earth that is mined or harvested from the earth, it cannot be regrown or replenished. Other examples include oil and natural gas (fossil fuels).

Temperature is measured in degrees Celsius (°C) or Kelvin (°K). Temperature should not be confused with heat. **Heat** is a form of energy: a change in temperature or a transfer of heat can also be a measure

of energy. The amount of energy measured by the change in temperature (or a transfer) is the measure of heat.

Heat energy (thermal energy) can be transferred through the following ways:

Conduction
Conduction is the heating of one object by another through the actual touching of molecules, in order to transfer heat across the objects involved. A spiral burner on an electric stovetop heats from one molecule touching another to transfer the heat via conduction.

Convection
Heat transfer due to the movement/flow of molecules from areas of high concentration to ones of low concentration. Warmer molecules tend to rise, while colder molecules tend to sink. The heat in a house will rise from the vents in the floor to the upper levels of the structure and circulate in that manner, rising and falling with the movement of the molecules. This molecular movement helps to heat or cool a house and is often called **convection current**.

Radiation
The sun warms the earth through **radiation** or radiant energy. Radiation does not need any medium for the heat to travel; therefore, the heat from the sun can radiate to the earth across space.

Greenhouse Effect
The sun transfers heat into the earth's atmosphere through radiation traveling in waves. The atmosphere helps protect the earth from extreme exposure to the sun, while reflecting some of the waves continuously within the atmosphere, creating habitable temperatures. The rest of the waves are meant to dissipate out through the atmosphere and back into space. However, humans have created pollutants and released an overabundance of certain gasses into the earth's atmosphere, causing a layer of blockage. So, the waves that should be leaving the atmosphere continue to bounce back upon the earth repeatedly, thus contributing to global warming. This is a negative effect from the extra re-radiation of the sun's energy and causes planetary overheating.

This additional warming is not something easily or quickly reversed. Because the rate of reflection within the atmosphere only multiplies the more a light wave is bounced around, it will take a concerted effort to undue past reflectance and stop future reflectance of the light waves in the earth's atmosphere. Once the re-reflectance occurs, it duplicates exponentially, along with the additional compounding of more waves. Each degree the atmospheric temperature increases has a profound effect on the delicate balance of our planet, including the melting of polar ice caps, the rise of tidal currents—which cause strong weather systems—and the depletion of specific ecosystems necessary to sustain certain species of animals or insects, to name a few.

Energy can be harnessed to operate objects, and this energy is obtained from various sources such as electricity, food, gasoline, batteries, wind, and sun. For example, wind turbines out in a field are turned by the natural power of the wind. The turbines then store that energy internally in power cells; that stored energy can be used to power the lights on a farm or run machinery.

Potential Energy vs. Kinetic Energy

Potential energy (gravitational potential energy, or PE) is stored energy, or energy due to an object's height above the ground. **Kinetic energy** (KE) is the energy of motion. If an object is moving, it has some amount of kinetic energy.

Consider a rollercoaster car sitting still on the tracks at the top of a hill. The rollercoaster has all potential energy and no kinetic energy. As it travels down the hill, the energy transfers from potential energy into kinetic energy. At the bottom of the hill, where the car is going the fastest, it has all kinetic energy, but no potential energy. If energy losses to the environment (friction, heat, sound) are ignored, the amount of potential energy at the top of the hill equals the amount of kinetic energy at the bottom of the hill.

Mechanical Energy

Mechanical energy is the sum of the potential energy plus the kinetic energy in a system, minus energy lost to non-conservative forces. Often, the effects of non-conservative forces are small enough that they can be ignored. The total mechanical energy of a system is conserved or always the same. The amount of potential energy and the amount of kinetic energy can vary to add up to this total, but the total mechanical energy in the situation remains the same.

$$ME = PE + KE$$

$$Mechanical\ Energy = Potential\ Energy + Kinetic\ Energy$$

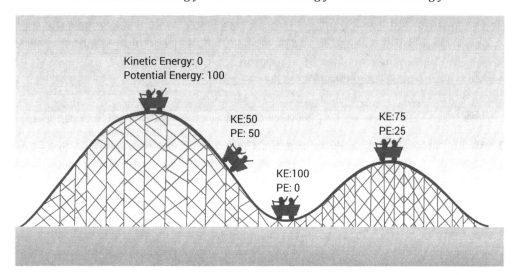

An illustration of a rollercoaster going down a hill demonstrates this point. At the top of the hill a label of $ME = PE$ describes the rollercoaster, halfway down the hill the label $ME = \frac{1}{2}PE + \frac{1}{2}KE$ describes the rollercoaster, and at the bottom of the hill, $ME = KE$ describes the rollercoaster.

Remember, energy can transfer or change forms, but it cannot be created or destroyed. This transfer can take place through waves (including light waves and sound waves), heat, impact, etc.

Simple Machines

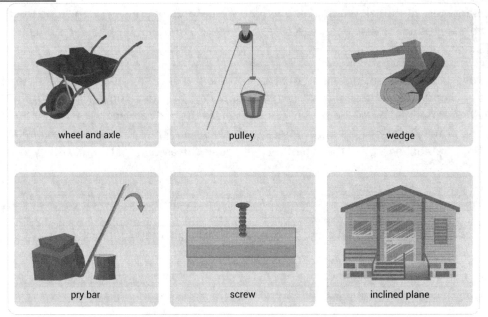

The use of simple machines can help by requiring less force to perform a task with the same result. This is also referred to as **mechanical advantage**.

Trying to lift a child into the air to pick an apple from a tree would require less force if the child was placed on the end of a teeter-totter and the adult pushed the other end of the teeter-totter down, in order to elevate the child to the same height to pick the apple. In this instance, the teeter-totter is a lever and provides a mechanical advantage to make the job easier.

Interactions of Energy

There is a fundamental law of **thermodynamics** (the study of heat and movement) called **Conservation of Energy**. This law states that energy cannot be created or destroyed, but rather energy is transferred to different forms involved in a process. For instance, a car pushed beginning at one end of a street will not continue down that street forever; it will gradually come to a stop some distance away from where it was originally pushed. This does not mean the energy has disappeared or has been exhausted; it means the energy has been transferred to different mediums surrounding the car.

The frictional force from the road on the tires dissipates some of the energy, the air resistance from the movement of the car dissipates some of the energy, the sound from the tires on the road dissipates some of the energy, and the force of gravity pulling on the car dissipates some of the energy. Each value can be calculated in a number of ways including measuring the sound waves from the tires, measuring the temperature change in the tires, measuring the distance moved by the car from start to finish, etc. It is important to understand that many processes factor into such a small situation, but all situations follow the conservation of energy.

As in the earlier example, the rollercoaster at the top of a hill has a measurable amount of potential energy, and when it rolls down the hill, it converts most of that energy into kinetic energy. There are still

224

additional factors like friction and air resistance working on the rollercoaster and dissipating some of the energy, but energy transfers in every situation.

Electrostatics

Electrostatics is the study of electric charges at rest. A charge comes from an atom having more or fewer electrons than protons. If an atom has more electrons than protons, it has a negative charge. If an atom has fewer electrons than protons, it has a positive charge. It is important to remember that opposite charges attract each other, while like charges repel each other. So, a negative attracts a positive, a negative repels a negative, and similarly, a positive repels a positive. Just as energy cannot be created or destroyed, neither can charge; charge is transferred. This transfer can be done through touch.

If a person wears socks and scuffs their feet across carpeting, they are transferring electrons to the carpeting through friction. If that person then goes to touch a light switch, they will receive a small shock, which is the electrons transferring from the switch to their hand. The person lost electrons to the carpet, which left them with a positive charge; therefore, the electrons from the switch attract to the person for the transfer. The shock is the electrons jumping from the switch to the person's finger.

Another method of charging an object is through induction. **Induction** is when a charged object is brought near, but not touched to, a neutral conducting object. The charged object will cause the electrons within the conductor to move. If the charged object is negative, the electrons will be induced away from the charged object and vice versa.

Yet another way to charge an object is through polarization. **Polarization** can be achieved by simply reconfiguring the electrons on an object. If a person were to rub a balloon on their hair, the balloon would then stick to a wall. This is because rubbing the balloon causes it to become negatively charged and when the balloon is held against a neutral wall, the negatively charged balloon repels all of the wall's electrons, causing a positively charged surface on the wall. This type of charge would be temporary, due to the massive size of the wall, and the charges would quickly redistribute.

Electric Current

Electrical current is the process by which electrons carry charge. In order to make the electrons move so that they can carry a charge, a change in voltage must be present. On a small scale, this is demonstrated through the electrons travelling from the light switch to a person's finger in the example where the person scuffed their socks on a carpet. The difference between the switch and the finger caused the electrons to move. On a larger and more sustained scale, this movement would need to be more controlled. This can be achieved through batteries/cells and generators. Batteries or cells have a chemical reaction that takes place inside, causing energy to be released and a charge to be able to move freely. Generators convert mechanical energy into electric energy.

If a wire is run from touching the end of a battery to the end of a light bulb, and then another is run from touching the base of the light bulb to the opposite end of the original battery, the light bulb will light up. This is due to a complete circuit being formed with the battery and the electrons being carried across the voltage drop (the two ends of the battery). The appearance of the light from the bulb is the visible heat caused by the friction of the electrons moving through the filament.

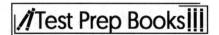

Electric Energy

Electric energy can be derived from a number of sources including coal, wind, sun, and nuclear reactions. Electricity has numerous applications, including being able to transfer into light, sound, heat, or magnetic forces.

Magnetic Forces

Magnetic forces can occur naturally in certain types of materials. If two straight rods are made from iron, they will naturally have a negative end (pole) and a positive end (pole). These charged poles react just like any charged item: opposite charges attract and like charges repel. They will attract each other when set up positive to negative, but if one rod is turned around, the two rods will repel each other due to the alignment of negative to negative and positive to positive.

These types of forces can also be created and amplified by using an electric current.

The relationship between magnetic forces and electrical forces can be explored by sending an electric current through a stretch of wire, which creates an electromagnetic force around the wire from the charge of the current, as long as the flow of electricity is sustained. This magnetic force can also attract and repel other items with magnetic properties. Depending upon the strength of the current in the wire, a smaller or larger magnetic force can be generated around this wire. As soon as the current is cut off, the magnetic force also stops.

Magnetic Energy

Magnetic energy can be harnessed, or controlled, from natural sources or from a generated source (a wire carrying electric current). Magnetic forces are used in many modern applications, including the creation of super-speed transportation. Super-magnets are used in rail systems and supply a cleaner form of energy than coal or gasoline.

Sound/Acoustic Energy

Just like light, sound travels in waves and both are forms of energy. The transmittance of a sound wave produced when plucking a guitar string sends vibrations at a specific frequency through the air, resulting in one's ear hearing a specific note or sets of notes that form a chord. If the same guitar is plugged into an electric amplifier, the strength of the wave is increased, producing what is perceived as a "louder" note. If a glass of water is set on the amplifier, the production of the sound wave can also be visually observed in the vibrations in the water. If the guitar were being plucked loudly enough and in great succession, the force created by the vibrations of the sound waves could even knock the glass off of the amplifier.

Waves can travel through different mediums. When they reach a different material (i.e., light traveling from air to water), they can bend around and through the new material. This is called **refraction**.

If one observes a straw in half a glass of water from above, the straw appears to be bent at the height of the water. The straw is still straight, but the observation of light passing from air to water (different materials) makes the straw seem as though it bends at the water line. This illusion occurs because the human eye can perceive the light travels differently through the two materials. The light might slow down in one material, or refract or reflect off of the material, causing differences in an object's appearance.

In another example, imagine a car driving straight along a paved road. If one or two of the tires hit the gravel along the side of the road, the entire car will pull in that direction, due to the tires in the gravel now traveling slower than the tires on the paved road. This is what happens when light travels from one medium to another: its path becomes warped, like the path of the car, rather than traveling in a straight line. This is why a straw appears to be bent when the light travels from water to air; the path is warped.

When waves encounter a barrier, like a closed door, parts of the wave may travel through tiny openings. Once a wave has moved through a narrow opening, the wave begins to spread out and may cause interference. This process is called **diffraction**.

Science as an Endeavor, Process, and Career

People of all cultures around the world utilize science in order to explore questions and find solutions to problems. The systematic process of designing, conducting, and analyzing experiments is universally known and respected. These processes are time-consuming and require specific knowledge and skills. Therefore, the pursuit of science is its own career path, with many smaller paths for each respective area of study (i.e., life sciences, chemical sciences, physical sciences). Of course, each of those paths splits into even more refined areas and requires much study and dedication. Men and women alike pursue scientific questions; some are driven by pure curiosity and others are compelled by finding a faster, or even a more economical way, of performing a task or producing an object.

Not all ideas, methods, or results are popular or accepted by society. Thus, the pursuit of science is often riddled with controversy. This has been an underlying theme since the early days of astronomical discovery. Copernicus was excommunicated from his religious establishment when he announced the belief that the sun, not the Earth, was the controlling body of the heavens known to humans at the time. Despite his having documented observations and calculations, those opposed to his theory could not be convinced. Copernicus experienced great ridicule and suffering due to his scientific research and assertions. In addition, other scientists have faced adverse scrutiny for their assertions including Galileo, Albert Einstein, and Stephen Hawking. In each case, logical thought, observations, and calculations have been used to demonstrate their ideas, yet opposition to their scientific beliefs still exists.

The possibilities for careers involving science range from conducting research, to the application of science and research (engineering), to academia (teaching). All of these avenues require intensive study and a thorough understanding of the respective branch of science and its components. An important factor of studying and applying science is being able to concisely and accurately communicate knowledge to other people. Many times this is done utilizing mathematics or even through demonstration. The necessity of communicating ideas, research, and results brings people from all nationalities together. This often lends to different cultures finding common ground for research and investigation, and opens lines of communication and cooperation.

Science as Inquiry

Scientific questions can be derived from a multitude of sources including observation, experience, or even just wondering how something is made or works. In order to answer these questions, experiments should be designed and conducted to try to achieve a solution. At the end of an experiment, there often is no clear solution and a new experiment must be designed to test the same question. If a sound, logical solution is reached through experimentation, then it must be repeatable, by the experimenter and any

other person wishing to test this solution. This entire process is commonly referred to as the **scientific method**.

A question or situation exists, a **hypothesis** (or a well-educated guess) is formulated, an **experiment** is designed to test this guess, a prediction is made as to what the outcome might be based upon research, and a conclusion is formed (either the guess was correct or not). This simple method is repeated over and over, as much as necessary for each question, idea, or proposed investigation.

An experiment must be carefully designed to include concerns for safety, use of proper instrumentation for measurement, systematic methods of documentation or data collection, appropriate mathematics for analysis of data and for the interpretation to draw valid conclusions. These conclusions must be explainable and verifiable by an outside source.

The importance of having an independent party test a solution is one of the critical parts of scientific inquiry. This ensures an experiment is free from bias, truly repeatable, and documentable to multiple sources. Without this confirmation, people could make erroneous claims and cause disastrous results. There would be no order to the inquiry of science.

In scientific experimentation, safety, respect for living things, and the effect on an environment must be acknowledged and protected, as necessary. There exist universal rules for research in order to preserve these underlying tenets. Most researchers or facilities that demonstrate an adherence to these rules garner the most support from others in the scientific community when accepting ideas.

Research

Part of the process of scientific inquiry is researching a problem or question. Before an experiment can be designed, proper research should be conducted into the question. The initial question needs to be well formed and based in logical reasoning. A literature review should be conducted on existing material pertaining to the subject in question, and confirmation of any experimentation on the question that has been conducted prior should be made. If prior experimentation exists, what were the results obtained and were any conclusions drawn from those results? In addition, research should be done on all possible information regarding the initial question, the experiment, how to investigate the question, and what tools will be necessary to draw conclusions and explain any findings. Just as an experiment must be unbiased, so should any research regarding the experiment. All sources of information need to be proven reliable and accredited. For instance, a person's account of their opinion on a situation does not constitute as a valid source for research. Sources should be free of opinion or speculation.

During experimentation, research should be conducted with appropriate mechanisms for observation and measurement. Knowing the proper tools and units for accurately measuring a volume or a mass is a fundamental skill of research. Researchers also need to be held to standards of ethics and honesty. The independent repetition of an experiment helps to ensure this level of accountability. Often, the most reliable resources are those of accredited experimenters, universities, and other research laboratories. In order for such sources to publish information, they should demonstrate strict adherence to scientific methods, precise measurements for observations, and specific mathematical reporting.

It is often common for different scientists in the same place, or even separate countries, to be conducting experiments to test the same hypothesis. This does not always lead to a race to see who finishes first, but it can lead to cooperative research and shared accolades if the results prove successful.

Awards for research, discoveries, and scientific application are often used by the scientific community to show appreciation for advancements in science.

Unifying Process of Science

Following the scientific method, and keeping to the standards of proper research and reporting, lends to easier communication of data and results. When information can be conveyed to multiple audiences in a manner of common understanding (i.e., mathematics), it increases the possibilities for the use of such information. Having other scientists understand an idea can also lead to further experimentation and discovery in that area. This leads to the further organization of information and a deeper understanding of our universe.

It is more systematic to group, sort, and organize information for commonalities in order to increase understanding. The organization of groups can also serve as a reference point when attempting to identify other members of that group. For instance, a newly discovered type of rock can be compared to known rocks and then better categorized as to its uses or properties, based upon how it appears and responds in experiments, when measured against known rocks. This occurs regularly when varying crystal rock structures are developed for use in super-cooled or super-conductive experiments because certain properties are more useful with regard to conduction and strength. In order to have knowledge and access to this type of variation of information, societies are formed and people from all over the world find ways to communicate and share in the scientific endeavor.

The communication of research can further questions and explorations across the world. This common goal of reaching new discoveries or uses for the application of science can bring people together. Oftentimes, the quest for scientific discovery is spawned by competition or the race to create something before another society or country. Examples of this include the race to explore space, the race for nuclear armaments, and the race to create and cure strains of deadly bacteria. In these situations, the urge to push scientific discovery ahead may not be for the most humanitarian motives; however, oftentimes these research prompts result in accidental discoveries that can solve other problems. The discoveries of vaccinations, stronger materials such as plastics, and cleaner forms of energy through superconducting crystals have all been accidental discoveries along the way of competitive scientific research. Whatever the motive for scientific discovery, it can be seen as a common thread across many nations with a potential to create unity through its demand for structure and organization.

Practice Questions

1. How many daughter cells are formed from one parent cell during meiosis?
   a. One
   b. Two
   c. Three
   d. Four

2. What is the total mechanical energy of a system?
   a. The total potential energy
   b. The total kinetic energy
   c. Kinetic energy plus potential energy
   d. Kinetic energy minus potential energy

3. What does the Lewis Dot structure of an element represent?
   a. The outer electron valence shell population
   b. The inner electron valence shell population
   c. The positioning of the element's protons
   d. The positioning of the element's neutrons

4. Which rock is formed from cooling magma underneath the Earth's surface?
   a. Extrusive sedimentary rocks
   b. Sedimentary rocks
   c. Igneous rocks
   d. Metamorphic rocks

5. Which of the following is most abundant in the Earth's atmosphere?
   a. Carbon dioxide
   b. Oxygen
   c. Nitrogen
   d. Water

See answers on next page.

Answer Explanations

1. D: Meiosis has the same phases as mitosis, except that they occur twice—once in meiosis I and once in meiosis II. During meiosis I, the cell splits into two. Each cell contains two sets of chromosomes. Next, during meiosis II, the two intermediate daughter cells divide again, producing four total haploid cells that each contain one set of chromosomes.

2. C: In any system, the total mechanical energy is the sum of the potential energy and the kinetic energy. Either value could be zero, but it still must be included in the total. Choices *A* and *B* only give the total potential or kinetic energy, respectively. Choice *D* gives the difference in the kinetic and potential energy.

3. A: A Lewis Dot structure shows the alignment of the valence (outer) shell electrons and how readily they can pair or bond with the valence shell electrons of other atoms to form a compound. Choice B is incorrect because the Lewis Dot structure aids in understanding how likely an atom is to bond or not bond with another atom, so the inner shell would add no relevance to understanding this likelihood. The positioning of protons and neutrons concerns the nucleus of the atom, which again would not lend information to the likelihood of bonding.

4. C: Igneous rocks are formed from the cooling of magma, both on and below the Earth's surface, which are classified as extrusive and intrusive, respectively. Sedimentary rocks are formed from deposition and cementation on the surface, and metamorphic rocks are formed from the transformation of sedimentary or igneous rocks through heat and pressure.

5. C: Nitrogen is the most abundant element in the atmosphere at 78%. Carbon dioxide and water don't make up a large percentage. Oxygen makes up only 21% of the atmosphere.

Practice Test #1

Reading and Language Arts

1. What area of study involves mechanics, usage, and sentence formation?
   a. Word analysis
   b. Spelling conventions
   c. Morphemes
   d. Phonics

2. How do the majority of high-frequency sight words differ from decodable words?
   a. They do not rhyme.
   b. They do not follow the Alphabetic Principle.
   c. They do not contain onsets.
   d. They contain rimes.

3. Reading fluency involves what key areas?
   a. Accuracy, rate, and prosody
   b. Accuracy, rate, and consistency
   c. Prosody, accuracy, and clarity
   d. Rate, prosody, and comprehension

4. Which of the following is a pre-reading strategy used to support comprehension?
   a. Skimming the text for content
   b. Summarizing the text effectively
   c. Organizing the main ideas and supporting details
   d. Clarifying unfamiliar ideas in the text

5. Which best describes the *plot* in fiction?
   a. What happens in the story or the storyline
   b. Character development
   c. The time and place of the story
   d. The events in the story that are true

6. Which option best portrays *second person point of view*?
   a. I went down the road, hoping to catch a glimpse of his retreating figure.
   b. You, my dear reader, can understand loss and grief, too.
   c. He left her standing there, alone to face the world.
   d. There's nothing wrong with Margaret.

7. Which option best defines a *fable*?
   a. A melancholy poem lamenting its subject's death
   b. An oral tradition influenced by culture
   c. A story with events that occur in threes and in sevens
   d. A short story with animals, fantastic creatures, or other forces within nature

8. Which of the following describes the organizational pattern of chronological or sequence order?
   a. Text organized by describing a dilemma and a possible solution
   b. Text organized by observing the consequences of an action
   c. Text organized by the timing of events or actions
   d. Text organized by analyzing the relative placement of an object or event

9. Read the following poem. Which option best describes the use of the spider?

   The spider as an artist
   Has never been employed
   Though his surpassing merit
   Is freely certified

   By every broom and Bridget
   Throughout a Christian land.
   Neglected son of genius,
   I take thee by the hand—Emily Dickinson, "Cobwebs"

   a. Idiom
   b. Haiku
   c. ABBA rhyming convention
   d. Simile

10. Which option best exemplifies an author's use of *alliteration* and *personification*?
    a. Her mood hung about her like a weary cape, very dull from wear.
    b. It shuddered, swayed, shook, and screamed its way into dust under hot flames.
    c. Driving past the still, silent house always sent a shiver down his spine.
    d. At its shoreline, visitors swore they heard the siren call of the cliffs above.

11. Read the following poem. Which option best depicts the rhyme scheme?

    A slumber did my spirit seal;
    I had no human fears:
    She seemed a thing that could not feel
    The touch of earthly years.—from William Wordsworth, "A Slumber Did My Spirit Seal"

    a. BAC BAC
    b. ABAB
    c. ABBA
    d. AB CD AB

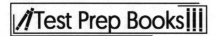

12. Read the following poem. Which option describes its corresponding meter?

> Half a league, half a league
> Half a league onward,
> All in the valley of Death
> Rode the six hundred.
> 'Forward, the Light Brigade!
> Charge for the guns!' he said:
> Into the valley of Death
> Rode the six hundred.—Alfred Lord Tennyson "The Charge of the Light Brigade"

a. Iambic (unstressed/stressed syllables)
b. Anapest (unstressed/unstressed/stressed syllables)
c. Spondee (stressed/stressed syllables)
d. Dactyl (stressed/unstressed/unstressed syllables)

13. Which phrase best completes the definition of a *memoir*?
a. A historical account of a person's life written by one who has intimate knowledge of the person's life
b. A historical account of a person's life written by the person himself or herself
c. A fictional account about a famous person
d. A nonfictional account about a famous person without factual reference

14. Which of the following is an example of a rhetorical strategy?
a. Cause and effect
b. Antimetabole
c. Individual vs. Self
d. Ad hominem

15. Which word serves as the best example of the poetic device, *onomatopoeia*?
a. Crackle
b. Eat
c. Provide
d. Walking

16. Which term best defines a *sonnet*?
a. A Japanese love poem
b. An eight-line stanza or poem
c. A fourteen-line poem written in iambic pentameter
d. A ceremonious, lyric poem

17. Every week, Cindy volunteers time at the local shelter. She always has a smile on her face, and she always talks to others with kindness and patience. Considering that her current job is very taxing, that two of her three children are still in diapers, and that her husband, Steve, the old curmudgeon, is the opposite of her in temperament, it's amazing that no one has ever seen her angry.

Based on the context in this passage, the best substitute for *curmudgeon* would be:
   a. Stingy
   b. Surly
   c. Scared
   d. Shy

The next question is based on the following passage.

Annabelle Rice started having trouble sleeping. Her biological clock was suddenly amiss and she began to lead a nocturnal schedule. She thought her insomnia was due to spending nights writing a horror story, but then she realized that even the idea of going outside into the bright world scared her to bits. She concluded she was now suffering from <u>heliophobia</u>.

18. Which of the following most accurately describes the meaning of the underlined word in the sentence above?
   a. Fear of dreams
   b. Fear of sunlight
   c. Fear of strangers
   d. Anxiety spectrum disorder

19. At the top of an encyclopedia's page are the following two guide terms: kingcraft and klieg light. Which one of the following words will be found on this page?
   a. Kleptomania
   b. Knead
   c. Kinesthesia
   d. Kickback

20. Which of the following is a primary source? *Select all that apply.*
   a. A critic's summary and review of a new book on the life of Abraham Lincoln
   b. A peer-reviewed scientific journal's table of contents
   c. A personal journal from a commander during World War II
   d. An encyclopedia entry discussing the Industrial Revolution

Question 21 refers to the following paragraph.

The Brookside area is an older part of Kansas City, developed mainly in the 1920s and 30s, and is considered one of the nation's first "planned" communities with shops, restaurants, parks, and churches all within a quick walk. A stroll down any street reveals charming two-story Tudor and Colonial homes with smaller bungalows sprinkled throughout the beautiful tree-lined streets. It is common to see lemonade stands on the corners and baseball games in the numerous "pocket" parks tucked neatly behind rows of well-manicured houses. The Brookside shops on 63rd street between Wornall Road and Oak Street are a hub of commerce and entertainment where residents freely shop

and dine with their pets (and children) in tow. This is also a common "hangout" spot for younger teenagers because it is easily accessible by bike for most. In short, it is an idyllic neighborhood just minutes from downtown Kansas City.

21. In what kind of publication might you read the above paragraph?
a. Fictional novel
b. Community profile
c. Newspaper article
d. Movie review

22. David Foster Wallace's *Infinite Jest* is the holy grail of modern literature. It will stand the test of time in its relevance. Every single person who starts reading *Infinite Jest* cannot physically put down the book until completing it.

Which of the following is the main point of the passage?
a. David Foster Wallace's *Infinite Jest* is the holy grail of modern literature.
b. *Infinite Jest* is a page-turner.
c. David Foster Wallace wrote *Infinite Jest*.
d. *Infinite Jest* is a modern classic for good reason, and everybody should read it.

Question 23 is based on the following two passages.

Passage 1

In the modern classroom, cell phones have become indispensable. Cell phones, which are essentially handheld computers, allow students to take notes, connect to the web, perform complex computations, teleconference, and participate in surveys. Most importantly, though, due to their mobility and excellent reception, cell phones are necessary in emergencies. Unlike tablets, laptops, or computers, cell phones are a readily available and free resource—most school district budgets are already strained to begin with—and since today's student is already strongly rooted in technology, when teachers incorporate cell phones, they're "speaking" the student's language, which increases the chance of higher engagement.

Passage 2

As with most forms of technology, there is an appropriate time and place for the use of cell phones. Students are comfortable with cell phones, so it makes sense when teachers allow cell phone use at their discretion. Allowing cell phone use can prove advantageous if done correctly. Unfortunately, if that's not the case—and often it isn't—then a sizable percentage of students pretend to pay attention while *surreptitiously* playing on their phones. This type of disrespectful behavior is often justified by the argument that cell phones are not only a privilege but also a right. Under this logic, confiscating phones is akin to rummaging through students' backpacks. This is in stark contrast to several decades ago when teachers regulated where and when students accessed information.

23. With which of the following statements would both the authors of Passages 1 and 2 agree?
    a. Teachers should incorporate cell phones into curriculum whenever possible.
    b. Cell phones are useful only when an experienced teacher uses them properly.
    c. Cell phones and, moreover, technology, are a strong part of today's culture.
    d. Despite a good lesson plan, cell phone disruptions are impossible to avoid.

The next four questions are based on the timeline of the life of Alexander Graham Bell.

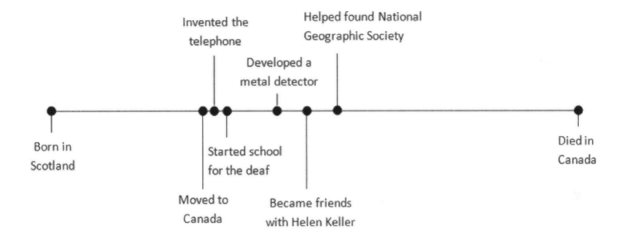

24. Which of the following is the event that occurred fourth on the timeline?
    a. Helped found National Geographic Society
    b. Developed a metal detector
    c. Moved to Canada
    d. Started a school for the deaf

25. Of the pairings in the answer choices, which has the longest gap between the two events?
    a. Moved to Canada and Became friends with Helen Keller
    b. Became friends with Helen Keller and Died in Canada
    c. Started school for the deaf and Developed a metal detector
    d. Born in Scotland and Started school for the deaf

26. Which one of the following statements is accurate based on the timeline?
    a. Bell did nothing significant after he helped found the National Geographic Society.
    b. Bell started a school for the deaf in Canada.
    c. Bell lived in at least two countries.
    d. Developing a metal detector allowed Bell to meet Helen Keller.

27. Which one of the following events occurred most recently?
    a. Bell's invention of the telephone
    b. Bell's founding of the school
    c. Bell's birth
    d. Bell's move to Canada

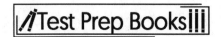

28. A student is starting a research assignment on Japanese-American internment camps during World War II, but she is unsure of how to gather relevant resources. Which of the following would be helpful advice for the student? *Select all that apply.*
   a. Conduct a broad internet search to get a wide view of the subject.
   b. Locate digital or print interviews of individuals interned in the camps.
   c. Find websites about Japanese culture such as fashion and politics.
   d. Locate texts in the library related to World War II in America and look for references to internment camps in the index.

29. When selecting a career path, it's important to explore the various options available. Many students entering college may shy away from a major because they don't know much about it. For example, many students won't opt for a career as an actuary, because they aren't exactly sure what it entails. But in doing so, they are missing out on a career that is very lucrative and in high demand. Actuaries work in the insurance field and assess risks and premiums. The average salary of an actuary is $100,000 per year. Another career option students may avoid, due to lack of knowledge of the field, is a hospitalist. This is a physician that specializes in the care of patients in a hospital, as opposed to those seen in private practices. The average salary of a hospitalist is upwards of $200,000. It pays to do some digging and find out more about these lesser-known career fields.
An actuary is:
   a. A doctor who works in a hospital
   b. The same as a hospitalist
   c. An insurance agent who works in a hospital
   d. A person who assesses insurance risks and premiums

30. Which of the following sentences has an error in capitalization?
   a. The East Coast has experienced very unpredictable weather this year.
   b. My Uncle owns a home in Florida, where he lives in the winter.
   c. I am taking English Composition II on campus this fall.
   d. There are several nice beaches we can visit on our trip to the Jersey Shore this summer.

31. Which of the following sentences uses correct punctuation?
   a. Carole is not currently working; her focus is on her children at the moment.
   b. Carole is not currently working and her focus is on her children at the moment.
   c. Carole is not currently working, her focus is on her children at the moment.
   d. Carole is not currently working her focus is on her children at the moment.

32. Which of these examples is a compound sentence?
   a. Alex and Shane spent the morning coloring and later took a walk down to the park.
   b. After coloring all morning, Alex and Shane spent the afternoon at the park.
   c. Alex and Shane spent the morning coloring, and then they took a walk down to the park.
   d. After coloring all morning and spending part of the day at the park, Alex and Shane took a nap.

33. Which of these examples shows incorrect use of subject-verb agreement?
   a. Neither of the cars are parked on the street.
   b. Both of my kids are going to camp this summer.
   c. Any of your friends are welcome to join us on the trip in November.
   d. Each of the clothing options is appropriate for the job interview.

238

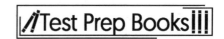

34. Which example shows correct comma usage for dates?
    a. The due date for the final paper in the course is Monday, May 16, 2016.
    b. The due date for the final paper in the course is Monday, May 16 2016.
    c. The due date for the final project in the course is Monday, May, 16, 2016.
    d. The due date for the final project in the course is Monday May 16, 2016.

35. Which of the following passages best displays clarity, fluency, and parallelism?
    a. Ernest Hemingway is probably the most noteworthy of expatriate authors. Hemingway's concise writing style, void of emotion and stream of consciousness, had a lasting impact, one which resonates to this very day. In Hemingway's novels, much like in American cinema, the hero acts without thinking, is living in the moment, and is repressing physical and emotional pain.
    b. Ernest Hemingway is probably the most noteworthy of expatriate authors since his concise writing style is void of emotion and stream of consciousness and has had a lasting impact on Americans which has resonated to this very day, and Hemingway's novels are much like in American cinema. The hero acts. He doesn't think. He lives in the moment. He represses physical and emotional pain.
    c. Ernest Hemingway is probably the most noteworthy of authors. His concise writing style, void of emotion and consciousness, had a lasting impact, one which resonates to this very day. In Hemingway's novels, much like in American cinema, the hero acts without thinking, lives in the moment, and represses physical and emotional pain.
    d. Ernest Hemingway is probably the most noteworthy of expatriate authors. His concise writing style, void of emotion and stream of consciousness, had a lasting impact, one which resonates to this very day. In Hemingway's novels, much like in American cinema, the hero acts without thinking, lives in the moment, and represses physical and emotional pain.

36. When giving a presentation, one should have three to five bullet points per slide. It is impossible for a presenter to memorize an entire speech, but if you can memorize the main ideas connected to the bullet points, then your speech will be more natural and fluid.
The point(s) of view represented in this passage is/are:
    a. First person only
    b. Third person only
    c. Second person and third person
    d. First person and third person

37. Based on the words *transfer, transact, translation, transport*, what is the meaning of the prefix *trans*?
    a. Separation
    b. All, everywhere
    c. Forward
    d. Across, beyond, over

38. An antibiotic is prescribed to eliminate bacterial infections; someone who is antisocial ignores society and laws. Based on these two definitions, the Latin prefix *anti-* would most likely mean:
    a. Reduce
    b. Revolt
    c. Oppose
    d. Without

239

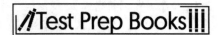
39. *Conform* means to adjust one's behavior to better fit in with social norms. Inform means to communicate new knowledge to another. Based on these definitions, the Latin suffix *-form* most likely means:
   a. Match
   b. Relay
   c. Negate
   d. Shape

40. Volume, articulation, and awareness of audience help with what practice?
   a. Effective instruction
   b. Communication
   c. Active listening
   d. Oral presentations

41. Offering a presenter with undivided attention and asking relevant and timely questions are examples of what skill set?
   a. Active listening skills
   b. Effective speaking
   c. Formal communication
   d. Informal communication

42. What is the method called that teachers use before and after reading to improve critical thinking and comprehension?
   a. Self-monitoring comprehension
   b. KWL charts
   c. Metacognitive skills
   d. Directed reading-thinking activities

The next question is based on the following passage.

> A famous children's author recently published a historical fiction novel under a pseudonym; however, it did not sell as many copies as her children's books. In her earlier years, she had majored in history and earned a graduate degree in Antebellum American History, which is the time frame of her new novel. Critics praised this newest work far more than the children's series that made her famous. In fact, her new novel was nominated for the prestigious Albert J. Beveridge Award but still isn't selling like her children's books, which fly off the shelves because of her name alone.

43. Which one of the following statements might be accurately inferred based on the above passage?
   a. The famous children's author produced an inferior book under her pseudonym.
   b. The famous children's author is the foremost expert on Antebellum America.
   c. The famous children's author did not receive the bump in publicity for her historical novel that it would have received if it were written under her given name.
   d. People generally prefer to read children's series than historical fiction.

44. Which of the following sentences uses second person point of view?
    a. I don't want to make plans for the weekend before I see my work schedule.
    b. She had to miss the last three yoga classes due to illness.
    c. Pluto is no longer considered a planet because it is not gravitationally dominant.
    d. Be sure to turn off all of the lights before locking up for the night.

45. What is the most valuable strategy for helping children understand new words?
    a. Phonics instruction
    b. Pre-teaching
    c. Self-monitoring
    d. Context clues

46. Context clues assist vocabulary development by providing:
    a. A knowledge of roots, prefixes, and suffixes that are used to determine the meaning a word
    b. Information within the sentence that surrounds an unknown word and is used to determine the word's meaning
    c. Content learned in previous grades that serves as a bridge to the new term
    d. Background knowledge to fill in a missing word within a sentence

47. Which organizational style is used in the following passage?

    There are several reasons why the new student café has not been as successful as expected. One factor is that prices are higher than originally advertised, so many students cannot afford to buy food and beverages there. Also, the café closes rather early; as a result, students go out in town to other late-night gathering places rather than meeting friends at the café on campus.

    a. Cause and effect order
    b. Compare and contrast order
    c. Spatial order
    d. Time order

48. The assassination of Archduke Franz Ferdinand of Austria is often ascribed as the cause of World War I. However, the assassination merely lit the fuse in a combustible situation since many of the world powers were in complicated and convoluted military alliances. For example, England, France, and Russia entered into a mutual defense treaty seven years prior to World War I. Even without Franz Ferdinand's assassination _____.
Which of the following most logically completes the passage?
    a. A war between the world powers was extremely likely.
    b. World War I never would have happened.
    c. England, France, and Russia would have started the war.
    d. Austria would have started the war.

The next question is based on the following passage.

    In 2015, 28 countries, including Estonia, Portugal, Slovenia, and Latvia, scored significantly higher than the United States on standardized high school math tests. In the 1960s, the United States consistently ranked first in the world. Today, the United States spends more than $800 billion dollars on education, which exceeds the next highest

241

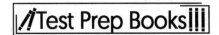
country by more than $600 billion dollars. The United States also leads the world in spending per school-aged child by an enormous margin.

49. If these statements above are factual, which of the following statements must be correct?
   a. Outspending other countries on education has benefits beyond standardized math tests.
   b. The United States' education system is corrupt and broken.
   c. The standardized math tests are not representative of American academic prowess.
   d. Spending more money does not guarantee success on standardized math tests.

50. Philadelphia is home to some excellent walking tours where visitors can learn more about the culture and rich history of the city of brotherly love.

   What are the adjectives in the preceding sentence?

   a. Philadelphia, tours, visitors, culture, history, city, love
   b. Excellent, walking, rich, brotherly
   c. Is, can, learn
   d. To, about, of

51. The realtor showed _____ and _____ a house on Wednesday afternoon. Which of the following pronoun pairs should be used in the blanks above?
   a. she, I
   b. she, me
   c. me, her
   d. her, me

52. Which of the following examples uses correct punctuation?
   a. Recommended supplies for the hunting trip include the following: rain gear, large backpack, hiking boots, flashlight, and non-perishable foods.
   b. I left the store, because I forgot my wallet.
   c. As soon as the team checked into the hotel; they met in the lobby for a group photo.
   d. None of the furniture came in on time: so they weren't able to move in to the new apartment.

53. Which of the following sentences shows correct word usage?
   a. Your going to have to put you're jacket over their.
   b. You're going to have to put your jacket over there.
   c. Your going to have to put you're jacket over they're.
   d. You're going to have to put your jacket over their.

54. A teacher notices that, when students are talking to each other between classes, they are using their own unique vocabulary words and expressions to talk about their daily lives. When the teacher hears these non-standard words that are specific to one age or cultural group, what type of language is she listening to?
   a. Slang
   b. Jargon
   c. Dialect
   d. Vernacular

55. Which of the following should be evaluated to ensure the credibility of a source?
   a. The publisher, the author, and the references
   b. The subject, the title, and the audience
   c. The organization, stylistic choices, and transition words
   d. The length, the tone, and the contributions of multiple authors

56. Which of the following is true of using citations in a research paper?
   a. If a source is cited in the bibliography, it is not necessary to cite it in the paper as well.
   b. In-text citations differ in format from bibliographic citations.
   c. Students should learn one standard method of citing sources.
   d. Books and articles need to be cited, but not websites or multimedia sources.

57. Which of the following is true regarding the integration of source material to maintain the flow of ideas in a research project or paper?
   a. There should be at least one quotation in every paragraph.
   b. If a source is paraphrased instead of being directly quoted, it is not necessary to include a citation.
   c. An author's full name must be used in every signal phrase.
   d. In-text citations should be used to support the paper's argument without overwhelming the student's writing.

Questions 58-62 are based on the following passage:

> The Middle Ages were a time of great superstition and theological debate. Many beliefs were developed and practiced, while some died out or were listed as heresy. Boethianism is a Medieval theological philosophy that attributes sin to gratification and righteousness with virtue and God's providence. Boethianism holds that sin, greed, and corruption are means to attain temporary pleasure, but that they inherently harm the person's soul as well as other human beings.
>
> In *The Canterbury Tales,* we observe more instances of bad actions punished than goodness being rewarded. This would appear to be some reflection of Boethianism. In the "Pardoner's Tale," all three thieves wind up dead, which is a result of their desire for wealth. Each wrong doer pays with their life, and they are unable to enjoy the wealth they worked to steal. Within his tales, Chaucer gives reprieve to people undergoing struggle, but also interweaves stories of contemptible individuals being cosmically punished for their wickedness. The thieves idolize physical wealth, which leads to their downfall. This same theme and ideological principle of Boethianism is repeated in the "Friar's Tale," whose summoner character attempts to gain further wealth by partnering with a demon. The summoner's refusal to repent for his avarice and corruption leads to the demon dragging his soul to Hell. Again, we see the theme of the individual who puts faith and morality aside in favor for a physical prize. The result, of course, is that the summoner loses everything.
>
> The examples of the righteous being rewarded tend to appear in a spiritual context within the *Canterbury Tales*. However, there are a few instances where we see goodness resulting in physical reward. In the Prioress' Tale, we see corporal punishment for barbarism *and* a reward for goodness. The Jews are punished for their murder of the

243

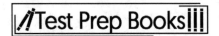

child, giving a sense of law and order (though racist) to the plot. While the boy does die, he is granted a lasting reward by being able to sing even after his death, a miracle that marks that the murdered youth led a pure life. Here, the miracle represents eternal favor with God.

Again, we see the theological philosophy of Boethianism in Chaucer's *The Canterbury Tales* through acts of sin and righteousness and the consequences that follow. When pleasures of the world are sought instead of God's favor, we see characters being punished in tragic ways. However, the absence of worldly lust has its own set of consequences for the characters seeking to obtain God's favor.

58. What would be a potential reward for living a good life, as described in Boethianism?
    a.   A long life sustained by the good deeds one has done over a lifetime
    b.   Wealth and fertility for oneself and the extension of one's family line
    c.   Vengeance for those who have been persecuted by others who have a capacity for committing wrongdoing
    d.   God's divine favor for one's righteousness

59. What might be the main reason why the author chose to discuss Boethianism through examining The Canterbury Tales?
    a.   *The Canterbury Tales* is a well-known text.
    b.   *The Canterbury Tales* is the only known fictional text that contains use of Boethianism.
    c.   *The Canterbury Tales* presents a manuscript written in the medieval period that can help illustrate Boethianism through stories and show how people of the time might have responded to the idea.
    d.   Within each individual tale in *The Canterbury Tales*, the reader can read about different levels of Boethianism and how each level leads to greater enlightenment.

60. What "ideological principle" is the author referring to in the middle of the second paragraph when talking about the "Friar's Tale"?
    a.   The principle that the act of ravaging another's possessions is the same as ravaging one's soul.
    b.   The principle that thieves who idolize physical wealth will be punished in an earthly sense as well as eternally.
    c.   The principle that fraternization with a demon will result in one losing everything, including their life.
    d.   The principle that a desire for material goods leads to moral malfeasance punishable by a higher being.

61. Which of the following words, if substituted for the word *avarice* in paragraph two, would LEAST change the meaning of the sentence?
    a.   Perniciousness
    b.   Pithiness
    c.   Covetousness
    d.   Precariousness

62. Based on the passage, what view does Boethianism take on desire?
    a. Desire does not exist in the context of Boethianism
    b. Desire is a virtue and should be welcomed
    c. Having desire is evidence of demonic possession
    d. Desire for pleasure can lead toward sin

Questions 63-68 are based upon the following passage:

This excerpt is an adaptation from Abraham Lincoln's Address Delivered at the Dedication of the Cemetery at Gettysburg, November 19, 1863.

Four score and seven years ago our fathers brought forth on this continent, a new nation, conceived in Liberty, and dedicated to the proposition that all men are created equal.

Now we are engaged in a great civil war, testing whether that nation, or any nation so conceived and so dedicated, can long endure. We are met on a great battle-field of that war. We have come to dedicate a portion of that field, as a final resting place for those who here gave their lives that that nation might live. It is altogether fitting and proper that we should do this.

But, in a larger sense, we can not dedicate—we can not consecrate—we cannot hallow—this ground. The brave men, living and dead, who struggled here, have consecrated it, far above our poor power to add or detract. The world will little note, nor long remember what we say here, but it can never forget what they did here. It is for us the living, rather, to be dedicated here to the unfinished work which they who fought here have thus far so nobly advanced. It is rather for us to be here dedicated to the great task remaining before us—that from these honored dead we take increased devotion to that cause for which they gave the last full measure of devotion—that we here highly resolve that these dead shall not have died in vain—that this nation, under God, shall have a new birth of freedom—and that government of the people, by the people, for the people, shall not perish from the earth.

63. The best description for the phrase *four score and seven years ago* is which of the following?
    a. A unit of measurement
    b. A period of time
    c. A literary movement
    d. A statement of political reform

64. What is the setting of this text?
    a. A battleship off of the coast of France
    b. A desert plain on the Sahara Desert
    c. A battlefield in North America
    d. The residence of Abraham Lincoln

245

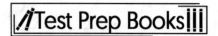
65. Which war is Abraham Lincoln referring to in the following passage?

> Now we are engaged in a great civil war, testing whether that nation, or any nation so conceived and so dedicated, can long endure.

a. World War I
b. The War of the Spanish Succession
c. World War II
d. The American Civil War

66. What message is the author trying to convey through this address?
a. The audience should perpetuate the ideals of freedom that the soldiers died fighting for.
b. The audience should honor the dead by establishing an annual memorial service.
c. The audience should form a militia that would overturn the current political structure.
d. The audience should forget the lives that were lost and discredit the soldiers.

67. Which rhetorical device is being used in the following passage?

> ...we here highly resolve that these dead shall not have died in vain—that this nation, under God, shall have a new birth of freedom—and that government of the people, by the people, for the people, shall not perish from the earth.

a. Antimetabole
b. Antiphrasis
c. Anaphora
d. Epiphora

68. What is the effect of Lincoln's statement in the following passage?

> But, in a larger sense, we can not dedicate—we can not consecrate—we can not hallow—this ground. The brave men, living and dead, who struggled here, have consecrated it, far above our poor power to add or detract.

a. His comparison emphasizes the great sacrifice of the soldiers who fought in the war.
b. His comparison serves as a reminder of the inadequacies of his audience.
c. His comparison serves as a catalyst for guilt and shame among audience members.
d. His comparison attempts to illuminate the great differences between soldiers and civilians.

69. Julia Robinson, an avid photographer in her spare time, was able to capture stunning shots of the local wildlife on her last business trip to Australia.

Which of the following is an adjective in the preceding sentence?

a. Time
b. Capture
c. Avid
d. Photographer

70. When it gets warm in the spring, _____ and _____ like to go fishing at Cobbs Creek.

Which of the following word pairs should be used in the blanks above?

a. me, him
b. he, I
c. him, I
d. he, me

71. At last night's company function, in honor of Mr. Robertson's retirement, several employees spoke kindly about his career achievements.
In the preceding sentence, what part of speech is the word *function*?
a. Adjective
b. Adverb
c. Verb
d. Noun

72. Which of the examples uses the correct plural form?
a. Tomatos
b. Analysis
c. Cacti
d. Criterion

73. Which of the following examples uses correct punctuation?
a. The moderator asked the candidates, "Is each of you prepared to discuss your position on global warming?".
b. The moderator asked the candidates, "Is each of you prepared to discuss your position on global warming?"
c. The moderator asked the candidates, 'Is each of you prepared to discuss your position on global warming?'
d. The moderator asked the candidates, "Is each of you prepared to discuss your position on global warming"?

74. In which of the following sentences does the word *part* function as an adjective?
a. The part Brian was asked to play required many hours of research.
b. She parts ways with the woodsman at the end of the book.
c. The entire team played a part in the success of the project.
d. Ronaldo is part Irish on his mother's side of the family.

75. All of Shannon's family and friends helped her to celebrate her 50th birthday at Café Sorrento.

Which of the following is the complete subject of the preceding sentence?

a. Family and friends
b. All
c. All of Shannon's family and friends
d. Shannon's family and friends

76. Which of the following examples correctly uses quotation marks?
 a. "Where the Red Fern Grows" was one of my favorite novels as a child.
 b. Though he is famous for his roles in films like "The Great Gatsby" and "Titanic," Leonardo DiCaprio never won an Oscar until 2016 for his work in "The Revenant".
 c. Sylvia Plath's poem, "Daddy" will be the subject of this week's group discussion.
 d. "The New York Times" reported that many fans are disappointed in some of the trades made by the Yankees this off-season.

77. Which of the following sentences shows correct word usage?
 a. It's often been said that work is better then rest.
 b. Its often been said that work is better then rest.
 c. It's often been said that work is better than rest.
 d. Its often been said that work is better than rest.

78. Which of the following is an imperative sentence?
 a. Pennsylvania's state flag includes two draft horses and an eagle.
 b. Go down to the basement and check the hot water heater for signs of a leak.
 c. You must be so excited to have a new baby on the way!
 d. How many countries speak Spanish?

79. Which of the following examples is a compound sentence?
 a. Shawn and Jerome played soccer in the backyard for two hours.
 b. Marissa last saw Elena and talked to her this morning.
 c. The baby was sick, so I decided to stay home from work.
 d. Denise, Kurt, and Eric went for a run after dinner.

80. Which of the following sentences uses correct subject-verb agreement?
 a. There is two constellations that can be seen from the back of the house.
 b. At least four of the sheep needs to be sheared before the end of summer.
 c. Lots of people were auditioning for the singing competition on Saturday.
 d. Everyone in the group have completed the assignment on time.

Mathematics

1. Which of the following numbers has the greatest value?
 a. 1.43785
 b. 1.07548
 c. 1.43592
 d. 0.89409

2. The value of 6×12 is the same as:
 a. $2 \times 4 \times 4 \times 2$
 b. $7 \times 4 \times 3$
 c. $6 \times 6 \times 3$
 d. $3 \times 3 \times 4 \times 2$

3. Which of the following is largest?
   a. 0.45
   b. 0.096
   c. 0.3
   d. 0.313

4. What is the value of b in this equation?

$$5b - 4 = 2b + 17$$

   a. 13
   b. 24
   c. 7
   d. 21

5. In 2015, it was estimated that there were 7,350,000,000 people living on Earth. Express this value in scientific notation.
   a. 7.35×10^7
   b. 7.35×10^9
   c. 73.5×10^8
   d. 73.5×10^9

6. Express the solution to the following problem in decimal form:

$$\frac{3}{5} \times \frac{7}{10} \div \frac{1}{2}$$

   a. 0.042
   b. 84%
   c. 0.84
   d. 0.42

7. What is the product of two irrational numbers?
   a. Irrational
   b. Rational
   c. Irrational or rational
   d. Complex and imaginary

8. How is the number -4 classified?
   a. Real, rational, integer, whole, natural
   b. Real, rational, integer, natural
   c. Real, rational, integer
   d. Real, irrational

9. Twenty is 40% of what number?
   a. 50
   b. 8
   c. 200
   d. 5,000

249

10. What is the product of the following expression?

$$(4x - 8)(5x^2 + x + 6)$$

    a. $20x^3 - 36x^2 + 16x - 48$
    b. $6x^3 - 41x^2 + 12x + 15$
    c. $20x^3 + 11x^2 - 37x - 12$
    d. $2x^3 - 11x^2 - 32x + 20$

11. What is the solution for the following equation?

$$\frac{x^2 + x - 30}{x - 5} = 11$$

    a. $x = -6$
    b. There is no solution.
    c. $x = 16$
    d. $x = 5$

12. What is the simplified form of the expression $1.2 \times 10^{12} \div 3.0 \times 10^8$?
    a. 0.4×10^4
    b. 4.0×10^4
    c. 4.0×10^3
    d. 3.6×10^{20}

13. Write the expression for six less than three times the sum of twice a number and one.
    a. $2x + 1 - 6$
    b. $3x + 1 - 6$
    c. $3(x + 1) - 6$
    d. $3(2x + 1) - 6$

14. What is the solution to $4 \times 7 + (25 - 21)^2 \div 2$?
    a. 512
    b. 36
    c. 60.5
    d. 22

15. What value of x would solve the following equation?

$$9x + x - 7 = 16 + 2x$$

    a. $x = -4$
    b. $x = 3$
    c. $x = \frac{9}{8}$
    d. $x = \frac{23}{8}$

16. Arrange the following numbers from least to greatest value:

$$0.85, \frac{4}{5}, \frac{2}{3}, \frac{91}{100}$$

   a. $0.85, \frac{4}{5}, \frac{2}{3}, \frac{91}{100}$

   b. $\frac{4}{5}, 0.85, \frac{91}{100}, \frac{2}{3}$

   c. $\frac{2}{3}, \frac{4}{5}, 0.85, \frac{91}{100}$

   d. $0.85, \frac{91}{100}, \frac{4}{5}, \frac{2}{3}$

17. Keith's bakery had 252 customers go through its doors last week. This week, that number increased to 378. Express this increase as a percentage.

   a. 26%

   b. 50%

   c. 35%

   d. 12%

18. Simplify the following fraction:

$$\frac{\frac{5}{7}}{\frac{9}{11}}$$

   a. $\frac{55}{63}$

   b. $\frac{7}{1,000}$

   c. $\frac{13}{15}$

   d. $\frac{5}{11}$

19. If $\frac{5}{2} \div \frac{1}{3} = n$, then n is between:

   a. 5 and 7

   b. 7 and 9

   c. 9 and 11

   d. 3 and 5

20. This chart indicates how many sales of CDs, vinyl records, and MP3 downloads occurred over the last year. Approximately what percentage of the total sales was from CDs?

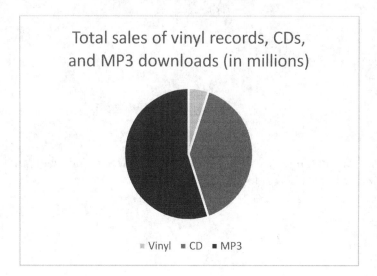

Total sales of vinyl records, CDs, and MP3 downloads (in millions)

▤ Vinyl   ▪ CD   ▪ MP3

    a. 55%
    b. 25%
    c. 40%
    d. 5%

21. Express as a reduced mixed number 54/15.
    a. 3 3/5
    b. 3 1/15
    c. 3 3/54
    d. 3 1/54

22. Express as an improper fraction 8 3/7.
    a. 11/7
    b. 21/8
    c. 5/3
    d. 59/7

23. $52.3 \times 10^{-3} =$
    a. 0.00523
    b. 0.0523
    c. 0.523
    d. 523

24. Mom's car drove 72 miles in 90 minutes. How fast did she drive in feet per second?
    a. 0.8 feet per second
    b. 48.9 feet per second
    c. 0.009 feet per second
    d. 70.4 feet per second

25. For the following similar triangles, what are the values of x and y (rounded to one decimal place)?

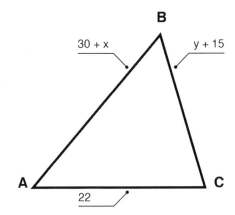
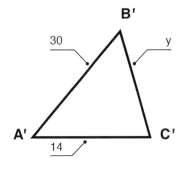

    a. $x = 16.5, y = 25.1$
    b. $x = 19.5, y = 24.1$
    c. $x = 17.1, y = 26.3$
    d. $x = 26.3, y = 17.1$

26. The triangle shown below is a right triangle. What's the value of x?

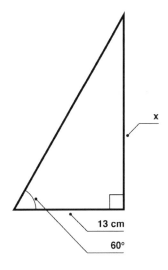

    a. $x = 1.73$
    b. $x = 0.57$
    c. $x = 13$
    d. $x = 22.52$

27. Given the following triangle, what's the length of the missing side? Round the answer to the nearest tenth.

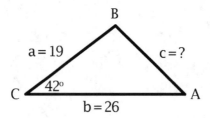

a. 17.0
b. 17.4
c. 18.0
d. 18.4

28. The total perimeter of a rectangle is 36 cm. If the length is 12 cm, what is the width?
a. 3 cm
b. 12 cm
c. 6 cm
d. 8 cm

29. What's the probability of rolling a 6 exactly once in two rolls of a die?
a. $\frac{1}{3}$
b. $\frac{1}{36}$
c. $\frac{1}{6}$
d. $\frac{11}{36}$

30. Two cards are drawn from a shuffled deck of 52 cards. What's the probability that both cards are kings if the first card isn't replaced after it's drawn?
a. $\frac{1}{169}$
b. $\frac{1}{221}$
c. $\frac{1}{13}$
d. $\frac{4}{13}$

31. For a group of 20 men, the median weight is 180 pounds and the range is 30 pounds. If each man gains 10 pounds, which of the following would be true?
a. The median weight will increase, and the range will remain the same.
b. The median weight and range will both remain the same.
c. The median weight will stay the same, and the range will increase.
d. The median weight and range will both increase.

32. Five of six numbers have a sum of 25. The average of all six numbers is 6. What is the sixth number?
   a. 8
   b. 10
   c. 11
   d. 12

33. If the ordered pair $(-3, -4)$ is reflected over the x-axis, what's the new ordered pair?
   a. $(-3, -4)$
   b. $(3, -4)$
   c. $(3, 4)$
   d. $(-3, 4)$

34. The graph shows the position of a car over a 10-second time interval. Which of the following is the correct interpretation of the graph for the interval 1 to 3 seconds?

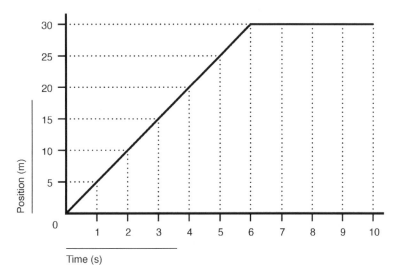

   a. The car remains in the same position.
   b. The car is traveling at a speed of 5 m/s.
   c. The car is traveling up a hill.
   d. The car is traveling at 5 mph.

35. An equilateral triangle has a perimeter of 18 feet. If a square whose sides have the same length as one side of the triangle is built, what will be the area of the square?
   a. 6 square feet
   b. 36 square feet
   c. 256 square feet
   d. 1,000 square feet

36. A cube has sides that are 7 inches long. What is the cube's volume?
   a. 49 in^3
   b. 343 in^3
   c. 294 in^3
   d. 28 in^3

255

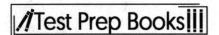

37. Approximately how many kilometers is 4,382 feet? There are 0.3048 meters in 1 foot.
   a. 1.336 kilometers
   b. 14,376 kilometers
   c. 1.437 kilometers
   d. 13,336 kilometers

38. What is the length of the other leg of a right triangle with a hypotenuse of 10 inches and a leg of 8 inches?
   a. 6 in
   b. 18 in
   c. 80 in
   d. 13 in

39. Five students take a test. The scores of the first four students are 80, 85, 75, and 60. If the median score is 80, which of the following could NOT be the score of the fifth student?
   a. 60
   b. 80
   c. 85
   d. 100

40. If Sarah reads at an average rate of 21 pages in four nights, how long will it take her to read 140 pages?
   a. 6 nights
   b. 26 nights
   c. 8 nights
   d. 27 nights

41. Alan currently weighs 200 pounds, but he wants to lose weight to get down to 175 pounds. What is this difference in kilograms? (1 pound is approximately equal to 0.45 kilograms.)
   a. 9 kg
   b. 11.25 kg
   c. 78.75 kg
   d. 90 kg

42. Johnny earns $2,334.50 from his job each month. He pays $1,437 for monthly expenses. Johnny is planning a vacation in 3 months that he estimates will cost $1,750 total. How much will Johnny have left over from three months of saving once he pays for his vacation?
   a. $948.50
   b. $584.50
   c. $852.50
   d. $942.50

43. Kimberley earns $10 an hour babysitting, and after 10 p.m., she earns $12 an hour, with the amount paid being rounded to the nearest hour accordingly. On her last job, she worked from 5:30 p.m. to 11 p.m. In total, how much did Kimberley earn on her last job?

    a. $45
    b. $57
    c. $62
    d. $42

44. A line that travels from the bottom-left of a graph to the upper-right of the graph indicates what kind of relationship between an independent and a dependent variable?

    a. Positive
    b. Negative
    c. Exponential
    d. Logarithmic

45. Which of the following is the best description of the relationship between x and y?

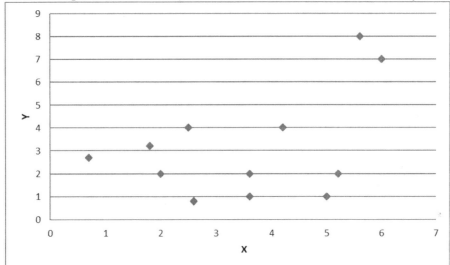

    a. The data has normal distribution.
    b. x and y have a negative relationship.
    c. No relationship
    d. x and y have a positive relationship.

46. How do you solve $V = lwh$ for h?

    a. $lwV = h$
    b. $h = \dfrac{V}{lw}$
    c. $h = \dfrac{Vl}{w}$
    d. $h = \dfrac{Vw}{l}$

47. What type of function is modeled by the values in the following table?

x	$f(x)$
1	2
2	4
3	8
4	16
5	32

a. Linear
b. Exponential
c. Quadratic
d. Cubic

48. Which of the following is a factor of both $x^2 + 4x + 4$ and $x^2 - x - 6$?
a. $x - 3$
b. $x + 2$
c. $x - 2$
d. $x + 3$

49. If $4x - 3 = 5$, what is the value of x?
a. 1
b. 2
c. 3
d. 4

50. A ball is drawn at random from a ball pit containing 8 red balls, 7 yellow balls, 6 green balls, and 5 purple balls. What's the probability that the ball drawn is yellow?
a. $\frac{1}{26}$
b. $\frac{19}{26}$
c. $\frac{7}{26}$
d. 1

Social Studies

1. An elementary teacher is planning a social studies lesson on individuals who have had an important historical influence to the state of Georgia. All EXCEPT which of the following individuals should be discussed in this lesson?
a. Andrew Jackson
b. John White
c. William T. Sherman
d. Booker T. Washington

2. What is NOT a responsibility for citizens of democracy?
    a. To stay aware of current issues and history
    b. To avoid political action
    c. To actively vote in elections
    d. To understand and obey laws

Question 3 is based on the following passage:

> We hold these Truths to be self-evident: that all Men are created equal; that they are endowed by their creator with certain inalienable rights; that among these are life, liberty, and the pursuit of happiness: that to secure these rights, governments are instituted among men, deriving their just powers from the consent of the governed; that whenever any form of government becomes destructive of these ends, it is the right of the people to alter or abolish it, and to institute new government, laying its foundation on such principles, and organizing its powers in such form, as to them shall seem most likely to affect their safety and happiness.

> Prudence indeed will dictate that governments long established should not be changed for light and transient causes; and accordingly all experience hath shown that mankind are more disposed to suffer while evils are sufferable, than to right themselves by abolishing the forms to which they are accustomed. But when a long train of abuses and usurpations begun at a distinguished period and pursuing invariably the same object, evinces a design to reduce them under absolute despotism, it is their right, it is their duty to throw off such government, and to provide new guards for their future security

> Declaration of Independence, adopted July 4, 1776

3. What is the main purpose of the excerpt?
    a. Provide a justification for revolution when the government infringes on "certain inalienable rights"
    b. Provide specific evidence of the "train of abuses"
    c. Provide an argument why "all Men are created equal"
    d. Provide an analysis of the importance of "life, liberty, and the pursuit of happiness"

4. Which member of British parliament convinced King George II in 1732 to colonize the area that is now Georgia with individuals from Britain's overflowing debtor prisons?
    a. James Oglethorpe
    b. Button Gwinnett
    c. George Walton
    d. Lyman Hall

5. A fourth-grade teacher is having students work in small groups to research and present about historical figures instrumental in leading the charge for discussion at the Constitutional Convention held in Philadelphia in 1787. Which of the following gentlemen would NOT be assigned to a group for this project?
    a. George Washington
    b. Alexander Hamilton
    c. Thomas Jefferson
    d. James Madison

259

6. A text read in a third-grade classroom is introducing readers to an American Indian tribe that led a nomadic lifestyle and lived in teepees that were easily moved from place to place. In which region did this tribe likely live?
   a. Plains
   b. Southwest
   c. Eastern
   d. Northwest

7. What was Britain's first permanent settlement in North America?
   a. Plymouth, Massachusetts
   b. Roanoke, Virginia
   c. Jamestown, Virginia
   d. L'Anse Meadows, Newfoundland

8. Fourth-grade students are creating timelines with landmark events of the American Revolution. Under which of the following events should they notate as where the first shot took place?
   a. At the Boston Massacre
   b. During the Boston Tea Party
   c. On Lexington Green
   d. At the Battle of Trenton

9. How many times has the U.S. Constitution been amended in order to accommodate changes and updates?
   a. Fourteen
   b. Eighteen
   c. Twenty-one
   d. Twenty-seven

10. Which type of map illustrates the world's climatological regions?
   a. Topographic Map
   b. Conformal Projection
   c. Isoline Map
   d. Thematic Map

11. In which manner is absolute location expressed?
   a. The cardinal directions (north, south, east, and west)
   b. Through latitudinal and longitudinal coordinates
   c. Location nearest to a more well-known location
   d. Hemispherical position on the globe

12. Which of these is NOT a true statement about culture?
   a. Culture derives from the beliefs, values, and behaviors of people in a community.
   b. All people are born into a certain culture.
   c. Cultures are stagnant and cannot be changed.
   d. Culture can be embedded within families, schools, businesses, social classes, and religions.

13. Latitudinal lines are used to measure distance in which direction?
    a. East to west
    b. North to south
    c. Between two sets of coordinates
    d. In an inexact manner

14. Which of the following statements most accurately describes the Achaemenid Empire in Persia until the fourth century BCE?
    a. Islam was the official religion.
    b. Achaemenid emperors constructed the entire Silk Road network.
    c. The Achaemenid Empire successfully conquered Greece.
    d. None of the above

15. The Silk Roads had which of the following results?
    a. Spread of Buddhism from India to China
    b. The devastation of European economies
    c. Introduction of the Bubonic Plague to the New World
    d. The Great War

16. What caused the end of the Western Roman Empire in 476 CE?
    a. Invasions by Germanic tribes
    b. The Mongol invasion
    c. The assassination of Julius Caesar
    d. Introduction of Taoism in Rome

17. Which of the following statements most accurately describes the Mongol Empire?
    a. The Mongol army was largely a cavalry force.
    b. Mongol rulers did not tolerate other religions.
    c. Mongol rulers neglected foreign trade.
    d. The Mongol Empire is known for its discouragement of literacy and the arts.

18. Renaissance scholars and artists were inspired by which classical civilization?
    a. Ancient Greece
    b. Ancient Egypt
    c. The Zhou Dynasty
    c. The Ottoman Empire

19. Which of the following was a consequence of increasing nationalism in Europe in the 1800s?
    a. The unification of Spain
    b. The unification of France
    c. Increasing competition and tension between European powers
    d. More efficient trade between nations

20. Which of the following led to the American Revolution?
    a. The Stamp Act
    b. The Boston Massacre
    c. The Boston Tea Party
    d. All of the above

21. Which political concept describes a ruling body's ability to influence the actions, behaviors, or attitudes of a person or community?
   a. Authority
   b. Sovereignty
   c. Power
   d. Legitimacy

22. Which feature differentiates a state from a nation?
   a. Shared history
   b. Common language
   c. Population
   d. Sovereignty

23. Which of the following was a consequence of World War II?
   a. The collapse of British and French empires in Asia and Africa
   b. A Communist revolution in Russia
   c. The end of the Cold War
   d. The death of Franz Ferdinand, the Archduke of Austria

24. Which best describes ethnic groups?
   a. Subgroups within a population who share a common history, language, or religion
   b. Divisive groups within a nation's boundaries seeking independence
   c. People who choose to leave a location
   d. Any minority group within a nation's boundaries

25. In recent years, agricultural production has been affected by which of the following?
   a. The prevalence of biotechnology and GMOs
   b. Weaker crop yields due to poor soil
   c. Plagues of pests, which have limited food production
   d. Revolutions in irrigation, which utilize salinated water

26. Which of the following is true of political boundaries?
   a. They have remained static for centuries.
   b. They are generally visible on Earth.
   c. They are constantly changing.
   d. They are never disputed among nations.

27. Which of the following is the subgroup of economics that studies large-scale economic issues such as unemployment, interest rates, price levels, and national income?
   a. Microeconomics
   b. Macroeconomics
   c. Scarcity
   d. Supply and demand

28. Which kind of market does not involve government interventions or monopolies while trades are made between suppliers and buyers?
   a. Free
   b. Command
   c. Gross
   d. Exchange

29. Which is NOT an indicator of economic growth?
   a. GDP (Gross Domestic Product)
   b. Unemployment
   c. Inflation
   d. Theory of the Firm

30. Which of the following consequences did NOT result from the discovery of the New World in 1492 CE?
   a. Proof that the world was round instead of flat
   b. The deaths of millions of Native Americans
   c. Biological exchange between Europe and the New World
   d. The creation of new syncretic religions

31. Which of the following was NOT a consequence of industrialization in Europe during the 1800s?
   a. The birth of the working class
   b. The expansion of European empires in Africa and Asia
   c. Improved transportation and economic efficiency
   d. The reduction of child labor.

32. Which check does the legislative branch possess over the judicial branch?
   a. Appoint judges
   b. Call special sessions of Congress
   c. Rule legislation unconstitutional
   d. Determine the number of Supreme Court judges

33. Which of the following is NOT included in the Bill of Rights?
   a. Freedom to assemble
   b. Freedom against unlawful search
   c. Freedom to vote
   d. Reservation of non-enumerated powers to the states or the people

34. The United States elects the president by which of the following ways?
   a. Popular majority vote
   b. Plurality vote
   c. Electoral College
   d. Party list system

Question 35 is based on the following passage:

> Hand in hand with this we must frankly recognize the overbalance of population in our industrial centers and, by engaging on a national scale in a redistribution, endeavor to provide a better use of the land for those best fitted for the land. The task can be helped

263

by definite efforts to raise the values of agricultural products and with this the power to purchase the output of our cities. It can be helped by preventing realistically the tragedy of the growing loss through foreclosure of our small homes and our farms. It can be helped by insistence that the Federal, State, and local governments act forthwith on the demand that their cost be drastically reduced. It can be helped by the unifying of relief activities which today are often scattered, uneconomical, and unequal. It can be helped by national planning for and supervision of all forms of transportation and of communications and other utilities which have a definitely public character. There are many ways in which it can be helped, but it can never be helped merely by talking about it. We must act and act quickly.

Finally, in our progress toward a resumption of work we require two safeguards against a return of the evils of the old order; there must be a strict supervision of all banking and credits and investments; there must be an end to speculation with other people's money, and there must be provision for an adequate but sound currency.

President Franklin D. Roosevelt, Inaugural Address, March 4, 1933

35. Which of the following best describes President Roosevelt's underlying approach to government?
   a. Government must be focused on redistribution of land.
   b. Government must "act and act quickly" to intervene and regulate the economy.
   c. Government must exercise "strict supervision of all banking."
   d. Government must prevent the "growing loss through foreclosure."

36. In the American election system, where do the candidates ultimately receive the nomination from their party?
   a. At the primary
   b. At the caucus
   c. At the debates
   d. At the party convention

37. Which part of the legislative process differs in the House and the Senate?
   a. Who may introduce the bill
   b. How debates about a bill are conducted
   c. Who may veto the bill
   d. What wording the bill contains

38. Which of the following is the primary problem with map projections?
   a. They are not detailed.
   b. They do not include physical features.
   c. They distort areas near the poles.
   d. They only focus on the Northern Hemisphere.

39. Literacy rates are more likely to be higher in which area?
   a. Developing nations
   b. Northern Hemispherical Nations
   c. Developed Nations
   d. Near centers of trade

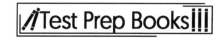
40. All of the following are negative demographic indicators EXCEPT which of the following?
    a. High Infant Mortality Rates
    b. Low Literacy Rates
    c. High Population Density
    d. Low Life Expectancy

41. Which of the following is NOT a factor in a location's climate?
    a. Latitudinal position
    b. Elevation
    c. Longitudinal position
    d. Proximity to mountains

42. All but which of the following are true of the Tropics?
    a. They are consistently hit with direct rays of the sun.
    b. They fall between the Tropics of Cancer and Capricorn.
    c. They are nearer the Equator than the Middle Latitudes.
    d. They are always warmer than other parts of the Globe.

43. What is the term for the ability of a ruling body to influence the actions, behavior, and attitude of a person or group of people?
    a. Politics
    b. Power
    c. Authority
    d. Legitimacy

44. Which of the following is a function of a nation AFTER it has been formed rather than a shared characteristic that would be helpful in the formation of a nation?
    a. Culture and traditions
    b. History
    c. Sovereignty
    d. Beliefs and religion

45. Of the following ideologies, which one advocates for the most radical government intervention to achieve social and economic equality?
    a. Socialism
    b. Liberalism
    c. Libertarianism
    d. Fascism

46. Of the following ideologies, which one prioritizes stability and traditional institutions within a culture?
    a. Socialism
    b. Liberalism
    c. Conservatism
    d. Libertarianism

47. The central government established under the Articles of Confederation held which of the following powers?
    a. The power to impose taxes
    b. The power to declare war
    c. The power to regulate trade
    d. The power to enforce laws enacted by Congress

48. What was a consequence of the industrialization that followed the Civil War?
    a. Decreased immigration
    b. Increased urbanization
    c. Decreased socioeconomic inequality
    d. Increased rights for workers

49. Which of the following best describes how the Treaty of Versailles contributed to the outbreak of World War II?
    a. Forced Germany to assume responsibility for all damage incurred during the war and pay billions of dollars in reparations.
    b. Failed to adequately end the violence of World War I.
    c. Left large tracts of territory unclaimed by any nation-state.
    d. Created the League of Nations.

Question 50 is based on the following passage:

> Now, therefore I, Abraham Lincoln, President of the United States, by virtue of the power in me vested as Commander-in-Chief, of the Army and Navy of the United States in time of actual armed rebellion against the authority and government of the United States, and as a fit and necessary war measure for suppressing said rebellion...
>
> And by virtue of the power, and for the purpose aforesaid, I do order and declare that all persons held as slaves within said designated States, and parts of States, are, and henceforward shall be free; and that the Executive government of the United States, including the military and naval authorities thereof, will recognize and maintain the freedom of said persons.

President Abraham Lincoln, Emancipation Proclamation, January 1, 1863

50. How does President Lincoln justify freeing the slaves in designated areas of the South?
    a. Emancipation is necessary since slavery is evil.
    b. Emancipation is necessary to boost the morale of the North.
    c. Emancipation is necessary to punish for the South seceding from the Union.
    d. Emancipation is necessary to strengthen the war effort of the North.

51. Federalism is described as the relationship between the federal government and which of the following?
    a. The people
    b. State governments
    c. The branches of government
    d. The Constitution

52. The case of Brown v. Board of Education reversed what landmark Supreme Court doctrine?
    a. Judicial review doctrine
    b. Public safety exception
    c. Due process doctrine
    d. Separate but equal doctrine

53. All EXCEPT which of the following are true of an area with an extremely high population density?
    a. Competition for resources is intense
    b. Greater strain on public services exists
    c. More people live in rural areas
    d. More people live in urban areas

54. Which of the following characteristics best defines a formal region?
    a. Homogeneity
    b. Diversity
    c. Multilingualism
    d. Social Mobility

55. The process of globalization can best be described as what?
    a. The integration of the world's economic systems into a singular entity
    b. The emergence of powerful nations seeking world dominance
    c. The absence of nation-states who seek to control certain areas
    d. Efforts to establish a singular world government for the world's citizens

56. What is the name of the central bank that controls the value of money in the United States?
    a. Commodity Reserve
    b. Central Reserve
    c. Federal Reserve
    d. Bank Reserve

57. How is economic growth measured?
    a. By the rise in the inflation of a country
    b. By the amount of reserves that a country holds
    c. By the amount of exports that a country has
    d. By the GDP of a country

58. A developing nation is more likely to have which of the following?
    a. Complex highway networks
    b. Higher rates of subsistence farmers
    c. Stable government systems
    d. Little economic instability

59. Which constitutional amendment gave women the right to vote in the United States?
    a. 15th
    b. 18th
    c. 19th
    d. 20th

60. What consequences did the Great Migration have?
   a. It led to conflict with Native Americans in the West in the 1800s.
   b. It led to increased racial tension in the North in the early 1900s.
   c. It led to increased conflict with Mexican immigrants in the 1900s.
   d. It led to increased conflict with Irish and German immigrants in the 1800s.

Science

1. An ecosystem that normally has moderate summers with high rainfall is experiencing a heat wave and a drought. How does this affect the rate of photosynthesis of the producers in this ecosystem?
   a. The decrease in transpiration from the high heat and the drop in rainfall decreases the number of chloroplasts, so photosynthesis rates decrease.
   b. The increase in transpiration from the high heat and the drop in rainfall results in less water. Since photosynthesis creates water, the rate increases to meet increased water demands.
   c. Increased temperature increases the number of mitochondria, so photosynthesis rates increase.
   d. The increase in transpiration from the high heat and the drop in rainfall results in less water available for photosynthesis. The rate decreases.

2. A farmer grows all of his tomato plants by vegetative propagation. He finds that one clone produces tomatoes that sell much better than any other clone. He then uses this clone to plant his entire field. Two years later a fungus wipes out his entire crop. What could the farmer have done to prevent this?

   I. Plant tomatoes that sell poorly. They are more resistant to fungus.
   II. Plant a variety of tomatoes. Genetic variation would have left some of the crop less susceptible to the fungus.
   III. Plant a variety of crops. Plants other than tomatoes might not be affected by the fungus.

   a. Choice I only
   b. Choice II only
   c. Choice I or III
   d. Choice II or III

3. What object in the solar system becomes dim during a lunar eclipse?
   a. Sun
   b. Earth
   c. Moon
   d. Earth and moon

4. Which statement about white blood cells is true?
   a. B cells are responsible for antibody production.
   b. White blood cells are made in the white/yellow cartilage before they enter the bloodstream.
   c. Platelets, a special class of white blood cell, function to clot blood and stop bleeding.
   d. The majority of white blood cells only activate during the age of puberty, which explains why children and the elderly are particularly susceptible to disease.

5. Which locations in the digestive system are sites of chemical digestion?
   1. Mouth
   2. Stomach
   3. Small Intestine

   a. II only
   b. III only
   c. II and III only
   d. I, II, and III

6. What is the theory that certain physical and behavioral survival traits give a species an evolutionary advantage?
   a. Gradualism
   b. Evolutionary advantage
   c. Punctuated equilibrium
   d. Natural selection

7. Which of the following structures is unique to eukaryotic cells?
   a. Cell walls
   b. Nuclei
   c. Cell membranes
   d. Organelles

8. Which is the cellular organelle used for digestion to recycle materials?
   a. The Golgi apparatus
   b. The lysosome
   c. The centrioles
   d. The mitochondria

9. Which of the following leads to diversity in meiotic division but not mitotic division?
   a. Tetrad formation
   b. Disassembly of the mitotic spindle
   c. Extra/fewer chromosomes due to nondisjunction
   d. Fertilization by multiple sperm

10. The sun is a major external source of energy. Which of the following is the best demonstration of this?
   a. Flowers tend to bloom in the morning, after dawn.
   b. Large animals like bears do not need to eat food when hibernating.
   c. Deserts can reach scorching temperatures in daylight but subzero temperatures at night.
   d. The tides of the ocean are highly dependent on the movement of the Moon, the celestial body that is highly reflective to sunlight.

11. Which of the following describes a typical gas?
   a. Indefinite shape and indefinite volume
   b. Indefinite shape and definite volume
   c. Definite shape and definite volume
   d. Definite shape and indefinite volume

12. What information does a genotype give that a phenotype does not?
   a. The genotype necessarily includes the proteins coded for by its alleles.
   b. The genotype will always show an organism's recessive alleles.
   c. The genotype must include the organism's physical characteristics.
   d. The genotype shows what an organism's parents looked like.

13. Which statement is supported by the Punnett square below, if "*T*" = tall and "*t*" = short?

	T	t
T		
t		

   a. Both parents are homozygous tall.
   b. 100% of the offspring will be tall because both parents are tall.
   c. There is a 25% chance that an offspring will be short.
   d. The short allele will soon die out.

14. Which of the following is a chief difference between evaporation and boiling?
   a. Liquids boil only at the surface, while they evaporate equally throughout the liquid.
   b. Evaporating substances change from gas to liquid, while boiling substances change from liquid to gas.
   c. Evaporation happens in nature, while boiling is a manmade phenomenon.
   d. Evaporation can happen below a liquid's boiling point.

15. Which of the following is a special property of water?
   a. Water easily flows through phospholipid bilayers.
   b. A water molecule's oxygen atom allows fish to breathe.
   c. Water is highly cohesive which explains its high boiling point.
   d. Water can self-hydrolyze and decompose into hydrogen and oxygen.

16. A student believes that there is an inverse relationship between sugar consumption and test scores. To test this hypothesis, he recruits several people to eat sugar, wait one hour, and take a short aptitude test afterwards. The student will compile the participants' sugar intake levels and test scores. How should the student conduct the experiment?
   a. One round of testing, where each participant consumes a different level of sugar.
   b. Two rounds of testing: The first, where each participant consumes a different level of sugar, and the second, where each participant consumes the same level as they did in Round 1.
   c. Two rounds of testing: The first, where each participant consumes the same level of sugar as each other, and the second, where each participant consumes the same level of sugar as each other but at higher levels than in Round 1.
   d. One round of testing, where each participant consumes the same level of sugar.

17. Which of the following is a standard or series of standards to which the results from an experiment are compared?
    a. A control
    b. A variable
    c. A constant
    d. Collected data

18. What is the LAST phase of mitosis?
    a. Prophase
    b. Telophase
    c. Anaphase
    d. Metaphase

19. Which of the following is a type of boundary between two tectonic plates?
    a. Continental
    b. Oceanic
    c. Convergent
    d. Fault

20. Volcanic activity can occur in which of the following?
    a. Convergent boundaries
    b. Divergent boundaries
    c. The middle of a tectonic plate
    d. All of the above

21. Where is most of the Earth's weather generated?
    a. The troposphere
    b. The ionosphere
    c. The thermosphere
    d. The stratosphere

22. What type of cloud is seen when looking at the sky during a heavy rainstorm?
    a. High-Clouds
    b. Altocumulus
    c. Stratus
    d. Nimbostratus

23. What is the largest planet in our solar system and what is it mostly made of?
    a. Saturn, rocks
    b. Jupiter, ammonia
    c. Jupiter, hydrogen
    d. Saturn, helium

24. Viruses belong to which of the following classifications?
    a. Domain Archaea
    b. Kingdom Monera
    c. Kingdom Protista
    d. None of the above

25. Considering a gas in a closed system, at a constant volume, what will happen to the temperature if the pressure is increased?
    a. The temperature will stay the same.
    b. The temperature will decrease.
    c. The temperature will increase.
    d. It cannot be determined with the information given.

26. According to Newton's three laws of motion, which of the following is true?
    a. Two objects cannot exert a force on each other without touching.
    b. An object at rest has no inertia.
    c. The weight of an object is the same as the mass of the object.
    d. The weight of an object is equal to the mass of an object multiplied by gravity.

27. The Sun transferring heat to the Earth through space is an example of which of the following?
    a. Convection
    b. Conduction
    c. Induction
    d. Radiation

28. Which of the Earth's layers is thickest?
    a. The crust
    b. The shell
    c. The mantle
    d. The inner core

29. What is the process called in which a tectonic plate moves over another plate?
    a. Fault
    b. Diversion
    c. Subduction
    d. Drift

30. What is transpiration?
    a. Evaporation from moving water
    b. Evaporation from plant life
    c. Movement of water through the ground
    d. Precipitation that falls on trees

31. Which of the following will freeze last?
    a. Freshwater from a pond
    b. Pure water
    c. Seawater from the Pacific Ocean
    d. Seawater from the Dead Sea

32. Which of the following is true of glaciers?
    a. They form in water.
    b. They float.
    c. They form on land.
    d. They are formed from icebergs.

33. What is the broadest, or LEAST specialized, classification of the Linnaean taxonomic system?
    a. Species
    b. Family
    c. Domain
    d. Phylum

34. Which statement is true about the pH of a solution?
    a. A solution cannot have a pH less than 1.
    b. The more hydroxide ions in the solution, the higher the pH.
    c. If an acid has a pH of greater than 2, it is considered a weak base.
    d. A solution with a pH of 2 has ten times more hydrogen ions than a solution with a pH of 1.

35. Salts like sodium iodide (NaI) and potassium chloride (KCl) use what type of bond?
    a. Ionic bonds
    b. Disulfide bridges
    c. Covalent bonds
    d. London dispersion forces

36. Which of the following is unique to covalent bonds?
    a. Most covalent bonds are formed between the elements H, F, N, and O.
    b. Covalent bonds are dependent on forming dipoles.
    c. Bonding electrons are shared between two or more atoms.
    d. Molecules with covalent bonds tend to have a crystalline solid structure.

37. For any given element, an isotope is an atom with which of the following?
    a. A different atomic number
    b. A different number of protons
    c. A different number of electrons
    d. A different mass number

38. What is the electrical charge of the nucleus?
    a. A nucleus always has a positive charge.
    b. A stable nucleus has a positive charge, but a radioactive nucleus may have no charge and instead be neutral.
    c. A nucleus always has no charge and is instead neutral.
    d. A stable nucleus has no charge and is instead neutral, but a radioactive nucleus may have a charge.

39. Which of the following is a representation of a natural pattern or occurrence that's difficult or impossible to experience directly?
    a. A theory
    b. A model
    c. A law
    d. An observation

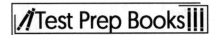

40. "This flower is dead; someone must have forgotten to water it." This statement is an example of which of the following?
    a. A classification
    b. An observation
    c. An inference
    d. A collection

41. Which statement is true regarding atomic structure?
    a. Protons orbit around a nucleus.
    b. Neutrons have a positive charge.
    c. Electrons are in the nucleus.
    d. Protons have a positive charge.

42. What is ionization energy?
    a. One-half the distance between the nuclei of atoms of the same element.
    b. A measurement of the tendency of an atom to form a chemical bond.
    c. The amount of energy needed to remove a valence electron from a gas or ion.
    d. The ability or tendency of an atom to accept an electron into its valence shell.

43. The process of breaking large molecules into smaller molecules to provide energy is known as which of the following?
    a. Metabolism
    b. Bioenergetics
    c. Anabolism
    d. Catabolism

44. The Human Genome Project is a worldwide research project launched in 1990 to map the entire human genome. Although the Project was faced with the monumental challenge of analyzing tons and tons of data, its objective was completed in 2003 and ahead of its deadline by two years. Which of the following inventions likely had the greatest impact on this project?
    a. The sonogram
    b. X-ray diffraction
    c. The microprocessor
    d. Magnetic Resonance Imaging (MRI)

45. Which of the following inventions likely had the greatest improvement on the ability to combat nutrition deficiencies in developing countries?
    a. Food products fortified with dietary vitamins and minerals
    b. Integrated statistical models of fish populations
    c. Advances so that microscopes can use thicker tissue samples
    d. Refrigerated train cars for transportation of food

46. Which element's atoms have the greatest number of electrons?
    a. Hydrogen
    b. Iron
    c. Copper
    d. Iodine

47. A teacher presents a science lesson to her class of second graders about physical and chemical properties. After the lesson, students create posters that highlight examples of each. Which of the following would fall off the list of examples of chemical properties?
    a. Color
    b. Malleability
    c. Reactivity
    d. Luster

48. Which of the following happens first in the scientific method?
    a. Procedure
    b. Hypothesis
    c. Observation
    d. Data collection

49. Students in a fourth-grade class are brainstorming testable hypotheses. Which of the following suggestions offered by a student is a valid hypothesis?
    a. If a cat is happy, then it purrs.
    b. If pants are softer, then they feel more comfortable.
    c. If light exposure increases, then plant height will increase.
    d. If calories are added to a dog's diet, then it will grow.

50. An elementary teacher is about to begin a new science unit of seasons and weather. As part of various a activities to gauge students' background knowledge, he asks. Each student to share what they believe to be the difference between seasons and weather. The responses of four students are presented below. Which of these students is most accurate?
    a. Carter: Seasons depend on wind and heat patterns.
    b. Darrel: Weather depends on proximity to the sun.
    c. Gloria: Seasons are day-to-day weather.
    d. Dimitri: Weather involves the water cycle.

51. Which is the best way to teach the concept of day and night to early childhood students?
    a. Showing an animated PowerPoint
    b. Going outside and talking about the Sun's location
    c. Modeling with flashlights and tennis balls
    d. Reading a book where the Sun and moon are friends

52. Why is Florida hotter than Alaska?
    a. Florida is next to the ocean.
    b. Florida is a peninsula.
    c. Alaska is farther from the equator.
    d. Alaska is larger than Florida.

53. Which of the following weather phenomena do NOT directly involve the water cycle?
    a. Hurricanes
    b. Tornadoes
    c. Snow
    d. Rain

54. Plate tectonic movement contributes to the Earth's topography by doing which of the following?
    a. Causing volcanoes
    b. Stimulating evaporation
    c. Forming deltas
    d. Stopping tornadoes

55. Which type of fossil is considered a "trace fossil"?
    a. Bone
    b. Footprint
    c. Shell
    d. Tooth

Answer Explanations #1

Reading and Language Arts

1. B: Spelling conventions is the area of study that involves mechanics, usage, and sentence formation. Mechanics refers to spelling, punctuation, and capitalization. Usage refers to the use of the various parts of speech within sentences, and sentence formation is the order in which the various words in a sentence appear. Generally speaking, word analysis is the breaking down of words into morphemes and word units in order to arrive at the word's meaning. Morphemes are the smallest units of a written language that carry meaning, and phonics refers to the study of letter-sound relationships.

2. B: Although some high-frequency sight words are decodable, the majority of them are not, so they do not follow the Alphabetic Principle, which relies on specific letter-sound correspondence. High-frequency sight words appear often in children's literature and are studied and memorized in order to strengthen a child's spelling and reading fluency. High-frequency sight words, as well as decodable words, may or may not rhyme and may or may not contain onsets and rimes.

3. A: Reading fluency involves how accurately a child reads each individual word within a sentence, the speed at which a child reads, and the expression the child applies while reading. Therefore, accuracy, rate, and prosody are the three key areas of reading fluency.

4. A: The correct answer is skimming the text for content. Skimming text for content is an important pre-reading strategy where readers identify important ideas and words without reading every line of the text. Summarizing text effectively, organizing main ideas and supporting details, and clarifying unfamiliar ideas in the text are all reading strategies to be used during or after reading a text.

5. A: The correct answer is "what happens" or the storyline. Choice *B* refers to characters in fiction. Choice *C* defines the setting. Choice *D* is incomplete. It may be partially true, but it isn't always the case. Most fiction is based on the imaginary.

6. B: The correct answer is *B* as the author is speaking directly to the reader and uses the pronoun *you*. Choice *A* uses first person point of view, which uses the pronoun *I*. Choice *C* uses third person point of view which utilizes pronouns such as *he*, *she*, or *we*. Choice *D* is unclear.

7. D: The correct answer is a short story with animals, fantastic creatures, or other forces within nature. Choice *A* defines an elegy. Choice *B* partially alludes to folklore. Choice *C* defines a fairytale.

8. C: The correct answer is text organized by the timing of events or actions. Chronological or sequence order is the organizational pattern that structures text to show the passage of time or movement through steps in a certain order. Choice *A* demonstrates the problem/solution structure. Choice *B* defines the cause/effect pattern. Choice *D* represents the spatial order structure.

9. D: The correct answer is simile. Choice *A* is incorrect because the poem does not contain an idiom. Choice *B* is incorrect since the poem is not haiku. Choice *C* is incorrect as it does not use the ABBA rhyming convention.

10. B: Only Choice *B* uses both repetitive beginning sounds (alliteration) and personification—the portrayal of a building as a human crumbling under a fire. Choice *A* is a simile and does not utilize

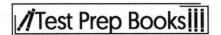

alliteration or the use of consistent consonant sounds for effect. Although Choice *C* does use alliteration, it does not use personification to describe the house. Choice *D* describes neither alliteration nor personification.

11. B: The correct answer is ABAB. Choice *A* is not a valid rhyme scheme. Choice *C* would require the second and third lines to rhyme, so it is incorrect. Choice *D* would require the first and fifth lines rhyme, then the second and sixth. This is also incorrect as the passage only contains four lines.

12. D: The correct answer is dactyl. If read with a combination of stressed and unstressed syllables as Tennyson intended and as the poem naturally flows, the reader will stumble upon the stressed/unstressed/unstressed rhythmic, dactyl meter similar to a waltz beat. Choices *A*, *B*, and *C* describe meters that do not follow the dactyl pattern.

13. A: The correct answer is a historical account of a person's life written by one who has intimate knowledge of the person's life. Choice *B* is not applicable since it is the definition of an autobiography. Choice *C* strictly refers to fiction and is not applicable to nonfiction. Choice *D* indicates that a memoir is not based on historical fact. In many instances, it is.

14. A: The correct answer is cause and effect. A writer may use cause and effect as a strategy to illustrate a point in order to convince an audience. Choice *B* is a rhetorical device, not a strategy. Choice *C* refers to a narrative conflict, and Choice *D* is a logical fallacy.

15. A: The correct answer is *crackle* as it is the only option that reflects the sound that the action would make. The other options do not.

16. C: The correct answer is a fourteen-line poem written in iambic pentameter. Choice *A* is incorrect as it incorrectly alludes to the haiku form. Choice *B* defines the octave poetic structure. Choice *D* defines what a poetic ode is.

17. B: To arrive at the best answer (*surly*), all the character traits for Cindy must be analyzed. She's described as *happy* ("always has a smile on her face"), *kind* ("volunteers at the local shelter"), and *patient* ("no one has ever seen her angry"). Since Cindy's husband is the *opposite* of her, these adjectives must be converted to antonyms. Someone who is *surly* is *unhappy*, *rude*, and *impatient*. Choice *A* (*stingy*) is too narrow of a word. Someone could be *happy* and *kind*, for instance, but still be *stingy*. For Choice *C*, *scared*, to be plausible, the rest of the passage would need instances of Cindy being *bold* or *courageous*. Though she's certainly *kind* and *helpful*, none of those traits are modeled. Choice *D* (*shy*) also doesn't match. Someone who is *shy* could still be *happy*, *kind*, and *patient*.

18. B: The passage indicates that Annabelle has a fear of going outside into the daylight. Thus *heliophobia* must refer to a fear of bright lights or sunlight. Choice *B* is the only answer that describes this.

19. A: The guide words indicate that all of the other words on the page will be found between those words when listed alphabetically. The two guide words are *kingcraft* and *klieg light*, so the correct answer will fit between the two when ordering them alphabetically. Choice *B*, *knead*, comes after *klieg light*; Choice *C*, *kinesthesia*, and Choice *D*, *kickback*, both come before *kingcraft*. The correct answer is Choice *A*, *kleptomania*.

278

20. C: A primary source is an artifact, document, recording, or other source of information that is created at the time under study. Think of a primary source as the original representation of the information. In contrast, secondary sources make conclusions or draw inferences based on primary sources, as well as other secondary sources. Choice *C* is correct because a personal journal from World War II is a historical document and is, therefore, a primary source. Choice *A*, a critic's summary and review of a new book, is a secondary source. Choice *B*, a table of contents, is a secondary source, since it refers to other information. Choice *D* is also a secondary source.

21. B: A passage like this one would likely appear in some sort of community profile, highlighting the benefits of living or working there. Choice *A* is incorrect because nothing in this passage suggests that it is fictional. It reads as non-fiction, if anything. Choice *C* is incorrect because it does not report anything particularly newsworthy, and Choice *D* is incorrect because it has absolutely nothing to do with a movie review.

22. D: Choice *D* looks like a strong answer. This answer choice references the argument's main points—*Infinite Jest* is a modern classic, the book deserves its praise, and everybody should read it. In contrast, Choice *A* restates the author's conclusion. The correct answer to main point questions will often be closely related to the conclusion. Choice *B* restates a premise. Is the author's main point that *Infinite Jest* is a page-turner? No, he uses readers' obsession with the book as a premise. Eliminate this choice. Choice *C* is definitely not the main point of the passage. It's a simple fact underlying the argument. It certainly cannot be considered the main point. Eliminate this choice.

23. C: Despite the opposite stances in Passages 1 and 2, both authors establish that cell phones are a strong part of culture. In Passage 1 the author states, "Today's student is already strongly rooted in technology." In Passage 2 the author states, "Students are comfortable with cell phones." The author of Passage 2 states that cell phones have a "time and place." The author of Passage 2 would disagree with the statement that *teachers should incorporate cell phones into curriculum whenever possible. Cell phones are useful only when an experienced teacher uses them properly*—this statement is implied in Passage 2, but the author in Passage 1 says cell phones are "indispensable." In other words, no teacher can do without them. *Despite a good lesson plan, cell phone disruptions are impossible to avoid.* This is not supported by either passage. Even though the author in the second passage is more cautionary, the author states, "This can prove advantageous if done correctly." Therefore, there is a possibility that a classroom can run properly with cell phones.

24. D: This question is testing whether you realize how a timeline illustrates information in chronological order from left to right. "Started school for the deaf" is fourth on the timeline from the left, which means that it is the fourth event on the timeline. Thus, Choice *D* is the correct answer.

25. B: This question is asking you to determine the length of time between the pairs of events listed as answer choices. Events in timelines are arranged proportional to time. To determine the answer to this question, one must find the largest space between two events. Visually, this can be seen between the events of befriending Helen Keller and dying in Canada. Thus, Choice *B* is the correct answer.

26. C: This question is testing whether you can discern accurate conclusions from a timeline. Although the incorrect answer choices can seem correct, they cannot be confirmed from the information presented on the timeline. Choice *A* is incorrect; while it may be reasonable to assume that the timeline documents all major life events, we do not know for certain that Bell did not engage in any notable activities after founding the National Geographic Society. Choice *B* is incorrect because the timeline

279

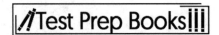

does not confirm that the school was in Canada; Bell actually started it in the United States. Choice D is incorrect because nothing on the timeline shows causation between the two events. According to the timeline, answer choice "C" is the only verifiable statement based on the timeline. Thus, Choice C is the correct answer.

27. B: The founding of the school is the event listed farthest to the right of the events in the answer choices. This means it occurred most recently. Thus, Choice B is the correct answer.

28. B, D: Relevant information refers to information that is closely related to the subject being researched. Students might get overwhelmed by information when they first begin researching, so they should learn how to narrow down search terms for their field of study. Choice A is incorrect because it starts with a range that is far too wide; the student will spend too much time sifting through unrelated information to gather only a few related facts. Choice C introduces a more limited range, but it is not closely related to the topic that is being researched. Choices B and D are correct because the student is choosing media and books that are closely related to the topic.

29. D: An actuary assesses risks and sets insurance premiums. While an actuary does work in insurance, the passage does not suggest that actuaries have any affiliation with hospitalists or working in a hospital, so all other choices are incorrect.

30. B: In Choice B the word Uncle should not be capitalized, because it is not functioning as a proper noun. If the word named a specific uncle, such as *Uncle Jerry*, then it would be considered a proper noun and should be capitalized. Choice A correctly capitalizes the proper noun East Coast, and does not capitalize winter, which functions as a common noun in the sentence. Choice C correctly capitalizes the name of a specific college course, which is considered a proper noun. Choice D correctly capitalizes the proper noun *Jersey Shore*.

31. A: Choice A is correctly punctuated because it uses a semicolon to join two independent clauses that are related in meaning. Each of these clauses could function as an independent sentence. Choice B is incorrect because the conjunction is not preceded by a comma. A comma and conjunction should be used together to join independent clauses. Choice C is incorrect because a comma should only be used to join independent sentences when it also includes a coordinating conjunction such as *and* or *so*. Choice D does not use punctuation to join the independent clauses, so it is considered a fused (same as a run-on) sentence.

32. C: Choice C is a compound sentence because it joins two independent clauses with a comma and the coordinating conjunction *and*. The sentences in Choices B and D include one independent clause and one dependent clause, so they are complex sentences, not compound sentences. The sentence in Choice A has both a compound subject, *Alex and Shane*, and a compound verb, *spent and took*, but the entire sentence itself is one independent clause.

33. A: Choice A uses incorrect subject-verb agreement because the indefinite pronoun *neither* is singular and must use the singular verb form *is*. The pronoun *both* is plural and uses the plural verb form of *are*. The pronoun *any* can be either singular or plural. In this example, it is used as a plural, so the plural verb form *are* is used. The pronoun *each* is singular and uses the singular verb form *is*.

34. A: It is necessary to put a comma between the date and the year. It is also required to put a comma between the day of the week and the month. Choice B is incorrect because it is missing the comma

280

between the day and year. Choice *C* is incorrect because it adds an unnecessary comma between the month and date. Choice *D* is missing the necessary comma between day of the week and the month.

35. D: This passage displays clarity (the author states precisely what he or she intended), fluency (the sentences run smoothly together), and parallelism (words are used in a similar fashion to help provide rhythm). Choice *A* lacks parallelism. When the author states, "the hero acts without thinking, is living in the moment, and is repressing physical and emotional pain," the words *acts, is living* and *is repressing* are in different tenses, and, consequently, jarring to one's ears. Choice *B* runs on endlessly in the first half ("Ernest Hemingway is probably the most noteworthy of expatriate authors since his concise writing style is void of emotion and stream of consciousness and has had a lasting impact on Americans which has resonated to this very day, and Hemingway's novels are much like in American cinema.")

It demands some type of pause and strains the readers' eyes. The second half of the passage is choppy: "The hero acts. He doesn't think. He lives in the moment. He represses physical and emotional pain." For Choice *C*, leaving out *expatriate* is, first, vague, and second, alters the meaning. The correct version claims that Hemingway was the most notable of the expatriate authors while the second version claims he's the most notable of any author *ever*, a very bold claim indeed. Also, leaving out *stream of* in "stream of consciousness" no longer references the non-sequential manner in which most people think. Instead, this version sounds like all the characters in the novel are in a coma!

36. C: Both second and third person points of view are represented. The phrases *one should have* and *it is* are in the third person. Typical third-person subjects include *he, she, him, her, they, one, person, people*, and *someone*. Second person voice is indicated in the second half of the passage by the words *you* and *your*. Second person is simple to identify because it is the *you* voice, in which the reader is directly addressed.

37. D: The prefix *trans* means across, beyond, over. Choices A, B, and C are incorrect because they are the meanings of other prefixes. Choice *A* is a meaning of the prefix *de*. Choice *B* is the meaning of the prefix *omni*. Choice *C* is one of the meanings of the prefix *pro*. The example words are helpful in determining the meaning of *trans*. All of the example words—*transfer, transact, translation, transport*—indicate something being *across, beyond*, or *over* something else. For example, *translation* refers to text going across languages. If no example words were given, you could think of words starting with *trans* and then compare their meanings to try to determine a common definition.

38. C: For the prefix *anti-* to work in both situations, it must have the same meaning, one that generalizes to any word in the English language. *Oppose* makes sense in both instances. Antibiotics *oppose* bacteria, and antisocials *oppose* society. Choice *A* is illogical. *Reducing* the number of bacteria is somewhat logical, but *reducing* society doesn't make sense when considering the definition of antisocial. Choice *B* is not the best match for bacteria. *Revolt*, a word normally reserved for human opposition, sounds odd when paired with bacteria. Choice *D* might work for antibiotic (without bacteria) but doesn't work for antisocial (without society).

39. D: Shape is the best answer. If *conform* means to adjust behavior, *shape* could replace *conform*, as in the behavior was *re-shaped* or modified. The same goes for *inform*. New information *re-shapes* how one thinks about the world. Also, the word *shape* gives rise to the abstract idea that both behavior and information are malleable, like modeling clay, and can be molded into new forms. Choice *A* (*match*) works for *conform* (matching to society), but it doesn't work for *inform* (one cannot *match* information to a person). Choice *B* (*relay*) doesn't work for *conform* (there's no way to pass on new behavior), but it

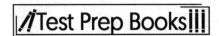

does work for *inform*, as to pass on new information. Choice C (*negate*) works for neither *conform* (the behavior is not being completely cancelled out) nor *inform* (the information is not being rescinded).

40. D: In order for oral presentations to be effective, the presenter's volume should match the size of audience and the location of the presentation. The presenter should also practice articulation—how clearly the words are being said. The third most important element of oral presentations is how well the presenter is engaging the audience. Making eye contact, moving around the room, and involving the audience, when appropriate, are all part of audience awareness skills.

41. A: Active listening skills are very important in all forms of communication, whether one is at home, among friends, in school, or at work. An active listener is one who pays close attention to what is being said, maintains eye contact, uses body language to indicate respect, asks relevant questions, and shares information that directly pertains to the subject.

42. D: Teachers use directed reading-thinking activities before and after reading to improve critical thinking and reading comprehension. Metacognitive skills are when learners think about thinking. Self-monitoring is when children are asked to think as they read and ask themselves if what they have just read makes sense. KWL charts help guide students to identify what they already know about a given topic.

43. C: We are looking for an inference—a conclusion that is reached on the basis of evidence and reasoning—from the passage that will likely explain why the famous children's author did not achieve her usual success with the new genre (despite the book's acclaim). Choice A is wrong because the statement is false according to the passage. Choice B is wrong because, although the passage says the author has a graduate degree on the subject, it would be an unrealistic leap to infer that she is the foremost expert on Antebellum America. Choice D is wrong because there is nothing in the passage to lead us to infer that people generally prefer a children's series to historical fiction. In contrast, Choice C can be logically inferred since the passage speaks of the great success of the children's series and the declaration that the fame of the author's name causes the children's books to "fly off the shelves." Thus, she did not receive any bump from her name since she published the historical novel under a pseudonym, which makes Choice C correct.

44. D: Choice D directly addresses the reader, so it is in second person point of view. This is an imperative sentence since it issues a command; imperative sentences have an *understood you* as the subject. Choice A uses first person pronouns *I* and *my*. Choices B and C are incorrect because they use third person point of view.

45. B: Pre-teaching is the most valuable strategy for helping children understand new words. Educators select what they evaluate to be the unfamiliar words in the text and then introduce them to the class before reading. Educators using this method should be careful not to simply ask the children to read the text and then spell the new words correctly.

46. B: When using contextual strategies, students are indirectly introduced to new words within a sentence or paragraph. Contextual strategies require students to infer the meaning(s) of new words. Word meaning is developed by utilizing semantic and contextual clues of the reading in which the word is located.

47. A: The passage describes a situation and then explains the causes that led to it. Also, it utilizes cause and effect signal words, such as *causes, factors, so,* and *as a result*. B is incorrect because a compare and

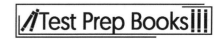

contrast order considers the similarities and differences of two or more things. *C* is incorrect because spatial order describes where things are located in relation to each other. Finally, *D* is incorrect because time order describes when things occurred chronologically.

48. A: Choice *A* is consistent with the argument's logic. The argument asserts that the world powers' military alliances amounted to a lit fuse, and the assassination merely lit it. The main point of the argument is that any event involving the military alliances would have led to a world war. Choice *B* runs counter to the argument's tone and reasoning. It can immediately be eliminated. Choice *C* is also clearly incorrect. At no point does the argument blame any single or group of countries for starting World War I. Choice *D* is incorrect for the same reason as Choice *C*. Eliminate this choice.

49. D: Outspending other countries on education could have other benefits, but there is no reference to this in the passage, so Choice *A* is incorrect. Choice *B* is incorrect because the author does not mention corruption. Choice *C* is incorrect because there is nothing in the passage stating that the tests are not genuinely representative. Choice *D* is accurate because spending more money has not brought success. The United States already spends the most money, and the country is not excelling on these tests. Choice *D* is the correct answer.

50. B: *Excellent* and *walking* are adjectives modifying the noun *tours*. *Rich* is an adjective modifying the noun *history*, and *brotherly* is an adjective modifying the noun *love*. Choice *A* is incorrect because all of these words are functioning as nouns in the sentence. Choice *C* is incorrect because all of these words are functioning as verbs in the sentence. Choice *D* is incorrect because all of these words are considered prepositions, not adjectives.

51. D: The object pronouns *her* and *me* act as the indirect objects of the sentence. If *me* is in a series of object pronouns, it should always come last in the series. Choice *A* is incorrect because it uses subject pronouns *she* and *I*. Choice *B* is incorrect because it uses the subject pronoun *she.* Choice *C* uses the correct object pronouns, but they are in the wrong order.

52. A: In this example, a colon is correctly used to introduce a series of items. Choice *B* places an unnecessary comma before the word *because.* A comma is not needed before the word *because* when it introduces a dependent clause at the end of a sentence and provides necessary information to understand the sentence. Choice *C* is incorrect because it uses a semi-colon instead of a comma to join a dependent clause and an independent clause. Choice *D* is incorrect because it uses a colon in place of a comma and coordinating conjunction to join two independent clauses.

53. B: Choice *B* correctly uses the contraction for *you are* as the subject of the sentence, and it correctly uses the possessive pronoun *your* to indicate ownership of the jacket. It also correctly uses the adverb *there*, indicating place. Choice *A* is incorrect because it reverses the possessive pronoun *your* and the contraction for *you are.* It also uses the possessive pronoun *their* instead of the adverb *there.* Choice *C* is incorrect because it reverses *your* and *you're* and uses the contraction for *they are* in place of the adverb *there.* Choice *D* incorrectly uses the possessive pronoun *their* instead of the adverb *there.*

54. A: *Slang* refers to non-standard expressions that are not used in elevated speech and writing. *Slang* tends to be specific to one group or time period and is commonly used within groups of young people during their conversations with each other. *Jargon* refers to the language used in a specialized field. The *vernacular* is the native language of a local area, and a *dialect* is one form of a language in a certain region. Thus, Choices *B*, *C*, and *D* are incorrect.

283

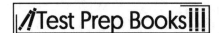

55. A: The publisher, author, and references are elements of a resource that determine credibility. If the publisher has published more than one work, the author has written more than one piece on the subject, or the work references other recognized research, the credibility of a source will be stronger. Choice *B* is incorrect because the subject and title may be used to determine relevancy, not credibility, and the audience does not have much to do with the credibility of a source. Choice *C* is incorrect because the organization, stylistic choices, and transition words are all components of an effectively-written piece, but they have less to do with credibility, other than to ensure that the author knows how to write. The length and tone of a piece are a matter of author's preference, and a work does not have to be written by multiple people to be considered a credible source.

56. B: In-text citations are much shorter and usually only include the author's last name, page numbers being referenced, and for some styles, the publication year. Bibliographic citations contain much more detailed reference information. *B* is incorrect because citations are necessary both in the text and in a bibliography. *C* is incorrect because there are several different citation styles depending on the type of paper or article being written. Rather, students should learn when it is appropriate to apply each different style. Choice *D* is incorrect because all sources need to be cited regardless of medium.

57. D: The purpose of integrating research is to add support and credibility to the student's ideas, not to replace the student's own ideas altogether. Choice *A* is incorrect as the bulk of the paper or project should be comprised of the author's own words, and quotations and paraphrases should be used to support them. Outside sources should be included when they enhance the writer's argument, but they are not required in every single paragraph. Choice *B* is also incorrect because regardless of whether ideas are directly quoted or paraphrased, it is essential to always credit authors for their ideas. The use of the author's full name in every signal phrase is unnecessary, so Choice *C* is also incorrect.

58. D: The author explains that Boethianism is a Medieval theological philosophy that attributes sin to temporary pleasure and righteousness with virtue and God's providence. Besides Choice *D,* the choices listed are all physical things. While these could still be divine rewards, Boethianism holds that the true reward for being virtuous is in God's favor. It is also stressed in the article that physical pleasures cannot be taken into the afterlife. Therefore, the best choice is *D*, God's favor.

59. C: *The Canterbury Tales* presents a manuscript written in the medieval period that can help illustrate Boethianism through stories and show how people of the time might have responded to the idea. Choices *A* and *B* are generalized statements, and we have no evidence to support Choice *B*. Choice *D* is very compelling, but it looks at Boethianism in a way that the author does not. The author does not mention "different levels of Boethianism" when discussing the tales, only that the concept appears differently in different tales. Boethianism also doesn't focus on enlightenment.

60. D: The author is referring to the principle that a desire for material goods leads to moral malfeasance punishable by a higher being. Choice *A* is incorrect; while the text does mention thieves ravaging others' possessions, it is only meant as an example and not as the principle itself. Choice *B* is incorrect for the same reason as *A*. Choice *C* is mentioned in the text and is part of the example that proves the principle, and also not the principle itself.

61. C: The word *avarice* most nearly means *covetousness*, or extremely desirous of money or wealth. Choice *A* means *evil* or *mischief* and does not relate to the context of the sentence. Choice *B* is also incorrect, because *pithiness* means *shortness* or *conciseness.* Choice *D* is close because *precariousness*

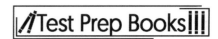

means dangerous or instability, which goes well with the context. However, we are told of the summoner's specific characteristic of greed, which makes Choice *C* the best answer.

62. D: Desire for pleasure can lead toward sin. Boethianism acknowledges desire as something that leads out of holiness, so Choice *A* is incorrect. Choice *B* is incorrect because in the passage, Boethianism is depicted as being wary of desire and anything that binds people to the physical world. Choice *C* can be eliminated because the author never says that desire indicates demonic possession.

63. B: It denotes a period of time. It is apparent that Lincoln is referring to a period of time within the context of the passage because the sentence contains the words years and ago. Choices *A*, *C*, and *D* do not fit the language or context of the sentence and are therefore incorrect.

64. C: Lincoln's reference to *the brave men, living and dead, who struggled here,* proves that he is referring to a battlefield. Choices *A* and *B* are incorrect, as a *civil war* is mentioned and not a war with France or a war in the Sahara Desert. Choice *D* is incorrect because it does not make sense to consecrate a President's ground instead of a battlefield ground for soldiers who died during the American Civil War.

65. D: Abraham Lincoln is a former president of the United States, and he referenced a "civil war" during his address.

66. A: Lincoln doesn't address any of the topics outlined in Choices *B*, *C*, or *D*. Therefore, Choice *A* is the correct answer.

67. D: Choice *D* is the correct answer because of the repetition of the word *people* at the end of the passage. Choice *A*, *antimetatabole*, is the repetition of words in a succession. Choice *B*, *antiphrasis*, is a form of denial of an assertion in a text. Choice *C*, *anaphora*, is the repetition that occurs at the beginning of sentences.

68. A: Choice *A* is correct because Lincoln's intention was to memorialize the soldiers who had fallen as a result of war as well as celebrate those who had put their lives in danger for the sake of their country. Choices *B*, *C,* and *D* are incorrect because Lincoln's speech was supposed to foster a sense of pride among the members of the audience while connecting them to the soldiers' experiences.

69. C: In Choice *C*, *avid* is functioning as an adjective that modifies the word photographer. *Avid* describes the photographer Julia Robinson's style. The words *time* and *photographer* are functioning as nouns, and the word *capture* is functioning as a verb in the sentence. Other words functioning as adjectives in the sentence include, *local, business,* and *spare*, as they all describe the nouns they precede.

70. B: Choice *B* is correct because the pronouns *he* and *I* are in the subjective case. *He* and *I* are the subjects of the verb *like* in the independent clause of the sentence. Choices *A, C,* and *D* are incorrect because they all contain at least one objective pronoun (*me* and *him*). Objective pronouns should not be used as the subject of the sentence, but rather, they should come as an object of a verb. To test for correct pronoun usage, try reading the pronouns as if they were the only pronoun in the sentence. For example, *he* and *me* may appear to be the correct answer choices, but try reading them as the only pronoun.

He like[s] to go fishing...

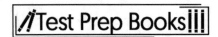

Me like to go fishing...

When looked at that way, *me* is an obviously incorrect choice.

71. D: In Choice *D*, the word function is a noun. While the word *function* can also act as a verb, in this particular sentence it is acting as a noun as the object of the preposition *at*. Choices *A* and *B* are incorrect because the word *function* cannot be used as an adjective or adverb.

72. C: Cacti is the correct plural form of the word *cactus*. Choice *A* (*tomatos*) includes an incorrect spelling of the plural of *tomato*. Both Choice *B* (*analysis*) and Choice *D* (*criterion*) are incorrect because they are in singular form. The correct plural form for these choices would be *criteria* and *analyses*.

73. B: Quotation marks are used to indicate something someone said. The example sentences feature a direct quotation that requires the use of double quotation marks. Also, the end punctuation, in this case a question mark, should always be contained within the quotation marks. Choice *A* is incorrect because there is an unnecessary period after the quotation mark. Choice *C* is incorrect because it uses single quotation marks, which are used for a quote within a quote. Choice *D* is incorrect because it places the punctuation outside of the quotation marks.

74. D: In Choice *D*, the word *part* functions as an adjective that modifies the word *Irish*. Choices *A* and *C* are incorrect because the word *part* functions as a noun in these sentences. Choice *B* is incorrect because the word *part* functions as a verb.

75. C: *All of Shannon's family and friends* is the complete subject because it includes who or what is doing the action in the sentence as well as the modifiers that go with it. Choice *A* is incorrect because it only includes the simple subject of the sentence. Choices *B* and *D* are incorrect because they only include part of the complete subject.

76. C: Choice *C* is correct because quotation marks should be used for the title of a short work such as a poem. Choices *A*, *B*, and *D* are incorrect because the titles of novels, films, and newspapers should be placed in italics, not quotation marks.

77. C: This question focuses on the correct usage of the commonly confused word pairs of *it's/its* and *then/than*. *It's* is a contraction for *it is* or *it has*. *Its* is a possessive pronoun. The word *than* shows comparison between two things. *Then* is an adverb that conveys time. Choice *C* correctly uses *it's* and *than*. *It's* is a contraction for *it has* in this sentence, and *than* shows comparison between *work* and *rest*. None of the other answers choices use both of the correct words.

78. B: Choice *B* is an imperative sentence because it issues a command. In addition, it ends with a period, and an imperative sentence must end in a period or exclamation mark. Choice *A* is a declarative sentence that states a fact and ends with a period. Choice *C* is an exclamatory sentence that shows strong emotion and ends with an exclamation point. Choice *D* is an interrogative sentence that asks a question and ends with a question mark.

79. C: Choice *C* is a compound sentence because it joins two independent clauses—*The baby was sick* and *I decided to stay home from work*—with a comma and the coordinating conjunction *so*. Choices *A, B,* and *D* are all simple sentences, each containing one independent clause with a complete subject and predicate. Choices *A* and *D* each contain a compound subject, or more than one subject, but they are still simple sentences that only contain one independent clause. Choice *B* contains a compound verb (more than one verb), but it's still a simple sentence.

80. C: The simple subject of this sentence, the word *lots*, is plural. It agrees with the plural verb form *were*. Choice *A* is incorrect, because the simple subject *there*, referring to the two constellations, is considered plural. It does not agree with the singular verb form *is*. In Choice *B*, the plural subject *four*, does not agree with the singular verb form *needs*. In Choice *D* the singular subject *everyone* does not agree with the third person plural verb form *have*.

Mathematics

1. A: Compare each number after the decimal point to figure out which overall number is greatest. In Choices *A* (1.43785) and *C* (1.43592), both have the same tenths place (4) and hundredths place (3). However, the thousandths place is greater in Choice *A* (7), so *A* has the greatest value overall.

2. D: By grouping the four numbers in the answer into factors of the two numbers of the question (6 and 12), it can be determined that:

$$(3 \times 2) \times (4 \times 3) = 6 \times 12$$

Alternatively, you could find the prime factorization of each answer choices and compare it to the original value. The product of 6×12 is 72 and has a prime factorization of $2^3 \times 3^2$. The answer choices respectively have values of 64, 84, 108, and 72 and prime factorizations of 2^6, $2^2 \times 3 \times 7$, $2^2 \times 3^3$, and $2^3 \times 3^2$, so Choice *D* is the correct choice.

3. A: To figure out which is largest, look at the first non-zero digits. Choice *B*'s first nonzero digit is in the hundredths place. The other three all have nonzero digits in the tenths place, so it must be *A, C,* or *D*. Of these, *A* has the largest first nonzero digit.

4. C: To solve for the value of b, isolate the variable b on one side of the equation.

Start by moving the lower value of -4 to the other side by adding 4 to both sides:

$$5b - 4 = 2b + 17$$

$$5b - 4 + 4 = 2b + 17 + 4$$

$$5b = 2b + 21$$

Then subtract $2b$ from both sides:

$$5b - 2b = 2b + 21 - 2b$$

$$3b = 21$$

Then divide both sides by 3 to get the value of b:

$$\frac{3b}{3} = \frac{21}{3}$$

$$b = 7$$

5. D: The total faculty is:

$$15 + 20 = 35$$

So, the ratio is $35 : 200$. Then, divide both of these numbers by 5, since 5 is a common factor to both, with a result of $7 : 40$.

6. C: The first step in solving this problem is expressing the result in fraction form. Multiplication and division are typically performed in order from left to right but they can be performed in any order. For this problem, let's start by solving the division operation of the last two fractions. When dividing one fraction by another, invert or flip the second fraction and then multiply the numerator and denominator.

$$\frac{7}{10} \times \frac{2}{1} = \frac{14}{10}$$

Next, multiply the first fraction with this value:

$$\frac{3}{5} \times \frac{14}{10} = \frac{42}{50}$$

In this instance, you can find the decimal form by converting the fraction into $\frac{x}{100}$, where x is the number from which the final decimal is found. Multiply both the numerator and denominator by 2 to get the fraction as an expression of $\frac{x}{100}$.

$$\frac{42}{50} \times \frac{2}{2} = \frac{84}{100}$$

In decimal form, this would be expressed as 0.84.

7. C: The product of two irrational numbers can be rational or irrational. Sometimes the irrational parts of the two numbers cancel each other out, leaving a rational number. For example, $\sqrt{2} \times \sqrt{2} = 2$ because the roots cancel each other out. Technically, the product of two irrational numbers can be complex because complex numbers can have either the real or imaginary part (in this case, the imaginary part) equal zero and still be considered a complex number. However, Choice D is incorrect because the product of two irrational numbers is not an imaginary number so saying the product is complex and imaginary is incorrect.

8. C: The number negative four is classified as a real number because it exists and is not imaginary. It is rational because it does not have a decimal that never ends. It is an integer because it does not have a fractional component. The next classification would be whole numbers, for which negative four does not qualify because it is negative. Choice *D* is wrong because -4 is not considered an irrational number because it does not have a never-ending decimal component.

288

9. A: Setting up a proportion is the easiest way to represent this situation. The proportion becomes $\frac{20}{x} = \frac{40}{100}$, where cross-multiplication can be used to solve for x. Here, $40x = 2000$, so $x = 50$.

10. A: Finding the product means distributing one polynomial to the other so that each term in the first is multiplied by each term in the second. Then, like terms can be collected. Multiplying the factors yields the expression:

$$20x^3 + 4x^2 + 24x - 40x^2 - 8x - 48$$

Collecting like terms means adding the x^2 terms and adding the x-terms. The final answer after simplifying the expression is:

$$20x^3 - 36x^2 + 16x - 48$$

11. B: The equation can be solved by factoring the numerator into:

$$(x + 6)(x - 5)$$

Since that same factor $(x - 5)$ exists on top and bottom, that factor cancels. This leaves the equation $x + 6 = 11$. Solving the equation gives the answer $x = 5$. When this value is plugged into the equation, it yields a zero in the denominator of the fraction. Since this is undefined, there is no solution.

12. C: Scientific notation division can be solved by grouping the first terms together and grouping the tens together. The first terms can be divided, and the tens terms can be simplified using the rules for exponents. The initial expression becomes 0.4×10^4. This is not in scientific notation because first number is not a positive whole number less than 10. Shifting the decimal and subtracting one from the exponent, the answer becomes 4.0×10^3.

13. D: The expression is three times the sum of twice a number and 1, which is $3(2x + 1)$. Then, 6 is subtracted from this expression.

14. B: To solve this correctly, keep in mind the order of operations with the mnemonic PEMDAS (Please Excuse My Dear Aunt Sally). This stands for Parentheses, Exponents, Multiplication, Division, Addition, Subtraction. Taking it step by step, solve the parentheses first:

$$4 \times 7 + (4)^2 \div 2$$

Then, apply the exponent:

$$4 \times 7 + 16 \div 2$$

Multiplication and division are both performed next:

$$28 + 8$$

Then finally, addition:

$$28 + 8 = 36$$

289

15. D:

$9x + x - 7 = 16 + 2x$	Combine $9x$ and x
$10x - 7 = 16 + 2x$	
$10x - 7 + 7 = 16 + 2x + 7$	Add 7 to both sides to remove (-7).
$10x = 23 + 2x$	
$10x - 2x = 23 + 2x - 2x$	Subtract $2x$ from both sides to move it to the other side of the equation.
$8x = 23$	
$\dfrac{8x}{8} = \dfrac{23}{8}$	Divide by 8 to get x by itself.
$x = \dfrac{23}{8}$	

16. C: The first step is to depict each number using decimals:

$$\frac{91}{100} = 0.91$$

Dividing the numerator by denominator of $\frac{4}{5}$ to convert it to a decimal yields 0.80, while $\frac{2}{3}$ becomes 0.66 recurring. Rearrange each expression in ascending order, as found in Choice *C*.

17. B: First, calculate the difference between the larger value and the smaller value:

$$378 - 252 = 126$$

To calculate this difference as a percentage of the original value, and thus calculate the percentage *increase*, divide 126 by 252, then multiply by 100 to reach the percentage 50%, Choice *B*.

18. A: First, simplify the larger fraction by separating it into two. When dividing one fraction by another, remember to *invert* the second fraction and multiply the two, as follows:

$$\frac{5}{7} \times \frac{11}{9}$$

The resulting fraction $\frac{55}{63}$ cannot be simplified further, so this is the answer to the problem.

19. B: $\frac{5}{2} \div \frac{1}{3} = \frac{5}{2} \times \frac{3}{1} = \frac{15}{2} = 7.5$.

20. C: The sum total percentage of a pie chart must equal 100%. Since the CD sales take up less than half of the chart (50%) and more than a quarter (25%), it can be determined to be 40% overall. This can also be measured with a protractor. The angle of a circle is 360°. Since 25% of 360° would be 90° and 50% would be 180°, the angle percentage of CD sales falls in between; therefore, it would be Choice *C*.

21. A: $3\frac{3}{5}$. Divide 54 by 15:

$$15\overline{)54} \\ \,\underline{-45} \\ \;\;9$$

$$\begin{array}{r} 3 \\ 15\overline{)54} \\ -45 \\ \hline 9 \end{array}$$

The result is $3\frac{9}{15}$. Reduce the remainder for the final answer, $3\frac{3}{5}$.

22. D: $\frac{59}{7}$

The original number was $8\frac{3}{7}$. Multiply the denominator by the whole number portion. Add the numerator and put the total over the original denominator.

$$\frac{(8 \times 7) + 3}{7} = \frac{59}{7}$$

23. B: Multiplying by 10^{-3} means moving the decimal point three places to the left, putting in zeros as necessary.

24. D: This problem can be solved by using unit conversions. The initial units are miles per minute. The final units need to be feet per second. Converting miles to feet uses the equivalence statement 1 mile = 5,280 feet. Converting minutes to seconds uses the equivalence statement 1 minute = 60 seconds. Setting up the ratios to convert the units is shown in the following equation:

$$\frac{72 \text{ miles}}{90 \text{ minutes}} \times \frac{1 \text{ minute}}{60 \text{ seconds}} \times \frac{5{,}280 \text{ feet}}{1 \text{ mile}} = 70.4 \text{ feet per second}$$

The initial units cancel out, and the new, desired units are left.

25. C: Because the triangles are similar, the lengths of the corresponding sides are proportional. Therefore:

$$\frac{30 + x}{30} = \frac{22}{14} = \frac{y + 15}{y}$$

This results in the equation:

$$14(30 + x) = 22 \times 30$$

When solved, this gives:

$$x = 17.1$$

The proportion also results in the equation:

$$14(y + 15) = 22y$$

When solved, this gives:

$$y = 26.3$$

26. D: SOHCAHTOA is used to find the missing side length. Because the angle and adjacent side are known, $\tan 60 = \frac{x}{13}$. Making sure to evaluate tangent with an argument in degrees, this equation gives:

$$x = 13 \tan 60 = 13 \times \sqrt{3} = 22.52$$

27. B: Because this isn't a right triangle, SOHCAHTOA can't be used. However, the law of cosines can be used. Therefore:

$$c^2 = a^2 + b^2 - 2ab \cos C$$

$$c^2 = 19^2 + 26^2 - 2 \times 19 \times 26 \times \cos 42° = 302.773$$

Taking the square root and rounding to the nearest tenth results in $c = 17.4$.

28. C: The formula for the perimeter of a rectangle is $P = 2L + 2W$, where P is the perimeter, L is the length, and W is the width. The first step is to substitute all of the data into the formula:

$$36 = 2(12) + 2W$$

Simplify by multiplying 2×12:

$$36 = 24 + 2W$$

Simplifying this further by subtracting 24 on each side gives:

$$36 - 24 = 24 - 24 + 2W$$

$$12 = 2W$$

Divide by 2:

$$6 = W$$

The width is 6 cm. Remember to test this answer by substituting this value into the original formula:

$$36 = 2(12) + 2(6)$$

29. D: The addition rule is necessary to determine the probability because a 6 can be rolled on either roll of the die but not both. The rule used is:

$$P(A \text{ or } B) = P(A) + P(B) - P(A \text{ and } B)$$

The probability of a 6 being individually rolled is $\frac{1}{6}$ and the probability of a 6 being rolled twice is:

$$\frac{1}{6} \times \frac{1}{6} = \frac{1}{36}$$

Therefore, the probability that a 6 is rolled at least once is:

$$\frac{1}{6} + \frac{1}{6} - \frac{1}{36} = \frac{11}{36}$$

30. B: For the first card drawn, the probability of a king being pulled is $\frac{4}{52}$. Since this card isn't replaced, if a king is drawn first, the probability of a king being drawn second is $\frac{3}{51}$. The probability of a king being drawn in both the first and second draw is the product of the two probabilities:

$$\frac{4}{52} \times \frac{3}{51} = \frac{12}{2,652}$$

This fraction, when divided by $\frac{12}{12}$, equals $\frac{1}{221}$.

31. A: If each man gains 10 pounds, every original data point will increase by 10 pounds. Therefore, the man with the original median will still have the median value, but that value will increase by 10. The smallest value and largest value will also increase by 10 and, therefore, the difference between the two won't change. The range does not change in value and, thus, remains the same.

32. C: The average is calculated by adding all six numbers, then dividing by 6. The first five numbers have a sum of 25. If the total divided by 6 is equal to 6, then the total itself must be 36. The sixth number must be $36 - 25 = 11$.

33. D: When an ordered pair is reflected over an axis, the sign of at least one of the coordinates must change. When it's reflected over the x-axis, the sign of the y-coordinate must change. The x-value remains the same. Therefore, the new ordered pair is $(-3, 4)$.

34. B: The car is traveling at a speed of five meters per second. On the interval from one to three seconds, the position changes by ten meters. By making this change in position over time into a rate, the speed becomes ten meters in two seconds, or five meters in one second.

35. B: An equilateral triangle has three sides of equal length, so if the total perimeter is 18 feet, each side must be 6 feet long. A square with sides of 6 feet will have an area of $6^2 = 36$ square feet.

36. B: The formula for the volume of a cube is $V = s^3$. Substitute the side length of 7 in to get:

$$V = 7^3 = 343 \text{ in}^3$$

37. A: The conversion can be obtained by setting up and solving the following equation:

$$4,382 \text{ ft} \times \frac{0.3048 \text{ m}}{1 \text{ ft}} \times \frac{1 \text{ km}}{1,000 \text{ m}} = 1.336 \text{ km}$$

38. A: This answer is correct because $100 - 64$ is 36 and taking the square root of 36 is 6. Choice *B* is not the correct answer because that is $10 + 8$. Choice *C* is not the correct answer because that is 8×10. Choice *D* is also not the correct answer because there is no reason to arrive at that number.

39. A: Lining up the given scores provides the following list: 60, 75, 80, 85, and one unknown. Because the median needs to be 80, it means 80 must be the middle data point out of these five. Therefore, the

unknown data point must be the fourth or fifth data point, meaning it must be greater than or equal to 80. The only answer that fails to meet this condition is 60.

40. D: This problem can be solved by setting up a proportion involving the given information and the unknown value. The proportion is:

$$\frac{21 \text{ pages}}{4 \text{ nights}} = \frac{140 \text{ pages}}{x \text{ nights}}$$

Solving the proportion by cross-multiplying, the equation becomes $21x = 4 \times 140$, where $x = 26.67$. Since it is not an exact number of nights, the answer is rounded up to 27 nights. Twenty-six nights would not give Sarah enough time.

41. B: Using the conversion rate, multiply the projected weight loss of 25 lb by $0.45 \frac{\text{kg}}{\text{lb}}$ to get the amount in kilograms (11.25 kg).

42. D: First, subtract $1,437 from $2,334.50 to find Johnny's monthly savings; this equals $897.50. Then, multiply this amount by 3 to find out how much he will have (in three months) before he pays for his vacation: this equals $2,692.50. Finally, subtract the cost of the vacation ($1,750) from this amount to find how much Johnny will have left: $942.50.

43. C: Kimberley worked 4.5 hours at the rate of $10/h and 1 hour at the rate of $12/h. The problem states that her pay is rounded to the nearest hour, so the 4.5 hours would round up to 5 hours at the rate of $10/h.

$$(5 \text{ h}) \times (\$10/\text{h}) + (1 \text{ h}) \times (\$12/\text{h}) = \$50 + \$12 = \$62$$

44. A: This vector indicates a positive relationship. A negative relationship would show points traveling from the top-left of the graph to the bottom-right. Exponential and logarithmic functions aren't linear (don't create a straight line), so these options can be immediately eliminated.

45. C: There is no verifiable relationship between the two variables. While it may seem to have somewhat of a negative correlation because of the last two data points: $(5.6, 8)$ and $(6, 7)$, you must also take into account the two data points before those $(5, 1)$ and $(5.2, 2)$ that have low y-values despite high x-values. Data with a normal distribution, Choice A, has an arc to it while this data does not.

46. B: The formula can be manipulated by dividing both sides by the length, l, and the width, w. The length and width will cancel on the right, leaving height by itself.

47. B: The table shows values that are increasing exponentially. The differences between the inputs are the same, while the differences in the outputs are changing by a factor of 2. The values in the table can be modeled by the equation $f(x) = 2^x$.

48. B: To factor $x^2 + 4x + 4$, the numbers needed are those that add to 4 and multiply to 4. Therefore, both numbers must be 2, and the expression factors to:

$$x^2 + 4x + 4 = (x + 2)^2$$

Similarly, the second expression factors to $x^2 - x - 6 = (x - 3)(x + 2)$, so that they have $x + 2$ in common.

49. B: Add 3 to both sides to get $4x = 8$. Then divide both sides by 4 to get $x = 2$.

50. C: The sample space is made up of:

$$8 + 7 + 6 + 5 = 26 \text{ balls}$$

The probability of pulling each individual ball is $\frac{1}{26}$. Since there are 7 yellow balls, the probability of pulling a yellow ball is $\frac{7}{26}$.

Social Studies

1. B: John White does not have an important historical influence to the state of Georgia. White was the leader of the Roanoke colony founded under the authority of Sir Walter Raleigh in what was then called Virginia and later became North Carolina. White went back to England for supplies in 1587 and when he returned, all of the colonists had mysteriously disappeared.

2. B: To avoid involvement in political processes such as voting is antithetical to the principles of a democracy. Therefore, the principal responsibility of citizens is the opposite, and they should be steadily engaged in the political processes that determine the course of government.

3. A: Choice *A* is correct. Heavily influenced by the Enlightenment, the Declaration of Independence repudiated the colonies' allegiance to Great Britain. The main purpose of the excerpt is to justify the colonists' revolutionary stance due to Great Britain's tyranny and the role of consent in government to protect the natural rights of citizens. Choice B is incorrect because, although the excerpt alludes to abuses, the purpose isn't to list specific evidence. This occurs later in the Declaration of Independence. Choices C and D are supporting evidence for the main purpose.

4. A: James Oglethorpe convinced King George II to colonize the area that is now Georgia with individuals from Britain's overflowing debtor's prisons. Button Gwinnett, George Walton, and Lyman Hall were the three Georgians who signed the Declaration of Independence in 1776. Thus, Choices B, C, and D are incorrect.

5. C: At the time of the Constitutional Convention, Thomas Jefferson was in Paris serving as America's foreign minister to France. Therefore, he is not a good fit for this project. George Washington led the meeting, and Alexander Hamilton and James Madison set the tone for debate, rendering A, B, and D incorrect.

6. A: Plains Indians followed the buffalo across the prairies, living in tent-like teepees that were easily moved from place to place. Choice *B* is incorrect because Indians in the Southwest relied on farming for much of their food and built adobes, which are houses made out of dried clay or earth. Indians in the Eastern and Northwest sections of North America survived by hunting, gathering, farming, and fishing, and lived in wooden longhouses, plank houses, or wigwams. Thus, Choices C and D are incorrect.

7. C: Established in 1607, Jamestown, Virginia was the first permanent British settlement in the New World. Plymouth was founded a bit later in 1620 when a group of Pilgrims founded the first permanent European settlement in New England, making Choice A incorrect. Choice B is incorrect because although the Roanoke Colony was founded in 1585, it isn't considered permanent – the colony's leader, John White, went back to England for supplies two years later, and he returned to find that all of the colonists

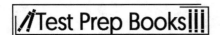

had mysteriously disappeared. Choice *D* is incorrect because L'Anse Meadows was an area in Newfoundland that was briefly settled by Scandinavian Vikings around 1000 A.D.

8. C: The first shot took place on Lexington Green. When the British heard that colonists were stockpiling weapons they sent troops to Concord to seize them. However, a group of approximately seventy Minutemen confronted the British soldiers on Lexington green. British troops killed five protesting colonists during the Boston Massacre in 1770, but this is not considered the first shot of the Revolution. Thus, Choice *A* is incorrect. Choice *B* is incorrect because the Boston Tea Party was when colonists dumped 342 chests of expensive tea into the Boston Harbor in defiance of the tea tax. The Revolution had already started when the Battle of Trenton took place on December 25, 1776, making Choice *D* incorrect.

9. D: There are twenty-seven amendments to the U.S. Constitution. The 14th Amendment was adopted in 1868 to abolish slavery. The 18th Amendment was passed in 1919 and prohibited the production and sale of alcoholic beverages, but the 21st Amendment repealed it in 1933.

10. D: Thematic maps create certain themes in which they attempt to illustrate a certain phenomenon or pattern. The obvious theme of a climate map is the climates in the represented areas. Thematic maps are very extensive and can include thousands of different themes, which makes them quite useful for students of geography. Topographic maps (Choice *A*) are utilized to show physical features, conformal projections (Choice *B*) attempt to illustrate the globe in an undistorted fashion, and isoline maps (Choice *C*) illustrate differences in variables between two points on a map.

11. B: Latitudinal and longitudinal coordinates delineate absolute location. In contrast to relative location, which describes a location as compared to another, better-known place, absolute location provides an exact place on the globe through the latitude and longitude system. Choice A, cardinal directions (north, south, east, west) are used in absolute location, but coordinates must be added in order to have an absolute location. Using other, better-known locations to find a location, Choice *C*, is referred to as relative location, and absolute location is far more precise than simply finding hemispherical position on the globe.

12. C: Each statement about culture is correct except for Choice *C*. Cultures often will adapt to the settings in which they are found. Improvements in technology, changes in social values, and interactions with other cultures all contribute to cultural change.

13. B: Lines of latitude measure distance north and south. The equator is zero degrees, and the Tropic of Cancer is 23 ½ degrees north of the equator. The distance between those two lines measures degrees north to south, as with any other two lines of latitude. Longitudinal lines, or meridians, measure distance east and west, even though they run north and south down the Globe. Latitude is not inexact, in that there are set distances between the lines. Furthermore, coordinates can only exist with the use of longitude and latitude.

14. D: During the Achaemenid Empire, Persians practiced the Zoroastrian faith and worshipped two gods. Islam only came about one thousand years later. The Achaemenids built a Royal Road that stretched across their empire, but the Silk Roads expanded throughout Asia. The Achaemenids twice tried to conquer Greece but failed both times.

15. A: The Silk Roads were a network of trade routes between Asia and the Mediterranean. Merchants and Pilgrims traveled along the Silk Roads and brought new ideas and technologies, as well as trade

296

goods. For example, Buddhism spread from India to China. Chinese technologies also spread westward, including gunpowder and the printing press. The Silk Roads also spread the Bubonic Plague to Europe, but it did not arrive in the New World until Columbus landed there in 1492.

16. A: Invasions by Germanic tribes. Large numbers of Franks, Goths, Vandals, and other Germanic peoples began moving south in the fifth century CE. They conquered Rome twice, and the Western Roman Empire finally disintegrated. The Mongol invasion, Choice *B*, pushed westward in the thirteenth century, long after the western Roman Empire was gone. The assassination of Julius Caesar, Choice *C*, led to the end of the Roman Republic and the birth of the Roman Empire. Taoism never spread to Rome, making Choice *D* incorrect.

17. A: The Mongol army was largely a cavalry force. The Mongols were a nomadic people who trained as horsemen from a young age. They used their highly mobile army to build a huge empire in Asia, the Middle East, and Eastern Europe. Mongol rulers were relatively tolerant of other religions because they wanted to reduce conflict within their empire, making Choice *B* incorrect. They also encouraged trade because they produced few of their own goods, making Choice *C* incorrect. The Mongol rulers also encouraged literacy and appreciated visual art, making Choice *D* incorrect.

18. A: Renaissance scholars and artists sought to emulate classical Greek and Roman culture. They translated Greek and Roman political philosophers and literature. They also copied classical architecture. Europeans had little direct contact with China until the thirteenth century, which was long after the Zhou Dynasty collapsed, making Choice *C* incorrect. The Renaissance Era occurred within the continent of Europe and drew from other European styles, so nations of northern Africa and the Middle East, such as ancient Egypt and the Ottoman Empire, had little to no inspiration on Renaissance scholars and artists at that time. Therefore, Choices *B* and *D* are incorrect.

19. C: In the 1800s, nationalists in different parts of Europe encouraged their countrymen to take pride in their shared backgrounds. This led to tension between different nations, as each sought to increase its status and prestige. The French and British nearly came to blows in Africa, and nationalism ultimately led to World War I in 1914. France and Spain were unified several centuries before the 1800s.

20. D: All three events led to increasing tension and conflict between the colonists and the British government, which finally exploded at the Battle of Lexington and Concord in 1775. The Stamp Act of 1765 imposed a tax on documents. It was repealed after colonists organized protests. The Boston Massacre resulted in the death of five colonists in 1770. The Boston Tea Party was a protest in 1773 against a law that hurt colonial tea merchants. The British responded to the tea party by punishing the colony of Massachusetts, which created fear among the other colonies and united them against the British government.

21. C: Power is the ability of a ruling body or political entity to influence the actions, behavior, and attitude of a person or group of people. Authority, Choice *A*, is the right and justification of the government to exercise power as recognized by the citizens or influential elites. Similarly, legitimacy, Choice *D*, is another way of expressing the concept of authority. Sovereignty, Choice *B*, refers to the ability of a state to determine and control their territory without foreign interference.

22. D: Sovereignty is the feature that differentiates a state from a nation. Nations have no sovereignty, as they are unable to enact and enforce laws independently of their state. A state must possess sovereignty over the population of a territory in order to be legitimized as a state. Both a nation and a

297

state must have a population, Choice *C*. Although sometimes present, shared history and common language are not requirements for a state, making Choices *A* and *B* incorrect.

23. A: Devastated by World War II, Britain and France were unable to maintain their empires. Japan and Germany were also weak, which left only the United States and USSR as superpowers. The Russian Revolution had occurred during World War I, in 1917, making Choice *B* incorrect. Ideological and economic conflict between the U.S. and the USSR led to the start of the Cold War shortly after World War II ended, making Choice *C* incorrect. Choice *D* is also incorrect; the death of Franz Ferdinand marked the beginning of World War I.

24. A: Although some ethnic groups throughout the world do engage in armed conflicts, the vast majority do not. Most ethnic groups tend to live in relative harmony with others with whom they share differences. Ethnic groups are simply a group of people with a religious, cultural, economic, or linguistic commonality. Additionally, ethnic groups don't always choose to leave places. Many have called certain locations home for centuries. Also, some ethnic groups actually make up the majority in some countries and are not always minority groups.

25. A: The use of biotechnology and GMOs has increased the total amount of food on Earth. Additionally, it has helped to sustain the Earth's growing population; however, many activists assert that scientists are creating crops that, in the long run, will be destructive to human health, even though not enough evidence exists to prove such an allegation. Agricultural production has not been affected by poorer soil, plagues of pests, or the use of saline for irrigation purposes.

26. C: Like the boundaries of the United States, political boundaries are constantly changing due to war (South Sudan), religious conflict (India and Pakistan, Israel, East Timor), and differing political ideologies (North and South Korea, Reunification of Germany after the Cold War). The only constant with political boundaries is change. It is not possible to see manmade lines separating countries on Earth, unless they are natural boundaries. Additionally, boundaries are always under dispute, and they have not remained static for centuries.

27. B: Macroeconomics. Macroeconomics studies the economy on a large scale and focuses on issues such as unemployment, interest rates, price levels, and national income. Microeconomics studies more individual or small group behaviors such as scarcity or supply and demand. Scarcity is incorrect because it refers to the availability of goods and services. Supply and demand is also incorrect because it refers to the quantity of goods and services that is produced and/or needed.

28. A: Free. A free market does not involve government interventions or monopolies while trading between buyers and suppliers. However, in a command market, the government determines the price of goods and services. Gross and exchange markets refer to situations where brokers and traders make exchanges in the financial realm.

29. D: Theory of The Firm. Behaviors of firms is not an indicator of economic growth because it refers to the behavior that firms follow to reach their desired outcome. GDP, unemployment, and inflation are all indicators that help determine economic growth.

30. A: Most scholars already knew the world was round by 1492. On the other hand, the arrival of Europeans in North and South America introduced deadly diseases that killed millions of native peoples. Europeans had developed immunity to diseases such as smallpox, while Native Americans had not. In addition, Europeans introduced a number of new plants and animals to the New World, but they also

adopted many new foods as well, including potatoes, tomatoes, chocolate, and tobacco. Finally, Europeans tried to convert Native Americans to Christianity, but Indians did not completely give up their traditional beliefs. Instead, they blended Christianity with indigenous and African beliefs to create new syncretic religions.

31. D: The Industrial Revolution is probably one of the most important turning points in world history. The United States and Western Europe, especially Britain, were the first areas to industrialize. Steam engines were used to improve economic and transportation efficiency. They also gave western empires a military advantage over less developed countries in Asia and Africa. Finally, industrialization required large amounts of unskilled labor, which created the working class.

32. D: The Constitution granted Congress the power to decide how many justices should be on the court, and Congress first decided on six judges in the Judiciary Act of 1789. The Constitution granted the power to appoint judges and to call special sessions of Congress to the president. Only the Supreme Court may interpret the laws enacted by Congress and rule a law unconstitutional and subsequently overturn the law.

33. C: The first ten amendments to the Constitution are collectively referred to as the Bill of Rights. The Founding Fathers did not support universal suffrage, and as such, the Bill of Rights did not encompass the freedom to vote. The Fifteenth Amendment provided that the right to vote shall not be denied on the basis of race, color, or previous condition of servitude, and women did not receive the right to vote until passage of the Nineteenth Amendment. The other three answer choices are included in the Bill of Rights—the freedom to assembly is established in the First Amendment; the freedom against unlawful search is established in the Fourth Amendment; and the reservation of non-enumerated powers to the states or the people is established in the Tenth Amendment.

34. C: The president of the United States is elected by the Electoral College. The number of electors for each state depends on the state's total number of senators and representatives. The president must receive a majority (270) of the electoral votes (538), and if this doesn't occur, the Twelfth Amendment empowers the House of Representatives to elect the president. Choices *A, B,* and *C* are different methods for electing candidates.

35. B: Choice *B* is correct. President Franklin D. Roosevelt introduced the New Deal, a series of executive orders and laws passed by Congress in response to the Great Depression. The excerpt describes how President Roosevelt intended to fight poverty by using the government's power to intervene and regulate the economy. Although Choices A, C, and D correctly identify specific activities referenced in the excerpt, they are specific examples of the underlying philosophy in action. The underlying philosophy is an active role for government in the nation's economic affairs.

36. D: The two major political parties hold conventions to nominate their presidential candidate. The delegates are awarded based on candidates' performance in the primary elections or caucuses vote at the party convention to select the nominee. Primaries and caucuses are the democratic contests held by each state to award their delegates. The candidates participate in debates on the campaign issues, but they do not receive the nomination at debates.

37. B: The process by which the House and Senate may debate a bill differs. In the House, how long a speaker may debate a bill is limited, while in the Senate, speakers may debate the bill indefinitely and delay voting on the bill by filibuster—a practice in which a speaker refuses to stop speaking until a

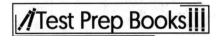

majority vote stops the filibuster or the time for the vote passes. In both the House and the Senate, anyone may introduce a bill. Only the president of the United States may veto the bill, so neither the House nor Senate holds that power. Before the bill may be presented to the president to be signed, the wording of the bill must be identical in both houses. Another procedural difference is that the number of amendments is limited in the House but not the Senate; however, this does not appear as an answer choice.

38. C: Map projections, such as the Mercator Projection, are useful for finding positions on the globe, but they attempt to represent a spherical object on a flat surface. As a result, they distort areas nearest the poles, which misrepresent the size of Antarctica, Greenland, and other high latitudinal locations. Map projects can include great detail; some illustrate the physical features in an area, and most include both the northern and southern hemispheres.

39. C: Developed Nations have better infrastructural systems, which can include government, transportation, financial, and educational institutions. Consequently, its citizens tend to have higher rates of literacy, due to the sheer availability of educational resources and government sanctioned educational systems. In contrast, developing nations struggle to provide educational resources to their citizens. Nations in the Northern Hemisphere have no greater availability to educational resources than those in the Southern Hemisphere, and centers of trade don't necessarily equate to higher levels of education as many may exist in poorer nations with fewer resources.

40. C: Although it can place a strain on some resources, population density is not a negative demographic indicator. For example, New York City, one of the most densely populated places on Earth, enjoys one of the highest standards of living in the world. Other world cities such as Tokyo, Los Angeles, and Sydney also have tremendously high population densities and high standards of living. High infant mortality rates, low literacy rates, and low life expectancies are all poor demographic indicators that suggest a low quality of life for the citizens living in those areas.

41. C: Longitudinal position, or a place's location either east or west, has no bearing on the place's climate. In contrast, a place's latitudinal position, or its distance away from the direct rays of the sun in the Tropics, greatly affects its climate. Additionally, proximity to mountains, which can block wind patterns, and elevation, which generally lowers temperature by three degrees for every one thousand feet gained, also impacts climate.

42. D: Although nearest the direct rays of the sun, the Tropics are not always warm. In fact, the nations of Ecuador and Peru, which are entirely within the Tropics, are home to the Andes Mountains, which remain snowcapped the entire year. This climatological anomaly is also due to cooler ocean currents and the orographic effect. Choices *A, B,* and *C* are all true of the tropics.

43. B: Choice *B* is correct, as power is the ability of a ruling body to influence the actions, behavior, and attitude of a person or group of people. Choice *A* is incorrect, as politics is the process of governance typically exercised through the enactment and enforcement of laws over a community, such as a state. Although closely related to power, Choice *C* is incorrect, because authority refers to a political entity's justification to exercise power. Legitimacy is synonymous with authority, so Choice *D* is also incorrect.

44. C: Choice *C* is correct. Sovereignty is a characteristic of a nation that is self-governing, which can only happen after the nation has been formed. Choices *A, B,* and *D* are incorrect because, while there are no definitive requirements to form a nation, they typically begin with a group of people bound by some

shared characteristic. Examples include language, culture and traditions, history, beliefs and religion, homeland or geography, and ethnicity.

45. A: Choice *A* is correct. On the political spectrum, ideologies on the left side of the axis emphasize socioeconomic equality and advocate for government intervention, while ideologies on the right axis seek to preserve society's existing institutions or structures. Therefore, the correct answer will be the farthest left on the axis, making Choice *A* correct. Choice *B* is incorrect because Liberalism supports less government intervention than Socialism. Choice *C* is incorrect because Libertarianism strongly opposes government intervention. Choice *D* is incorrect because, while Fascism advocates for strong government intervention, it supports a hierarchical structure and opposes equality.

46. C: Choice *C* is correct, as it most closely corresponds to the provided definition. Conservatism prioritizes traditional institutions. In general, conservatives oppose modern developments and value stability. Choices *A* and *B* are incorrect because socialism and liberalism both feature the desire to change the government to increase equality. Choice *D* is incorrect because libertarianism is more concerned with establishing a limited government to maximize personal autonomy rather than prioritizing stability and traditional institutions.

47. B: Choice *B* is correct. The Articles of Confederation were the first form of government adopted in the American colonies. Under the Articles of Confederation, the central government (the Continental Congress) was granted very limited powers, rendering it largely ineffective. Although the choices describe what would appear to be basic functions of government, the central government could only declare war.

48. B: Choice *B* is correct. Industrialization directly caused an increase in urbanization. Factories were located near cities to draw upon a large pool of potential employees. Between 1860 and 1890, the urbanization rate increased from about 20 percent to 35 percent. The other three choices are factually incorrect. Immigration increased during industrialization, as immigrants flooded into America to search for work. Socioeconomic problems plagued the period due to the unequal distribution of wealth and the social ills caused by rapid urbanization. Labor unrest was common as unions advocated for workers' rights and organized national strikes.

49. A: Choice *A* is correct. The Treaty of Versailles contained a clause that required Germany to assume responsibility for damages incurred during the conflict. Thus, the Treaty ordered Germany to pay $31.4 billion, the equivalent of $442 billion in 2017. World War I ravaged the German economy, and the country couldn't afford the war debt. The resulting poverty contributed to the rise of the Nazi Party, leading to World War II.

50. D: Choice *D* is correct. President Lincoln issued the Emancipation Proclamation to free the slaves in the Confederacy, allowing the institution to continue in states and territories that didn't secede. The excerpt justifies the decision as a "fit and necessary war measure for suppressing said rebellion." Therefore, per the excerpt, emancipation was necessary to strengthen the war effort for the North. Choice *C* is the second-best answer, but the excerpt supports the contention that emancipation was part of an active war effort, rather than merely a punishment. Choices A and B are incorrect because nothing in the excerpt describes the evil of slavery or the effect of emancipation on morale in the North.

51. B: Federalism, at least as it was put forth by the Founders, describes the relationship between the federal and state governments wherein the powers of government are divided between the two. Choice

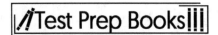

A is incorrect because Federalism does not refer to a relationship between the federal government and the people. Instead, the federal government interacts with the people through their state governments. Choice C is incorrect because the relationship between the branches of the federal government is defined by a system of checks and balances, not federalism. Choice D is incorrect because the Constitution lays out the system of federalism, but federalism does not describe the relationship between the federal government and the Constitution.

52. D: Separate but equal doctrine. Brown v. Board of Education set the stage for the fight for civil rights throughout the United States and was the first true rebuff to segregation. It overturned the separate but equal doctrine laid out in the Plessy v. Ferguson Supreme Court case. Choice A is incorrect because the doctrine of judicial review was established one hundred years earlier and has never been overturned. Choice B is incorrect because the public safety exception has to do with Miranda Rights. Choice C is incorrect because the due process doctrine doesn't apply here.

53. C: Population density, which is the total number of people divided by the total land area, generally tends to be much higher in urban areas than rural ones. This is true due to high-rise apartment complexes, sewage and freshwater infrastructure, and complex transportation systems, allowing for easy movement of food from nearby farms. Consequently, competition among citizens for resources is certainly higher in high-density areas, as are greater strains on infrastructure within urban centers.

54. A: Homogeneity, or the condition of similarity, is the unifying factor in most formal regions. Regions have one or more unifying characteristics such as language, religion, history, or economic similarities, which make the area a cohesive formal region. A good example is the Southern United States. In contrast, diversity and multilingualism, Choices B and C, are factors that may cause a region to lose homogeneity and be more difficult to classify as a region. Also, social mobility, Choice D, is a distractor that refers to one's ability to improve their economic standing in society and is not related to formal regions.

55. A: Globalization has put students and workers in direct conflict with one another despite their relative level of physical separation. For example, students who excel in mathematics and engineering may be recruited by multinational firms who want the best talent for their business despite where they are educated. Furthermore, products produced in other nations are also in competition with global manufacturers to ensure quality craftsmanship at an affordable price. Globalization does not refer to world domination, an absence of nation-states, or a singular world government.

56. C: Federal Reserve. The Federal Reserve is the bank of banks. It is the central bank of the United States and controls the value of money. A commodity is the value of goods such as precious metals. While the Central Reserve and Bank Reserve may sound like good options, the term "bank reserve" refers to the amount of money a bank deposits into a central bank, and the Central Reserve is simply a fictitious name.

57. D: The GDP is used to measure an economy's growth. The inflation of a country doesn't tell us anything about their growth. A country may hold a lot of money in reserves but this does not tell us if they are growing or not. The same can be said for having a lot of exports. It doesn't indicate that an economy is necessarily growing.

58. B: Developing nations tend to have higher levels of impoverished citizens. As a result, many of their citizens must rely on subsistence farming, or producing enough food to feed their families, in order to

survive. In contrast, developed nations tend to produce surpluses of food and very few, if any, of its citizens engage in subsistence farming. Developing nations are less likely to have complex highway systems, stable governments, and economic stability due to financial pressures.

59. C: The 19th amendment gave women the right to vote. The 15th Amendment, Choice *A*, gave blacks the right to vote. The 18th Amendment, Choice *B*, introduced alcohol prohibition. The 20th amendment, Choice *D*, repealed prohibition.

60. B: More than one million African Americans in the South went north in search of jobs during and after World War I. The Great Migration led to increased racial tension as blacks and whites competed for housing and jobs in northern cities. The Great Migration also led to the Harlem Renaissance.

Science

1. D: Water is essential for photosynthesis. Increasing temperatures increase transpiration and drought conditions result in less water available for photosynthesis. The rate of photosynthesis will decrease.

2. D: Genetic variety in a species allows them to be more resistant to stresses. Having genetic diversity increases resilience. Growing multiple strains of tomatoes or multiple types of crops could protect the farm.

3. C: During a lunar eclipse, the Sun and moon are on opposite sides of the Earth. They line up so that the Sun's light that normally illuminates the moon is blocked by the Earth. This causes the moon to become dim. Sunlight can still be seen, Choice *A*, and the Earth does not become dark, Choices *B* and *D*.

4. A: When activated, B cells create antibodies against specific antigens. White blood cells are generated in red and yellow bone marrow, not cartilage. Platelets are not a type of white blood cell and are typically cell fragments produced by megakaryocytes. White blood cells are active throughout nearly all of one's life and have not been shown to specially activate or deactivate because of life events like puberty or menopause.

5. D: Mechanical digestion is physical digestion of food and tearing it into smaller pieces using force. This occurs in the stomach and mouth. Chemical digestion involves chemically changing the food and breaking it down into small organic compounds that can be utilized by the cell to build molecules. The salivary glands in the mouth secrete amylase that breaks down starch, which begins chemical digestion. The stomach contains enzymes such as pepsinogen/pepsin and gastric lipase, which chemically digest protein and fats, respectively. The small intestine continues to digest protein using the enzymes trypsin and chymotrypsin. It also digests fats with the help of bile from the liver and lipase from the pancreas. These organs act as exocrine glands because they secrete substances through a duct. Carbohydrates are digested in the small intestine with the help of pancreatic amylase, gut bacterial flora and fauna, and brush border enzymes like lactose. Brush border enzymes are contained in the towel-like microvilli in the small intestine that soak up nutrients.

6. D: The theory that certain physical and behavioral traits give a species an evolutionary advantage is called natural selection. Charles Darwin developed the theory of natural selection that explains the evolutionary process. He postulated that heritable genetic differences could aid an organism's chance of survival in its environment. The organisms with favorable traits pass genes to their offspring, and because they have more reproductive success than those that do not contain the adaptation, the

favorable gene spreads throughout the population. Those that do not contain the adaptation often extinguish, thus their genes are not passed on. In this way, nature "selects" for the organisms that have more fitness in their environment. Birds with bright colored feathers and cacti with spines are examples of "fit" organisms.

7. B: The structure exclusively found in eukaryotic cells is the nucleus. Animal, plant, fungi, and protist cells are all eukaryotic. DNA is contained within the nucleus of eukaryotic cells, and they also have membrane-bound organelles that perform complex intracellular metabolic activities. Prokaryotic cells (archae and bacteria) do not have a nucleus or other membrane-bound organelles and are less complex than eukaryotic cells.

8. B: The cell structure responsible for cellular storage, digestion, and waste removal is the lysosome. Lysosomes are like recycle bins. They are filled with digestive enzymes that facilitate catabolic reactions to regenerate monomers. The Golgi apparatus is designed to tag, package, and ship out proteins destined for other cells or locations. The centrioles typically play a large role only in cell division when they ratchet the chromosomes from the mitotic plate to the poles of the cell. The mitochondria are involved in energy production and are the powerhouses of the cell.

9. A: Crossing over, or genetic recombination, is the rearrangement of chromosomal sections in tetrads during meiosis, and it results in each gamete having a different combination of alleles than other gametes. The disassembly of the mitotic spindle happens only after telophase and is not related to diversity. While nondisjunction does cause diversity in division and is highly noticeable in gametes formed through meiosis, it can also happen through mitotic division in somatic cells. Although an egg being fertilized by multiple sperm would lead to interesting diversity in the offspring (and possibly fraternal twins), this is not strictly a byproduct of meiotic division.

10. C: Deserts' temperatures are extremely hot in the day and cold at night because of the warming effects of the sun's solar rays, so this is the best example of the sun's energy. Although some flowers do tend to bloom after dawn, this is probably due to day/night cycles regulated by the presence of light rather than intense amounts of energy. Hibernating animals tend to use large repositories of stored nutrients as energy sources rather than relying on the sun's energy, and they may in fact be in caves or hidden underground to shelter them from the sun or weather. The tides are more dependent on the moon due to its gravity rather than any effects its albedo moonlight may have.

11. A: Gases like air will move and expand to fill their container, so they are considered to have an indefinite shape and indefinite volume. Liquids like water will move and flow freely, so their shapes change constantly, but do not change volume or density on their own. Solids change neither shape nor volume without external forces acting on them, so they have definite shapes and volumes.

12. B: Since the genotype is a depiction of the specific alleles that an organism's genes code for, it includes recessive genes that may or may not be otherwise expressed. The genotype does not have to name the proteins that its alleles code for; indeed, some of them may be unknown. The phenotype is the physical, visual manifestations of a gene, not the genotype. The genotype does not necessarily include any information about the organism's physical characteristics. Although some information about an organism's parents can be obtained from its genotype, its genotype does not actually show the parents' phenotypes.

13. C: One in four offspring (or 25%) will be short, so all four offspring cannot be tall. Although both of the parents are tall, they are hybrid or heterozygous tall, not homozygous. Although it may seem intuitive that the short allele will be expressed by lower numbers of the population than the tall allele, it still appears in 75% of the offspring (although its effects are masked in 2/3 of those). Besides, conditions could favor the recessive allele and kill off the tall offspring.

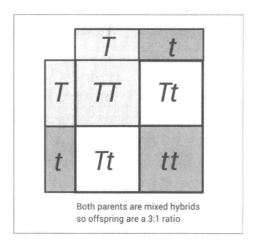

Both parents are mixed hybrids
so offspring are a 3:1 ratio

14. D: Evaporation takes place at the surface of a fluid while, boiling takes place throughout the fluid. The liquid will boil when it reaches its boiling or vaporization temperature, but evaporation can happen due to a liquid's volatility. Volatile substances often coexist as a liquid and as a gas, depending on the pressure forced on them. The phase change from gas to liquid is condensation, and both evaporation and boiling take place in nature.

15. C: Water's polarity lends it to be extremely cohesive and adhesive; this cohesion keeps its atoms very close together. Because of this, it takes a large amount of energy to boil its liquid form. Phospholipid bilayers are made of nonpolar lipids and water, a polar liquid, cannot easily flow through it. Cell membranes use proteins called aquaporins to solve this issue and let water flow in and out. Fish breathe by capturing dissolved oxygen through their gills. Water can self-ionize, wherein it decomposes into a hydrogen ion (H+) and a hydroxide ion (OH-), but it cannot self-hydrolyze.

16. C: To gather accurate data, the student must be able compare a participant's test score from round 1 with their test score from round 2. The differing levels of intellect among the participants means that comparing participants' test scores to those of other participants would be inaccurate. This requirement excludes Choices *A* and *D*, which involve only one round of testing. The experiment must also involve different levels of sugar consumption from round 1 to round 2. In this way, the effects of different levels of sugar consumption can be seen on the same subjects. Thus, Choice *B* is incorrect because the experiment provides for no variation of sugar consumption. Choice *C* is the correct answer because it allows the student to compare each participant's test score from round 1 with their test score from round 2 after different levels of sugar consumption.

17. A: A control is the component or group of the experimental design that isn't manipulated—it's the standard against which the resultant findings are compared, so Choice *A* is correct. A variable is an element of the experiment that is able to be manipulated, making Choice *B* false. A constant is a condition of the experiment outside of the hypothesis that remains unchanged in order to isolate the changes in the variables; therefore, Choice *C* is incorrect. Choice *D* is false because collected data are simply recordings of the observed phenomena that result from the experiment.

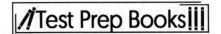

18. B: During telophase, two nuclei form at each end of the cell and nuclear envelopes begin to form around each nucleus. The nucleoli reappear, and the chromosomes become less compact. The microtubules are broken down by the cell, and mitosis is complete. The process begins with prophase as the mitotic spindles begin to form from centrosomes. Prometaphase follows, with the breakdown of the nuclear envelope and the further condensing of the chromosomes. Next, metaphase occurs when the microtubules are stretched across the cell and the chromosomes align at the metaphase plate. Finally, in the last step before telophase, anaphase occurs as the sister chromatids break apart and form chromosomes.

19. C: Convergent plate boundaries occur where two tectonic plates collide together. The denser oceanic plate will drop below the continental plate in a process called subduction.

20. D: Volcanic activity can occur at both fault lines and within the area of a tectonic plate at areas called hot spots. Volcanic activity is more common at fault lines because of cracks that allow the mantle's magma to more easily escape to the surface.

21. A: Technically, the troposphere is a layer of the atmosphere where the majority of the activity that creates weather conditions experienced on Earth occurs. The ozone layer is in the stratosphere; this is also where airplanes fly.

22. D: Stratus clouds are also grey, but nimbostratus clouds are the low clouds that appear during stormy weather. The other choices are usually seen on fair-weather days.

23. C: Jupiter is the largest planet in the solar system, and it is primarily composed of hydrogen and helium. Ammonia is in much lower quantity and usually found as a cloud within Jupiter's atmosphere.

24. D: Viruses are not classified as living organisms. They are neither prokaryotic or eukaryotic; therefore, they don't belong to any of the answer choices.

25. C: According to the *ideal gas law* ($PV = nRT$), if volume is constant, the temperature is directly related to the pressure in a system. Therefore, if the pressure increases, the temperature will increase in direct proportion. Choice *A* would not be possible, since the system is closed and a change is occurring, so the temperature will change. Choice *B* incorrectly exhibits an inverse relationship between pressure and temperature, or $P = 1/T$. Choice *D* is incorrect because even without actual values for the variables, the relationship and proportions can be determined.

26. D: The weight of an object is equal to the mass of the object multiplied by gravity. According to Newton's second law of motion, $F = m \times a$. Weight is the force resulting from a given situation, so the mass of the object needs to be multiplied by the acceleration of gravity on Earth: $W = m \times g$.

Choice *A* is incorrect because, according to Newton's first law, all objects exert some force on each other, based on their distance from each other and their masses. This is seen in planets, which affect each other's paths and those of their moons. Choice *B* is incorrect because an object in motion or at rest can have inertia; inertia is the resistance of a physical object to change its state of motion. Choice *C* is incorrect because the mass of an object is a measurement of how much substance there is to the object, while the weight is gravity's effect on the mass.

27. D: Radiation can be transmitted through electromagnetic waves and needs no medium to travel; it can travel in a vacuum. This is how the Sun warms the Earth and it typically applies to large objects with

306

great amounts of heat, or objects that have a large difference in their heat measurements. Choice *A*, convection, involves atoms or molecules traveling from areas of high concentration to those of low concentration and transferring energy or heat with them. Choice *B*, conduction, involves the touching or bumping of atoms or molecules to transfer energy or heat. Choice *C*, induction, deals with charges and does not apply to the transfer of energy or heat. Choices *A*, *B*, and *C* need a medium in which to travel, while radiation requires no medium.

28. C: The mantle is the Earth's thickest layer; it holds most of the Earth's material. The crust is thin, and the inner core is also small compared to the mantle. There is no such thing as Earth's shell.

29. C: Subduction occurs when one plate is pushed down by another. A fault is where two plates meet. Diversion occurs when two plates move apart. Drift isn't a term used with tectonic plates.

30. B: Transpiration is water that evaporates from pores in plants called stomata. Evaporation of moving water is still called evaporation. Infiltration is the process of water moving into the ground, and precipitation that falls on trees is called canopy interception.

31. D: Water with a higher salinity has more dissolved salt and a lower freezing point. Water from the Dead Sea has the highest salinity of the answer choices.

32. C: Glaciers are formed only on land and constantly move because of their own weight. Icebergs are formed from glaciers and float.

33. C: In the Linnaean system, organisms are classified as follows, moving from comprehensive and specific similarities to fewer and more general similarities: domain, kingdom, phylum, class, order, family, genus, and species. A popular mnemonic device to remember the Linnaean system is "Dear King Philip came over for good soup."

34. B: Substances with higher amounts of hydrogen ions will have lower pHs, while substances with higher amounts of hydroxide ions will have higher pHs. Choice *A* is incorrect because it is possible to have an extremely strong acid with a pH less than 1, as long as its molarity of hydrogen ions is greater than 1. Choice *C* is false because a weak base is determined by having a pH lower than some value, not higher. Substances with pHs greater than 2 include anything from neutral water to extremely caustic lye. Choice *D* is false because a solution with a pH of 2 has ten times fewer hydrogen ions than a solution of pH 1.

35. A: Salts are formed from compounds that use ionic bonds. Disulfide bridges are special bonds in protein synthesis which hold the protein in their secondary and tertiary structures. Covalent bonds are strong bonds formed through the sharing of electrons between atoms and are typically found in organic molecules like carbohydrates and lipids. London dispersion forces are fleeting, momentary bonds which occur between atoms that have instantaneous dipoles but quickly disintegrate.

36. C: As in the last question, covalent bonds are special because they share electrons between multiple atoms. Most covalent bonds are formed between the elements H, F, N, O, S, and C, while hydrogen bonds are formed nearly exclusively between H and either O, N, or F of other molecules. Covalent bonds may inadvertently form dipoles, but this does not necessarily happen. For instance, dipoles do not form with similarly electronegative atoms, like carbon and hydrogen. Crystal solids are typically formed by substances with ionic bonds like the salts sodium iodide and potassium chloride.

37. D: An isotope of an element has an atomic number equal to its number of protons, but a different mass number because of the additional neutrons. Even though there are differences in the nucleus, the behavior and properties of isotopes of a given element are identical. Atoms with different atomic numbers also have different numbers of protons and are different elements, so they cannot be isotopes.

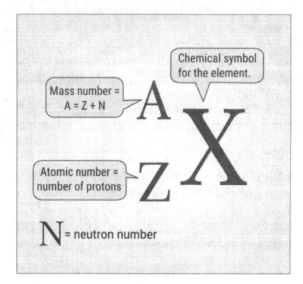

38. A: The neutrons and protons make up the nucleus of the atom. The nucleus is positively charged due to the presence of the protons. The negatively charged electrons are attracted to the positively charged nucleus by the electrostatic or Coulomb force; however, the electrons are not contained in the nucleus. The positively charged protons create the positive charge in the nucleus, and the neutrons are electrically neutral, so they have no effect. Radioactivity does not directly have a bearing on the charge of the nucleus.

39. B: Models are representations of concepts that are impossible to experience directly, such as the 3D representation of DNA, so Choice *B* is correct. Choice *A* is incorrect because theories simply explain why things happen. Choice *C* is incorrect because laws describe how things happen. Choice *D* is false because an observation analyzes situations using human senses.

40. C: An inference is a logical prediction of a why an event occurred based on previous experiences or education. The person in this example knows that plants need water to survive; therefore, the prediction that someone forgot to water the plant is a reasonable inference, hence Choice *C* is correct. A classification is the grouping of events or objects into categories, so Choice *A* is false. An observation analyzes situations using human senses, so Choice *B* is false. Choice *D* is incorrect because collecting is the act of gathering data for analysis.

41. D: Protons have a positive charge. An atom is structured with a nucleus in the center that contains neutral neutrons and positive protons. Surrounding the nucleus are orbiting electrons that are negatively charged. Choice *D* is the only correct answer.

42. C: The qualitative definition of a gas or element's ionization energy is the amount of energy needed to remove a valence electron, or the one most loosely bound, from that substance and form a cation. Choice A refers to atomic radius, Choice B refers to electronegativity, and Choice D refers to electron affinity. All four of these properties follow trends on the Periodic table.

43. D: Catabolism is the process of breaking large molecules into smaller molecules to release energy for work. Carbohydrates and fats are catabolized to provide energy for exercise and daily activities. Anabolism synthesizes larger molecules from smaller constituent building blocks. Bioenergetics and metabolism are more general terms involving overall energy production and usage.

44. C: Because of the vast amounts of data that needed to be processed and analyzed, technological breakthroughs like innovations to the microprocessor were directly responsible for the ease of computing handled by the Human Genome Project. Although the sonogram and MRI technology are helpful to the healthcare industry in general, they would not have provided a great deal of help for sequencing and comprehending DNA data, in general. X-ray diffraction is a technique that helps visualize the structures of crystallized proteins, but cannot determine DNA bases with enough precision to help sequence DNA.

45. A: Many foods from developed countries are grown from plants which have been processed or bioengineered to include increased amounts of nutrients like vitamins and minerals that otherwise would be lost during manufacturing or are uncommon to the human diet. White rice, for example, is typically enriched with niacin, iron, and folic acid, while salt has been fortified with iodine for nearly a century. These help to prevent nutrition deficiencies. While it can be useful for fisheries to maintain models of fish populations so that they don't overfish their stock, this is not as immediately important to nutrition as are fortified and enriched foods. Although innovations to microscopes could lead to improved healthcare, this also has no direct effect on nutrition deficiency. Refrigerated train carts were historically a crucial invention around Civil War times and were used to transport meat and dairy products long distances without spoiling, but dietary deficiencies could be more easily remedied by supplying people with fortified foods containing those nutrients rather than spoilable meats.

46. D: Iodine has the greatest number of electrons at 53 electrons. The number of electrons increases in elements going from left to right across the periodic table. Hydrogen, Choice *A*, is at the top left corner of the periodic table, so it has the fewest electrons (one electron). Iron has 26 electrons, copper has 29 electrons, Choices *B*, and *C*, respectively.

47. C: Reactivity. Chemical properties describe the behavior of substances, while physical properties describe their appearance. Reactivity is a behavior, and therefore it's the correct answer.

48. C: An observation typically kicks off the scientific method. The first step is to identify a problem based on an observation—the who, what, when, where, why, and how. An observation is the analysis of information using basic human senses: sight, sound, touch, taste, and smell. In this step of the scientific method, the problem is identified—the who, what, when, where, why, and how. Recall that designing a science investigation is based on the scientific method, which consists of the following steps making an observation, forming a question, conducting an experiment, collecting and analyzing data, and forming a conclusion.

49. C: If light exposure increases, then plant height will increase. Choices *A* and *B* are not good choices because it's impossible to measure a cat's happiness, and there's a subjective factor involved in determining the softness of pants. Feeling more comfortable isn't objective enough, and measuring growth should be clarified—will height or mass be measured? Measuring purring would also be difficult to do quantitatively; cats either do purr or don't purr. Volume could be measured with a scientific device, but that would have to be specified. Choice *C* has a valid independent and dependent variable, both which can be measured, so it's the correct choice.

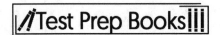

50. D: Dimitri because weather involves the water cycle. The other suggestions (ad thus, answer choices) reflect are misunderstandings. It's weather that's day-to-day and depends on wind and heat patterns, while seasons depend on proximity to the Sun. Weather patterns such as rain and snow definitely involve the water cycle, so that's the correct choice.

51. C: Modeling with flashlights and tennis balls. Early childhood educators should know that PowerPoint isn't an effective teaching method, and while going outside is fun, without modeling, the activity will be meaningless. The book idea would not be an effective teaching tool in this case because it's unable to model nearness, closeness, and general location. Modeling is the best option.

52. C: Alaska is farther from the equator. Climate has nothing to do with the size or shape of a state; it relates to exposure to the Sun. Places closer to the equator are hotter, so the answer is *C*.

53. B: Tornadoes. Hurricanes and rain are liquid precipitation, and snow is solid precipitation. Tornadoes only involve wind, so *B* is the correct answer.

54. A: Causing volcanoes. Plate tectonics involve movement in the Earth's crust that exposes areas for volcanic activities. Plates have nothing to do with evaporation or delta formation; both of those processes involve the water cycle. Plate movement also has nothing to do with tornado and wind movement.

55. B: Footprint. Trace fossils are *evidence* of an organism as opposed to the *remains* of an organism. Bones, shells, and teeth were all once part of an organism and are true fossils.

Practice Test #2

Reading and Language Arts

1. Which of the following statements is true regarding decoding and encoding?
   a.   Decoding is the spelling of words.
   b.   Encoding helps students to recognize and read words quickly.
   c.   Encoding is the application of letter-sound correspondences, letter patterns, and other phonics relationships.
   d.   Decoding and encoding are learned in opposite stages or steps.

2. Kimberly draws a picture of her family, and her instructor asks her to write what she drew on the line below the picture. She puts together a jumble of letter-like forms rather than a series of discrete letters. The instructor asks her what she wrote, and she replies, "My family." Which stage of spelling development is Kimberly in?
   a.   Pre-phonetic stage
   b.   Semiphonetic stage
   c.   Phonetic stage
   d.   Conventional stage

3. Which of the following is true of word walls?
   a.   Their primary purpose is to teach morphemes.
   b.   They help students sort words they know, want to know, and have learned.
   c.   They are primarily useful in the transitional phase of spelling.
   d.   They group words that share common consonant-vowel patterns or letter clusters.

4. Which of the following displays a correct matching of an orthographic pattern with an example of that pattern?
   a.   Vowel-vowel digraph that have the same sound: loud and wow
   b.   Vowel-vowel digraph that have the same sound: read and speed
   c.   Vowel-consonant digraphs with different sounds: stand and stair
   d.   Vowel-consonant digraphs with different sounds: harm and have

5. A local newspaper is looking for writers for a student column. A student would like to submit his article to the newspaper, but he isn't sure how to format his article according to journalistic standards. What resource should he use?
   a.   A thesaurus
   b.   A dictionary
   c.   A style guide
   d.   A grammar book

6. Which sentence is grammatically correct?
   a.   Every morning we would wake up, ate breakfast, and broke camp.
   b.   Every morning we would wake up, eat breakfast, and broke camp.
   c.   Every morning we would wake up, eat breakfast, and break camp.
   d.   Every morning we would wake up, ate breakfast, and break camp.

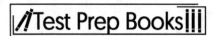

7. Polls show that more and more people in the US distrust the government and view it as dysfunctional and corrupt. Every election, the same people are voted back into office.
Which word or words would best link these sentences?
   a. Not surprisingly,
   b. Understandably,
   c. And yet,
   d. Therefore,

8. Which of the following terms refers to techniques that allow students to progress toward a greater level of understanding on an increasingly independent level?
   a. Discourse
   b. Differentiation
   c. Scaffolding
   d. Benchmarking

9. Which of the following statements about literacy development is true?
   a. Research shows that literacy development begins as early as 3 months of age.
   b. Between 3 and 6 months, babies begin to study a speaker's mouth and listen closely to speech sounds.
   c. Between 6 and 9 months, babies can generally recognize a growing number of commonly repeated words, utter simple words, respond appropriately to simple requests, and begin to attempt to group sounds.
   d. Between 9 and 12 months, babies rapidly strengthen their communication skills, connecting sounds to meanings and combining sounds to create coherent sentences.

10. Receptive language development refers to which of the following stages of literacy?
   a. Beginning literacy
   b. Early intermediate literacy
   c. Intermediate literacy
   d. Early advanced literacy

11. All EXCEPT which of the following are considered non-decodable sight words?
   a. None
   b. Who
   c. Runner
   d. Said

12. What is the noun phrase in the following sentence?

   Charlotte's new German shepherd puppy is energetic.

   a. Puppy
   b. Charlotte
   c. German shepherd puppy
   d. Charlotte's new German shepherd puppy

312

13. The following sentence contains what kind of error?

> Forgetting that he was supposed to meet his girlfriend for dinner, Anita was mad when Fred showed up late.

a. Parallelism
b. Run-on sentence
c. Misplaced modifier
d. Subject-verb agreement

Questions 14–18 are based upon the following passage:

This excerpt is adapted from *Our Vanishing Wildlife,* by William T. Hornaday

> Three years ago, I think there were not many bird-lovers in the United States who believed it possible to prevent the total extinction of both egrets from our fauna. All the known rookeries accessible to plume-hunters had been totally destroyed. Two years ago, the secret discovery of several small, hidden colonies prompted William Dutcher, President of the National Association of Audubon Societies, and Mr. T. Gilbert Pearson, Secretary, to attempt the protection of those colonies. With a fund contributed for the purpose, wardens were hired and duly commissioned. As previously stated, one of those wardens was shot dead in cold blood by a plume hunter. The task of guarding swamp rookeries from the attacks of money-hungry desperadoes to whom the accursed plumes were worth their weight in gold, is a very chancy proceeding. There is now one warden in Florida who says that "before they get my rookery they will first have to get me."

> Thus far the protective work of the Audubon Association has been successful. Now there are twenty colonies, which contain all told, about 5,000 egrets and about 120,000 herons and ibises which are guarded by the Audubon wardens. One of the most important is on Bird Island, a mile out in Orange Lake, central Florida, and it is ably defended by Oscar E. Baynard. To-day, the plume hunters who do not dare to raid the guarded rookeries are trying to study out the lines of flight of the birds, to and from their feeding-grounds, and shoot them in transit. Their motto is—"Anything to beat the law, and get the plumes." It is there that the state of Florida should take part in the war.

> The success of this campaign is attested by the fact that last year a number of egrets were seen in eastern Massachusetts—for the first time in many years. And so to-day the question is, can the wardens continue to hold the plume-hunters at bay?

313

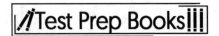

14. The author's use of first-person pronouns in the following text does NOT have which of the following effects?

> Three years ago, I think there were not many bird-lovers in the United States who believed it possible to prevent the total extinction of both egrets from our fauna.

    a. The phrase *I think* acts as a sort of hedging, where the author's tone is less direct and/or absolute.
    b. It allows the reader to more easily connect with the author.
    c. It encourages the reader to empathize with the egrets.
    d. It distances the reader from the text by overemphasizing the story.

15. What purpose does the quote serve at the end of the first paragraph?
    a. The quote shows proof of a hunter threatening one of the wardens.
    b. The quote lightens the mood by illustrating the colloquial language of the region.
    c. The quote provides an example of a warden protecting one of the colonies.
    d. The quote provides much needed comic relief in the form of a joke.

16. What is the meaning of the word *rookeries* in the following text?

> To-day, the plume hunters who do not dare to raid the guarded rookeries are trying to study out the lines of flight of the birds, to and from their feeding-grounds, and shoot them in transit.

    a. Houses in a slum area
    b. A place where hunters gather to trade tools
    c. A place where wardens go to trade stories
    d. A colony of breeding birds

17. What is on Bird Island?
    a. Hunters selling plumes
    b. An important bird colony
    c. Bird Island Battle between the hunters and the wardens
    d. An important egret with unique plumes

18. What is the main purpose of the passage?
    a. To persuade the audience to act in preservation of the bird colonies
    b. To show the effect hunting egrets has had on the environment
    c. To argue that the preservation of bird colonies has had a negative impact on the environment
    d. To demonstrate the success of the protective work of the Audubon Association

19. Which phrase below best defines the term *audience* as it is used in rhetoric?
    a. The group of readers to which the author is trying to appeal
    b. Students
    c. Subject matter experts
    d. Readers who already have formed subject matter opinions

20. Which of the following refers to what an author wants to express about a given subject?
   a. Primary purpose
   b. Plot
   c. Main idea
   d. Characterization

21. A student encounters the word *aficionado* and wants to learn more about it. It doesn't sound like other English words he knows, so the student is curious to identify the word's origin. What resource should he consult?
   a. A thesaurus
   b. A dictionary
   c. A style guide
   d. A grammar book

22. Which domain is likely to be used by a website run by a nonprofit group?
   a. .com
   b. .edu
   c. .org
   d. .gov

23. Which phrase below best defines *inference*?
   a. Reading between the lines
   b. Skimming a text for context clues
   c. Writing notes or questions that need answers during the reading experience
   d. Summarizing the text

24. Which mode of writing aims to inform the reader objectively about a particular subject or idea and typically contains definitions, instructions, or facts within its subject matter?
   a. Argumentative
   b. Informative
   c. Narrative
   d. Descriptive

25. The rhetorical appeal that elicits an emotional and/or sympathetic response from an audience is known as which of the following?
   a. Logos
   b. Ethos
   c. Pathos
   d. None of the above

Read the selection about traveling in an RV and answer Questions 26–32.

I have to admit that when my father bought a recreational vehicle (RV), I thought he was making a huge mistake. I didn't really know anything about RVs, but I knew that my dad was as big a "city slicker" as there was. In fact, I even thought he might have gone a little bit crazy. On trips to the beach, he preferred to swim at the pool, and whenever he went hiking, he avoided touching any plants for fear that they might be poison ivy. Why

315

would this man, with an almost irrational fear of the outdoors, want a 40-foot camping behemoth?

The RV was a great purchase for our family and brought us all closer together. Every morning we would wake up, eat breakfast, and broke camp. We laughed at our own comical attempts to back The Beast into spaces that seemed impossibly small. We rejoiced as "hackers." When things inevitably went wrong and we couldn't solve the problems on our own, we discovered the incredible helpfulness and friendliness of the RV community. We even made some new friends in the process.

Above all, it allowed us to share adventures. While traveling across America, which we could not have experienced in cars and hotels. Enjoying a campfire on a chilly summer evening with the mountains of Glacier National Park in the background, or waking up early in the morning to see the sun rising over the distant spires of Arches National Park are memories that will always stay with me and our entire family. Those are also memories that my siblings and me have now shared with our own children.

26. Which of the following would be the best choice for this sentence (reproduced below)?

In fact, I even thought he might have gone a little bit crazy.

a. Keep the sentence as it is.
b. Move the sentence so that it comes before the preceding sentence.
c. Move the sentence to the end of the first paragraph.
d. Omit the sentence.

27. In context, which is the best version of the underlined portion of this sentence (reproduced below)?

The RV was a great purchase for our family and brought us all closer together.

a. The RV
b. Not surprisingly, the RV
c. Furthermore, the RV
d. As it turns out, the RV

28. Which is the best version of the underlined portion of this sentence (reproduced below)?

Every morning we would wake up, eat breakfast, and broke camp.

a. we would wake up, eat breakfast, and broke camp.
b. we would wake up, eat breakfast, and break camp.
c. would we wake up, eat breakfast, and break camp?
d. we are waking up, eating breakfast, and breaking camp.

29. Which is the best version of the underlined portion of this sentence (reproduced below)?

We rejoiced as "hackers."

a. We rejoiced as "hackers."
b. To a nagging problem of technology, we rejoiced as "hackers."
c. We rejoiced when we figured out how to "hack" a solution to a nagging technological problem.
d. To "hack" our way to a solution, we had to rejoice.

30. Which is the best version of the underlined portion of this sentence (reproduced below)?

We even made some new friends in the process.

a. We even made some new friends in the process.
b. In the process was the friends we were making.
c. We are even making some new friends in the process.
d. We will make new friends in the process.

31. Which is the best version of the underlined portion of this sentence (reproduced below)?

Above all, it allowed us to share adventures. While traveling across America, which we could not have experienced in cars and hotels.

a. Above all, it allowed us to share adventures. While traveling across America
b. Above all, it allowed us to share adventures while traveling across America
c. Above all, it allowed us to share adventures; while traveling across America
d. Above all, it allowed us to share adventures—while traveling across America

32. Which is the best version of the underlined portion of this sentence (reproduced below)?

Those are also memories that my siblings and me have now shared with our own children.

a. Those are also memories that my siblings and me
b. Those are also memories that me and my siblings
c. Those are also memories that my siblings and I
d. Those are also memories that I and my siblings

Questions 33–36 are based on the following passage:

Becoming a successful leader in today's industry, government, and nonprofit sectors requires more than a high intelligence quotient (IQ). Emotional Intelligence (EI) includes developing the ability to know one's own emotions, to regulate impulses and emotions, and to use interpersonal communication skills with ease while dealing with other people. A combination of knowledge, skills, abilities, and mature emotional intelligence (EI) reflects the most effective leadership recipe. Successful leaders sharpen more than their talents and IQ levels; they practice the basic features of emotional intelligence. Some of the hallmark traits of a competent, emotionally intelligent leader include self-efficacy, drive, determination, collaboration, vision, humility, and openness to change. An unsuccessful leader exhibits opposite leadership traits: unclear directives, inconsistent vision and planning strategies, disrespect for followers, incompetence, and

317

an uncompromising transactional leadership style. There are ways to develop emotional intelligence for the person who wants to improve their leadership style. For example, an emotionally intelligent leader creates an affirmative environment by incorporating collaborative activities, using professional development training for employee self-awareness, communicating clearly about the organization's vision, and developing a variety of resources for working with emotions. Building relationships outside the institution with leadership coaches and with professional development trainers can also help leaders who want to grow their leadership success. Leaders in today's work environment need to strive for a combination of skill, knowledge, and mature emotional intelligence to lead followers to success and to promote the vision and mission of their respective institutions.

33. The passage suggests that the term *emotional intelligence (EI)* can be defined as which of the following?
   a.   A combination of knowledge, skills, abilities, and mature emotional intelligence reflects the most effective EI leadership recipe.
   b.   An emotionally intelligent leader creates an affirmative environment by incorporating collaborative activities, using professional development training for employee self-awareness, communicating clearly about the organization's vision, and developing a variety of resources for working with emotions.
   c.   EI includes developing the ability to know one's own emotions, to regulate impulses and emotions, and to use interpersonal communication skills with ease while dealing with other people.
   d.   Becoming a successful leader in today's industry, government, and nonprofit sectors requires more than a high IQ.

34. Based on the information in the passage, a successful leader must have a high EI quotient.
   a.   The above statement can be supported by the fact that Daniel Goldman conducted a scientific study.
   b.   The above statement can be supported by the example that emotionally intelligent people are highly successful leaders.
   c.   The above statement is not supported by the passage.
   d.   The above statement is supported by the illustration that claims, "Leaders in today's work environment need to strive for a combination of skill, knowledge, and mature emotional intelligence to lead followers to success and to promote the vision and mission of their respective institutions."

35. According to the passage above, some of the characteristics of an unsuccessful leader include which of the following?
   a.   Talent, IQ level, and abilities
   b.   Transactional leadership style
   c.   Loud, demeaning actions toward female employees
   d.   Outdated technological resources and strategies

36. According to the passage above, which of the following must be true?
   a.   The leader exhibits a healthy work/life balance lifestyle.
   b.   The leader is uncompromising in transactional directives for all employees, regardless of status.
   c.   The leader learns to strategize using future trends analysis to create a five-year plan.
   d.   The leader uses a combination of skill, knowledge, and mature reasoning to make decisions.

Choose the option that corrects an error in the underlined portion. If no error exists, choose Choice A.

37. Early in my career, <u>a master's teacher shared this thought with me "Education is the last bastion of civility."</u>
    a. a master's teacher shared this thought with me "Education is the last bastion of civility."
    b. a master's teacher shared this thought with me: "Education is the last bastion of civility."
    c. a master's teacher shared this thought with me: "Education is the last bastion of civility".
    d. a master's teacher shared this thought with me. "Education is the last bastion of civility."

38. Which of the following words is spelled incorrectly?

    It is really what <u>makes</u> us <u>human</u> and what <u>distinguishes</u> us as <u>civilised</u> creatures.

    a. makes
    b. human
    c. distinguishes
    d. civilised

39. Education should never discriminate on any basis, and it should create individuals who are self-sufficient, patriotic, and tolerant of <u>others' ideas.</u>
    a. others' ideas
    b. other's ideas
    c. others ideas
    d. others's ideas

40. <u>All children can learn. Although not all children learn in the same manner.</u>
    a. All children can learn. Although not all children learn in the same manner.
    b. All children can learn although not all children learn in the same manner.
    c. All children can learn although, not all children learn in the same manner.
    d. All children can learn, although not all children learn in the same manner.

41. If teachers set high expectations for <u>there students</u>, the students will rise to that high level.
    a. there students
    b. they're students
    c. their students
    d. his students

42. In the modern age of technology, a teacher's focus is no longer the "what" of the content, <u>but more importantly, the 'why.'</u>
    a. but more importantly, the 'why.'
    b. but more importantly, the "why."
    c. but more importantly, the 'why'.
    d. but more importantly, the "why".

319

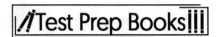

43. Students have to <u>read between the lines, identify bias, and determine</u> who they can trust in the milieu of ads, data, and texts presented to them.
   a. read between the lines, identify bias, and determine
   b. read between the lines, identify bias, and determining
   c. read between the lines, identifying bias, and determining
   d. reads between the lines, identifies bias, and determines

44. During their time in present-day Newfoundland, Leif's expedition made contact with the natives whom they referred to as Skraelings <u>(which translates to 'wretched ones' in Norse).</u>
   a. (which translates to 'wretched ones' in Norse).
   b. (which translates to "wretched ones" in Norse.)
   c. (which translates to 'wretched ones' in Norse.)
   d. (which translates to "wretched ones" in Norse).

Questions 45–48 are based on the following passage:

> Learning how to write a ten-minute play may seem like a monumental task at first; but, if you follow a simple creative writing strategy, similar to writing a narrative story, you will be able to write a successful drama. The first step is to open your story as if it is a puzzle to be solved. This will allow the reader a moment to engage with the story and to mentally solve the story with you, the author. Immediately provide descriptive details that steer the main idea, the tone, and the mood according to the overarching theme you have in mind. For example, if the play is about something ominous, you may open Scene One with a thunderclap. Next, use dialogue to reveal the attitudes and personalities of each of the characters who have a key part in the unfolding story. Keep the characters off balance in some way to create interest and dramatic effect. Maybe what the characters say does not match what they do. Show images on stage to speed up the narrative; remember, one picture speaks a thousand words. As the play progresses, the protagonist must cross the point of no return in some way; this is the climax of the story. Then, as in a written story, you create a resolution to the life-changing event of the protagonist. Let the characters experience some kind of self-discovery that can be understood and appreciated by the patient audience. Finally, make sure all things come together in the end so that every detail in the play makes sense right before the curtain falls.

45. Based on the passage above, which of the following statements is FALSE?
   a. Writing a ten-minute play may seem like an insurmountable task.
   b. Providing descriptive details is not necessary until after the climax of the story line.
   c. Engaging the audience by jumping into the story line immediately helps them solve the story's developing ideas with you, the writer.
   d. Descriptive details give clues to the play's intended mood and tone.

46. In the passage above, the writer suggests that writing a ten-minute play is accessible for a novice playwright because of which of the following reasons?
  a. It took the author of the passage only one week to write his first play.
  b. The format follows similar strategies of writing a narrative story.
  c. There are no particular themes or points to unravel; a playwright can use a stream of consciousness style to write a play.
  d. Dialogue that reveals the characters' particularities is uncommonly simple to write.

47. Based on the passage above, which basic feature of narrative writing is NOT mentioned with respect to writing a ten-minute play?
  a. Character development
  b. Descriptive details
  c. Dialogue
  d. Style

48. Based on the passage above, which of the following is true?
  a. The class of eighth graders quickly learned that it is not that difficult to write a ten-minute play.
  b. The playwrights of the twenty-first century all use the narrative writing basic feature guide to outline their initial scripts.
  c. In order to follow a simple structure, a person can write a ten-minute play based on some narrative writing features.
  d. Women find playwriting easier than men because they are used to communicating in writing.

49. Which sentence is grammatically correct?
  a. The baseball that is autographed belongs to whom?
  b. The baseball which is autographed belongs to who?
  c. Whom does the baseball which is autographed belong to?
  d. Whom does the baseball that is autographed belong to?

50. Which of the following words is spelled incorrectly?
  a. Caffiene
  b. Counterfeit
  c. Sleigh
  d. Receipt

51. Which sentence is grammatically incorrect?
  a. Will you please bring me the water before you take her the pizza?
  b. Can I put the box on the shelf where you can reach?
  c. Will you lend me your pen so I can sign for my loan?
  d. What if the two of us were to gather too many flowers?

52. Which word combination properly completes the following sentence:

  I hurt my ankle_____ but now it feels _____.

  a. badly/good
  b. bad/good
  c. bad/well
  d. badly/well

321

53. Which of the following sentences is a fragment?
   a. We went to the zoo to see the tigers and lions.
   b. Instead we saw elephants, zebras and giraffes.
   c. Because the lion and tiger habitat was closed.
   d. What sound does a giraffe make anyway?

54. Which of the following is a run-on sentence?
   a. I love to go water-skiing, I love alpine skiing, I also love Nordic skiing.
   b. The best way to learn to ski is to take lessons.
   c. All three types of skiing require different skills and different equipment.
   d. It takes a long time to learn how to ski; waterskiing takes the longest time.

55. Select the correct meaning of the italicized word in the following sentence:

   The nurse measured her *sublingual* temperature against her axillary temperature.

   a. In the ear
   b. In the rectum
   c. Under the armpit
   d. Under the tongue

56. What is the best definition of the word *dysfunction*?
   a. Exacerbate
   b. Abnormality
   c. Dilate
   d. Lethargic

57. What does *abstain* mean?
   a. To regurgitate
   b. To imbibe
   c. To refrain from something
   d. To prolong

58. Select the correct meaning of the underlined word in the following sentence:

   The surgeon was concerned about the patient's prognosis.

   a. Outlook
   b. Etiology
   c. Mechanism of transmission
   d. Incidence in the population

59. What word meaning "to widen or expand" best fits in the following sentence:

   The nitrous oxide was administered to _____ his blood vessels.

   a. Dilute
   b. Dilate
   c. Occlude
   d. Distill

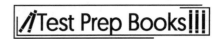

60. Which sentence that contains an error in punctuation or capitalization?
    a. "The show is on," Jackson said.
    b. The Grand Canyon is a national park.
    c. Lets celebrate tomorrow.
    d. Oliver, a social worker, got a new job this month.

61. Which of the following sentences contains an error in usage?
    a. Their words was followed by a signing document.
    b. No one came to the theater that evening.
    c. Several cats were living in the abandoned house down the road.
    d. It rained that morning; they had to cancel the kayaking trip.

62. What type of grammatical error does the following sentence contain?

    It was true, Lyla ate the last cupcake.

    a. Subject-verb agreement error
    b. Punctuation error
    c. Shift in verb tense
    d. Split infinitive

63. Which sentence below contains an error in punctuation or capitalization?
    a. Afterwards, we got ice cream down the road.
    b. The word "slacken" means to decrease.

    c. They started building the Hoover dam in 1931.
    d. Matthew got married to his best friend, Maria.

64. Choose the sentence that contains an error in usage. If there are no errors, select Choice *D*.
    a. After her swim, Jeanine saw a blue kid's shovel.
    b. Pistachios are my favorite kind of nut, although they're expensive.
    c. One apple is better than two lemons.
    d. We found three five-dollar bills on the way home.

Questions 65-69 are based on the following passage:

This excerpt is an adaptation of Jonathan Swift's Gulliver's Travels into Several Remote Nations of the World.

> My gentleness and good behaviour had gained so far on the emperor and his court, and indeed upon the army and people in general, that I began to conceive hopes of getting my liberty in a short time. I took all possible methods to cultivate this favourable disposition. The natives came, by degrees, to be less apprehensive of any danger from me. I would sometimes lie down, and let five or six of them dance on my hand; and at last the boys and girls would venture to come and play at hide-and-seek in my hair. I had now made a good progress in understanding and speaking the language. The emperor had a mind one day to entertain me with several of the country shows, wherein they exceed all nations I have known, both for dexterity and magnificence. I was diverted with none so much as that of the rope-dancers, performed upon a slender white thread,

323

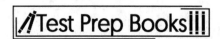
extended about two feet, and twelve inches from the ground. Upon which I shall desire liberty, with the reader's patience, to enlarge a little.

This diversion is only practised by those persons who are candidates for great employments, and high favour at court. They are trained in this art from their youth, and are not always of noble birth, or liberal education. When a great office is vacant, either by death or disgrace (which often happens,) five or six of those candidates petition the emperor to entertain his majesty and the court with a dance on the rope; and whoever jumps the highest, without falling, succeeds in the office. Very often the chief ministers themselves are commanded to show their skill, and to convince the emperor that they have not lost their faculty. Flimnap, the treasurer, is allowed to cut a caper on the straight rope, at least an inch higher than any other lord in the whole empire. I have seen him do the summerset several times together, upon a trencher fixed on a rope which is no thicker than a common packthread in England. My friend Reldresal, principal secretary for private affairs, is, in my opinion, if I am not partial, the second after the treasurer; the rest of the great officers are much upon a par.

65. Which of the following statements best summarizes the central purpose of this text?
    a. Gulliver details his fondness for the archaic yet interesting practices of his captors.
    b. Gulliver conjectures about the intentions of the aristocratic sector of society.
    c. Gulliver becomes acquainted with the people and practices of his new surroundings.
    d. Gulliver's differences cause him to become penitent around new acquaintances.

66. What is the word *principal* referring to in the following text?

My friend Reldresal, principal secretary for private affairs, is, in my opinion, if I am not partial, the second after the treasurer; the rest of the great officers are much upon a par.

    a. Primary or chief
    b. An acolyte
    c. An individual who provides nurturing
    d. One in a subordinate position

67. What can the reader infer from this passage?

I would sometimes lie down, and let five or six of them dance on my hand; and at last the boys and girls would venture to come and play at hide-and-seek in my hair.

    a. The children tortured Gulliver.
    b. Gulliver traveled because he wanted to meet new people.
    c. Gulliver is considerably larger than the children who are playing around him.
    d. Gulliver has a genuine love and enthusiasm for people of all sizes.

68. What is the significance of the word *mind* in the following passage?

> The emperor had a mind one day to entertain me with several of the country shows, wherein they exceed all nations I have known, both for dexterity and magnificence.

a. The ability to think
b. A collective vote
c. A definitive decision
d. A mythological question

69. Which of the following assertions does NOT support the fact that games are a commonplace event in this culture?
a. My gentleness and good behavior . . . short time.
b. They are trained in this art from their youth . . . liberal education.
c. Very often the chief ministers themselves are commanded to show their skill . . . not lost their faculty.
d. Flimnap, the treasurer, is allowed to cut a caper on the straight rope . . . higher than any other lord in the whole empire.

70. Select the best word for the blank in the following sentence:

> Tom couldn't decide which shirt to ___.

a. ware
b. where
c. wear
d. were

71. Identify the adjective clause in the following sentence.

> A boy who loves to ride bikes gets plenty of exercise.

a. a boy who loves
b. who loves to ride bikes
c. to ride bikes
d. gets plenty of exercise

72. Identify the adverbial clause in the following sentence.

> I want to work in the garden longer unless you are too tired.

a. I want to work in the garden
b. in the garden
c. are too tired
d. unless you are too tired

325

73. Identify the noun phrase in the following sentence.

   The actor and actress rode in the long black limousine.

   a. actor and actress
   b. rode in the
   c. the long black limousine
   d. actress rode in

74. Which sentence does NOT include a gerund phrase?
   a. Swimming several laps is a great way to get exercise.
   b. The best way to swim quickly is using the flippers.
   c. I can swim farther than the coach can in three minutes.
   d. Learning to swim is not as difficult as you imagine it to be.

Questions 75 and 76 are based on the following passage:

This excerpt is an adaptation from "The 'Hatchery' of the Sun-Fish"--- *Scientific American, #711*

   I have thought that an example of the intelligence (instinct?) of a class of fish which has come under my observation during my excursions into the Adirondack region of New York State might possibly be of interest to your readers, especially as I am not aware that any one except myself has noticed it, or, at least, has given it publicity.

   The female sun-fish (called, I believe, in England, the roach or bream) makes a "hatchery" for her eggs in this wise. Selecting a spot near the banks of the numerous lakes in which this region abounds, and where the water is about 4 inches deep, and still, she builds, with her tail and snout, a circular embankment 3 inches in height and 2 thick. The circle, which is as perfect a one as could be formed with mathematical instruments, is usually a foot and a half in diameter; and at one side of this circular wall an opening is left by the fish of just sufficient width to admit her body.

   The mother sun-fish, having now built or provided her "hatchery," deposits her spawn within the circular inclosure, and mounts guard at the entrance until the fry are hatched out and are sufficiently large to take charge of themselves. As the embankment, moreover, is built up to the surface of the water, no enemy can very easily obtain an entrance within the inclosure from the top; while there being only one entrance, the fish is able, with comparative ease, to keep out all intruders.

   I have, as I say, noticed this beautiful instinct of the sun-fish for the perpetuity of her species more particularly in the lakes of this region; but doubtless the same habit is common to these fish in other waters.

75. What is the purpose of this passage?
   a. To show the effects of fish hatcheries on the Adirondack region
   b. To persuade the audience to study Ichthyology (fish science)
   c. To depict the sequence of mating among sun-fish
   d. To enlighten the audience on the habits of sun-fish and their hatcheries

76. How is the circle that keeps the larvae of the sun-fish made?
    a. It is formed with mathematical instruments.
    b. The sun-fish builds it with her tail and snout.
    c. It is provided to her as a "hatchery" by Mother Nature.
    d. The sun-fish builds it with her larvae.

77. The author included the third paragraph in this passage to achieve which of the following effects?
    a. To complicate the subject matter
    b. To express a bias
    c. To insert a counterargument
    d. To conclude a sequence and add a final detail

78. Which sentence is an example of a double negative?
    a. She couldn't find anything to say.
    b. He did like something she said.
    c. They didn't like nothing I said.
    d. I cannot say I don't disapprove of that.

For the next two questions, select the answer choice that best corrects the underlined portion of the sentence:

79. It is necessary for instructors to offer tutoring <u>to any students who need extra help in the class.</u>
    a. to any students who need extra help in the class.
    b. for any students that need extra help in the class.
    c. with any students who need extra help in the class.
    d. for any students needing any extra help in their class.

80. <u>Because many people</u> feel there are too many distractions to get any work done, I actually enjoy working from home.
    a. Because many people
    b. While many people
    c. Maybe many people
    d. With most people

Mathematics

1. Convert $\frac{5}{8}$ to a decimal.
    a. 0.62
    b. 1.05
    c. 0.63
    d. 1.60

2. Subtract and express in reduced form $\frac{23}{24} - \frac{1}{6}$.

    a. $\frac{22}{18}$

    b. $\frac{11}{9}$

    c. $\frac{19}{24}$

    d. $\frac{4}{5}$

3. Subtract and express in reduced form $\frac{43}{45} - \frac{11}{15}$.

    a. $\frac{10}{45}$

    b. $\frac{16}{15}$

    c. $\frac{32}{30}$

    d. $\frac{2}{9}$

4. Change 0.56 to a fraction.

    a. $\frac{5.6}{100}$

    b. $\frac{14}{25}$

    c. $\frac{56}{1,000}$

    d. $\frac{56}{10}$

5. Multiply $13,114 \times 191$.

    a. 2,504,774

    b. 250,477

    c. 150,474

    d. 2,514,774

6. Marty wishes to save $150 over a 4-day period. How much must Marty save each day on average?

    a. $37.50

    b. $35

    c. $45.50

    d. $41

7. Multiply and reduce $\frac{15}{23} \times \frac{54}{127}$.

    a. $\frac{810}{2,921}$

    b. $\frac{81}{292}$

    c. $\frac{69}{150}$

    d. $\frac{810}{2929}$

328

8. Bernard can make $80 per day. If he needs to make $300 and only works full days, how many days will this take?

    a. 6
    b. 3
    c. 5
    d. 4

9. A couple buys a house for $150,000. They sell it for $165,000. By what percentage did the house's value increase?

    a. 18%
    b. 13%
    c. 15%
    d. 10%

10. Which is closest to 17.8×9.9?

    a. 140
    b. 180
    c. 200
    d. 350

11. Taylor works two jobs. The first pays $20,000 per year. The second pays $10,000 per year. She donates 15% of her income to charity. How much does she donate each year?

    a. $4,500
    b. $5,000
    c. $5,500
    d. $6,000

12. A box with rectangular sides is 24 inches wide, 18 inches deep, and 12 inches high. What is the volume of the box in cubic feet?

    a. 2
    b. 6
    c. 3
    d. 5

13. What is the solution to $9 \times 9 \div 9 + 9 - 9 \div 9$?

    a. 0
    b. 17
    c. 81
    d. 9

14. Solve for x:

$$\frac{2x}{5} - 1 = 59$$

    a. 60
    b. 145
    c. 150
    d. 115

15. A National Hockey League store in the state of Michigan advertises 50% off all items. Sales tax in Michigan is 6%. How much would a hat originally priced at $32.99 and a jersey originally priced at $64.99 cost during this sale? Round to the nearest penny.
    a. $97.98
    b. $103.86
    c. $51.93
    d. $48.99

16. Store brand coffee beans cost $1.23 per pound. A local coffee bean roaster charges $1.98 per $1\frac{1}{2}$ pounds. How much more would 5 pounds from the local roaster cost than 5 pounds of the store brand?
    a. $0.55
    b. $1.55
    c. $1.45
    d. $0.45

17. Paint Inc. charges $2,000 for painting the first 1,800 feet of trim on a house and $1.00 per foot for each foot after. How much would it cost to paint a house with 3,125 feet of trim?
    a. $3,125
    b. $2,000
    c. $5,125
    d. $3,325

18. A bucket can hold 11.4 liters of water. A kiddie pool needs 35 gallons of water to be full. How many times will the bucket need to be filled to fill the kiddie pool? 1 gallon = 3.78541 liters
    a. 12
    b. 35
    c. 11
    d. 45

19. The hospital has a nurse-to-patient ratio of 1:25. If there is a maximum of 325 patients admitted at a time, how many nurses are there?
    a. 13 nurses
    b. 25 nurses
    c. 325 nurses
    d. 12 nurses

20. A hospital has a bed to room ratio of 2: 1. If there are 145 rooms, how many beds are there?
    a. 145 beds
    b. 2 beds
    c. 90 beds
    d. 290 beds

21. Convert 0.351 to a percentage.
    a. 3.51%
    b. 35.1%
    c. $\frac{351}{100}$
    d. 0.00351%

330

22. Convert $\frac{2}{9}$ to a percentage.
   a. 22%
   b. 4.5%
   c. 450%
   d. 0.22%

23. If $6t + 4 = 16$, what is t?
   a. 1
   b. 2
   c. 3
   d. 4

24. The variable y is directly proportional to x. If $y = 3$ when $x = 5$, then what is y when $x = 20$?
   a. 10
   b. 12
   c. 14
   d. 16

25. There are $4x + 1$ treats in each party favor bag. If a total of $60x + 15$ treats are distributed, how many bags are given out?
   a. 15
   b. 16
   c. 20
   d. 22

26. The following stem-and-leaf plot shows plant growth in cm for a group of tomato plants.

Stem	Leaf
2	0 2 3 6 8 8 9
3	2 6 7 7
4	7 9
5	4 6 9

What is the range of measurements for the tomato plants' growth?
   a. 29 cm
   b. 37 cm
   c. 39 cm
   d. 59 cm

27. A rectangle has a length that is 5 feet longer than three times its width. If the perimeter is 90 feet, what is the length in feet?
   a. 10
   b. 20
   c. 25
   d. 35

28. In an office, there are 50 workers. A total of 60% of the workers are women, and the chances of a woman wearing a skirt is 50%. If no men wear skirts, how many workers are wearing skirts?
   a. 12
   b. 15
   c. 16
   d. 20

29. Ten students take a test. Five students get a 50. Four students get a 70. If the average score is 55, what was the last student's score?
   a. 20
   b. 40
   c. 50
   d. 60

30. A company invests $50,000 in a building where they can produce saws. If the cost of producing one saw is $40, then which function expresses the amount of money the company pays? The variable y is the money paid and x is the number of saws produced.
   a. $y = 40x + 50{,}000$
   b. $y + 40 = x - 50{,}000$
   c. $y = 40x - 50{,}000$
   d. $y = 50x - 400{,}000$

31. A six-sided die is rolled. What is the probability that the roll is 1 or 2?
   a. $\frac{1}{6}$
   b. $\frac{1}{4}$
   c. $\frac{1}{3}$
   d. $\frac{1}{2}$

32. Which of the following is NOT a way to write 40 percent of N?
   a. $(0.4)N$
   b. $\frac{2}{5}N$
   c. $40N$
   d. $\frac{4N}{10}$

332

33. At the store, Jan spends $90 on apples and oranges. Apples cost $1 each and oranges cost $2 each. If Jan buys the same number of apples as oranges, how many oranges did she buy?
   a. 20
   b. 25
   c. 30
   d. 35

34. What is the volume of a box with rectangular sides 5 feet long, 6 feet wide, and 3 feet high?
   a. 60 cubic feet
   b. 75 cubic feet
   c. 90 cubic feet
   d. 14 cubic feet

35. A train traveling 50 miles per hour takes a trip lasting 3 hours. If a map has a scale of 1 inch per 10 miles, how many inches apart are the train's starting point and ending point on the map?
   a. 14
   b. 12
   c. 13
   d. 15

36. A traveler takes an hour to drive to a museum, spends 3 hours and 30 minutes there, and takes half an hour to drive home. What percentage of their time was spent driving?
   a. 15%
   b. 30%
   c. 40%
   d. 60%

37. A truck is carrying three cylindrical barrels. Their bases have a diameter of 2 feet, and they have a height of 3 feet. What is the total volume of the three barrels in cubic feet?
   a. 3π
   b. 9π
   c. 12π
   d. 15π

38. What is the value of b in this equation?

$$5b - 4 = 2b + 17$$

   a. 13
   b. 24
   c. 7
   d. 21

39. A rectangle has a length that is 5 feet longer than three times its width. If the perimeter is 90 feet, what is the length in feet?
   a. 10
   b. 20
   c. 25
   d. 35

40. Which of the following equations best represents the problem below?

The width of a rectangle is 2 centimeters less than the length. If the perimeter of the rectangle is 44 centimeters, then what are the dimensions of the rectangle?

a. $2l + 2(l - 2) = 44$
b. $l + 2) + (l + 2) + l = 48$
c. $l \times (l - 2) = 44$
d. $(l + 2) + (l + 2) + l = 44$

41. What is the value of x in the diagram below?

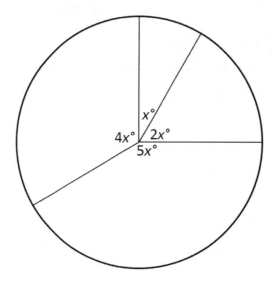

a. 60
b. 50
c. 30
d. 36

42. The width of a rectangular house is 22 feet. What is the perimeter of this house if it has the same area as a house that is 33 feet wide and 50 feet long?

a. 184 feet
b. 200 feet
c. 194 feet
d. 206 feet

43. What is the probability of randomly picking the winner and runner-up from a race of four horses and distinguishing which is the winner?

a. $\frac{1}{4}$
b. $\frac{1}{2}$
c. $\frac{1}{16}$
d. $\frac{1}{12}$

334

44. Kassidy drove for 3 hours at a speed of 60 miles per hour. Using the distance formula, $d = r \times t$ ($distance = rate \times time$), how far did Kassidy travel?

    a. 20 miles

    b. 180 miles

    c. 65 miles

    d. 120 miles

45. If Amanda can eat two times as many mini cupcakes as Marty, what would the missing values be for the following input-output table?

Input (number of cupcakes eaten by Marty)	Output (number of cupcakes eaten by Amanda)
1	2
3	
5	10
7	
9	18

    a. 6, 10

    b. 3, 11

    c. 6, 14

    d. 4, 12

46. The table below shows tickets purchased during the week for entry to the local zoo. What is the mean of adult tickets sold for the week?

Day of the Week	Age	Tickets Sold
Monday	Adult	22
Monday	Child	30
Tuesday	Adult	16
Tuesday	Child	15
Wednesday	Adult	24
Wednesday	Child	23
Thursday	Adult	19
Thursday	Child	26
Friday	Adult	29
Friday	Child	38

    a. 24.2

    b. 21

    c. 22

    d. 26.4

47. An accounting firm charted its income on the following pie graph. If the total income for the year was $500,000, how much of the income was received from Audit and Taxation Services?

Income

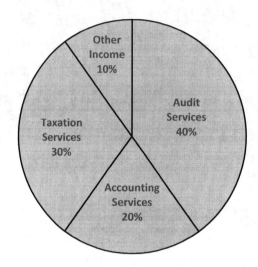

a. $200,000
b. $350,000
c. $150,000
d. $300,000

48. Which inequality represents the number line below?

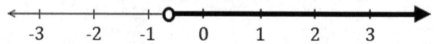

a. $4x + 5 < 8$
b. $-4x + 5 < 8$
c. $-4x + 5 > 8$
d. $4x - 5 > 8$

49. $x^4 - 16$ can be simplified to which of the following?
a. $(x^2 - 4)(x^2 + 4)$
b. $(x^2 + 4)(x^2 + 4)$
c. $(x^2 - 4)(x^2 - 4)$
d. $(x^2 - 2)(x^2 + 4)$

50. Which of the following is not a parallelogram?

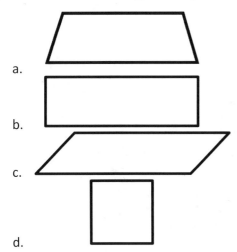

a.

b.

c.

d.

Social Studies

1. Which of these choices BEST describes a participatory democracy?
    a. A system in which only the educated and wealthy members of society vote and decide upon the leaders of the country
    b. A system in which groups come together to advance certain select interests
    c. A system that emphasizes everyone contributing to the political system
    d. A system in which one group makes decisions for the population at large

2. Which of the following types of government intervention lowers prices, reassures the supply, and creates opportunity to compete with foreign vendors?
    a. Income redistribution
    b. Price controls
    c. Taxes
    d. Subsidies

3. What type of map would be the most useful for calculating data and differentiating between the characteristics of two places?
    a. Topographic maps
    b. Dot-density maps
    c. Isoline maps
    d. Flow-line maps

Question 4 is based on the following map:

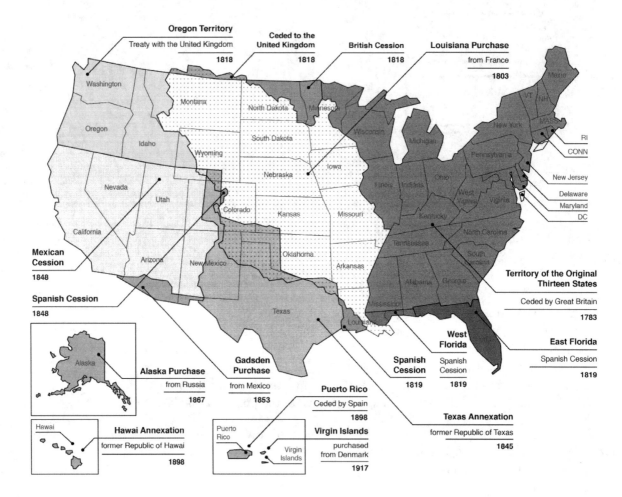

4. What current state did the United States gain through military force with a non-native nation-state?
   a. Nebraska
   b. Missouri
   c. Alaska
   d. Nevada

5. Nationalism had the LEAST influence on which one of the following world events?
   a. German unification
   b. Latin American wars of independence
   c. Russo-Turkish War
   d. War of the Spanish Succession

6. Which ONE of the following was NOT a cause of World War I?
   a. Communism
   b. Imperialism
   c. Militarism
   d. Nationalism

7. Which of the following is NOT a characteristic of cultural landscapes?
   a. Ethnocentrism
   b. Industrial practices
   c. Land use patterns
   d. Physical features

8. Which of the following is an ethnic religion?
   a. Buddhism
   b. Christianity
   c. Hinduism
   d. Islam

9. Which of the following best describes the relationship between sovereignty and territoriality?
   a. Sovereignty is held by central governments, whereas subnational units of government enjoy rights to territoriality.
   b. Territoriality refers to control over territory, whereas sovereignty is related to political organization.
   c. Political entities leverage territoriality to protect their sovereignty.
   d. Territoriality is generally more valuable to political entities than sovereignty.

10. Which is NOT true of nonrenewable resources?
    a. They tend to be used more frequently than renewables.
    b. They are thought to be responsible for climate change.
    c. They are relied upon heavily in developing economies.
    d. They have slowed industrial growth.

11. Which political orientation emphasizes maintaining traditions and stability over progress and change?
    a. Socialism
    b. Liberalism
    c. Conservatism
    d. Libertarianism

12. Governments deployed large-scale propaganda for the FIRST time during which one of the following military conflicts?
    a. Russo-Turkish War
    b. First Sino-Japanese War
    c. Spanish Civil War
    d. World War I

13. Which of the following was a long-term consequence of explorers looking for a northwest passage?
    a. European powers gained a faster route to the Pacific Ocean.
    b. European powers abandoned international trade networks.
    c. European powers forged alliances with Amerindian empires.
    d. European powers colonized the Americas.

14. Which of the following was NOT a problem presented by the Articles of Confederation?
   a. Infighting between branches of government
   b. The inability to implement and collect taxes to pay off debt
   c. Slow responses from the government toward rebellions
   d. Ineffective raising of armies for wartime

Question 15 refers to the diagram below.

Redistricting

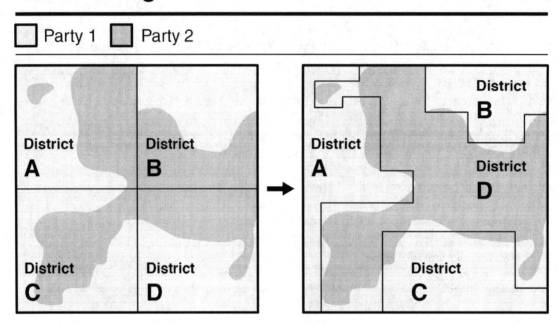

15. The diagram illustrates which of the following manipulative redistricting practices?
   a. Contiguity
   b. Gerrymandering
   c. Partisan fairness
   d. Proportional representation

16. Which of the following statements accurately describes the European Union?
   a. It was formed in 1945 after World War II.
   b. It was founded as a result of the Paris Peace Conference that ended the first World War.
   c. It aims to ensure free movement of people, goods, services and capital within the internal market.
   d. It was founded to avoid the repetitions of the Great War.

17. Which of the following nations saw their standing during the nineteenth century fall as other powers were rising?
   a. Ottoman Empire
   b. England
   c. Germany
   d. Russia

18. In 1850, the ten most populous cities in the United States, in order from most populous to least were: New York, NY; Baltimore, MD; Boston, MA; Philadelphia, PA; New Orleans, LA; Cincinnati, OH; Brooklyn, NY; St. Louis, MO, Spring Garden, PA; Albany, NY. How many of these cities are located in a state that was one of the original thirteen colonies?
   a. 6
   b. 7
   c. 8
   d. 9

19. Which term is best defined as a group of people joined by a common culture, language, heritage, history, and religion?
   a. State
   b. Nation
   c. Regime
   d. Government

20. During the 1960s–1980s, deindustrialization in cities in the Industrial North (now called the *Rust Belt*), including hubs like Buffalo, Cleveland, Chicago, and Milwaukee, would be considered an example of which of the following?
   a. Political push factor
   b. Political pull factor
   c. Economic push factor
   d. Economic pull factor

21. Which of the following best describes how culture is transmitted across society?
   a. Culture is almost always transmitted through hierarchical relationships, and it has a trickle-down effect.
   b. Culture is primarily transmitted through religion, economic activities, and government policies.
   c. Cultural exchanges on the internet have given rise to a global popular culture in recent years.
   d. Culture can be transmitted through an endless variety of activities, and the transmission can either be intentional or spontaneous.

22. Which of the following is NOT a purpose of the central bank?
   a. Manage interest rates
   b. Set the tax rate
   c. Backup the commercial banks
   d. Set reserve requirements

23. What is the name for the movement, started in the 1970s, that began the conservative pushback against the increasing role the government was taking in the economy?
   a. Fiscal policy
   b. Keynesian economics
   c. Fiscal responsibility
   d. Supply-side economics

24. Which ONE of the following best describes an economic benefit of free trade agreements?
   a. Free trade agreements increase international trade by reducing barriers to trade.
   b. Free trade agreements reduce the cost of reparations.
   c. Free trade agreements allow countries to protect domestic iron and steel production.
   d. Free trade agreements facilitate imperialism and the creation of lucrative empires.

25. What social consequence(s) did the Black Death have in Europe?
   a. It gave birth to the concept of absolute monarchy.
   b. It ignited the Protestant Reformation.
   c. It eroded serfdom.
   d. It gave rise to Child Labor Laws in England.

26. Nicolaus Copernicus was a key figure in which cultural phenomena?
   a. The Scientific Revolution
   b. The Age of Enlightenment
   c. The Renaissance
   d. The Protestant Reformation

27. Which of the following statements best describes King Louis XIV of France?
   a. He abdicated his throne during the French Revolution.
   b. He supported the American Revolution.
   c. He was the ultimate example of an absolute monarch.
   d. He created the concept of the Mandate of Heaven.

28. Which of the following resulted from the Age of Enlightenment?
   a. The discovery of the heliocentric theory
   b. The birth of Lutheranism
   c. The American Revolution
   d. The Renaissance

29. Which of the following statements best describes the relationship, if any, between the revolutions in America and France?
   a. The French Revolution inspired the American Revolution.
   b. The American Revolution inspired the French Revolution.
   c. They both occurred simultaneously.
   d. There was no connection between the French and American revolutions.

30. What impact, if any, did the introduction of the movable type printing press have in Europe?
    a. It increased the cost of books because the process was labor intensive.
    b. It led to an increase in literacy.
    c. The Catholic Church used it to effectively suppress the Protestant Reformation.
    d. It led to the Dark Ages.

31. Which of the following documents outlawed slavery throughout the United States?
    a. U.S. Constitution
    b. Compromise of 1850
    c. Emancipation Proclamation
    d. 13th Amendment

32. Which event(s) contributed to increasing sectional tension before the Civil War?
    a. Malcom X's death
    b. The Bleeding Kansas conflict
    c. The 13th Amendment
    d. Shay's Rebellion

33. Which of the following caused America to join World War I in 1917?
    a. Germany's unrestricted submarine warfare
    b. The destruction of the USS Maine
    c. The Japanese attack on Pearl Harbor
    d. Franz Ferdinand's death in 1914

34. Which event was the last major armed conflict between U.S. forces and Native Americans?
    a. Trail of Tears
    b. Tecumseh's War
    c. Massacre at Wounded Knee
    d. Battle of the Little Big Horn

Questions 35 and 36 are based on the following table:

Presidential Election of 1824			
Candidate	Electoral Votes	Popular Votes	State Votes in the House of Representatives
Andrew Jackson	99	153,544	7
John Quincy Adams	84	108,740	13
William H. Crawford	41	46,618	4
Henry Clay	37	47,136	0

35. Who won the presidential election of 1824?
    a. Andrew Jackson
    b. John Quincy Adams
    c. William H. Crawford
    d. Henry Clay

343

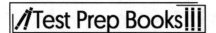

36. What electoral system can result in a second round of voting commonly referred to as a runoff?
   a. Majority systems
   b. Plurality systems
   c. Single transferable systems
   d. Party list systems

37. Which document established the first system of government in the United States?
   a. Declaration of Independence
   b. Constitution
   c. Articles of Confederation
   d. Bill of Rights

38. What consequences did the New Deal have?
   a. It established a number of federal agencies and programs that continue to function in the 21st century.
   b. It led to a third political party.
   c. It established a two-term limit in the White House.
   d. It led to the Great Depression.

39. What advantage(s) did the North have over the South during the Civil War?
   a. The North was defending their homes from damage.
   b. The North had free labor at home.
   c. The North had a larger navy.
   d. The North had more experienced military leaders.

40. In which of the following areas did the United States achieve victory during the Cold War?
   a. The Korean War
   b. The Space Race
   c. The Vietnam War
   d. The Battle of Gettysburg

41. The presidential cabinet has which of the following duties?
   a. Advise the president.
   b. Act as spokesperson for the U.S. government administration.
   c. Solicit donations for the president's re-election campaign.
   d. Preside over the Senate.

42. Which of the following motivated Christopher Columbus to sail across the Atlantic Ocean?
   a. A desire to establish a direct trade route to Asia.
   b. A desire to confirm the existence of America.
   c. A desire to prove the world was round.
   d. A desire to spread Judaism.

43. Which of the following were characteristics of the American economy after World War II?
   a. A return to the Great Depression.
   b. Increased use of computers.
   c. The decline of the Sun Belt.
   d. The fall of the stock market.

44. Which of the following agreements allowed territories to vote on whether or not they would become free or slave states?
    a. The Connecticut Compromise
    b. The Missouri Compromise
    c. The Compromise of 1850
    d. The Three-Fifths Compromise

45. Which of the following could be considered a pull factor for a particular area?
    a. High rates of unemployment
    b. Low GDP
    c. Educational opportunity
    d. High population density

46. Differences in race, gender, sexual orientation, economic status, and language can be denoted as what?
    a. Behaviorism
    b. Peer pressure
    c. Adaptation
    d. Diversity

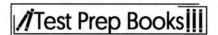
Questions 47 and 48 refer to the map below.

European NATO members (2019)

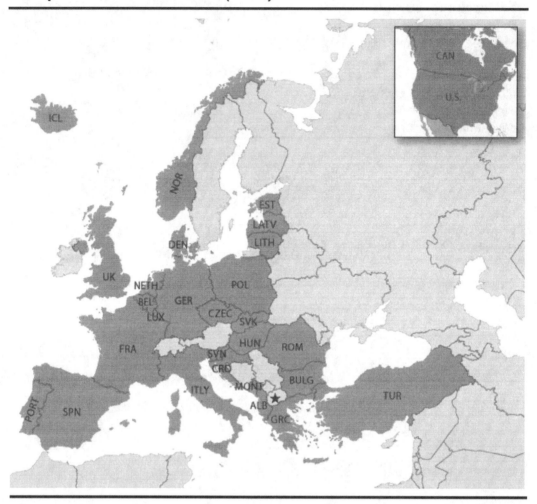

47. The map depicts which of the following types of organizations?
    a. Free-trade organization
    b. International financial organization
    c. Joint task force for transnational challenges
    d. Military alliance

48. Which of the following best explains why the members have joined this organization?
    a. The organization increases members' sovereignty by protecting their territorial integrity.
    b. The organization offers a framework for widespread international cooperation in economic, military, and political matters.
    c. The organization provides for the common defense of members and facilitates the transfer of sensitive technologies.
    d. The organization helps members secure greater levels of foreign direct investment.

49. Which political party was founded to advocate for the abolition of slavery?
    a. Constitutional Union
    b. Southern Democrat
    c. Republican
    d. Libertarian

50. The era following the Civil War is known as what?
    a. Antebellum Era
    b. Reconstruction
    c. Progressive Era
    d. Civil rights movement

51. What is the name of the policies developed by President Franklin Delano Roosevelt during the Great Depression?
    a. The Great Society
    b. The War Against Poverty
    c. Progressivism
    d. The New Deal

52. What were the consequences of the Spanish-American War?
    a. The U.S. acquired colonies in the Caribbean and Pacific oceans.
    b. The U.S. acquired large swaths of territory in the Southwestern United States.
    c. It led to the formation of the League of Nations.
    d. It ended the Great Depression.

53. Which Supreme Court decision struck down the separate but equal doctrine?
    a. *Roe vs. Wade*
    b. *Brown vs. Board of Education*
    c. *Plessy vs. Ferguson*
    d. *Marbury vs. Madison*

54. Which term is best defined as a group of people joined by a common culture, language, heritage, history, and religion?
    a. State
    b. Nation
    c. Regime
    d. Government

55. Which event helped sparked the gay and lesbian rights movement in 1969?
    a. The Stonewall Inn Riot
    b. The murder of Matthew Shepard
    c. The murder of Vincent Chin
    d. The emergence of AIDS

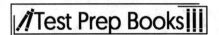

56. What became the scholarly capital of the Hellenistic world during the reign of Alexander the Great?
   a. Jerusalem
   b. Athens
   c. Alexandria
   d. Constantinople

57. The First Agricultural Revolution occurred how many years ago?
   a. 50
   b. 1000
   c. 200
   d. 10,000

58. Which of the following fields falls under the umbrella of the social sciences?
   a. Biology
   b. English
   c. Psychology
   d. Geometry

59. Which of the following are markets that establish a few large firms as the major sellers/distributors?
   a. Free enterprise economies
   b. Pure monopolies
   c. Oligopolies
   d. Command economies

60. Which of the following is the best definition for a pure monopoly?
   a. When there is only one seller of a particular product or commodity, and the sole seller attempts to restrict firms from exiting and entering the industry at will
   b. When prices are determined by consumer demand, and no supplier maintains any significant influence over prices
   c. When people are completely free to buy the goods and services they want/need
   d. When a few large firms become the major sellers/distributors of an industry

Science

1. What is an adaptation?
   a. The original traits found in a common ancestor
   b. Changes that occur in the environment
   c. When one species begins behaving like another species
   d. An inherited characteristic that enhances survival and reproduction

2. What organelle is the site of protein synthesis?
   a. Nucleus
   b. Smooth ER
   c. Ribosome
   d. Lysosome

3. The energy from electricity results from which of the following?
    a.   The atomic structure of matter
    b.   The ability to do work
    c.   The neutrons in an atom
    d.   Conductive materials like metals

4. Which is the cellular organelle used to tag, package, and ship out proteins destined for other cells or locations?
    a.   The Golgi apparatus
    b.   The lysosome
    c.   The centrioles
    d.   The mitochondria

5. What molecule serves as the hereditary material for prokaryotic and eukaryotic cells?
    a.   Proteins
    b.   Carbohydrates
    c.   Lipids
    d.   DNA

6. Which taxonomic system is commonly used to describe the hierarchy of similar organisms today?
    a.   Aristotle system
    b.   Linnaean system
    c.   Cesalpino system
    d.   Darwin system

7. What is the Latin specific name for humans?
    a.   *Homo sapiens*
    b.   *Homo erectus*
    c.   *Canis familiaris*
    d.   *Homo habilis*

8. Which is an organelle found in a plant cell but not an animal cell?
    a.   Mitochondria
    b.   Chloroplast
    c.   Golgi body
    d.   Nucleus

9. What kind of energy do plants use in photosynthesis to create chemical energy?
    a.   Light
    b.   Electric
    c.   Nuclear
    d.   Cellular

10. What does the cell membrane do?
    a.   Builds proteins
    b.   Breaks down large molecules
    c.   Contains the cell's DNA
    d.   Controls which molecules are allowed in and out of the cell

11. What gets converted to heat inside a greenhouse?
    a. Water
    b. Sunlight
    c. Plants
    d. Oxygen

12. Circular motion occurs around what?
    a. The center of mass
    b. The center of matter
    c. An elliptical
    d. An axis

13. Which statement is true regarding electrostatic charges?
    a. Like charges attract.
    b. Like charges repel.
    c. Like charges are neutral.
    d. Like charges neither attract nor repel.

14. Which of the following depicts a form of potential energy?
    a. The light given off by a lamp
    b. The gravitational pull of a black hole
    c. The heat from a microwaved burrito
    d. The motion of a pendulum

15. A car is traveling at a constant velocity of 25 m/s. How long does it take the car to travel 45 kilometers in a straight line?
    a. 1 hour
    b. 3600 seconds
    c. 1800 seconds
    d. 900 seconds

16. What is ONE feature that both prokaryotes and eukaryotes have in common?
    a. A plasma membrane
    b. A nucleus enclosed by a membrane
    c. Organelles
    d. A nucleoid

17. With which genotype would the recessive phenotype appear, if the dominant allele is marked with "A" and the recessive allele is marked with "a"?
    a. AA
    b. aa
    c. Aa
    d. aA

350

18. How are fungi similar to plants?
    a. They have a cell wall.
    b. They contain chloroplasts.
    c. They perform photosynthesis.
    d. They use carbon dioxide as a source of energy.

19. What important function are the roots of plants responsible for?
    a. Absorbing water from the surrounding environment
    b. Performing photosynthesis
    c. Conducting sugars downward through the leaves
    d. Supporting the plant body

20. Which subdiscipline of biology would a botanist study?
    a. Growth of an aloe plant
    b. Evolution of monkeys
    c. Genetic changes in human brain cancer
    d. Interaction between worker bees and a queen bee

21. What shape does a water molecule form?
    a. C-shape
    b. S-shape
    c. V-shape
    d. T-shape

22. Which type of biological molecule stores information?
    a. Carbohydrates
    b. Nucleic acids
    c. Proteins
    d. Lipids

23. If a molecule were trying to enter an animal cell, which organelle would it have to pass through first?
    a. Cell wall
    b. Cell membrane
    c. Nucleus
    d. Endoplasmic reticulum

24. Which of the following is identical in both mitosis and meiosis?
    a. The number of divisions
    b. The number of daughter cells produced
    c. The synapsis of homologous chromosomes
    d. When DNA replication occurs

25. Which of following about nuclear reactions is NOT true?
    a. They involve the release of energy
    b. The structure of the nucleus changes.
    c. They take place in the atom's nucleus.
    d. The reactants and products have equal mass.

26. What is the chemical reaction when a compound is broken down into its basic components called?
    a. A synthesis reaction
    b. A decomposition reaction
    c. An organic reaction
    d. An oxidation reaction

27. What is the name of this compound: CO?
    a. Carbonite oxide
    b. Carbonic dioxide
    c. Carbonic monoxide
    d. Carbon monoxide

28. According to the periodic table, which of the following elements is the least reactive?
    a. Fluorine
    b. Silicon
    c. Neon
    d. Gallium

29. Explain the Law of Conservation of Mass as it applies to this reaction: $2\,H_2 + O_2 \rightarrow 2\,H_2O$.
    a. Electrons are lost.
    b. The hydrogen loses mass.
    c. New oxygen atoms are formed.
    d. There is no decrease or increase of matter.

30. Dark storm clouds are usually located where?
    a. Between 5,000 and 13,000 meters above sea level
    b. Between 2,000 and 7,000 meters above sea level
    c. Below 2,000 meters above sea level
    d. Outer space

31. Which of the following best describes this moon phase?

a. Gibbous
b. Waxing
c. Waning
d. Crescent

32. The Big Bang theory helps explain which of the following?
a. The expanding universe
b. Dark matter
c. Life
d. Gravity

33. Currently, water can be found where?
a. On the Earth
b. Around Saturn
c. On Jupiter's moons
d. All of the above

34. Which of the following correctly displays 8,600,000,000,000 in scientific notation?
a. 8.6×10^{12}
b. 8.6×10^{-12}
c. 8.6×10^{11}
d. 86×10^{11}

35. Scientist A is observing an unknown substance in the lab. Which observation describes a chemical property of the substance?
    a. She sees that it is green in color.
    b. She weighs it and measures the volume and finds the density to be 10 g/L.
    c. She applies pressure to it and finds that it breaks apart easily.
    d. She passes it through a flame and finds that it burns.

36. Which of the following processes can be SOLELY categorized as a chemical reaction process?
    a. The condensation of water vapor around the container of an ice-cold beverage
    b. Baking brownies with chocolate chips
    c. The shattering of a glass mason jar after falling on the floor
    d. The combination of sand (SiO_2) in water

37. What is the force that opposes motion?
    a. Reactive force
    b. Responsive force
    c. Friction
    d. Momentum

38. Absolute dating involves which of the following?
    a. Measuring radioactive decay
    b. Comparing rock stratification
    c. Fossil location
    d. Fossil record

39. What is the basic unit of matter?
    a. Elementary particle
    b. Atom
    c. Molecule
    d. Photon

40. Which particle is responsible for all chemical reactions?
    a. Electrons
    b. Neutrons
    c. Protons
    d. Orbitals

41. Which of these give atoms a negative charge?
    a. Electrons
    b. Neutrons
    c. Protons
    d. Orbital

42. In a chemical equation, the reactants are on which side of the arrow?
    a. Right
    b. Left
    c. Neither right nor left
    d. Both right and left

43. Which of these is a substance that increases the rate of a chemical reaction?
    a. Catalyst
    b. Brine
    c. Solvent
    d. Inhibitor

44. What type of eclipse occurs when the moon comes between the Earth and Sun and covers the Sun's light completely?
    a. Total solar eclipse
    b. Partial lunar eclipse
    c. Total lunar eclipse
    d. Partial solar eclipse

45. The fact that the Earth is tilted as it revolves around the Sun creates which phenomenon?
    a. Life
    b. Plate tectonics
    c. Wind
    d. Seasonality

46. Water that has seeped into rock cracks and freezes will most likely result in what process?
    a. Chemical weathering
    b. Mechanical weathering
    c. Erosion
    d. Deposition

47. Which soil is the least permeable to water?
    a. Pure sand
    b. Pure silt
    c. Pure clay
    d. Loam

48. Which of the following is true regarding the Earth's southern geomagnetic pole?
    a. It's always around the same area
    b. It's near the North Pole
    c. It's near the South Pole
    d. It never moves

49. Which apparatus would be best to use to look at a solar eclipse?
    a. A telescope facing the eclipse
    b. A pinhole camera facing away from the eclipse
    c. Sunglasses facing the eclipse
    d. Binoculars facing the eclipse

50. Which type of eclipse is viewed during the daytime?
    a. Both solar and lunar
    b. Solar only
    c. Partial lunar
    d. Total lunar

51. The Sun transfers heat to the Earth through space via which mechanism?
    a. Convection
    b. Conduction
    c. Induction
    d. Radiation

52. Which period in history dramatically increased air, water, and soil pollution?
    a. The Paleolithic Era
    b. The Big Bang Era
    c. The Industrial Revolution
    d. The Medieval Ages

53. Which greenhouse gas is a common byproduct of landfills and concentrated animal feeding operations?
    a. Carbon
    b. Corn fumes
    c. Nitrogen
    d. Methane

54. Which of the following is a drawback of geothermal power?
    a. It is less efficient than other alternative energy sources
    b. It involves combustion, so it still contributes some amount of greenhouse gas emissions
    c. It requires land or roof space
    d. It requires a large amount of water

55. Which types of geological material can serve as natural filters for water?
    a. Clay and coal particles
    b. Leaf and limb particles
    c. Granite and quartz particles
    d. Shale and calcite particles

Answer Explanations #2

Reading and Language Arts

1. D: Choice *D* is correct because decoding and encoding are reciprocal phonological skills, meaning that the steps to each are opposite of one another. It is because of this reciprocal relationship that the development of phonics, vocabulary, and spelling are interrelated. The other answer choices are incorrect because they ascribe the wrong description to the given term.

2. A: Kimberly is in the pre-phonetic stage of spelling because she formed a jumble of letter-like forms rather than a series of discrete letters. This indicates that she only has precommunicative writing ability. Her letter-sound correspondence is limited. In the semiphonetic stage, she would have demonstrated a better understanding of the fact that letters represent sounds. She may have missed syllables in her words or used single letters to represent entire words, but she would have demonstrated letter formation and the alphabetic principle. The other choices list stages in which her spelling would be even further advanced.

3. D: Word walls are great tools for students as they learn to read, spell, and write. They help students learn unfamiliar words by visually grouping similar ones. Choice *A* is incorrect because the primary purpose of word walls is to provide visual groupings of words with similar letter patterns. Choice *B* is incorrect because it describes KWL charts typically used for reading. Choice *C* is incorrect because word walls are primarily useful in the phonetic stage.

4. B: Choice *B* is a correct match between *read* and *speed.* These two words are vowel-constant digraphs that have the same sound.

5. C: A style guide offers advice about proper formatting, punctuation, and usage when writing for a specific field, such as journalism or scientific research. The other resources would not offer similar information. A dictionary is useful for looking up definitions; a thesaurus is useful for looking up synonyms and antonyms. A grammar book is useful for looking up specific grammar topics. Thus, Choices *A, C,* and *D* are incorrect.

6. C: This sentence uses verbs in a parallel series, so each verb must follow the same pattern. In order to fit with the helping verb "would," each verb must be in the present tense. In Choices *A, B,* and *D,* one or more of the verbs switches to past tense. Only Choice *C* remains in the same tense, maintaining the pattern.

7. C: The second sentence tells of an unexpected outcome of the first sentence. Choice *A,* Choice *B,* and Choice *D* indicate a logical progression, which does not match this surprise. Only Choice *C* indicates this unexpected twist.

8. C: *Scaffolding* refers to techniques that allow students to progress toward a greater level of understanding on an increasingly independent level by incrementally increasing difficulty and independence. *Discourse* is a general term that refers to oral or written communication, so Choice *A* is incorrect. *Differentiation* refers to tailoring instructional methods and activities towards individual students or different levels. Therefore, Choice *B* is incorrect. Choice *D* is incorrect because *benchmarking* refers to setting measurable standards during the learning process.

9. B: Choice *B* is a correct statement about the generally accepted progression of normal literacy development. Choice *A* is incorrect because research indicates that literacy development begins from birth. Choices *C* and *D* are incorrect because those skills start developing a bit later than stated, between 9 and 12 months of age for Choice *C*, and in the toddler years for Choice *D*.

10. A: Receptive language development is a term used to describe the beginning literacy stage, during which children begin understanding the "input" of language. This means that they start developing the ability to connect words with their meanings and comprehend spoken language that others say or read.

11. C: The word *runner* is a decodable word because it follows the rules of phonics and is spelled phonetically. The other three choices are considered non-decodable sight words that students simply need to memorize because they are not spelled phonetically.

12. D: A noun phrase consists of the noun and all of its modifiers. In this case, the subject of the sentence is the noun *puppy*, but it is preceded by several modifiers—adjectives that give more information about what kind of puppy, which are also part of the noun phrase. Thus, *A* is incorrect. Charlotte is the owner of the puppy and a modifier of the puppy, so *B* is false. *C* is incorrect because it contains some, but not all, of the modifiers pertaining to the puppy. *D* is correct because it contains all of them.

13. C: In this sentence, the modifier is the phrase "Forgetting that he was supposed to meet his girlfriend for dinner." This phrase offers information about Fred's actions, but the noun that immediately follows it is Anita, creating some confusion about the "do-er" of the phrase. A more appropriate sentence arrangement would be "Forgetting that he was supposed to meet his girlfriend for dinner, Fred made Anita mad when he showed up late." *A* is incorrect as parallelism refers to the consistent use of sentence structure and verb tense, and this sentence is appropriately consistent. Choice *B* is incorrect as this sentence contains appropriate punctuation for the number of independent clauses presented; it is not a run-on sentence. *D* is incorrect because subject-verb agreement refers to the appropriate conjugation of a verb relative to the subject, and all verbs have been properly conjugated.

14. D: The use of "I" could serve to have a "hedging" effect, allow the reader to connect with the author in a more personal way, and cause the reader to empathize more with the egrets. However, it doesn't distance the reader from the text, making Choice *D* the answer to this question.

15. C: The quote provides an example of a warden protecting one of the colonies. Choice *A* is incorrect because the speaker of the quote is a warden, not a hunter. Choice B is incorrect because the quote does not lighten the mood but shows the danger of the situation between the wardens and the hunters. Choice *D* is incorrect because there is no humor found in the quote.

16. D: A *rookery* is a colony of breeding birds. Although *rookery* could mean Choice *A*, houses in a slum area, it does not make sense in this context. Choices *B* and *C* are both incorrect, as this is not a place for hunters to trade tools or for wardens to trade stories.

17. B: An important bird colony. The previous sentence is describing "twenty colonies" of birds, so what follows should be a bird colony. Choice *A* may be true, but we have no evidence of this in the text. Choice *C* does touch on the tension between the hunters and wardens, but there is no official "Bird Island Battle" mentioned in the text. Choice *D* does not exist in the text.

358

18. D: To demonstrate the success of the protective work of the Audubon Association. The text mentions several different times how and why the association has been successful and gives examples to back this fact. Choice *A* is incorrect because although the article, in some instances, calls certain people to act, it is not the purpose of the entire passage. There is no way to tell if Choices *B* and *C* are correct, as they are not mentioned in the text.

19. A: The correct answer is the group of readers to which the author is trying to appeal. Choice *B* could be a partial answer, but it is incorrect. Choice *C* assumes authors only write for experts, so it is incorrect. Choice *D* is not true. Rhetoric tries to appeal to readers and tries to convince them of a thesis.

20. C: The main idea of a piece is its central theme or subject and what the author wants readers to know or understand after they read. Choice *A* is incorrect because the primary purpose is the reason that a piece was written, and while the main idea is an important part of the primary purpose, the above elements are not developed with that intent. Choice *B* is incorrect because while the plot refers to the events that occur in a narrative, organization, tone, and supporting details are not used only to develop plot. Choice *D* is incorrect because characterization is the description of a person.

21. B: A word's origin is also known as its *etymology*. In addition to offering a detailed list of a word's various meanings, a dictionary also provides information about a word's history, such as when it first came into use, what language it originated from, and how its meaning may have changed over time. A thesaurus is for identifying synonyms and antonyms, so *A* is incorrect. A style guide provides formatting, punctuation, and syntactical advice for a specific field, and a grammar book is related to the appropriate placement of words and punctuation, which does not provide any insight into a word's meaning. Therefore, Choices *A*, *C*, and *D* are incorrect.

22. C: The .org domain on websites is generally used by nonprofit groups or community organizations. A government website uses .gov, and .edu is used for educational institutions. Private companies and businesses use .com, so Choices *A*, *B*, and *D* are incorrect.

23. A: Inferring is reading between the lines. Choice *B* describes the skimming technique. Choice *C* describes a questioning technique readers should employ, and Choice *D* is a simple statement regarding summary. It's an incomplete answer and not applicable to inference.

24. B: The key word here is "inform," which is the primary purpose of all informative modes. They contain facts, definitions, instructions, and other elements with the objective purpose of informing a reader—such as study guides, instruction manuals, and textbooks. Choice *A* is incorrect because an argumentative mode contains language that is subjective and is intended to persuade or to inform with a persuasive bias. Choice *C* is incorrect as a narrative mode is used primarily to tell a story and has no intention of informing, nor is the language inherently objective. Choice *D* is incorrect as descriptive modes possess no inherent intent to inform, and are used primarily to describe.

25. C: Pathos is the rhetorical appeal that draws on an audience's emotions and sympathies. Choice *A* is incorrect as logos appeals to the audience's logic, reason, and rational thinking, using facts and definitions. Choice *B* is incorrect because ethos appeals to the audience's sense of ethics and moral obligations. Choice *D* is incorrect because *C* contains the correct answer; thus, the answer cannot be "None of the above."

26. B: For this question, place the underlined sentence in each prospective choice's position. Leaving the sentence in place is incorrect because the father "going crazy" doesn't logically follow the fact that he

359

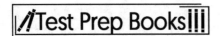

was a "city slicker." Choice *C* is incorrect because the sentence in question is not a concluding sentence and does not transition smoothly into the second paragraph. Choice *D* is incorrect because the sentence doesn't necessarily need to be omitted since it logically follows the very first sentence in the passage.

27. D: Choice *D* is correct because "As it turns out" indicates a contrast from the previous sentiment, that the RV was a great purchase. Choice *A* is incorrect because the sentence needs an effective transition from the paragraph before. Choice *B* is incorrect because the text indicates it *is* surprising that the RV was a great purchase because the author was skeptical beforehand. Choice *C* is incorrect because the transition "furthermore" does not indicate a contrast.

28. B: This sentence calls for parallel structure. Choice *B* is correct because the verbs "wake," "eat," and "break" are consistent in tense and parts of speech. Choice *A* is incorrect because the words "wake" and "eat" are present tense while the word "broke" is in past tense. Choice *C* is incorrect because this turns the sentence into a question, which doesn't make sense within the context. Choice *D* is incorrect because it breaks tense with the rest of the passage. "Waking," "eating," and "breaking" are all present participles, and the context around the sentence is in past tense.

29. C: Choice *C* is correct because it provides clarity and fits within the context of the passage. Choice *A* is incorrect because "We rejoiced as 'hackers'" does not explain what was meant by "hackers" or why it was a cause for rejoicing. Choice *B* is incorrect because it does not mention a solution being found and is therefore not specific enough. Choice *D* is incorrect because the meaning is eschewed by the helping verb "had to rejoice," and the sentence suggests that rejoicing was necessary to "hack" a solution.

30. A: The original sentence is correct because the verb tense, as well as the meaning, aligns with the rest of the passage. Choice *B* is incorrect because the order of the words makes the sentence more confusing than it otherwise would be. Choice *C* is incorrect because "We are even making" is in present tense. Choice *D* is incorrect because "We will make" is future tense. The surrounding text of the sentence is in past tense.

31. B: Choice *B* is correct because there is no punctuation needed if a dependent clause ("while traveling across America") is located behind the independent clause ("it allowed us to share adventures"). Choice *A* is incorrect because there are two dependent clauses connected and no independent clause, and a complete sentence requires at least one independent clause. Choice *C* is incorrect because of the same reason as Choice *A*. Semicolons have the same function as periods: there must be an independent clause on either side of the semicolon. Choice *D* is incorrect because the dash simply interrupts the complete sentence.

32. C: The rule for "me" and "I" is that one should use "I" when it is the subject pronoun of a sentence, and "me" when it is the object pronoun of the sentence. Break the sentence up to see if "I" or "me" should be used. To say "Those are memories that I have now shared" is correct, rather than "Those are memories that me have now shared." Choice *D* is incorrect because "my siblings" should come before "I."

33. C: Because the details in Choice *A* and Choice *B* are examples of how an emotionally intelligent leader operates, they are not the best choice for the definition of the term *emotional intelligence*. They are qualities observed in an EI leader. Choice *C* is true as noted in the second sentence of the passage: Emotional Intelligence (EI) includes developing the ability to know one's own emotions, to regulate impulses and emotions, and to use interpersonal communication skills with ease while dealing with

other people. It makes sense that someone with well-developed emotional intelligence will have a good handle on understanding their emotions, be able to regulate impulses and emotions, and use interpersonal communication skills. Choice *D* is not a definition of EI.

34. C: Choice *A* can be eliminated because it does not reflect an accurate fact. Choices *B* and *D* do not support claims about how to be a successful leader.

35. B: The qualities of an unsuccessful leader possessing a transactional leadership style are listed in the passage. Choice *A* is incorrect because it lists the qualities of a successful leader. Choices *C* and *D* are definitely not characteristics of a successful leader; however, they are not presented in the passage and readers should do their best to ignore such options.

36. D: Even though some choices may be true of successful leaders, the best answer must be supported by sub-points in the passage. Therefore, Choices *A* and *C* are incorrect. Choice *B* is incorrect because uncompromising transactional leadership styles squelch success.

37. B: Choice *B* is correct. Here, a colon is used to introduce an explanation. Colons either introduce explanations or lists. Additionally, the quote ends with the punctuation inside the quotes, unlike Choice *C*.

38. D: The word *civilised* should be spelled *civilized*. The words "makes," "human," and "distinguishes," are all spelled correctly.

39. A: Choice *A* is correct because the phrase "others' ideas" is both plural and indicates possession. Choice *B* is incorrect because "other's" indicates only one "other" that's in possession of "ideas," which is incorrect. Choice *C* is incorrect because no possession is indicated. Choice *D* is incorrect because the word "other" does not end in *s*. *Others's* is not a correct form of the plural possessive word.

40. D: This sentence must have a comma before "although" because the word "although" is connecting two independent clauses. Thus, Choices *B* and *C* are incorrect. Choice *A* is incorrect because the second sentence in the underlined section is a fragment.

41. C: Choice *C* is the correct choice because the word "their" indicates possession, and the text is talking about "their students," or the students of someone. Choice *A*, "there," means at a certain place and is incorrect. Choice *B*, "they're," is a contraction and means "they are." Choice *D* is incorrect because it contains a singular pronoun, and our noun, "teachers," is plural.

42. B: Choice *B* uses all punctuation correctly in this sentence. In American English, single quotes should only be used if they are quotes within a quote, making Choices *A* and *C* incorrect. Additionally, punctuation should go inside the quotation marks with a few exceptions, making Choice *D* incorrect.

43. A: Choice *A* has consistent parallel structure with the verbs "read," "identify," and "determine." Choices *B* and *C* have faulty parallel structure with the words "determining" and "identifying." Choice *D* has incorrect subject/verb agreement. The sentence should read, "Students have to read . . . identify . . . and determine."

44. D: Choice *D* uses the correct punctuation. American English uses double quotes unless placing quotes within a quote (which would then require single quotes). Thus, Choices *A* and *C* are incorrect. Choice *B* is incorrect because the period should go outside of the parenthesis, not inside.

361

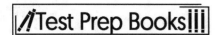

45. B: Readers should carefully focus their attention on the beginning of the passage to answer this series of questions. Even though the sentences may be worded a bit differently, all but one statement is true. It presents a false idea that descriptive details are not necessary until the climax of the story. Even if one does not read the passage, he or she probably knows that all good writing begins with descriptive details to develop the main theme the writer intends for the narrative.

46. B: To suggest that a ten-minute play is accessible does not imply any timeline, nor does the passage mention how long a playwright spends with revisions and rewrites. So, Choice *A* is incorrect. Choice *B* is correct because of the opening statement that reads, "Learning how to write a ten-minute play may seem like a monumental task at first; but, if you follow a simple creative writing strategy, similar to writing a narrative story, you will be able to write a successful drama." None of the remaining choices are supported by points in the passage.

47. D: Note that the only element not mentioned in the passage is the style feature that is part of a narrative writer's tool kit. It is not to say that ten-minute plays do not have style. The correct answer denotes only that the element of style was not illustrated in this particular passage.

48. C: This choice allows room for the fact that not all people who attempt to write a play will find it easy. If the writer follows the basic principles of narrative writing described in the passage, however, writing a play does not have to be an excruciating experience. None of the other options can be supported by points from the passage.

49. A: The clause *that is autographed* is essential to the sentence so the word *that* is appropriate. *Whom* is the object of the verb *belongs to,* so you would not use *who.* Choice *B* is incorrect because the clause *which is autographed* is not enclosed in commas, and you would not use *who* as the object in the sentence. Choice *C* is incorrect because you would not use *whom* as the subject of the sentence and the clause *which is autographed* is not enclosed in commas. Choice *D* is incorrect because you would not use *whom* as the subject of the sentence.

50. A: The correct spelling of this word is *caffeine.* This answer, along with Choices *B* and *C* are exceptions to the rule *i before e, except after c.* Choice *D* follows this rule because the letters *ie* follow the letter *c,* so the correct order would be *ei.*

51. B: Use the word *may* instead of *can* at the beginning of the sentence because it is asking for permission and *can* means "able to." Choice *A* is a proper sentence using the word *bring* (coming toward) and the word *take* (going away) correctly. Choice *C* is a proper sentence using the word *lend* as a verb and the word *loan* as a noun. Choice *D* is a proper sentence using the words *two* (the number), *to* (the infinitive) and *too* (meaning "very") in the correct placements.

52. A: *Badly* is an adverb describing how hurt and *good* is used with the sensory word *feels.* Choice *B* is incorrect because *bad* is an adjective not an adverb. Choice *C* is incorrect because *bad* is an adjective where an adverb is needed and *well* is an adverb where an adjective is needed. Choice *D* is incorrect because *badly* fits but *good* should be used instead of *well* because of the sensory word *feels.*

53. C: *Because the lion and tiger habitat was closed* is a dependent clause and needs a subject. Choice *A* is incorrect because the sentence is an independent clause with both a subject and a verb, therefore it creates a complete sentence. Choice *B* is incorrect because the sentence is also a complete independent clause. Choice *D* is incorrect because the sentence is a complete independent clause forming an interrogative sentence.

54. A: *I love to go water-skiing, I love alpine skiing,* and *I also love Nordic skiing* are all independent clauses and are not connected with coordinating conjunctions or separated with semi colons, colons, or dashes. This makes it a run-on sentence. Choice *B* is not a run-on sentence; it is a simple single independent clause. Choice *C* is incorrect; it is a complete independent clause with both a subject (*types of skiing*) and a verb (*require*). Choice *D* is incorrect. It contains two independent clauses but a semicolon correctly separates them, therefore it is a complete compound sentence.

55. D: The correct answer Choice is *D, under the tongue.* The root word of *sublingual* is *lingual,* which means *tongue.* The prefix is *sub,* which means *under.* Therefore, if we pay attention the prefix and how it relates to the root word, we get *under the tongue.* Choice *A, in the ear,* would be the word *tympanic.* Choice *B,* in the rectum, would be the word *rectal.* Choice *C,* under the armpit, would be the word *axillary.*

56. B: In the word *dysfunction,* we have the root word *function* and the prefix *dys. Function* means to work or operate in a particular way. The prefix *dys* denotes *bad* or *difficult.* Therefore, the word *dysfunction* would mean functioning with difficulty; the word closest to this is *abnormality,* which means the quality or state of being abnormal or defected, which is Choice *B.* Choice *A, exacerbate,* means something that becomes more intense in nature. Choice *C, dilate,* means to enlarge or extend. Choice *D, lethargic,* means sluggish or apathetic.

57. C: To refrain from something. For example, someone who chooses to *abstain* from alcohol does not drink alcohol.

58. A: Outlook. The *prognosis* is the expected likely course of an illness or injury.

59. B: Dilate. To *dilute* is to make a solution less concentrated, *occlude* means to block or obstruct, and *distill* means to purify a liquid or to extract the most important aspects or meaning of something.

60. C: The correct answer choice is "Lets celebrate tomorrow." "Lets" is supposed to be short for "let us," and therefore needs an apostrophe between the "t" and the "s": "Let's."

61. A: This error is marked by a subject/verb agreement. "Words" is plural, so the verb must be plural as well. The correct usage would be: "Their words were followed by a signing document."

62. B: There is a punctuation error. The comma creates a comma splice where a period or a semicolon should be since we have two independent clauses on either side of the comma.

63. C: Choice *C* is the problematic answer; the whole phrase "Hoover Dam" should be capitalized, not just "Hoover."

64. A: Choice *A* has the error in usage because we have a dangling modifier with the phrase "blue kid's shovel." The sentence indicates the kid is blue. We want the sentence to say that the shovel is blue. Therefore, it should be: "After her swim, Jeanine saw a kid's blue shovel."

65. C: Gulliver becomes acquainted with the people and practices of his new surroundings. Choice *C* is the correct answer because it most extensively summarizes the entire passage. While Choices *A* and *B* are reasonable possibilities, they reference portions of Gulliver's experiences, not the whole. Choice *D* is incorrect because Gulliver doesn't express repentance or sorrow in this particular passage.

363

66. A: Principal refers to *chief* or *primary* within the context of this text. Choice *A* is the answer that most closely aligns with this definition. Choices *B* and *D* make reference to a helper or followers while Choice *C* doesn't meet the description of Reldresal from the passage.

67. C: One can reasonably infer that Gulliver is considerably larger than the children who were playing around him because multiple children could fit into his hand. Choice *B* is incorrect because there is no indication of stress in Gulliver's tone. Choices *A* and *D* aren't the best answer because though Gulliver seems fond of his new acquaintances, he didn't travel there with the intentions of meeting new people or to express a definite love for them in this particular portion of the text.

68. C: The emperor made a *definitive decision* to expose Gulliver to their native customs. In this instance, the word *mind* was not related to a vote, question, or cognitive ability.

69. A: Choice *A* is correct. This assertion does *not* support the fact that games are a commonplace event in this culture because it mentions conduct, not games. Choices *B, C,* and *D* are incorrect because these do support the fact that games were a commonplace event.

70. C: While all of these words are spelled similarly and sound the same, the correct answer is Choice *C*, *wear*, which means to cover or equip. We *wear* clothes. Choice *A, ware,* refers to an item that is created or manufactured. Choice *B* is incorrect because *where* asks for a specific location. Choice *D, were,* is the second person plural version of *to be*, so it is completely irrelevant to the sentence.

71. B: The clause *who loves to ride bikes* is a restrictive adjective clause modifying the noun *boy*. Choice *A* is incorrect because *a boy who loves* is a phrase not a clause. Choice *C* is incorrect because *to ride bikes* is an infinitive phrase and does not have a subject. Choice *D* is incorrect because *gets plenty of exercise* is not a clause; it has no subject.

72. D: The adverbial clause *unless you are too tired* modifies the verb *want*. Choice *A* is incorrect because *I want to work in the garden* is an independent clause. Choice *B* is incorrect because *in the garden* has no subject and is a prepositional phrase. Choice *C* is incorrect because *are too tired* is not a clause because it has no subject.

73. C: A noun phrase is a noun and all of its modifiers; in this case, *long* and *black* are adjectives modifying the noun *limousine* and *the* is an article modifying *limousine*. Choice *A* is incorrect because it identifies the compound subject of the sentence. Choice *B* is incorrect because it includes the verb *rode*. Choice *D* is incorrect because it includes a subject and a verb, and phrases do not have both.

74. C: There is no gerund phrase in the sentence. Choice *A* is incorrect because *swimming several laps* is a gerund phrase serving as the noun subject of the sentence. Choice *B* is incorrect because *using the flippers* is a gerund phrase serving as the noun object of the sentence. Choice *D* is incorrect because *learning to swim* is a gerund phrase serving as the noun subject of the sentence.

75. D: To enlighten the audience on the habits of sun-fish and their hatcheries. Choice *A* is incorrect because although the Adirondack region is mentioned in the text, there is no cause or effect relationships between the region and fish hatcheries depicted here. Choice *B* is incorrect because the text does not have an agenda, but rather is meant to inform the audience. Finally, Choice *C* is incorrect because the text says nothing of how sun-fish mate.

76. B: The sun-fish builds it with her tail and snout. The text explains this in the second paragraph: "she builds, with her tail and snout, a circular embankment 3 inches in height and 2 thick." Choice *A* is used in the text as a simile.

77. D: To conclude a sequence and add a final detail. The concluding sequence is expressed in the phrase "[t]he mother sun-fish, having now built or provided her 'hatchery.'" The final detail is the way in which the sun-fish guards the "inclosure." Choices *A, B,* and *C* are incorrect.

78. C: The words *didn't* and *nothing* are both negatives. The sentence actually means a positive: *"They did like something I said."* Choice *A* is incorrect because it is a proper sentence with a single negative, *couldn't*. Choice *B* is incorrect because it is a proper sentence without any negatives. Choice *D* is incorrect because it is actually a triple negative; the words *cannot, don't,* and *disapprove* are all negatives. The sentence actually means: *"I disapprove of that."*

79. A: Answer Choice *A* uses the best, most concise word choice. Choice *B* uses the pronoun *that* to refer to people instead of *who*. *Choice C* incorrectly uses the preposition *with*. Choice *D* uses the preposition *for* and the additional word *any*, making the sentence wordy and less clear.

80. B: Choice *B* uses the best choice of words to create a subordinate and independent clause. In Choice *A, because* makes it seem like this is the reason they enjoy working from home, which is incorrect. In Choice *C,* the word *maybe* creates two independent clauses, which are not joined properly with a comma. Choice *D* uses *with,* which does not make grammatical sense.

Mathematics

1. C: 0.63

Divide 5 by 8, which results in 0.625. This rounds up to 0.63.

2. C: $\frac{19}{24}$

Set up the problem and find a common denominator for both fractions.

$$\frac{23}{24} - \frac{1}{6}$$

Multiply each fraction across by a fraction equivalent to 1 to convert to a common denominator.

$$\frac{23}{24} \times \frac{1}{1} - \frac{1}{6} \times \frac{4}{4}$$

Once over the same denominator, subtract across the top.

$$\frac{23 - 4}{24} = \frac{19}{24}$$

3. D: $\frac{2}{9}$

Set up the problem and find a common denominator for both fractions.

$$\frac{43}{45} - \frac{11}{15}$$

Multiply each fraction across by a fraction equivalent to 1 to convert to a common denominator.

$$\frac{43}{45} \times \frac{1}{1} - \frac{11}{15} \times \frac{3}{3}$$

Once over the same denominator, subtract across the top.

$$\frac{43 - 33}{45} = \frac{10}{45}$$

Reduce.

$$\frac{10 \div 5}{45 \div 5} = \frac{2}{9}$$

4. B: $\frac{14}{25}$

Since 0.56 goes to the hundredths place, it can be placed over 100:

$$\frac{56}{100}$$

Essentially, the way we got there is by multiplying the numerator and denominator by 100:

$$\frac{0.56}{1} \times \frac{100}{100} = \frac{56}{100}$$

Then, the fraction can be simplified down to $\frac{14}{25}$:

$$\frac{56}{100} \div \frac{4}{4} = \frac{14}{25}$$

5. A: 2,504,774

Line up the numbers (the number with the most digits on top) to multiply. Begin with the right column on top and the right column on bottom.

Move one column left on top and multiply by the far-right column on the bottom. Remember to add the carry over after you multiply. Continue that pattern for each of the numbers on the top row.

Starting on the far-right column on top repeat this pattern for the next number left on the bottom. Write the answers below the first line of answers; remember to begin with a zero placeholder. Continue for each number in the top row.

Starting on the far-right column on top, repeat this pattern for the next number left on the bottom. Write the answers below the first line of answers. Remember to begin with zero placeholders.

Once completed, ensure the answer rows are lined up correctly, then add.

6. A: In order to determine the savings needed per day, divide up $150 into four equal parts:

$$\frac{\$150}{4\,d} = \frac{\$37.5}{d}$$

So, she needs to save an average of $37.50 per day.

7. A: $\frac{810}{2,921}$

Line up the fractions.

$$\frac{15}{23} \times \frac{54}{127}$$

Multiply across the top and across the bottom.

$$\frac{15 \times 54}{23 \times 127} = \frac{810}{2,921}$$

8. D: The number of days can be found by taking the total amount Bernard needs to make and dividing it by the amount he earns per day:

$$\frac{300}{80} = \frac{30}{8} = \frac{15}{4} = 3.75$$

But Bernard is only working full days, so he will need to work 4 days, since 3 days is not a sufficient amount of time.

9. D: The value went up by $165,000 - \$150,000 = \$15,000$. Out of $150,000, this is:

$$\frac{15,000}{150,000} = \frac{1}{10}$$

Convert this to having a denominator of 100, the result is $\frac{10}{100}$, or 10%.

10. B: Instead of multiplying these out, the product can be estimated by using $18 \times 10 = 180$. The error here should be lower than 15, since it is rounded to the nearest integer, and the numbers add to something less than 30.

11. A: Taylor's total income is $\$20,000 + \$10,000 = \$30,000$. Fifteen percent as a fraction is $\frac{15}{100} = \frac{3}{20}$. So, 15% of $30,000 is:

$$\frac{3}{20} \times \$30,000 = \frac{\$90,000}{20}$$

$$\frac{\$9,000}{2} = \$4,500$$

12. C: Since the answer will be in cubic feet rather than inches, the first step is to convert from inches to feet for the dimensions of the box. There are 12 inches per foot, so the box is $\frac{24}{12} = 2$ feet wide, $\frac{18}{12} = 1.5$ feet deep, and $\frac{12}{12} = 1$ foot high. The volume is the product of these three together:

$$2 \times 1.5 \times 1 = 3 \text{ cubic feet}$$

13. B: According to the order of operations, multiplication and division must be completed first from left to right. Then, addition and subtraction are completed from left to right. Therefore:

$$9 \times 9 \div 9 + 9 - 9 \div 9$$

$$81 \div 9 + 9 - 9 \div 9$$

$$9 + 9 - 9 \div 9$$

$$9 + 9 - 1$$

$$18 - 1$$

$$17$$

14. C: $x = 150$

Set up the initial equation.

$$\frac{2x}{5} - 1 = 59$$

Add 1 to both sides.

$$\frac{2x}{5} - 1 + 1 = 59 + 1$$

Multiply both sides by $\frac{5}{2}$.

$$\frac{2x}{5} \times \frac{5}{2} = 60 \times \frac{5}{2} = 150$$

$$x = 150$$

15. C: $51.93

List the givens.

$$\text{Tax} = 6.0\% = 0.06$$

$$\text{Sale} = 50\% = 0.5$$

$$\text{Hat} = \$32.99$$

$$\text{Jersey} = \$64.99$$

Calculate the sales prices.

$$\text{Hat Sale} = 0.5\ (32.99) = 16.495$$

$$\text{Jersey Sale} = 0.5\ (64.99) = 32.495$$

Total the sales prices.

$$\text{Hat sale} + \text{jersey sale} = 16.495 + 32.495 = 48.99$$

Calculate the tax and add it to the total sales prices.

$$\text{Total after tax} = 48.99 + (48.99 \times 0.06) = \$51.93$$

16. D: $0.45

List the givens.

$$\text{Store coffee} = \$1.23/\text{lb}$$

$$\text{Local roaster coffee} = \$1.98/1.5\ \text{lb}$$

Calculate the cost for 5 pounds of store brand.

$$\frac{\$1.23}{1\ \text{lb}} \times 5\ \text{lb} = \$6.15$$

Calculate the cost for 5 pounds of the local roaster.

$$\frac{\$1.98}{1.5\ \text{lb}} \times 5\ \text{lb} = \$6.60$$

Subtract to find the difference in price for 5 pounds.

$$\begin{array}{r} \$6.60 \\ -\$6.15 \\ \hline \$0.45 \end{array}$$

17. D: $3,325

List the givens.

$$1{,}800\ \text{ft} = \$2{,}000$$

$$Cost\ after\ 1{,}800\ ft = \$1.00/\text{ft.}$$

Find how many feet left after the first 1,800 feet.

$$\begin{array}{r} 3{,}125\ \text{ft} \\ -1{,}800\ \text{ft} \\ \hline 1{,}325\ \text{ft} \end{array}$$

369

Calculate the cost for the feet over 1,800 feet.

$$1{,}325 \text{ ft} \times \frac{\$1.00}{1 \text{ ft}} = \$1{,}325$$

Add these together to find the total for the entire cost.

$$\$2{,}000 + \$1{,}325 = \$3{,}325$$

18. A: 12

Calculate how many gallons the bucket holds.

$$11.4 \text{ L} \times \frac{1 \text{ gal}}{3.8 \text{ L}} = 3 \text{ gal}$$

Next, calculate how many buckets are needed to fill the 35-gallon pool.

$$\frac{35}{3} = 11.67$$

Since the amount is more than 11 but less than 12, we must fill the bucket 12 times.

19. A: 13 nurses

Using the given information of 1 nurse to 25 patients and 325 patients, set up an equation to solve for number of nurses (N):

$$\frac{N}{325} = \frac{1}{25}$$

Multiply both sides by 325 to get N by itself on one side.

$$\frac{N}{1} = \frac{325}{25} = 13 \text{ nurses}$$

20. D: 290 beds

Using the given information of 2 beds to 1 room and 145 rooms, set up an equation to solve for number of beds (B):

$$\frac{B}{145} = \frac{2}{1}$$

Multiply both sides by 145 to get B by itself on one side.

$$\frac{B}{1} = \frac{290}{1} = 290 \text{ beds}$$

21. B: 35.1%

370

To convert from a decimal to a percentage, the decimal needs to be moved two places to right. In this case, that makes 0.351 become 35.1%.

22. A: 22%

Converting from a fraction to a percentage generally involves two steps. First, the fraction needs to be converted to a decimal.

Divide 2 by 9 which results in $0.\overline{22}$. The top line indicates that the decimal actually goes on forever with an endless amount of 2's.

Second, the decimal needs to be moved two places to the right:

$$22\%$$

23. B: First, subtract 4 from each side. This yields $6t = 12$. Now, divide both sides by 6 to obtain $t = 2$.

24. B: To be directly proportional means that $y = kx$. If x is changed from 5 to 20, the value of x is multiplied by 4. Applying the same rule to the y-value, also multiply the value of y by 4. Therefore:

$$y = 12$$

25. A: Each bag contributes $4x + 1$ treats. The total treats will be in the form $4nx + n$ where n is the total number of bags. The total is in the form $60x + 15$, from which it is known $n = 15$.

26. C: The range of the entire stem-and-leaf plot is found by subtracting the lowest value from the highest value, as follows: $59 - 20 = 39$ cm. All other choices are miscalculations read from the chart.

27. D: Denote the width as w and the length as l. Then:

$$l = 3w + 5$$

The perimeter is:

$$2w + 2l = 90$$

Substituting the first expression for l into the second equation yields:

$$2(3w + 5) + 2w = 90$$

$$6w + 10 + 2w = 90$$

$$8w = 80$$

$$w = 10$$

Putting this into the first equation, it yields:

$$l = 3(10) + 5 = 35$$

28. B: If 60% of 50 workers are women, then there are 30 women working in the office. If half of them are wearing skirts, then that means 15 women wear skirts. Since none of the men wear skirts, this means there are 15 people wearing skirts.

371

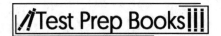

29. A: Let the unknown score be x. The average will be:

$$\frac{5 \times 50 + 4 \times 70 + x}{10} = \frac{530 + x}{10} = 55$$

Multiply both sides by 10 to get $530 + x = 550$, or $x = 20$.

30. A: For manufacturing costs, there is a linear relationship between the cost to the company and the number produced, with a y-intercept given by the base cost of acquiring the means of production and a slope given by the cost to produce one unit. In this case, that base cost is $50,000, while the cost per unit is $40. So:

$$y = 40x + 50,000$$

31. C: A die has an equal chance for each outcome. Since it has six sides, each outcome has a probability of $\frac{1}{6}$. The chance of a 1 or a 2 is therefore:

$$\frac{1}{6} + \frac{1}{6} = \frac{1}{3}$$

32. C: $40N$ would be 4,000% of N. $\frac{40}{100}$.

33. C: The best way to solve this problem is by using a system of equations. We know that Jan bought $90 worth of apples ($a$) and oranges ($o$) at $1 and $2 respectively. That means our first equation is:

$$1(a) + 2(o) = 90$$

We also know that she bought an equal number of apples and oranges, which gives us our second equation $a = o$. We can then replace a with o in the first equation to give:

$$1(o) + 2(o) = 90 \text{ or } 3(o) = 90$$

Which yields:

$$o = 30$$

Thus, Jan bought 30 oranges (and 30 apples).

34. C: The formula for the volume of a box with rectangular sides is the length times the width times the height, so:

$$5 \times 6 \times 3 = 90 \text{ cubic feet}$$

35. D: First, the train's journey in the real world is:

$$3\,\text{h} \times 50\,\frac{\text{mi}}{\text{h}} = 150\,\text{mi}$$

On the map, 1 inch corresponds to 10 miles, so that is equivalent to:

$$150 \text{ mi} \times \frac{1 \text{ in}}{10 \text{ mi}} = 15 \text{ in}$$

Therefore, the start and end points are 15 inches apart on the map.

36. B: The total trip time is $1 + 3.5 + 0.5 = 5$ hours. The total time driving is $1 + 0.5 = 1.5$ hours. So, the fraction of time spent driving is $\frac{1.5}{5}$ or $\frac{3}{10}$. To get the percentage, convert this to a fraction out of 100. The numerator and denominator are multiplied by 10, with a result of $\frac{30}{100}$. The percentage is the numerator in a fraction out of 100, so 30%.

37. B: The formula for the volume of a cylinder is $\pi r^2 h$, where r is the radius and h is the height. The diameter is twice the radius, so these barrels have a radius of 1 foot. That means each barrel has a volume of:

$$\pi \times 1^2 \times 3 = 3\pi \text{ ft}^3$$

Since there are three of them, the total is:

$$3 \times 3\pi = 9\pi \text{ ft}^3$$

38. C: To solve for the value of b, isolate the variable b on one side of the equation.

Start by moving the lower value of -4 to the other side by adding 4 to both sides:

$$5b - 4 = 2b + 17$$

$$5b - 4 + 4 = 2b + 17 + 4$$

$$5b = 2b + 21$$

Then subtract $2b$ from both sides:

$$5b - 2b = 2b + 21 - 2b$$

$$3b = 21$$

Then divide both sides by 3 to get the value of b:

$$\frac{3b}{3} = \frac{21}{3}$$

$$b = 7$$

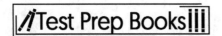

39. D: Denote the width as w and the length as l. Then, $l = 3w + 5$. The perimeter is $2w + 2l = 90$. Substituting the first expression for l into the second equation yields:

$$2(3w + 5) + 2w = 90$$

$$6w + 10 + 2w = 90$$

$$8w = 80$$

$$w = 10$$

Putting this into the first equation, it yields:

$$l = 3(10) + 5 = 35$$

40. A: The first step is to determine the unknown, which is in terms of the length, l.

The second step is to translate the problem into the equation using the perimeter of a rectangle, $P = 2l + 2w$. The width is the length minus 2 centimeters. The resulting equation is $2l + 2(l - 2) = 44$. The equation can be solved as follows:

$2l + 2l - 4 = 44$	Apply the distributive property on the left side of the equation
$4l - 4 = 44$	Combine like terms on the left side of the equation
$4l = 48$	Add 4 to both sides of the equation
$l = 12$	Divide both sides of the equation by 4

The length of the rectangle is 12 centimeters. The width is the length minus 2 centimeters, which is 10 centimeters. Checking the answers for length and width forms the following equation:

$$44 = 2(12) + 2(10)$$

The equation can be solved using the order of operations to form a true statement: $44 = 44$.

41. C: 30. A complete circle measures $360°$. This circle is broken up into 4 different parts with different measures for each part. Adding these parts should give a total of 360 degrees. The equation generated from this diagram is:

$$4x + 5x + x + 2x = 360$$

Collecting like terms gives the equation $12x = 360$, which can be solved by dividing by 12 to give $x = 30$. The value of x in the diagram is 30.

42. C: First, find the area of the second house. The area is:

$$A = l \times w = 33 \times 50 = 1,650 \text{ square feet}$$

Then, use the area formula to determine what length gives the first house an area of 1,650 square feet. So,

$$1{,}650 = 22 \times l$$

$$l = \frac{1{,}650}{22} = 75 \text{ feet}$$

Then, use the formula for perimeter to get:

$$75 + 75 + 22 + 22 = 194 \text{ feet}$$

43. D: $\frac{1}{12}$. The probability of picking the winner of the race is:

$$\frac{1}{4}\left(\frac{number\ of\ favorable\ outcomes}{number\ of\ total\ outcomes}\right)$$

Assuming the winner was picked on the first selection, three horses remain from which to choose the runner-up (these are dependent events). Therefore, the probability of picking the runner-up is $\frac{1}{3}$. To determine the probability of multiple events, the probability of each event is multiplied:

$$\frac{1}{4} \times \frac{1}{3} = \frac{1}{12}$$

44. B: 180 miles. The rate, 60 miles per hour, and time, 3 hours, are given for the scenario. To determine the distance traveled, the given values for the rate (r) and time (t) are substituted into the distance formula and evaluated:

$$d = r \times t$$

$$d = (60 \text{ mi/h}) \times (3 \text{ h}) \rightarrow d = 180 \text{ mi}$$

45. C: The situation can be described by the equation ? × 2. Filling in for the missing numbers would result in 3 × 2 = 6 and 7 × 2 = 14. Therefore, the missing numbers are 6 and 14. The other choices are miscalculations or misidentification of the pattern formed by the table.

46. C: To find the mean, or average, of a set of values, add the values together and then divide by the total number of values. Each day of the week has an adult ticket amount sold that must be added together. The equation is as follows:

$$\frac{22 + 16 + 24 + 19 + 29}{5} = 22$$

47. B: $350,000: Since the total income is $500,000, then a percentage of that can be found by multiplying the percent of Audit Services as a decimal, or 0.40, by the total of 500,000. This answer is found from the equation:

$$500000 \times 0.4 = 200000$$

The total income from Audit Services is $200,000.

For the income received from Taxation Services, the following equation can be used:

$$500000 \times 0.3 = 150000$$

The total income from Audit Services and Taxation Services is:

$$150,000 + 200,000 = 350,000$$

Another way of approaching the problem is to calculate the easy percentage of 10% then multiply it by 7 because the total percentage for Audit and Taxation Services was 70%. 10% of 500,000 is 50,000. Then multiplying this number by 7 yields the same income of $350,000.

48. B: The number line shows:

$$x > -\frac{3}{4}$$

Each inequality must be solved for x to determine if it matches the number line. Choice A of $4x + 5 < 8$ results in $x < -\frac{3}{4}$, which is incorrect. Choice C of $-4x + 5 > 8$ yields $x < -\frac{3}{4}$, which is also incorrect. Choice D of $4x - 5 > 8$ results in $x > \frac{13}{4}$, which is not correct. Choice B, $-4x + 5 < 8$ is the only choice that results in the correct answer of:

$$x > -\frac{3}{4}$$

49. A: This has the form $t^2 - y^2$, with $t = x^2$ and $y = 4$. It's also known that $t^2 - y^2 = (t + y)(t - y)$, and substituting the values for t and y into the right-hand side gives:

$$(x^2 - 4)(x^2 + 4)$$

50. A: A parallelogram has two sets of parallel sides. Choice A is a trapezoid and only has one set of parallel sides. The rest of the answer choices have two sets.

Social Studies

1. C: A participatory democracy in its truest form is a system in which everyone participates in the political system. Choice A describes an elite democracy, which was advocated by some of the Founders like James Madison. Choice B is a pluralist democracy—one where interest groups and advocacy for certain issues dominate the government. Choice D describes an aristocracy or an oligarchy rather than a participatory democracy.

2. D: Choice D is correct. By artificially increasing supply and lowering costs of production in various sectors of the economy, subsidies can lower prices, reassure the supply, and create opportunity to compete with foreign vendors. Choice A is incorrect because income redistribution moves wealth from some people in a society to others; it does not have the effects asked for in the question. Choice B is incorrect because, while price controls can lower prices, they do have the other effects asked for in the question. Choice C is incorrect because taxes increase government revenue but do not have the effects asked for in the question.

3. C: Choice *C* is correct. Isoline maps are used to calculate data and differentiate between the characteristics of two places. In an isoline map, symbols represent values, and lines can be drawn between two points to determine differences. The other answer choices are maps with different purposes. Choice *A* is incorrect because topographic maps display contour lines, which represent the relative elevation of a particular place. Choices *B* and *C* are incorrect because dot-density maps and flow-line maps are types of thematic maps. Dot-density maps illustrate the volume and density of a characteristic of an area. Flow-line maps use lines to illustrate the movement of goods, people, or even animals between two places.

4. D: Choice *D* is correct. Mexico ceded Nevada as part of the peace agreement ending the Mexican-American War. Choices *A*, *B*, and *C* are incorrect because they are territories gained via purchase when the question asks about military force. Missouri and Nebraska became American territories through the Louisiana Purchase, and the United States purchased Alaska from Russia.

5. D: The Prussian political leader Otto von Bismarck leveraged nationalism to rally support for German unification, which occurred in 1871. So, Choice *A* is incorrect. Mexican nationalists defeated Spanish colonizers in the Mexican Revolution, and Simon Bolivar led nationalist revolts across South America during the early nineteenth century. So, Choice *B* is incorrect. The Russo-Turkish War was largely caused by nationalist revolts in Bulgaria, Montenegro, and Romania against the Ottoman Empire, so Choice *C* is incorrect. The War of the Spanish Succession was fought in the early eighteenth century, which predates the rise of nationalism in continental Europe. Thus, Choice *D* is the correct answer.

6. A: World War I had a number of interrelated causes. European powers were in an intense struggle over the colonization of Africa and Asia, so Choice *B* is incorrect. Imperialism was supported through intense militarization, particularly in terms of naval spending. Therefore, Choice *C* is incorrect. Governments stoked nationalist sentiments to justify their imperial conquests and aggressive militarization. Furthermore, Bosnian nationalist Gavrilo Princip assassinated the Archduke Franz Ferdinand of Austria, and it was the inciting incident that led the complex alliance systems into World War I. So, Choice *D* is incorrect. Although communism had begun to attract significant support during the latter half of the nineteenth century, it was not a primary cause of World War I. Communists didn't control the government of a major global power until the Russian Revolution overthrew the Czar in 1917. Thus, Choice *A* is the correct answer.

7. A: Ethnocentrism is a perspective on cultural differences, and it's not traditionally a characteristic of cultural landscapes. Thus, Choice *A* is the correct answer. Cultural landscape is an extremely broad concept to describe the relationship between physical environments and human development. Cultural landscapes include forms of economic production, including industrial practices. Therefore, Choice *B* is incorrect. Cultural landscapes also incorporate innumerable cultural aspects, such as land use practices. Therefore, Choice *C* is incorrect. Physical features of the land are a critical aspect of cultural landscapes because they shape the natural environment. Therefore, Choice *D* is incorrect.

8. C: Ethnic religions don't claim to hold universal truths that are applicable to all people, so they expand less aggressively than universalizing religions. As a result, ethnic religions tend to remain most popular in their hearth region of origin, and if they expand at all, it's through relocation diffusion. Hinduism is a classic ethnic religion because it has only spread from its hearth region of origin through relocation diffusion. Thus, Choice *C* is the correct answer. Buddhism, Choice *A*, Christianity, Choice *B*, and Islam, Choice *D*, are all universalizing religions. These four religions assert universal truths, and they have all

spread through both relocation diffusion and expansion diffusion. Therefore, Choice *A*, Choice *B*, and Choice *D* are incorrect.

9. C: Sovereignty is government's ability to project political power and authority over its territories, and territoriality refers to people's cultural, economic, and historical connections to land. Political entities have sought to increase territoriality in order to unify the state and maintain sovereign claims. Thus, Choice *C* is the correct answer. Sovereignty isn't exclusively held by central governments. In federal states, the central government shares sovereignty with subnational units of government. So, Choice *A* is incorrect. Sovereignty is also closely related to territorial control, and territoriality is more strongly associated with people's connections to land than political organizations. As such, Choice *B* is incorrect. Choice *D* is incorrect because all states need to exercise sovereignty in order to have a functional government.

10. D: Most nonrenewable resources are easier to harness and utilize than renewable sources. That may sound counterintuitive, but the reality is that it is harder to develop solar, wind, and geothermal infrastructure than it is to build a coal-fired power plant for the production of electricity. Consequently, developing nations tend to rely on these reliable sources in order to fuel their equally developing economy.

11. C: Conservatism emphasizes maintaining traditions and believes political and social stability is more important than progress and reform. In general, Socialism, Choice *A*, seeks to establish a democratically elected government that owns the means of production, regulates the exchange of commodities, and distributes the wealth equally among citizens. Liberalism, Choice *B*, is based on individualism and equality, supporting the freedoms of speech, press, and religion, while Libertarian ideals, Choice *D*, emphasize individual liberties and freedom from government interference.

12. D: Governments first deployed large-scale propaganda during World War I. Propaganda was a critical part of the governments' total war strategy, which called for the mobilization of every possible resource for the war effort. In order to fight this unprecedented global conflict, governments had to convince the public to sacrifice their food, goods, and lives to the war effort like never before. Thus, Choice *D* is the correct answer. Propaganda was used in the Russo-Turkish War (1877–1878) and First Sino-Japanese War (1894–1895), but it was not widespread and orchestrated by the government. During World War I, nearly every government created official propaganda departments for the first time in history. So, Choices *A* and *B* are incorrect. Choice *C* is the second best answer choice. The Spanish, German, and Soviet governments all published a significant amount of propaganda. However, World War I (1914–1918) occurred several decades before the Spanish Civil War (1936–1939). Therefore, Choice *C* is incorrect.

13. D: European explorers never found the Northwest Passage, but the search uncovered the Americas' economic potential. European colonization started almost immediately after Columbus reached the Caribbean, and it spread across both continents as explorers continued to search for the elusive route to Asia. Thus, Choice *D* is the correct answer. Although Ferdinand Magellan found a passage to Asia through the southern Atlantic, it was much slower than sailing around the Cape of Good Hope. So, Choice *A* is incorrect. The search for a Northwest Passage exponentially increased international trade, so Choice *B* is incorrect. European powers occasionally made strategic short-term alliances with individual Amerindian tribes, but alliances weren't a long-term consequence of European exploration in the Americas. As such, Choice *C* is incorrect.

14. A: Despite all of the issues of the Articles of Confederation, infighting among the governmental branches was not one of them. This was mainly because there weren't many branches of government, but also because the federal government didn't meet very often. Problems with debt, slow military response, and an army were all problems of the Confederation that prompted the change to a more steadfast and central solution.

15. B: Prior to redistricting, the two political parties have relatively equal support in all four voting districts. Afterward, Political Party 1 gained a decisive advantage in three political districts by packing most of Political Party 2's supporters into a single district. This manipulative redistricting practice is commonly referred to as *gerrymandering*. Thus, Choice *B* is the correct answer. Nearly all states require voting districts to have contiguous borders, and all of the districts depicted in the diagram are contiguous. However, contiguity isn't a manipulative practice, so Choice *A* is incorrect. If redistricting had occurred in accordance with the principle of partisan fairness, the voting districts wouldn't have significantly changed. In fact, Political Party 2 likely dominated the redistricting process in order to achieve such a partisan victory. Therefore, Choice *C* is incorrect. Choice *D* is incorrect because proportional representation is an electoral system, not a redistricting practice.

16. C: The European Union aims to ensure free movement of people, goods, services, and capital within the internal market. The United Nations was formed in 1945 after World War II, making Choice *A* incorrect. The League of Nations was founded as a result of the Paris Peace Conference that ended the first World War and was also founded to avoid the repetitions of the first World War, making Choices *B* and *D* incorrect.

17. A: Throughout the nineteenth century, most European nations grew through trade and expansion. Germany saw unification and expansion as their trade power grew. England saw the largest growth, becoming the dominant European power by the end of the nineteenth century. Russia also grew, expanding through military might and trading alliances in the region. The Ottoman Empire, however, once a proud nation, saw war and trade deficits end their reign as a major European power.

18. B: The original thirteen colonies were Virginia, New York, Massachusetts, Maryland, Rhode Island, Connecticut, New Hampshire, Delaware, North Carolina, South Carolina, New Jersey, Pennsylvania, and Georgia. Thus, all but three cities on the list (New Orleans, Cincinnati, St. Louis) are in states that were one of the original thirteen colonies, so the correct answer is Choice *B, 7*.

19. B: A Nation is defined as a group of people who have common traits, such as heritage, history, language, culture, and religion. It has nothing to do with borders, sovereignty, power, people in office, or the rules by which a government operates (all of which are found in the other answer terms of state, government, constitution, and regime).

20. C: Deindustrialization in cities in the Industrial North during the 1960s–1980s pushed many residents away from industrial hubs like Buffalo, Cleveland, Chicago, and Milwaukee because the number of jobs dropped significantly. Thus, people needed to move elsewhere to find employment. This is an example of an economic push factor— pushing people out of the area because of an economic downturn. Choice *A* is incorrect because the situation described is an economic factor, not a political factor. Choice *B* is incorrect because the situation described is an economic factor, not a political factor, and because economic downturn is a push factor rather than a pull factor. Choice *D* is incorrect because an economic downturn is a push factor rather than a pull factor.

21. D: Culture can be transmitted in nearly endless ways, ranging from governmental policies to entertainment consumption. Furthermore, culture can be transmitted intentionally or spontaneously. For example, powerful institutions can sometimes unilaterally shift the culture to achieve a goal, but other times cultural change is a natural byproduct of social interactions that spirals in an unforeseen direction. Thus, Choice *D* is the correct answer. Culture is not always transmitted through hierarchical relationships. For example, relocation diffusion and contagious diffusion can occur outside of hierarchical relationships, so Choice *A* is incorrect. Religion, economic activities, and government policies play a powerful role in cultural development, but culture can be transmitted in other important ways, such as through social interactions and digital networks. Therefore, Choice *B* is incorrect. Choice *C* is a true statement, but it does not describe how culture is transmitted across society, so it's incorrect.

22. B: The central bank is responsible for all of these except for setting the tax rate. This is done by the government.

23. D: Fiscal policy is the term for what the government decides to do when it comes to its impact on the economy. Keynesian economics is the liberal economic belief that says that the government should have a role in the economy. Fiscal responsibility refers to taxation and government spending. Supply-side economics is the correct answer, as it refers to the pushback against government in the economy.

24. A: Free trade agreements seek to increase international trade by limiting or eliminating tariffs and subsidies for domestic industries. Overall, international trade increased dramatically after the signing of the General Agreement on Tariffs and Trade (1947) and formation of the World Trade Organization (1995). Thus, Choice *A* is the correct answer. Although Keynes issued proposals to reduce German reparations and establish a Free Trade Union, they are separate proposals. Reparations aren't directly related to free trade agreements. As such, Choice *B* is incorrect. Choice *C* is incorrect because free trade agreements generally prohibit countries from subsidizing or protecting domestic industries. Free trade agreements don't facilitate imperialism, so Choice *D* is incorrect.

25. C: It eroded serfdom. Millions of people died during the Black Death, but those who survived found that their standard of living had improved, especially serfs. Before the Black Death, serfs had few rights and were expected to work without pay for their lord. Because labor was in such short supply after the Black Death, serfs found they were in a much better bargaining position. The Protestant Reformation was a cultural phenomenon, and the rise of absolutism was a political change. Neither had any connection to the Black Death, making Choices *A* and *B* incorrect. Choice *D* is also incorrect; although Child Labor Laws came after the Black Death in the early 1800s, they weren't a direct result of the Black Death.

26. A: Copernicus exemplified the key techniques of the Scientific Revolution, including an emphasis on empirical data and the scientific method. He carefully observed the movement of the planets and found that his data did not match the contemporary geocentric theory, which stated that the earth was the center of the universe. He found that his data indicated that the planets revolved around the sun instead.

27. C: Louis the XIV was an absolute monarch who ruled during the sixteenth century. He concentrated power on the throne by forcing nobles to spend most of their time at the royal court. The French Revolution occurred about two hundred years after he died. Absolute monarchs like Louis the XIV bolstered their prestige by claiming they were appointed by God. The Mandate of Heaven was a similar

380

concept, but it was developed by the Zhou Dynasty in China about two thousand years before Louis XIV was born.

28. C: The Age of Enlightenment in the eighteenth century focused on political and economic philosophy as opposed to scientific discoveries. English philosopher John Locke introduced the concept of a social contract between the ruler and his subjects. His ideas helped inspire revolutions in the British colonies in North America and later France. Choice *A* is incorrect; the discovery of the heliocentric theory happened in 1543. Luther began to criticize the Catholic Church about two hundred years before the Age of Enlightenment began, making Choice *B* incorrect. Choice *D* is also incorrect, as the Renaissance happened before the Age of Enlightenment from approximately 1300-1600.

29. B: The American Revolution occurred first in 1775, and a number of European soldiers fought for the patriots. The American Revolution, in part, inspired the French Revolution. The Marquis de Lafayette came to America in 1777 and was wounded during the Battle of Brandywine. He returned to France after the American Revolution and became a leader in the French Revolution in 1789.

30. B: The printing press was much more efficient than previous methods, which required a single scribe to copy text by hand. This made books much more affordable and encouraged the growing middle class to read. No church or organization had a monopoly on the technology, so many different writers used it to spread the ideas of the Reformation, as well as the Renaissance, Scientific Revolution, and Age of Enlightenment.

31. D: 13th Amendment. The U.S. Constitution, Choice *A*, actually legalized slavery by counting slaves as three-fifths of a person. The Compromise of 1850, Choice *B*, banned the slave trade in Washington D.C. but also created a stronger fugitive slave law. The Emancipation Proclamation, Choice *C*, only banned slavery in the Confederacy. The 13th Amendment finally banned slavery throughout the country.

32. B: The Bleeding Kansas conflict contributed to sectional tension before the Civil War. The application of popular sovereignty in Kansas led to conflict as free-soil and pro-slavery forces rushed into the territory. Malcolm X's death, Choice *A*, was in 1965, almost 100 years after the Civil War ended. The 13th Amendment, Choice *C*, was ratified in 1865 and was approved at the very end of the Civil War. Shay's Rebellion, Choice *D*, was an uprising during 1786 and 1787 in Massachusetts.

33. A: Because the British naval blockade during World War I was so effective, Germany retaliated by using submarines to attack any ship bound for Britain or France. This led to the sinking of the RMS Lusitania in 1915, which killed more than 100 Americans. The destruction of the USS Maine, Choice *B*, sparked the Spanish-American War in 1898. The Japanese attack on Pearl Harbor in 1941, Choice *C*, brought America into World War II, not World War I. Franz Ferdinand's death in 1914, Choice *D*, sparked the outbreak of World War I, but America did not join the war until 1917.

34. C: Massacre at Wounded Knee. The Massacre at Wounded Knee in 1890 left at least 150 Native Americans dead, including many women and children, and was the last major engagement between Indians and American soldiers. The Trail of Tears, Choice *A*, involved the forced relocation of tribes from the American Southeast in the 1830s. Although thousands of Native Americans died along the way, it was not a battle. Tecumseh launched his uprising in 1811, Choice *B*, and conflict between Native Americans and U.S. soldiers would continue for decades as the country expanded further west. The Battle of Little Big Horn in 1876, Choice *D*, was a great Native American victory that led to the death of General Custer and more than 200 men.

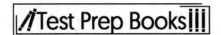

35. B: Choice *B* is correct. The Electoral College determines the winner of presidential races, but if a candidate doesn't win a majority of electoral votes, the Twelfth Amendment requires the House of Representatives to decide the presidency, with each state delegation voting as a single bloc. The candidate with the most votes in the House wins the election. The total number of Electoral Votes in the table provided is 261; because no candidate has a majority of the votes (131), the vote went to the House of Representatives. Choice *A* is incorrect because the table shows that Andrew Jackson won a plurality of electoral and popular votes, but he didn't receive a majority. Choices *C* and *D* are incorrect because John Quincy Adams received the most votes in the House of Representatives, so he won the presidency.

36. A: Choice *A* is correct. Electoral systems dictate how the members of the ruling body are selected, how votes translate into positions, and how seats are filled in the political offices at each level of government. In a majority system, a candidate must receive a majority of the total votes in order to be awarded a seat, but if none of the candidates reach a majority, a second round of voting occurs, commonly referred to as a runoff. Choice *B* is incorrect because in a plurality system the candidate with the most votes, regardless of the total number, wins the election.

Choice *C* is incorrect because in a single transferable system the voters each only have one ballot and rank the available candidates from most to least preferred. If a candidate is eliminated, the ballots that included him/her as the voter's first choice are transferred to each voter's second choice candidate rather than being wasted or lost because the first choice candidate is no longer eligible for election. Choice *D* is incorrect because in a party list system a political party makes a list of candidates and divides available electoral seats between the candidates on the list based on a variety of voting systems. There would be no need for a runoff election in any of these three types of electoral system.

37. C: Articles of Confederation. Issued in 1776, the Declaration of Independence, Choice *A*, explained why the colonists decided to break away from England but did not establish a government. That was left to the Articles of Confederation, which were adopted in 1781. The Articles of Confederation established a very weak central government that was replaced by the Constitution, Choice *B*, in 1789. It established a stronger executive branch. In 1791, the Bill of Rights, Choice *D*, amended the Constitution by guaranteeing individual rights.

38. A: The New Deal introduced a number of programs designed to increase regulation and boost the economy. Many of them remain in effect today, such as the Social Security Administration and the Securities and Exchange Commission. The New Deal also led to the Republican and Democratic parties to reverse their ideological positions on government intervention. It did not lead to a third party, Choice *B*. President Franklin D. Roosevelt was actually elected to four terms in office and the official two-term limit was not established until the 22nd Amendment was ratified in 1951. Until then, the two-term limit had been an informal custom established by President George Washington when he left office in 1797. Thus, Choice *C* is incorrect. Choice *D* is also incorrect. The Great Depression led to the New Deal, and not the other way around.

39. C: The North had a population of about 18.5 million while the South had only 5.5 million citizens and 3.5 million slaves. This meant the Union could more easily replace men while the Confederacy could not. The South was defending their homes from damage, since most of the war happened in the South, so Choice *A* is incorrect. Choice *B* is incorrect—the South had free labor at home, so they didn't have to worry about leaving their farms to go to war. Finally, Choice *D* is incorrect; the South had more experienced military leaders due to their participation in the Mexican-American War.

40. B: Although the United States initially lagged behind the Soviets, the U.S. successfully landed the first man on the Moon in 1969. However, the Korean War resulted in a stalemate in 1953, leaving Choice *A* incorrect. The Vietnam War, Choice *C*, was a defeat for U.S. forces. Despite sending more than 500,000 troops to Vietnam, the Vietnam War became increasingly unpopular and the United States eventually withdrew in 1973. The communist North Vietnamese eventually captured the southern capital of Saigon in 1975. Choice *D*, Battle of Gettysburg, is part of the Civil War.

41. A: Although the Constitution makes no provisions for a presidential cabinet, President George Washington created one when he took office. Members of the cabinet advise the president on a wide variety of issues including, but not limited to, defense, transportation, and education. The White House Press Secretary acts as spokesperson for the U.S. government administration, Choice *B*. The cabinet members are not required to raise money for the president's re-election effort, Choice *C*. The Vice President, not the cabinet, is who presides over the Senate, Choice *D*.

42. A: King Ferdinand and Queen Isabella agreed to support his mission because he promised to establish a direct trade route to Asia that would allow European merchants to bypass Middle Eastern middlemen. Columbus had no idea that America existed, Choice *B*, and he believed he had landed in India when he arrived in the Caribbean. That's why he mistakenly called the natives *Indians*. It is a common myth that Columbus sought to prove experts wrong by showing them the world was round, not flat. Most European thinkers already knew the world was round, making Choice *C* incorrect. Choice *D* is also incorrect; Christopher Columbus practiced the Christian faith, not Judaism.

43. B: World War II brought about an end to the Great Depression by switching over to wartime production. After the end of World War II, consumer demand remained high and unemployment was usually low. Computers began to become more powerful, efficient, and inexpensive in the latter part of the 20th century, and they became more common in business. The Sun Belt actually expanded after World War II as the traditional manufacturing base in the North and Midwest fell into decline. Land was cheaper in the South and West and wages were also lower too, so these regions were very attractive to businesses.

44. C: The Compromise of 1850. The Connecticut Compromise, Choice *A*, formed the basis for the Constitution by proposing a bicameral Congress. The Missouri Compromise, Choice *B*, banned slavery north of the 36°30' parallel in the Louisiana Territory. The Compromise of 1850 essentially undid the Missouri Compromise by introducing popular sovereignty, which allowed voters in territories to decide whether or not the state constitution would ban slavery. The Three-Fifths Compromise, Choice *D*, counted slaves as three-fifths of a human being when allocating representatives.

45. C: Pull factors are reasons people immigrate to a particular area. Obviously, educational opportunities attract thousands of people on a global level and on a local level. For example, generally areas with strong schools have higher property values, due to the relative demand for housing in those districts. The same is true for nations with better educational opportunities. Unemployment, low GDP, and incredibly high population densities may serve to deter people from moving to a certain place and can be considered push factors.

46. D: Diversity. Diversity refers to how everything and everyone is uniquely different. Choice *A* (behaviorism) is the study of how behavior influences the way human beings interact with their environment. Choice *B* (peer pressure) is when a group uses the majority vote to try to persuade the minority into changing their minds. Finally, Choice *C* (adaptation) is also incorrect because adaptation

refs to how a human being adjusts to their surroundings to create a desired outcome. Therefore, Choice *D* (diversity) is correct.

47. D: The map depicts European members of the North Atlantic Treaty Organization (NATO), which is a military organization. NATO originally formed in the aftermath of World War II to protect against a Soviet invasion of Western Europe. Thus, Choice *D* is the correct answer. Free-trade organizations seek to reduce barriers to trade, such as tariffs and domestic subsidies, and NATO isn't involved in free trade. So, Choice *A* is incorrect. Likewise, NATO isn't similar to international financial organizations, such as the World Bank and International Monetary Fund. In general, international financial organizations facilitate investment and development projects. As such, Choice *B* is incorrect. Many NATO members participate in joint task forces on transnational challenges, especially terrorism. However, Choice *D* is the better answer because all of the highlighted countries are members, so Choice *C* is incorrect.

48. C: Like most defense alliances, the North Atlantic Treaty Organization (NATO) involves a common defense agreement. In addition, NATO facilitates the transfer of sensitive technologies, such as digital communication tools and missile defense systems, between members. Thus, Choice *C* is the correct answer. NATO is a supranational organization, and membership requires the transfer of some sovereignty to the organization. For example, under NATO's common defense agreement, if one member is attacked, all members are legally obligated to join the conflict. So, Choice *A* is incorrect. NATO isn't directly involved with members' economic or political issues, so Choice *B* is incorrect. Similarly, Choice *D* is incorrect because NATO is more concerned with military issues than foreign direct investment.

49. C: The Republican Party emerged as the abolitionist party during the antebellum period and succeeded in abolishing slavery after the North's victory in the Civil War. The Constitutional Union Party supported slavery but opposed Southern secession, while the Southern Democrats supported slavery and secession. The Whig Party splintered in the 1850s as a result of tension over slavery, leading to the creation of the Republican Party and Constitutional Union Party.

50. B: Reconstruction was the Postbellum Era in which the United States tried to reinstate former Confederate states into the Union and rebuild the South through occupation. The Antebellum Era, Choice *A*, was the time frame that preceded the Civil War. The Progressive Era, Choice *C*, was the era of widespread reform in the late nineteenth and early twentieth century that set the stage for Prohibition. The civil rights movement, Choice *D*, is the era of U.S. history that witnessed desegregation, reaching its culmination in the mid-1960s under the presidency of Lyndon B. Johnson.

51. D: Following his election during the Great Depression, Franklin Delano Roosevelt pledged a *New Deal* for the American people, inaugurating an era of social welfare and public works programs. The Great Society, Choice *A*, also set forth social welfare and public works programs, but under the presidency of Lyndon B. Johnson (LBJ). The War Against Poverty, Choice *B*, was a subcategory of LBJ's Great Society—it promised to declare war on poverty like any nation would declare war on a foreign threat. Progressivism, Choice *C*, brought about reforms much like the New Deal, but during the early twentieth century, prior to the Great Depression and FDR's administration.

52. A: The Spanish-American War of 1898 made the U.S. a colonial power because it acquired many former Spanish colonies. The Mexican-American War of 1846-48 led to the acquisition of California, Nevada, Utah, Arizona, and New Mexico, Choice *B*. World War I led to the formation of the League of

384

Nations in 1919, Choice *C*. The Great Depression ended when Americans joined World War II in 1941, Choice *D*.

53. B: *Brown vs. Board of Education* ruled that separate schools for blacks and whites were inherently unequal and sparked demands for more civil rights. *Roe v. Wade* in 1973, Choice *A*, increased access to abortion. *Plessy vs. Ferguson*, Choice *C*, established the separate but equal doctrine. *Marbury vs. Madison* in 1803, Choice *D*, established the doctrine of judicial review.

54. B: A Nation is defined as a group of people who have common traits, such as heritage, history, language, culture, and religion. It has nothing to do with borders, sovereignty, power, people in office, or the rules by which a government operates (all of which are found in the other answer terms of state, government, constitution, and regime).

55. A: The Stonewall Inn Riot in 1969 helped ignite the gay and lesbian rights movement when patrons fought back against a police raid. The site became a national monument in 2016. Although he became an icon of the gay and lesbian rights movement, Matthew Shepard was murdered in 1998. Thus, Choice *B* is incorrect. The murder of Vincent Chin, Choice *C*, in 1982, became a rallying cry for Asian American activists. The gay and lesbian rights movement was well established when activists campaigned to raise awareness of AIDS during the 1980s and 1990s, making Choice *D* incorrect.

56. C: Alexandria became the capital. Jerusalem, Choice *A*, although the epicenter of Judaism and Christianity, did not host as many scholars as Alexandria during the Hellenistic period. Constantinople, Choice *D*, is incorrect because it was not yet created during the Hellenistic period. And Athens, Choice *B*, the former capital of Greek scholarship, is not the answer because scholarly culture shifted from Athens to Alexandria during this period.

57. D: The First Agricultural Revolution occurred 10,000 years ago. Choice *A* and Choice *C* respectively point to the Second Agricultural Revolution (200 years) and the Green Revolution (50 years). Choice *B*—1000 years—is just an erroneous number listed to trick the test takers.

58. C: Psychology is a social science that studies the ways in which the mind and cognition affect social relationships and identities. Biology, Choice *A*, is a hard science that studies life. English, Choice *B*, would be placed under the umbrella of the humanities. Geometry, Choice *D*, would fall under the category of mathematics.

59. C: Oligopolies are markets that establish a few large firms as the major sellers/distributors. Free market economies, Choice *A*, allow for more competition, while command economies, Choice *D*, allow for greater government control. Choice *B* is incorrect because pure monopolies are typically dominated by one firm rather than a few.

60. A: A pure monopoly is when there is only one seller of a particular product or commodity, and the sole seller attempts to restrict firms from exiting and entering the industry at will. Choices *B* and *C* describe a free enterprise economy. Choice *D* describes an oligopoly.

Science

1. D: Charles Darwin based the idea of adaptation around his original concept of natural selection. He believed that evolution occurred based on three observations: the unity of life, the diversity of life, and the suitability of organisms to their environments. There was unity in life based on the idea that all

organisms descended from a common ancestor. Then, as the descendants of common ancestors faced changes in their environments or moved to new environments, they began adapting new features to help them. This concept explained the diversity of life and how organisms were matched to their environments. Natural selection helps to improve the fit between organisms and their environments by increasing the frequency of features that enhance survival and reproduction.

2. C: Proteins are synthesized on ribosomes. The ribosome uses messenger RNA as a template and transfer RNA brings amino acids to the ribosome where they are synthesized into peptide strands using the genetic code provided by the messenger RNA.

3. A: The physical structure of the atoms that compose matter lends itself to the production of electricity. The arrangement of the subatomic particles and the associated charges — mainly the negatively charged electrons in the cloud — are associated with the ability to create an electric current, which can be harnessed to do work.

4. A: The Golgi apparatus is designed to tag, package, and ship out proteins destined for other cells or locations. The centrioles typically play a large role only in cell division when they ratchet the chromosomes from the mitotic plate to the poles of the cell. The mitochondria are involved in energy production and are the powerhouses of the cell. The cell structure responsible for cellular storage, digestion and waste removal is the lysosome. Lysosomes are like recycle bins. They are filled with digestive enzymes that facilitate catabolic reactions to regenerate monomers.

5. D: DNA serves as the hereditary material for prokaryotic and eukaryotic cells.

6. B: The Linnaean system is the commonly used taxonomic system today. It classifies species based on their similarities and moves from comprehensive to more general similarities. The system is based on the following order: species, genus, family, order, class, phylum, and kingdom.

7. A: Homo is the human genus. Sapiens are the only remaining species in the homo genus.

8. B: Plants use chloroplasts to turn light energy into glucose. Animal cells do not have this ability. Chloroplasts can be found in the plant cell but not the animal cell.

9. A: Photosynthesis is the process of converting light energy into chemical energy, which is then stored in sugar and other organic molecules. The photosynthetic process takes place in the thylakoids inside chloroplast in plants. Chlorophyll is a green pigment that lives in the thylakoid membranes and absorbs photons from light.

10. D: The cell membrane surrounds the cell and regulates which molecules can move in and out of the cell. Ribosomes build proteins, Choice *A*. Lysosomes, Choice *B*, break down large molecules. The nucleus, Choice *C*, contains the cell's DNA.

11. B: Sunlight enters the greenhouse as short-wavelength IR and gets converted to long-wavelength IR. This process also gives off heat and makes the greenhouse feel warmer than the outside climate. Water and oxygen, Choices *A* and *D*, are not involved in this reaction. The plants remain the same and do not get converted into anything else, Choice *C*.

12. D: Circular motion occurs around an invisible line around which an object can rotate. This invisible line is called an axis. Choice *A*, center of mass, is the average location of an object's mass. Choice *B*, the

386

center of matter, is not a real term. Choice *C*, elliptical, describes an elongated circle and is not a viable selection.

13. B: For charges, *like charges repel* each other and *opposite charges attract* each other. Negatives and positives will attract, while two positive charges or two negative charges will repel each other. Charges have an effect on each other, so Choices *C* and *D* are incorrect.

14. B: In broad terms, energy is divided into kinetic and potential energy. Kinetic energy refers to an object in motion. It is the product of mass and velocity ($KE = \frac{1}{2}mv^2$). Potential energy refers to the capacity for doing work. Its gravitational configuration is the product of mass, acceleration due to gravity, and height ($PE = mgh$). Examples of kinetic energy include heat (which is the thermal energy from atoms and molecules moving around), waves like light, and physical motion. Potential energy examples include gravitational energy and chemical energy stored in bonds.

15. C: The answer is 1,800 seconds:

$$\frac{45 \text{ km} \times \frac{1,000 \text{ m}}{\text{km}}}{25 \frac{\text{m}}{\text{s}}} = 1,800 \text{ seconds}$$

16. A: Both types of cells are enclosed by a cell membrane, which is selectively permeable. Selective permeability means essentially that it is a gatekeeper, allowing certain molecules and ions in and out, and keeping unwanted ones at bay, at least until they are ready for use. Prokaryotes contain a nucleoid and do not have organelles; eukaryotes contain a nucleus enclosed by a membrane, as well as organelles.

17. B: Dominant alleles are considered to have stronger phenotypes and, when mixed with recessive alleles, will mask the recessive trait. The recessive trait would only appear as the phenotype when the allele combination is "aa" because a dominant allele is not present to mask it.

18. A: Fungal cells have a cell wall, similar to plant cells; however, they use oxygen as a source of energy and cannot perform photosynthesis. Because they do not perform photosynthesis, fungal cells do not contain chloroplasts.

19. A: Roots are responsible for absorbing water and nutrients that will get transported up through the plant. They also anchor the plant to the ground. Photosynthesis occurs in leaves, stems transport materials through the plant and support the plant body, and phloem moves sugars downward to the leaves.

20. A: The correct answer is Choice *A*. Botanists study the field of botany, which is the study of plants. Neither the evolution of monkeys nor the genetic changes in human brain cancer, Choices *B* and *C*, involve studying plants. An ecologist would study how worker bees interact with a queen bee, Choice *D*, because that subdiscipline involves analyzing how organisms interact with each other.

21. C: The best answer is Choice *C*. Water molecules form a V-shape because of the uneven sharing of electrons between the atoms. The oxygen atom is slightly negatively charged, and the hydrogen atoms are slightly positively charged, so they pull away from each other and the molecule forms a V-shape.

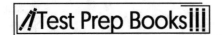

22. B: The correct answer is Choice *B*. Nucleic acids include DNA and RNA, which store an organism's genetic information. Carbohydrates, Choice *A*, are used as an energy source for an organism. Proteins, Choice *C*, are important for the structure and function of organisms. Lipids, Choice *D*, are important for energy storage and insulation.

23. B: The correct answer is Choice *B*. An animal cell is surrounded by a cell membrane. The cell membrane contains proteins that regulate which molecules are allowed in and out of the cell. Only plant cells are surrounded by a cell wall, so Choice *A* is incorrect. The nucleus, Choice *C*, is located in middle of the cell and would not be the first organelle that a molecule would encounter. The endoplasmic reticulum, Choice *D*, is located within the cytoplasm, inside the cell membrane.

24. D: The correct answer is Choice *D*. In both mitosis and meiosis, DNA replication occurs during interphase. Mitosis has one cell division whereas meiosis has two cell divisions; therefore, Choice *A*, the number of divisions, is incorrect. Mitosis produces two daughter cells whereas meiosis produces four daughter cells; therefore, Choice *B* is incorrect. Synapsis of homologous chromosomes, Choice *C*, does not occur in mitosis.

25. D: Nuclear reactions take place in the nucleus of certain unstable atoms. They involve a change in the structure of the nucleus, through some type of decomposition, and energy is released. Unlike in regular chemical reactions where mass is conserved, in nuclear reactions, there is a change in mass between the reactants and products.

26. B: A decomposition reaction breaks down a compound into its constituent elemental components. Choice *A* is incorrect because a synthesis reaction joins two or more elements into a single compound. Choice *C*, an organic reaction, is a type of reaction involving organic compounds, primarily those containing carbon and hydrogen. Choice *D*, oxidation/reduction (redox or half) reaction, is incorrect because it involves the loss of electrons from one species (oxidation) and the gain of electrons to the other species (reduction). There is no mention of this occurring within the given reaction, so it is incorrect.

27. D: The naming of compounds focuses on the second element in a chemical compound. Elements from the non-metal category are written with an "ide" at the end. The compound CO has one carbon and one oxygen, so it is called carbon monoxide. Choice *B* represents that there are two oxygen atoms, and Choices *A, B,* and *C* incorrectly alter the name of the first element, which should remain as carbon.

28. C: Neon, one of the noble gases, is chemically inert or not reactive because it contains eight valence electrons in the outermost shell. The atomic number is 10, with a 2.8 electron arrangement, meaning that there are 2 electrons in the inner shell and the remaining 8 electrons in the outer shell. This is extremely stable for the atom, so it will not want to add or subtract any of its electrons and will not react under typical circumstances.

29. D: The law states that matter cannot be created or destroyed in a closed system. In this equation, there are the same number of molecules of each element on either side of the equation. Matter is not gained or lost, although a new compound is formed. As there are no ions on either side of the equation, no electrons are lost. The law prevents the hydrogen from losing mass and prevents oxygen atoms from being spontaneously spawned.

30. C: Dark storm clouds are considered nimbostratus clouds, which are located below 2,000 meters above sea level. There are no atmospheric clouds in outer space.

31. C: When the left side of the Moon is illuminated, as it is in the given figure, it's in the waning phase. In contrast, when the right side of the Moon is illuminated, it's in its waxing phase. Gibbous describes a moon that's more than half-illuminated, and a crescent is less than half-illuminated.

32. A: The Big Bang theory explains how the universe was created from a large explosion, resulting in an expanding cloud of cosmic dust that clumped together to form stars and planets. Dark matter and life are found within the universe, and gravity is a universal law that helps explain how the Big Bang occurred.

33. D: Ice (solid water) can be found in Saturn's rings. Liquid water may have recently been discovered on Jupiter's moons Europa and Callisto.

34. A: The decimal point for this value is located after the final zero. Because the decimal is moved 12 places to the left in order to get it between the *8* and the *6*, then the resulting exponent is positive, so Choice *A* is the correct answer. Choice *B* is false because the decimal has been moved in the wrong direction. Choice *C* is incorrect because the decimal has been moved an incorrect number of times. Choice *D* is false because the decimal needs to be moved to after the first non-zero number. This will always result in a significand which is less than 10.

$$8,600,000,000,000$$

12 11 10 9   8 7   6   5 4   3   2 1

35. D: Chemical properties of a substance describe how they react with another substance, whereas physical properties describe the appearance of the substance by itself. Choice *D* is the correct answer because it describes how the substance reacts while burning and interacting with oxygen molecules. It is flammable because it does burn. The physical properties of color, density, and fragility are described by Choices *A, B,* and *C* respectively.

36. B: Recall that chemical changes involve changes to the molecular structure, whereas physical changes have to do with the appearance of the substance.

For Choice *A*, the condensation of water is represented by:

$$H_2O(g) \leftrightarrow H_2O(l)$$

This process is considered a physical change because there is no change in the identity of the substance. The process is reversible and is a common occurrence. The water vapor, or humidity, in the air tends to condense around cooler objects. If you are wearing glasses and walking from a cold building or car to the outside where it's warm, your glasses will quickly fog up due to condensation. When a glass mason jar is broken, which is the same as a glass cup, there are chemical bonds that break; however, the nature of the substance (glass, or SiO_2) is still the same. In other words, the glass is still glass. Therefore, this process is characterized as a physical change. In Choice *D,* mixing sand in water will not change the chemical structure of sand.

The process is reversible if you were to evaporate out the water, leaving only sand. In Choice *B,* baking is considered a chemical process for many reasons. For example, most people have smelled the aroma that is associated with baking brownies or a cake. There is also a color change in the batter (eggs, flour,

389

butter, chocolate chips) as its heated. This process is not reversible, which is a key characteristic of a chemical change, because once we make the brownies, there is no way to get the eggs or butter back. New chemical bonds form as the mixture is heated, e.g., the flaky crust and slightly burnt edges around the brownie.

37. C: The force that opposes motion is called *friction*. It also provides the resistance necessary for walking, running, braking, etc. In order for something to slide down a ramp, it must be acted upon by a force stronger than that of friction. Choices *A* and *B* are not actual terms, and Choice *D* is the measure of mass multiplied by velocity ($p = mv$).

38. A: Absolute dating involves measuring radioactive decay of elements such as carbon-14 trapped in rocks or minerals and using the known rate of decay to determine how much time has passed. Another element used is uranium-lead, which allows dating for some of the oldest rocks on the Earth.

39. B: The basic unit of matter is the atom. Each element is identified by a letter symbol for that element and an atomic number, which indicates the number of protons in that element. Atoms are the building block of each element and are comprised of a nucleus that contains protons (positive charge) and neutrons (no charge). Orbiting around the nucleus at varying distances are negatively-charged electrons. An electrically-neutral atom contains equal numbers of protons and electrons. Atomic mass is the combined mass of protons and neutrons in the nucleus. Electrons have such negligible mass that they are not considered in the atomic mass. Although the nucleus is compact, the electrons orbit in energy levels at great relative distances to it, making an atom mostly empty space.

40. A: Nuclear reactions involve the nucleus, and chemical reactions involve electron behavior alone. If electrons are transferred between atoms, they form ionic bonds. If they are shared between atoms, they form covalent bonds. Unequal sharing within a covalent bond results in intermolecular attractions, including hydrogen bonding. Metallic bonding involves a "sea of electrons," where they float around non-specifically, resulting in metal ductility and malleability, due to their glue-like effect of sticking neighboring atoms together. Their metallic bonding also contributes to electrical conductivity and low specific heats, due to electrons' quick response to charge and heat, given to their mobility. Their floating also results in metals' property of luster as light reflects off the mobile electrons. Electron movement in any type of bond is enhanced by photon and heat energy investments, increasing their likelihood to jump energy levels. Valence electron status is the ultimate contributor to electron behavior as it determines their likelihood to be transferred or shared.

41. A: Electrons give atoms their negative charge. Electron behavior determines their bonding, and bonding can either be covalent (electrons are shared) or ionic (electrons are transferred). The charge of an atom is determined by the electrons in its orbitals. Electrons give atoms their chemical and electromagnetic properties. Unequal numbers of protons and electrons lend either a positive or negative charge to the atom. Ions are atoms with a charge, either positive or negative.

42. B: In chemical equations, the reactants are on the left side of the arrow. The direction of the reaction is in the direction of the arrow, although sometimes reactions will be shown with arrows in both directions, meaning the reaction is reversible. The reactants are on the left, and the products of the reaction are on the right side of the arrow. Chemical equations indicate atomic and molecular bond formations, rearrangements, and dissolutions. The numbers in front of the elements are called coefficients, and they designate the number of moles of that element accounted for in the reaction. The subscript numbers tell how many atoms of that element are in the molecule, with the number "1" being

understood. In H_2O, for example, there are two atoms of hydrogen bound to one atom of oxygen. The ionic charge of the element is shown in superscripts and can be either positive or negative.

43. A: A catalyst increases the rate of a chemical reaction by lowering the activation energy. Enzymes are biological protein catalysts that are utilized by organisms to facilitate anabolic and catabolic reactions. They speed up the rate of reaction by making the reaction easier (perhaps by orienting a molecule more favorably upon induced fit, for example). Catalysts are not used up by the reaction and can be used over and over again.

44. A: When the moon comes between the Earth and Sun, a solar eclipse occurs. If the sun is far enough away and is completely blocked by the moon, it is a total solar eclipse. If it is only partially blocked by the moon, it is a partial solar eclipse, Choice *D*. A lunar eclipse occurs when the moon is on the opposite side of the Earth as the Sun and the Sun creates a shadow of the Earth on the moon, so that the moon becomes completely dark, Choice *C*, or partially dark, Choice *B*.

45. D: This is the only answer choice created by Earth's tilt. The Earth rotates around the Sun at an axis of 23.5 degrees, which causes different latitudes to receive varying amounts of direct sunlight throughout the year.

46. B: Freezing water expands because ice is less dense than liquid water. This expansion can break up solid rocks, which describes a form of mechanical weathering. Chemical weathering occurs when water dissolves rocks. Erosion is the movement of broken rock, and deposition is the process of laying down rocks from erosion.

47. C: Pure clay has small particles that pack together tightly and are impermeable to water. Sand is the most permeable type of soil because it has the largest grains. Loam is a combination of all three types of soil in relatively equal proportions.

48. B: Earth's northern geomagnetic pole is located near Greenland. It constantly moves around the same area, but it can intermittently flip or reverse every 100,000 years or so.

49. B: Solar eclipses should not be looked at directly. The rays of the Sun do not seem as bright as normal but can still cause damage to the eyes. A pinhole camera facing away from the eclipse allows the viewer to see a reflection of the eclipse instead of the actual eclipse. Choices *A, C,* and *D* all require looking directly at the solar eclipse.

50. B: Solar eclipses are viewed during the daytime because they involve viewing the Sun while it is out during normal daytime hours. Lunar eclipses, Choices *C* and *D*, are viewed at nighttime when the moon is in the sky during its normal hours. The moon is normally illuminated by the Sun that is on the other side of the Earth. When the Sun is on the other side of the earth, it is nighttime for people looking at the moon.

51. D: Radiation can be transmitted through electromagnetic waves and needs no medium to travel. Radiation can travel in a vacuum. This is how the Sun warms the Earth and typically applies to large objects with great amounts of heat, or objects that have a large difference in their heat measurements. Choice *A*, convection, involves atoms or molecules traveling from areas of high concentration to those of low concentration and they transfer energy or heat with them. Choice *B*, conduction, involves the touching or bumping of atoms or molecules in order to transfer energy or heat. Choice *C*, induction,

deals with charges and does not apply to the transfer of energy or heat. Choices *A*, *B*, and *C* need a medium in which to travel, while radiation requires no medium.

52. C: The Industrial Revolution switched the economical focus for most of the world from agriculture to manufacturing. This period produced factories and many machines, which required the combustion of coal and other fuel sources. As a new industry, the lack of regulation did not combat the air pollution from these factories, nor were there rules on where to dump waste. While some pollution likely did occur in the other periods listed, the period of the Industrial Revolution, from approximately the mid-1760s to the early 1800s, caused a dramatic spike.

53. D: Landfills and animal waste are large contributors to methane. They do not cause significant amounts of the other greenhouse gases listed. Corn fumes are not a greenhouse gas.

54. C: Geothermal power is a renewable resource that uses the Earth's core temperature to generate energy. Unlike solar energy, which requires land or roof space for panels, geothermal energy's main drawback is that it requires a lot of water because water is injected deep underground where it is heated. As it turns to steam, it turns turbines that generate electric power. It can also cause underground and well water damage. Additionally, emergency events, such as geyser eruptions and landslides, have a high risk of being catastrophic to life. Geothermal energy does not involve combustion, so there is no greenhouse gas emission. It is also said to be three-to-five times more efficient than other alternative energy sources.

55. A: Clay and coal particles are known for their filtration properties in aquifers, as they are porous enough to let water molecules through but keep debris from passing. The other items listed typically are not porous enough for adequate filtration; rather, they just block all water.

Practice Test #3

Reading and Language Arts

1. When children begin to negotiate the sounds that make up words in their language independently, what skill(s) are they demonstrating?
    a. Phonological awareness
    b. Phonemes
    c. Phoneme substitution
    d. Blending skills

2. What is phonics?
    a. The study of syllabication
    b. The study of onsets and rimes
    c. The study of sound-letter relationships
    d. The study of graphemes

3. Word analysis skills are NOT critical for the development of what area of literacy?
    a. Vocabulary
    b. Reading fluency
    c. Spelling
    d. Articulation

4. What is scaffolding?
    a. Breaking words down into parts.
    b. Dividing words into syllables.
    c. Analyzing individual morphemes.
    d. Dividing texts into digestible sections.

5. Which of the following is the best way to utilize a reading center or corner in a classroom?
    a. As a spot for students to play games
    b. As a private and quiet place to chat about books
    c. As a location to provide reading options above students' reading level
    d. As a place for students to take a break from the rigors of the classroom

6. What is the study of what words mean in certain situations?
    a. Morphology
    b. Pragmatics
    c. Syntax
    d. Semantics

7. When students study character development, setting, and plot, what are they most likely studying?
    a. Word analysis
    b. Point of view
    c. Literary analysis of a fictional text
    d. Fluency

393

8. The author's purpose, major ideas, supporting details, visual aids, and vocabulary are the five key elements of what type of text?
   a. Fictional texts
   b. Narratives
   c. Persuasive texts
   d. Informational texts

9. When students use inference, what are they able to do?
   a. Make logical assumptions based on contextual clues
   b. Independently navigate various types of text
   c. Summarize a text's main idea
   d. Paraphrase a text's main idea

10. Story maps, an effective instructional tool, do NOT help children in what way?
    a. Analyze relationships among characters, events, and ideas in literature
    b. Understand key details of a story
    c. Follow the story's development
    d. Read at a faster pace

11. Which text feature does NOT help a reader locate information in printed or digital text?
    a. Hyperlink
    b. Sidebar
    c. Glossary
    d. Heading

12. Read the following passage to answer the question below:

    He is a kind and generous man who wants nothing more than the best for his community, thought Michael as the board members discussed the nominees for head of council. Lana June, however, was far more critical. He is just saying those things to get elected, she thought.

What is the author's point of view?
    a. First person
    b. Third person limited
    c. Third person omniscient
    d. Objective

13. What do *quantitative*, *qualitative*, and *reader and task* measure?
    a. Text complexity
    b. Genres of writing
    c. Points of view
    d. Reading comprehension

14. Autobiographies and memoirs are examples of what form of writing?
    a. Fiction
    b. Narrative
    c. Informational text
    d. Research papers

15. Rating scales, student logs, and the POWER method are effective assessment practices for what area of literacy development?
   a. Reading
   b. Writing
   c. Spelling
   d. Listening

16. Which effective writing area engages and connects with the audience, igniting emotion?
   a. Ethos
   b. Logos
   c. Pathos
   d. Kairos

17. When children begin to leave spaces between words with a mixture of uppercase and lowercase letters, what developmental stage of writing are they demonstrating?
   a. Emergence of beginning sound
   b. Strings of letters
   c. Words represented by consonants
   d. Transitional phase

18. First-hand accounts of an event, subject matter, time period, or an individual are referred to as what type of source?
   a. Primary sources
   b. Secondary sources
   c. Direct sources
   d. Indirect sources

19. The following is an example of what type of sentence?

   Although I wished it were summer, I accepted the change of seasons, and I started to appreciate the fall.

   a. Compound
   b. Simple
   c. Complex
   d. Compound-complex

20. Read the following sentence to answer the question below:

   The teacher directed the children's attention to the diagram, but the children couldn't understand the information.

This is an example of what type of sentence?
   a. Complex
   b. Compound
   c. Simple
   d. Compound-complex

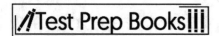
21. Read the following sentences to answer the question below:

Give me a shout back when you can.

Please return my call at your earliest convenience.

What is the main difference in these two sentences?
a. Point of view
b. Dialect
c. Accent
d. Register

22. What type of literary device is being used in this sentence?

I worked a billion hours this week!

a. Idiom
b. Metaphor
c. Hyperbole
d. Alliteration

23. What are the three tiers of vocabulary?
a. Conversational, academic, and domain-specific language
b. Informal, formal, and academic
c. Social, professional, and academic
d. Phonics, fluency, and rate

Questions 24-26 are based on the following passage, which is an adaptation of Robert Louis Stevenson's The Strange Case of Dr. Jekyll and Mr. Hyde*:*

"Did you ever come across a protégé of his—one Hyde?" He asked.

"Hyde?" repeated Lanyon. "No. Never heard of him. Since my time."

That was the amount of information that the lawyer carried back with him to the great, dark bed on which he tossed to and fro until the small hours of the morning began to grow large. It was a night of little ease to his toiling mind, toiling in mere darkness and besieged by questions.

Six o'clock struck on the bells of the church that was so conveniently near to Mr. Utterson's dwelling, and still he was digging at the problem. Hitherto it had touched him on the intellectual side alone; but now his imagination also was engaged, or rather enslaved; and as he lay and tossed in the gross darkness of the night in the curtained room, Mr. Enfield's tale went by before his mind in a scroll of lighted pictures. He would be aware of the great field of lamps in a nocturnal city; then of the figure of a man walking swiftly; then of a child running from the doctor's; and then these met, and that human Juggernaut trod the child down and passed on regardless of her screams. Or else he would see a room in a rich house, where his friend lay asleep, dreaming and smiling at his dreams; and then the door of that room would be opened, the curtains of the bed plucked apart, the sleeper recalled, and, lo! There would stand by his side a

396

figure to whom power was given, and even at that dead hour he must rise and do its bidding. The figure in these two phases haunted the lawyer all night; and if at any time he dozed over, it was but to see it glide more stealthily through sleeping houses, or move the more swiftly, and still the more smoothly, even to dizziness, through wider labyrinths of lamplighted city, and at every street corner crush a child and leave her screaming. And still the figure had no face by which he might know it; even in his dreams it had no face, or one that baffled him and melted before his eyes; and thus it was that there sprung up and grew apace in the lawyer's mind a singularly strong, almost an inordinate, curiosity to behold the features of the real Mr. Hyde. If he could but once set eyes on him, he thought the mystery would lighten and perhaps roll altogether away, as was the habit of mysterious things when well examined. He might see a reason for his friend's strange preference or bondage, and even for the startling clauses of the will. And at least it would be a face worth seeing: the face of a man who was without bowels of mercy: a face which had but to show itself to raise up, in the mind of the unimpressionable Enfield, a spirit of enduring hatred.

From that time forward, Mr. Utterson began to haunt the door in the by-street of shops. In the morning before office hours, at noon when business was plenty and time scarce, at night under the face of the fogged city moon, by all lights and at all hours of solitude or concourse, the lawyer was to be found on his chosen post.

"If he be Mr. Hyde," he had thought, "I should be Mr. Seek."

24. What can one infer about the meaning of the word *Juggernaut* from the author's use of it in the passage?
   a. It is an apparition that appears at daybreak.
   b. It scares children.
   c. It is associated with space travel.
   d. Mr. Utterson finds it soothing.

25. What is the definition of the word *haunt* in the following passage?

   From that time forward, Mr. Utterson began to haunt the door in the by-street of shops. In the morning before office hours, at noon when business was plenty and time scarce, at night under the face of the fogged city moon, by all lights and at all hours of solitude or concourse, the lawyer was to be found on his chosen post.

   a. To levitate
   b. To constantly visit
   c. To terrorize
   d. To daunt

26. What can one reasonably conclude from the final comment of this passage:

"If he be Mr. Hyde," he had thought, "I should be Mr. Seek."

    a.   The speaker is considering a name change.
    b.   The speaker is experiencing an identity crisis.
    c.   The speaker has mistakenly been looking for the wrong person.
    d.   The speaker intends to continue to look for Hyde.

27. When a student looks back at a previous reading section for information, he or she is using which of the following?
    a.   Self-monitoring comprehension
    b.   KWL charts
    c.   Metacognitive skills
    d.   Directed reading-thinking activities

28. Which choice of skills is NOT part of Bloom's Taxonomy?
    a.   Remembering and understanding
    b.   Applying and analyzing
    c.   Listening and speaking
    d.   Evaluating and creating

29. When a student looks at a word and is able to tell the teacher that the letters spell C-A-T, but the student cannot actually say the word, what is the spelling stage of the student?
    a.   Alphabetic Spelling
    b.   Within Word Pattern Spelling
    c.   Derivational Relations Spelling
    d.   Emergent Spelling

30. Predicting, Summarizing, Questioning, and Clarifying are steps of what?
    a.   Reciprocal teaching
    b.   Comprehensive teaching
    c.   Activation teaching
    d.   Summative teaching

31. When a student asks, "What do I know?" "What do I want to know?" and "What have I learned?" and records the answers in a table, he or she is using which of the following?
    a.   Self-monitoring comprehension
    b.   KWL charts
    c.   Metacognitive skills
    d.   Directed reading-thinking activities

32. What technique might an author use to let the reader know that the main character was in a car crash as a child?
    a.   Point of view
    b.   Characterization
    c.   Figurative language
    d.   Flashback

33. A graphic organizer is a method of achieving what?
   a. Integrating knowledge and ideas
   b. Generating questions
   c. Determining point of view
   d. Determining the author's purpose

34. A student is trying to decide if a character is telling the truth about having stolen candy. After the student reads that the character is playing with an empty candy wrapper in her pocket, the student decides the character is guilty. This is an example of what?
   a. Flashback
   b. Making inferences
   c. Style
   d. Figurative language

35. What is the method of categorizing text by its structure and literary elements called?
   a. Fiction
   b. Non-Fiction
   c. Genre
   d. Plot

36. A reader is distracted from following a story because they are having trouble understanding why a character has decided to cut school, so the reader jumps to the next page to find out where the character is headed. This is an example of what?
   a. Self-monitoring comprehension
   b. KWL charts
   c. Metacognitive skills
   d. Directed reading-thinking activities

37. Phonemic awareness, phonics, fluency, vocabulary, and comprehension are the five basic elements of what?
   a. Bloom's Taxonomy
   b. Spelling instruction
   c. Reading education
   d. Genre

38. A child reads the story Little Red Riding Hood aloud. He easily pronounces the words, uses an apprehensive tone to show that the main character should not be leaving the path, adds a scary voice for the Big Bad Wolf, and reads the story at a pace that engages the class. What are these promising signs of?
   a. Reading fluency
   b. Phonemic awareness
   c. Reading comprehension
   d. Working memory

39. A student is trying to read the word "preferred." She first recognizes the word "red" at the end, then sounds out the rest of the word by breaking it down into "pre," then "fer," then "red." Finally she puts it together and says "preferred." This student is displaying what attribute?
   a. Phonemic awareness
   b. Phonics
   c. Fluency
   d. Vocabulary

40. A class silently reads a passage on the American Revolution. Once they are done, the teacher asks who were the two sides fighting, why were they fighting, and who won. What skill is the teacher gauging?
   a. Orthographic development
   b. Fluency
   c. Comprehension
   d. Phonics

41. Poems are often an effective device when teaching what skill?
   a. Fluency
   b. Spelling
   c. Writing
   d. Word decoding

42. What allows readers to effectively translate print into recognizable speech?
   a. Fluency
   b. Spelling
   c. Phonics
   d. Word decoding

43. A teacher wants to help her students write a nonfiction essay on how the Pueblos built their homes. Before they write, she helps the students make clay from cornstarch and water, draw a plan for the house with a ruler, and build it using the clay and leaves from the schoolyard. These exercises are examples of what?
   a. Proficiency
   b. Collaboration
   c. Constructive writing
   d. Cross-curricular integration

44. A student has quickly written a story and turned it in without reading it. To help reinforce the POWER strategy, the teacher tells the student go back and read his story. This POWER stage is called what?
   a. Prewriting
   b. Evaluating
   c. Organizing
   d. Revising

45. During which stage of the POWER strategy are graphic organizers used?
   a. Pre-writing
   b. Organizing
   c. Writing
   d. Evaluating

46. A teacher wants his students to write a story over two weeks. They are instructed to write a draft the first day. On each of the following days, he asks the students to develop and edit the story for one of the following: ideas, organization, voice, word choice, sentence fluency, conventions, and presentation. What does this teaching technique incorporate?
   a. Ideas
   b. POWER strategy
   c. Cross-curricular integration
   d. 6+1 Traits

47. Which trait teaches students to build the framework of their writing?
   a. Conventions
   b. Word choice
   c. Ideas
   d. Organization

48. Which trait ultimately forms the content of the writing?
   a. Conventions
   b. Word choice
   c. Ideas
   d. Voice

49. Which trait is most commonly associated with giving individuality and style to writing?
   a. Voice
   b. Word choice
   c. Presentation
   d. Ideas

50. A teacher asks a student to describe a beautiful day. The student says the flowers were pretty, the air was warm, and animals were running. The teacher asks the student to specify how many flowers there were—just a few hopeful buds or an abundance of blossoms? Was the air still or breezy? How did it feel? The teacher is developing which trait in the student?
   a. Voice
   b. Word choice
   c. Organization
   d. Presentation

51. Writing practice for the sole purpose of communicating refers to what kind of writing?
   a. Persuasive
   b. Informational
   c. Narrative
   d. Purposeful

52. A second-grade student brings a book to read to a group. It is about a caterpillar counting its food each day of the week before becoming a butterfly. Realizing the group is very familiar with their days and numbers, the teacher uses the story to explore the "moral" of the story and proper nutrition. This is an example of what?

    a. Modeling
    b. Encouragement
    c. Acknowledgement
    d. Challenging

53. A student is struggling with reading, especially aloud. When it is his turn to read to the class, the teacher offers an easier book she knows the student likes and is very familiar with. When the student reads aloud well and with enthusiasm, the teacher praises him to the class, then gives a more challenging book the next time. What is this called?

    a. Acknowledgement
    b. Providing feedback
    c. Encouragement
    d. Effective assistance

54. Preparation, Presentation, Application, and Evaluation are the four steps of what?

    a. Demonstration
    b. Modeling
    c. Explanation
    d. Challenging

55. Students are asked to pretend to prepare a meal. At various classroom stations, they must draw a picture, engage in pretend play, or write a list of instructions: one for grocery shopping, cooking, and cleanup. The teacher helps each student choose which task to pair with which station, encouraging autonomy and self-motivation. This is an example of what instruction technique?

    a. Challenging
    b. Modeling
    c. Giving feedback
    d. Giving assistance

56. Throughout the day, a teacher used language priority, beginning each subject by asking students to volunteer five related words that start with the letter "P." Then, during a reading exercise, the teacher partnered with a small group to turn their words from the day into a cover illustration for a story. This is an example of what?

    a. Giving directions
    b. The Abecedarian Approach
    c. Developmentally appropriate practice
    d. Autonomy

57. Speaking, listening, reading, and writing are four essential elements of what?

    a. Developmentally appropriate practice
    b. The Abecedarian Approach
    c. Literacy development
    d. Task, purpose, and audience

58. A teacher is about to read a story. He tells the class they will be quizzed and need to pay attention. He instructs them to focus by clearing everything else from their desks, to look at his face for clues about the story's tone, and to think about the adjectives used to describe the characters to learn more about them. What skill is he teaching?
    a. Writing
    b. Reading
    c. Speaking
    d. Listening

59. Since teachers must be communicators, educators, evaluators, models, and agents of socialization, this is considered to be mastery of what?
    a. Conventions
    b. Spelling
    c. Speaking
    d. Listening

60. Synonyms, Antonyms, and Homonyms are examples of what?
    a. Syntax relationships
    b. Pragmatic relationships
    c. Semantic relationships
    d. Morphology relationships

61. In the word *shut*, the *sh* is an example of what?
    a. Consonant digraph
    b. Sound segmentation
    c. Vowel digraph
    d. Rime

62. When students identify the phonemes in spoken words, they are practicing which of the following?
    a. Sound blending
    b. Substitution
    c. Rhyming
    d. Segmentation

63. What is the alphabetic principle?
    a. The understanding that letters represent sounds in words
    b. The ability to combine letters to correctly spell words
    c. The proper use of punctuation within writing
    d. The memorization of all the letters in the alphabet

64. Print awareness includes all EXCEPT which of the following concepts?
    a. The differentiation of uppercase and lowercase letters
    b. The identification of word boundaries
    c. The proper tracking of words
    d. The spelling of sight words

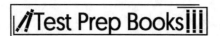

65. When teachers point to words during shared readings, what are they modeling?

      I. Word boundaries
      II. Directionality
      III. One-to-one correspondence

   a. I and II
   b. I and III
   c. II and III
   d. I, II, and III

66. Structural analysis would be the most appropriate strategy in determining the meaning of which of the following words?
   a. Extra
   b. Improbable
   c. Likely
   d. Wonder

67. A student spells *eagle* as *EGL*. This student is performing at which stage of spelling?
   a. Conventional
   b. Phonetic
   c. Semiphonetic
   d. Transitional

68. Spelling instruction should include which of the following?

      I. Word walls
      II. Daily reading opportunities
      III. Daily writing opportunities
      IV. Weekly spelling inventories with words students have studied during the week

   a. I and IV
   b. I, II, and III
   c. I, II, and IV
   d. I, II, III, and IV

69. A kindergarten student is having difficulty distinguishing the letters *b* and *d*. The teacher should do which of the following?
   a. Have the student use a think-aloud to verbalize the directions of the shapes used when writing each letter.
   b. Have the student identify the letters within grade-appropriate texts.
   c. Have the student write each letter five times.
   d. Have the student write a sentence in which all of the letters start with either *b* or *d*.

70. When differentiating phonics instruction for English-language learners (ELLs), teachers should do which of the following?
   a. Increase the rate of instruction
   b. Begin with the identification of word boundaries
   c. Focus on syllabication
   d. Capitalize on the transfer of relevant skills from the learners' original language(s)

71. Which of the following is the most appropriate assessment of spelling for students who are performing at the pre-phonetic stage?
    a. Sight word drills
    b. Phonemic awareness tests
    c. Writing samples
    d. Concepts about print (CAP) test

72. Phonological awareness is best assessed through which of the following?
    a. Identification of rimes or onsets within words
    b. Identification of letter-sound correspondences
    c. Comprehension of an audio book
    d. Writing samples

73. The identification of morphemes within words occurs during the instruction of what?
    a. Structural analysis
    b. Syllabic analysis
    c. Phonics
    d. The alphabetic principle

74. Which of the following pairs of words are homophones?
    a. Playful and replay
    b. To and too
    c. Was and were
    d. Gloomy and sad

75. Nursery rhymes are used in kindergarten to develop what?
    a. Print awareness
    b. Phoneme recognition
    c. Syllabication
    d. Structural analysis

76. High-frequency words such as *be, the*, and *or* are taught during the instruction of what?
    a. Phonics skills
    b. Sight word recognition
    c. Vocabulary development
    d. Structural analysis

77. To thoroughly assess students' phonics skills, teachers should administer assessments that require students to do which of the following?
    a. Decode in context only
    b. Decode in isolation only
    c. Both A and B
    d. Neither A nor B

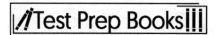

78. A student is having difficulty pronouncing a word that she comes across when reading aloud. Which of the following is most likely NOT a reason for the difficulty that the student is experiencing?
    a. Poor word recognition
    b. A lack of content vocabulary
    c. Inadequate background knowledge
    d. Repeated readings

79. Which is the largest contributor to the development of students' written vocabulary?
    a. Reading
    b. Directed reading
    c. Direct teaching
    d. Modeling

80. The study of roots, suffixes, and prefixes is called what?
    a. Listening comprehension
    b. Word consciousness
    c. Word morphology
    d. Textual analysis

Mathematics

1. Which of the following could be used in the classroom to show $\frac{3}{7} < \frac{5}{6}$ is a true statement?
    a. A bar graph
    b. A number line
    c. An area model
    d. Base 10 blocks

2. A teacher is showing students how to evaluate $5 \times 6 + 4 \div 2 - 1$. Which operation should be completed first?
    a. Multiplication
    b. Addition
    c. Division
    d. Subtraction

3. What is the definition of a factor of the number 36?
    a. A number that can be divided by 36 and have no remainder
    b. A number that 36 can be divided by and have no remainder
    c. A prime number that is multiplied times 36
    d. An even number that is multiplied times 36

4. Which of the following is the definition of a prime number?
    a. A number that factors only into itself and 1
    b. A number greater than one that factors only into itself and 1
    c. A number less than 10
    d. A number divisible by 10

406

5. What is the next number in the following series: $1, 3, 6, 10, 15, 21, \dots$?
   a. 26
   b. 27
   c. 28
   d. 29

6. Which of the following is the correct order of operations that could be used on a difficult math problem that contained grouping symbols?
   a. Parentheses, Exponents, Multiplication, Division, Addition, Subtraction
   b. Exponents, Parentheses, Multiplication, Division, Addition, Subtraction
   c. Parentheses, Exponents, Addition, Multiplication, Division, Subtraction
   d. Parentheses, Exponents, Division, Addition, Subtraction, Multiplication

7. If Danny takes 48 minutes to walk 3 miles, how long should it take him to walk 5 miles maintaining the same speed?
   a. 32 min
   b. 64 min
   c. 80 min
   d. 96 min

8. Rewriting mixed numbers as improper fractions can help students perform operations on mixed numbers. Which of the following is a mixed number?
   a. $16\frac{1}{2}$
   b. 16
   c. $\frac{16}{3}$
   d. $\frac{1}{4}$

9. If a teacher was showing a class how to round 245.2678 to the nearest thousandth, which place value would be used to decide whether to round up or round down?
   a. Ten-thousandth
   b. Thousandth
   c. Hundredth
   d. Thousand

10. Carey bought 184 pounds of fertilizer to use on her lawn. Each segment of her lawn required $11\frac{1}{2}$ pounds of fertilizer to do a sufficient job. If a student were asked to determine how many segments could be fertilized with the amount purchased, what operation would be necessary to solve this problem?
   a. Multiplication
   b. Division
   c. Addition
   d. Subtraction

11. Students should line up decimal places within the given numbers before performing which of the following?
    a. Multiplication
    b. Division
    c. Subtraction
    d. Exponents

12. Which of the following expressions best exemplifies the additive and subtractive identity?
    a. $5 + 2 - 0 = 5 + 2 + 0$
    b. $6 + x = 6 - 6$
    c. $9 - 9 = 0$
    d. $8 + 2 = 10$

13. Which of the following is an equivalent measurement for 1.3 cm?
    a. 0.13 m
    b. 0.013 m
    c. 0.13 mm
    d. 0.013 mm

14. Using the following diagram, calculate the total circumference, rounding to the nearest tenth.

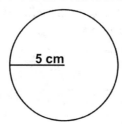

5 cm

    a. 25.0 cm
    b. 15.7 cm
    c. 78.5 cm
    d. 31.4 cm

15. Which four-sided shape is always a rectangle?
    a. Rhombus
    b. Square
    c. Parallelogram
    d. Quadrilateral

16. A rectangle was formed out of pipe cleaner. Its length was $\frac{1}{2}$ feet and its width was $\frac{11}{2}$ inches. What is its area in square inches?
    a. $\frac{11}{4}$ inch^2
    b. $\frac{11}{2}$ inch^2
    c. 22 inch^2
    d. 33 inch^2

17. A teacher cuts a pie into 6 equal pieces and takes one away. What topic would she be introducing to the class by using such a visual?
    a. Decimals
    b. Addition
    c. Fractions
    d. Measurement

18. Which item taught in the classroom would allow students to correctly find the solution to the following problem: A clock reads 5:00 am. What is the measure of the angle formed by the two hands of that clock?
    a. Each time increment on an analog clock measures 90 degrees.
    b. Each time increment on an analog clock measures 30 degrees.
    c. Two adjacent angles sum up to 180 degrees.
    d. Two complementary angles sum up to 180 degrees.

19. Which of the following represent one hundred eighty-two billion, thirty-six thousand, four hundred twenty-one and three hundred fifty-six thousandths?
    a. 182,036,421.356
    b. 182,036,421.0356
    c. 182,000,036,421.0356
    d. 182,000,036,421.356

20. A solution needs 5 mL of saline for every 8 mL of medicine given. How much saline is needed for 45 mL of medicine?
    a. $\frac{225}{8}$ mL
    b. 72 mL
    c. 28 mL
    d. $\frac{45}{8}$ mL

21. What other operation could be utilized to teach the process of dividing 9453 by 24 besides division?
    a. Multiplication
    b. Addition
    c. Exponents
    d. Subtraction

409

22. What unit of volume is used to describe the following 3-dimensional shape?

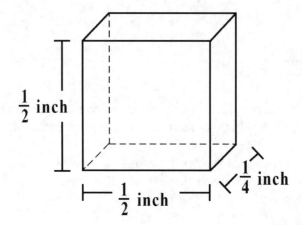

a. Square inches
b. Inches
c. Cubic inches
d. Squares

23. Which common denominator would be used to evaluate $\frac{2}{3} + \frac{4}{5}$?
a. 15
b. 3
c. 5
d. 10

24. What operation are students taught to repeat to evaluate an expression involving an exponent?
a. Addition
b. Multiplication
c. Division
d. Subtraction

25. Which of the following formulas would correctly calculate the perimeter of a legal-sized piece of paper that is 14 inches long and $8\frac{1}{2}$ inches wide?
a. $P = 14 + 8\frac{1}{2}$
b. $P = 14 + 8\frac{1}{2} + 14 + 8\frac{1}{2}$
c. $P = 14 \times 8\frac{1}{2}$
d. $P = 14 \times \frac{17}{2}$

26. Which of the following are units that would be taught in a lecture covering the metric system?
a. Inches, feet, miles, pounds
b. Millimeters, centimeters, meters, pounds
c. Kilograms, grams, kilometers, meters
d. Teaspoons, tablespoons, ounces

410

27. Which important mathematical property is shown in the expression: $(7 \times 3) \times 2 = 7 \times (3 \times 2)$?
   a. Distributive property
   b. Commutative property
   c. Associative property
   d. Multiplicative inverse

28. A grocery store is selling individual bottles of water, and each bottle contains 750 milliliters of water. If 12 bottles are purchased, what conversion will correctly determine how many liters that customer will take home?
   a. 100 milliliters equals 1 liter
   b. 1,000 milliliters equals 1 liter
   c. 1,000 liters equals 1 milliliter
   d. 10 liters equals 1 milliliter

29. If a student evaluated the expression $(3 + 7) - 6 \div 2$ to equal 2 on an exam, what error did she most likely make?
   a. She performed the operations from left to right instead of following order of operations.
   b. There was no error. 2 is the correct answer.
   c. She did not perform the operation within the grouping symbol first.
   d. She divided first instead of the addition within the grouping symbol.

30. What is the solution to $(2 \times 20) \div (7 + 1) + (6 \times 0.01) + (4 \times 0.001)$?
   a. 5.064
   b. 5.64
   c. 5.0064
   d. 48.064

31. A cereal box has a base 3 inches by 5 inches and is 10 inches tall. Another box has a base 5 inches by 6 inches. What formula is necessary for students to use to find out how tall the second box would need to be in order to hold the same amount of cereal?
   a. Area of a rectangle
   b. Volume of a rectangular solid
   c. Volume of a cube
   d. Perimeter of a square

32. An angle measures 54 degrees. In order to correctly determine the measure of its complementary angle, what concept is necessary?
   a. Two complementary angles sum up to 180 degrees.
   b. Complementary angles are always acute.
   c. Two complementary angles sum up to 90 degrees.
   d. Complementary angles sum up to 360 degrees.

33. The diameter of a circle measures 5.75 centimeters. What tool could be used in the classroom to draw such a circle?
   a. Ruler
   b. Meter stick
   c. Compass
   d. Yard stick

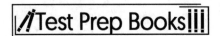

34. A piggy bank contains 12 dollars' worth of nickels. A nickel weighs 5 grams, and the empty piggy bank weighs 1,050 grams. What is the total weight of the full piggy bank?
    a. 1,110 grams
    b. 1,200 grams
    c. 2,250 grams
    d. 2,200 grams

35. $\frac{3}{4}$ of a pizza remains on the stove. Katie eats $\frac{1}{3}$ of the remaining pizza. In order to determine how much of the pizza is left, what topic must be introduced to the students?
    a. Converting fractions to decimals
    b. Subtraction of fractions with like denominators
    c. Addition of fractions with unlike denominators
    d. Division of fractions

36. Last year, the New York City area received approximately $27\frac{3}{4}$ inches of snow. The Denver area received approximately 3 times as much snow as New York City. How much snow fell in Denver?
    a. 60 inches
    b. $27\frac{1}{4}$ inches
    c. $9\frac{1}{4}$ inches
    d. $83\frac{1}{4}$ inches

37. Joshua has collected 12,345 nickels over a span of 8 years. He took them to bank to deposit into his bank account. If the students were asked to determine how much money he deposited, for what mathematical topic would this problem be a good introduction?
    a. Adding decimals
    b. Multiplying decimals
    c. Geometry
    d. The metric system

38. Which of the following would be an instance in which ordinal numbers are used in the classroom?
    a. Katie scored a 9 out of 10 on her quiz.
    b. Matthew finished second in the spelling bee.
    c. Jacob missed 1 day of school last month.
    d. Kim was 5 minutes late to school this morning.

39. What is the solution to $9 \times 9 \div 9 + 9 - 9 \div 9$?
    a. 0
    b. 17
    c. 81
    d. 9

40. A student answers a problem with the following fraction: $\frac{3}{15}$. Why would this be considered incorrect?
    a. It is not expressed in decimal form.
    b. It is not simplified. The correct answer would be $\frac{1}{5}$.
    c. It needs to be converted to a mixed number.
    d. It is in the correct form, and there is no problem with it.

41. Which of the following statements is true about the two lines below?

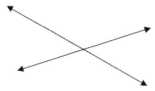

    a. The two lines are parallel but not perpendicular.
    b. The two lines are perpendicular but not parallel.
    c. The two lines are both parallel and perpendicular.
    d. The two lines are neither parallel nor perpendicular.

42. Which of the following figures is not a polygon?
    a. Decagon
    b. Cone
    c. Triangle
    d. Rhombus

43. What is the area of the regular hexagon shown below?

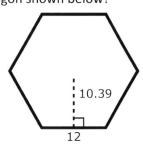

    a. 72
    b. 124.68
    c. 374.04
    d. 748.08

44. The area of a given rectangle is 24 square centimeters. If the measure of each side is multiplied by 3, what is the area of the new figure?
    a. $48\ cm^2$
    b. $72\ cm^2$
    c. $216\ cm^2$
    d. $13,824\ cm^2$

413

45. What are the coordinates of the point plotted on the grid?

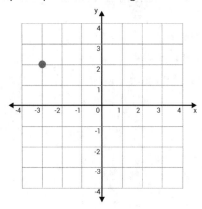

a. $(-3, 2)$
b. $(2, -3)$
c. $(-3, -2)$
d. $(2, 3)$

46. The perimeter of a 6-sided polygon is 56 cm. The lengths of three sides are 9 cm each. The lengths of two other sides are 8 cm each. What is the length of the missing side?
a. 11 cm
b. 12 cm
c. 13 cm
d. 10 cm

47. Katie works at a clothing company and sold 192 shirts over the weekend. One third of the shirts that were sold were patterned, and the rest were solid. Which mathematical expression would calculate the number of solid shirts Katie sold over the weekend?
a. $192 \times \frac{1}{3}$
b. $192 \div \frac{1}{3}$
c. $192 \times (1 - \frac{1}{3})$
d. $192 \div 3$

48. Which measure for the center of a small sample set is most affected by outliers?
a. Mean
b. Median
c. Mode
d. None of the above

49. Given the value of a given stock at monthly intervals, which graph should be used to best represent the trend of the stock?
a. Box plot
b. Line plot
c. Line graph
d. Circle graph

50. What is the probability of randomly picking the winner and runner-up from a race of four horses and distinguishing which is the winner?

    a. $\frac{1}{4}$

    b. $\frac{1}{2}$

    c. $\frac{1}{16}$

    d. $\frac{1}{12}$

51. Which of the following is equivalent to the value of the digit 3 in the number 792.134?

    a. 3×10

    b. 3×100

    c. $\frac{3}{10}$

    d. $\frac{3}{100}$

52. How will the following number be written in standard form: $(1 \times 10^4) + (3 \times 10^3) + (7 \times 10^1) + (8 \times 10^0)$

    a. 137

    b. 13,078

    c. 1,378

    d. 8,731

53. How will the number 847.89632 be written if rounded to the nearest hundredth?

    a. 847.90

    b. 900

    c. 847.89

    d. 847.896

54. What is the value of the sum of $\frac{1}{3}$ and $\frac{2}{5}$?

    a. $\frac{3}{8}$

    b. $\frac{11}{15}$

    c. $\frac{11}{30}$

    d. $\frac{4}{5}$

55. What is the value of the expression: $7^2 - 3 \times (4 + 2) + 15 \div 5$?

    a. 12.2

    b. 40.2

    c. 34

    d. 58.2

56. How will $\frac{4}{5}$ be written as a percent?

    a. 40%

    b. 125%

    c. 90%

    d. 80%

57. What are all the factors of 12?
    a. 12, 24, 36
    b. 1, 2, 4, 6, 12
    c. 12, 24, 36, 48
    d. 1, 2, 3, 4, 6, 12

58. A construction company is building a new housing development with the property of each house measuring 30 feet wide. If the length of the street is zoned off at 345 feet, how many houses can be built on the street?
    a. 11
    b. 115
    c. 11.5
    d. 12

59. How will the following algebraic expression be simplified: $(5x^2 - 3x + 4) - (2x^2 - 7)$?
    a. x^5
    b. $3x^2 - 3x + 11$
    c. $3x^2 - 3x - 3$
    d. $x - 3$

60. Karen gets paid a weekly salary and a commission for every sale that she makes. The table below shows the number of sales and her pay for different weeks.

Sales	2	7	4	8
Pay	$380	$580	$460	$620

Which of the following equations represents Karen's weekly pay?
    a. $y = 90x + 200$
    b. $y = 90x - 200$
    c. $y = 40x + 300$
    d. $y = 40x - 300$

Social Studies

1. Which of the following correctly lists the Thirteen Colonies?
    a. Connecticut, Delaware, Georgia, Maryland, Massachusetts, New Hampshire, New Jersey, New York, North Carolina, Pennsylvania, Rhode Island, South Carolina, Virginia
    b. Carolina, Connecticut, Delaware, Maryland, Massachusetts, New Hampshire, New Jersey, New York, Ohio, Pennsylvania, Rhode Island, Virginia, West Virginia
    c. Connecticut, Delaware, Georgia, Maine, Massachusetts, New Hampshire, New Jersey, New York, North Carolina, South Carolina, Pennsylvania, Vermont, Virginia
    d. Canada, Connecticut, Delaware, Georgia, Florida, Maryland, Massachusetts, New Hampshire, New York, North Carolina, Rhode Island, South Carolina, Virginia

2. Which of the following was NOT an issue contributing to the American Revolution?
   a. Increased taxes on the colonies
   b. Britain's defeat in the French and Indian War
   c. The stationing of British soldiers in colonists' homes
   d. Changes in class relations

3. The election of a presidential candidate from which party led to the Civil War?
   a. Democrat
   b. Whig
   c. Republican
   d. Federalist

4. Which of the following was NOT an important invention in the twentieth century?
   a. Airplanes
   b. Telegraph
   c. Television
   d. Computers

5. A teacher is working on a lesson describing cause and effect. Which of the following sets might the teacher use as an example using a primary cause and effect of the American Revolution?
   a. A cause was the taxation of the colonies, and an effect was the civil rights movement.
   b. A cause was the Declaration of Independence, and an effect was the Constitution.
   c. A cause was the French and Indian War, and an effect was the Bill of Rights.
   d. A cause was the debate over slavery, and an effect was the Seven Years' War.

6. What are the two main parts of the federal legislative branch?
   a. President and vice president
   b. Federal and state
   c. District court and court of appeals
   d. Senate and House of Representatives

7. What was a concern that George Washington warned of in his Farewell Address?
   a. The danger of political parties
   b. To be prepared to intervene in Europe's affairs
   c. The abolition of slavery
   d. To protect states' rights through sectionalism

8. Fourth graders are brainstorming ideas about responsibilities of citizens of democracy. Which of the following suggested responsibilities is NOT correct and could warrant further discussion as a class?
   a. To stay aware of current issues and history
   b. To avoid political action
   c. To actively vote in elections
   d. To understand and obey laws

9. Which of the following statements is true?
   a. Times zones are defined by their latitude.
   b. Eastern and Western hemispheres are defined by the prime meridian.
   c. A place is constant, while a location is changeable with the movement of people.
   d. A continent is one of six especially large landmasses in the world.

10. Which of the following statements is true?
    a. Water usage has largely shifted from appropriation to riparian.
    b. Native Americans lived in harmony with nature by never disrupting it.
    c. Cities are fully isolated environments.
    d. Invasive species can have catastrophic impacts on ecosystems.

11. A fifth grader wants to know why geography is important to the examination of history. Which of the following are valid reasons that a teacher could share with this student?

   I. Historians make use of maps in their studies to get a clear picture of how history unfolded.
   II. Knowing the borders of different lands helps historians learn different cultures' interactions.
   III. Geography is closely linked with the flow of resources, technology, and population in societies.
   IV. Environmental factors, such as access to water and proximity of mountains, help shape the course of civilization.

   a. I, II, and III only
   b. II, III, and IV only
   c. I, II, and IV only
   d. I, III, and IV only

12. Which of the following statements is true?
    a. All Native American tribes are matrilineal.
    b. Japan is struggling to manage its high birthrate.
    c. Shi'a Muslims traditionally follow imams.
    d. Mexico's culture is deeply tied to its Protestant roots.

13. Which of the following advancements was NOT invented by Greek culture?
    a. The alphabet
    b. The Hippocratic Oath
    c. Democratic government
    d. Theater

14. Which of the following was an important development in the twentieth century?
    a. The United States and the Soviet Union officially declared war on each other in the Cold War.
    b. The League of Nations signed the Kyoto Protocol.
    c. World War I ended when the United States defeated Japan.
    d. India violently partitioned into India and Pakistan after the end of colonialism.

15. A second grade teacher is discussing cross-cultural interactions. Which of the following is NOT an example that he or she should share with the class?
   a.   Egyptian and Mayan pyramids
   b.   The Spanish language
   c.   Styles of sushi
   d.   Study of Chinese culture

16. Which of the following is true?
   a.   The barter system no longer exists.
   b.   Economic resources can be divided into four categories: natural, capital, manufactured, and nonrenewable.
   c.   Individuals help to determine the scarcity of items through their choices.
   d.   According to the law of supply, as the price of a product increases, the supply of the product will decrease.

17. What is NOT an effect of monopolies?
   a.   Promote a diverse variety of independent businesses
   b.   Inhibit developments that would be problematic for business
   c.   Control the supply of resources
   d.   Limit the degree of choice for consumers

18. Which method is NOT a way that governments manage economies in a market system?
   a.   Laissez-faire
   b.   Absolute Monarchy
   c.   Capitalism
   d.   Self-interest

19. Which of the following nations did NOT establish colonies in what would become the United States?
   a.   Italy
   b.   England
   c.   France
   d.   Spain

20. Which of the following statements about the U.S. Constitution is true?
   a.   It was signed on July 4, 1776.
   b.   It was enacted at the end of the Revolutionary War.
   c.   New York failed to ratify it, but it still passed by majority.
   d.   It replaced the Articles of Confederation.

21. Which of the following locations was NOT subjected to American imperialism?
   a.   Philippines
   b.   Puerto Rico
   c.   Canada
   d.   Guam

419

22. What is a power that Congress has?
   a. To appoint the cabinet
   b. Right of nullification
   c. To impeach the president
   d. To interpret laws through courts

23. Which of the following is true?
   a. The Emancipation Proclamation ended slavery in the United States.
   b. President Wilson called for the foundation of the United Nations in his Fourteen Points.
   c. The Constitution of 1787 and the Bill of Rights were ratified simultaneously.
   d. The Declaration of Independence was primarily concerned with the colonists' complaints against King George III.

24. *The entire Roman Empire was destroyed in the fifth century A.D.* Is this statement true or false?
   a. True; it was conquered by barbarians in that era.
   b. True; it was destroyed by a civil war during that time period.
   c. False; the western half survived as the Holy Roman Empire.
   d. False; the eastern half, known as the Byzantine Empire, survived until 1453 A.D.

25. Which of the statements about the United Nations is false?
   a. It ensured the continuance of an alliance between the United States and Soviet Union.
   b. It was based on the idea for the League of Nations.
   c. It helps to promote human rights.
   d. It includes many former colonies from around the world.

26. Which of the following gentlemen was not instrumental in leading the charge for discussion at the Constitutional Convention held in Philadelphia in 1787?
   a. George Washington
   b. Alexander Hamilton
   c. Thomas Jefferson
   d. James Madison

27. Which American Indian tribe led a nomadic lifestyle and lived in teepees that were easily moved from place to place?
   a. Plains
   b. Southwest
   c. Eastern
   d. Northwest

28. A third grade teacher is planning a lesson on life in the United States during WWII. Which of the following would be an applicable primary source to include in the lesson?
   a. A recording of one of FDR's Fireside chats
   b. A picture book about the Treaty of Versailles
   c. A movie about life in Germany under the Nazi regime
   d. A documentary of Eisenhower's Inaugural Address

29. What was the controlling act imposed by the British on American colonists that taxed imported lead, glass, paints, paper, and tea, and prompted the colonies to unite against British rule?
    a. The Stamp Act
    b. The Sugar Act
    c. The Currency Act
    d. The Townsend Act

30. Where did the first shot of the American Revolution take place?
    a. At the Boston Massacre
    b. During the Boston Tea Party
    c. On Lexington Green
    d. At the Battle of Trenton

31. The Revolutionary War's final battle took place on October 19, 1781, when British General Lord Cornwallis surrendered to Washington's troops at what location?
    a. Yorktown, Virginia
    b. Valley Forge, Pennsylvania
    c. Trenton, New Jersey
    d. Saratoga, New York

32. What important U.S. structure was burned during the War of 1812?
    a. The Washington Monument
    b. Independence Hall
    c. The White House
    d. The Statue of Liberty

33. Who was elected President of the Confederate States of America during the Civil War?
    a. Robert E. Lee
    b. Jefferson Davis
    c. William T. Sherman
    d. Abraham Lincoln

34. The period of business and industrial growth from 1876 through the turn of the twentieth century was deemed by author Mark Twain as what?
    a. Manifest Destiny
    b. The Columbian Exchange
    c. The New Deal
    d. The Gilded Age

35. When did World War I begin?
    a. 1915
    b. 1917
    c. 1914
    d. 1918

36. Which of the following countries was a U.S. ally during World War II?
    a. The Soviet Union
    b. Italy
    c. Germany
    d. Japan

37. The North Atlantic Treaty Organization (NATO) was formed between which countries or regions?
    a. Canada, the U.S., and South America
    b. Western Europe, the U.S., and Canada
    c. The U.S., Western Europe, Canada, and the Soviet Union
    d. Asia, the U.S., and Western Europe

38. A fifth grade student is giving a report on events that served as driving forces for the passage of the Civil Rights Act in 1964. She has cited the following four events. As her teacher, upon completion of her report, you acknowledge her successes and then inform her that which of the following was actually NOT a driving force?
    a. *Brown vs. the Board of Education*
    b. Freedom rides
    c. The G.I. Bill
    d. The Montgomery bus boycott

39. What program launched by the U.S. government under President Ronald Reagan was designed to shield the U.S. from nuclear attack by the Soviet Union?
    a. The Strategic Arms Limitation Talks (SALT I and II)
    b. The Strategic Defense Initiative (SDI)
    c. The Iran-Contra Affair
    d. *Glasnost*

40. After the terrorist attacks initiated by Islamic fundamentalist Osama bin Laden on September 11, 2001, President George W. Bush ordered bombing raids on various locations in what country in an attempt to bring down bin Laden and his al-Qaeda network?
    a. Afghanistan
    b. Iraq
    c. Kuwait
    d. Pakistan

41. What are the two largest rivers in the U.S. called?
    a. The Mississippi and the Colorado
    b. The Mississippi and the Missouri
    c. The Missouri and the Ohio
    d. The Mississippi and the Ohio

42. What is used to pinpoint location on a map?
    a. Scale and longitude
    b. Contour lines and scale
    c. Latitude and longitude
    d. Latitude and contour lines

43. Third grader students are debating what are the obligations of citizens under America's democratic form of government. Which of the following is NOT one of these such obligations?
    a. Obey the law
    b. Pay taxes
    c. Serve on a jury if asked to do so
    d. Vote in elections

44. A teacher is preparing a lesson about the dynamic nature of history. Which of the following is a good example of this principle?
    a. The fact that GPS technology was first implemented in the 1960s but now is available on smartphones.
    b. The fact there are checks and balances built into the various branches of government.
    c. The fact that there are contradictory accounts of certain historical events, such as when Europeans first came to America.
    d. The fact that there are twenty-seven amendments to the U.S. Constitution

45. What is interaction of consumers, households, and companies within individual markets and the relationships between them called?
    a. Macroeconomics
    b. Microeconomics
    c. Boom and bust
    d. Economic output

46. What are the types of productive resources used to create products, such as machinery, tools, buildings, and equipment called?
    a. Natural resources
    b. Human resources
    c. Capital resources
    d. Entrepreneurship

47. What is the business sector of the economy that provides consumer or business services, including industries such as entertainment, travel and tourism, and banking called?
    a. Primary
    b. Secondary
    c. Tertiary
    d. Quaternary

48. Consumers must make choices regarding the goods and services to buy with their limited income. By purchasing one good or service, they are giving up the chance to purchase another. This is referred to as which of the following?
    a. The circular flow model
    b. Opportunity cost
    c. Savings account
    d. Assets

423

49. Which of the following is one way teachers can move beyond traditional direct instruction in the social studies classroom?
   a. Textbook work
   b. Lectures
   c. PowerPoints
   d. Field experiences

50. Which of the following geographic tools best allows teachers and students to use satellite technology in the classroom?
   a. Globes
   b. GPS
   c. Timelines
   d. Map projections

Science

1. At what point in its swing does a pendulum have the most mechanical energy?
   a. At the top of its swing, just before going into motion
   b. At the bottom of its swing, in full motion
   c. Halfway between the top of its swing and the bottom of its swing
   d. It has the same amount of mechanical energy throughout its path

2. What does the scientific method describe?
   a. How to review a scientific paper
   b. How to organize a science laboratory
   c. The steps utilized to conduct an inquiry into a scientific question
   d. How to use science to earn money in society

3. The energy of motion is also referred to as what?
   a. Potential energy
   b. Kinetic energy
   c. Solar energy
   d. Heat energy

4. Burning a piece of paper is what type of change?
   a. Chemical change
   b. Physical change
   c. Sedimentary change
   d. Potential change

5. A ramp leading up to a loading dock would be considered which type of simple machine?
   a. Screw
   b. Lever
   c. Inclined plane
   d. Pulley

6. Who is credited for simplifying the laws of motion?
   a. Einstein
   b. Hawking
   c. Copernicus
   d. Newton

7. The heat transfer due to the movement of gas molecules from an area of higher concentration to one of lower concentration is known as what?
   a. Conduction
   b. Convection
   c. Solarization
   d. Radiation

8. Which of the following is true of an object at rest on earth?
   a. It has no forces acting upon it.
   b. It has no gravity acting upon it.
   c. It is in transition.
   d. It is in equilibrium.

9. When researching a problem in science, what are the best sources to use?
   a. People you have seen on television
   b. Anyone with a Ph.D.
   c. Accredited laboratories and universities
   d. Any source with an internet webpage

10. What is a change in state from a solid to a gas called?
    a. Evaporation
    b. Melting
    c. Condensation
    d. Sublimation

11. The forces acting upon an object can be illustrated using what?
    a. A Venn diagram
    b. A periodic table
    c. A force diagram
    d. A stress-strain diagram

12. Which is not a form of Energy?
    a. Light
    b. Sound
    c. Heat
    d. Mass

13. A projectile at a point along its path has 30 Joules of potential energy and 20 Joules of kinetic energy. What is the total mechanical energy for the projectile?
    a. 50 Joules
    b. 30 Joules
    c. 20 Joules
    d. 10 Joules

14. What factors can prompt scientific inquiry and progress?
    a. Curiosity
    b. Competition
    c. Greed
    d. All of the above

15. Which of the following is considered a force?
    a. Weight
    b. Mass
    c. Acceleration
    d. Gravity

16. Why would a pencil appear to bend at the water line in a glass of water?
    a. The wood of the pencil becomes warped from being in the water.
    b. It appears to bend because of the refraction of light traveling from air to water.
    c. The pencil temporarily bends because of its immersion into separate mediums.
    d. The reflection of the light from water to a human's pupil creates the illusion of a warping object.

17. Which of the following is NOT one of Newton's three laws of motion?
    a. Inertia: an object at rest tends to stay at rest, and an object in motion tends to stay in motion
    b. $E = mc^2$
    c. For every action there is an equal and opposite reaction
    d. $F = ma$

18. The law of the conservation of energy states which of the following?
    a. Energy should be stored in power cells for future use.
    b. Energy will replenish itself once exhausted.
    c. Energy cannot be created or destroyed.
    d. Energy should be saved because it can run out.

19. Which of the following is true regarding magnets?
    a. Opposite charges attract
    b. Like charges attract
    c. Opposite charges repel
    d. Like charges do not repel or attract

20. Running electricity through a wire generates which of the following?
    a. A gravitational field
    b. A frictional field
    c. An acoustic field
    d. A magnetic field

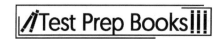

21. When an ice skater spins on one skate in a circle, what happens if they extend their arms out like the letter "T"?
    a. They spin faster.
    b. They spin slower.
    c. They stop spinning.
    d. Nothing changes.

22. For circular motion, what is the name of the actual force pulling toward the axis of rotation?
    a. Centrifugal force
    b. Gravity
    c. Centripetal force
    d. No force is acting.

23. Which is not a method for transferring electrostatic charge?
    a. Polarization
    b. Touch
    c. Election
    d. Induction

24. What does the re-radiation of solar waves trapped in the earth's atmosphere contribute to?
    a. Global warming
    b. Greenhouse effect
    c. Climate change
    d. All of the above

25. Velocity is a measure of which of the following?
    a. Speed with direction
    b. The change in position over the change in time
    c. Meters covered over seconds elapsed
    d. All of the above

26. Which of the following sources of energy are non-renewable?
    a. Wind energy
    b. Solar energy
    c. Fossil fuel energy
    d. Geothermal energy

Use the following image to answer question 27.

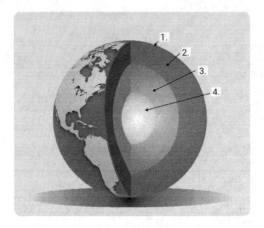

27. Which choice describes layer 4?
    a. Inner core: solid
    b. Inner core: liquid
    c. Outer core: solid
    d. Outer core: liquid

28. Which type of rock accumulates in layers at the bottom of the ocean due to run-off?
    a. Igneous
    b. Sedimentary
    c. Metamorphic
    d. Minerals

29. The water cycle involves phase changes. Which example below is evaporation?
    a. Clouds forming in the sky
    b. Rain, snow, or ice storms
    c. River water flowing to the ocean
    d. Sunlight's effect on morning dew

30. Which of the following is NOT directly caused by tectonic plate movement?
    a. Spreading of the ocean floor
    b. Earthquakes
    c. Mountain formation
    d. Precipitation

31. Which of the following statements is false?
    a. Magma circulates in the upper mantle.
    b. All volcanoes have explosive eruptions.
    b. Igneous rocks are formed by crystallized lava.
    c. Igneous rocks recycle and form magma.

Use the following image to answer questions 32 and 33.

32. Which fossil is the oldest?
    a. Dinosaur head
    b. Seashell
    c. Skeleton
    d. Grass

33. The fossils in the figure are embedded in which type of rock?
    a. Metamorphic
    b. Igneous
    c. Sedimentary
    d. Magma

Use the following image to answer question 34.

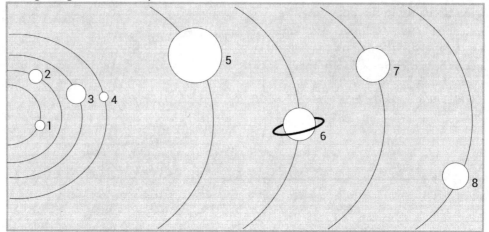

34. Where is the asteroid belt located in the figure above?
    a. Between structures #2 and #3
    b. Between structures #3 and #4
    c. Between structures #4 and #5
    d. Between each planet

35. Why is a year on Mars shorter than a year on Jupiter?
    a. Mars is much smaller than Jupiter.
    b. Mars is a rocky planet, while Jupiter is made of gas.
    c. Mars has a smaller orbit around the Sun.
    d. Mars is inside the asteroid belt.

Use the following image to answer question 36.

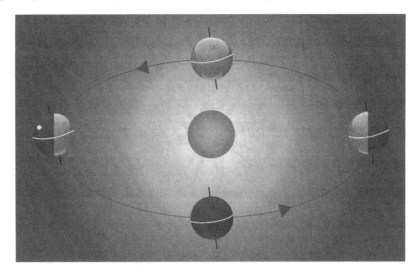

36. The figure above illustrates earth's orbit around the sun. What season is it where the dot is located?
    a. Summer
    b. Winter
    c. Fall
    d. Spring

37. Which statement(s) are true about the phases of the moon?
    a. Full moons are farther away from the sun than new moons.
    b. Crescent moons are smaller than half moons.
    c. Gibbous moons are larger than half moons.
    d. All of the above are true.

38. Why are greenhouse gases important?
    a. They allow UV rays to penetrate the troposphere.
    b. They insulate earth and keep it warm.
    c. They reflect light so that the sky looks blue.
    d. They form clouds and directly participate in the water cycle.

39. How is a theory different from a hypothesis?
    a. Theories are predictions based on previous research, and hypotheses are proven.
    b. Hypotheses can change, while theories cannot.
    c. Theories are accepted by scientists, while hypotheses remain to be proven.
    d. Hypotheses are always wrong, while theories are always true.

40. Which scientist is correctly paired with what he or she studies?
    a. Paleontologist: earth's crust
    b. Meteorologist: fossils
    c. Seismologist: earthquakes
    d. Geologist: weather

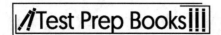
41. What part of most plants performs photosynthesis?
    a. Root
    b. Stem
    c. Leaf
    d. Flower

42. Which definition describes an ecosystem?
    a. One individual organism
    b. Rocks, soil, and atmosphere within an area
    c. All the organisms in a food web
    d. All living and nonliving things in an area

Use the following image to answer questions 43 and 44.

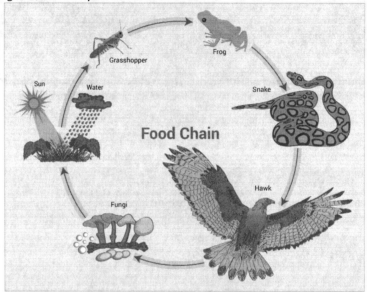

43. Which is the decomposer in the food chain above?
    a. Sun
    b. Grass
    c. Frog
    d. Fungi

44. Which is the herbivore in the food chain above?
    a. Grass
    b. Grasshopper
    c. Frog
    d. Fungi

45. What is a product of photosynthesis?
    a. Water
    b. Sunlight
    c. Oxygen
    d. Carbon Dioxide

46. What is cellular respiration?
    a. Making high-energy sugars
    b. Breathing
    c. Breaking down food to release energy
    d. Sweating

47. Which is true regarding DNA?
    a. It is the genetic code.
    b. It provides energy.
    c. It is single-stranded.
    d. All of the above.

48. Which one of the following can perform photosynthesis?
    a. Mold
    b. Ant
    c. Mushroom
    d. Algae

49. What happens at stomata?
    a. Carbon dioxide enters.
    b. Water exits due to transpiration.
    c. Oxygen exits.
    d. Glucose exits.

50. Which of the following represents a helpful inherited adaptation?
    a. A male elephant defending his territory by chasing another elephant away.
    b. A female dog that has a permanent strong odor that other male dogs tend to avoid.
    c. A male moose born with bigger horns that enable him to reduce competition for mating.
    d. A monkey learning to peel a banana after several tries.

51. Esther is left-handed. Hand dominance is a genetic factor. If being right-handed is a dominant trait over being left-handed, which of the following cannot be true about Esther's parents?
    a. Her parents are both right-handed.
    b. Her parents are both left-handed.
    c. Only one parent is right-handed.
    d. All of the above can be true.

52. What structures are made by the body's white blood cells that fight bacterial infections?
    a. Antibodies
    b. Antibiotics
    c. Vaccines
    d. Red blood cells

433

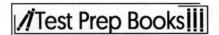
53. Cell -> ___1___ -> ___2___ -> organ system -> organism

Fill in blank #2 with the correct structure and a possible example in the circulatory system.

    a. Organ: heart

    b. Organ: blood vessel

    c. Tissue: heart

    d. Tissue: blood vessel

Use the following image to answer question 54.

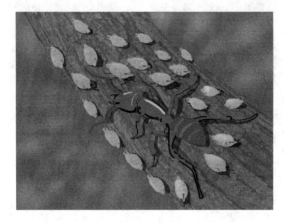

54. Ants and aphids are organisms commonly found in nature. The ant doesn't eat the aphid, nor does the aphid eat the ant, so they have a different type of relationship than predator-prey. When aphids feed on plants, they simultaneously secrete a sugary substance that ants like to snack on. Ants in return protect the aphids from predators. What kind of relationship do the ant and the aphid demonstrate?

    a. Competition

    b. Parasitism

    c. Mutualism

    d. Commensalism

55. Jackson wants to open a dog-training business. He wants to see which dog treat is most effective in training dogs to sit. If he wants to design an experiment testing twenty dogs to figure out which treats to use, what would be a good dependent variable?

    a. Type of food

    b. Time in seconds the dogs sit

    c. How many times the dog wags its tail

    d. Shape of food

Answer Explanations #3

Reading and Language Arts

1. A: Phonological awareness refers to a child's ability to understand and use familiar sounds in their social environment in order to form coherent words. Phonemes are defined as distinct sound units in any given language. Phonemic substitution is part of phonological awareness—a child's ability to substitute specific phonemes for others. Blending skills refers to the ability to construct or build words from individual phonemes by blending the sounds together in a unique sequence.

2. C: When children begin to recognize and apply sound-letter relationships independently and accurately, they are demonstrating a growing mastery of phonics. Phonics is the most commonly used method for teaching people to read and write by associating sounds with their corresponding letters or groups of letters, using a language's alphabetic writing system. Syllabication refers to the ability to break down words into their individual syllables. The study of onsets and rimes strives to help students recognize and separate a word's beginning consonant or consonant-cluster sound, the onset, from the word's rime, the vowel and/or consonants that follow the onset. A grapheme is a letter or a group of letters in a language that represent a sound.

3. D: Breaking down words into their individual parts, studying prefixes, suffixes, root words, rimes, and onsets, are all examples of word analysis. When children analyze words, they develop their vocabulary and strengthen their spelling and reading fluency.

4. D: Scaffolding is breaking texts down into sections and dissecting their key points. Breaking words down into parts and analyzing individual morphemes are both parts of morphology. Dividing words into syllables is syllabication.

5. B: A reading corner is not designed to be a "hang out" for students, nor is it supposed to be a break location. Rather, it is a place for students to share thoughts on books or discuss recommendations. A reading corner should have books that are of appropriate reading level for students in the classroom.

6. B: Pragmatics is the study of what words mean in certain situations. Choice *A*, morphology, involves the structure and formation of words. Choice *C*, syntax, refers to the order of words in a sentence. Choice *D*, semantics, addresses the distinct meanings of words.

7. C: Literary analysis of a fictional text involves several areas of study, including character development, setting, and plot. Although point of view refers to a specific area of study in literary analysis, it is only one area. Word analysis does not involve the study of elements within a fictional text.

8. D: Informational texts generally contain five key elements in order to be considered informative. These five elements include the author's purpose, the major ideas, supporting details, visual aids, and key vocabulary. Narratives are accounts—either spoken or written—of an event or a story. Persuasive texts, such as advertisements, use persuasive language to try to convince the reader to act or feel a certain way. Informational texts strive to share factual information about a given subject in order to advance a reader's knowledge.

9. A: When a person infers something, he or she is demonstrating the ability to extract key information and make logical assumptions based on that information. The information provided is not direct, but

implied. Being able to navigate a variety of texts independently has nothing to do with inference; it demonstrates a student's reading comprehension and fluency. Successfully summarizing and paraphrasing texts are advanced literacy skills that demonstrate a student's reading comprehension and writing proficiency.

10. D: Story maps are a specific type of visual aid that helps younger children develop a clearer understanding of a story being read. Story maps may represent the beginning, middle, and ending of a story, or they may be used to develop a clearer picture of each character's personality and traits, unfold the story's plot, or establish the setting.

11. C: Informational texts organized with headings, subheadings, sidebars, hyperlinks and other features help strengthen the reader's reading comprehension and vocabulary knowledge. A glossary defines terms and words used within a text.

12. C: Third person is a term used to refer to a specific point of view in literature. A third person omniscient point of view develops the point of view of each character within a given story and allows the reader to understand each character's feelings as well as their interpretation of a story's events. Third person limited only offers insight into one character, usually the main character.

13. A: These are all measures of a text's complexity. Quantitative measures determine a text's level of difficulty. There are several ways to measure this level of difficulty, some of which are sentence length, number of unfamiliar words, and even syllable count within words. Qualitative measures examine a text's attributes, including clarity of language, figurative versus literal language, and a text's overall meaning. Since each reader has unique background knowledge, skill set, and level of reading motivation, reader and task refers to how likely a reader is to engage in and comprehend a given text. Thus, all three of these components comprise a text's complexity. A genre of writing is simply the style of writing that the author employs. Authors will always reveal a given point of view in fictional writing. Sometimes, the author offers readers several points of view, and sometimes, the points of view are limited. Reading comprehension refers to how well a student demonstrates understanding or mastery of the text.

14. B: Narratives are personal accounts of a time period, event, or an individual, with the purpose of documenting, recording, or sharing such factual information. By contrast, fiction is a genre of writing that is fabricated. Informational texts are academic texts used to further a student's mastery of a given subject. Research papers are reports that students research and write to demonstrate their understanding of an area of study.

15. B: There are several effective assessments to evaluate a child's overall writing progress. Rating scales, student logs, and the POWER method are just some of these assessment methods. Although educators can create rating scales and student logs to assess and help students assess reading and spelling, the POWER method is specific to writing:

P—Prewriting

O—Organizing

W—Writing a rough draft

E—Evaluating

436

R—Revise and Rewrite

16. C: Pathos refers to the author's appeal to the audience or reader's emotions. Ethos refers to the level of credibility of a piece of writing. Logos refers to the author's appeal to the audience or reader's logic. Kairos refers to the most opportune moment to do something. Therefore, the correct answer is pathos.

17. C: There are eight developmental writing stages:

- Scribbling
- Letter-like symbols
- Strings of letters
- The emergence of beginning sounds
- Words represented by consonants
- Initial, middle, and final sounds
- Transitional phase
- Standard spelling

When children begin to leave visible spacing between words, even if those words are incorrectly spelled or if there is a mixture of upper and lower case letters, they are considered to be at the *Words represented by consonants* stage.

18. A: Firsthand accounts are given by primary sources—individuals who provide personal or expert accounts of an event, subject matter, time period, or of an individual. They are viewed more as objective accounts than subjective. Secondary sources are accounts given by an individual or group of individuals who were not physically present at the event or who did not have firsthand knowledge of an individual or time period. Secondary sources are sources that have used research in order to create a written work. Direct and indirect sources are not terms used in literary circles.

19. D: Since the sentence contains two independent clauses and a dependent clause, the sentence is categorized as compound-complex:

Independent clause: *I accepted the change of seasons*

Independent clause: *I started to appreciate the fall*

Dependent clause: *Although I wished it were summer*

20. B: Since the sentence contains two independent clauses connected by a conjunction, it is referred to as a compound sentence.

Independent clause: The teacher directed the children's attention to the diagram
Independent clause: The children couldn't understand the information
Conjunction: But

21. D: The first sentence is written quite informally and gives a clear impression that the exchange is on a socially relaxed level. The second sentence is written quite formally and gives a clear impression that the exchange is academic or professional in nature. Although both sentences carry the same message—to respond to the messenger as quickly as possible—the register, or level of formality, is very different.

Accent refers to the way in which certain words are pronounced by an individual and is usually dependent on where a person resides. Dialect refers to how groups of people from a specific geographical region manipulate their language. Point of view refers to a person's interpretation of or feelings toward an event. In literature, a point of view refers to a character's interpretation of or feelings toward an event.

22. C: When authors use hyperbole, they are using extreme exaggeration to strongly state a point or evoke a specific emotion in the reader. Idioms can be in the form of words, phrases, or sentences that are expressed figuratively, but they carry a literal meaning that readers must infer. Metaphors are literary devices that compare two unlike entities, as in "The United States is a melting pot." Alliteration is a poetic device that repeats the beginning consonant sound throughout a sentence or phrase strictly for entertainment—"The **b**all **b**ounced along the **b**lue **b**alcony."

23. A: The three tiers of vocabulary are as follows:

> Conversational: informal, more relaxed
> Academic: more professional, with vocabulary intended to challenge critical thinking skills
> Domain-specific language: a unique vocabulary inventory that focuses around a given discipline or computer language

24. B: The passage states that the Juggernaut causes the children to scream. Choices *A* and *D* don't apply because the text doesn't mention either of these instances specifically. Choice *C* is incorrect because there is nothing in the text that mentions space travel.

25. B: To constantly visit. The mention of *morning*, *noon*, and *night* make it clear that the word *haunt* refers to frequent appearances at various times. Choice *A* doesn't work because the text makes no mention of levitating. Choices *C* and *D* are not correct because the text makes mention of Mr. Utterson's anguish and disheartenment because of his failure to find Hyde but does not make mention of Mr. Utterson's feelings negatively affecting anyone else.

26. D: The speaker invokes the game of hide and seek to indicate they will continue their search for Hyde. Choices *A* and *B* are not possible answers because the text doesn't refer to any name changes or an identity crisis, despite Mr. Utterson's extreme obsession with finding Hyde. The text also makes no mention of a mistaken identity when referring to Hyde, so Choice *C* is also incorrect.

27. C: Asking oneself a comprehension question is a metacognition skill. Readers with metacognitive skills have learned to think about thinking. It gives students control over their learning while they read. KWL charts help students to identify what they already know about a given topic.

28. C: Listening and speaking are not part of Bloom's Taxonomy. The six parts are remembering, understanding, applying, analyzing, evaluating, and creating.

29. D: During the Emergent Spelling stage, children can identify letters but not the corresponding sounds. The other choices are all fictitious.

30. A: Reciprocal teaching involves predicting, summarizing, questioning, and clarifying. The other choices are all fictitious.

31. B: KWL charts are an effective method of activating prior knowledge and taking advantage of students' curiosity. Students can create a KWL (*Know/Want to know/Learned*) chart to prepare for any unit of instruction and to generate questions about a topic.

32. D: Flashback is a technique used to give more background information in a story. None of the other concepts are directly related to going back in time.

33. A: Graphic organizers are a method of integrating knowledge and ideas. These include many different visual tools for connecting concepts to help students understand information.

34. B: Making inferences is a method of deriving meaning that is intended by the author but not explicitly stated in the text. A flashback is a scene set earlier than the main story. Style is a general term for the way something is done. Figurative language is text that is not to be taken literally.

35. C: Genre is a means of categorizing text by its structure and literary elements. Fiction and non-fiction are both genre categories. Plot is the sequence of events that makes a story happen.

36. A: Scanning future portions of the text for information that helps resolve a question is an example of self-monitoring. Self-monitoring takes advantage of a natural ability of students to recognize when they understand the reading and when they do not. KWL charts are used to help guide students to identify what they already know about a given topic. Metacognitive skills are when learners think about thinking. Directed reading-thinking activities are done before and after reading to improve critical thinking and reading comprehension.

37. C: The five basic components of reading education are phonemic awareness, phonics, fluency, vocabulary, and comprehension.

38. A: If a child can accurately read text with consistent speed and appropriate expression while demonstrating comprehension, the child is said to have reading fluency skills. Without the ability to read fluently, a child's reading comprehension, Choice *C*, will be limited.

39. B: Phonics is the ability to apply letter-sound relationships and letter patterns in order to accurately pronounce written words. Phonemic awareness is the understanding that words are comprised of a combination of sounds. Fluency is an automatic recognition and accurate interpretation of text. Vocabulary is the body of words known to a person.

40. C: Comprehension is the level of content understanding that a student demonstrates after reading. Orthographic development is a cumulative process for learning to read, with each skill building on the previously mastered skill. Fluency is an automatic recognition and accurate interpretation of text. Phonics is the ability to apply letter-sound relationships and letter patterns in order to accurately pronounce written words.

41. A: Poems are an effective method for teaching fluency, since rhythmic sounds and rhyming words build a child's understanding of phonemic awareness.

42. C: Phonics allows readers to effectively translate print into recognizable speech. If children lack proficiency in phonics, their ability to read fluently and to increase vocabulary will be limited.

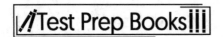

43. D: Cross-curricular integration is choosing to teach writing projects that include the subjects of science, social studies, mathematics, reading, etc.

44. B: Students should carefully read what they've written during the Evaluating stage of the POWER strategy.

45. B: Graphic organizers are used during the Organizing stage of the POWER strategy. They help students to examine, analyze, and summarize selections they have read and can be used individually or collaboratively in the classroom. Graphic organizers may be sequencing charts, graphs, Venn diagrams, timelines, chain of events organizers, story maps, concept maps, mind maps, webs, outlines, or other visual tools for connecting concepts to achieve understanding.

46. D: 6+1 Traits is a model for teaching writing that uses common language to explain writing standards. The 6+1 Traits are the characteristics that make writing readable and effective no matter what genre of writing is being used. These seven traits are ideas, organization, voice, word choice, sentence fluency, conventions, and presentation.

47. D: Organization is the trait that teaches students how to build the framework of their writing. Students choose an organizational strategy or purpose for the writing and build the details upon that structure. There are many purposes for writing, and they all have different frameworks.

48. C: Ideas ultimately form the content of the writing. The Ideas Trait is one of the 6+1 Traits model and is where students learn to select an important topic for their writing. They are taught to narrow down and focus their idea before further developing it.

49. A: Voice is the primary trait that shows the individual writing style of an author. It is based on an author's choice of common syntax, diction, punctuation, character development, dialogue, etc.

50. B: Word choice is the trait that teaches the use of precise language. Teachers can enhance this trait in students by helping them to use exact language that is accurate, concise, precise, and lively.

51. D: Intentional writing practice for the purpose of communicating refers to purposeful writing. Students can use this as a method of thinking through issues and solving problems related to writing.

52. C: Considering prior knowledge before instruction is part of Acknowledgement. For teachers, it begins with understanding where students are coming from and the experiences they bring with them to the classroom. When a teacher considers prior knowledge before beginning instruction, they are being considerate of each student's time and intellect.

53. B: Providing feedback is a way to build positive self-image and encourage success. A positive self-image is fostered by repeated success. Giving clear and effective feedback communicates to the student that their work is worthwhile, and that someone cares enough to review and consider it.

54. A: Demonstration includes the four steps: Preparation, Presentation, Application and Evaluation. Demonstration is when a teacher not only models and explains how to do a task but also engages in thinking through the task with the students. Effective teachers narrate their thinking processes when modeling a strategy.

55. D: Autonomy and self-motivation are the goals of giving assistance. Students need assistance and guidance in a classroom; however, knowing how much help to offer is always a balancing act. If teachers

440

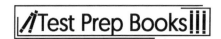

give too much assistance, they end up doing the work for students, who then do not learn. If teachers do not offer enough assistance, students become lost, overwhelmed, and do not learn.

56. B: Conversational reading and language priority are premises of the Abecedarian Approach. Conversational reading involves a conversational-style of reading instruction in which the educator plays an active role by partnering in shared reading activities. By emphasizing language throughout the day, the language priority strategy creates endless occasions for meaningful conversations. Educators work to extend conversations from a variety of different angles, promoting higher cognitive thinking and engagement.

57. C: Speaking, Listening, Reading, and Writing are the four elements of literacy development. As social beings, children begin to recognize that with effective literacy skills, their social, emotional, and physical needs can be met, and their curiosity can be satisfied.

58. D: Four concepts that teach listening skills are focusing, looking, non-verbal cues, and verbal cues. Behaviors that enable good listening skills should not be expected. They need to be taught. Students need to learn the difference between what an excellent listener does and what poor listening behaviors are.

59. A: Teachers must master conventions because they are communicators, educators, evaluators, models, and agents of socialization. Teachers serve several key roles in the classroom. Students will not be able to learn properly unless their teachers have mastered these conventions.

60. C: Synonyms, Antonyms, and Homonyms are examples of semantic relationships. There are five types of semantic relationships, including the three noted in the question. The other two are Hyponyms and Meronyms.

61. A: The *sh* is an example of a consonant digraph. Consonant digraphs are combinations of two or three consonants that work together to make a single sound. Examples of consonant digraphs are *sh*, *ch*, and *th*. Choice *B*, sound segmentation, is used to identify component phonemes in a word, such as separating the /t/, /u/, and /b/ for *tub*. Choice *C*, vowel digraph, is a set of two vowels that make up a single sound, such as *ow*, *ae*, or *ie*. Choice *D*, rime, is the sound that follows a word's onset, such as the /at/ in *cat*.

62. D: Sound segmentation is the identification of all the component phonemes in a word. An example would be the student identifying each separate sound, /t/, /u/, and /b/, in the word *tub*. Choice *A*, sound blending, is the blending together of two or more sounds in a word, such as /ch/ or /sh/. Choice *B*, substitution, occurs when a phoneme is substituted within a word for another phoneme, such as substituting the sound /b/ in *bun* to /r/ to create *run*. Choice *C*, rhyming, is an effective tool to utilize during the analytic phase of phonics development because rhyming words are often identical except for their beginning letters.

63. A: The alphabetical principle is the understanding that letters represent sounds in words. It is through the alphabetic principle that students learn the interrelationships between letter-sound (grapheme-phoneme) correspondences, phonemic awareness, and early decoding skills (such as sounding out and blending letter sounds).

64. D: Print awareness includes all of the answer choices except the spelling of sight words. Print awareness includes Choice *A*, the differentiation of uppercase and lowercase letters, so that students

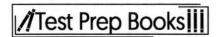

can understand which words begin a sentence. Choice *B*, the identification of word boundaries, is also included in print awareness; that is, students should be made aware that words are made up of letters and that spaces appear between words, etc. Choice *C*, the proper tracking of words, is also included in print awareness; this is the realization that print is organized in a particular way, so books must be tracked and held accordingly.

65. D: Word boundaries is included as one of the factors modeled because students should be able to identify which letters make up a word as well as the spaces before and after the letters that make up words. Directionality is the ability to track words as they are being read, so this is also modeled. One-to-one correspondence, the last factor listed, is the ability to match written letters to words to spoken words when reading. It is another thing teachers model when they point to words while they read.

66. B: Structural analysis focuses on the meaning of morphemes. Morphemes include base words, prefixes, and word endings (inflections and suffixes) that are found within longer words. Students can use structural analysis skill to find familiar word parts within an unfamiliar word in order to decode the word and determine the definition of the new word. The prefix *im-* (meaning not) in the word "improbable" can help students derive the definition of an event that is not likely to occur.

67. B: The student is performing at the phonetic stage. Phonetic spellers will spell a word as it sounds. The speller perceives and represents all of the phonemes in a word. However, because phonetic spellers have limited sight word vocabulary, irregular words are often spelled incorrectly.

68. B: The creation of word walls, Choice *I*, is advantageous during the phonetic stage of spelling development. On a word wall, words that share common consonant-vowel patterns or letter clusters are written in groups. Choices *II* and *III*, daily reading and writing opportunities, are also important in spelling instructions. Students need daily opportunities in order to review and practice spelling development. Daily journals or exit tickets are cognitive writing strategies effective in helping students reflect on what they have learned. A spelling inventory, Choice *IV*, is different than a traditional spelling test because students are not allowed to study the words prior to the administration of a spelling inventory. Therefore, this option is incorrect as it mentions the inventory contains words students have studied all week.

69. A: The teacher should have the student use a think-aloud to verbalize the directions of the shapes used when writing each letter. During think-alouds, teachers voice the metacognitive process that occurs when writing each part of a given letter. Students should be encouraged to do likewise when practicing writing the letters.

70. D: Teachers should capitalize on the transfer of relevant skills from the learner's original language(s). In this way, extra attention and instructional emphasis can be applied toward the teaching of sounds and meanings of words that are nontransferable between the two languages.

71. C: Writing samples are the most appropriate assessment of spelling for students who are performing at the pre-phonetic stages. During this stage, students participate in pre-communicative writing, which appears to be a jumble of letter-like forms rather than a series of discrete letters. Samples of students' pre-communicative writing can be used to assess their understanding of the alphabetic principle and their knowledge of letter-sound correspondences.

72. A: Phonological awareness is best assessed through identification of rimes or onsets within words. Instruction of **phonological awareness** includes detecting and identifying word boundaries, onsets/rimes, syllables, and rhyming words.

73. A: The identification of morphemes within words occurs during the instruction of structural analysis. Structural analysis is a word recognition skill that focuses on the meanings of word parts, or morphemes, during the introduction of a new word. Choice *B*, syllabic analysis, is a word analysis skill that helps students split words into syllables. Choice *C*, phonics, is the direct correspondence between and blending of letters and sounds. Choice *D*, the alphabetic principle, teaches that letters or other characters represent sounds.

74. B: Homophones are words that are pronounced the same way but differ in meaning and/or spelling. The pair *to* and *too* is an example of a homophone because they are pronounced the same way, but differ in both meaning and spelling. Choices *A*, *C*, and *D* are not homophones because they do not sound the same when spoken aloud.

75. B: Nursery rhymes are used in kindergarten to develop phoneme recognition. Rhyming words are often almost identical except for their beginning letter(s), so rhyming is a great strategy to implement during the analytic phase of phoneme development.

76. B: High-frequency words are taught during the instruction of sight word recognition. Sight words, sometimes referred to as high-frequency words, are words that are used often but may not follow the regular principles of phonics. Sight words may also be defined as words that students are able to recognize and read without having to sound out.

77. C: Both *A* and *B*. Decoding should be assessed in context in addition to isolation. During such assessments, the students read passages from reading-level appropriate texts aloud to the teacher so that the teacher is better able to analyze a student's approach to figuring out unknown words. Decoding should also be assessed in isolation. In these types of assessments, students are given a list of words and/or phonics patterns. Initially, high-frequency words that follow predictable phonics patterns are presented. The words that are presented become more challenging as a student masters less difficult words.

78. D: An individual's sight vocabulary includes the words that he or she can recognize and correctly pronounce when reading. Limited sight vocabulary can be caused by poor word recognition, a lack of content vocabulary, and inadequate background knowledge. Although proper pronunciation may affect the ability to spell a word, the ability to properly spell a word is less likely to affect a student's ability to properly pronounce that word.

79. A: There is a positive correlation between a student's exposure to text and the academic achievement of that individual. Therefore, students should be given ample opportunities to read as much text as possible independently in order to gain vocabulary and background knowledge.

80. C: By definition, morphology is the identification and use of morphemes such as root words and affixes. Listening comprehension refers to the processes involved in understanding spoken language. Word consciousness refers to the knowledge required for students to learn and effectively utilize language. Textual analysis is an approach that researchers use to gain information and describe the characteristics of a recorded or visual message.

443

Mathematics

1. B: This inequality can be seen with the use of a number line. $\frac{3}{7}$ is close to $\frac{1}{2}$. $\frac{5}{6}$ is close to 1, but less than 1, and $\frac{8}{7}$ is greater than 1. Therefore, $\frac{3}{7}$ is less than $\frac{5}{6}$.

2. A: Using the order of operations, multiplication and division are computed first from left to right. Multiplication is on the left; therefore, multiplication should be performed first.

3. B: A factor of 36 is any number that can be divided into 36 and have no remainder. $36 = 36 \times 1$, 18×2, 9×4, and 6×6. Therefore, it has 7 unique factors: 36, 18, 9, 6, 4, 2, and 1.

4. B: A number is prime because its only factors are itself and 1. Positive numbers (greater than one) can be prime numbers.

5. C: Each number in the sequence is adding one more than the difference between the previous two. For example:

$$10 - 6 = 4, 4 + 1 = 5$$

Therefore, the next number after 10 is $10 + 5 = 15$.

Going forward:

$$21 - 15 = 6, 6 + 1 = 7$$

The next number is $21 + 7 = 28$. Therefore, the difference between numbers is the set of whole numbers starting at 2: 2, 3, 4, 5, 6, 7....

6. A: Order of operations follows PEMDAS—Parentheses, Exponents, Multiplication and Division from left to right, and Addition and Subtraction from left to right.

7. C: 80 min. To solve the problem, a proportion is written consisting of ratios comparing distance and time. One way to set up the proportion is:

$$\frac{3}{48} = \frac{5}{x} \left(\frac{distance}{time} = \frac{distance}{time} \right)$$

x represents the unknown value of time. To solve a proportion, the ratios are cross-multiplied:

$$(3)(x) = (5)(48) \rightarrow 3x = 240$$

The equation is solved by isolating the variable, or dividing by 3 on both sides, to produce $x = 80$.

8. A: A mixed number contains both a whole number and either a fraction or a decimal. Therefore, the mixed number is $16\frac{1}{2}$.

9. A: The place value to the right of the thousandth place, which would be the ten-thousandth place, is what gets used. The value in the thousandth place is 7. The number in the place value to its right is 5 or greater, so the 7 gets bumped up to 8. Everything to its right turns to a zero, and the final zero is dropped because it is part of the decimal. 245.2678 rounded to the nearest thousandth is 245.268.

444

10. B: This is a division problem because the original amount needs to be split up into equal amounts. The mixed number $11\frac{1}{2}$ should be converted to an improper fraction first:

$$11\frac{1}{2} = \frac{(11 \times 2) + 1}{2} = \frac{23}{2}$$

Carey needs to determine how many times $\frac{23}{2}$ goes into 184. This is a division problem:

$$184 \div \frac{23}{2} = ?$$

The fraction can be flipped, and the problem turns into the multiplication:

$$184 \times \frac{2}{23} = \frac{368}{23}$$

This improper fraction can be simplified into 16 because $368 \div 23 = 16$. The answer is 16 lawn segments.

11. C: Numbers should be lined up by decimal places before subtraction is performed. This is because subtraction is performed within each place value. The other operations, such as multiplication, division, and exponents (which is a form of multiplication), involve ignoring the decimal places at first and then including them at the end.

12. A: The additive and subtractive identity is 0. When added or subtracted to any number, 0 does not change the original number.

13. B: 100 cm is equal to 1 m. 1.3 divided by 100 is 0.013. Therefore, 1.3 cm is equal to 0.013 m. Because 1 cm is equal to 10 mm, 1.3 cm is equal to 13 mm.

14. D: To calculate the circumference of a circle, use the formula $2\pi r$, where r equals the radius, or half of the diameter, of the circle and $\pi \approx 3.14$. Substitute the given information to get:

$$2 \times 3.14 \times 5 = 31.4$$

15. B: A rectangle is a specific type of parallelogram. It has 4 right angles. A square is a rhombus that has 4 right angles. Therefore, a square is always a rectangle because it has two sets of parallel lines and 4 right angles.

16. D: Recall the formula for area, area = length × width. The answer must be in square inches, so all values must be converted to inches. Half of a foot is equal to 6 inches. Therefore, the area of the rectangle is equal to:

$$6 \text{ in} \times \frac{11}{2}\text{ in} = \frac{66}{2}\text{ in}^2 = 33 \text{ in}^2$$

17. C: The teacher would be introducing fractions. If a pie was cut into 6 pieces, each piece would represent $\frac{1}{6}$ of the pie. If one piece was taken away, $\frac{5}{6}$ of the pie would be left over.

18. B: Each hour on the clock represents 30 degrees. For example, 3:00 represents a right angle. Therefore, 5:00 represents 150 degrees.

19. D: There are no millions, so the millions period consists of all zeros. 182 is in the billions period, 36 is in the thousands period, 421 is in the hundreds period, and 356 is the decimal.

20. A: Every 8 mL of medicine requires 5 mL. The 45 mL first needs to be split into portions of 8 mL. This results in $\frac{45}{8}$ portions. Each portion requires 5 mL. Therefore,

$$\frac{45}{8} \times 5 = \frac{45 \times 5}{8} = \frac{225}{8} \text{ mL is necessary}$$

21. D: Division can be computed as a repetition of subtraction problems by subtracting multiples of 24.

22. C: Volume of this three-dimensional figure is calculated using $length \times width \times height$. Each measure of length is in inches. Therefore, the answer would be labeled in cubic inches.

23. A: A common denominator must be found. The least common denominator is 15 because it has both 5 and 3 as factors. The fractions must be rewritten using 15 as the denominator.

24. B: A number raised to an exponent is a compressed form of multiplication. For example,

$$10^3 = 10 \times 10 \times 10$$

25. B: The perimeter of a rectangle is the sum of all four sides. Therefore, the answer is:

$$P = 14 + 8\frac{1}{2} + 14 + 8\frac{1}{2}$$

$$14 + 14 + 8 + \frac{1}{2} + 8 + \frac{1}{2}$$

45 square inches

26. C: Inches, pounds, and baking measurements, such as tablespoons, are not part of the metric system. Kilograms, grams, kilometers, and meters are part of the metric system.

27. C: It shows the associative property of multiplication. The order of multiplication does not matter, and the grouping symbols do not change the final result once the expression is evaluated.

28. B: $12 \times 750 = 9,000$. Therefore, there are 9,000 milliliters of water, which must be converted to liters. 1,000 milliliters equals 1 liter; therefore, 9 liters of water are purchased.

29. A: According to order of operations, the operation within the parentheses must be completed first. Next, division is completed and then subtraction. Therefore, the expression is evaluated as:

$$(3 + 7) - 6 \div 2$$

$$10 - 6 \div 2$$

$$10 - 3 = 7$$

446

In order to incorrectly obtain 2 as the answer, the operations would have been performed from left to right, instead of following PEMDAS.

30. A: Operations within the parentheses must be completed first. Then, division is completed. Finally, addition is the last operation to complete. When adding decimals, digits within each place value are added together. Therefore, the expression is evaluated as:

$$(2 \times 20) \div (7 + 1) + (6 \times 0.01) + (4 \times 0.001)$$

$$40 \div 8 + 0.06 + 0.004$$

$$5 + 0.06 + 0.004 = 5.064$$

31. B: The formula for the volume of a rectangular solid would need to be used. The volume of the first box is:

$$V = 3 \times 5 \times 10 = 150 \text{ cubic inches}$$

The second box needs to hold cereal that would take up the same space. The volume of the second box is:

$$V = 5 \times 6 \times h = 30 \times h$$

In order for this to equal 150, h must equal 5 inches.

32. C: The measure of two complementary angles sums up to 90 degrees. $90 - 54 = 36$. Therefore, the complementary angle is $36°$.

33. C: A compass is a tool that can be used to draw a circle. The circle would be drawn by using the length of the radius, which is half of the diameter.

34. C: A dollar contains 20 nickels. Therefore, if there are 12 dollars' worth of nickels, there are:

$$12 \times 20 = 240 \text{ nickels}$$

Each nickel weighs 5 grams. Therefore, the weight of the nickels is:

$$240 \times 5 = 1,200 \text{ grams}$$

Adding in the weight of the empty piggy bank, the filled bank weighs 2,250 grams.

35. B: Katie eats $\frac{1}{3}$ of $\frac{3}{4}$ of the pizza. That means she eats:

$$\frac{1}{3} \times \frac{3}{4} = \frac{3}{12} = \frac{1}{4} \text{ of the pizza}$$

Therefore,

$$\frac{3}{4} - \frac{1}{4} = \frac{2}{4} = \frac{1}{2} \text{ of the pizza remains}$$

This problem involves subtraction of fractions with like denominators.

36. D: To find Denver's total snowfall, 3 must be multiplied by $27\frac{3}{4}$. In order to easily do this, the mixed number should be converted into an improper fraction.

$$27\frac{3}{4} = \frac{27 \times 4 + 3}{4} = \frac{111}{4}$$

Therefore, Denver had approximately $\frac{3 \times 111}{4} = \frac{333}{4}$ inches of snow. The improper fraction can be converted back into a mixed number through division.

$$\frac{333}{4} = 83\frac{1}{4} \text{ inches}$$

37. B: Each nickel is worth $0.05. Therefore, Joshua deposited:

$$12{,}345 \times \$0.05 = \$617.25$$

Working with change is a great way to teach decimals to children, so this problem would be a good introduction to multiplying decimals.

38. B: Ordinal numbers represent a ranking. Placing second in a competition is a ranking among the other participants of the spelling bee.

39. B: According to the order of operations, multiplication and division must be completed first from left to right. Then, addition and subtraction are completed from left to right. Therefore:

$$9 \times 9 \div 9 + 9 - 9 \div 9$$

$$81 \div 9 + 9 - 9 \div 9$$

$$9 + 9 - 9 \div 9$$

$$9 + 9 - 1 = 18 - 1 = 17$$

40. B: When giving an answer to a math problem that is in fraction form, it always should be simplified. Both 3 and 15 have a common factor of 3 that can be divided out, so the correct answer is:

$$\frac{3 \div 3}{15 \div 3} = \frac{1}{5}$$

41. D: The two lines are neither parallel nor perpendicular. Parallel lines will never intersect or meet. Therefore, the lines are not parallel. Perpendicular lines intersect to form a right angle (90°). Although the lines intersect, they do not form a right angle, which is usually indicated with a box at the intersection point. Therefore, the lines are not perpendicular.

42. B: Cone. A polygon is a closed two-dimensional figure consisting of three or more sides. A decagon is a polygon with 10 sides. A triangle is a polygon with three sides. A rhombus is a polygon with 4 sides. A cone is a three-dimensional figure and is classified as a solid.

43. C: 374.04. The formula for finding the area of a regular polygon is $A = \frac{1}{2} \times a \times P$ where a is the length of the apothem (from the center to any side at a right angle), and P is the perimeter of the figure.

448

The apothem a is given as 10.39, and the perimeter can be found by multiplying the length of one side by the number of sides (since the polygon is regular):

$$P = 12 \times 6 \rightarrow P = 72$$

To find the area, substitute the values for a and P into the formula:

$$A = \frac{1}{2} \times a \times P$$

$$A = \frac{1}{2} \times (10.39) \times (72)$$

$$A = 374.04$$

44. C: 216 cm^2. Because area is a two-dimensional measurement, the dimensions are multiplied by a scale factor that is squared to determine the scale factor of the corresponding areas. The dimensions of the rectangle are multiplied by a scale factor of 3. Therefore, the area is multiplied by a scale factor of 3^2 (which is equal to 9):

$$24 \text{ cm}^2 \times 9 = 216 \text{ cm}^2$$

45. A: $(-3, 2)$. The coordinates of a point are written as an ordered pair (x, y). To determine the x-coordinate, a line is traced directly above or below the point until reaching the x-axis. This step notes the value on the x-axis. In this case, the x-coordinate is -3. To determine the y-coordinate, a line is traced directly to the right or left of the point until reaching the y-axis, which notes the value on the y-axis. In this case, the y-coordinate is 2. Therefore, the ordered pair is written $(-3, 2)$.

46. C: The perimeter is found by calculating the sum of all sides of the polygon:

$$9 + 9 + 9 + 8 + 8 + s = 56$$

s is the missing side length. Therefore, $43 + s = 56$. The missing side length is 13 cm.

47. C: $\frac{1}{3}$ of the shirts sold were patterned. Therefore, $1 - \frac{1}{3} = \frac{2}{3}$ of the shirts sold were solid. Anytime "of" a quantity appears in a word problem, multiplication should be used. Therefore:

$$192 \times \frac{2}{3} = \frac{192 \times 2}{3} = \frac{384}{3} = 128 \text{ solid shirts were sold}$$

The entire expression is:

$$192 \times \left(1 - \frac{1}{3}\right)$$

48. A: Mean. An outlier is a data value that is either far above or far below the majority of values in a sample set. The mean is the average of all the values in the set. In a small sample set, a very high or very low number could drastically change the average of the data points. Outliers will have no more of an effect on the median (the middle value when arranged from lowest to highest) than any other value above or below the median. If the same outlier does not repeat, outliers will have no effect on the mode (value that repeats most often).

449

49. C: Line graph. The scenario involves data consisting of two variables, month and stock value. Box plots display data consisting of values for one variable. Therefore, a box plot is not an appropriate choice. Both line plots and circle graphs are used to display frequencies within categorical data. Neither can be used for the given scenario. Line graphs display two numerical variables on a coordinate grid and show trends among the variables.

50. D: $\frac{1}{12}$. The probability of picking the winner of the race is $\frac{1}{4}$, or $\left(\frac{number\ of\ favorable\ outcomes}{number\ of\ total\ outcomes}\right)$. Assuming the winner was picked on the first selection, three horses remain from which to choose the runner-up (these are dependent events). Therefore, the probability of picking the runner-up is $\frac{1}{3}$. To determine the probability of multiple events, the probability of each event is multiplied:

$$\frac{1}{4} \times \frac{1}{3} = \frac{1}{12}$$

51. D: $\frac{3}{100}$. Each digit to the left of the decimal point represents a higher multiple of 10 and each digit to the right of the decimal point represents a quotient of a higher multiple of 10 for the divisor. The first digit to the right of the decimal point is equal to the value $\div 10$. The second digit to the right of the decimal point is equal to the value $\div (10 \times 10)$, or the value $\div 100$.

52. B: 13,078. The power of 10 by which a digit is multiplied corresponds with the number of zeros following the digit when expressing its value in standard form. Therefore,

$$(1 \times 10^4) + (3 \times 10^3) + (7 \times 10^1) + (8 \times 10^0) = 10,000 + 3,000 + 70 + 8 = 13,078$$

53. A: 847.90. The hundredths place value is located two digits to the right of the decimal point (the digit 9 in the original number). The digit to the right of the place value is examined to decide whether to round up or keep the digit. In this case, the digit 6 is 5 or greater, so the hundredths place is rounded up. When rounding up, if the digit to be increased is a 9, the digit to its left is increased by one and the digit in the desired place value is made a zero. Therefore, the number is rounded to 847.90.

54. B: $\frac{11}{15}$. Fractions must have like denominators to be added. We are trying to add a fraction with a denominator of 3 to a fraction with a denominator of 5, so we have to convert both fractions to equivalent fractions that have a common denominator. The common denominator is the least common multiple (LCM) of the two original denominators. In this case, the LCM is 15, so both fractions should be changed to equivalent fractions with a denominator of 15.

To determine the numerator of the new fraction, the old numerator is multiplied by the same number by which the old denominator is multiplied to obtain the new denominator.

For the fraction $\frac{1}{3}$, 3 multiplied by 5 will produce 15.

Therefore, the numerator is multiplied by 5 to produce the new numerator:

$$\frac{1 \times 5}{3 \times 5} = \frac{5}{15}$$

For the fraction $\frac{2}{5}$, multiplying both the numerator and denominator by 3 produces $\frac{6}{15}$. When fractions have like denominators, they are added by adding the numerators and keeping the denominator the same:

$$\frac{5}{15} + \frac{6}{15} = \frac{11}{15}$$

55. C: When performing calculations consisting of more than one operation, the order of operations should be followed: Parentheses, Exponents, Multiplication/Division, Addition/Subtraction.

Parentheses:

$$7^2 - 3 \times (4 + 2) + 15 \div 5$$

$$7^2 - 3 \times (6) + 15 \div 5$$

Exponents:

$$49 - 3 \times 6 + 15 \div 5$$

Multiplication/Division (from left to right):

$$49 - 18 + 3$$

Addition/Subtraction (from left to right):

$$49 - 18 + 3 = 34$$

56. D: 80%. To convert a fraction to a percent, the fraction is first converted to a decimal. To do so, the numerator is divided by the denominator: $4 \div 5 = 0.8$. To convert a decimal to a percent, the number is multiplied by 100:

$$0.8 \times 100 = 80\%.$$

57. D: 1, 2, 3, 4, 6, 12. A given number divides evenly by each of its factors to produce an integer (no decimals). To find the factors of 12, determine what integers multiply to 12. 1×12, 2×6, and 3×4 are all the ways to multiply to 12 using integers, so the factors of 12 are: 1, 2, 3, 4, 6, 12.

58. A: 11. To determine the number of houses that can fit on the street, the length of the street is divided by the width of each house: $345 \div 30 = 11.5$. Although the mathematical calculation of 11.5 is correct, this answer is not reasonable. Half of a house cannot be built, so the company will need to either build 11 or 12 houses. Since the width of 12 houses (360 feet) will extend past the length of the street, only 11 houses can be built.

59. B: $3x^2 - 3x + 11$. By distributing the implied one in front of the first set of parentheses and the -1 in front of the second set of parentheses, the parentheses can be eliminated:

$$1(5x^2 - 3x + 4) - 1(2x^2 - 7) = 5x^2 - 3x + 4 - 2x^2 + 7$$

451

Next, like terms (same variables with same exponents) are combined by adding the coefficients and keeping the variables and their powers the same:

$$5x^2 - 3x + 4 - 2x^2 + 7 = 3x^2 - 3x + 11$$

60. C: $y = 40x + 300$. In this scenario, the variables are the number of sales and Karen's weekly pay. The weekly pay depends on the number of sales. Therefore, weekly pay is the dependent variable (y), and the number of sales is the independent variable (x). Each pair of values from the table can be written as an ordered pair (x, y): $(2, 380)$, $(7, 580)$, $(4, 460)$, $(8, 620)$. The ordered pairs can be substituted into the equations to see which creates true statements (both sides equal) for each pair. Even if one ordered pair produces equal values for a given equation, the other three ordered pairs must be checked.

The only equation which is true for all four ordered pairs is $y = 40x + 300$:

$$380 = 40(2) + 300 \rightarrow 380 = 380$$

$$580 = 40(7) + 300 \rightarrow 580 = 580$$

$$460 = 40(4) + 300 \rightarrow 460 = 460$$

$$620 = 40(8) + 300 \rightarrow 620 = 620$$

Social Studies

1. A: Carolina is divided into two separate states—North and South. Maine was part of Nova Scotia and did not become an American territory until the War of 1812. Likewise, Vermont was not one of the original Thirteen Colonies. Canada remained a separate British colony. Finally, Florida was a Spanish territory. Therefore, by process of elimination, A is the correct list.

2. B: Britain was not defeated in the French and Indian War, and, in fact, disputes with the colonies over the new territories it won contributed to the growing tensions. All of the other options were key motivations behind the Revolutionary War.

3. C: Abraham Lincoln was elected president as part of the new Republican Party, and his plans to limit and potentially abolish slavery led the southern states to secede from the Union.

4. B: Out of the four inventions mentioned, the first telegraphs were invented in the 1830s, and did not have as great of an impact during the twentieth century. In contrast, the other inventions had considerable influence over the course of the twentieth century.

5. C: Cause and effect is an important concept in social sciences. The Declaration of Independence occurred during the American Revolution, so it should therefore be considered an effect, not a cause. Similarly, slavery was a cause for the later Civil War, but it was not a primary instigator for the Revolutionary War. Although a single event can have many effects long into the future, it is also important to not overstate the influence of these individual causes; the civil rights movement was only tangentially connected to the War of Independence among many other factors, and therefore it should not be considered a primary effect of it. The French and Indian War (which was part of the Seven Years' War) and the Bill of Rights, on the other hand, were respectively a cause and effect from the American Revolution, making Choice C the correct answer.

6. D: The president and vice president are part of the executive branch, not the legislative branch. The question focuses specifically on the federal level, so state government should be excluded from consideration. As for the district court and the court of appeals, they are part of the judicial branch. The legislative branch is made up of Congress, which consists of the House of Representatives and the Senate.

7. A: George Washington was a slave owner himself in life, so he did not make abolition a theme in his Farewell Address. On the other hand, he was concerned that sectionalism could potentially destroy the United States, and he warned against it. Furthermore, he believed that Americans should avoid getting involved in European affairs. However, one issue that he felt was especially problematic was the formation of political parties, and he urged against it in his farewell.

8. B: It is not a responsibility to avoid involvement in political processes such as voting is antithetical to the principles of a democracy. Therefore, the principal responsibility of citizens is the opposite, and they should be steadily engaged in the political processes that determine the course of government.

9. B: Time zones are determined by longitude, not latitude. Locations are defined in absolute terms, while places are in part defined by the population, which is subject to movement. There are seven continents in the world, not six. On the other hand, it is true that the prime meridian determines the border for the Eastern and Western hemispheres.

10. D: Riparian water usage was common in the past, but modern usage has shifted to appropriation. While often practicing sustainable methods, Native Americans used fire, agriculture, and other tools to shape the landscape for their own ends. Due to the importance of trade in providing essential resources to cities, a city is never truly separated from the outside world. However, invasive species are a formidable threat to native environments, making *D* the correct answer.

11. C: I, II, and IV only. Historians make use of maps in their studies to get a clear picture of how history unfolded, knowing the borders of different lands helps historians learn different cultures' interactions, and environmental factors, such as access to water and the proximity of mountains, help determine the course of civilization. The phrase "Geography is closely linked with the flow of resources, technology, and population in societies" is a characteristic of economics.

12. C: While many Native American tribes are matrilineal, not all of them are. Japan is currently coping with an especially low birthrate, not a high one. Mexico's religion, like that of Spain, is primarily Roman Catholic rather than Protestant. On the other hand, Shi'a Islam is based on the view that imams should be honored as Muhammad's chosen heirs to the Caliphate, making *C* correct.

13. A: Although Greeks used the alphabet as the basis for their written language, leading to a diverse array of literature, they learned about the alphabet from Phoenician traders. All the other options, in contrast, were invented in Greece.

14. D: It is important to realize that the Cold War was never an official war and that the United States and the Soviet Union instead funded proxy conflicts. The Kyoto Protocol was signed by members of the United Nations, as the League of Nations was long since defunct. While Japan was a minor participant in World War I, it was not defeated by America until World War II. The correct answer is *D*: India's partition between Hindu India and Islamic Pakistan led to large outbreaks of religious violence.

15. A: Although Egyptian and Mayan civilizations are an interesting subject for comparisons, the two cultures never interacted; therefore, the teacher should not use this as an example of cross-cultural interactions. The other answers are all examples of interactions between different cultures; a study of Chinese culture, for instance, would require examination of the multiple ethnic groups throughout China.

16. C: Although monetary systems were invented to solve problems with barter systems, it is wrong to assume that barter systems have ceased to exist; bartering remains a common practice throughout the world, albeit less common than money. The four main categories for economic resources are land, labor, capital, and entrepreneurship. The law of supply says that supplies will increase, not decrease, as prices increase. The correct answer is *C,* as scarcity is determined by human choice.

17. A: Rather than competition, a monopoly prevents other businesses from offering a certain product or service to consumers.

18. B: Absolute monarchies often use command system economies, but they do not represent a way that governments manage economies. Laissez-faire, capitalism, and self-interest, in contrast, are all fundamental concepts behind the market system.

19. A: England, France, and Spain all established North American colonies that would later be absorbed into the United States, but Italy, despite Christopher Columbus' role as an explorer, never established a colony in America.

20. D: The Constitution was signed in 1787; the Declaration of Independence was signed in 1776. It was successfully ratified by all the current states, including New York. Finally, the Articles of Confederation was established at the end of the American Revolution; the Constitution would replace the articles years later due to issues with the government's structure.

21. C: Although American forces made several early attempts to take Canada from Britain, the United States was never able to successfully seize this territory. On the other hand, the United States did control the Philippines, Puerto Rico, and Guam.

22. C: The executive branch determines the cabinet, while the judicial branch has the responsibility of interpreting the Constitution and laws. Even so, the legislative branch can check the president's power by impeaching him.

23. D: The Emancipation Proclamation only freed slaves in Confederate-held territories; southern states still loyal to the Union kept their slaves for the time being. Although Wilson succeeded in instituting the League of Nations, the United Nations would not emerge until decades later. The Bill of Rights was ratified after the Constitution to provide additional protection for individual liberties. However, it is true that the main body of the Declaration of Independence consisted of grievances that the colonies had against British rule.

24. D: While it is true that Rome fell to barbarians in the fifth century A.D., it would be inaccurate to say the Roman Empire had been completely destroyed. The Byzantine Empire considered itself the heir of the Roman Empire. The western sections, on the other hand, certainly collapsed; the later Holy Roman Empire tried to draw on Rome's past glory but was not a true successor.

25. A: Based on the prior League of Nations, the United Nations included many nations in postcolonial Africa and Asia and worked to support human rights. However, it failed to maintain the World War II alliance between the United States and the Soviet Union, leading to the unofficial Cold War.

26. C: At the time of the Constitutional Convention, Thomas Jefferson was in Paris serving as America's foreign minister to France. George Washington led the meeting, and Alexander Hamilton and James Madison set the tone for debate, rendering *A*, *B*, and *D* incorrect.

27. A: Plains Indians followed the buffalo across the prairies, living in tent-like teepees that were easily moved from place to place. Choice *B* is incorrect because Indians in the Southwest relied on farming for much of their food and built adobes, which are houses made out of dried clay or earth. Indians in the Eastern and Northwest sections of North America survived by hunting, gathering, farming, and fishing, and lived in wooden longhouses, plank houses, or wigwams. Thus, Choices *C* and *D* are incorrect.

28. A: President Franklin Roosevelt is notorious for his Fireside chats during his presidency, particularly surrounding WWII. A recording of one of these radio broadcasts is a good example of a primary source. Primary sources are context-specific, first-hand accounts. They don't have to be in the form of written words, so a radio recording that is a first-hand account of life during that time would be a great example for a third-grade class. Choices *B* and *C* might be useful during WWII lessons, but they are not examples of primary sources. Moreover, Choice *C* is not about life in the United States. Choice *D* is incorrect because Eisenhower took to office after WWII had ended.

29. D: The British issued the Townsend Act in 1767, which taxed imported lead, glass, paints, paper, and tea, and increased the colonists' anger and further strained the relationship between England and the colonies. Choice *A*, the Stamp Act of 1765, taxed printed items, including playing cards and newspapers printed in the colonies. Choice *B*, the Sugar Act of 1764, placed import duties on items such as molasses, sugar, coffee, and wine. Choice *C*, the Currency Act, banned the issuing of paper money in the colonies and mandated the use of gold in business dealings.

30. C: The first shot took place on Lexington Green. When the British heard that colonists were stockpiling weapons, they sent troops to Concord to seize them. However, a group of approximately seventy Minutemen confronted the British soldiers on Lexington green. British troops killed five protesting colonists during the Boston Massacre in 1770, but this is not considered the first shot of the Revolution. Thus, Choice *A* is incorrect. Choice *B* is incorrect because the Boston Tea Party was when colonists dumped 342 chests of expensive tea into the Boston Harbor in defiance of the tea tax. The Revolution had already started when the Battle of Trenton took place on December 25, 1776, making Choice *D* incorrect.

31. A: British General Lord Cornwallis surrendered to Washington's troops at Yorktown, Virginia. No battles occurred at Valley Forge, but Washington's troops suffered major losses as a result of starvation, disease, and exposure to the cold, making Choice *B* incorrect. Choice *C* is incorrect because the Battle of Trenton was the first major battle of the Revolution, which occurred when Washington led his troops across the Delaware River to wage a surprise attack on British and Hessian soldiers stationed in Trenton on December 25, 1776. Choice *D*, Saratoga, New York, was the site of a major victory by General John Burgoyne in October 1777 and prompted European countries to help support the American cause.

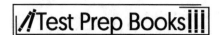

32. C: British soldiers burned the White House during the War of 1812. Neither the Washington Monument nor the Statue of Liberty – Choices *A* and *D* – were built at the time, and Philadelphia's Independence Hall, Choice *B*, escaped conflict during this war.

33. B: Jefferson Davis was elected president of the Confederate States of America in November 1861. Choice *A*, General Robert E. Lee, was the leader of the Confederate Army. Choice *C*, William T. Sherman, was a union general famous for his march through Georgia and the burning of Atlanta in 1864. Choice *D*, Abraham Lincoln, was President of the U.S. during the Civil War.

34. D: This period was called the Gilded Age since it appeared shiny and golden on the surface, but was fueled by undercurrents of corruption led by big businessmen known as robber barons. Choice *A*, Manifest Destiny, is the concept referring to the pursuit and acquisition of new lands by the U.S., which led to the purchase of Alaska from Russia in 1867 and the annexation of Hawaii in 1898. The Columbian Exchange, Choice *B*, was an era of discovery, conquest, and colonization of the Americas by the Europeans. The New Deal, Choice *C*, was a plan launched by President Franklin Delano Roosevelt to help rebuild America's economy after the Great Depression.

35. C: World War I began in 1914 when a Serbian assassin killed Archduke Franz Ferdinand of Austria and prompted Austria-Hungary to declare war on Serbia. 1915, Choice *A*, is the year when German submarines sank the passenger ship *Lusitania*, killing 128 Americans and leading many to support U.S. efforts to enter the war. 1917, Choice *B*, is the year the U.S. entered World War I, declaring war on Germany. 1918, Choice *D*, signaled the end of the war when American troops helped defeat the German army that September. Fighting ended in November after Germany signed a peace agreement.

36. A: The Soviet Union was invaded by Germany in 1941 and allied with Britain and subsequently the U.S. President Roosevelt, British Prime Minister Winston Churchill, and Soviet director Joseph Stalin met in 1945 to plan their final assault on Germany and discuss postwar strategies. Germany aligned with Italy and Japan in 1940 to form the Axis Alliance. Their goal was to establish a German empire in Europe and place Japan in control over Asia. Thus, Choices *B*, *C*, and *D* are incorrect.

37. B: The North Atlantic Treaty Organization (NATO) was formed between Western Europe, Canada, and the U.S. in defense of Soviet hostility after the Soviet Union introduced Communism into Eastern Europe. The Soviet Union countered by creating the Warsaw Pact.

38. C: You inform her that the G.I. Bill was a government program started in the 1950s that gave military veterans a free education. In the revolutionary 1954 case, *Brown vs. the Board of Education,* the Supreme Court ruled that school segregation was illegal, thereby setting the Civil Rights Movement in motion, making Choice *A* incorrect. *Freedom Rides*, Choice *B*, and the Montgomery bus boycott, Choice *D*, were among the non-violent protests against segregation that took place in the U.S. in the 1960s.

39. B: President Reagan advocated *peace through strength*, building up the U.S. military and launching the Strategic Defense Initiative (SDI), also called *Star Wars*. Choice *A*, the Strategic Arms Limitation Talks (SALT I and II), negotiated between 1972 and 1979, resulted in limits on nuclear weapons for both the U.S. and Russia. Choice *C*, the Iran-Contra Affair, was a scandal involving the secret sale of weapons to Iran in exchange for American hostages. Choice *D*, *Glasnost*, was a policy of political openness launched by Soviet leader Mikhail Gorbachev.

40. A: Afghanistan was the site of the bombing raids. Bush invaded Iraq, Choice *B*, in 2003 when Iraqi dictator Saddam Hussein defied the terms of the truce agreed upon in 1991 after the Gulf War. Kuwait,

456

Choice *C*, was invaded by Iraq in 1990, sparking the Gulf War. Pakistan, Choice *D*, is where Osama bin Laden was killed by a group of Navy SEALs under orders from President Obama.

41. B: The Mississippi and the Missouri are the two largest rivers in the U.S., winding through the Great Plains in the center of the country. The Colorado and Ohio Rivers are about half the length of the Mississippi and Missouri.

42. C: Latitude – imaginary lines covering the globe from east to west – and longitude – imaginary lines running north to south – are used to pinpoint location on a map. Scale is used to show the relationship between the map measurements and the equivalent distance on the world's surface. Contour lines are used to show detailed elevation on a map.

43. D: Under America's democratic form of government, voting is a *right*, but it is not an *obligation*. U.S. citizens are *obliged* to obey the law, pay taxes, and serve on a jury if asked to do so, making Choices *A*, *B*, and *C* incorrect.

44. D: History is dynamic, meaning that it can change over time. A good example of this is that there are twenty-seven amendments to the U.S. Constitution. The document was not created and then set permanently in stone. It has been changed to reflect changing thoughts and circumstances in the country. The 14th Amendment was adopted in 1868 to abolish slavery. The 18th Amendment was passed in 1919 and prohibited the production and sale of alcoholic beverages, but the 21st Amendment repealed it in 1933. It is true that GPS technology was first implemented in the 1960s and now is available on smartphones, but this is more about improvements in technology and not how the field of history and social sciences itself changes. There are checks and balances built into the various branches of government, but this is an example of balancing power rather than change. Lastly, there are contradictory accounts of certain historical events, such as when Europeans first came to America. This is a good example of considering sources, perspectives, reliability, and circumstances when studying social sciences.

45. **B:** Microeconomics looks at the interplay of consumers, households, and companies within individual markets and the relationships between them. Macroeconomics, Choice *A*, is the study of entire economies. Booms and busts, Choice *C*, are terms used to describe the cyclical nature of economic activity, typically prompted by extreme changes in the economy. Economic output, Choice *D*, is the total amount of goods and services produced by an ***economy.***

46. C: Capital resources are the man-made physical resources used to create products, such as machinery, tools, buildings, and equipment. Natural resources, Choice *A*, are raw materials taken from the land, such as corn, beef, lumber, water, oil, and iron. Human resources, Choice *B*, refer to the human labor—both mental and physical—required to produce goods. Entrepreneurship, Choice *D*, is the capability and motivation to cultivate, organize, and oversee the other three resources into a business venture.

47. C: The tertiary sector provides consumer or business services, including industries such as entertainment, retail sales, and restaurants. The primary sector, Choice *A*, takes raw materials from the Earth, such as coal, timber, copper, and wheat. The secondary sector, Choice *B*, converts raw materials into goods, such as textile manufacturing, food processing, and car manufacturing. The quaternary sector, Choice *D*, provides informational and knowledge services, such as education, business consulting, and financial services.

457

48. B: Opportunity cost is the term used to describe the choices that determine how consumers spend or save their money. Choice *A*, the circular flow model, is used by economists to describe the movement of supply, demand, and payment between businesses and consumers. A savings account, Choice *C*, is considered low-risk because the bank will pay the saver a low interest rate to keep it safe. Assets, Choice *D*, are valuable items purchased by investors in the hopes that they will increase in worth over time and yield returns or profits.

49. D: Field experiences. The FTCE guide recommends that teachers move beyond traditional, direct instruction to enhance student learning and better prepare students for work in secondary school and college. Field experiences can enhance student learning by exposing them to real-world objects, ideas, and issues. Field experiences prepare students to become young social scientists who can carry out qualitative and quantitative research.

50. B: GPS uses satellite technology to analyze and display geographic features. In an increasingly technological world, students must know how to use GPS technology to their advantage in the classroom. Other tools, such as globes, timelines, and map projections can also be useful, but none of these employ satellite technologies.

Science

1. D: It has the same amount of mechanical energy throughout its path. Mechanical energy is the total amount of energy in the situation; it is the sum of the potential energy and the kinetic energy. The amount of potential and kinetic energy both vary by the position of an object, but the mechanical energy remains constant.

2. C: The scientific method refers to how to conduct a proper scientific inquiry, including recognizing a question/problem, formulating a hypothesis, making a prediction of what will happen based on research, experimenting, and deciding whether the outcome confirmed or denied the hypothesis.

3. B: Kinetic energy is energy an object has while moving. Potential energy is energy an object has based on its position or height. Solar energy is energy that comes from the sun. Heat energy is the energy produced from moving atoms, molecules, or ions, and can transfer between substances.

4. A: A chemical change alters the chemical makeup of the original object. When a piece of paper burns it cannot be returned to its original chemical makeup because it has formed new materials. Physical change refers to changing a substance's form, but not the composition of that substance. In physical science, "sedimentary change" and "potential change" are not terms used to describe any particular process.

5. C: An inclined plane is a simple machine that can make it easier to raise or lower an object in height. Simple machines offer a mechanical advantage to performing tasks. While a screw, a level, and a pulley are also simple machines, they would be used to offer a mechanical advantage in other situations.

6. D: Sir Isaac Newton simplified the laws of motion into three basic rules, based upon his observations in experimentation and advanced mathematical calculations. Albert Einstein was known for his theories involving electricity and magnetism, relativity, energy, light, and gravitational waves. Stephen Hawking is known for his theories and studies of space, dark matter, black holes, and relativity. Copernicus was

458

known for his observations and theories regarding the movements of the planets in our universe; specifically, that the sun was the center of our solar system, not earth.

7. B: Convection is the transfer of heat due to the movement of molecules from an area of higher concentration to that of lower concentration; this is also how heat can travel throughout a house to warm each room. Conduction is the transfer of energy from one molecule to another molecule through actually touching or making contact with each other. Radiation is how the sun warms the earth; no medium is needed for this type of transfer.

8. D: An object at rest has forces acting upon it, including gravitational, normal, and frictional forces. All of these forces are in balance with each other and cause no movement in the object's position. This is equilibrium. An object in constant motion is also considered to be in equilibrium or a state of balanced forces.

9. C: When conducting scientific research, it is best to rely on sources that are known for honest, ethical, and unbiased research and experimentation. Most laboratories and universities must have their work validated through independent means in order to publish or claim results. Anyone can publish things on the Internet—it does not mean their work has been validated, and therefore, their work may not be correct.

10. D: Sublimation is a change in state from a solid to a gas. Evaporation is a change in state from a liquid to a gas, melting is a change in state from a solid to a liquid, and condensation is a change in state from a gas to a liquid.

11. C: A force diagram shows all of the forces acting upon an object in a situation. The direction of arrows pointing around the object shows the direction of each force. A Venn diagram is used to show mathematical sets, a periodic table shows how the elements are categorized, and a stress-strain diagram is used in engineering.

12. D: Mass refers to the amount or quantity there is of an object. Light, sound, and heat are all forms of energy that can travel in waves.

13. A: The mechanical energy is the total (or sum) of the potential energy and the kinetic energy at any given point in a system.

$$ME = PE + KE; 50 \text{ Joules} = 30 \text{ Joules} + 20 \text{ Joules}$$

14. D: Scientific inquiry can be prompted by simple curiosity as to how or why something works. As seen in the race to enter outer space, scientific progress can be driven by competition. Many inventors are motivated by the idea of finding a better, faster, or more economical way of doing or producing something so that they can prosper from their discovery.

15. A: Using Newton's equation for motion, $F = ma$, and substituting gravity in for acceleration (a), the weight, or force could be calculated for an object having mass (m). Weight is a force, mass is the amount of a substance, and acceleration and gravity are rate of speed over time.

16. B: It appears to bend because of the refraction of light traveling from air to water. When light travels from one material to another it can reflect, refract, and go through different materials. Choice *A* is incorrect, as the pencil does not actually become warped but only *appears* to be warped. Choice *C* is

incorrect; although the pencil appears to bend because of its immersion into separate mediums where speed is different, the pencil does not become temporarily warped—it only appears to be warped. Choice *D* is incorrect; it is the refraction of light, not reflection. The latter happens within the same medium, which makes the answer choice incorrect.

17. B: While this is Einstein's application of Newton's theory to that of light, it is not one of Newton's original three laws of motion. Newton's three laws are $F = ma$, the law of inertia, and for every action there is an equal and opposite reaction.

18. C: This is a fundamental law of thermodynamics. Energy can only transfer, transform, or travel. The amount of energy in a system is always the same.

19. A: The ends (or poles) of a straight magnet are different charges. One end is positive and one end is negative. Therefore, the positive end of magnet #1 would attract the negative end of magnet #2 and repel magnet #2's positive end.

20. D: When electricity is run through a wire, it is carrying current and current has a charge. Therefore, there is a charge running down the wire, which creates a magnetic field that can attract and repel just like any magnet.

21. B: The ice skater is demonstrating the conservation of angular momentum. This means that the amount of momentum for the situation will remain the same. If the skater is redistributing the mass (their arms), then the angular speed will compensate for that alteration. In this case, the mass is extended out away from the axis of rotation, so the rate of rotation is slowed down. If their arms were brought back in near their body, then the rate of rotation would increase, making the skater spin faster.

22. C: This is the actual force recognized in a rotational situation. The reactive force acting opposite of the centripetal force is named the centrifugal force, but it is not an actual force on its own. A common mistake is to interchange the two terms. But the real force acting in a rotational situation is pulling in toward the axis of rotation and is called the centripetal force.

23. C: Electric charge can be transferred through touch of one physical object to another, induction by bringing a charged object near another object, and polarization, or the forcing of one charge to the end of an object in a centralized area.

24. D: The solar waves from the sun warm the earth. Many of the waves are meant to reflect back off of the atmosphere to keep the earth warm, and the rest of the waves are meant to reflect back out into space through the atmosphere. This is known as the greenhouse effect. However, when the atmosphere has become too dense (polluted by gases), the waves meant to escape are trapped and re-radiate in the earth's atmosphere, causing an overall warming of the climate, known as global warming.

25. D: Velocity is a measure of speed with direction. To calculate velocity, find the distance covered and the time it took to cover that distance; change in position over the change in time. A standard measurement for velocity is in meters per second (m/s).

26. C: Fossil fuel energy. Wind energy from turbines, solar energy from sun panels, and geothermal energy are all considered renewable and preferable alternatives to fossil fuel, of which there is a limited supply.

The following image is the answer to question 27.

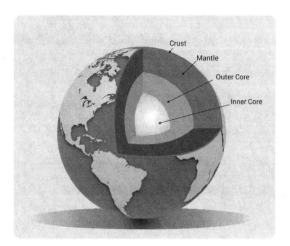

27. A: Inner core: solid. Layer 4 is the inner core; therefore, Choices *C* and *D* are incorrect. The inner core is solid due to the intense pressure upon it, making Choice *B* incorrect.

28. B: Sedimentary. Choice *A* (igneous) is incorrect, because that is crystallized magma found on land. Choice *C* (metamorphic) is incorrect, because that is unified, solid rock close to earth's mantle. Choice *D* (minerals) isn't a type of rock, but what composes rock.

29. D: Sunlight evaporates dew from plants. Choice *A* is incorrect because cloud formation is condensation. Choice *B* is incorrect because rain, snow, and ice storms are different forms of precipitation. Choice *C* is incorrect because rivers flowing into the oceans are examples of run-off.

30. D: Precipitation. Precipitation has nothing to do with plate tectonic theory. Plate movement causes ocean floor spreading, mountain formation, and earthquakes; therefore, all other answer choices are correct.

31. B: All volcanoes have explosive eruptions. This isn't true; shield volcanoes have thin magma that oozes out gently. Choice *A* is correct because magma circulates in the upper mantle. Choice *C* is correct because igneous rock is cooled lava. Choice *D* is correct because igneous rock goes through the rock cycle and will eventually become magma again.

The following image is for questions 32 and 33.

32. B: Seashells. The oldest rock layer is on the bottom. Choice *D* doesn't show a fossil—the grass is a living organism. Choices *A* and *C* show fossils in higher layers, so these are not the correct answers.

33. C: Sedimentary rock. Fossils are only found in sedimentary rock. Igneous rock, metamorphic rock, and liquid magma don't contain fossils, so Choices *A*, *B*, and *D* are incorrect.

The following image is for question 34.

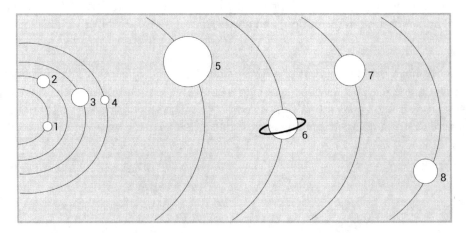

34. C: Between structures #4 and #5. The asteroid belt is rock orbiting between the inner, solid planets and the outer, gassy planets. More precisely, it is between Mars (planet #4) and Jupiter (planet #5). It is not Choice *A* (between Venus and Earth), nor is it Choice *B* (between Earth and Mars). Choice *D* is incorrect since it is not between every planet.

35. C: Mars has a smaller orbit around the Sun. This question requires critical thinking because every answer choice is true, but only one of them has to do with orbiting time. A year is the time it takes a

462

planet to orbit the Sun, and because Mars is closer to the Sun and has a smaller orbit, its year is significantly shorter than a year on Jupiter.

The following image is for question 36.

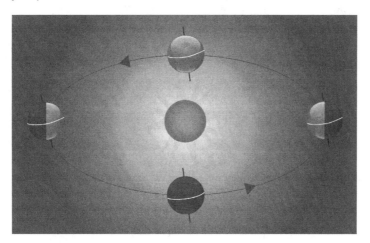

36. B: Winter. Students must identify the lateral equator and know the difference between North and South. They should recognize that because the top hemisphere is tilted away from the Sun; it would be winter at that time. Spring and fall, Choices *D* and *C*, are incorrect because both hemispheres have the same exposure to the sun, and summer, Choice *A*, is incorrect since the top hemisphere is tilted toward the sun.

37. D: All of the above. All choices are correct. New moons are closest to the sun and full moons are farthest, Choice *A*. Crescent moons are smaller than half-moons, Choice *B*, and gibbous moons are larger than half-moons, Choice *C*.

38. B: They insulate earth and keep it warm. Greenhouse gases serve as a blanket and allow earth to exist at livable temperatures. Choice *D* is incorrect because greenhouse gases do not form clouds; clouds are formed by condensed water vapor. Choice *C* is incorrect because while it is true that particles in the atmosphere reflect light so that the sky appears blue, this isn't an important function of the particles in the troposphere. The blue appearance is just cosmetic. Choice *A* is incorrect because ozone in the stratosphere actually prevents UV rays from passing.

39. C: Theories are accepted by scientists, while hypotheses remain to be proven. Choice *A* is incorrect because theories are far more than predictions; they are actually highly supported and accepted as truth. Choice *B* is incorrect because theories can change with new technology and understanding. Choice *D* is also incorrect because theories may not always be true and can change. Also, hypotheses can be and often are supported.

40. C: Seismologist: earthquakes. All other choices have been mixed up. Paleontologists study fossils, meteorologists study weather, and geologists study the earth's crust.

41. C: Leaf. Leaves are the part of the plant that contain chloroplast (due to their green appearance), thus they are the parts that perform photosynthesis. Roots, Choice *A*, suck up water. Seeds and flowers are reproductive structures, Choices *B* and *D*.

42. D: All living and nonliving things in an area. Choice *C* (all the organisms in a food web) describes feeding relationships and not symbiosis. Choice *B* (rocks, soil, and atmosphere in an area) includes nonliving factors in an ecosystem. Choice *A*, one organism, is too small to be considered an ecosystem.

The following image is for questions 43 and 44.

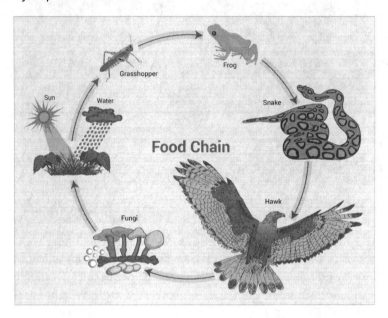

43. D: Fungi. Choice *A* (the sun) is not even a living thing. Grass (*B*) is a producer, and the frog (*C*) is a consumer. The fungi break down dead organisms and are the only decomposer shown.

44. B: Grasshopper. An herbivore is an organism that eats only plants, and that's the grasshopper's niche in this particular food chain. Grass (*A*) is a producer, the frog (*C*) is a consumer, and the fungi (*D*) is a decomposer.

45. C: Oxygen. Water (*A*) is a reactant that gets sucked up by the roots. Carbon dioxide (*D*) is a reactant that goes into the stomata, and sunlight (*B*) inputs energy into the reaction in order to create the high-energy sugar.

46. C: Breaking down food to release energy. Breathing (*B*) is not cellular respiration; breathing is an action that takes place at the organism level with the respiratory system. Making high-energy sugars (*A*) is photosynthesis, not cellular respiration. Perspiration (*D*) is sweating, and has nothing to do with cellular respiration.

47. A: It is the genetic code. Choice *B* is incorrect because DNA does not provide energy—that's the job of carbohydrates and glucose. Choice *C* is incorrect because DNA is double-stranded. Because Choices *B* and *C* are incorrect, Choice *D*, all of the above, is incorrect.

48. D: Algae can perform photosynthesis. One indicator that a plant is able to perform photosynthesis is the color green. Plants with the pigment chlorophyll are able to absorb the warmer colors of the light spectrum, but are unable to absorb green. That's why they appear green. Choices *A* and *C* are types of fungi, and are therefore not able to perform photosynthesis. Fungi obtain energy from food in their environment. Choice *B*, ant, is also unable to perform photosynthesis, since it is an animal.

49. D: Glucose exits. The stomata are pores at the bottom of the leaf, and carbon dioxide enters (it is a reactant for photosynthesis) and oxygen exits (it is a product for photosynthesis), so Choices *A* and *C* are correct. Water exits through the stomata in the process of transpiration, so Choice *B* is correct as well. Glucose is the sugar that is either broken down by the plant for its own energy usage or eaten by other organisms for energy.

50. C: A male moose with horns that enable him to reduce competition for mating. Choices *A* and *D* (elephant and monkey) are not caused by genes. These are learned behaviors from other animals. Choice *B* (smelly dog) is actually a detriment because the dog will be less likely to mate, so she will not pass on her smelly genes.

51. D: All of the above. Let's label *R* as the right-handed allele and *r* as the left-handed allele. Esther has to have the combination rr since she's left-handed. She had to get at least one recessive allele from each parent. So, mom could either be Rr or rr (right-handed or left-handed), and dad can also be Rr or rr. As long as each parent carries one recessive allele, it is possible that Esther is left-handed. Therefore, all answer choices are possible.

52. A: Antibodies. Antibiotics (*B*) fight bacteria, but the body does not make them naturally. White blood cells, not red blood cells (*D*) are the blood cells produced that fight the bacteria. Vaccines (*C*) are given to create antibodies and prevent future illness.

53. A: Organ: Heart. Blank #1 is tissue and blank #2 is organ, so Choices *C* and *D* are automatically incorrect. Blood vessels (*B*) are a type of smooth muscle tissue. The heart is an organ.

The following image is for question 54.

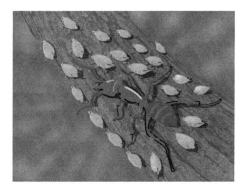

54. C: Mutualism. In the ant-aphid case, both organisms benefit, as the ants are getting food and the aphids are getting protection. Competition (*A*) is when organisms want the same thing (food, water, shelter, space), which is clearly not the case here. Parasitism (*B*) involves one organism getting hurt in the relationship at the expense of the other, while commensalism (*D*) involves an organism that is benefited connected to an indifferent party.

55. B: Time in seconds the dogs sit. This is a better choice than Choice *C* (tail wagging) because it is a measurable, meaningful, and relevant dependent variable. Tail wagging, although quantitative, is not a valid measure of anything. Choices *A* and *D* could be independent variables in the experiment.

Index

Dear Praxis II Elementary Education Test Taker,

We would like to start by thanking you for purchasing this study guide for your Praxis II Elementary Education exam. We hope that we exceeded your expectations.

Our goal in creating this study guide was to cover all of the topics that you will see on the test. We also strove to make our practice questions as similar as possible to what you will encounter on test day. With that being said, if you found something that you feel was not up to your standards, please send us an email and let us know.

We would also like to let you know about other books in our catalog that may interest you.

Praxis II Social Studies

This can be found on Amazon: amazon.com/dp/1628457686

Praxis II English Language Arts

amazon.com/dp/1628458895

Praxis II General Science

amazon.com/dp/1628458550

Praxis II Mathematics

amazon.com/dp/1628458496

Praxis Core Study Guide

amazon.com/dp/1637753470

We have study guides in a wide variety of fields. If the one you are looking for isn't listed above, then try searching for it on Amazon or send us an email.

Thanks Again and Happy Testing!
Product Development Team
info@studyguideteam.com

FREE Test Taking Tips Video/DVD Offer

To better serve you, we created videos covering test taking tips that we want to give you for FREE. **These videos cover world-class tips that will help you succeed on your test.**

We just ask that you send us feedback about this product. Please let us know what you thought about it—whether good, bad, or indifferent.

To get your **FREE videos**, you can use the QR code below or email freevideos@studyguideteam.com with "Free Videos" in the subject line and the following information in the body of the email:

    a. The title of your product

    b. Your product rating on a scale of 1-5, with 5 being the highest

    c. Your feedback about the product

If you have any questions or concerns, please don't hesitate to contact us at info@studyguideteam.com.

Thank you!